ENTREPRENEURSHIP
Strategies and
Resources

SECOND EDITION

ENTREPRENEURSHIP
Strategies and Resources

Marc J. Dollinger

Indiana University

Prentice Hall, Upper Saddle River, New Jersey 07458

Acquisitions Editor: Stephanie Johnson
Editorial Assistant: Hersch Doby
Editor-in-Chief: Natalie Anderson
Marketing Manager: Tami Wederbrand
Production Coordinator: Maureen Wilson
Managing Editor: Dee Josephson
Manufacturing Buyer: Diane Peirano
Manufacturing Supervisor: Arnold Vila
Manufacturing Manager: Vincent Scelta
Design Manager: Patricia Smythe
Cover Design: Bruce Kenselaar
Cover Photo: Annabelle Breakey/Tony Stone Images
Composition: UG

Library of Congress Cataloging-in-Publication Data
Dollinger, Marc J.
    Entrepreneurship: strategies and resources / Marc J. Dollinger—
2nd ed.
      p. cm.
    Includes bibliographical references and index.
    ISBN 0-13-745993-9
    1. New business enterprises. 2. Entrepreneurship. I. Title.
HD62. 5.065 1999
658.4'21—dc21   98-23829
                                          CIP

Prentice-Hall International (UK) Limited, London
Prentice-Hall of Australia Pty. Limited, Sydney
Prentice-Hall Canada, Inc., Toronto
Prentice-Hall Hispanoamericana, S.A., Mexico
Prentice-Hall of India Private Limited, New Delhi
Prentice-Hall of Japan, Inc., Tokyo
Simon & Schuster Asia Pte. Ltd., Singapore
Editora Prentice-Hall do Brasil, Ltda., Rio de Janeiro

Printed in the United States of America

10 9 8 7 6 5 4 3 2 1

Brief Contents

Contents

Preface

Since the publication of the first edition of *Entrepreneurship: Strategies and Resources,* the field of entrepreneurship has grown even faster than I would have predicted. There are more courses and schools teaching entrepreneurship than ever. The major business periodicals, *Business Week, Fortune*, and *Wall Street Journal* continue expanding their coverage of entrepreneurs and their companies. *Success* magazine has begun a ranking of top business school entrepreneurship programs. Business plan competitions at the graduate and undergraduate level continue to proliferate and the prizes get larger and larger. International interest in new venture creation has grown exponentially and some of this has been delivered through the internet in distance learning formats. I personally participated in one such effort between Indiana University and City University of Hong Kong. The technology enabled us to form joint ventures between students in the United States and Hong Kong for the purpose of starting businesses. It was marvelous.

In this second edition of *Entrepreneurship: Strategies and Resources*, I have tried to improve upon the foundation set in the first edition. This book is designed to be friendlier to the user, beginning with its new design and softcover. A number of new features will help make the text easier to read and understand. Dozens of new examples and mini-cases, called "Street Stories," have been added. International examples and applications are integrated throughout the book.

Organization of the Book

Entrepreneurship: Strategies and Resources is organized into three parts. Part I introduces the major themes and theory of the book. Chapter 1 describes the roles that new venture creation plays in the international economy, defines entrepreneurship, and shows how three factors—individuals, environments, and organizations—come together to create the entrepreneurial event.

Chapter 2 sets this textbook apart from others because it casts entrepreneurial phenomena in terms of the predictive theory of the resource-based framework. In this chapter we present the basic concepts and model of the resource-based theory. There are six types of resources in our theory: financial, physical, technological, human, organizational, and reputational. The theory says that entrepreneurs can create sustainable competitive advantage for their ventures when they possess or can acquire and control resources that are rare, valuable, hard to duplicate, and nonsubstitutable. Here we emphasize the importance of human resources, especially the entrepreneur.

We then explain how these resources are a source of profit and rent for the entrepreneur and how the new venture needs to protect these rents and profits through isolating mechanisms and first mover advantages. Lastly, we offer a model of resource-based feasibility analysis to guide the student throughout the rest of the book.

Part II of *Entrepreneurship: Strategies and Resources* describes the environment for entrepreneurship. It presents the tools and techniques for analyzing business and competitive conditions and evaluating entrepreneurial opportunities. It is comparable to the strategy formulation phase of corporate strategic management. The purpose of this section is to show how the environment affects, directs, and impinges on the strategy formulation problem in new venture creation. It does this in two ways that can be expressed by the resource-based model: the environment helps determine what is rare, valuable, imitable, and substitutable **and** it is the source of resources that possess these four attributes. The strategy formulation problem in new venture creation can be stated as follows: What configuration of resources will provide the new firm with the best chances of achieving a competitive advantage?

Chapter 3 covers the aspects of the macro and micro environment that affect entrepreneurship and new venture creation. We present a process model for environmental analysis and then describe a six-element model of the macro environment: political, economic, technological, socio-demographic, and ecological factors. Next we offer the elements of the competitive environment. We incorporate the Porter Model (5-forces model) into the analysis. We begin by asking two questions of utmost importance to the entrepreneur in the early stages of new venture creation:

1. Is the industry the entrepreneur about to enter an attractive one?
2. What are the best ways to compete to increase the chances of creating a high profitability venture?

To address the first question, the chapter depicts an industry's profitability as a function of buyer and supplier power, the threat of substitutes, entry barriers, and the state of inter-firm rivalry. Students are shown how to do this analysis in sufficient depth and with limited data by resorting to the basics of microeconomic theory. To address the second question we discuss the ways that the possession and acquisition of the four-attribute resource-base provides the entrepreneur with tools to overcome strong industry forces and exploit weak industry forces. The resource-based model is incorporated into this discussion by demonstrating its applicability as a screening device for new venture ideas. We create and describe a resource-based implementation matrix—the four attributes of sustainable competitive advantage by the six types of resources: financial, physical, technological, reputational, human, and organizational resources.

Chapter 4 presents types of new venture strategies and examines different positions that entrepreneurs take regarding the resources required for their firms. We present the basic entry wedges available to the new venture and develop the set of resource-based strategies. We look at how the industry life cycle influences strategy choice. New ventures can be created successfully across the life cycle, but each poses its special challenges. The chapter concludes with an overview of strategic postures and orientations that entrepreneurs can take.

Chapter 5 presents the major tool for formulating and creating new ventures: the business plan. We offer an in-depth outline for a business plan, including all the key sections and tips on how to structure the plan and the financial proposal for maximum effectiveness. The chapter continues with a discussion of the criteria and techniques for evaluating business plans. At the end of the chapter we offer proven tips for the format and presentation, writing, and editing of successful business plans.

Part III of *Entrepreneurship: Strategies and Resources* makes the transition from the formulation of entrepreneurial strategy to the implementation stage. The section covers strategic choice, implementation issues, and the problems of securing resources.

Chapter 6 discusses the implementation of a marketing strategy for the new venture. The special problems of marketing a new venture are covered. In addition, the traditional "4 Ps" of marketing are refocused as problems of resource acquisition: access to markets, products, channels of distribution, and creative promotional campaigns. Chapter 6 provides the link between market analysis and marketing. The chapter concludes with a series of methodologies that can be employed by entrepreneurs to make sales forecasts. We complete the chapter with a comprehensive case showing an example of effective sales forecasting for a start-up business.

Chapter 7 begins where Chapter 6 leaves off—the first element of any financial analysis begins with the top line, the sales forecasts. We discuss how financial resources can and cannot be a source of advantage for the new venture. Then we show how the venture can determine its financial and cash flow needs. After reviewing the types and sources of potential financing, we present three methods of new venture valuation. The chapter has two appendices: a case depicting the actual calculation of start-up expenses for a new venture, and a brief introduction into the process of going public.

Chapter 8 shows how entrepreneurs actually obtain investors and structure the financial deal. We look at the characteristics of various types of investors and how to appeal to their needs. The basic elements of the deal structure are presented, and then more advanced elements, such as phased financing and the use of options, are introduced. The chapter concludes with a review of the legal and tax issues raised by seeking outside investors. This chapter has an appendix describing the negotiable terms to a financial agreement .

Chapter 9 examines the creation and development of the organization. We begin with a discussion of the top management team and provide guidelines for effective top management processes. We do the same for boards of directors. Then we discuss the design of the new venture. The organizational design question is: What are the boundaries of the new venture? What things should the new venture do for itself and what things should it subcontract and procure on the market? Similarly, the physical resource question is: What things should the firm own for itself and which things should it lease or contract for? Both of these questions can be handled within the resource-based theory. Last we offer a vision of the entrepreneurial workplace. We discuss how culture, ethics, and personnel practices can help make organizations unique and therefore provide a competitive advantage.

Chapter 10 discusses corporate entrepreneurship (intrapreneurship) and the factors that lead to successful intrapreneurship and those that hinder large corporations from being entrepreneurial. The second section discusses franchising. We discuss what elements make a business concept a legitimate franchise opportunity, and what factors potential franchisees should evaluate before buying a franchise. For both sections we offer guidelines for effective decision making.

Pedagogic Features

The second edition of *Entrepreneurship: Strategies and Resources* provides several features that are designed to aid the learning process:

- **Chapter outlines** at the beginning of each chapter inform the students about what they should know about entrepreneurship when they complete the reading.
- **Chapter objectives** blueprint concepts the student should understand upon completion of the chapter.
- **E-Notes** capsulize important entrepreneurship concepts for the student in a boxed format throughout each chapter.
- **Theory-based text** enables the student to analyze, evaluate, and predict the prospects for various business concepts and plans and make recommendations that increase the venture's chances.
- **Practical applications and guidelines** are offered in all the chapters to show the student how to deal with the real-world of entrepreneurs, markets, and competitors.
- **Street Stories** is the name of our boxed series of mini-cases. Each chapter contains these real-life examples drawn from the pages of the business press. Each Street Story illustrates the application of good theory to everyday new venture creation.
- **Tables and figures** throughout the book help illustrate difficult points and summarize the material for the student.
- **Extensive references** at the end of each chapter provide documentation for all of the arguments offered and enable the student to follow-up with additional reading.
- **End of chapter case and questions** provide the basis for stimulating discussion. Adapted from real situations described in the business press, these short cases are provocative illustrations of what can go right and what can go wrong in the process of new venture creation.
- **Key terms** are listed at the end of each chapter so that the student can be familiar with the language in use of entrepreneurship.
- **Chapter discussion questions** can provide the basis of classroom debate as well as be used for written assignments.
- **Chapter exercises** are designed for two purposes. The first is to aid the student in the development of his or her own business plan. The exercises guide the students to complete the portion of their plan covered in the chapter. Chapter exercises can also be used to complement the classroom experience by having the student go out into the business community to observe entrepreneurship first hand.
- **End of text cases** provide an in-depth learning exercise for the student. We have prepared 10 cases for analysis. The cases deal with the problems and opportunities of new venture creation, of securing resources, of building reputations, and of operating in a competitive market. The instructor's manual offers a comprehensive teaching note for each case.
- **Venture capital simulation** is a hands-on, multiple period, interpersonal team exercise that simulates the preparation, presentation, and negotiation of the terms of a venture capital investment. This gives the students the opportunity for personal and emotional learning, since the simulation produces much of the

same sort of tension, frustration, excitement, and exhilaration that entrepreneurs report. Detailed instructions on how to use the simulation and tips on making it a success are included in the instructor's manual.
- **Name and subject indexes** at the end of the book aid in finding topics and key people and companies.
- **State-of-the-art design** makes the book more readable and enhances learning.

Acknowledgments

As with the first edition, there are many people to thank for helping to bring this work together. From Prentice Hall there are major contributions and much support from my editor Stephanie Johnson, production manager Maureen Wilson, and Natalie Anderson who believed in the value of the book from the start.

I have been very fortunate to work for deans and department chairs who have supported my efforts. I thank Dean Dan Dalton and my Department Chair Harve Hegarty of the Kelley School of Business, Indiana University. I also thank Anne Tsui, the Department Head of Hong Kong University of Science and Technology, and Dean Ushio Sumita, Dean of International Management, International University of Japan.

A special thank you goes to my wife Mimi who helped with editing, proofreading, organizing materials, and wholehearted enthusiasm for the project.

Finally I would like to thank the reviewers of this book and the adopters of the first edition of the book for their many helpful comments and suggestions. All errors of commission and omission are mine alone.

Sol Ahiarah, Buffalo State University
John Butler, University of Washington
William B. Gartner, University of Southern California
Armand Gilinsky, Sonoma State University
Charles Hofer, University of Georgia
Roger Hutt, Arizona State University
Jane Ives, University of Massachusetts
Jack Kaplan, Columbia University
Katherine Klein, University of Maryland
Rahul Kochar, Metropolitan State College
Dennis Logue, Amos Tuck School, Dartmouth University
Walter W. Manley II, Florida State University
Richard L. McCline, San Francisco State University
Jim Nolen, University of Texas at Austin
John O'Del, Averett College
Jerry Osteryoung, Florida State University
Thomas Parkinson, Northwestern University
Edward Rogoff, Baruch College
William R. Soukup, University of San Diego
Justin Tan, California State University—San Marcos
Warren C. Weber, California Polytechnic University—Pomona

Marc Dollinger

About the Author

Marc J. Dollinger is Professor of Management in the School of Business, Indiana University. He is also a Fellow of Indiana University's Center for Entrepreneurship and Innovation. He received his PhD in Business and Economics from Lehigh University in 1983. Prior to receiving his doctorate, he was the Program Administrator of Lehigh's Small Business Development Center. Professor Dollinger conducts research in entrepreneurship and small business and teaches undergraduate and MBA entrepreneurship, venture growth management, new venture business planning, and small firm creativity and innovation classes. He has published articles in the *Academy of Management Journal, Academy of Management Review, Strategic Management Journal, Journal of Management, Entrepreneurship: Theory and Practice, Journal of Small Business Management*, and many others. He has served on the editorial review board of the *Academy of Management Review, Entrepreneurship: Theory and Practice, Journal of Small Business Management*, and the *Journal of Small Business Strategy*. In 1990, Professor Dollinger's research was recognized by the *Academy of Management Review* when he received the Best Paper Award. In 1993 he received the Alpha Kappa Psi award for Teaching Excellence in Management. He is a participant in the national Entrepreneurship Research Consortium, which is currently conducting the largest study of nascent entrepreneurs ever attempted. His students have frequently been finalists in national business plan competitions.

ENTREPRENEURSHIP
Strategies and Resources

CHAPTER 1

A Framework for Entrepreneurship

In school, getting one right out of one is an A, whereas getting two right out of twenty is an F. In business, two for twenty is an A, whereas one for one is probably luck.

—CARY ROSEN
executive director of the National Center for Employee Ownership, Oakland, California

Outline

1

Learning Objectives

After reading this chapter you will understand:

■ How to define *entrepreneurship*,

■ How entrepreneurship may affect *your future*, whether you're an employee, a venture creator, or a consumer,

■ How to define the *resource-based theory* of sustained competitive advantage,

■ The *paradoxes* of entrepreneurship,

■ The basics of *quality* in entrepreneurial firms,

■ The components of an entrepreneur's *economic organization*.

Entrepreneurship and Your Future

A recent best-selling book on the future of business organizations, work environments, and the nature of change, *The Age of Unreason,* presented the following visions for firms and products in the twenty-first century:

- Portable phones linked to faxes and laptop computers will turn cars, trains, and airport terminals into offices.
- Monoclonal antibodies and scavenger proteins designed to locate blood fats, cancers, and viruses will be available, prolonging life and the quality of life.
- A transgenic pig developed to produce organs for human transplant will populate pig farms, transforming agriculture into medical science.
- Genetically engineered crops will be able to take nitrogen directly from the air instead of the ground, reducing the need for most fertilizer and increasing usable acreage immensely.
- Microbes that can change waste materials into energy sources are under investigation. Previously unproductive ores will be usable.
- Computerized medical expert systems will be available to all physicians; expert systems will increase the productivity of all professionals, technicians, and even the supermarkets' purchasing departments.
- Voice-sensitive computers will make keyboards and keyboarding skills irrelevant.
- Irradiated food will make all food safe to eat and fresh year round. Appetite-reducing drugs and healthier foods will let people have it both ways.
- Telecatalogues, already available in some areas, will become commonplace. Shopping at home will be standard practice, with a small charge for delivery. Personal shopping will take place on leisure and hobby functions.
- Smart cards will replace credit cards, debit cards, and keys for home and auto.
- Genetic mapping will be employed as identification devices, replacing easily overcome Personal Identification Numbers (PINs).
- Windshield maps will act as guidance screens in an auto so the driver can maintain eye contact with the road at all times.

- Mileage bills will replace road usage taxes, as cables under the roads read meters in the cars and charge different rates for different parts of the city and different times, producing the equivalent of a phone bill for your car.[1]

The resources, technologies, organizations, and people who will soon bring the world these innovations already exist. It is only a matter of time before these changes are felt in our lives. The spirit of entrepreneurship—the notion of human progress, development, achievement, and change—motivates and energizes the people and organizations that improve our lives. We need entrepreneurship to reach this future.

Each of the innovations listed will result from entrepreneurship, but even more, each creates opportunities. The changes in the way we work and play, travel and eat, start families and raise our children all create opportunities for other entrepreneurs to build businesses and organizations that exploit the new technology and trends. You might say that entrepreneurship is a self-perpetuating phenomenon: If a society has it, it is likely to get more. For societies without it, the barriers seem to be insurmountable.

A second best-seller, *Workplace 2000,* argues that entrepreneurship not only affects our lives through innovation but represents the working future for many of us.[2] As large corporations continue to lay off middle managers to realize their goals of flatter, more responsive organizations, these middle managers must "go"—and the place that they will go is into business for themselves. What will they do? They will fill the niches and markets of servicing their former employers—providing consulting, aftermarket service, and other support functions. These former middle managers will operate small entrepreneurial firms that provide high quality and value to their customers in a way that working inside the bureaucracy of a large corporation made impossible.

There are other entrepreneurial alternatives as well. In a business environment where large corporations try to stay flat, lean, and responsive, there will be a burst of growth in "micro business" firms—firms with four or fewer employees. Some of these will be started by former middle managers and executives who have been let go. Some will be started by current managers trying to beat the clock to the next wave of layoffs. Many will be started by people who have never and will never work for Fortune 1000 companies.

In addition to micro businesses, there will be more corporate-backed ventures: spinoffs, joint ventures, intrapreneurial units, and partnering arrangements. Although these organizations originate in larger corporations, they are being formed specifically to stay small and entrepreneurial, to avoid bureaucracy, and to maintain their innovative edge.

> "Throughout the 1990s, companies will be looking for business opportunities. Many companies will provide financial backing for innovative employees who are willing to take a risk and develop an idea for a new product or service . . . [people with] the greatest chance of developing an idea that can turn into a growth business will be those who get wide exposure . . . [and this exposure] will greatly increase the chance that they will identify an emerging trend or market niche that can be filled with a start-up business."[3]

You really do not need to be a futurist, however, to see that entrepreneurship will play a large and increasing role in the future of our nation's and our individual working lives. The nature of organizations, work, and employment is changing, and individuals who recognize these changes and prepare for them will be best able to succeed in the new environment. So, most people will encounter entrepreneurship through the marketplace, in new products, services, or technologies, or through their own employment. The better they understand the marketplace, the better they will be able to survive and thrive in the new entrepreneurial environment.

What is Entrepreneurship?

There have been as many definitions of entrepreneurship as there have been writers on the subject. It has been suggested that trying to define entrepreneurship may be fruitless because the term is too vague and imprecise to be useful.[4] Table 1–1 provides a short selection of definitions that have been offered.

If we examine the common elements in these definitions, we might find the following characteristics:

- Creativity and innovation
- Resource gathering and the founding of an economic organization
- The chance for gain (or increase) under risk and uncertainty

Entrepreneurship, then, is the creation of an innovative economic organization (or network of organizations) for the purpose of gain or growth under conditions of risk and uncertainty.[5] What are the implications of this definition?

TABLE 1–1 Definitions of Entrepreneurship	
Source	*Definition*
Knight (1921)	Profits from bearing uncertainty and risk
Schumpeter (1934)	Carrying out of new combinations of firm organization—new products, new services, new sources of raw material, new methods of production, new markets, new forms of organization
Hoselitz (1952)	Uncertainty bearing . . . coordination of productive resources . . . introduction of innovations and the provision of capital
Cole (1959)	Purposeful activity to initiate and develop a profit-oriented business
McClelland (1961)	Moderate risk taking
Casson (1982)	Decisions and judgments about the coordination of scarce resources
Gartner (1985)	Creation of new organizations
Stevenson, Roberts & Grousbeck (1989)	The pursuit of opportunity without regard to resources currently controlled

Sources: Knight, F. *Risk, Uncertainty and Profit.* Boston: Houghton Mifflin, 1921. Schumpeter, J. *The Theory of Economic Development.* Cambridge, MA: Harvard University Press, 1934. Hoselitz, B. "Entrepreneurship and Economic Growth." *American Journal of Economic Sociology,* 1952. Cole, A. *Business Enterprise in its Social Setting.* Cambridge, MA: Harvard University, 1959, McClelland, D. *The Achieving Society,* New York: John Wiley, 1961. Casson, M. *The Entrepreneur.* Totowa, NJ: Barnes and Noble, 1982. Gartner, W. "A Conceptual Framework for Describing the Phenomenon of New Venture Creation." *Academy of Management Review* 10 (1985): 696–706. Stevenson, H., M. Roberts, and H. Grousbeck. *New Business Venture and the Entrepreneur,* Homewood, IL: Irwin, 1989.

CREATION

The term **creation** implies a founding and an origin. Therefore, technically speaking, the purchase of an existing firm or its transfer to new owners does not represent entrepreneurship. As one group of authors point out, if founding were the only criterion for entrepreneurship, then neither Watson of IBM nor Kroc of McDonald's would qualify.[6] It is rare for an organization to change ownership without a change in its management and resource configuration; however, the degree of change and innovation determines whether entrepreneurship is present. To see how large a change is needed, we can rely on Schumpeter's categories of "new combinations." Is:

- A new product or service offered?
- A new method or technology employed?
- A new market targeted and opened?
- A new source of supply of raw materials and resources used?
- A new form of industrial organization created?
  (Perhaps the rarest of all innovations.)

Now we can see how Watson and Kroc can reapply for membership in the entrepreneur's club.

ECONOMIC ORGANIZATION

The term **economic organization** means an organization whose purpose is to allocate scarce resources. This can be a firm, a business unit within a firm, a network of independent organizations, or a not-for-profit organization (NPO).[7] In what may seem paradoxical to many people, even governments can create entrepreneurial organizations under the right conditions. The business organization can, of course, pursue gain and growth as its motivations. In fact, some firms use both profit and size as their main objectives.[8] Other businesses do not seek growth, which distinguishes entrepreneurial firms from small businesses.[9] Do NPOs seek gain and growth? You bet they do. Although NPOs may be prohibited by law from making profits for stockholders, they are allowed to accumulate surpluses in their accounts. And NPOs certainly seek growth: more members, more services performed, more clients served—the list may be endless.

RISK AND UNCERTAINTY

Entrepreneurship exists under conditions of **risk** and **uncertainty.** The two terms are not the same. Risk refers to the variability of outcomes (or returns). If there is no risk, the returns are certain. A firm operating in a risk-free environment would continue to expand forever, since a negative outcome could not occur. Therefore, risk is a limit to ever-expanding entrepreneurship.[10] Uncertainty refers to the confidence entrepreneurs have in their estimates of how the world works, their understanding of the causes and effects in the environment. If there is no uncertainty, then the environment can be perfectly known. If this is true, then everyone can know it (at least for a price), and it could be a source of lasting profit for anyone. Uncertainty is what makes markets and poker games. Who would continue to place bets on a hand if all the cards were face up?

> **E-NOTES 1–1 ENTREPRENEURSHIP**
> A definition of entrepreneurship includes:
> - innovation,
> - economic organization,
> - growth during risk and/or uncertainty.

Where Is Entrepreneurship?

Two conditions must exist in order for entrepreneurship to flourish. First, there must be freedom: freedom to establish an economic venture, and freedom to be creative and innovative with that enterprise. Second, there must be prosperity: favorable economic conditions that give an entrepreneurial organization the opportunity to gain and grow.

ECONOMIC GROWTH AND FREEDOM

An annual Index of Economic Freedom published by the Heritage Foundation and the *Wall Street Journal* examines the trade policies, taxation, government intervention, monetary policies, and six other categories of 150 countries in order to rank them according to their level of economic freedom. In the 1997 edition, Hong Kong was rated the economically freest country in the world. (Of course, this ranking was based on conditions evaluated prior to the June 30, 1997 return of Hong Kong to the PRC.) Other countries included in the top ten Index of Economic Freedom include Singapore, Bahrain, New Zealand, Switzerland, the United States, the United Kingdom, Taiwan, the Bahamas, and the Netherlands. The ten countries with the lowest level of economic freedom were Angola, Azerbaijan, Iran, Libya, Somalia, Vietnam, Iraq, Cuba, and Laos, with North Korea being the country rated with the least amount of economic freedom.[11] Data collected by the Index supports several conclusions that are important for entrepreneurs and the study of entrepreneurship. First, the study demonstrates there is a strong correlation between a high level of economic freedom and a high standard of living. Second, a comparison of Index data over several years indicates that as wealthy countries become rich, they often impose fiscal restrictions that reduce economic freedom, such as higher taxation and social welfare programs. Four of the top ten countries in the 1996 Index (Switzerland, the Netherlands, Denmark, and Luxembourg) had lower ranking scores in the 1997 Index for this reason. Index data also suggests that countries with low standards of living are not poor because their wealthier neighbors fail to provide aid programs and investment capital. These countries are poor because their governments limit the economic freedom which would allow free enterprise to prosper. While the Index does not evaluate political freedom, many of the countries at the bottom of the economic freedom ranking also have a poor record on human rights.

Two examples from formerly communist economies illustrate how important economic freedom can be to entrepreneurship. After years of exile in France, Anoa Dussol-Perran returned to her native Vietnam to open a passenger-helicopter service in Hanoi. To avoid a possible three-year wait for government approval, Ms. Dussol attempted to smuggle her first helicopter into Vietnam without filing the proper paperwork. The helicopter was discovered and impounded by the Vietnamese government. It was released to Ms. Dussol only after a long wait, followed by a grueling 6-hour interview. When the time came to add a second helicopter to her service, Ms. Dussol elected to fly the new equipment from Paris to Hanoi herself rather than risk importing another machine.[12]

In contrast Jake Weinstock and his two partners have enjoyed relatively smooth sailing as they set up a Gold's Gym franchise in Moscow. While Russia is still ranked as relatively unfree in the Index of Economic Freedom, it did place 29 slots above Vietnam in the 1997 survey. Weinstock was able to avoid customs problems with his imported equipment—reportedly the toughest hurdle for new businesses in Russia—by letting his Russian partner, a former athlete and sporting goods trader, handle those negotiations. He has also been able to avoid the organized crime threats that plague other foreign businesses. "We built up many relationships and alliances, which meant we were less susceptible to shakedowns," explains Weinstock. "We made sure important people were interested in our success."[13]

Both Dussol and Weinstock are optimistic about their businesses' prospects for success. But we can see that Weinstock has a slight entrepreneurial advantage, because he's operating in an economy where he can be a little looser and a little more innovative. In Street Stories 1–1 we'll see that many young Americans are now interested in flexing their creative business muscles outside the United States.

STREET STORIES 1–1

Young Entrepreneurs Abroad

"The Iron Curtain's collapse was not just about politics," explains 33-year-old Daniel Arbess, an attorney with the prestigious New York law firm of White & Case. "It was also an unprecedented business opportunity."

Arbess should know, because the loosening of communist controls in Czechoslovakia transformed him into the youngest partner ever at White & Case. While vacationing in Prague in 1989, Arbess perceived that significant foreign investment was about to occur in the emerging democracy, and he boldly convinced the Czech government to hire his firm to handle the legal work for the $6.4 billion-dollar sale of the Skoda Auto Company to Volkswagen.

In 1989, there were less than 100 Americans living in the Czech Republic. Today, it is estimated there are 30,000 Americans living there. "We have more students interested in going to Prague than Chicago," says Colleen Troy, director of communications at NYU's Stern School of Business. White & Case has a dozen lawyers assigned to the Czech Republic now, and Daniel Arbess shuttles between its New York and Prague offices, unless he's off to Morocco, Turkey, or Vietnam pursuing new deals.

Many young entrepreneurs find the lure of foreign lands to be irresistible. It is estimated there are 250,000 U.S. citizens now living abroad. Many business schools report the same phenomenon as Northwestern's Kellogg School of Management: more than a third of their students now include a trip abroad as part of their studies, whereas virtually none of them traveled overseas for study five years ago. While the United States and other developed countries are experiencing slow or modest growth, regions such as Eastern Europe, Southeast Asia, Latin America, and South Africa seem to be poised on the brink of rapid expansion. Entrepreneurs willing to relocate there are placed on the fast track, too. "Here I am responsible for multimillion-dollar deals," says Eric Woo, who took a job with AT&T in Hong Kong after receiving his M.B.A. from Northwestern. "If I return home, I will be far ahead."

Some of the most promising new ventures abroad have decidedly American roots. Michael Giles and his Quick-Wash-Dry Clean USA corporation are building a chain of 108 coin-operated laundromats to serve Soweto and other black townships near Johannesburg, South Africa. Eugene Matthews has an $18 million dollar deal to import 20,000 dairy cattle and establish two state-of-the-art dairy farms in Vietnam. Harvard grads Robert Brooker and Adam Haven-Weiss have opened three bagel restaurants in Budapest. "In the United States there is so much competition," observes Brooker. "Here you don't have to reinvent the wheel."

Americans heading abroad have some distinct advantages. Start-up costs, including labor and material expenses, tend to be lower than costs in the United States. In many places there's a definite demand for American law, accounting, and business techniques. "Americans bring a special know-how in management, commerce, and contact building," observes Martin Procel, director of the U.S.-Argentinean Chamber of Commerce in Buenos Aires. According to David Wheeling, an analyst with Baring Securities in Brazil, just being an American is a plus. "You can get to talk to a company CEO a lot more easily than in the U.S.," he says.

American entrepreneurs are bound to have an even better experience abroad now that some of their compatriots have established a beachhead. "New expatriates have it easy," according to Kenneth Nash, a cartoonist living in Prague. "I remember when you couldn't get a decent *caffe latte* in this town."

Source: Adapted from William Echikson, "Young Americans Go Abroad to Strike It Rich," *Fortune,* October 17, 1994, 185–194.

AROUND THE WORLD

With high levels of freedom and prosperity, conditions are obviously favorable for entrepreneurship in the United States. Many examples throughout this book demonstrate this. However, in some parts of the United States, there are more opportunities than entrepreneurs. South Central Los Angeles in California is one of those places. Virtually gutted by riots in 1992, this area is now rebuilding slowly. A community-development bank set up by the Clinton Administration has placed only $23 million of the $400 million in federal funds they had hoped to lend to small businesses. Studies show that the purchasing power of area residents is far greater than existing businesses can serve, meaning that residents often leave the community to shop elsewhere. The density of competition is low, and the city of Los Angeles has been cooperative with permits,[14] but the level of risk and uncertainty in a place that has become famous for unrest is obviously too high for many would-be entrepreneurs.

The New Entrepreneur

Ask any group of businesspeople today if they consider themselves to be entrepreneurs. According to Bill Sahlman, professor and senior associate dean at the Harvard Business School, "most of them will raise their hands. That doesn't mean that they are entrepreneurial, but they would certainly not like you to think they aren't."[15]

If entrepreneurship is one of the hot labels today, it's because the concept of being an entrepreneur has changed. Fifteen years ago an entrepreneur might have been described as a business version of a John Wayne cowboy (tough and gutsy and significantly male) who steered his business through the rodeo of commerce without the help of training or education, and without the assistance of bankers or other experts. Entrepreneurs were once seen as small business founders with a strong independent streak, and maybe a flair for the dramatic. Entrepreneurs were once born, not made.

Things are different now (see Table 1–2). What is emerging today is a class of *professional entrepreneurs* who rely more upon their brains than their guts—and who have been trained to use both methods and technology to analyze the business envi-

TABLE 1–2 Entrepreneurs	
Then	*and Now*
Small-business founder	True entrepreneur
Boss	Leader
Lone Ranger	Networker
Secretive	Open
Self-reliant	Inquisitive
Seat-of-the-pants	Business Plan
Snap decisions	Consensus
Male ownership	Mixed ownership
	In 1993 women owned one-third of all sole proprietorships, up from one-quarter in 1980
Idea	*Execution*
In 1982, 80% of the CEO's of the *Inc.* 500 believed their companies' success was based on novel, unique or proprietary ideas	1992, 80% of the CEOs of *Inc.* 500 said that the ideas for their companies were ordinary, and that they owned their success of superior execution
Knows the Trade	*Knows the Business*
Eastern, one of the first airlines in the United States, was founded by pilot Eddie Rickenbacker	Federal Express, an overnight delivery service utilizing airplanes, was developed from a business plan written by Fred Smith while he was studying for his M.B.A.
Automation	*Innovation*
Technology lets business automate the work people had always done	Technology lets people do things never done before

Source: Adapted from Tom Richman, "The Evolution of the Professional Entrepreneur," *Inc.'s The State of Small Business Special Issue,* 1997, pp. 50–53.

A Compulsion to Create

The desire to create new businesses "is something I can't turn off," says serial entrepreneur Stuart D. Edwards. "It's a compulsion."

That compulsion has driven Edwards to create or co-found seven medical devices companies, one on the heels of another, during a five-year period in California's Silicon Valley. "I enjoy (managing) a company up to a point," he explains. "Then I want to go and do another thing."

Serial entrepreneurship is a relatively recent phenomenon, but one that is popular with investors. Seasoned business launchers are considered less risky than neophytes without a track record. Moreover, successful entrepreneurs often have plenty of cash of their own from sellouts and IPOs to invest in a new venture. Veteran start-up creators like Edwards usually have an established group of managers and advisers who travel with them from company to company. And sometimes they can even contribute technology to a new project. Two years after he created VidaMed Inc., a company whose product treats enlarged prostates, Edwards spun off some of that technology into a new firm which created a similar product to treat urological disorders.

Edwards' start-up method requires lots of cash. He likes to invest a lot of money up front in equipment in order to build and improve his medical devices internally, rather than outsourcing production like many new ventures. It's a financial gamble because it means that the company must either go public quickly or sell out at a very high price to avoid being saddled with unmanageable debt. "But he gets a product from first generation to fourth generation faster than any other entrepreneur I've been involved with," says David Douglass, general partner with the Delphi Ventures capital firm who has invested in three Edwards start-ups.

Edwards' compulsion to create businesses apparently grew out of his compulsion to simply create. A mechanical engineer by training, Edwards has now patented over 200 inventions. Born in England, Edwards spent almost 20 years working as an engineer for U.S. health-care giants including Abbott Laboratories and Baxter International before signing on as a senior manager for a start-up company called EP Technologies. While there, Edwards helped develop a line of products that utilize radio-frequency energy to shrink tissue. Edwards left in 1992 to start VitaMed, after filing suit against EP Technologies for an equity stake.

Despite Edwards' obsession to move on and start new businesses, he says that each of his start-ups is "like one of my offspring." In addition to VitaMed, the Edwards family includes Rita Medical Systems Inc., Oratec Interventions Inc., and Somnus Medical Technologies, Inc., which creates products to relieve severe snoring problems. Edwards serves on the board of directors for each company and continues to offer informal advice. And like other good offspring, each of the seven companies is still located within minutes of Edwards' Portola Valley, California home.

Source: Adapted from Stephanie N. Mehta, "Inventory Thrives on Founding Start-Ups," *Wall Street Journal,* April 29, 1997, B1.

ronment. According to Bill Wetzel, professor at the University of New Hampshire, the difference is like night and day. Wetzel says that the old-style entrepreneur of business founders was thought primarily to be about earning a living, while today's entrepreneur "has the intention of building a significant company that can create wealth for the entrepreneur and investors."[16]

The new entrepreneurs come from different sources, too. Many of them are corporate-track dropouts, pushed out by downsizing or lured out by the quest for status, big money, or control of their personal lives. Globalization has promoted an entrepreneurial spirit in both big and small companies, while information technology now enables many small start-ups to compete against big business.

Academia has contributed to the creation of this new professional entrepreneur class, too. Harvard Business School, which once had three or four professors teaching courses about small business, now has 17 full-time faculty in its entrepreneurial-studies program. Staffing at other colleges and universities reflects the same trend. The content of many finance, marketing, and other business courses has also been adjusted to reflect new venture concerns and development methods. The new class of entrepreneurs don't just do, they understand what they're doing.[17]

Entrepreneurial activity often leads to more of the same. In Street Stories 1–2 we see how the thrill of creating new products and new companies has led to a string of new ventures for one of the new class of entrepreneurs.

Dimensions of Entrepreneurship

NEW VENTURE CREATION

This book is concerned with entrepreneurship as the formation of a new business enterprise. This is most often called simply **new venture creation.** It contains theory and research about, and descriptions of, practice and techniques of entrepreneurship. We take an economic and managerial perspective on entrepreneurship and new venture creation, although at times we borrow important material from other disciplines. Much has been written about the phenomenon of entrepreneurship and new venture creation from the economic and managerial perspectives. There have been numerous descriptive studies and some valuable empirical research. But no textbook, including this one, can offer prospective entrepreneurs advice that will ensure their success. As the introductory quote illustrates, not enough is known about entrepreneurship (or business in general) for it to be considered a "sure thing." In fact, any guidance obtained from a book is probably of little long-term value to a potential entrepreneur.[18] However, the insights a reader gains by comparing personal experience with the material in this book may be invaluable.

RESOURCES, CAPABILITIES, AND STRATEGIES

The foundation for this book is the **resource-based theory** of sustained competitive advantage.[19] The resource-based theory is the most appropriate to understand new venture creation because it best describes how entrepreneurs themselves build their businesses from the resources and capabilities they currently possess or can realistically acquire. Successful entrepreneurship is not simply an analytical exercise. Industry and competitor analysis—the application of the theory of industrial organization economics—alone is insufficient. The resource-based theory argues that the choice of which industry to enter and what business to be in is not enough to ensure success. The theory says that the nature and quality of the resources, capabilities, and strategies the entrepreneur possesses and can acquire can lead to long-term success.

Using resources that are rare, valuable, hard to copy, and have no good substitutes[20] in favorable industry conditions provides sustainable competitive advantage. Choosing the appropriate resources is ultimately a matter of entrepreneurial vision and intuition. The creative act underlying such vision is a subject that has so far not been a central focus of resource-based theory. This book extends the theory and views entrepreneurship within the context of resource-based theory of the firm.[21]

E-NOTES 1–2   RESOURCE-BASED THEORY

The resource-based theory utilized in this book states that an entrepreneur uses resources that are:

- rare,
- valuable,
- hard-to-copy,
- have no good substitutes to obtain a sustainable competitive advantage.

Intelligence Versus Business Success   The resource-based theory of entrepreneurship also helps explain two of the paradoxes of entrepreneurship in ways that other theories cannot. The first paradox is often stated as, "If you are so smart, why aren't you rich?" Certainly professors and researchers can testify that there are a great many more smart people than rich people. A good theory of entrepreneurship needs to explain why intelligence does not always lead to success in business. Common logic seems to dictate that the better we understand a phenomenon such as new venture creation, the more likely we are to be successful in its practice. Textbook presentations of entrepreneurship that provide facts without examining cause and effect may make the student smarter (in some narrow sense), but these approaches are unlikely to make anyone (except the authors) richer.

The resource-based approach acknowledges that keen analysis (strategy formulation) and fact accumulation are necessary but insufficient tasks for entrepreneurs. Also, the resource-based theory follows the reality that some aspects of entrepreneurship cannot be analyzed; they are hard to copy because no one, including the founders, quite understands how or why they work. This inability to be duplicated or explained is actually a business advantage because competitors cannot copy the entrepreneur's strategy if they can't understand it. In simple language, what is known (or knowable) to all is an advantage to none. So you can get smarter without getting richer if the knowledge you possess lacks any of the four characteristics (rare, valuable, hard to copy, no substitutes).[22]

Barriers to Entry   The second paradox is summed up by the old punch line, "You wouldn't want to belong to any club that would have you as a member." The parallel application of this saying to new venture creation is that "you wouldn't want to enter any industry that would have you" (low-entry barriers) because if you could get in, then anyone could. Therefore, the opportunity will appear unattractive. This is the traditional economic analysis that examines the height of the entry

Sam Walton's Ten Best Rules

Sam Walton was born in 1918 and died in 1992. In between he built the largest, most successful retail organization in the world and became America's richest person. His chosen path to empire was either "overlooked or under-estimated by his rivals."

He began his life in humble beginnings but graduated from the University of Missouri and went right to work for J.C. Penney in 1940 for $75 per month. He loved retailing and the competitiveness of it. He bought his own store, a Ben Franklin, when he was mustered out of the Army in 1945. But it was not until 1962 that the first Wal-Mart was opened.

In between, Mr. Sam developed many of the habits and garnered the experience that was to serve him so well later. He says his big lesson came early when he found that if he "bought an item for 80 cents . . . and priced it at a dollar, [he] could sell three times more of it than by pricing it at $1.20. I might have made only half the profit per item but because I was selling three times as many, the overall profit was much greater."

In the early 1960s, Mr. Sam discovered that others were beginning to develop large discount stores and chains. He did his homework and spent many nights on the road visiting these other merchants' stores. He admits that he "borrowed" quite a bit from Sol Price, founder of Fedmart. He finally decided that the future was discounting, and the first Wal-Mart was opened in 1962. In that year, K mart, the first Target, and Woolco stores were also opened.

Ten years after the opening of the first Wal-Mart, the scoreboard read: K mart, 500 stores and $3 billion sales; Wal-Mart, 50 stores and $80 million sales. In addition, the four leading retailers of the first half of the century—Sears, J.C. Penney, Woolworth, and Montgomery Ward—were still flourishing, and every urban area had a regional department store or chain to compete with. Many had resources far in excess of Walton's. So how did Mr. Sam become number one?

In a book written shortly before his death in 1992, Mr. Sam was asked about this. He said that the keys were (1) going head to head with K mart, because the pressure of the competition made everyone a better retailer and encouraged innovation and change; (2) going small-town (under 50,000 people), because it was an underserved niche; (3) employee profit sharing, because it made everyone an owner directed toward the same goal; and (4) communication and sharing information with all people inside the organization, because it empowered people and pushed responsibility for decision making down. Sam wouldn't say it, but a fifth factor was his tireless and unceasing dedication to keeping costs down and spirits up. His leadership was unparalleled by any of his competitors.

So it's clear that Mr. Sam possessed personal experience, values, vision, and dedication in heroic proportions, unequaled by any of his rivals. But were his business decisions so unique that they cannot or could not be duplicated by another firm? When asked this question Mr. Sam came up with his ten rules to follow, rules that worked for him. If you follow these rules, can you be the next Sam Walton?

Rule 1:   Commit to your business and believe in it.

Rule 2:   Share your profits with your partners (employees).

Rule 3:   Motivate your partners, challenge them, and keep score.

Rule 4:   Communicate everything.

Rule 5:   Appreciate your associates with well-chosen words.

Rule 6:   Celebrate your successes.

Rule 7:   Listen to everyone and get them talking.

Rule 8:   Exceed your customer' expectations.

Rule 9:   Control your expenses.

Rule 10: BREAK ALL THE RULES. Swim upstream. Go the other way.

Rule 10 is a doozy (as well as a paradox). It suggests that rules 1 through 9 may not be for everyone. And it suggests that Mr. Sam himself knew that if you followed everyone's advice on everything, you could never achieve much more than everyone else did. Just as Mr. Sam visited as many K marts as he could, everyone who paid attention could have visited all the Wal-Marts and copied what they did. You could easily duplicate rules 1–9, but you could never duplicate precisely the decisions that were made following rule 10. This is the unique and idiosyncratic aspect that made Mr. Sam the world's greatest merchant.

Source: Fortune, March 23, 1992, pp. 113–114, and June 29, 1992, pp. 98–106.

barriers and weighs the cost of entry against the profit potential (margins) of firms in the industry and the probability of retaliation by incumbents.[23] One implication of this analysis is that, for the vast majority of economic organizations, the existing firms have the edge. Yet, experience indicates that certain individuals create businesses in industries with seemingly insurmountable barriers, and these individuals achieve superior and sometimes spectacular results. Analysis of industry structure fails to explain this because it cannot explain why everyone cannot follow. The resource-based theory can explain the likes of Sam Walton founder of Wal-Mart (see Street Story 1–3), Ted Turner of Turner Broadcasting, and Dave Thomas of Wendy's as individuals with unique personal resources. They were able to enter industries that appeared to have powerful predatory competitors and go against the odds to build major influential organizations.

There are three significant dimensions used to study entrepreneurship: individuals, environments, and organizations. These are required to flesh out the arguments and examples.[24] The interactions among individual, environments, and organizations make each new venture unique and must be considered.

INDIVIDUALS

The role that individuals play in entrepreneurship is undeniable. Each person's psychological, sociological, and demographic characteristics contribute to or detract from his or her abilities to be an entrepreneur. Personal experience, knowledge, education, and training are the accumulated human resources that the founder contributes to the enterprise. The personal integrity of the entrepreneur and the way the entrepreneur and the new venture are viewed by others is captured in the reputation of the firm. The risk profile of the entrepreneur determines the initial configuration of the venture—for example, financing, product offerings, and staffing. And although we speak now of the individual entrepreneur, frequently the entrepreneur is not alone. Entrepreneurs rely on a network of other people, other businesspeople, and other entrepreneurs. These contacts are personal resources that help them acquire additional resources and start their business. So it is true that "who you know" and "who knows you" are sometimes very valuable resources in new venture creation.

One of the most important responsibilities of the entrepreneur as an individual is the establishment of the ethical climate for the new venture.

Business **ethics** has been defined in many ways by many people. One definition of ethical behavior is: any business decision that creates value for the customer by matching quality and price. Why is this so? Ethical decisions (1) provide the customer with valid data about the product and service, (2) enable the customer to make a free and informed choice, and (3) generate customer commitment to the product and the organization that provides it. Violations of these three rules produce unethical behavior—invalid and false data, coerced and manipulated decisions, and low integrity and poor reputation for the firm.[25]

How important are ethics and a good reputation? According to one advertising executive, "The only sustainable competitive advantage any business has is its reputation."[26] Entrepreneurs are sometimes placed in situations where ethical decision making appears hard. It is tempting to cut corners, look for the edge by shading the truth, and adopt a *caveat emptor* (let the buyer beware) attitude. If entrepreneurs see themselves as outsiders, underdogs, overworked, and underappreciated, they may make decisions employing the premise that the ends justify the means. Caution is advised. The means will become known, and if the means fail the tests for ethical conduct, the fine reputation of the product and the entrepreneurial team will be irreparably tarnished.

ENVIRONMENT

The environment poses both opportunities and threats for new venture creation. The opportunities come mostly in the form of resources—money, people, technology. The entrepreneurial challenge is to acquire resources from the environment, combine them with other resources already possessed, and configure the new venture into a successful organization. The threats, or constraints, imposed by the environment are those inherent in any competitive marketplace. The entrepreneur can overcome these constraints, or protect against their worst effects, by developing strategies that exploit the firm's resources. The key elements of the environment are the government and politics, the economy, technology (i.e., innovation and invention), sociodemographics, and the ecosystem. Since the environment is characterized by change, uncertainty, and complexity, entrepreneurs must continually monitor events and trends and make adjustments to their organizations and strategies.

ORGANIZATIONS

The result of nearly all entrepreneurial start-ups is the creation of a new organization. The organization has a form and structure. It has a strategy that enables it to penetrate or create a market (entry wedges) and protect its position (isolating mechanisms). It possesses resources that it transforms into value for its customers.

But an organization can be even more than this. An organization is made up of people, who have skills and talents, values and beliefs, and maybe a recognition that by working together they can create something special. The organization can have a culture that supports high performance, and high quality.

Quality is a difficult concept to grasp, yet it is critical to success. Garvin identified five different approaches to the concept of **quality:** transcendent, product-based, user-based, manufacturing-based, and value-based.[27]

The Transcendent Approach   The transcendent approach to quality is philosophical and asks questions about the nature of things. From this viewpoint, quality is concerned with "innate excellence."[28] Some experts dismiss this approach as being of little practical value for the businessperson, but we believe it can offer some guidance. A product's or service's quality concerns the function that it is intended to serve. Anything that inhibits that function detracts from quality. For example, consider quality in terms of a restaurant meal. Its quality includes its nutritional value, premium ingredients, taste, aroma, presentation, and timeliness. A poor-quality meal lacks what is necessary and also has other qualities attached, such as slow service, foreign ingredients, poor presentation, and careless preparation. So the high-quality meal is distinguished from the poor-quality meal because it has only the elements it should and none of the detracting elements.

Product-based Approach   The product-based concept of quality focuses on an attribute of the product that is held in high regard—for example, the high butterfat content in ice cream, the tightness and intensity of evenness (consistency) of stitches in a garment, or the durability of a washing machine. Quality of this sort can be ranked because it lends itself to quantitative measurement. Because the assessment of these attributes can be made independently of the user, product-based quality is sometimes referred to as "objective" quality.[29]

User-based Approach   User-based quality is "subjective"—it exists in the eye of the beholder. Customers have different preferences, wants, and needs and therefore judge a product's quality by its usefulness to them. Are producers who meet these needs, but do so in nonquantitative ways (perhaps through advertising or superior product distribution), producing quality products? And when "subjective" quality competes with "objective" quality, is "good enough" really enough?

Manufacturing-based Approach   Manufacturing-based quality, or process quality, concerns the attention to detail in the construction and delivery of the product or service. It is linked to customer wants and needs and to objective quality because it presumes that someone defined "conformance standards" for the product or service. So

FIGURE 1-1 Dimensions of New Venture Creation

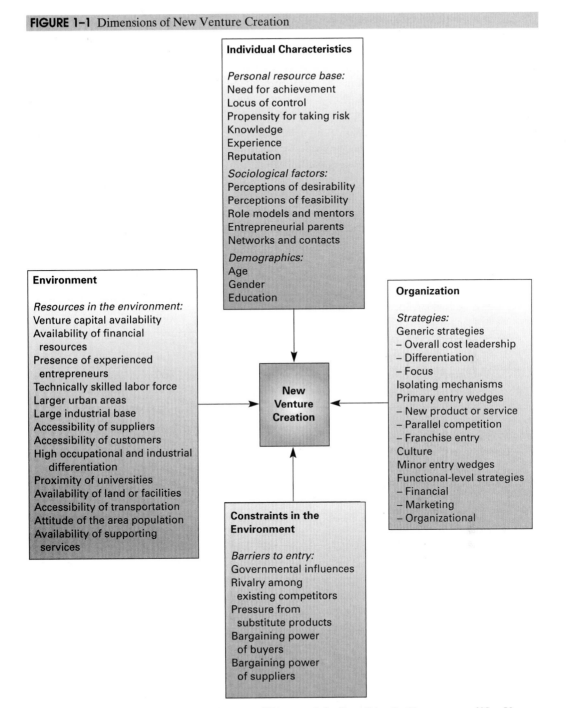

Source: Adapted from W. Gartner, "The Conceptual Framework for Describing the Phenomenon of New Venture Creation." *Academy of Management Review* 10 (1985): 696–706.

quality is defined as the degree to which the product conforms to set standards or the service to set levels and times. In other words, high reliability and zero manufacturing defects are important. The problem with this definition is that the link between standards and customer preferences was established in the past, perhaps long ago, and is not responsive to changes in the environment. Manufacturing-based quality shifts attention internally, on how things are done. At its worst, it leads to doing the wrong things but doing them very well.

Garvin's last category of quality is value-based. This approach takes the concept of quality farther than the previous definitions. **Value** evaluates quality in terms of price. This is what customers consider when they decide whether to buy a product or service. If money were not scarce, nothing would be valuable, not even quality, because everyone could buy anything. But this is, of course, not true. Therefore, in business where prices are signals and money is scarce, value, not pure quality, is critical.

Which is the correct perspective on quality and value for the entrepreneur? We believe that entrepreneurs should understand all these perspectives and be able to make decisions based on their current situations. The ability to understand many facets of quality improves the entrepreneur's decision making. It enables an entrepreneur to meet the challenges posed by complex problems. Figure 1–1 illustrates the dimensions of entrepreneurship and new venture creation.

E-NOTES 1–3 ORGANIZATIONS

An economic organization has:

- something of value to offer customers (generic strategies),
- form and structure (functional-level strategies),
- entry wedges (to penetrate or create a market),
- isolating mechanisms (to protect its position),
- a culture that determines performance and quality.

Organization of the Book

Chapter 1 provided the framework for the study of entrepreneurship, beginning with the theme that entrepreneurs succeed because of the resources that they possess and acquire, and the strategies they employ. This resource-based theory is described in greater detail in Chapter 2, where we also examine different types of resources and capabilities, and explore the relative importance of each.

Chapter 3 portrays the environment for entrepreneurship as two interrelated components: first, a remote environment which cannot be controlled by the entrepreneur, and second, a competitive environment in which the entrepreneur executes his or her strategies and plans. The importance of environmental scanning and a model for scanning are also presented in this chapter. Chapter 4 details exactly how entrepreneurs go into business by outlining methods including entry wedges, resource-based strategies, business level strategies, and international strategies, and presents a plan for evaluating those strategies.

Chapter 5 explains the basics of writing the business plan that is required for all new ventures, and depicts the transition from strategy formulation to implementation. Chapter 6 illustrates the development of a marketing plan, and discusses pricing, new product development, promotion, and sales forecasting. Chapter 7 describes the foundations of new venture financing, including debt, equity, and cash flow.

Chapter 8 shows how investors and entrepreneurs view each other, and describes how they are likely to want to structure a financial deal. This chapter also covers legal and tax issues. Chapter 9 explores building the new venture's organization and top management team. Chapter 10 describes corporate venturing, including intrapreneurship, and how large firms stay innovative and entrepreneurial.

The ten chapters are followed by a selection of cases drawn from real situations and business plans. These cases illustrate the possibilities and opportunities facing entrepreneurs—many who were once students just like you.

A Final Word

Not everyone will succeed as an entrepreneur, and sometimes the people who do succeed do so only after a number of painful attempts. As the introductory quote illustrates, studying entrepreneurship and being an entrepreneur are two different things. The odds of success are quite different in these two endeavors, and the outcomes are evaluated by different criteria. But the student of entrepreneurship should realize that he or she can be a successful entrepreneur. Previous academic achievement is not a requirement. Many of the students who excel in accounting, marketing, or finance will spend most of their careers working for entrepreneurs—people who were better at seizing opportunity than taking classroom examinations.

And try not to be too concerned about the grades you receive in this class. Consider the story of Fred Smith, founder of Federal Express. It is said that when he took the entrepreneurship course in which he proposed a nationwide delivery system for packages that would compete with the U.S. Post Office, he received the grade of C for his efforts. Sometimes the teachers of entrepreneurship have limits to their vision as well. The true test of your entrepreneurial potential is in the marketplace, not in the classroom.

Summary

The future is full of entrepreneurial opportunities, and new venture creation and entrepreneurship are changing the face of the world's businesses and economies. Historically, entrepreneurship has taken many different turns. In today's market-based economies, new venture creation is the key to technological and economic progress. Through entrepreneurship, people will continue to live better, longer, and more rewarding lives.

We have defined entrepreneurship as "the creation of an innovative economic organization (or network of organizations) for the purpose of gain or growth under conditions of risk and uncertainty." This definition enables us to make distinctions between entrepreneurship and other wealth- and income-generating activities.

Although entrepreneurs and entrepreneurship have been studied from many different perspectives, we take an economic and managerial perspective in this book. The guiding framework for our discussion and analysis of entrepreneurial opportunities is the resource-based theory of sustainable competitive advantage. This theory enables us to understand what is unique about the new venture and how the new enterprise will create value for its customers and subsequently its founders. The managerial dimensions of entrepreneurship are individuals, environments, and organizations. These dimensions provide us with a useful organizing framework to view the complex forces and interactions that produce entrepreneurial activity.

Key Terms

- Entrepreneurship
- Creation
- Economic organization
- Risk
- Uncertainty

- New venture creation
- Resource-based theory
- Quality
- Value
- Ethics

Discussion Questions

1. What would it be like to work for an entrepreneurial firm? A microbusiness? Compare this to working for a Fortune 500 firm.
2. What are Schumpeter's definitions for an entrepreneurial new venture? Give examples of businesses you know that meet these criteria.
3. What can modern societies that have little or no history of entrepreneurship (like Russia) do to encourage and sustain it?
4. What kind of changes might have to occur in a country like Vietnam or Cuba to make them more accessible to entrepreneurs?

5. What kind of American-style ventures do you think would prosper abroad, especially in those countries with a low level of economic freedom?
6. Do you think entrepreneurs are *born* or *made?*
7. Why doesn't "being smart" easily translate into "being rich"?
8. How do entrepreneurial dimensions of individuals, environments, and organizations interact to produce new ventures?
9. Discuss the different forms of quality. Why is quality important for an entrepreneur?
10. What is value? How is it created?

Exercises

1. Search the business press (*Business Week, Fortune,* The *Wall Street Journal,* and others) to identify future entrepreneurial opportunities. These could fulfill any of Schumpeter's criteria. What different options would an entrepreneur have in developing these opportunities? Could you develop these?
2. Take any of the future entrepreneurship examples at the beginning of the chapter and describe what kinds of businesses could be created from these opportunities. How would these businesses be developed? Could you develop these?
3. Interview an entrepreneur. Find out

what "rules" he or she followed to become a successful entrepreneur. Ask your entrepreneur if he or she agrees with Sam Walton's Rule 10.
4. Interview a government official in your city or county. How does this person view entrepreneurship? What does the government do to encourage or discourage entrepreneurship? Why do they do this?
5. Read a nonbusiness book or article about entrepreneurship. (Hint: Go to the library.) How is entrepreneurship treated in this material? How does it add to the economic and managerial approach we take in the business school?

Invasion on the Internet

Once Web surfing became popular, it was only matter of time until the Internet was transformed into a huge, thundering pipeline of . . . advertising! Billboard-style banner ads are spread across many Web pages, and you can purchase everything from astrological predictions to vacuum cleaners via the Internet. And in case you're one of the many Web cruisers who have learned to tune out those bright but passive banner ads, some electronic entrepreneurs have now developed new interactive ways to deliver their commercial messages.

Ad robots are perhaps the most obnoxious—oops! advanced—new method of Internet advertising. If you like to spend some of your Internet time in chat rooms, be forewarned that what you type gives listeners information about you and your lifestyle. For example, if you enter a chat room sponsored by Planet Direct of Wilmington, Massachusetts, and you happen to type in a word like *dirty,* you may receive an on-screen visit from Dusty, a cartoon character that wants to tell you all about products made by Black & Decker. Dusty looks suspiciously like one of that company's dustbuster appliances, and because this ad robot has identified you as a neatness freak, Dusty is just full of cleaning tips and product pitches from his producer.

Less obtrusive but just as tricky is the advertising method known as push technology. An example of this is the Game Ticker developed by Yoyodyne, Inc., an Internet promotions and marketing company from Irvington, New York. Game Ticker is a kind of virtual slot machine that spins new matches every four minutes in a small window on a viewer's screen. You may not have to search for Game Ticker; thanks to computer technology, it may pop up unrequested on your PC as part of a screen saver or as a companion to weather information. Every time your eyes glance at the Game Ticker you can't help but notice the small box ads from sponsors such as Duracell and Tinactin directly beneath the slot window. If Game Ticker spins three symbols in a row while you're watching, you win a prize. But the advertiser is the real winner, because you have to provide your e-mail address to claim the prize, guaranteeing that you'll also receive a lot more advertising sent directly to your computer address.

Of course you can't really get something for nothing, even on the Internet. In cyberspace you may be asked to pay in advance with your patience and undivided attention. "We didn't think the banner ads had much value" because they are easily ignored, says Michael Paolucci, CEO of Interactive Imaginations Inc. of New York. Paolucci's company produces Riddler, an Internet trivia and word game site which reports that it has about 65,000 visitors each day. While each visitor is waiting for Riddler's games to download onto their computer, they are forced to watch full-page computer screen ads from companies such as Master-Card and Snapple. Bingo Zone, an interactive bingo game site from nineCo Inc. of Boston, makes viewers sit through a succession of computer ads before they are allowed to play the game.

Innovative as these new electronic pitches may be, potential advertisers are somewhat nervous about how consumers will react. "Publishers and advertisers have the real potential to ruin their brand if they're too over the top," says Evan Neufeld, an on-line advertising analyst for the media-tracking firm of Jupiter Communications LLC of New York. Black Sun Interactive Inc. of San Francisco, creator of the server which makes the ad robots possible, claims to have a "consumer bill of rights" which any advertiser using the robots must agree to uphold. These rights stipulate that a robot must identify itself as advertising as soon as it starts talking, and that viewers must have the ability to mute the robot. Even the advertising agency which arranged for the Black & Decker ad robots isn't completely comfortable with the concept. "My mind is far from made up," says Rob Goergen, supervisor at McCann-Erickson Worldwide in New York.

Both agencies and advertisers are keeping a close watch on how consumers respond to this new interactive technology. After all, there are some people who said that the public would never tolerate any advertising on the Internet . . . and some who said that TV advertising would never work, either.

CASE QUESTIONS

1. As a consumer, how do you feel about this new advertising technology?
2. What ethical standards do you think Internet advertisers should adhere to?
3. Would you predict that interactive computer advertising will become commonplace or not?
4. Do you think the creators of these new advertising methods are entrepreneurs? Why or why not?

Source: Adapted from Rebecca Quick, "Web Sites Start Using A Much Harder Sell," *Wall Street Journal,* April 24, 1997.

Notes

1. C. Handy, *The Age of Unreason* (Cambridge, MA: Harvard Business School, 1990).
2. J. Boyette and H. Conn, *Workplace 2000* (New York, Dutton, 1991).
3. Boyette and Conn, *Workplace 2000,* p. 44.
4. M. Low and J. MacMillan, "Entrepreneurship: Past Research and Future Challengers," *Journal of Management* 14 (1988): 139–161.
5. The term "network" was added here to anticipate the possibility that the entrepreneur could create a "virtual" organization. This is an organization that employs other organizations, almost exclusively, to carry out the functions that are ordinarily thought of as within the enterprise. This will be explained in more detail in Chapter 9 in the section on organizational boundaries.
6. H. Stevenson, M. Roberts, and H. Grousbeck, *New Business Ventures and the Entrepreneur* (Homewood, IL: Irwin, 1989).
7. Some of the most entrepreneurial events happen in NPOs. Peter Drucker has written extensively about the Girl Scouts, and Max Wortman has studied entrepreneurship in church organiza-

tions. Even universities have been known to launch entrepreneurial efforts, especially recent attempts to exploit research in electronics and biotechnology.

8. W. Baumol, *Business Behavior: Value and Growth* (New York: Harcourt Brace, 1967).

9. J. Carland, F. Hoy, W. Boulton, and J. Carland, "Differentiating Entrepreneurs from Small Business Owners: A Conceptualization" *Academy of Management Review* 9 (1984): 354–359.

10. F. Penrose, *The Theory of the Growth of the Firm* (New York: John Wiley, 1959), especially pp. 56–57. This book was the precursor of the development of the resource-based theory that is the foundation for this text.

11. K. R. Holmes, "Freedom and Growth," *Wall Street Journal,* December 16, 1996, 10.

12. M. Jordan, "How One Woman Stormed Vietnam to Realize a Dream," *Wall Street Journal,* May 5, 1994, 1.

13. J. Vitullo-Martin, "Moscow Entrepreneurs Seize Golden Opportunity," *Wall Street Journal,* January 20, 1997, A11.

14. B. A. Holden and J. R. Emshwiller, "Selling Paint, Salsa and Cappuccino on Site of L.A. Riot," *Wall Street Journal,* April 24, 1997, B1.

15. T. Richman, "Creators of the New Economy," *Inc.'s The State of Small Business* (1997): 44–48.

16. Ibid.

17. Ibid.

18. In fact, one professor of entrepreneurship referred to the teaching and taking of entrepreneurship courses as oxymoronic—the juxtaposition of two incompatible ideas.

19. Although a case can be made that the origins of the theory can be claimed by E. Penrose in her 1959 book, *The Theory of the Growth of the Firm* (New York: Wiley), it really is not until the mid-1980s that the resource-based theory of sustained competitive advantage began to be explored and developed in management terms. Two particularly salient articles are: J. Barney, "Firm Resources and Sustained Competitive Advantage," *Journal of Management* 17 (1991): 99–120, and K. Conner, "A Historical Comparison of Resource-based Theory and Five Schools of Thought within Industrial Organization Economics: Do We Have a New Theory of the Firm?" *Journal of Management* 17 (1991): 121–154. Barney and Conner make the initial claim that this theory may supersede others as a theory of the firm.

20. These terms will be defined and their meanings elaborated in the next chapter.

21. Conner, 1991.

22. Rather than repeat the four desirable attributes of resources over and over throughout the book, we will adopt the convention of calling them "the four attributes" of the resource-based model.

23. J. Bain, "Economics of Scale, Concentration, and the Conditions of Entry in Twenty Manufacturing Industries," *American Economic Review* 44 (1954): 15–39; M. Porter, *Competitive Strategy* (New York: Free Press, 1980).

24. W. Gartner, "A Conceptual Framework for Describing the Phenomenon of New Venture Creation," *Academy of Management Review* 10 (1985): 696–706.

25. This brief discussion owes its genesis to Chris Argyris' discussion of the ethics of a consultant in *Intervention Theory and Method: A Behavioral Science View* (Reading, MA: Addison Wesley, 1973).

26. S. Caminiti, "A Payoff from a Good Reputation," *Fortune,* February 10, 1992, pp. 74–77. This is a quote from Laurel Cutler.

27. D. Garvin, *Managing Quality* (New York: Free Press, 1988). See Chapters 3 and 4 for a detailed discussion. This is one of the seminal books that launched the "quality" revolution in the United States.

28. Garvin, 1988, p. 41.

29. Garvin, 1988, p. 43.

CHAPTER

2

Resources
and Capabilities

Outline

There is nothing as practical as a good theory.
—KARL POPPER

Learning Objectives

After reading this chapter you will understand:

- Various approaches and theories about *entrepreneurship*.

- The *resource-based theory of entrepreneurship*, which explains how new firms can obtain and sustain competitive advantage.

- *Strategic resources*, and how these resources influence success.

- Some of the misconceptions about *personality traits* and the entrepreneurial personality.

- Why and how an entrepreneur is the primary *human resource* for a new venture.

- The components of the *entrepreneurial event*, which is the creation of a new venture.

Why do entrepreneurs need a theory of entrepreneurship? Because it enables its user to be efficient. Efficiency for the entrepreneur means recognizing what kinds of information are helpful and knowing where it can be obtained. The efficient entrepreneur uses the theory to translate this raw information into usable data and process the data into categories and variables. A good theory tells the user how things and events are related—which are likely to be external causes and independent, and which are likely to be internal results and controllable. A good theory also tells us the probable direction of causality. Elements may vary in a positive direction (go up or down together), in a negative direction (move in opposite ways), or be unrelated. Finally, a theory tells the user the timing and sequencing of events. Some things occur before others and these are leading variables, others occur after and these lag. When events happen at the same time, they are concurrent.

Therefore, an entrepreneur with a good theory of how entrepreneurship works is practical and efficient. This is crucial because entrepreneurship can be expensive. Real-time failures cost money and the irreplaceable time of many people as well as their hopes and reputations. There are thousands of opportunities for entrepreneurship, but we cannot try them all. Which will we pursue? By employing a good theory, we can think about all of the problems and issues of new venture creation without having to start business after business to see what works and what does not.

A warning is in order. A theory is not a law. A theory does not pretend to explain precisely what will happen with absolute certainty in all cases. It deals with hypotheses and propositions—educated guesses about the chances that certain relationships exist and the strength and nature of these relationships. If there were a "law of entrepreneurship," then once it was known, everyone could apply it and experience unlimited success. This does not make sense in any market-based economy where competition is prevalent. And besides, if everyone could succeed, there would not be much profit in it. So, we should be pleased that we have a theory and not a law of entrepreneurship.

Some people say that there have been a great many successful entrepreneurs and most of them did not have a theory. How did they do it? One serious possibility (we will discuss it further later in the chapter) is luck.[1] Another possibility is that they succeeded after many failures, an expensive and time-consuming method. But the most likely explanation is that their success was the result of a tacit, or unspoken and unverbalized, theory of how their businesses and industries operate. Like Sam Walton, the entrepreneur who created Walmart and Sam's Club, and his rules in Chapter 1 (Street Stories 1–1), a lifetime of experience can help to summarize the theory, but some pieces are still so complex and intuitive that they are unknown even to the theorist.

This chapter introduces the fundamentals of the resource-based theory of entrepreneurship. The resource-based theory is efficient and practical because it focuses on the strengths, assets, and capabilities of entrepreneurs and their ventures. It incorporates market opportunity and competition into the model, but it emphasizes resources. The entrepreneur may already control these resources or may be able to obtain them in the future. But without resources to exploit a situation, even the best situation cannot create an entrepreneur.[2] First, we present the basic terminology and concepts of the theory. Then we look at the relative importance of the different types of resources the entrepreneur will need to start the business. We then take a more in-depth look at how the entrepreneur is a key human resource for the new venture.

E-NOTES 2–1 THEORIES

A good theory:

- identifies useful information and tells where it can be obtained,
- explains how variables can be related,
- forecasts what may happen (causality) when elements are positive or negative,
- predicts timing and sequencing of events.

Identifying Attributes of Strategic Resources

What is a resource? A **resource*** is any thing or quality that is useful.[3] No two entrepreneurs are alike, and no two new firms are identical, either. Our resource-based theory of entrepreneurship makes sense for the study of new venture creation because it focuses on the differences that characterize entrepreneurs and the founding of their companies. Entrepreneurs are individuals and they are unique resources to the new firm, resources that money cannot buy. The theory says that firms have different starting points for resources (called resource heterogeneity) and other firms cannot get them (called resource immobility). Our theory values creativity, uniqueness, entrepreneurial vision and intuition, and the initial conditions (history) under which new ventures are created.[4]

What are the origins of new firms? Economic organizations that have their origins in the resources of the entrepreneur and the assets that entrepreneurial team controls,

---

*To improve the readability of the text, at various times we will use the terms "resource," "capital," and "asset" interchangeably. Also, when we say resource we intend it to include "skill" and "capability." **Capability** and **skill** in this context mean the ability to do something useful.

can potentially acquire, and, finally, combine and assemble. Firms usually begin their history with a relatively small amount of strategically relevant resources and skills, and each company's uniqueness shows how these resources are expected to perform in the marketplace.[5] Our theory has a rather simple formula:

Buy (or acquire) resources and skills cheaply→

Transform (the resource or skill) into a product or service
deploy and implement (the strategy)→
Sell dearly (for more than you paid).

However, this is only possible if cheap or undervalued resources and skills exist. And their availability depends on market imperfections and differences of opinion about prices and events. These are not limitations, because perfect agreement seldom exists, and the key to an entrepreneur's vision is insight into the future.[6]

Our resource-based theory holds that sustainable competitive advantage (SCA) is created when firms possess and employ resources and capabilities that are:

1. *Valuable* because they exploit some environmental opportunity,
2. *Rare* in the sense that there are not enough for all competitors,
3. *Hard to copy* so that competitors cannot merely duplicate them,
4. *Nonsubstitutable* with other resources.

Why are these four characteristics so important? When a firm possesses and controls resources with these four characteristics, it can withstand competitive pressures. If the new enterprise can protect these resources and maintain these four qualities, it will have competitive advantage over the long term. New ventures that form with some of these characteristics but not others have short-term or minor advantages. Firms with all these qualities, but not in full measure and without a plan to protect the resources, will have a competitive advantage until other firms are able to copy and imitate them. If the entrepreneur's goal is to achieve SCA for the new venture, then he or she must create a venture that is forgiving, rewarding, and enduring.[7] If not, the entrepreneur fades into an also-ran whose bundle of resources and skills may soon be depleted by the forces of destructive capitalism and go out of business.[8]

What are strategic resources? Strategic resources create competitive advantage. There is a distinction between strategic and nonstrategic, or common, resources. Not all capital resources are strategically important for the entrepreneur. Many can be considered "common" because they are necessary for carrying out the firm's usual activities but provide no specific advantage. Ordinary desks and chairs and office furniture are examples. And some resources may prevent the formulation and implementation of valuable strategies by their shoddiness, imperfections, and lack of quality. Still others may prevent beneficial strategies by blinding the entrepreneur to alternative possibilities because he or she focuses too narrowly on resources already controlled rather than resources potentially controllable.[9]

It is also important to distinguish between **competitive advantage** and **sustained competitive advantage**. Competitive advantage occurs when the entrepreneur "is implementing a value-creating strategy not simultaneously being implemented by any current or potential competitors."[10] "Value creating" in this definition refers to above-normal gain or growth. Sustained competitive advantage is competitive advantage with a very important addition: Current and potential firms are unable to duplicate the benefits of the strategy. Although SCA cannot be competed away by duplication, this does not mean that it can last forever. Changes in the environment or industry structure can make what once was SCA obsolete. Important strategic factors in one setting may be barriers to change in another or simple irrelevant.

VALUABLE RESOURCES

What makes resources valuable? Resources are **valuable** when they help the organization implement its strategy effectively and efficiently. This means that in a "strengths, weaknesses, opportunities, and threats" model of firm performance, a valuable resource exploits opportunities or minimizes threats in the firm's environment. A valuable resource is useful for the operation of the venture.[11] Examples of valuable resources and capabilities are property, equipment, people, and skills such as marketing, financing, and accounting. But all of these are pretty general, so we must look at other factors.

RARE RESOURCES

Valuable resources shared by a large number of firms cannot be a source of competitive advantage or SCA. Because of their widespread availability, they are not rare. An example might be legal resources, either independent professionals on retainer or staff. Their major purpose is to minimize threats of lawsuits from a contentious environment. Clearly these are valuable resources in the sense that they neutralize a threat. But lawyers are not rare, and most, if not all, firms have access to approximately the same legal talent (at a price, of course). So, retaining legal counsel or building a corporate legal staff cannot be the source of an advantage. Common resources like these may be necessary under certain conditions and may improve chances for survival, but they are not a source of SCA.

How rare does a resource need to be to generate a competitive advantage? A unique and valuable resource clearly gives the firm SCA. But does it need to be one of a kind? Probably not. A resource can be considered **rare** as long as it is not widely available to all competitors. If supply and demand are in equilibrium, and the market-clearing of the resource is generally affordable, it would cease to be rare. Examples of resources that may be considered rare are things like a good location, managers that are also considered good leaders, or the control of natural resources like oil reserves (if you are in the oil business).

HARD TO COPY RESOURCES

Firms with rare and valuable resources clearly have advantages over firms lacking such assets. Indeed, such strategic endowments often lead to innovation and market leadership.[12] However, at some price even rare resources can be obtained. If the price is so high that no profit is made, there is no SCA because the firm has spent its advantage on the resource. Where duplication is not possible at a price low enough to leave profits, the resource is said to be **hard to copy** (also called imperfectly imitable). There are three factors which make it difficult for firms to copy each other's skills and resources: unique historical conditions, causal ambiguity, and social complexity.

Unique Historical Conditions   The defining moment for many organizations is their founding. At birth organizations are imprinted with the vision and purpose of their founders. The initial assets and resources that accompany the organization's origin are unique for that place and time. Firms founded at different times in other places cannot obtain these resources; thus, the resources cannot be duplicated. Examples of unique historical foundings abound, for example, starting a company in a great location that was unrecognized by others at the time. Another example might be the creation of a new venture by scientists and engineers whose special knowledge represents human capital. Recently this has been true for companies in genetic engineering or software development.

Ambiguous Causes and Effects   Causal ambiguity exists when the relationship between cause and effect is not well understood or ambiguous.[13] In business this means that there is doubt about what caused what and why things happened. When these things are imperfectly understood, it is difficult for other firms to duplicate it. Even though the pieces may look the same as in the original, the rules of congruence are unknown, so the imitator cannot make it work. Entrepreneurs themselves often cannot explain their own success, so how can imitators hope to duplicate their operations?

It may seem odd that a firm with the high-performance skills and resources has no better idea why things work than the potential imitator. How is that possible? Economic organizations can be very complex. The relationships among product design, development, manufacturing, and marketing are not subject to complete quantitative analysis. They often depend on the complex interaction of social, psychological, economic, and technical factors. Even when organizations have all the information about their competitors, they often are unable to answer such questions as

- What makes one firm's sales force more effective?
- What makes its production more efficient?
- Why are its designs more appealing to the customer?

These are but a few of the areas that are ambiguous. Nobody can answer these questions.

What if there is no causal ambiguity? Consider a firm that understands the causes and effects between its resources and its performance. Can it keep that secret from its competitors? Not in the long run. Competitors have strategies to unearth the information they need. Among these are hiring workers and managers away from the advantaged organization and devising schemes to extract the needed information. It may take time and money, but in the long run the vital secrets will be known throughout the industry. The entrepreneur who started with an advantage will not be able to sustain it indefinitely.

Complex Social Relationships   Social complexity is the third reason a firm's capabilities and resources may not be easily duplicated. As long as a firm uses human and organizational resources, social complexity may serve as a barrier to imitation. Why? The interpersonal relationships of managers, customers, and suppliers are all complex. Someone, for example, could identify that our customers like our salespeople, but knowing this does not make it possible for competitors to copy the likability of our salespeople. The competitor could even hire away our whole sales force, but even this may not reproduce the original relationship, since the sales force may now work under different conditions, with different managers, and for different incentives.

Perhaps the most complex social phenomenon is **organizational culture**.[14] The new venture's culture is a complex combination of the founder's values, habits, and beliefs

---

STREET STORIES 2–1

A Success Story in Social Expression

Back in 1973 three young men, Mike Fitzgerald, Craig Aurness, and Stanley Jones, all recent graduates of Indiana University, were sitting around contemplating their future. As Fitzgerald recalls, "We all tried to think about what to do next. Craig was a photographer. He wanted some of his pictures done as greeting cards. That was the idea that started us off." The three had originally met in a class entitled "Religious Traditions of the North American Indians." The experience had exposed them to the art and drawings of Native Americans. As an afterthought they also decided the simple kind of illustrations that appear in children's books might also appeal to young yuppie consumers like themselves. "[The company] really began with those three elements: art photos, Indians, and drawings for kids' books," says Fitzgerald. The company these three unlikely entrepreneurs founded is Sunrise Publications, a success story that is today one of the leaders in the "social expression" business, and the fifth largest greeting card company in the world. Sunrise's special niche is known as "contemporary." While a traditional greeting card will offer six to ten lines of saccharine poetry inside, a contemporary card is distinguished by its artwork and the simplicity of its prose.

Once their mission and their concept was in place, the next step for the three partners was to raise the money, produce the products, and piece together an organization that could sell and distribute their cards. They scraped together $80,000, rented a six-unit garage, and broke down a few walls. They bought a second-hand press that could print black and white and sepia. They hired a commercial printer to do their four-color work. With handmade racks to store their cards, catalogues, and sales materials, they (with the help of Fitzgerald's wife, Judy, and another religion student, Jeffrey Willsey) flew to the California Card Show and laid out their merchandise.

Fitzgerald, now chairman, president, and CEO of Sunrise Publications, recalls: "We got orders, but we realized we had to cover the country. The three of us couldn't do that so at every other show we went to we found sales representatives. Some worked well, others didn't. It was a grinding start."

But the hard work paid off for these entrepreneurs. Today Sunrise sells over 33 million cards a year, including 18 million of the popular "Mary Engelbreit" cards. Sunrise's product line is distributed at over 20,000 outlets in the United States and overseas, and includes more than 5,000 different cards, stationary, and gift wrap designs.

What were the secrets that led to their success? They found a niche, they were one of the first entrants into the contemporary card market, and they combined their personal skills, resources, and vision in a rare, valuable, and hard-to-duplicate way.

Source: Adapted from J. Douglas Johnson, "Greetings from Bloomington," *Indiana Business Magazine,* December 1991.

and interaction of these elements with the newly created organization and the market. The culture might be, among other things, very supportive, highly authoritarian, very aggressive, extremely thrifty, or combinations of all these and additional factors. As organizations grow, subcultures form, adding additional complexity. Organizational cultures are difficult to "know" from the outside; they cannot be directly observed and resist quantitative measurement. And that makes them almost impossible to copy.

NONSUBSTITUTABLE RESOURCES

Nonsubstitutable resources are strategic resources that cannot be replaced by common. For example, let us say that there are two firms, A and B. A has a rare and valuable resource, and employs this resource to implement its strategy. If B has a common resource that can be substituted for the valuable and rare resources of A, and these common resources do basically the same things, then the rare and valuable resources of A do not confer strategic advantage. In fact, if B can obtain common resources that threaten the competitive advantage of A, then so can many other firms, thereby ensuring that A has no advantage.

Very different resources can be substitutes for each other. An expert-system computer program may substitute for a manager. A charismatic leader may substitute for a well-designed strategic-planning system. A well-designed programmed-learning module may substitute for an inspirational teacher. Figure 2–1 summarizes the four resource attributes needed for competitive advantage.

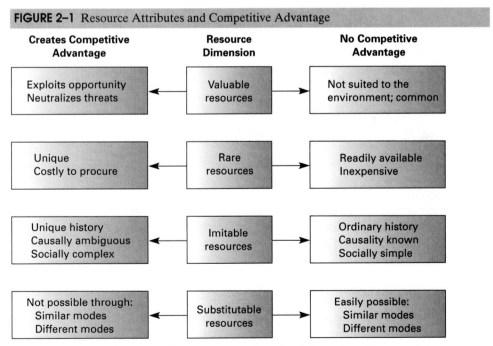

FIGURE 2–1 Resource Attributes and Competitive Advantage

Creates Competitive Advantage	Resource Dimension	No Competitive Advantage
Exploits opportunity / Neutralizes threats	Valuable resources	Not suited to the environment; common
Unique / Costly to procure	Rare resources	Readily available / Inexpensive
Unique history / Causally ambiguous / Socially complex	Imitable resources	Ordinary history / Causality known / Socially simple
Not possible through: Similar modes / Different modes	Substitutable resources	Easily possible: Similar modes / Different modes

Source: Adapted from J. Barney, "Firm Resources and Sustained Competitive Advantage," *Journal of Management* 17 (1991): 99–120

E-NOTES 2–2   RESOURCES

A resource is:

- any thing or quality that is useful

In our resource-based theory of entrepreneurship, a resource also:

- can help an organization implement its strategy (valuable),
- may not be available to all competitors (rare),
- may not be able to be duplicated easily or inexpensively (hard-to-copy),
- may not be the same as the resources of another firm (nonsubstitutable).

Resource Types

Our resource-based theory recognizes six types of resources: **P**hysical, **R**eputational, **O**rganizational, **F**inancial, **I**ntellectual/human and **T**echnological. These can be called our **PROFIT** factors. These six types are broadly drawn and include all "assets, capabilities, organizational processes, firm attributes, information and knowledge."[15] We review these six types and note the special situations where these resources may confer particular advantage, or no advantage at all.

E-NOTES 2–3   TYPES OF STRATEGIC RESOURCES: THE PROFIT FACTORS

We have identified six types of business resources:

- **P**hysical
- **R**eputational
- **O**rganizational
- **F**inancial
- **I**ntellectual and Human
- **T**echnological

PHYSICAL RESOURCES

Physical resources are the tangible property the firm uses in production and administration. These include the firm's plant and equipment, its location, and the amenities available at that location. Some firms also have natural resources such as minerals, energy resources, or land. These natural resources can affect the quality of its physical inputs and raw materials.

Physical resources can be the source of SCA if they have the four attributes previously described. But since most physical things can be manufactured and purchased they are probably not rare or hard to copy. Only in special circumstances, like a unique historical situation, will physical resources be a source of SCA.

REPUTATIONAL RESOURCES

Reputational resources are the perceptions that people in the firm's environment have of the company. Reputation can exist at the product level as brand loyalty or at the corporate level as a global image. While technological resources may be short-lived because of innovations and inventions, reputational capital may be relatively long-lived. Many organizations maintain high reputations over long periods of time. *Fortune* magazine's annual survey of corporate reputation indicates that seven of the top ten corporations in any given year have appeared in the top ten many times before. The *Fortune* survey uses eight different criteria for their rankings:

- The quality of management
- The use of corporate assets
- The firm's financial soundness
- The firm's value as an investment
- The quality of products and services
- Innovativeness
- The ability to attract, develop, and retain top people
- The extent of community and environmental responsibility

Our own research indicates that the most important of these are product quality, management integrity, and financial soundness.[16] The value of reputational relationships goes beyond personal relationships because these reputations continue even after the individuals originally responsible for them are no longer around (either in that job or with the firm).

ORGANIZATIONAL RESOURCES

Organizational resources include the firm's structure, routines, and systems.[17] The term ordinarily refers to the firm's formal reporting systems, its information-generation and decision-making systems, and formal or informal planning.

The organization's structure is an intangible resource that can make the difference between the organization and its competitors. A structure that promotes speed can be the entrepreneur's most valuable resource. In the postindustrial economy, organizations will be required to make decisions, innovate, and acquire and distribute information more quickly and more frequently than ever before.[18]

Organizational structures that separate the innovation from the production function speed up innovation, while those that separate marketing from production speed up marketing. The appropriateness of designs depends on the complexity and turbulence in the environment.[19] Organizational resources also show up as the skills and capabilities of the people. Street Story 2–2 shows how smaller firms can excel at manufacturing and gain advantage.

For new ventures that have emerged from the embryonic stage or those that are a spinoff or business development effort of an ongoing firm, other intangible resources are available. Collective remembered history (myth) and recorded history (files and archives) may also be considered organizational resources. These are part of the organization's past, and to the extent that "past is prologue," organizational history will be incorporated into the culture of the new venture, providing a set of rules, norms, policies, and guides for current and future behavior.

FINANCIAL RESOURCES

Financial resources represent money-assets. Financial resources are generally the firm's borrowing capacity, the ability to raise new equity, and the amount of cash generated by internal operations.[20] Being able to raise money at below-average cost

---

Speed and Agility Equals Capability for Small Manufacturers

In addition to resources, entrepreneurs and their companies need capabilities, they need to be able to do things well . . . and that means doing things that are rare, valuable, and hard to copy. In a forest of large companies, sometimes it is the smaller tree that is more agile and can use the capability of speed to establish a competitive advantage.

For example, Ultra Pac of Rogers, Minnesota has grown in six years to a 300-employee, $27-million-in-revenue company while competing with Mobil Corp. and Tenneco Inc. Using specialized equipment, Ultra Pac can turn out between 400 and 500 different designs of customized packaging products. And they claim that they can deliver within three days of an order, about one third of the time it takes their larger competitors. Calvin Krupa, Ultra Pac's founder, chairman, and CEO says, "We saw that if we reacted and made better decisions faster, we could get a nice chunk of the market."

Spartan Motors of Charlotte, Michigan is another example of how smaller ventures compete through speed and flexibility. Spartan is a manufacturer of truck chassis with less than 30 employees. Founded by Polish-born entrepreneur George Sztykiel, Spartan thrives by tailoring products to special customer needs for premium prices. Sztykiel, who worked as a truck engineer for Chrysler for 18 years, supervises a manufacturing line that offers at least 300 options—10 transmissions, more than a dozen engines, and a choice of more than 30 suspensions. This is not mass production, and therefore Sztykiel also has to watch his costs very closely. In each of these ventures, the capabilities include speed, customization, cost control, closeness to the customer, strong organizational communication, and the ability to innovate on the fly. Spartan has been so successful that one of its major competitors reorganized itself in 1989 to try to copy Spartan's capabilities. Oshkosh Truck divided itself up into business units in an attempt to capture Spartan's small, flexible style. Says Oshkosh's vice president and general manager of components, Ron Ziebel, we did it "in recognition that everybody wants stronger focus on customer response and customer input." But can everybody do it?

Adapted from: M. Selz, "Agility gives an edge to small companies," *Asian Wall Street Journal*, December 30, 1993, 1.

---

is an advantage attributable to the firm's credit rating and previous financial performance. Various indicators of a venture's financial resources and financial management skills are its debt-to-equity ratio, its cash-to-capital investment ratio, and its external credit rating. Yet while start-up entrepreneurs see that access to financial resources is the key to getting into business (it is certainly a necessary component),

TABLE 2–1   Sources of Sustainable Competitive Advantage

Factor	High Tech[a]	Service
Reputation for quality	38	44
Customer service/product support	34	35
Name recognition/profile	12	37
Good management	25	38
Low cost production	25	13
Financial resources	**16**	**23**
Customer orientation/market research	19	23
Product line depth	16	22
Technical superiority	44	6
Installed base of satisfied customers	28	19
Product innovation	22	18

[a]The numbers represent the frequency of mention by respondents. Numbers can add to more than 100 percent.

Source: Adapted from D. Aaker, "Managing Assets and Skills: The Key to Sustainable Competitive Advantage," *California Management Review* 31 (Winter 1989): 91–106. Abridged list of 20 factors from a study of 248 Californian businesses.

most agree that financial resources are seldom the source of sustainable competitive advantage. Why is it, then, that fledgling entrepreneurs see money and financial resources as the key to success but established businesses seldom do? Table 2–1 summarizes the results of a survey that compares high-tech and service industry entrepreneurs' perceptions of the sources of sustainable competitive advantage. Financial resources did not rank near the top. In fact, financial resources were named by just 16 percent of high-tech manufacturing firms and 23 percent of service firms. Out of 20 different factors mentioned, financial resources were ranked twelfth by manufacturers and 6th by the service firms.

Limitations of Financial Resources

Why do entrepreneurs think that financial resources are not the most important? To shed light on these findings, we can examine financial resources by the four attributes of resources.

Are Financial Resources Valuable?   No doubt about it. Valuable resources enable a firm to lower its costs, increase its revenue, and produce its product or service. Without financial resources—that is, money—no firm can get very far. Start-up incurs real financial costs even for micro businesses and home-based businesses. The axiom that you have to spend money to make money is true, and the entrepreneur who cannot acquire any financial resources may find that the dream never becomes reality.

Are Financial Resources Rare?   Sometimes yes and sometimes no. At various times in the business cycle credit crunches deter banks and other lending institutions from making loans and extending credit. (However, since banks do not often finance pure start-ups, this rarity applies to going concerns.) Similarly, the economic climate that governs initial public offerings (the IPO market) sometimes favors new issues (when the stock market is high and climbing) and at other times discounts new issues heavily (when the market is low and falling). For firms that must spend money before collecting receipts, financial resources are rarer than for firms who can collect receipts and deposits before expenses are paid. However, overall financial resources are not rare. It is estimated that each year as much as $6 billion is available through formal investors and an additional $60 billion through informal investors, or angels. This does not include the money invested by the entrepreneur and the top management team themselves.[21]

Are Financial Resources Hard to Copy?   No. One person's money looks and spends the same as another's. It yields competitive advantage in trading markets only for large transactions.[22] For example, the leveraged buyout of RJR Nabisco required about $25 billion in financing. Only a few organizations had the connections and were capable of securing that much money: Shearson-American Express; Kohlberg, Kravis, and Roberts; and Forstmann Little. In such a situation, the absolute size of the financial resource is an advantage. Most deals, however, are settled at amounts below $25 billion, and on a strictly financial basis, money is a perfect copy of itself.[23]

Are Financial Resources Nonsubstitutable with Resources That Are Common? Once again the technical answer is no. A few entrepreneurs succeed on the basis of sweat equity, and nothing is more common than sweat. This means that they start very small, on little capital other than their own hard work and effort. This is called bootstrapping. Through frugality, efficient operations, and reinvestment, they are able to grow. Eventually they can cross the threshold that makes them attractive to investors. Under certain circumstances, hard work substitutes for outside financing. Another alternative is a relationship with another firm. Strategic alliances can replace financing because they enable the firm to meet its goals without additional investment by piggybacking on the investment of another firm.

To summarize, financial resources are valuable and necessary, but because financial resources are not rare, hard to duplicate, or nonsubstitutable, they are insufficient (in most cases) to be a source of sustainable competitive advantage.

However, the *management* of financial resources—the firm's organization, processes, and routines that enable it to use its resources more effectively—*can be a source of SCA*. This is because capable financial management involves complexity and a human element that is valuable, rare, hard to copy, and nonsubstitutable. So while money as a resource is inert and static, the ability and skill to manage money is dynamic, complex, and creative.

INTELLECTUAL AND HUMAN RESOURCES

Intellectual and human resources include the knowledge, training, and experience of the entrepreneur and his or her team of employees and managers. It includes the judgment, insight, creativity, vision, and intelligence of the individual members of an organization. Entrepreneurs often perceive great opportunities where others see only competition or chaos; therefore, entrepreneurial perception is a resource. The values of the entrepreneurs and their beliefs about cause and effect can form the initial imprint of the firm's culture.

In addition, human capital includes **relationship capital** as a subset. Relationship capital refers not to *what* the organization's members know but rather to *who* the organization's members know and what information these people possess. Networking gives the entrepreneur access to resources without controlling them. This minimizes the potential risk of ownership and keeps overhead down. Entrepreneurial networking has become standard practice, and the old view of the "entrepreneur as the rugged individualist" has been modified to reflect the realities of today's complex business environment.[24]

Frequently, the most important and valuable resource that the new venture has is the founding entrepreneur. These are unique people with their own special characteristics, histories that cannot be duplicated, and complex social relationships. For the rest of this chapter we will focus on the entrepreneur as a human resource. The management of human resources will be covered in Chapter 9.

TECHNOLOGICAL RESOURCES

Technological resources are made up of processes, systems, or physical transformations. These may include labs, research and development facilities, and testing and quality control technologies. Knowledge generated by research and development and then protected by patents is a resource, as are formulae, licenses, trademarks, and copyrights. Technological secrets and proprietary processes are resources as well. There is a distinction between technological capital and intellectual capital. Intellectual capital is embodied in a person or persons and is mobile. If the person or persons leave the firm, so does the capital. Technological resources are physical, intangible, or legal entities and are owned by the organization.

Can complex physical technology provide a basis for SCA? The answer in general must be no. Technological resources—machines, computer systems, equipment, machine tools, robots, complicated electronics, and so on—cannot be the basis for SCA because they can be duplicated and reproduced. There is enough mobile and capable engineering and scientific human resources to take apart and put together any of this complex technology. A patent, however, might make it illegal for the competition to commercially develop an exact copy.

However, complex technology is not worthless as a source of competitive advantage. Although several firms can all have the same complex technology, one firm may be more adept at exploiting this technology through its human or organizational resources. If the method of exploiting the technology is not easy to copy (assuming it is valuable, rare, and difficult to substitute), then other resources can augment technology to provide SCA.[25]

E-NOTES 2–4 STRATEGIC RESOURCES OUTLINE				
Resources	*Valuable*	*Rare*	*Hard-to-Copy*	*Nonsubstitutable*
Physical	yes	sometimes	not usually	sometimes
Reputational	yes	yes	yes	yes
Organizational	yes	yes	yes	yes
Financial	yes	sometimes	no	no
Intellectual	yes	yes	usually	sometimes
Technological	yes	sometimes	sometimes	sometimes

A Psychological Approach

PERSONALITY CHARACTERISTICS

Are there personality characteristics that help us predict who will be an entrepreneur and who will not? Who will be a successful entrepreneur and who will not? Over the past few decades, entrepreneurial research has identified a number of personality characteristics that differentiate entrepreneurs from others.[26] Among the most frequently discussed are the need for achievement, locus of control, and risk-taking propensity.

The Need for Achievement   The entrepreneurial need for achievement, or **n Ach**, was first identified as a personality trait by McClelland in his work on economic development.[27] People with high levels of n Ach have a strong desire to solve problems on their own, enjoy setting goals and achieving them through their own efforts, and like receiving feedback on how they are doing. They are moderate risk takers.

However, the link between n Ach and entrepreneurship has not always held up in empirical testing. Researchers who have attempted to replicate McClelland's findings or apply them in other settings have occasionally been disappointed. For example, n Ach is a weak predictor of a person's tendency to start a business, and people specially trained to have high n Ach sometimes perform no differently from a control group that receives no training. The causal link between n Ach and small business ownership has not been proven.[28]

Locus of Control   A second trait often associated with entrepreneurship is **locus of control**.[29] In locus-of-control theory, there are two types of people: (1) **externals**, those who believe that what happens to them is a result of fate, chance, luck, or forces beyond their control; and (2) **internals**, those who believe that for the most part the future is theirs to control through their own effort. Clearly, people who undertake a new business must believe that their efforts will have something to do with the business's future performance.

A logical prediction of this theory would be that internals are more entrepreneurial than externals. But evidence supporting this hypothesis has been inconclusive.[30] Some studies have shown that there are more internals among entrepreneurs but others show no difference between entrepreneurs and others. In fact, it could be argued that any good manager must also possess the qualities of an internal: a person who believes that efforts affect outcomes. So, while locus of control might distinguish people who believe in astrology and those who do not, it may not differentiate potential entrepreneurs from potential managers or just plain business students.

Risk-taking Propensity   Related to the need for achievement is **risk-taking propensity**. Since the task of new venture creation is apparently fraught with risk and the financing of these ventures is often called risk capital, researchers have tried to determine whether entrepreneurs take more risks than other businesspeople. That hypothesis has been tested in a number of ways, but the work by Brockhaus has been most incisive.[31]

In Brockhaus's research, the risk-taking propensities of entrepreneurs were tested objectively using a series of decision scenarios. The results obtained from the entrepreneurs were compared with those obtained from a sample of managers. The conclusion was that risk-taking propensity is not a distinguishing characteristic of entrepreneurs.

INADEQUACY OF THE TRAIT APPROACH

Overall, the trait approach has failed to provide the decisive criteria for distinguishing entrepreneurs from others. What distinguishes entrepreneurs from nonentrepreneurs is that entrepreneurs start new businesses and others do not.[32] In Street Stories 2–3 we take a look at two entrepreneurs who start businesses—over and over again.

STREET STORIES 2–3

Entrepreneurs Start Businesses . . . Again and Again and Again

Debbie Nigro's latest business is a company that syndicates radio talk shows targeted at busy mothers. And although Debbie is still struggling, this business looks like it has promise and may fulfill its potential. That is more than you can say for her previous attempts, because Sweet Talk Productions is the fourth business that the 38-year-old businesswoman has founded. The other three no longer exist. But entrepreneurs like Debbie do not have failures, they have learning experiences.

As the stigma for business "nonsuccess" has declined, more and more entrepreneurs are trying again and again. Like many repeat entrepreneurs, it was hard to come up with finance at first. Debbie scraped up a few hundred dollars in cash and used up to $15,000 in credit card charges. After persuading a couple of radio stations to carry her show (Debbie is also the host), she raised additional money by splitting advertising revenue with them. And customers helped with the financing too, Avon (a sponsor) agreed to invest $3,000 in exchange for low advertising rates and lead sponsorship.

Now Debbie's weekly program is carried on 130 stations and she has attracted additional sponsors and advertisers, including big names like Proctor and Gamble. For 1997, she anticipates that revenue will double to about $1,000,000—not bad for an entrepreneur on her fourth life.

But Debbie is just an amateur compared with Courtland "Corky" L. Logue of Austin, Texas. He has started twenty-eight businesses—and he is only 47 years old. He has had a sign business, an air conditioner factory, a drywall supply house, and a chain of pawnshops, just to name a few. If entrepreneurs can be defined as folks who start businesses, Corky is an ENTREPRENEUR.

What lessons can be gained from a man who has started so many ventures? First, he says, obtain good people. "Remember, .200 hitters don't win championships, .300 hitters do." And if you don't have good people, it's your own fault. Next, Logue says that you should stick to what you know. Knowledge of the products, the markets, and the processes are key. He recalls that one of his worst losses was in the air-conditioning business. "I didn't understand manufacturing and I lost $400,000 on that one." Lastly, you must be a hands-on entrepreneur and watch the numbers like a hawk. "I know entrepreneurs who say they'll look at the numbers at the end of the year. Never wait until the end of the year, or you'll learn about trouble too late to act." And that is good advice from a man who starts businesses, over and over again.

Adapted from: R. Ricklefs, "More entrepreneurs follow adage to 'try, try again'," *Wall Street Journal*, February 13, 1996, B1–B2; P. Nulty, "Serial entrepreneur: Tips from a man who has started 28 businesses," *Fortune*, July 10, 1995, 182.

One researcher described the search of the entrepreneurial trait this way: "My own personal experience was that for ten years we ran a research center in entrepreneurial history, for ten years we tried to define the entrepreneur. We never succeeded. Each of us had some notion of it—what he thought was, for his purposes, a useful definition. And I don't think you're going to get farther than that."[33]

The trait approach looks for similarity among entrepreneurs. But as our resource-based theory suggests, if all entrepreneurs have a certain trait or characteristic, it is not an advantage to any of them, for it is neither rare nor hard to duplicate. To understand entrepreneurship, we must look for circumstances that produce differences, not similarities. For this we turn to a sociological framework that emphasizes personal history and the uniqueness of an individual's path to new venture creation.

A Sociological Approach

How are entrepreneurs unique? Each has a unique background, history, and biography. The sociological approach tries to explain the social conditions from which entrepreneurs emerge and the social factors that influence the decision. A sociological model is presented in Figure 2–2.[34] It depicts the decision to become an entrepreneur as a function of two factors: the impetus factors and the situational factors. The model is multiplicative: A zero on either of the causes means a failure to produce the entrepreneurial event.

IMPETUS FOR ENTREPRENEURSHIP

What propels entrepreneurs forward toward self-employment? There are four factors: negative displacement, being between things, positive push, and positive pull.

Negative Displacement

Figure 2–2 begins with the notion that people who find themselves displaced in some negative way may become entrepreneurs. **Negative displacement** is the alienation of individuals or groups of individuals from the core of society. These individuals or groups may be seen as "not fitting in" to the main flow of social and economic life. Because they are on the outer fringes of the economy and of society, they are sensitive to the allure of self-employment; having no one to depend on, they depend on no one. An example of this phenomenon is the tendency of immigrants to become entrepreneurs. In societies where economic rights are more easily exercised than political rights, immigrants turn to entrepreneurship. Throughout the world, for example, Asian and Jewish immigrants, wherever they have settled, have gone into business for themselves. Recent trends in the United States demonstrate high levels of entrepreneurship in the Vietnamese and Korean populations. One statistical estimate of Ko-

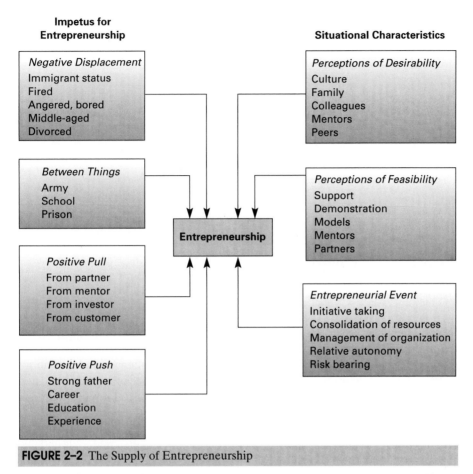

Impetus for Entrepreneurship

Situational Characteristics

Negative Displacement
Immigrant status
Fired
Angered, bored
Middle-aged
Divorced

Perceptions of Desirability
Culture
Family
Colleagues
Mentors
Peers

Between Things
Army
School
Prison

Entrepreneurship

Perceptions of Feasibility
Support
Demonstration
Models
Mentors
Partners

Positive Pull
From partner
From mentor
From investor
From customer

Entrepreneurial Event
Initiative taking
Consolidation of resources
Management of organization
Relative autonomy
Risk bearing

Positive Push
Strong father
Career
Education
Experience

FIGURE 2–2 The Supply of Entrepreneurship

Source: Adapted from A. Shapero and L. Sokol, "The Social Dimensions of Entrepreneurship," in C. Kent, D. Sexton, and K. Vesper, eds., *Encyclopedia of Entrepreneurship* (Englewood Cliffs, NJ: Prentice Hall, 1982), pp. 72–90.

rean immigrants in the New York City area concludes that 65 percent of Korean families own at least one business.[35] Indeed, as Table 2–2 indicates, the recent wave of Asian Americans is creating new businesses at a faster rate than any other immigrant group. Take the example of Jung Pack, a Korean who immigrated to the United States in 1982.[32] Jung works 16 hours a day in his own grocery business even though he has a college degree in business administration and was in construction management back in Korea. Jung says he left Korea because it was too rural and he wanted to live in a big "cosmopolitan" country. But when he arrived in the United States, downward mobility forced him to give up thoughts of a white-collar career to become a self-employed shopkeeper. His career in the United States has been blocked by the language barrier and skepticism about the value of his academic degree. But Jung can probably expect his two children, who will be U.S. citizens, to pursue either professional careers or entrepreneurial opportunities in business services like data processing or management consulting. Meanwhile, Jung says he still dreams of "a better life."

TABLE 2–2	Immigrant Entrepreneurs: Percentage of Immigrant Group Members Who Own a Business	
National Group	*1982*	*1987*
Korean	6.8%	10.2%
Asian Indian	6.6	7.6
Japanese	5.9	6.6
Chinese	4.9	6.3
Cuban	4.1	6.3
Vietnamese	1.5	4.9
Filipino	2.6	3.3
Other Hispanic	1.4	2.3
Mexican	1.7	1.9

Source: From "Asian-Americans Take Lead in Starting U.S. Businesses," *The Wall Street Journal*, August 2, 1991. Reprinted by permission of the Wall Street Journal. Copyright © 1991 Dow Jones & Company, Inc. All Rights Reserved Worldwide.

Other negative displacements result from being fired from a job or being angered or bored by current employment. Many bored managers and stifled executives in large corporations are leaving their white-collar jobs looking for challenges and autonomy. According to Harry Levinson, a Harvard psychologist who specializes in career and life-cycle issues, "The entrepreneur, psychologically speaking, has a lot more freedom than anybody in a big corporation."[36] To illustrate this, consider the case of Philip Schwartz, who was an executive with Olin Corporation and Airco Inc. He left his middle-level managerial career to start a business as a wholesaler of packaging materials and cleaning supplies and to find out "who and what I am." He reports that he enjoys the autonomy and action of drumming up business and interacting with customers. He enjoys putting his own personal stamp on his company. Having only four employees, he can create a family atmosphere, relaxed and friendly. He imprints his own values of honesty and dependability on the business, something that no middle-level corporate manager can do.[37]

Middle age or divorce can also provide the impetus for new venture creation. In an unusual example, one entrepreneur recreated his business because of a midlife crisis. Tom Chappell co-founded a personal-care and health-products business, Tom's of Maine Inc. A number of years ago he realized that he was not happy running this business even though he was successful. He went back to school and obtained a master's degree from Harvard Divinity School. His studies there led him to examine his values and his motivation for managing his own firm. He changed the company's goals, setting its mission to "address community concerns, in Maine and around the globe, by devoting a portion of our time, talent and resources to the environment, human needs, the arts and education."[38]

"Between Things"

People who are **between things** are also more likely to seek entrepreneurial outlets than those who are in the "middle of things." Like immigrants, people who are between things are sometimes outsiders. Three examples are offered in the model in

Figure 2–2: between military and civilian life, between student life and a career, and between prison and freedom.

Positive Pull

Positive influences also lead to the decision to investigate entrepreneurship, and these are called **positive pull** influences. They can come from a potential partner, a mentor, a parent, an investor, or a customer. The potential partner encourages the individual with the offer of sharing the experience, helping with the work, and spreading the risk. The mentor raises self-esteem and confidence. Mentors and partners can also introduce the entrepreneur to people inside the social and economic network for new venture activity.[39] There also appears to be a relationship between a parent's occupation and offspring entrepreneurship: Many entrepreneurs have a strong self-employed father figure in the family.[40] Investors that provide the initial financing can convince the individual that "there may be more where that came from." The prospect of a potential customer pulling the entrepreneur into business raises some difficult ethical and economic issues.[41] However, having a guaranteed market for the products or services is a temptation few can resist.

Positive Push

The final category of situations that provide impetus and momentum for entrepreneurship is termed **positive push**. Positive-push factors include such things as a career path that offers entrepreneurial opportunities or an education that gives the individual the appropriate knowledge and opportunity.

What types of career choices can people make that put them in good position to become entrepreneurs? Two types of career paths can lead to entrepreneurship. The first is the **industry path**. A person prepares himself for a job or career in a particular industry and learns everything there is to know about that industry. Since all industries display some sort of dynamics, or change, over time, entrepreneurial opportunities that exploit that change come and go. A person with a deep knowledge of the industry is an excellent position to develop a business that fills a niche or gap created by industry change.

People taking the industry path to new venture creation emphasize that specialized knowledge is the key resource. That knowledge may be embodied in particular people, a technology, or a system or process. The new firm may be a head-to-head competitor, it may serve a new niche not served by the former employer, or it may be an upstream firm (a supplier) or a downstream firm (a distributor or retailer). Whatever its functional form, a spin-off is a knowledge-based business; its primary resources are the competencies and experiences and the networks and contacts being transferred to a new venture.[42] The challenge for these people is to procure the other resources, financial and physical, that will enable them to make their plan a reality.

A different approach, the **sentry path**, emphasizes the money and the deal. People with careers in sentry positions see many different opportunities in many different industries. They tend to be lawyers, accountants, consultants, bankers (especially business loan officers), and brokers. These people learn how to make deals and find money. They have contacts that enable them to raise money quickly when the right property comes along. The challenge for these people, because they are experts in the "art of the deal" and not part of any particular industry, is to locate and retain good managers.

SITUATIONAL CHARACTERISTICS

Once the individual's inclination for entrepreneurship has been activated, situational characteristics help determine if the new venture will take place. The two situational factors are perceptions of desirability and perceptions of feasibility.

Perceptions of the Situation

Perceptions of Desirability   Entrepreneurship must be seen as desirable in order to be pursued. The factors that affect the perceptions of desirability can come from the individual's culture, family, peers and colleagues, or mentors. For example, the Sikhs and Punjabis who dominate the service station business in New York City also dominate the transportation and mechanics business in their native country. Sometimes religion can spark entrepreneurship and legitimize the perception of desirability. For example, Zen Buddhist communities are historically self-sufficient economically and provide the background for the story of an unusual entrepreneur, Bernard Glassman.

Glassman was born the son of immigrant Jewish parents and trained as a systems engineer. But now he is building a better world by combining Zen entrepreneurship with a mission to help people at the bottom of the economic ladder. After Glassman's introduction to Buddhism, he found that meditation alone could not meet his spiritual needs. So he chose the Way of Entrepreneurship. In 1983, he and his Zen community launched Greyston Bakery in Yonkers, New York, supplying high-priced pies and cakes to wealthy consumers. He received his early training as a baker from another Zen sect in San Francisco. Today his bakery grosses $1.2 million and employs 200 people, many previously considered unemployable. Many entrepreneurs say that they want to help the poor and needy, but Glassman has made it happen. Through Greyston's profits, he has been able to renovate buildings, provide counseling services, and open a day-care center. He still has to pay close attention to the bottom line, however; the bakery is his mandala and he must concentrate intensely to make it a success.[43]

Perceptions of Feasibility   Entrepreneurship must be seen as feasible if the process is to continue. Readiness and desirability are not enough. Potential entrepreneurs need models and examples of what can be accomplished. They require support from others— emotional, financial, and physical support. Again, ethnic and immigrant networks provide examples. Not only do the Koreans and Indians help train and employ each other in their businesses, but they demonstrate by their perseverance that it can be done.

E-NOTES 2–5   THE ENTREPRENEUR AS A HUMAN RESOURCE
The sociological approach theorizes that an entrepreneur's inclinations are propelled by:
- negative displacement (losing a job, etc.),
- being between things (transition from school to career, etc.),
- positive pull (example made by parent, mentor, etc.),
- positive push (a job, education, etc.),

> ... and activated by situations which positive affect:
> - perceptions of desirability (message from culture, peers, etc.),
> - perceptions of feasibility (demonstration, etc.),
> **... and culminate in an entrepreneurial event.**

So what happens next? At the end of the process depicted in Figure 2–2, the new venture creation process begins. The pre-entrepreneurial conditions described end in the entrepreneurial event, that is, in the creation and management of a new venture. One model of this process comprises five components:[44]

- *Initiative.* An individual or team, having been brought to the state of readiness by personal factors and by perceptions of desirability and feasibility, begin to act. Evidence of initiative usually includes scanning the environment for opportunities, searching for information, and doing research.
- *Consolidation of resources.* Levels of resource needs are estimated, alternatives for procurement are considered, and timing of resource arrival is charted and eventually consolidated into a pattern of business activity that could be called an organization.
- *Management of the organization.* The business's resource acquisition, transformation, and disposal are routinized and systemized. Those elements that are not easily systematized are managed separately.
- *Autonomous action.* The management of the new venture is characterized by free choice of strategy, structure, and processes.
- *Risk taking.* The initiators have put themselves at risk. They are personally affected by the variability of returns of the business and by its possible success or failure.

Another process-oriented model by Stevenson emphasizes entrepreneurial behavior toward resources. This model makes two valuable contributions to our understanding of the entrepreneurial process: (1) It recognizes that no entrepreneur behaves in an entrepreneurlike manner all the time. There are forces acting upon the individual that sometimes make entrepreneurial behavior appropriate and that at other times make administrative or managerial behavior appropriate. (2) It emphasizes that the commitment and control of resources are as important to the process as environmental scanning and opportunity recognition.[45] Each entrepreneur assesses the forces pushing for entrepreneurial action and those requiring administrative action and then makes the choice that is best for the new venture.

Summary

This chapter presents the basic concepts of the resource-based theory, including the four attributes of resources necessary to achieve sustainable competitive advantage: They must be rare, valuable, hard to copy, and nonsubstitutable. Our resource-based theory allows that certain aspects of entrepreneurship are not analyzable—they are causally ambiguous because no one, including the founders, quite understands how or why they work. New ventures created around the possession and controllability of resources with these characteristics have the potential to be rewarding, forgiving, and enduring.

The chapter also describes the six types of resources: physical, reputational, organizational, financial, intellectual/human, and technological. These are the basic profit factors to be used in assessing the potential of the new venture. All of the resources are important for the new venture, but the ones that are most likely to lead to competitive advantage are organizational, reputational and human resources.

The entrepreneur is the primary human resource for the new venture. While it is uncertain what, if any, personality traits make the best entrepreneurs, the entrepreneur's life history, experience, and knowledge make each founder a unique resource.

Key Terms

- Resources
- Capability
- Valuable
- Rare
- Hard to copy
- Nonsubstitutable
- Competitive advantage
- Sustained competitive advantage
- Need for achievement
- n ach
- Locus of control
- Externals
- Internals
- Risk-taking propensity
- Negative displacement

- "Between things"
- Positive pull
- Positive push
- Organizational culture
- Financial resources
- Bootstrapping
- Physical resources
- Relationship capital
- Technological resources
- Reputational resources
- Organizational resources
- Relationship capital
- Intellectual and human resources
- Industry path
- Sentry path

Discussion Questions

1. What are the characteristics of a good theory? What makes a theory practical? How can an entrepreneur use the resource-based theory for his or her advantage?
2. Explain the problems we would have if there were a "law of entrepreneurship."
3. How do each of the four attributes of resources contribute to SCA?
4. What is the difference between competitive advantage and sustainable competitive advantage?
5. How can an organization's culture be a source of SCA?
6. Describe how each of the six types of resources can be a source of SCA. What are the strengths and weaknesses of each type?

7. Why are personality traits not sufficient for evaluating and predicting successful entrepreneurship?
8. Describe the sociological approach to entrepreneurship. How can this approach be used to promote more entrepreneurship within the economy?
9. If immigrants are a major source of entrepreneurship in the economy, why do most countries limit the number of immigrants they allow in each year?
10. How are entrepreneurs behaviorally different from managers? When can we expect entrepreneurs to behave managerially? When can we expect managers to behave as entrepreneurs?

Exercises

1. Research a company and inventory its resource base using the six types of resources discussed in the chapter. Evaluate these resources in terms of the four attributes of resources necessary for SCA. Does the company have a competitive advantage? A sustainable competitive advantage? What recom-

mendations about resource procurement and development would you make for this company?

2. Interview an entrepreneur. Ask the entrepreneur to describe the "keys to successful entrepreneurship." Ask the entrepreneur to estimate how much of his or her success was the result of luck or unknown factors. Do the answers seem to fit the resource-based model?

3. Inventory your personal resource base using the six types of resources described in the chapter. Evaluate these resources employing the four criteria. Comment on your individual potential to start a business that has the prospect of achieving SCA.

4. If you are in a group with other students, inventory the group's resources and repeat Exercise 3 above.

5. Assume you have access to your college or university's resources. Redo your inventories (see Exercises 3 and 4). How have you increased your potential for competitive advantage?

Exercises for Writing a Business Plan

Beginning with this chapter, the exercises are designed to prepare the student to develop and write a business plan. These exercises can be done either individually or in a group setting.

1. Exercise envisioning. Sit in a quiet and dark room and begin to think about what kind of business you would like to start. Close your eyes and let your mind's eye see yourself working in that business. What do you see? Is it a manufacturing business, a service or retail outlet, a construction site, or something else? Notice the physical setting and the people around. What are they doing? Which are employees and which are customers? Are the people happy? Busy? Confused?

2. Develop 20 ideas for a new business. Make the 20 ideas into 100 ideas, no matter how unusual or apparently strange. Sort the ideas into the 10 best, and make the concepts more original. At the end of the exercise you should have 20 to 30 truly creative new business ideas.

3. For each of the group's or individual's best ideas, do the following short assignment:

   a. Describe the business in 25 words or less. The description should include the product/service, the customer, and the technology employed.

   b. Describe the opportunity that you believe this business exploits. In other words, why do you think this is a great business idea?

   c. Describe the resources you believe you would need to execute this new venture idea. Use the six categories from Chapter 2. Which resource(s) will be the source of competitive advantage?

   d. Estimate how much money it would cost to actually get this business started. The estimate will be very rough, but try to make an educated guess.

DISCUSSION CASE

If You Can't Eat It, Sell It

Entrepreneur Ed Alfke is hungry for success. In fact, Alfke is so hungry he's invested $5 million in Biofoam, an Arizona company founded in the mid 1980s that produces an all-natural packing material as an alternative to styrofoam. Biofoam's pellets, which look like pale cheese doodles and are popped from pellets of grain sorghum, are sometimes dished out to unsuspecting customers around a big bowl of salsa at trade shows. It may not taste good, but unlike its plastic- and chemical-based competitors, Biofoam dissolves in water and won't clog landfills.

Alfke is no stranger to success. He founded both the car rental firm Rent-A-Wreck and the Canadian retail chain Jean Jungle, becoming a multimillionaire in the process. Then he started looking for a new investment, saying that he wanted a firm with the potential for a big customer base and a large profit margin that could be sensitive to environmental issues at the same time. According to Alfke, "The writing is on the wall for companies that are not environmentally friendly."

When Alfke became CEO of Biofoam in May 1995, he immediately recruited a high profile Board of Directors which included a former deputy secretary of the interior and a past chairman of the Canadian National Railroad. He also raised $8 million, inaugurated a national sales campaign, and developed an innovative way to manufacture and distribute Biofoam peanuts. His innovation was to install a $250,000 Biofoam production unit free-of-charge at key customers' sites. Biofoam even provides an insured and bonded employee to operate the equipment.

For the customer, the pluses include an environmentally sensitive profile, reliable just-in-time delivery with no inventory, on-site maintenance, and a competitive price (Biofoam sweetens the deal by throwing in a 5-year price guarantee). But there are drawbacks, too. Biofoam is three times as heavy, creates more dust, and is less resilient than its synthetic competitors. The production units are hot, noisy, and smelly, and consume a lot of electricity. And some customers object to Biofoam's plan to market the excess created by the production unit at their site to neighboring businesses.

Biofoam sales increased five times during Alfke's first year. But real success still eludes him. After a year and a half, the company has only five production units in place, while Alfke says they need 16 to be profitable. One of their major customers, the Fuller Brush Company, is dissatisfied with the way the pellets crumble. And last year Biofoam was slapped with a patent infringement suit, and now reports repeated industrial espionage attempts and "smear tactics" from their synthetic-based competitors.

Alfke forecasts that Biofoam's sales will climb from $2.5 million in fiscal 1996 to a staggering $80 million by the year 2000, with a pretax profit of almost 30 percent. Part of his game plan is new applications for Biofoam, including oil-spill clean-ups, and molded packing materials, cafeteria trays, and fast-food sandwich clamshells. Alfke is still hungry. "I see a lot of deals," he says, "and I've never, *ever* seen a deal as good as this one."

Adapted from David Whitford, "The Snack Food That's Packing America," *Inc.*, October 1996, pp. 51–55.

CASE QUESTIONS

1. What are Biofoam's resources? To what extent are they valuable, rare, hard to copy, and nonsubstitutable?

2. Referring to the factors listed in Table 2–1, how would you rate Biofoam's sources of sustainable competitive advantage? Specifically, how important do you think Biofoam's financial resources will be to the firm's success?

3. Would you invest in this business? Why or why not?

Notes

1. J. Barney, "Strategic Factor Markets: Expectations, Luck and Business Strategy," *Management Science* 32 (1986): 1231–1241.

2. Here is a personal example. Two business professors teaching in Hong Kong, one an expert in management, the other in marketing, have endlessly discussed how to make money in China. After all, the rumor is that everyone is getting rich in China and these two professors are smart, talented, and even speak Chinese. But in spite of the myriad of opportunities, they are unable to create a new venture. Why? Because they have no resources and all they know how to do is teach class and write academic papers.

3. S. Winter, "Knowledge and Competence in Strategic Assets," in D. Teece, ed., *The Competitive Challenge* (Cambridge, MA: Ballinger, 1987), pp. 159–184.

4. History is often not studied when it comes to the social sciences such as psychology and sociology and even to some extent economics. One of the finest works in management and organization theory is a set of histories by A. Chandler, *Strategy and Structure* (Cambridge, MA: MIT Press, 1962); and entrepreneurial histories abounded as an early form of study. See II. Livesay, "Entrepreneurial History," in C. Kent, D. Sexton and K. Vesper, eds., *Encyclopedia of Entrepreneurship* (Englewood Cliffs, NJ: Prentice-Hall, 1982). To understand how history and science are related, see any works by Stephen Jay Gould.

5. Barney, 1986.

6. Barney, 1986. Barney also makes a case that "luck" has a much larger role in entrepreneurship and business success in general. This can also explain why there is an incongruence between "rich" and "smart."

7. J. Timmons, *New Venture Creation* (Homewood, IL: Irwin, 1990). Timmons uses these three general criteria for assessing the worthiness of an entrepreneurial effort. We will discuss in more detail the evaluation of business opportunities and business plans in this and later chapters.

8. J. Schumpeter, *Capitalism, Socialism and Democracy*, 3rd ed. (New York: Harper & Row, 1950). Schumpeter first coined this phrase "destructive capitalism" in his description of entrepreneurship as the force that initiates change in capitalistic systems.

9. H. Stevenson, M. Roberts, and I. Grosbeck, *New Business Ventures and the Entrepreneur* (Homewood, IL: Irwin, 1989). Especially Chapter 1.

10. J. Barney, "Firm Resources and Sustained Competitive Advantage." *Journal of Management* 17 (1991): 99–120.

11. See, for example, A. Thompson and A. Strickland, *Strategic Management: Concepts and Cases* (Homewood, IL: Irwin, 1992).

12. Barney, 1991.

13. Barney, 1991.

14. For more on culture and its effects see: C. Enz, *Power and Shared Values in the*

Corporate Culture (Ann Arbor, MI: UNI Research Press, 1986); and G. Hofstede, *Culture's Consequences: International Differences in Work-Related Values* (Beverly Hills: Sage Publications, 1984).

15. Barney, 1991.
16. M. Dollinger, P. Golden, and T. Saxton, 1997. The effects of reputation on the decision to joint venture." *Strategic Management Journal* 18,2, 127–140. See also C. Fombrun and M. Shanley, "What's in a name?" Reputation building and corporate strategy." *Academy of Management Journal* 33 (1990): 233–258.
17. Prahalad and Hamel refer to organizational resources, particularly those that confer strategic advantage on the firm as "core competencies." See C. Prahalad and G. Hamel, "The core competencies of the organization." *Harvard Business Review* (1990), May–June, 79–91.
18. G. Huber, "The nature and design of post-industrial organizations," *Management Science* 30 (1984): 929–959. This article takes a futuristic approach to organizational design and is still ahead of its time.
19. Huber, 1984.
20. R. Grant, *Contemporary Strategy Analysis* (Cambridge, MA: Blackwell, 1992).
21. J. Freear and W. Wetzel, "The Informal Venture Capital Market in the 1990s," in D. Sexton and J. Kasarda, eds., *The State of the Art of Entrepreneurship* (Boston: PWS-Kent, 1992), pp. 462–486.
22. Grant, 1992.
23. We qualify this a bit when we say, " on a strictly financial basis." Clearly, money raised from organized crime activities is neither morally nor contractually equivalent to a loan from the local commercial bank.
24. Sometimes relational capital is referred to as networking. For more information, see S. Birley, "The Role of Networks in the Entrepreneurial Process," *Journal of Business Venturing* 2 (1985): 155–165; M. Dollinger and P. Golden, "Interorganizational and Collective Strategies in Small Firms: Environmental Effects and Performance," *Journal of Management* 18 (1992): 696–717.

25. Barney, 1991.
26. J. Carland, F. Hoy, W. Boulton, and J. Carland, "Differentiating Entrepreneurs from Small Business Owners: A Conceptualization," *Academy of Management Review* 9 (1984): 354–359.
27. D. McClelland, *The Achieving Society* (Princeton: D. Van Nostrand, 1961).
28. See R. Brockhaus, "The Psychology of the Entrepreneur," in C. Kent, D. Sexton, and K. Vesper, eds. *Encyclopedia of Entrepreneurship* (Englewood Cliffs, NJ: Prentice Hall, 1982), pp. 39–71.
29. J. Rotter, "Generalized Expectancies for Internal versus External Control of Reinforcement," *Psychological Monographs* 80 (1966): Paper 609.
30. Brockhaus, 1982.
31. R. Brockhaus, "Risk-Taking Propensity of Entrepreneur," *Academy of Management Journal* 23 (1980): 509–520.
32. W. Gartner, "Who is the Entrepreneur? Is the Wrong Question," *American Journal of Small Business* 12 (1988): 11–32.
33. A. Cole, "Definition of Entrepreneurship," in J. Komives, ed., *Karl A. Bostrum Seminar in the Study of Enterprise* (Milwaukee: Center for Venture Management, 1969), pp. 10–22.
34. A. Shapero and L. Sokol, "The Social Dimensions of Entrepreneurship," in C. Kent, D. Sexton, and K. Vesper, eds., *Encyclopedia of Entrepreneurship* (Englewood Cliffs, NJ: Prentice Hall, 1982), pp. 72–90.
35. Professor Pyong Gap Min, quoted in D. Lorch, "Ethnic Niches Creating Jobs That Fuel Immigrant Growth," *New York Times*, January 12, 1992.
36. Based on a story by Timothy Noah that appeared in the *Wall Street Journal*, August 2, 1992.
37. Noah, 1992.
38. Noah, 1992.
39. S. Birley, "The Role of Networks in the Entrepreneurial Process," *Journal of Business Venturing* 1 (1985): 107–118. We will return to this topic in a later chapter.
40. For a discussion of this and other background characteristics, see Chapter 3 of

R. Hisrich and M. Peers, *Entrepreneurship* (Homewood, IL: Irwin, 1991).

41. This is not an uncommon situation, but it is a difficult one. Consider the employee (for example, an accountant, salesperson, or consultant) who services a customer who then encourages the employee to go into business for himself. Implicit here is the notion that the customer will switch to the new entrepreneur. This is a common situation. But is it ethical? Does the employee have a responsibility to an employer not to steal the customer? Should the employee report the offer and try to do a better job servicing the customer within the current employment relationship? There is an economic side as well. A firm with a single customer is vulnerable. The customer may feel the entrepreneur is in some way obligated to give the customer the best deal because of the history between them. The new firm's employees will, of course, know the circumstances of their firm's founding and may replicate it when their time comes.

42. Much of the discussion on spin-offs is adapted from D. Garvin, "Spin-offs and the New Firm Formation," *California Management Review* 25 (1983): 3–20.

43. U. Gupta, "Blending Zen and the Art of Philanthropic Pastry Chefs," *Wall Street Journal*, January 2, 1992.

44. Shapero and Sokol, 1982.

45. H. Stevenson, M. Roberts, and H. Grousbeck, *New Business Ventures and the Entrepreneur* (Homewood, IL: Irwin, 1989).

CHAPTER 3

The Environment for Entrepreneurship

Outline

The central task facing an organization which has entrepreneurial aspirations is to take advantage of the opportunities from change that appear in its environment.
—S. OSTER

Learning Objectives

After reading this chapter you will understand:

- The components of the *business environment.*

- The *process* of business environment.

- The five segments of the *macroenvironment*, and the issues presented by each of them.

- What changes in the macroenvironment can become *sources of opportunity* for the entrepreneur.

- The seven elements of the *industry environment*, and the components that affect each of those segments.

Schematic of the New Venture's Environment

What does the world look like to the entrepreneur? What parts of that world are important for making entrepreneurial decisions and finding opportunities for the new venture? Figure 3–1 shows the business environment as it might appear to an entrepreneur as a series of concentric circles. The innermost circle represents the firm and its resources. This is the core of the entrepreneur's world. The next circle holds all the elements that are part of the firm's industry but not part of the firm itself. The largest

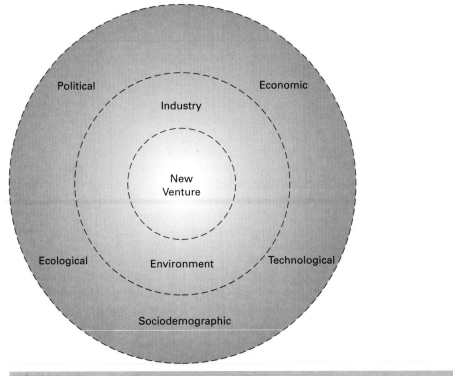

FIGURE 3–1 Schematic of the New Venture's Environment

circle represents everything that is not part of the firm's industry, but is still important for the new venture. This is the **macroenvironment** in which the firm operates. Five identifiable, though overlapping, segments are within the macroenvironment:

1. Politics and government
2. Macroeconomy
3. Technology
4. Sociodemography
5. Ecology

In this chapter we describe the characteristics and segments of the macroenvironment, and also the characteristics and segments for the industry or competitive environment. The distinction between the two environments is somewhat artificial because in the long run all the productive resources merge together. That is, they are interchangeable between organizations and institutions. Indeed, the organizations and institutions themselves are also exchangeable. They come and go as society, technology, and the rules of law dictate. As new industries are created from new technologies or the desires of consumers, resources from deteriorating industries are converted for their use. The purchasing power of a declining industry's customers can be redirected either to a new industry or to another more stable industry. Thus, the concentric circles representing the business environment appear as broken lines to depict the permeability of environmental boundaries and the possibility, indeed the necessity, of flow and exchange.

In the second half of this chapter we examine the competitive environment for entrepreneurship. To do this, we employ the model of competitive industry analysis popularized by Michael Porter of the Harvard Business School.[1] We conclude the chapter by discussing how competitor analysis based on our resource-based model can exploit industry opportunities and lessen the threats arising from unfavorable industry conditions.

Processes of Business Environment Analysis

Most of the time, thinking and analyzing are done very quickly and we are quite unaware that we are doing it. But sometimes it is necessary to be more conscious of our thinking and to do our analyzing in systematic ways. This is true when we are thinking about the environment for entrepreneurship. We want to make sure we are being comprehensive and analytical. Four separate (although sequentially related) tasks are required for a comprehensive entrepreneurial analysis: scanning, monitoring, forecasting, and assessing.[2]

E-NOTES 3–1   ENVIRONMENTAL ANALYSIS
Analysis of the business environment includes:

- scanning to detect change,
- monitoring to track development,
- forecasting to project the future,
- assessing to interpret data.

SCANNING

How does this comprehensive process begin? It begins by looking around. **Scanning** the environment is the process by which the entrepreneur first identifies the key elements and their characteristics. It is a surveillance system for early detection. The goal of scanning is to detect change that is already underway. Successful scanning catches important changes early, giving the new venture enough lead time to adapt.

The entrepreneur scans innumerable sources of data. The *Wall Street Journal*, *Business Week*, and *The Economist* are solid sources for the broad picture. Television provides a general and continuous source of data through Cable News Network (CNN), network news, special reports, and documentaries. More specialized business programming is becoming increasingly popular on cable channels like MSNBC. Surfing the Internet has become an important scanning activity. In addition, through "people-to-people" interactive scanning, entrepreneurs consult with a wide variety of professionals and experts outside their field of expertise. Accountants, lawyers, engineers, consultants, and, yes, even professors are available to the entrepreneur for information and advice. Scanning gives the entrepreneur a sensitivity to environmental conditions that sometimes looks like intuition.

MONITORING

Monitoring is the process of tracking the evolution, development, and sequence of critical events that affect the survival and profitability of the future new business. Data from the scanning process are input into the monitoring process. Specific trends and events identified for the new venture are monitored in real time to confirm or disprove predictions about how they will affect the firm. Monitoring is less general and therefore more focused than scanning. The entrepreneur follows specific periodicals, consults selected experts, and even convenes focus groups.[3] The outcome of the monitoring process is a detailed model of how various elements in the macroenvironment influence and affect the firm. The model, however, is not reality, but a workable version of cause and effect.

FORECASTING

Forecasting enables the entrepreneur to develop plausible projections for the future. These can be projections for elements such as the level of prices, the direction of interest rates, or future scenarios for cause and effect; for example, a typical forecast might be—if the money supply grows at above-target rates, then inflation will occur. Thus inputs for forecasts are the data from monitoring.

Forecasting uses a series of techniques to provide insight into the future. The specific techniques chosen for a task should correspond to the type of data used as input and the nature of the desired forecast. When forecasting is used to help search for new business opportunities and to uncover potential macroenvironmental constraints on these opportunities, the following five-step process is suggested.[4]

1. *Choose* the macroenvironmental variables that are critical to the new venture. These will probably relate to the resource base of the firm.
2. *Select* the sources of data for the forecast. These will probably be those you have been monitoring.
3. *Evaluate* various forecasting techniques.
4. *Integrate* forecast results into your plan for the creation of the new venture. These will probably concern resource levels and availability and sales forecasts.
5. *Keep track* of the critical aspects of your forecast. This will mean comparing actual results with forecasted results. If and when a gap appears, it is time for another forecast, beginning at step 1.

TABLE 3–1 Quantitative and Judgmental Forecasting Methods for Emerging Industries, New Ventures, New Products

Method	Description	Cost	Complexity
1. Sales force estimate	A bottom-up approach that aggregates unit demand.	Low	Low
2. Juries of executive opinion	Forecasts jointly prepared by experts in a functional area.	Low	Low
3. Customer surveys: market research focus groups	Learning about intentions of potential customers and final users.	Medium	Medium
4. Scenario development	Effects of anticipated conditions imagined by forecasters.	Medium	Low
5. Delphi method	Experts guided to consensus.	Low	Medium
6. Brainstorming	Idea generation in a noncritical group situation.	Low	Medium

Source: Adapted from J. Pearce and R. Robinson, *Strategic Management,* 4th ed. (Homewood, IL: Irwin, 1991).

Table 3–1 summarizes the costs and benefits of six quantitative and judgmental forecasting techniques.

ASSESSING

Assessing the environment is the most difficult and important of the four tasks of environmental analysis. Here the entrepreneur has to answer that most difficult of questions: "What does it all mean?" Interpretation is an art form, and so is assessment. In a poker game, players can agree on what cards are showing, the previous bets made, and the value of the cards they are holding. Yet some players hold, some fold, and others raise. Because their assessments are different, their behavior is different. So also, in assessing most entrepreneurial opportunities, there are few facts that people would agree can be generalized.

Political and Governmental Analysis

Politics is the art of the possible. You could say the same thing about entrepreneurship. Analyzing the political scene will give the entrepreneur a feeling for what is possible, what is probable, and what is unlikely. The political and governmental segment of the business environment is the arena where different interest groups compete for attention and resources to advance their own interests, establish their own values, and achieve their own goals. It is the arena in which particular individuals and groups exercise political power. To a large extent, the individual entrepreneur is forced to accept the current political environment of the new venture. Collectively and over time, however, an organized group of entrepreneurs can influence the political sector. One such group, the National Federation of Independent Business (NFIB) lobbies hard for issues that effect entrepreneurs and small businesses.

STAKEHOLDER ANALYSIS

How many different individuals, groups, and interests can influence the survival, development, and profitability of the new venture? Quite a few, and these are its **stakeholders**. Their influences can be both positive and negative. Not all stakeholders are alike. Stakeholders may vary along the following seven dimensions.[5]

- *Degree of organization.* The extent to which stakeholders are organized for collective action locally, regionally, and nationally. Some stakeholders are very well organized and influential. Others are disorganized or have their organization incompetently managed and are less of a threat.
- *Resource capability.* The degree to which stakeholders have access to resources that help influence businesses or agencies and that can be categorized in the same way as described in Chapter 2: financial, physical, technical, reputational, human, and organizational; rare, valuable, hard to copy, and nonsubstitutable.
- *Extent of influence.* The degree to which the interest group is able to promote its agenda. Some stakeholders are organized as lobbying groups and have enormous influence—for example, the National Rifle Association or Mothers Against Drunk Driving.[6]
- *Nature of interest.* The type of agenda the interest group has; a specific agenda (e.g., cleaning up toxic waste sites) or a general agenda (e.g., making business responsive to people's needs).

- *Duration.* The length of time the interest group has been active and its potential staying power. Sometimes stakeholders are interested in issues that prove to be fads or of passing interest. This is especially true in areas affecting consumer goods and travel and leisure industries.
- *Degree of manifestation.* The ability of the interest group to take its case directly to the public or to the media.
- *Bases of influence.* The extent to which an interest group can gain support from other interest groups that share an affinity for similar causes.

Stakeholders analysis helps the entrepreneur identify which groups and interests are friendly to the new venture and which are hostile. It enables the entrepreneur to see whether any groups have an immediate affinity for the product or service, and whether this affinity can be translated into a market. The analysis also reveals trends regarding consumer attitudes and behavior for the new venture's products, competing products, and complementary goods.

GLOBAL AND INTERNATIONAL ISSUES

Although it may seem to the entrepreneur that her business is strictly local, in truth very few businesses are. We are all interconnected in a global economy and events that occur thousands of miles away can influence our business. At the global level the main issues are trade barriers, tariffs, political risks, and bilateral and multilateral relationships. All of these issues are interrelated.

Trade Barriers and Tariffs Trade barriers and tariffs hinder the free flow of resources across national boundaries. They are the result of economic interest groups within a country attempting to prevent transnational competition. The trend is the reduction of trade barriers worldwide.

Trade Agreements Since World War II and especially since the end of the cold war, the trend has been toward increased trade agreements. These country-to-country and regional agreements have set the economic rules businesses follow when they are interacting with businesses within the cosigning group of nations.

Political Risk Political risk refers to the potential for instability, corruption, and violence in a country or region. It is an important variable because in areas where political risk is high, it is difficult and costly to procure, protect, and dispose of resources. There is always the risk of governmental nationalization and legal appropriation. (Even in a stable democracy, people can vote to take away other people's money.) But as Street Story 3–1 illustrates, government efforts to stabilize political risk can bring entrepreneurs economic rewards.

NATIONAL ISSUES

Political and governmental analysis on the national level are concerned with taxation, regulation, antitrust legislation, government spending, and patent protection.

Taxation At the national level the primary political factor facing the entrepreneur is taxation. Governments require large amounts of money to promote the public good and to carry out the will of the people (stakeholders) who exercise political power.

Post-Apartheid Potential

When Nelson Mandela was elected President of South Africa in May 1994, he promised that this new multiracial government would work to reverse the social and economic problems caused in his country by apartheid. As it turns out, that promise opened up a wealth of opportunities not only for Blacks in South Africa, but also for African-American entrepreneurs from the United States. The changes in government policy stabilized the environment for investment and new ventures and reduced the political risk.

Economic development had high priority for President Mandela from the start. Five months after his election he made his first investment-seeking tour of the United States. The Clinton Administration responded enthusiastically by creating a $100-million venture capital fund under the U.S. Agency for International Development, and by backing the establishment of two separate $75-million private equity funds by the Overseas Private Investment Corp., a federally supported investment agency. One fund provided capital to South African businesses with an economic connection to the United States, while the other was focused on U.S. businesses reentering the South African market. The United States also sponsored a variety of trade fairs and trade missions to South Africa, including one led by the late Commerce Secretary Ron Brown.

"The trade and investment opportunities emerging in the new South Africa represent enormous potential for African-American entrepreneurs," noted Secretary Brown at the time. Donald Keene, regional legal adviser for Southern Africa at the U.S. Aid office in Pretoria, observed that those entrepreneurs responded eagerly. "In all my 10 years of working in Africa I have never seen such an influx of African-American businesses," said Keene.

Black Entertainment Television (BET), the only black-owned cable TV network in the United States, was among the first African-American entrepreneurs to invest in South Africa. Working with the NNTV network, in 1994 they began broadcasting eight hours of U.S.-produced news and entertainment programs each night to 500,000 subscribers. Other early investors included Tydow Inc., a Washington D.C. joint venture that combined software and training skills to help implement South Africa's first national on-line lottery, and Global Diamond Resources, Inc., a diamond-exploration venture that secured the rights to an abandoned diamond mine with its start-up find of $1 million. The company hopes to grow to nearly 2,000 employees, including mine workers, diamond cutters, and marketing professionals.

South Africa has some distinct advantages for foreign entrepreneurs. Unlike other countries with emerging markets, South Africa already has a business infrastructure in place. Unlike countries such as India and China, business development isn't hampered by poor communications, weak transportation links, and scarce capital. Political risk has been significantly reduced since apartheid ended, and Nelson Mandela's government has pledged to lower tariffs and ease other trade restrictions. Some barriers remain, however, including foreign-exchange controls and the country's widespread poverty.

But more and more African-American investors are becoming bullish on the new democracy's potential. "South Africa is a big new market with millions of untapped consumers," notes John Tyson, one of the Global Diamond Resources partners.

Source: Adapted from Udayan Gupta, "African-American Firms Gain Foothold in South Africa," *Wall Street Journal*, October 3, 1994.

But taxation reduces the cash available to the firm for reinvestment. Thus, the entrepreneur is able to invest or reinvest not the economically rational amount but an amount somewhat less than that, known as earnings after taxes. The outside investor is also left to calculate returns after taxes, which means that required rates of return must be high enough to cover the government's share. Some new ventures are not able to generate outside financing because their after-tax returns to investors will simply be too low to justify the investment.

Taxation affects not only each business individually but also the relationships between businesses, giving some firms advantages over others. Special tax breaks for certain industries, like depreciation and depletion allowances, work to the benefit of the firms that receive them. Capital intensive companies, like manufacturers, benefit disproportionately from the tax shield that depreciation affords, whereas service businesses with large investments in training and development cannot depreciate their employees. The differential tax treatment given to interest and dividends under the U.S. tax code favors firms that can obtain bank loans and other forms of debt over equity-financed firms that pay dividends and whose investors receive capital gains. Since "bankable" businesses—those to whom a loan is likely to be offered—are generally older firms that are likely to have physical assets than can serve as collateral, new ventures, especially service businesses, are disadvantaged by the current tax code.

There is a global perspective to taxation as well. Different countries treat dividends, interest, and capital gains in different ways. For example, Japanese firms pay very low dividends relative to their German and U.S. counterparts because dividends are more highly taxed in Japan. Thus, the Japanese investor prefers capital gains, which are not taxed at all. This enables Japanese firms to keep more of their cash for reinvestment.[7]

Regulation   The government controls the flow of resources to firms and the property rights of business owners through federal agency regulation. These agencies are created by government in response to some special-interest group or group of stakeholders to protect their interests, values, and goals. This is not an inherently bad thing because we all belong to some special-interest groups. For example, we all eat and take medicine at some time. The Food and Drug Administration helps protect our interests in these matters.

The effects of regulation on business, however, are sometimes negative. Regulatory agencies impose significant costs on firms in the form of paperwork, testing and monitoring, and compliance. These costs may or may not be recoverable through higher prices. If the industry being regulated has good substitutes for its products and the substitute industry is less regulated, the firms in the more highly regulated industry have to absorb the costs, and profitability suffers. This results in less reinvestment and overall lower output in the regulated industry. If higher prices can be charged, then the public eventually pays for the protection and services it receives from the regulations.

Antitrust Legislation   Each national government determines the level of antitrust activity it will enforce. The United States has the toughest antitrust laws in the world. The antitrust division of the United States Justice Department was a driving force in the breakup of AT&T and in IBM's change in strategy. Currently they are investigating Microsoft. Other countries, most notably Japan, have a different view of the antitrust problem. In these countries the zeal of regulatory enforcement may be a function of national economic interests (such as balance of trade or currency exchange). When national interests collide with consumer or entrepreneurial interests, national interests have priority. Generally, it is unlikely that new ventures will be in danger of violating antitrust laws. New firms are more likely to be victims of lax antitrust enforcement.

Patent Protection   National governments grant patents and enforce patent laws. A patent is legal property that enables its holder to prevent others from employing this property for their own use for a specified period of time. There are three types of patents:

1. **Utility patents** for new articles, processes, machines, and techniques.
2. **Design patents** covering new and original ornamental designs for manufactured products.
3. **Plant patents** covering various forms of life and genetically engineered organisms.

A patent is a resource and therefore can be analyzed using our resource-based model. In countries where patent enforcement is lax, the firm may need to consider the costs of publicly divulging the technology versus the benefits of the protection (such as it is) before applying for a patent. In many cases small changes to a product or design erode the patent protection enough to make the patent worthless.

Government Spending   In most countries the national government is the largest purchaser and consumer of goods and services. The government is therefore a large market, and it displays preferences for products, services, and suppliers. These preferences are influenced by pressures from the various interest groups, stakeholders, and political organizations that constantly lobby the government. At times it appears that the political winds are favoring defense spending, and therefore new entrants into defense and related industries benefit. At other times government priorities may be set on building infrastructure or developing social programs. Construction contractors, consultants, and related service industries would then benefit.

STATE, REGIONAL, AND LOCAL ISSUES

State, regional, or local level, tax policies can create opportunities or disadvantages for the entrepreneur. At the state level three other areas affect business: licensing, securities and incorporation laws, and economic development and incentives.

Licensing   Licenses are economic privileges granted to individuals and firms that enable them to legally conduct a business. Not all businesses require licenses, but many do. At one time licenses were valuable franchises and a way of limiting entry and raising quality within a particular industry. Today, however, state and local authorities often consider licenses as a revenue source and do little to monitor the performance level of the licensees. The entrepreneur must still be watchful of current regulation and potential changes that would affect the new venture.

Securities and Incorporation Laws   Many security regulations and incorporation laws are written and enforced by the states. Because the U.S. Constitution does not specifically grant to the federal government the power to regulate business incorporation, this is one of the major regulatory roles left to the states. Although the federal government does have an important regulatory role under the Securities Act of 1934, which created the Securities and Exchange Commission, new incorporations are granted and monitored at the state level. Most early financing that the firm receives is covered by state securities regulations. Entrepreneurs need to employ lawyers and accountants to ensure that the firm complies with all state regulations.

Incentives   State and local authorities control the granting of economic development incentives and tax abatements to new businesses or to old businesses relocating within their jurisdiction. These incentives can be a powerful stimulus for new firms. They can include subsidized job-training programs, real estate improvements and favorable real estate tax treatment, and improved infrastructure (e.g., roads and interchanges, sidewalks, water and sewer improvements). Local governments also control zoning ordinances and laws, which determine how property can be used and developed. Every firm has a local component. Entrepreneurs can scan and monitor these developments, especially when considering location.

At the municipal level, taxation again erodes the firm's ability to finance itself and reward its investors. Local taxes include income and property, sewer, water, and waste disposal. If local taxes can be allocated to particular services provided by local government for business use, they are not really taxes but fees for service.

To summarize, the entrepreneur must be knowledgeable about a wide variety of political issues, particularly those related to securing, protecting, and disposing of resources. Of primary concern is the effect of political power on property rights. Table 3–2 presents the three levels at which political and governmental analysis should be performed.

TABLE 3–2 Political and Governmental Issues			
Global	*National*	*State and Region*	*Local*
Trade barriers	Taxation	Taxation	Taxation
Trade agreements	Regulation	Securities Law	Zoning
Tariffs and duties	Antitrust legislation	Licensing	
Political Risk	Patent protection	Incentives	
	Government spending		

Macroeconomic Analysis

The macroeconomy is the total of all goods and services produced, distributed, sold, and consumed. Where does all of this activity take place? At the global, national, and local levels. Each level has its own macroeconomy, and the sum of all the lower levels is the global economy. These geographic distinctions are important to policymakers because policymakers usually have geographic limits to their power and influence. The geographic distinctions are also important to the entrepreneur because to a greater or lesser degree, every business is entwined in all three macroeconomics. The entrepreneur should analyze all three macroeconomies, but the time spent on any one should be proportional to its potential impact on the firm's performance. Macroeconomic change can occur at any of the three geographic levels discussed previously.[8]

There are two types of macroeconomic change: structural change and cyclical change.

STRUCTURAL CHANGE

Structural change in the macroeconomy are major, permanent shifts of resources and customers from one sector of the economy to another. As these shifts occur, the financial capital, physical resources, and employees diminish in an industry that is fading and flow to the emerging industry.

CYCLICAL CHANGE

The second type of macroeconomic change is **cyclical change**. The macroeconomy enjoys periods of growth and then sustains periods of contraction. These alternating time periods form what is called the **business cycle**. Business cyclicality is the degree to which the new firm follows the trend of the business cycle. A venture that grows and contracts as the economy does is **procyclical**; one that runs against the business cycle is **countercyclical**. A venture that is unaffected by the business cycle is **acyclical**.

Understanding the new venture's relationship to the business cycle is crucial to the entrepreneur because it is difficult, if not impossible, for the new business to run counter to its natural cyclicality. This, if the firm is in a procyclical industry, and current trends in the business cycle are downward, the firm will have a difficult time going against this trend and expanding. Clearly the entrepreneur needs to scan and monitor the economic variables that indicate the direction of economic trends.

E-NOTES 3–2 ECONOMIC ANALYSIS

Analysis of the economic segment of the macroenvironment explore the impact of:

- structural change (major shifts of resources),
- cyclical changes, including:
  procyclical (mirrors the economy),
  countercyclical (runs against the economy),
  acyclical (unaffected by economy).

Technological Analysis

What is technology? **Technology** can be defined as "the branch of knowledge that deals with industrial arts, applied science, and engineering," and "a process, an invention, or a method." The first part of the definition tells us that technological analysis is concerned with the "what" of science. Technological analysis, then, requires scanning and monitoring from the time of basic research through product development and commercialization. The second part of the definition implies that technology is also concerned with the "how" of science. Therefore, a complete technological analysis also includes scanning of operations and manufacturing techniques.[9] Technological change takes place in two ways: through pure invention (and scientific discovery) and through process innovation.

PURE INVENTION

Pure invention is the creation of something radically different from existing technologies or products. Because it is different, it has certain characteristics that are economically interesting. An invention may have no competitors at its birth, thereby giving a monopoly to the individuals who hold the legal rights to the invention. The disadvantage is that the invention also has no market at the time of its invention, and there may never be a market for the commercial version of the invention. The combination of the monopolist upside with the no-ready-market downside makes the economic aspect of invention risky because the outcomes are potentially so variable.

New inventions can create new industries. The invention of the semiconductor created the computer industry in all its forms. The scientific discoveries made by geneticists created the biotech industry with all of its niches and segments. In the initial phase of such technologies and discoveries—in the creation of products and markets—entrepreneurs play the most important role. Over the product's life cycle, large organizational units develop to exploit these products and markets as they mature.

PROCESS INNOVATION

After the invention is successfully commercialized, the second type of technological change, **process innovation,** becomes dominant. Whereas invention is radical and revolutionary, carrying with it the potential to create new industries, process innovation is incremental and evolutionary. Its purpose is to make existing industries more efficient. Process innovation refers to the small changes in design, product formulation and manufacturing, materials, and service delivery that firms make to keep their product up-to-date and their costs down. Table 3–3 shows how technology and key related variables change over the course of the product life cycle. Scanning and monitoring the technological environment is difficult. Early in the life of a scientific discovery or breakthrough, much of the information relating to it is accessible only to highly trained scientists. Sometimes the information is purely conceptual, appearing only in scientific journals. Sometimes the information is simply private and not accessible to anyone but the research team. Aside from conferences and meetings of academicians and scientists, the most accessible sources of information are government databases such as those maintained by NASA or the National Technical Information Service (NTIS). Many of these are accessible on the Internet.

TABLE 3–3 Forms of Technological Change Over the Product Life Cycle Stages

	Product Life Cycle Stage			
	Introduction	*Shakeout*	*Growth*	*Mature*
Type of Innovation	Major product innovation or invention	→	→ Incremental product/major process innovation	→ Incremental product/process innovation
Location of Innovation	Entrepreneur	→ Marketing/R&D	→ Marketing/production	→ Production
Bases of Competition	Product, performance, or novelty	→	→ Product differentiation price	→ Price, image, minor differences
Production Process	Job shop	→ Batch	→ Islands of automation	→ Assembly line → Continuous flow
Dominant Function	Entrepreneur	→ Marketing/R&D	→ Marketing/production	→ Production/sales (promotion)
Management Role	Entrepreneur	→ Sophisticated market manager	→ Administrator/integrator	→ Steward
Modes of Integration	Informal communication	→ Informal communication, task forces, teams	→ Informal communication, teams, project manager	→ Formal communication, senior management committees
Organizational Structure	Free form	→ Functional organic	→ Project/matrix	→ Functional/bureaucratic

Source: Adapted from W. L. Moore, and M. L. Tushman, "Managing Innovation over the Product Life Cycle," in M. L. Tushman and W. L. Moore, eds., *Readings in the Management of Innovation* (Boston: Pitman Press, 1982), 143.

One Click, No Waiting

Friends say that 35-year-old Kim Polese has a knack for going to the heart of a problem. When she applied that knack to Internet headaches, the result was the formation of the new venture, Marimba, Inc., to produce a technology innovation that enables the speedy transfer of graphics and software on the Internet. Silicon Valley pundits say that Polese's insight may make Marimba the next hot technology company.

"No one likes to click and wait," observes Ms. Polese. Marimba's main product, a technology known as Castanet, relies upon a downloading method originally created by Sun Microsystems, Inc. to distribute programming to interactive television. Kim Polese was previously employed as product manager for the Sun division that developed that downloading method. In fact, it was Polese who christened that technology "Java," and who first spotted that it could be applied to on-line computer services and the Internet when interactive TV trials ran into problems.

Despite support from some of Sun's top executives, Kim Polese was passed over for promotion when Sun announced the creative of a Java business unit in May 1995. She resigned shortly thereafter, and formed Marimba with three other former Sun employees. To form the start-up, each of the four partners invested $15,000 in personal savings, and agreed not to draw salaries or accept outside funding from venture capitalists for six months. In July 1996, the company finally accepted $4 million in financing from Cleaner, Perking, Coalfield & Byers. Marimba's Castanet is an answer to one of the computer industry's hottest debates. While most computer users now buy their software in shrink-wrapped packages from companies like the Microsoft Corp., in the future they could buy and download much of their software from computer networks. This approach would also enable computer users to customize their software by selecting mix-and-match components from several companies.

The problem is that the Internet was created to move text and graphics, not software. Downloading even simple programs takes a lot of time. Castanet reduces that wait time dramatically, and offers software producers a way to distribute updates to users automatically over the Internet, even if the users' computers are engaged in other tasks. James Barksdale, CEO for Netscape Communications, recognizes Castanet as one of the "new wave" technologies that will transform the way information is retrieved from the Internet in the future. While hot technology processes like Castanet will undoubtedly attract competitors, Polese and Marimba have definite first-mover advantage.

Unlike other Silicon Valley stars, Kim Polese is a biophysicist by training, not a computer programmer. She says that the desire to start her own company was the real reason she left Sun, and that she realized that she could do it when she was setting prices for Sun's Java technology in 1995. When she studied other pricing models and consulted senior industry experts, Polese realized, "they were all making it up I realized if they were making it up, so could I." So now Kim Polese is a CEO in her own right, making up the price models and marketing plan for one of the hottest computer companies in town.

Source: Adapted from Joan Indiana Rigdon, "Hot Marimba Product Puts Focus on CEO," *Wall Street Journal,* December 13, 1996.

Frequently process innovation improvements are made by people working for large companies. If these companies are not the best place to fully exploit these improvements, the people who develop the changes may decide to become entrepreneurs. They literally spin themselves and their new product off into a new venture. Street Story 3–2 illustrates how and why this happens.

E-NOTES 3–3   TECHNOLOGICAL ANALYSIS

Analysis of technology studies the changes which occur from:

- pure invention,
- process invention.

Sociodemographic Analysis

The sociodemographic phase of business environment analysis has two highly related aspects: demographics and social trends (sometimes referred to as lifestyle trends). The interaction of these produce popular culture. Within a society's popular culture reside enormous business opportunities in consumer and durable goods, retailing and services, leisure and entertainment, and housing and construction.

DEMOGRAPHICS

Demographic changes are a major source of long-term social change. **Demography** is the study of trends in human populations: the size of the population and its various subgroups; the population's age structure, geographic distribution, and ethnic and racial mix; and the distribution of income and wealth within the population. Demographic change refers to changes in any of these variables and changes in the relationships between them. Demography is destiny, since all of these factors form the essence of consumer demand, industrial capacities, and purchasing power. From demographic analysis markets are created.

SOCIAL TRENDS AND VALUES

Social trends refer to the modes and manners in which people live their lives. Lifestyles reflect people's tastes and preferences in an economic sense. Lifestyle-related variables that affect new venture creation include household formation, work modes and labor force participation rates, education levels and attainments, patterns of consumption, and patterns of leisure.

Scanning and monitoring lifestyle changes is relatively easy because many diverse sources of data are available. Much of the data is aggregated and therefore suggests trends. There are both public and private sources for demographic data. The national government, through its agencies, bureaus, and regulatory bodies, collects vast amounts of data. Trade publications and specialist magazines and newspapers contribute demographic analysis. Consumer reports and the annual reports of corporations furnish additional details. One publication, *American Demographics*, is specifically designed to ferret out unusual and important trends.

Social values and social change together form an important component of sociodemographic analysis. "A **value** is a conception, explicit or implicit, distinctive of an individual or characteristic of a group of the desirable which influences the selection of available means and ends of action.[10] This means, simply, that the choices we make reflect our values. The values that individuals and groups hold cluster around the dimensions of the macroenvironment discussed earlier in this chapter. People hold political values relating to the role of government, political participation, and distributive justice.[11] They hold regulatory values concerning issues like consumerism and energy policy. Their social values reflect their choices concerning work, the relationship between races, and gender. Economic values are reflected in the choices they make relating to growth and taxation. Some of these values are at the core of the individual's belief systems, and other values are on the periphery.

E-NOTES 3–3   SOCIODEMOGRAPHIC ANALYSIS

Analysis of the sociodemographic investigates the impact of changes in:

- demographics,
- social trends and values.

Ecological Analysis

Ecological analysis is the study of the current state of the ecology. The **ecology** pertains to such issues as pollution and waste disposal, recycling of usable materials, protection of wildlife and wilderness preserve areas, workplace safety and hazards, and the general quality of life. Ecological analysis cuts across all the other areas already discussed: politics and government, the macroeconomy, technology, and lifestyle values. Ecological issues are bottom-line issues, and the entrepreneur must be as accountable as any other businessperson or citizen. Ecological awareness goes beyond simply addressing the manufacturing issues of pollution and waste.

The entrepreneur is part of the world movement toward **sustainable development**, that is, meeting the needs of the present generation without compromising the needs of future generations.[12] Future economic progress must be guided by ecological conservation. The ecosystem and its protection enters into all major entrepreneurial and business development decisions. For example, product development and design issues take into account the rate of usage and transformation of natural resources and the disposal of waste products. These decisions should be made in the planning stage of a business, not at the crisis stage. Also, financial calculations should fully value natural resources for their current worth and their potential value to future generations. Undervaluation of natural resources causes waste and overdemand.

The time when entrepreneurs could run the earth like a business in liquidation has long since passed.[13]

E-NOTES 3–4   MACROENVIRONMENT

The five segments of the business macroenvironment are:

- Politics and government,
- Economy,
- Technology,
- Sociodemographics,
- Ecology.

Sources of Opportunity

What is the most important thing to notice about the business environment? **Change.** Changes in the business environment offer opportunities for entrepreneurs. Existing firms have their resources, strategy, and organization structure geared for the past or current macroenvironment. When a change occurs, it is frequently easier for the new firm to spot the change and configure a set of resources and an organization to meet the new needs and the new realities. There are seven sources of opportunity to look for in the macroenvironment.[14]

THE UNEXPECTED

When current businesses are surprised by an unanticipated event, they are often unable to adapt quickly enough to take advantage. The event can be an unexpected success (good news) or an unexpected failure (bad news). For example, if war breaks out where it is unexpected, it changes the economics and demand structure of the warring parties and their populations. This can provide opportunity if it is ethically pursued. Similarly, a breakthrough in a peace negotiation also provides opportunity, since it changes the economies of the former combatants.

THE INCONGRUOUS

Incongruity is dissonance, things that "ought to be" but are not. It creates instability and opportunity. For example, it is incongruous for a growing industry with increasing sales not to be profitable. But it happens and is happening now on the Internet. Some key to the industry's economics has yet to be discovered. When reality and conventional wisdom collide, incongruity exists. Listen for "expert old-timers" who use the words "never" and "always" to explain how things should be. These unexamined assumptions have once been right but may now be wrong, and therefore provide opportunities for the responsive entrepreneur.

THE PROCESS NEED

This opportunity has its source in technology's inability to provide the "big breakthrough." Technicians often need to work out a way to get from point A to point B in some process. Currently, efforts are being made in the areas of superconductivity, fusion, interconnectivity, and the search for a treatment and cure for AIDS. Thomas Edison and others knew that in order to start the electric energy industry, they needed to solve a process need—to develop a light bulb that worked. Process need opportunities are often addressed by program research projects, which are the systematic research and analysis efforts designed to solve a single problem, such as the effort against AIDS.

INDUSTRY AND MARKET STRUCTURES

Changes in technology, both innovation and invention, change market and industry structures by altering costs, quality requirements, and volume capabilities. This alteration can potentially make existing firms obsolete if they are not attuned to it and are inflexible. Similarly, changes in social values and consumer tastes as well as demographics shift the economics of industries to new equilibria. The markets of firms that do not adapt are fair game for the entrepreneur.

DEMOGRAPHICS

Demographic changes are changes in the population or subpopulations of society. They can be changes in the size, age, structure, employment, education, or incomes of these groups. Such changes influence all industries and firms by changing the mix of products and services demanded, the volume of products and services, and the buying power of customers. Some of these changes are predictable, since people who will be older are already alive and birth and death rates stay fairly stable over time. Other changes are not predictable and are caused by natural disasters, war, social change, and immigration. Population statistics are available for assessment, but opportunities can be found before the data are published by observing what is happening in the street and being reported in the newspaper.

CHANGES IN PERCEPTION

"Is the glass half full or half empty?" The two perceptions are logically equivalent but reflect significantly different attitudes and behaviors. People hold different perceptions of the same reality, and these differences affect the products and services they demand and the amounts they spend. Some groups feel powerful and rich, others disenfranchised and poor. Some people think they are thin when they are not, others think they are too fat when they are not. The entrepreneur can sell power and status to the rich and powerful, and sell relief and comfort to the poor and oppressed. Whether people are rich or poor, if they perceive that they are middle class, they will demand education for their children, good housing for their family, and travel for their vacations.

NEW KNOWLEDGE

New knowledge is often seen as the "superstar" of entrepreneurial opportunity. Yet it can be "temperamental, capricious, and hard to manage."[15] It is not enough to have new knowledge; there must also be a way to make products from it and to protect the profits of those products from competition as the knowledge is spread to others. In addition, timing is critical. It frequently takes the convergence of many pieces of new knowledge to make a product. For example,

> A number of knowledges came together to make possible the computer. The earliest was the binary theorem, a mathematical theory going back to the seventeenth century that enables all numbers to be expressed by two numbers

only: one and zero. It was applied to a calculating machine by Charles Babbage in the first half of the nineteenth century. In 1890, Hermann Hollerith invented the punchcard going back to the invention in the early nineteenth century by Frenchman J-M. Jacquard. The punchcard makes it possible to convert numbers into "instructions." In 1906 an American, Lee de Forest, invented the audion tube, and with it created electronics. Then, between 1910 and 1913, Bertrand Russell and Alfred North Whitehead, in the *Principia Mathematica*, created symbolic logic, which enables us to express all logical concepts as numbers. Finally, during World War I, the concepts of programming and feedback were developed, primarily for the purposes of antiaircraft gunnery. By 1918, in other words, all the knowledge needed to develop the computer was available. The first computer became operational in 1946.[16]

E-NOTES 3–5   ENTREPRENEURIAL OPPORTUNITIES
Sources of opportunity in the macroenvironment can originate with:
- The unexpected,
- The incongruous,
- The process need,
- Industry and market structures,
- Demographics,
- Changes in perception,
- New knowledge.

COMPETITIVE ANALYSIS

The tools of competitive analysis are derived from economics, the so-called dismal science. Jokes are sometimes told to illustrate how deflating economics can be to entrepreneurs. So, let us begin with a joke.[17] A student and her economics professor, while walking together across campus, were engaged in a serious discussion concerning the price elasticity of demand for a college education. As they walked, the student's eyes fell on a piece of paper on the walk ahead of them. As they got closer, the student could see that the paper was a $20 bill. When they were upon the bill, the student bent down to pick it up. "What are you doing?" asked the economics professor. "There's a $20 bill on the walk," replied the student. "Nonsense," said the professor. "If there were a $20 bill on the ground, someone would have picked it up by now."

The joke demonstrates that a strong belief in the all-powerful, efficient-market model of economics can prevent a person from seeing an opportunity, even when it is right under his nose. The economics professor cannot believe that a $20 bill (an opportunity) would be lying on the walk, because under the assumptions of the efficient market opportunities disappear instantly.[18] And yet, current reality and economic history show that there are truly many opportunities for individuals who follow their instincts and act on them intelligently.

However, we should not dismiss the model of efficient markets too quickly. Although it is conceivable that the first mover, the initiator, or the innovator can earn the high returns of entrepreneurship by identifying and retrieving the $20 bill that no one else has seen, few business opportunities are of the once-and-done variety. Most ventures must be managed and operated over the foreseeable future, if not indefinitely. This is the point of our introductory quote. The key for the new venture is to find a measure of distinctiveness and develop a strategy to protect it. Therefore, the microeconomics of the firm and of that firm's industry are crucial to determining the venture's profit potential and the strategies most appropriate for realizing it.

Industry Analysis

The purpose of industry analysis is to determine what makes an industry attractive, and to decide which segments of the industry are most attractive. This analysis reveals appropriate strategies and resources to be procured or developed. Industry attractiveness is generally indicated either by above-normal profits or high growth. It depends on the resources and cost positions of the firms in the industry. For example, hard-to-replicate efficiency levels (resources) lead to high industry profitability, but they also make the industry less attractive for inefficient firms. On the other hand, high-growth industries are relatively more attractive for less-efficient firms than for efficient firms.[19] Research has shown that some industries are more profitable over the long run than others. Each year, *Fortune* magazine surveys all major industry groups and publishes the data. The results are remarkably stable over time. One-year results might be spectacularly bad or good, but overall profitability within an industry is constrained by the industry's characteristics.

The firm's ultimate objective is to earn above-normal profits. It does this in one of two ways: (1) developing a product that is distinctive enough that the customer will be willing to pay a price high enough to produce attractive margins, or (2) if it has a product identical to the competition's, being able to produce it at a cost low enough to produce attractive margins and profitability. These two strategies are broadly referred to as **differentiation strategy** and **low cost strategy**, respectively. When a firm pursues either the differentiation or the low-cost position for a subsegment of a market (as opposed to the general market), the strategy is called a **focus strategy**.[20]

A comprehensive analytical tool for determining the attractiveness of an industry is the *model of competitive analysis*.[21] This model describes five forces that determine the price/cost relationships within an industry and therefore define the industry's margins:

1. The **bargaining power of buyers**.
2. The **bargaining power of suppliers**.
3. The **threat of** relevant **substitutes**.
4. The threat of new entrants into the industry (presence of **entry barriers**).
5. The **rivalry** among existing firms (influenced by the other four factors).

Figure 3–2 provides a schematic of the five forces at work. The industry under analysis is referred to as the **focal industry** to distinguish it from the buyer, supplier, and substitute industries that exert pressure on it.

Buyer Power

In perfectly competitive markets, buyers or customers have no power other than to accept or reject the product offered. All products are the same, so there is no shopping around for quality, service, or other characteristics. All have the same price, so no haggling is possible. In fact, it is almost ironic that the model is known as the "com-

FIGURE 3–2 Elements of Industry Structure

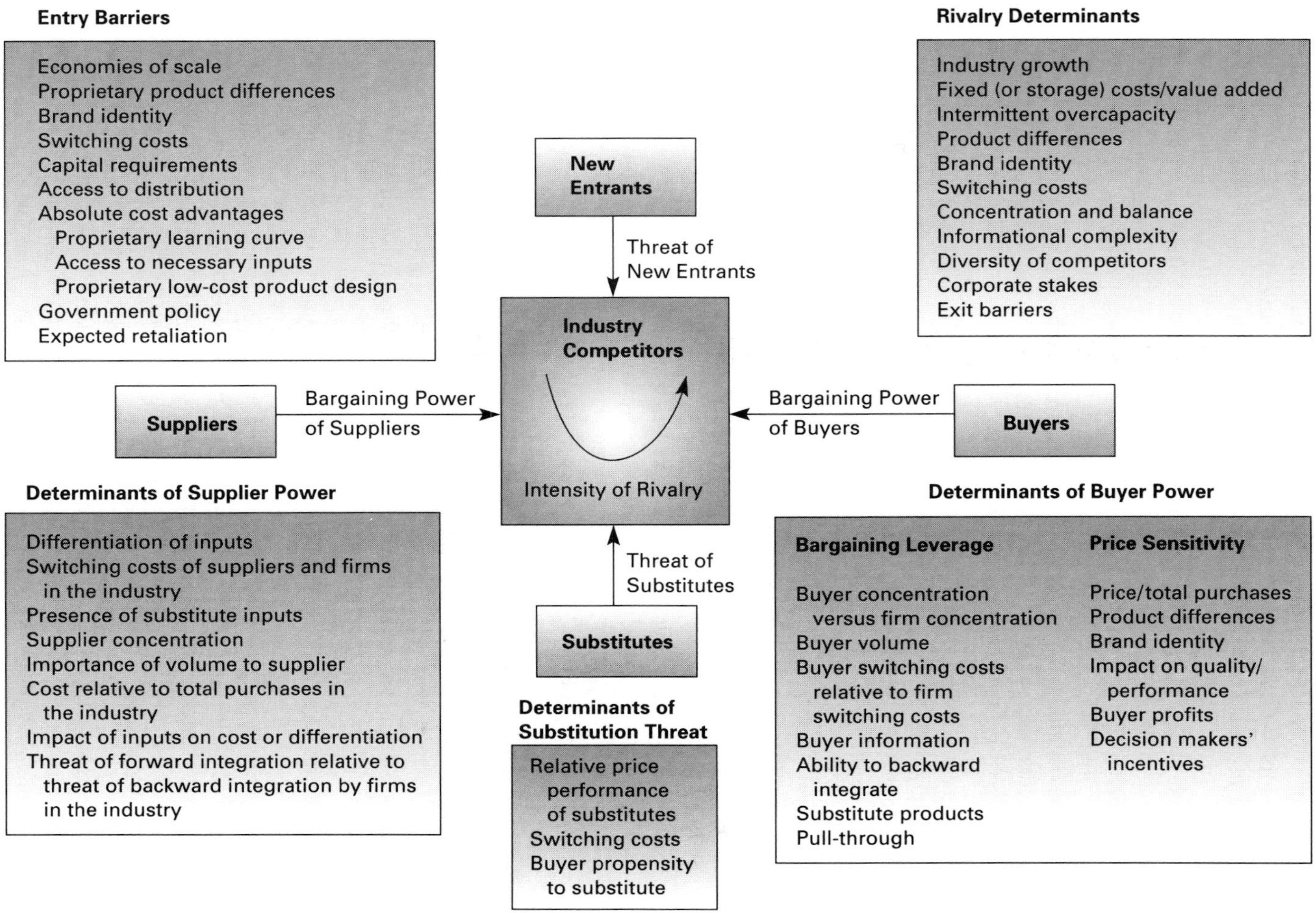

Entry Barriers

Economies of scale
Proprietary product differences
Brand identity
Switching costs
Capital requirements
Access to distribution
Absolute cost advantages
Proprietary learning curve
Access to necessary inputs
Proprietary low-cost product design
Government policy
Expected retaliation

Rivalry Determinants

Industry growth
Fixed (or storage) costs/value added
Intermittent overcapacity
Product differences
Brand identity
Switching costs
Concentration and balance
Informational complexity
Diversity of competitors
Corporate stakes
Exit barriers

Determinants of Buyer Power

Bargaining Leverage

Buyer concentration
versus firm concentration
Buyer volume
Buyer switching costs
relative to firm
switching costs
Buyer information
Ability to backward
integrate
Substitute products
Pull-through

Price Sensitivity

Price/total purchases
Product differences
Brand identity
Impact on quality/
performance
Buyer profits
Decision makers'
incentives

Determinants of Supplier Power

Differentiation of inputs
Switching costs of suppliers and firms
in the industry
Presence of substitute inputs
Supplier concentration
Importance of volume to supplier
Cost relative to total purchases in
the industry
Impact of inputs on cost or differentiation
Threat of forward integration relative to
threat of backward integration by firms
in the industry

Determinants of Substitution Threat

Relative price
performance
of substitutes
Switching costs
Buyer propensity
to substitute

New Entrants — Threat of New Entrants

Suppliers — Bargaining Power of Suppliers

Industry Competitors — Intensity of Rivalry

Buyers — Bargaining Power of Buyers

Substitutes — Threat of Substitutes

Adapted with the permission of The Free Press, A Division of Simon & Schuster from Competitive Advantage: Creating and Sustaining Superior Performance by Michael E. Porter. Copyright © 1985 by Michael E. Porter.

petitive" model, because sellers do not actually compete directly for customers. Products are produced for the market and are either purchased or not purchased depending on the buyer's utility function (for a final consumer) or on the production function (for a producer).

When we relax this condition, we find that in a number of scenarios the buyer has a great deal of bargaining power. The two issues that are dearest to the buyer in bargaining situations are (1) decreases in price for the product, and (2) increases in the product's quality. Both of these buyer bargaining positions decrease the producer firm's margins. Price concessions squeeze margins from the revenue side, while increases in quality squeeze margins by increasing the seller's costs.[22]

Once the conditions for perfect competition are relaxed, a buyer group can become powerful in several circumstances.

1. **Buyer Group Concentration.** If there are more sellers selling than there are buyers buying, the natural tendency is for the sellers to reduce prices to make a sale. Even if they do not reduce prices, they offer additional services to make quality improvements to their products, both of which have the same effect of squeezing margins. If the buying group makes large purchases, in an absolute as well as a relative sense, it will bargain for volume discounts. The bases for these discounts are (1) the threat to withhold the order and disrupt production, (2) lower per-unit costs of billing and shipping large orders, and (3) lower production costs resulting from long production runs.

2. **Buyer's Costs.** If the products represent a significant share of the buyer's total costs or total income, the buyer becomes extremely price sensitive. When purchases are large, small concessions in price produce large benefits for the buyer. Most consumers are familiar with this situation, since bargaining over the price of cars and homes is the primary consumer bargaining experience. The automobile and residential real estate industries allow people to bargain over the prices of these items because they know their customers are price sensitive owing to the size of the purchase. These industries have, of course, adapted to this sensitivity by hiding the true reservation prices (the lowest price the seller will take) of the products from the customer at all times. So consumers bargain a little, but they still pay enough to salvage the margins of the sellers.[23]

3. **Similar Products.** If the buyer is indifferent among sellers because the products available for purchase are basically alike, the buyer has power. If buyers can procure alternatives, they naturally look for a reason to buy from a particular seller, and one good reason is a lower price. The implication here is that the selling firm may believe it has a product that should command a premium price because of its high quality and special features. But if these features are unimportant or not communicated to the buyer, the buyer will still shop on price.

4. **Switching Costs.** If the buyer faces few switching costs and can shop around for price or quality without incurring high transaction costs, the buyer is powerful. Switching costs are costs that lock the buyer into an ongoing relationship with the seller. An example is frequent-flyer miles. Travelers will fly higher-priced, less-convenient air routes to accumulate these miles. The cost of switching airlines is the loss of the frequent-flyer miles.[24] Sometimes high transaction costs also result from switching

vendors or searching for information. Faced with these costs, the buyer remains passive in the current relationship, enabling the seller to maintain profitable margins.

5. **Buyer Income.** The buyer who earns low profits or has a low income is price sensitive. Sensitivity is increased when the buyer is short of funds, either personal income (for consumers) or profits from operations (for industrial buyers). Although rich people sometimes haggle over a price and purchasing agents of profitable companies search for a penny-saving agreement, more often, when the buyer has enough funds, the cost of negotiating a tough deal outweighs the minor savings.

6. **Threat of Integration.** If the buyer firm can make a credible threat to fabricate a product or provide a service itself if it chooses not to buy it on the open market, it increases its power by gaining bargaining leverage over the sellers in the industry. This factor brings into play the classic make-or-buy decision, and it does so on a strategic level. If it can provide all the product itself, it is a credible threat for full **backward integration**. If it can provide some of the input, the process is known as **tapered integration**. The reasons for increased buyer power are as follows: (1) the buyer can make a take-it-or-leave-it offer to the seller with the full knowledge that if the seller "leaves it," the firm can still supply itself; (2) the buyer knows the actual costs of producing the product of delivering the service and can negotiate more effectively down to the seller's reservation price. The major offsetting factor for the seller is the credibility of its threat of **forward integration**.

7. **Indifference to Quality.** If the products or services in an industry are not distinguished by quality, cost is a determining factor in consumer choice. In the presence of indifference to quality, the major reason for distinguishing between sellers is price. Increased price sensitivity causes buyers to shop around and will negatively affect the industry's margins.

8. **Full Information.** The more information the buyer group has about product prices, manufacturing costs, comparative product attributes, and the negotiating strategies of sellers, the more bargaining leverage it has. In young industries, where buyers and sellers are new at dealing with one another, certain cost and price data can be kept secret. This makes firms in young industries less likely to face pressure on margins. In mature industries, as firms build up long records and files of information on each other, they are more likely to have full information, causing downward pressure on prices.

Seldom does an industry's products have only one type of buyer. Certainly, for consumer products, market segmentation analysis demonstrates that there are many types of buyers. Each segment possesses its own utility functions and is therefore subject to strategic product-positioning tactics. The same is true in industrial marketing. This makes **buyer selection** a key strategic variable. Firms strive to hold a portfolio of buyers, each with a different degree of bargaining power. If a firm has only weak buyers, its short-term margins may be good, but the firm is not producing high-quality products and is probably not investing enough in the kind of product improvements and innovation that more powerful buyers demand. These deficiencies make the venture potentially vulnerable to an innovative competitor that produces high-quality products or services. If the venture has only strong buyers in its portfolio, it will have low margins and will always be a captive of its customers. Such a firm is vulnerable to the whims of its customers and to their desire to increase their own profits.

Supplier Power

Like buyers, suppliers exert bargaining power over an industry in two ways. Suppliers seek to (1) increase the prices they charge for the products and services they sell or (2) decrease the quality of those products and services for the current market-clearing prices. Either of these bargaining objectives has the net effect of squeezing the margins in the focal industry and, other things being equal, making the industry less attractive. If the supplier industry is successful in the use of these tactics, it shifts profits from the focal industry to its own industry, capturing the economic power that the focal industry may have with its own buyers and appropriating the gains for itself. Entrepreneurs who concentrate all their energy and analysis on their buyers and none on the supplier industry may well find that profits are quickly eroded by cost-squeeze pressures.

Supplier power is basically the other side of the buyer-power coin. The same principles apply, only this time the focal industry is the buyer. Suppliers can exert pressure on margins under several conditions.

1. **Supplier Concentration.** When the supplying industry is dominated by a few companies and is more concentrated than the focal industry, suppliers have power.

2. **Role of Substitutes.** Suppliers are powerful when there are few good substitutes for the supplying industry's products. Even large, powerful suppliers cannot maintain high prices and low quality if good substitutes for their products are available.

3. **Purchasing Power.** If the focal industry is not an important customer for the suppliers, the suppliers have power. If the total dollars spent by the focal industry is small relative to the supplying industry's total sales, it will be difficult for the focal industry to obtain price concessions, quality improvements, or extra services such as delivery, warranties, and on-site repair.

4. **Importance of Quality.** When the product or service being purchased is crucial to the success of the industry's product or service, this input must be high quality. Focal industry firms often pay dearly for this high quality. Without substitutes of similar quality, the focal industry can expect cost increases for the product or service, which could severely diminish its profitability.

5. **Switching Costs.** Switching costs prevent buyers from playing suppliers off against each other in an attempt to bargain for price concessions or improvements in quality. This is, of course, analogous to the buyer-power conditions mentioned in the preceding section.

6. **Threat of Integration.** Again, the analogy to the buyer-power situation is apparent. If suppliers can do for themselves what the focal industry does, the focal industry cannot expect to exert much bargaining power. For suppliers, this is a use-or-sell decision. They have the option to either sell their input to another firm or use that input themselves to produce a final product. Also, tapered integration, where the supplier uses only some of the input internally, can be used to generate data on costs, which enhances the supplier's bargaining power.

Although it is natural to think of suppliers only as firms that sell the entrepreneur goods and services, other supplier industries may require analysis. For example, labor, capital, land, information, and business services are all suppliers. Each can be analyzed using the framework described previously. Every new venture has a portfolio of suppliers—some can be influenced by strategy and some are too powerful to be influenced. **Supplier selection strategy** minimizes the possibility that profits made in output markets will be lost in input decisions.

The Threat of Substitutes

Every industry competes against other industries for customers. Sometimes the competition is fairly direct, such as with fiberglass insulation versus rock wool, cellulose, or plastic foam.[25] At other times the substitute-product rivalry is indirect, though still real. For example, the "eat at home" food-processing industry and its distribution chain—the grocery stores and supermarkets—competes with the "meals away from home" restaurant industry and all its many segments. There are times when it is difficult to tell whether another industry is a factor. For example, does the motor home industry compete with other vehicles (cars, trucks, and boats), or does it compete with motels located along interstate highways and near campgrounds and parks? Clearly the substitute product is defined by its function, not by the way it looks, by how it is produced, or even by what it costs.

It is important for the entrepreneur to understand the nature of substitute products for three reasons. First, when the entrepreneurs are the first to market a new product or product type, they sometimes believe they have no competition because "we're the first ones doing this." However, competition often exists in *function*, and a competitive challenge from a substitute industry is likely to surface. Second, substitutes can limit the potential returns to the focal industry by placing a price ceiling on what the industry can charge. There is always a price so high that it will force customers to switch from one industry's product to another's. The more attractive the value of the substitute (its price/performance relationship), the lower the price ceiling.

Last, existing firms often disparage the threat of substitutes because of psychological factors that block quick action. For the entrepreneur, this can be an advantage. The entrepreneur usually has a period of time to maneuver before established firms recognize the threat. In Street Story 3–3 we see the competitive effects of buyer power, supplier power, and substitutes on a group of new ventures in a new industry—website publishing.

Entry Barriers

Why is it that the professor of economics is so certain that the $20 bill (remember our little joke) is not there? It is because nothing prevents someone else from picking it up first. There are no entry barriers to the "found $20 opportunity." Entry barriers are a crucial factor for entrepreneurs in analyzing industry structure.[26] The entrepreneur must overcome entry barriers as they currently exist and later attempt to create entry barriers to prevent others from following and diminishing the found opportunity.

Reality Bites the Internet

To many it seemed like the perfect new venture: a business with low-entry barriers and eager buyers, with lots of opportunity for innovation and creativity. Plus it was cool, because it was a way to do business on the World Wide Web. So hundreds of companies, both large and small, scurried to join the communication revolution by developing electronic publications such as on-line magazines, chat rooms, talk shows, and soap operas.

"A lot of people out there thought the Internet was a one-way ticket to a pot of gold," observes Halsey Minor, chief executive of CNET Inc., a large San Francisco Web publisher. "But the vast majority of companies that are trying to do content on the Web won't become profitable."

Those on-line entrepreneurs thought the rapidly expanding number of computer users meant they would be able to attract subscription-paying viewers to their on-line publications, plus lure advertisers who wanted to reach those viewers. It is now estimated that there are PCs in more than one third of U.S. homes. But a mere 15 percent of those homes are connected to an on-line service, and only another 10 percent to 15 percent of that number are classified as heavy users who sign on daily. According to a recent survey by the research firm Odyssey Ventures Inc., a heavy Internet user spends about 6 1/2 hours on line each week compared to the 35 hours he or she spends tuned in to the TV.

The competition for paid subscribers has been harder than most expected. The Dow Jones's Wall Street Journal Interactive Edition fell from 600,000 to 50,000 registered users when the newspaper started charging for subscriptions in September 1996. "Right now there are too many people who are too damned cheap ... er, we mean ... engaged by the novelty of the medium to pay extra for content," says Michael Kinsley, editor of Slate, Microsoft's on-line political journal. Microsoft has now abandoned its plan to collect an annual fee for Slate.

The competition for advertising dollars has been intense, too. Jupiter Research LLC estimates there were more than 900 companies competing for $300 million Web advertising dollars in 1996, but that two thirds of those ads went to the 10 biggest companies. Many of the successful but smaller Web sites are attracting less than $3,000 a month in sales. Analysts predict that sales will reach $5 billion by the year 2000, but Web publishers will continue to face small audiences, stiff competition, and increasing production costs.

The computer waves are littered with casualties. Global Network Navigator, known to many as the first commercial Web site, has already been terminated by its parent, America Online Inc. Turner Network Television was forced to cancel its electronic magazine after only seven months. TNT now has a movie-only site to promote its cable-TV programs. Publications including The Spot, the Web's first soap opera, and Happy Puppy, a popular site to preview and download games, have been forced to pare personnel, scrounge for new investors, and even scuttle dreams of going public. Even media giants Time Warner and Knight-Ridder are rumored to be losing millions in order to keep their Web sites afloat.

Time and technology may make a difference. The growing number of on-line users, along with super-fast transmission lines and more powerful PCs, may make Web publishing more attractive in the next few years. That's why well-heeled companies like Knight-Ridder are willing to invest $20 million a year and hold on to their Web ventures. "We don't have a choice," notes Bob Ingle, Knight-Ridder's president of new media. "This is the future."

Source: Adapted from Don Clark, "Facing Early Loses, Some Web Publishers Begin to Pull the Plug," *Wall Street Journal*, January 14, 1997.

This is the **paradox of entrepreneurship**. If the entrepreneur can find an industry that is easy to enter, then it may be similarly easy for others to enter. This makes the opportunity a fleeting one, since, as we show below, low entry barriers are a characteristic of unprofitable industries. If the entrepreneur finds an industry that is difficult to enter (and by implication profitable), all its profit potential might have to be expended in high initial start-up costs to overcome the barriers.[27] The conclusion might therefore be: No profit can be made in an industry with low-entry barriers, and no profit can be made in an industry with high-entry barriers (the conclusion is the same for intermediate situations). In other words, "What $20 bill?" The answer to the paradox is that new entrant resources and strategic differences between new firms and existing firms allow entry despite high barriers.

Table 3–4 presents the major entry barriers that face a new venture entering an existing industry. There are two general types: (1) **structural barriers**, which result from the industry's history, technology, and macroenvironment, and (2) **retaliatory barriers**, which are a function of current competitor's anticipated reactions.

TABLE 3–4 Entry Barriers

Structural Barriers	*Retaliatory Barriers*
Economies of scale	Competitors' reputation
Excess capacity	Industry history
Product differentiation core	Attack on competitors' business
Specific assets	Slow industry growth rate
Capital requirements	Competitors with substantial resources
Switching costs	Price cutting
Access to distribution channels	Legal challenges
Cost disadvantages unrelated to size	

STRUCTURAL BARRIERS TO ENTRY

The structural barriers prevent the entrepreneur from getting started, and that represents a lost opportunity. But more dangerous to the entrepreneur are the retaliating barriers, because these can destroy the entrepreneurs chances of success after a large investment of time, money, and resources.

RETALIATORY BARRIERS TO ENTRY

Usually, when a new firm, especially one that is relatively small, enters an industry, there is little response from that firm's large, well-established competitors. Sometimes, however, entry by a new venture provokes a strong response from larger and more powerful firms. Because retaliation becomes an immediate threat to the survival of the new venture, the owners of new firms should understand when they may provoke retaliation. Large, established firms retaliate under the following three conditions:

1. ***When they have a reputation to uphold and a history of retaliation.*** Firms that are historically known as aggressive competitors do not want to lose that reputation, even if the competition is a new venture of small size. This is because that reputation is an asset (rare, valuable, imperfectly imitable, and nonsubstitutable) that helps protect the competitor from other aggressive strategies and tactics. If the reputation is tarnished, other firms may decide to attack.
2. ***If the attack is at the core business.*** When a newcomer attacks the core business of an established firm, that firm feels the greatest threat and will most likely retaliate.
3. ***If the entry occurs in a slow-growth industry.*** When an industry is growing slowly, in terms of total sales dollars and unit volume, each new entrant takes away a small percentage of sales that an established firm was counting on. The slow-growth industry has the elements of a zero-sum game: Sales garnered by one firm are forever lost to all other firms.

PRICE CUTTING

Retaliation can be expected in two additional situations: when the product is commodity-like and when the industry has high fixed costs. Both are likely to cause price-cutting retaliation in an attempt to force the new firm out of business by driving the industry price level down to the entry-deterring price, the hypothetical price that will just balance the rewards and cost of entry. In other words, it is the product or service price that makes the entrepreneur forecast zero profits for the proposed new venture. When an industry's prices are above the entry-deterring level, no rational entrepreneur would start a new business in that industry. The existing firms will allow prices to rise again when the threat of entry has subsided. If the threat is persistent, these firms have to use other methods or concede that their industry imposes low-entry barriers and therefore, other things being equal, is not an attractive industry to be in.

In some situations the small, new venture is protected from entry-deterring price cuts. Table 3–5 lists the factors that both encourage and inhibit the use of price cutting as a competitive tactic. The table illustrates that when price cutting is not likely to work—when it is likely to cause major losses for the price cutter and probably provoke large, existing competitors to follow suit—the new firm can operate under the **price umbrella** of the existing competition without fear of price retaliation.

TABLE 3-5 Factors Affecting Retaliatory Pricing	
Encouraging Factors	*Discouraging Factors*
Elastic demand	Inelastic demand
Cost advantages	No cost advantages
Excess capacity	Tight capacity
Small competitors	Large competitors
New competitors	Long-time rivalry
Single-product markets	Market interdependency

LEGAL CHALLENGES TO NEW VENTURES

The new firm can expect retaliation to take forms other than just price cutting, especially when price cutting is not advisable for the larger firms. Legal attacks have become common. The basis for a court battle could be patent, copyright, or trademark infringement, violation of a former-employee non-compete clause, claims of defective products, violation of environmental laws, or, in the case of a foreign new venture entrant, claims of dumping and unfair competition.

Let us conclude our discussion of entry barriers by returning to the anecdote that led off this chapter—that of the economics professor and the $20 bill. The professor refuses to pick up the money because he cannot believe it is still there. Why? Because there are no entry barriers that would prevent somebody else from picking it up first. And since the professor is nothing if not rational, and the odds that he got there first minuscule, the bill cannot exist. This is a case of his assumptions preventing him from seeing the opportunity. But before we condemn the professor for his blindness, let us consider this: If he would look down and see the bill, so might others at approximately the same time. And they might rush over and contest the ownership of that $20 bill. Some would be loud, and others might use force. A deal would then be struck giving each competitor for the money just enough to reward him or her for the trouble it took to strike the bargain. In some sense, they would all be even and the costs would equal the rewards. Thus, it is not only the professor's assumption but also the competitors' reactions that lead him to keep walking.

Rivalry between Firms

The effects of strong buyer power, strong supplier power, good substitutes, and low entry barriers on an industry make the industry more competitive. Each force, by itself, can cause costs to rise or prices to fall, or both. This cost push or price squeeze reduces the operating margins of the firms in the industry. Reduced margins force less-efficient firms to go out of business (if exit barriers are low),[28] the modestly efficient firms to break even, and the most efficient firms to endure low profitability until industry conditions are altered.

The rivalry and competitiveness between firms increase when the other four forces in the model are negative. However, additional conditions lead to rivalry and low industry attractiveness. These conditions focus on the status of the existing firms.

Rivalry among firms increases (and, other things being equal, margins and profitability decreases) when the following conditions prevail.

1. **Numerous and Balanced Competitors.** The more competitors there are, the more likely it is that some of them will "misbehave" by slashing prices and quality. This causes problems for everyone. When competitors are balanced and all are about the same size, there is no clear leader in the industry to whom the others can look for direction. An industry leader helps maintain price discipline and keeps the industry from engaging in destructive price wars.

2. **Slow Industry Growth.** When an industry is growing, there are enough customers to go around and fill most firms' capacity. Slow growth causes firms to compete for customers, either with price decreases or quality increases. Also, as growth slows, the need for advertising may increase, adding an additional expense and hurting margins.

3. **High Fixed Costs.** Firms with high fixed costs have high operating leverage. This means that they need high volumes to break even, but after the break-even point has been reached, each unit sold adds significantly to the bottom line. Therefore, industries with high fixed costs have strong incentives to fill capacity any way they can. This may lead to price cutting. Examples of this are the recent history of the airline and automobile industries.

4. **Commodity-type Products.** When the product is a commodity, or is perceived by the public as a commodity because the industry cannot differentiate products, pressures for intense price and service competition grow. Related to this condition is the absence of switching costs and increased buyer power.[29] It is time to address the "all things being equal" assumption interspersed in our discussion. In this context, "all things being equal" refers to the firms' resource-based strategies. That is, industries are attractive or unattractive for entry without considering the resources the new entrant may bring to the venture. The type of resources and the extent to which they possess the four attributes of competitive advantage do make a difference. An unattractive industry might be a profitable opportunity for a firm with a winning configuration of resources. An attractive industry might produce mediocre results for a firm without any resource advantages.

Competitor Analysis

So what is the new entrepreneur to do with all of this analysis? The new entrant in an industry must perform a detailed analysis of its competition. The industry analysis, discussed previously, precedes the competitor analysis and is more general. The data required for the industry analysis were aggregated; in their disaggregated (firm-level) form, these data provide the raw material needed to assess the strategy and resource base of the competition.

IDENTIFYING THE COMPETITION

The first step is to determine who the competition is. This is the equivalent of asking, "What business am I in?" and "What needs does my product/service fulfill for the customer?" The competition consists of firms that fulfill the same customer needs or have the potential to serve those customers. How can this competition be determined?

Current competitors can be identified in a number of ways. A direct method is to ask customers (of existing firms) or potential customers (of new ventures) where else they would consider procuring the product or service. Indirect methods include scanning trade and business directories and the Yellow Pages and the Internet. To discover the larger competitors, the entrepreneur should check *Value Line, Standard & Poor's* classifications, and the *Disclosure* database that identifies firms by the U.S. government's four-digit Standard Industrial Classification code.[30]

RANKING COMPETITORS

The next step is to evaluate a set of relevant current and potential competitors on the basis of the qualities of their resources. This analysis will give a picture of the competitors' relative strengths and weaknesses and will present a comparative framework enabling the entrepreneur to position the new venture. Weaker competitors may be attacked head-on. Competitors with characteristics similar to the new entrant's may be candidates for alliances that would strengthen both firms. Or the entrepreneur may be required to position the new venture around powerful competitors to avoid head-to-head conflict.

A useful tool for competitor analysis is the resource-based grid in Figure 3–3. The grid presents the six types of resources by attribute for each relevant competitor and requires the entrepreneur to assign a score for each dimension.[31] The entrepreneur's own venture is included in the analysis.

The initial information derived from the competitor analysis will rank the competitors on each type of resource, producing a grand ranking of all competitors. The next step is to examine how the competitors use their resource bases to confront industry forces. That is, how do the competitors' strategies influence buyer power, supplier power, threats of substitutes, entry barriers, and rivalry among firms? The competitors' strategies are revealed by studying their deployment of resources.[32] This examination enables the entrepreneur to answer the second question posed earlier in the chapter: What is the best way to compete in the industry for the highest profitability? The answer is: *Look for ways to employ your resource base that reduce the forces threatening firm profitability, and position your firm for leadership in that area.*

E-NOTES 3–6 INDUSTRY ENVIRONMENT

Analysis of the industry or competitive environment involves issues including:

- Competitive analysis,
- Industry analysis,
- Buyer power,
- Supplier power,
- The threat of substitutes,
- Entry barriers,
- Rivalry between firms.

Instructions On a scale of 1 through 7 evaluate the competition's resource base. A value of 1 indicates that the firm has absolutely no advantage in the resource area; a value of 4 indicates that the firm possesses about the same resource capabilities as other industry participants; a value of 7 indicates that the firm possesses an absolute advantage in the resource category.

Resource type and attribute	Own firm	Competitors #1	#2	#3	#4	#5
Financial resources						
Rare						
Valuable						
Imperfectly imitable						
Nonsubstitutable						
Physical resources						
Rare						
Valuable						
Imperfectly imitable						
Nonsubstitutable						
Human resources						
Rare						
Valuable						
Imperfectly imitable						
Nonsubstitutable						
Technical resources						
Rare						
Valuable						
Imperfectly imitable						
Nonsubstitutable						
Reputational resources						
Rare						
Valuable						
Imperfectly imitable						
Nonsubstitutable						
Organizational resources						
Rare						
Valuable						
Imperfectly imitable						
Nonsubstitutable						

Total Scores _____

Grand Mean _____

+/– from Mean _____

FIGURE 3–3 Resource-Based Competitive Analysis Grid

Summary

One way of looking at the business environment is as a stock of resources: financial, physical, technological, reputational, human, and organizational. The entrepreneur with an effective strategy for acquiring resources can control some of these resources, with others being controlled by competitors and potential competitors. No single entrepreneur can control all the resources. Larger forces are at work, and it is unlikely that the trends in the macroenvironment will be influenced by any single firm.

The entrepreneur must understand the macroenvironment, for it establishes the political, economic, technological, sociodemographic, and ecological rules under which the new firm is created and must operate. The entrepreneur must be able to scan and monitor the macroenvironment and to recognize the contingencies and constraints the macroenvironment imposes. This analysis, however, is not enough for the firm's success. The entrepreneur must be able to forecast and assess development, using as a knowledge resource the four attributes required for competitive advantage. Also required is the ability to marshal the resources necessary to overcome the constraints or effectively deal with the contingencies.

Understanding the elements and the processes of the competitive market enable us to discover the forces that make an industry attractive to the entrepreneur. These forces are power of buyers, the power of suppliers, the threat of substitutes, the height of the entry barriers, and the nature of the rivalry between competitors. When buyers and suppliers are powerful, when good substitutes exist for the firm's products, and when entry barriers are low and rivalry is intense, the industry is not attractive because profits are likely to be low.

However, the resource configuration of the entrepreneur occasionally enables entry into an unattractive industry. If an entrepreneur can configure his or her resource base and design a strategy that offsets the profit-reducing forces within an industry, the new venture can achieve a sustainable competitive advantage.

Attractive industries provide opportunities for profitability. The forces that determine rivalry in attractive industries are not strong forces, and the rivalry is not cutthroat. Firms compete on the level of product innovations, advertising and brand loyalty, and distribution channels, a level that enables firms to differentiate and position their products. There is little pressure on prices, and increased costs are passed along to the customer as increased value. Operating margins are generous and sufficient for reinvestment and shareholder distributions. An industry characterized by high profitability and good returns to investors is attractive for entry, all things being equal.

Key Terms

- Macroenvironment
- Scanning
- Monitoring business cycle
- Forecasting
- Assessing
- Stakeholders
- Trade barriers
- Political risk
- Utility patents
- Design patents
- Plant patents
- Differentiation strategy
- Low-cost strategy
- Focus strategy
- Bargaining power of buyers
- Bargaining power of suppliers
- Threat of substitutes
- Entry barriers

- Structural change
- Cyclical change
- Procyclical price umbrella
- Countercyclical
- Acyclical
- Technology
- Pure invention
- Process innovation
- Demography
- Values
- Rivalry
- Focal industry
- Backward integration
- Tapered integration
- Forward integration
- Buyer selection strategy
- Paradox of entrepreneurship
- Ecology

- Sustainable development
- Retaliatory barriers
- Supplier selection strategy
- Structural barriers

Discussion Questions

1. Perform "thought experiments" on the following businesses using the five dimensions of the macroenvironment: politics, macroeconomy, technology, sociodemography, and ecology factors.
   a. Video game designer
   b. Pizza restaurant
   c. Manufacturer of woman's sweaters
2. What are the costs and benefits of the process model of environmental analysis? How could an "ordinary" entrepreneur set up and manage such a process?
3. Discuss the primary factors in political and governmental analysis. Compare and contrast these factors for the following countries: United States, Russia, China, Nigeria.
4. Identify the stakeholders of the university or college that you attend. Which are the most powerful? Why and when? Which are the least powerful? Why and when?
5. Discuss how technological change creates entrepreneurial opportunities. What are some current changes under way and what opportunities do they create?
6. Discuss how demographic change creates entrepreneurial opportunities. What are some current changes underway and what opportunities do they create?
7. Discuss how ecological change creates entrepreneurial opportunities. What are some current changes under way and what opportunities do they create?
8. How do challenging old assumptions and traditions lead to entrepreneurial opportunities?
9. How can the entrepreneur influence the power of buyers and suppliers to make them more favorable or overcome them?
10. How do substitutes influence industry attractiveness and profitability?
11. How do entry barriers influence industry attractiveness and profitability?
12. Explain the paradox of entrepreneurship.
13. How can the entrepreneur employ resources to obtain a sustainable competitive advantage? Refer to the elements of the Porter model in your answer.

Exercises

1. Return to the business treatments and business ideas that you developed in the Chapter 2 exercises.
   a. Set up a system for analyzing the business environment for that business. Where does the information come from and how will you assess and evaluate it?
   b. Evaluate the five dimensions for your business:
      Political-governmental
      Macroeconomy
      Technology
      Sociodemographics
      Ecology
2. Return to the business treatments and ideas that you developed in the Chapter 2 exercises. In what ways do these ideas emerge from the business environment? How does the business environment support these ideas? What resources are available from the business environment that will support these business ideas?
3. Scan the business press. Identify the entrepreneurial opportunity from each of the seven sources described in the chapter.
4. Perform an analysis of the industry that you (and your team) are consider-

ing for your new venture. Use outside sources for data, such as the library, computer databases, and industry experts.

5. Perform an analysis of the competitors for your new venture. Use Figure 3–3 as a summary sheet to guide you in your research.

DISCUSSION CASE

The Meter Is Ticking

Change is coming to the parking meter industry, and Vincent Yost and his "smart meter" are prepared to lead the charge, assuming that Yost can keep on dropping the quarters into his own meter of opportunity.

There are currently more than 5 million parking meters lining the streets of the United States. Most of those meters aren't mechanically much different from the very first parking meter, which debuted in Oklahoma City in 1935. A mere ten percent of meters today are electronic, meaning that they feature digital readouts and more reliable innards, and most significant of all, have the capacity to count coins and therefore safeguard against theft by the employees who empty the meters. Within the next ten years it is estimated that those electronic meters will dominate the industry.

Vincent Yost has a high-tech meter that can do all that his electronic competitors can do, and more. He has developed a meter that is equipped with an infrared detection system to sense when a car enters and leaves a parking spot. When a car leaves, his product responds by zeroing the meter's clock and wiping out any remaining time, meaning that the parking authority is then free to resell time the previous user may already have paid for. This feature alone increased parking revenues by as much at 50 percent in field tests in New Jersey and Pennsylvania. Yost also has a software package that worked with hand-held remote units to track expired meters, compute average parking time, and collect other key parking data. "If the mechanical meter is a single, and the electronic meter is a double, this is a home run or a grand slam, even," says Leonard Bier, acting executive director of parking for the city of Camden, New Jersey.

Then why is it that Yost's company, Intelligent Devices, Inc., has yet to receive a single coin from sales? A large part of the problem is his customer base. Parking meters are purchased by municipal governments, notoriously slow-moving and risk-avoiding customers. "Bureaucrats try to do one thing, and that's not rock the boat," explains Scott A. Clark, a one-time government vendor. The Pittsburgh Parking Authority recently ordered 1,000 meters from one of Yost's competitors, overriding the endorsement of their own executive director, simply because Pittsburgh didn't want to be the first big city to install smart meters. Timing a sale to a city government can be a bureaucratic nightmare, too. "You miss an annual budget, you lose a whole year, and it's not unusual for that to happen two or three times," observes David L. McNeff, vice-president of sales for Printrak International Inc., which sells automated fingerprint-ID systems to some city agencies. Yost has been working with cities like Hoboken and New York for almost two years without a sale, despite the fact that he has demonstrated in both cities that smart meters will increase revenue.

Price is the second obstacle for Intelligent Devices. Their parking meters cost about $400 apiece, three times the cost of competing electronic meters. The company is now offering cities a five-year lease plan, and is armed with data to demonstrate that financing will enable a city to pay for the meters and turn a profit. But even under the lease plan, their only sale to date has been an order for 58 parking meters from the little town of New Hope, Pennsylvania, and the lease company still hasn't paid Intelligent Devices.

"I didn't expect this," admits Yost, who was president of a computerized cash register company when he created the smart meter. He traded his stake in that company for the rights to the parking meter and six months severance pay, and then used that money to set up the business in his home in 1994. But Yost admits he didn't understand that selling to governments would be different than selling to businesses, and also didn't realize the time lag for parking meter orders could be so long.

"The worry is absolutely crushing," says Yost, who has now invested $350,000 out of his pocket in the company. "But I use it to drive me. Bill Gates said it—the paranoid makes the money. And I worry a lot." Vincent Yost reevaluates a lot, too. He has now made refinements in his parking meter prototype (including the addition of 10 minutes grace time before the meter resets itself) and has ordered 200 of these new meters to use in demonstrations in Beverly Hills and other cities. Armed with these more friendly smart meters and some additional financing from his manufacturer, Yost hopes to sell 2,000 to 5,000 meters in 1997, and to double that number in 1998.

CASE QUESTIONS

1. How would you evaluate Vincent Yost's environmental analysis efforts?
2. How could his environmental analysis have been improved?
3. What could Vincent Yost do to influence the macroenvironment in his favor?
4. What factors in the competitive environment help or hurt this business?
5. Would you invest in his business? Why or why not?

Source: Adapted from John Grossmann, "Running Out of Time," *Inc.*, February 1997.

Notes

1. The model has antecedents in the work of many industrial organization economists, but it was Michael Porter's book *Competitive Strategy* (New York: Free Press, 1980) that made the analysis compulsory for noneconomics majors in all business schools.
2. L. Fahey and V. K. Narayanan, Macroenvironmental Analysis for Strategic Management (St. Paul, MN: West Publishing, 1986).
3. Focus groups are small panels of experts or interested individuals who have special knowledge of the problem at hand.
4. J. Pearce and R. Robinson, *Strategic Management* 4th ed. (Homewood, IL: Irwin, 1991).
5. Fahey and Narayanan, 1986.
6. In a totalitarian state, the property of others can be confiscated by the state by force. We recognize this as immoral, although there may not be much, short of

risking life and limb, that an individual can do about it. In a democracy, one group of people can vote itself the rights to the money and economic productivity of another group. Few of us consider this immoral, yet it has the same effect.

7. "Japanese Business Methods," *The Economist*, April 4, 1992, 19–22.

8. This section is largely derived from Fahey and Narayanan, *Macroenvironmental Analysis*, 1986.

9. There is an extensive literature on technological change, technological diffusion and the adoption of innovations, and the role of technology in society. However, these topics are beyond the scope of this book.

10. C. Kluckhorn, "Values and Value-Orientation," in T. Parsons and E. Shils, eds., *Toward a General Theory of Action* (Cambridge, MA: Harvard University Press, 1962), 338–433.

11. Distributive justice refers to the desirable distribution of the wealth of society among its members.

12. The World Commission on Environment, 1987.

13. Comments by Frank Popoff, CEO and chairman of Dow Chemical Company, at the Graduate Business Conference, April 3, 1992, Indiana University, Bloomington, Indiana.

14. P. Drucker, *Innovation and Entrepreneurship* (New York: Harper & Row, 1985).

15. Drucker, 1985.

16. Drucker, 1985, 108.

17. The story is an old one and often makes the rounds in graduate economics classes. However, I was reminded of it by reading S. Oster, *Modern Competitive Analysis* (Oxford University Press: New York, 1990).

18. A frequently heard question when challenging a new venture opportunity is: "If this is such a good idea, why has not someone already done it?" As we can see, this is actually an economic question in sheep's clothing. The correct answer to this line of questioning is: "Because no one else has been smart enough, until now."

19. B. Wernerfelt and C. Montgomery, "What Is an Attractive Industry? *Management Science* 32 (1986): 1223–1230.

20. These three strategies are known as "generic" strategies because other strategies are derivatives of these three. Porter originally argued that a firm must choose to pursue one of the three strategies because the firm could not adhere to more than one strategy within a single market. He called this being "stuck in the middle." Empirical research has demonstrated that sometimes firms can achieve differentiation and the low-cost position simultaneously. C. Hill, "Differentiation versus Low Cost or Differentiation and Low Cost: A Contingency Framework," *Academy of Management Review* 13 (1988): 401–412; A. Murray, "A Contingency View of Porter's 'Generic Strategies,' " *Academy of Management Review* 13 (1988): 390–400; P. Wright, "A Refinement of Porter's Strategies," *Strategic Management Journal* 9 (1980): 93–101.

21. This is the model developed and popularized by Michael Porter in his two books, *Competitive Strategy* (New York: Free Press, 1980) and *Competitive Advantage* (New York: Free Press, 1985). Although this chapter borrows heavily from these two books and relates the Porter analysis to the problems of new venture creation, there is really no substitute for reading the originals.

22. Often the argument is offered that quality improvements pay for themselves, either by increasing customer loyalty or increasing customer base. All this may be true if the increased loyalty decreases the price elasticity of demand and the cost increases can be passed on to the new customers.

23. There are some interesting counter-examples, however. When competition heats up in the automobile industry, factory rebates (price concessions from manufacturers) plus the normal bargaining process within the dealerships can produce final sales prices lower than the average variable cost for the combina-

tion of manufacturer and dealer. In an overheated housing market, buyers often bid up the price of the house against each other instead of bargaining for lower prices. This can be true even if the supply of houses is greater than the demand. It is the inflationary expectations that drive this process. People feel that the prices will be even higher if they do not buy quickly. Of course, this is a self-fulfilling prophesy for the group of buyers, even if it benefits a particular buyer.

24. This is especially true when a third party is paying for the airline ticket (for example, your employer), but the flyer receives private credit for the miles.

25. Example from Porter, 1980.

26. The presence of entry barriers is prima facie evidence that perfect competition does not exist. But does actual entry have to occur to keep incumbents from earning above-normal returns? It can be argued that the threat of entry is itself sufficient, as long as that entry is relatively costless and irreversible. This is known as the "contestability theory." This theory makes a distinction between competitive markets, where actual entry enforces price discipline, and contestable markets, where the threat of entry enforces discipline even though the industry looks like an oligopoly. See W. Baumol, J. Panzer, and R. Willig, *Contestable Markets and the Theory of Industry Structure* (New York: Harcourt, Brace, Jovanovich, 1982).

27. The general model to determine if entry will be profitable can be written as an equation where the sum of all future discounted cast flows from the new venture is set against the sum of the direct investment attributable to the new venture, plus the sum of the expenses related to overcoming the structural

barriers, plus the sum of the expenses related to retaliation costs (such as price concessions, marketing and legal expenses). All too often entrepreneurs make their calculations and include only the direct investment costs (property, plant equipment, and initial organization costs). An opportunity that looks profitable based on direct costs might not be profitable when the barrier and retaliation costs are factored in.

28. Exit barriers are those structural impediments that prevent inefficient firms from leaving an industry even when the firms are unprofitable and have little prospect of achieving profitability. Examples of exit barriers are psychological commitment by the firm's owners, specialized assets, fixed costs of exit (e.g., labor agreements), and government policy (e.g., Chrysler and Lockheed in the United States).

29. Porter, 1980, 18–20.

30. The Federal Trade Commission maintains a classification scheme for all businesses known as the Standard Industrial Classification code, or SIC code for short. All products and services are assigned codes that range from two to seven digits. Two- and three-digit SIC codes are too broad and general to identify competitors, and five- through seven-digit codes may be too narrow. The four-digit SIC code is the generally accepted level for current and potential competitor analysis.

31. See Chapter 2 for complete definitions and descriptions of the resources and their attributes.

32. Included in the general term *strategy* here would be such elements as the firm's goals and future goals, its assumptions about itself and its industry, and its own assessment of its strengths and weaknesses.

C H A P T E R

Entrepreneurial Strategies

Outline

> *Profits are not made by differential cleverness, but by differential stupidity.*
> —Attributed to David Ricardo, economist, by Peter Drucker

Learning Objectives

After reading this chapter you will understand:

- How entrepreneurship is related to *strategic management.*

- Five different *hierarchies of strategy* that an entrepreneur can employ.

- What an *entry wedge* is, and the different major and minor entry wedges.

- Three *resource-based strategies* an entrepreneur can utilize to achieve sustainable competitive advantage.

- *First mover advantage.*

- Six different *industry environments*, each with its own unique *life cycle.*

- How to evaluate *entrepreneurial strategies.*

What is the most common criticism that entrepreneurs hear about their business ideas, and their new venture strategies? It is "If that's such a good idea, why hasn't someone else already done it?" The answer implied by David Ricardo in the introductory quote is that most people never have a good idea, and many who do lack the faintest clue what to do next. Human intelligence and energy are the scarce resources. There are countless strategies for creating and operating profitable enterprises, but most of them have not yet been conceived.

In this chapter we examine some of the strategies entrepreneurs have already conceived to create and guide their new ventures. However, many entrepreneurs are unaware that they are following any strategy. Often the strategy is not written or spoken by the founders. For example, the founders of Cisco Systems, a computer networking firm with over $4 billion in sales, reported that they started their firm "without a particular business vision."[1] And it certainly would not surprise the publishers of this book to find that many entrepreneurs had not read it before launching their enterprises. Further, this chapter cannot tell you what strategy to employ to become successful. If we really had that information, then (1) we would not be writing textbooks about it, and (2) by releasing the information, we would make the strategy easy to imitate and it would cease to be rare. Once everyone has the keys to success, the locks must be changed.

What this chapter *can* do is describe a wide range of entrepreneurial strategies called entry wedges. Then we examine some of the strategic choices available to new ventures. Next we introduce the industry life cycle and see how the different stages influence new venture strategy. We also look at the effects of fragmented and global environment. At the end of the chapter we present a model for assessing entrepreneurial opportunities and evaluating the strategies chosen.

Entrepreneurship and Strategy

How is entrepreneurship like business strategy? Some of the concepts presented in this chapter are borrowed and adapted from the strategic management literature.[2] In this literature, **strategy** is defined as "the patterns of decisions that shape the venture's internal resource configuration and deployment and guide alignment with the environment."[3] This definition has two major implications. The first is that "patterns of decisions" means both **strategy formulation** and **strategy implementation.** Formulation includes planning and analysis. Implementation is the execution and evaluation of the activities that make up the strategy. The second implication is that the entrepreneur has to consider both internal factors such as the firm's resources and competencies, and external factors such as the market environment. That is what we did in Chapters 2 and 3.

One of the core assumptions of strategic management is that strategy exists on different levels within the firm. In descending order, these are the enterprise, corporate, business, functional, and subfunctional levels. Part of the environment for each level is the level above it; lower and higher levels must be aligned, with the higher levels leading the way. One result of this hierarchy is a cascading effect. Strategy formulation starts at the top of the hierarchy and flows down to each level. As it does, strategy formulation is increasingly replaced by implementation. The cascade effect contributes to consistency, and helps hold together organizations that are sometimes large and far-flung.

E-NOTES 4–1   STRATEGIC MANAGEMENT

Strategic management can be defined as patterns of decisions which:

- determine a business venture's internal resource structure and implementation,
- influence its interaction with the macroenvironment.

Strategic management includes:

- strategy formulation,
- planning,
- analysis,
- strategy implementation,
- execution,
- evaluation.

Enterprise-level strategy is at the top of the hierarchy. It is concerned with the relationships between the firm and society at large. The context for analyzing this strategy was presented in Chapter 3. **Corporate strategy** focuses on the problems of diversification and the management of a portfolio of business. Because the new venture is most often a single business, corporate strategy is not discussed in this book. **Business-level strategy** is oriented toward competing within a single industry. It deals with the acquisition, organization, and employment of resources. Industry analysis was examined in Chapter 3. The strategies that correspond to industry conditions are the subject of this chapter. In other words, this chapter is about business-level strategy. **Functional** and **sub-functional strategies** involve marketing, finance and accounting, and human resource policies, which will be examined in Chapters 6 through 9.

E-NOTES 4–2   STRATEGY HIERARCHY

A business venture can employ 5 different levels of strategy:

- **Enterprise level**—to relate to society,
- **Corporate level**—to manage diversification within the firm,
- **Business level**—to relate to competitors,
- **Functional level**—to manage marketing, finance and accounting,
- **Subfunctional level**—to manage human resources.

Entry Wedges

Entry wedges are momentum factors.[4] They are not really full-blown strategies but are rather the methods the founders use to get their initial foothold in a business. Because the entry wedge becomes an important part of the firm's history, it may influence later strategic decisions. Since each founding is unique, the entry wedge can therefore be part of the firm's sustainable competitive advantage.

MAJOR WEDGES

All new ventures employ one or more of three major entry wedges: new product or service, parallel competition, and franchising.

New Product or Service   A new produce or service is one of the most potent entry wedges. Truly new products and services are relatively rare. If they employ a new technology as well, they may be hard to imitate. Typically, new products have a lower failure rate than new services, primarily because most service organizations face lower entry barriers. Firms that do employ the new service wedge are likely to offer or introduce a related product if the firm gains a foothold in the industry. Ventures that initially offer a new product sometimes follow up with a related service, but this is less common.[5]

The new product or new service wedge is what Drucker has called the "being first with the most" strategy.[6] The strategy is aimed at achieving a permanent leadership position either within an existing industry or by creating a new industry. Success in this strategy requires a concentrated effort at being comprehensive and innovative. "Being first," like the first-mover advantage, gives the firm a head start and possibly an insurmountable lead in market share, in low-cost manufacture and supply, and in public awareness and recognition. This is the strategy that Intel employs in manufacturing microprocessors. "With the most" requires that the product or service be comprehensive. If it is missing something (for example, service, warranty, delivery, or functional components that customers require), the door is left open for competitors. This is the high-risk, high-reward entry wedge.

New technology can be the source of product innovation. In Street Story 4–1, an innovative product in a mature industry provides the entry wedge.

A New Kind of Philately

Every year the U.S. Postal Service delivers $20 billion in metered mail, and most of that mail bears the inky eagle imprint of Pitney Bowes postage meter. Thanks to strong patents and a close relationship with the Postal Service, Pitney Bowes Inc. manufactures 85 percent of the postage meters now in use, and dominates the industry with sales totaling $3.9 billion in 1996.

But the E-Stamp Corporation has found an entry wedge into the postage meter business, and that wedge is technology. Mail fraud is now stalking Pitney Bowes' market share. The Postal Service estimates that it loses a whopping $100 million each year from mechanical meters, which can be rigged to print unpaid postage. About half of the meters currently in use are digital or electronic postage meters, which are more tamper resistant, but these machines are still unpopular with many businesses because they have to be carted to the local Post Office to have their postage "bank" increased.

To combat both fraud and inconvenience, E-Stamp has developed a computer-based electronic mail meter. Their system includes security hardware which attaches to the computer and verifies that the stamp is real (the electronic "stamp" is actually a big bar code below the usual postmark). E-Stamp originally designed a meter than could be refilled by phone or regular mail, and is now working on a system where the postage could be downloaded over the Internet. The company reports that at a recent Postal Service trade show, "We had more Pitney Bowes executives in the booth at one point than E-Stamp people manning it."

Breaking into the postage meter industry hasn't been easy for E-Stamp. While the Postal Service appears anxious to enlist technology to combat fraud, the company had to wait six months for their first meeting with top officials. The agency, which must test and approve proposed electronic stamps, did approve a basic E-Stamp design in 1995, but since then has specified new security requirements which have cost E-Stamp millions of dollars to incorporate into their system.

Right now E-Stamp enjoys a "first with the most" advantage in electronic mail. "If you're on the right side of the fence, you have a uniquely defensible position," says Sunir Kapoor, a Microsoft Corporation veteran hired by E-Stamp to redesign their system. But they won't be lonely for long. Other companies, including Micro General Corp. and Pitney Bowes, are racing to develop their own systems. "We have no plans to be complacent," notes a Pitney Bowes spokesman.

Source: Adapted from Rodney Ho, "Postage-Meter Firms Seek Market's Stamp of Approval," *Wall Street Journal,* February 10, 1997.

Parallel Competition   Parallel competition is a "me too" strategy that introduces competitive duplications into the market. These duplications are parallel, not identical, to existing products or services. They represent an attempt to fill a niche, a small hole in the market. This can be done with a small innovation or variation in an already well-accepted and well-understood product line or service system. An entrepreneur who notes that the present customers of a firm are unhappy and conceives a strategy to make them happy, would be entering with a parallel wedge strategy. Marginal firms always risk being replaced by others that do basically the same things but do them better.

Most retailing start-ups, for example, enter with the parallel competition wedge. The only difference between one retail operation and another might be location or minor variations in merchandising and marketing. The typical retail store carries the same or similar products from the same suppliers and charges approximately the same markups. This type of entry is fairly easy, since entry barriers are low. Firms of this type can produce stable income and profits over a long time if they possess some distinctive competence. More likely, though, these firms are low-sales/low-profit operations. For the entrepreneur they are alternatives to other jobs and replace income from other employment. Without a distinctive competence, these small retailers quickly become marginal and risk being replaced by another firm using the parallel wedge strategy.

However, if used with creativity and vision, the parallel wedge can lead to superior payoffs. Drucker calls this form of the parallel strategy "creative imitation."[7] Creative imitation combines the common business configuration of the competition (the imitation part) with a new twist or variation (the creative part). Two types of competitors are susceptible to a new venture's creative imitation: those with weak spots and those with blind spots. Firms with weak spots may have the same resources as others but not employ them well. The new venture, without different assets but knowing how to use the assets it does have, has an advantage. Some entrepreneurs also have blind spots—things they do not see about the market, the competition, or themselves—that make them vulnerable to creative imitation. Examples include:

- *The "not invented here" syndrome.* Firms are sometimes slow to adapt innovations or are reluctant to change because they did not initiate the idea themselves. This makes them easy to target for the new venture that is quick to adopt the new standard.
- *The "skim the market" blind spot.* Firms that charge high prices and attempt to capture only the most profitable business are vulnerable. Other firms can operate under their price umbrella, gain market share, and become close to their customers. The creative imitators learn how to add value by serving the tougher customers.
- *Technological tunnel vision.* Firms that emphasize produce- and manufacturing-based quality to the exclusion of user-based quality have technological tunnel vision. They are vulnerable as minor changes in customer needs and perceptions go unnoticed by them but are obvious to the imitator.
- *The maximizer complex.* Firms that try to do too much, that serve all types of customers with all types of products and services, are vulnerable because they may serve no customers particularly well. A parallel competitor who carves a niche to serve a specialized customer base can succeed here.

Franchising   The third major wedge is franchising. Franchising takes a proven formula for success and expands it. The entrepreneur may be either the franchisor or the franchisee. The **franchisor** is the seller of franchises. For the franchisor, franchising is a means of expanding by using other people's money, time, and energy to sell the product or service. These other people are the **franchisees.** In return for a franchise fee and royalties (usually based on sales), they gain the expertise, knowledge, support (training, marketing, operations), and experience of the franchisor. This reduces the risk of failure for the new entrepreneur.

The key to franchising's power is that it is a geographic expansion under a license agreement. Geographic expansion enables the franchise system to saturate markets. Saturation gives the franchise the benefits of visibility and recognition, logistical cost savings, volume buying power, lower employment and training costs, and the ability to use the mass media for advertising efficiently. The license agreement gives the franchise system a mechanism for standardizing its products or services, incentives for growth, and barriers to entry. All three parties to the franchise system (franchisor, franchisee, and customer) benefit, which explains why franchising has become the most prevalent form of new business start-up.

MINOR WEDGES

A number of other entry wedges are designated as minor because they can be classified under the three major categories. Four categories of minor wedges, each with several variations, include exploiting partial momentum, customer sponsorship, parent company sponsorship, and government sponsorship. Table 4–1 cross-references the major entry wedges with the minor ones.

TABLE 4–1 Major and Minor Entry Wedges

	Major Entry Wedges		
Minor Entry Wedges	*New Product/ Service*	*Parallel Competition*	*Franchise System*
Exploiting Partial Momentum			
1. Geographic transfer			X
2. Supply shortage		X	
3. Tapping underutilized resources	X	X	
Customer Sponsorship			
4. Customer contract		X	
5. Second sourcing		X	
Parent Company Sponsorship			
6. Joint venture	X		
7. Licensing		X	
8. Market relinquishment		X	
9. Spin-off	X		
Government Sponsorship			
10. Favored purchasing		X	
11. Rule change	X		
12. Direct assistance	X	X	

Source: Adapted from K. Vesper, *New Venture Strategies* (Englewood Cliffs, NJ: Prentice Hall, 1980).

Exploiting Partial Momentum   Sometimes the entrepreneur already has market and product information that indicates the new venture will be successful. This information acts as the impetus for the launch. The entrepreneur can exploit this existing momentum in three ways: by geographic transfer, by filling a supply shortage, or by putting an underutilized resource to work. A **geographic transfer** occurs when a business that works in one area is started in another. For example, a restaurant concept that is successful in Los Angeles might be tried by a different entrepreneur in New York City. The New York City entrepreneur gains partial momentum by studying the Los Angeles venture. The major wedge that more fully exploits this factor is franchising.

Entrepreneurs can launch new ventures by filling market gaps such as **supply shortages.** Sometimes the product or service in short supply must be physically transferred from one area to another. In this case, filling the supply shortage resembles geographic transfer. A purer example is the entrepreneur who organizes resources to fill a shortage within an area. For example, recent trends indicate that for various tasks at varying times of the year, many firms prefer to hire temporary workers rather than full-time employees. But there is a shortage of people available for temporary positions, because most people prefer to work full-time if they can. New ventures have been developed that specialize in personnel services for temporaries. These firms organize the resource that is in short supply (temps) to meet market demand. They also meet the demands of the temporary personnel by scheduling additional work after each temporary assignment expires. For the firm, the shortage is relieved; for the personnel, they have full-time work (in various temporary assignments).

An **underutilized resource** is one with an economic value that is not recognized or one that is not being employed in its best use. Many times people are the most underutilized resource, and entrepreneurs who can more fully realize their economic value are called "leaders." The underutilized resource can also be physical, financial, reputational, technological, or organizational. For example, entrepreneurs in the financial sector find ways to better use nonperforming financial assets, such as cash or bonds. Entrepreneurs have helped large organizations with strong positive reputations—for example, Disney and Coca-Cola—gain additional income by licensing their brand names, trademarks, and copyrights. Underutilized physical resources are often somebody's junk, waste, by-product, or worn-out product. These are the core of the recycling and remanufacturing industries. For example, entrepreneurs are building businesses by finding new uses for the mountains of worn-out tires dumped across the United States. Others are building vending machines that take in aluminum cans for recycling and dispense store and manufacturers' coupons.

Customer Sponsorship   A new venture's launch may depend on the momentum supplied by the firm's first customers. A customer can encourage an entrepreneur in either of two ways. **A customer contract** can guarantee the new firm sales and help it obtain its initial financing. Since the customer is not assumed to have altruistic motives, the entrepreneur should look to expand the customer base once the venture is up and running. Sometimes customers encourage entrepreneurs to become **a second source.** If the customer has previously had difficulty working with a single supplier, good purchasing practice would suggest that the customer rebid the contract. However, a good alternative for obtaining the product or service is not always available.

When this is the case, the customer can encourage and even provide assistance (managerial, technical, financial) to an entrepreneur who can supply the customer's needs. Both customer-contract and second-source sponsorships generally lead the firm to employ parallel competition as the major wedge.

Parent Company Sponsorship   A parent company can help launch a new venture in four ways. Two of these require ongoing parent company relationships: **licensing** and **joint venturing.** The other two methods may continue the parent-new venture relationship, but it is optional. These are **market relinquishment** and the **spin-off.**

Under a licensing agreement, the entrepreneur contracts with the parent company to produce a product or service or to employ a system or technology. The connection between the entrepreneur and the parent provides momentum for the new venture because the founders have previous organizational experience with the parent and technical experience with the product or technology. The joint venture differs from the license in two significant ways: (1) resources are commingled when the joint venture is formed, and (2) the ownership rights in a joint venture require negotiation. These differences make the joint venture more difficult to manage, but the benefits of having two (or more) organizational parents can outweigh the cost.

Market relinquishment means that the parent company decides to stop serving a market or producing a product. Although the parent's motivation for this can vary, usually it is because the parent is not cost-efficient. This is especially likely to be true if the product volume or market niche is small, for a large company's overhead can be high enough to make a small niche unprofitable. However, such a niche may be profitable for a small firm. The most likely candidates to start that small firm are the large firm's former managers of that product/market niche. So when the larger corporation relinquishes the market, the former managers may have the opportunity to purchase the larger firm's specialized assets and continue in their jobs, but this time as owner/managers instead of just managers. This provides the new venture strong momentum: The change may not be visible to customers and suppliers, but the new firm can be much more profitable (and perhaps strategically more flexible) without the need to support the corporate bureaucracy.

E-NOTES 4–3   MAJOR AND MINOR ENTRY WEDGES

Major entry wedges include:

- new products or services,
- parallel competition,
- franchising.

Minor entry wedges include:

- exploiting partial momentum,
- customer sponsorship,
- parent company sponsorship,
- government sponsorship.

One of the most common starting points for new venture creation based on previously acquired knowledge is the **spin-off.** A spin-off is a new firm created by a person or persons leaving an existing firm and starting a new firm in the same industry. The most frequent examples of spin-offs today are in high-tech businesses, biotechnology, semiconductors and computers, consulting, law, and medicine (and medical devices). What do these diverse industries have in common? Both emerging industries and growing industries are prime breeding grounds for spin-offs. In these industries pockets of information possessed by employees can be disseminated throughout the market. This information is mobile; it is embodied not in a machine or particular location but in individuals, a process, or a technique. Both the knowledge and the individuals can be transferred at very low cost to just about any place on earth.

The knowledge assets transferred to the new firm in a spin-off have certain dimensions that can be analyzed to determine whether they possess the four attributes of competitive advantage. Table 4–2 displays the opposing poles of the dimensions of knowledge.[8] The characteristics on the right-hand side of the table are more difficult to transfer, but if the new management team is able to successfully transfer them, the firm will gain momentum toward competitive advantage.

For example, tacit skills, knowledge, and competencies are based on rules and behaviors that are unknown to the person performing the tasks. Individual skills are often tacit; people cannot explain the process they go through in applying their skills. Evidence even suggests that there are different brain structures for procedural (process) knowledge and declarative (content) knowledge.[9] For the organization, tacit knowledge comes embedded in the people who work for the firm. Other members of the firm may have articulated knowledge of the kind reflected in: "Oh, yes, we have someone working here who knows how to do that." Much of the relational skill and knowledge in an organization is tacit; some people know some things about who can get things done under what conditions, but most company participants do not know the details of these relationships.

Knowledge that is not teachable is also difficult to transfer to the spin-off, but it is also rare and hard to duplicate if it comes with the new venture management team. Skills and competencies that are observable in use can be copied and transferred. Complex knowledge is more difficult to copy than simple knowledge; an independent skill is easier to transfer than one that requires cooperation, teamwork, or coordination.

When individuals leave one firm to start another in a related industry, they take with them the knowledge and competencies they acquired and developed. The most important elements for the new business are the hardest to transfer, yet they are also the most valuable, rarest, and hardest to duplicate.

TABLE 4–2 Taxonomy of Knowledge Assets in the Resource-Based Theory		
Easy to Copy		*Hard to Copy*
Articulated knowledge	⟵⟶	Tacit knowledge
Teachable knowledge	⟵⟶	Nonteachable knowledge
Skills observable in use	⟵⟶	Nonobservable in use
Simple and singular knowledge	⟵⟶	Complex and multidimensional knowledge
Independent skills	⟵⟶	Interdependent skills

Source: Adapted from S. Winter, "Knowledge and Competence as Strategic Assets," in D. Teece, ed., *The Competitive Challenge* (Cambridge, MA: Ballinger, 1988), pp. 159–184.

We see, then, that knowledge and competencies that are widely available and easily taught and transferred cannot be the source of competitive advantage for a new venture. But this does not mean that entrepreneurship cannot be taught.

Government Sponsorship   In Chapter 3 we discussed the impediments and constraints that government often imposes on new ventures. But the government can also act as a sponsor for new ventures and provide entrepreneurs with launch momentum. We saw this in Street Story 4–1. There are three mechanisms for this: direct assistance, favored purchasing, and rule changes.

Direct assistance.   "They're from the government, how can they help you?" A number of local, state, and federally supported programs can aid the entrepreneur in starting or managing a new business. Most provide managerial or technical assistance; a few, like the Small Business Administration, may also on occasion provide financial assistance. One of the less well-known sources of technical assistance is the federal research laboratory system. At these labs, such as the Oak Ridge National Laboratory in Oak Ridge, Tennessee, scientists and engineers help businesses solve difficult technical problems. Other federal agencies have started programs to help small and medium-sized businesses. NASA offers free consulting advice in cooperation with state agencies in Tennessee, Mississippi, and Louisiana. The Sandia National Laboratory in Albuquerque, New Mexico, also has a program.[10]

Favored purchasing.   Favored purchasing rules enable some firms to enter the marketplace with an edge. The federal government's own procurement policies often mandate set-asides and quotas for small businesses, minority and woman-owned firms, firms started and managed by physically disabled people, and Vietnam era veterans. Many of these favored purchasing rules have also been incorporated into procurement policies and practices at other government levels and throughout corporate America.

Rule changes.   As government regulatory practices change and as new laws are implemented, opportunities for new firms arise. For example, one of the fastest-growing environmental business segments is in energy-efficiency ventures. Pressure and rule changes from local utility commissions have mandated that utility companies encourage their customers to become more energy efficient. These companies are spending billions of dollars managing demand to get customers to use less electricity. Increasingly, they are hiring outside consulting and installation firms to do the work of these programs. Xenergy Inc. of Burlington, Massachusetts, is one company formed to take advantage of this momentum. The company, launched in 1975, was one of the first in the energy conservation business. Growth exploded, with revenue in 1992 rising to more than $20 million. Today Xenergy has more than 20 offices throughout the United States and Canada, and works with industrial and commercial facilities. It has become an independently operated, wholly owned subsidiary of NGI Enterprises, Inc., which is owned by New York State Electric and Gas Co.

Resource-Based Strategies

How can our resource-based theory help us to create entrepreneurial strategy? We have already discussed the fundamentals of competitive strategy in terms of our resource-based theory. Briefly, resource-based theory says that for firms to have a sustainable competitive advantage, they must possess resources and capabilities that are rare, valuable, hard to copy, and nonsubstitutable (with resources that are neither rare nor valuable). There are three strategies that relate directly to the resources and capabilities of the new venture. These are rent-seeking, growth, and quality.

RENT-SEEKING STRATEGIES

Strategy in the resource-based framework is rentseeking.[11] There are four types of rents, and the strategies available to obtain them are different. Firms can attempt to capture more than one type of rent simultaneously. The four types of rents are:

- **Ricardian rent.** Rents derived from acquiring, owning, and controlling a scarce and valuable resource. These are most often derived from ownership of land or natural resources or from a preferred location. This type of rent can be collected as long as ownership and control exist, possibly in perpetuity.
- **Monopoly rent.** Rents collected from government protection, collusive agreements, or structural entry barriers. Examples of government protection include patents and copyrights, restrictive licenses, and government-granted franchises. Many collusive practices such as price-fixing and conspiracies in restraint of trade are illegal in the United States, but enforcement varies by time and place.
- **Entrepreneurial rent.** Rents accrued from risk-taking behavior or insights into complex and uncertain environments. This is also known as Schumpeterian rent, and is the type most closely associated with new venture creation. Schumpeterian rents are not as long-lasting as Ricardian and monopoly rents because of the eventual diffusion of knowledge and entry by competing firms into the market.
- **Quasi-rent.** Rents earned by employing firm-specific assets in a manner that other firms cannot copy. These rents are often based on idiosyncratic capital and dedicated assets. They are derived from a distinctive competence in how to use the resource as opposed to mere control.

Resource-based strategies are geared toward rent-seeking behavior. The most prevalent of the four rent-seeking behaviors is the entrepreneurial strategy; a firm enters with a new resource configuration or implementation strategy and makes above-average profits until, through technological diffusion and increased knowledge, competitors are able to enter and compete away those profits. This describes the cycle of "destructive capitalism" that constantly redeploys capital to its most economic use.

Ventures that possess the four attributes required for sustainable competitive advantage are positioned to employ strategy to collect one or more of the four types of rents. The more types of rent the firm can accumulate, the better its overall long-term performance will be. Rents of any of the four types require ways for the firm to protect its advantage. These protective devices are called isolating mechanisms. The absence of isolating mechanisms means that others (workers, investors, customers, competitors, governments) can work out strategies to claim the rents for their own.

Isolating Mechanisms and First-Mover Advantage

An entrepreneur who is fortunate enough to create a new venture must expect that competitors will attempt to retaliate and protect their own positions.[12] Therefore, it is important for the entrepreneur to find ways to increase these benefits and cash flows for either future investment or personal incentives. The methods the entrepreneur employs to prevent the rents generated from the new venture from leaking out are known as **isolating mechanisms.**

TYPES OF ISOLATING MECHANISMS

Isolating mechanisms can take a number of forms. Most obvious are **property rights,** which take the form of patents, trademarks, and copyrights. Any secrets, proprietary information, or proprietary technology also help isolate the firm from competitive attack. But as discussed before, these mechanisms will not last indefinitely; therefore, the entrepreneur must be prepared to move quickly and establish a strong position. This is known as **first-mover advantage.**

SOURCES OF FIRST-MOVER ADVANTAGE

First-mover advantages are isolating mechanisms that prevent the erosion of the new venture's competitive advantage.[13] The first use of a technology, known as **technological leadership,** can provide first-mover advantages. The first mover in a particular technology can, of course, obtain the initial patents, but these are seldom decisive.[14] More importantly, the first mover builds up a research and development base that can lead to further innovations and improvement, keeping the venture ahead of the pack. As production (either *through* the new technology or *of* the new technology) increases, the learning curve is pushed ahead of competitors', often conferring cost advantages and economies of scale that can preempt or delay competition.

Being the first mover may mean obtaining valuable and scarce resources ahead of others. It may mean getting rights to natural resources, securing the best locations, or crowding distribution channels (distribution space is a valuable and rare resource).[15]

The final source of first-mover advantage is imposing switching costs on buyers.[16] **Switching costs** can be developed through marketing or contractual obligations. When a new venture creates brand loyalty through effective advertising, high buyer learning and evaluation costs, or complementary products, the firm makes it difficult for others to compete away the venture's profit.

First-mover advantages can also be a disadvantage in certain situations. In some cases, the first mover must reveal the underlying business concept, and others may copy this using different resource combinations. The first mover invests in resolving the technological and production problems that go with any new venture. Other firms can then benefit from these investments. Also, being first once does not guarantee that you will always be first. Indeed, inertia can make the successful first mover resist abandoning a strategy when it is no longer effective. Later in the chapter, Figure 4–2 summarizes the entrepreneurial process of strategic choice.

E-NOTES 4–4 FIRST MOVER ADVANTAGE

First-Mover Advantage is a rent-seeking strategy that operates as an isolating mechanism, and may include:

- technological leadership,
- obtaining resources more quickly than others,
- switching costs.

GROWTH STRATEGIES

So far we have seen how new ventures enter using their wedges and how they seek to collect rents based on their capabilities and resources. We can also use our resource-based model to account for the rate and direction of a venture's growth strategies. Firms grow in the direction of underutilized resources and toward their areas of expertise. The rate of growth is a step function, not a smooth path, since resources are usually employable only in bulky, discrete increments.[17] Basically, the limits to firm growth are limits to resources. Resources determine the industry the firm will enter and the levels of profit it can attain. For example, labor shortages and finance and technological barriers all limit growth.

In the long run, however, the most important limit of all may be the scarcity of management capacity. There are two demands on managerial capacity: (1) to run the firm at its current size, and (2) to expand and grow. Current managers recruit new managers to increase the growth potential of the venture. However, these new managers need to be trained and integrated into the firm's current activities, and this takes time away from existing managers. While ingesting these new managers, the firm's growth slows. When the new managers have been incorporated into the venture's structure and systems, growth begins again. This implies that "management is both the accelerator and brake for the growth process."[18] This rubber-band process, called the "Penrose effect" after the theorist who first proposed it, suggests that fast growth in one period will be followed by slow growth in the next period (that is, there is a negative correlation between period growth rates).[19]

Motivation for Growth   In addition, the resource-based view helps explain the motivation for growth. A firm seldom employs all six types of resources (physical, financial, technological, human, reputational, and organizational) at the same rates. This means that capacity use differs among resources. This produces excess capacity in some assets and capabilities. Where excess resource capacity exists, especially in human resources, managers are motivated to expand to use this excess capacity. The activities designed to fill this capacity seldom stop when the current limits are reached. Therefore, additional resources are required to complement the full employment of current resources. The optimal growth rate for the new venture involves a balance between the full exploitation of existing resources and the development of new ones.[20]

Furthermore, these existing resources are not completely applicable to any and all tasks. They are specialized to some degree, and almost certainly this specialization is related to the firm's primary competencies and market niche. New resources, added to complement existing resources, also are likely to be highly specialized. Thus, as the firm grows, it is most likely to grow (and/or diversify) in a direction related to its original core mission. This may mean market-related growth, product-related growth, or both. Diversification and growth do not occur at random.[21]

Focus Effect and Synergy Effect   The final insight concerns performance. It is now also well established that growth by related diversification produces the highest levels of profitability.[22] This high level of performance can come from two sources: the focus effect and synergy effects. The **focus effect** indicates that a firm is better able to transfer a key capability to closely related products and markets. Unrelated products and markets are too different for the firm to competently deal with them. Growth outside the firm's core competence does not employ those highly specialized resources that generate higher levels of rent (the less specialized, the easier to copy and substitute). In other words, a venture should "stick to its knitting."

The **synergy effect** is a result of the combination of technology and marketing. Synergy that involves acquiring and employing resources which create value but can be imitated by others is called **contestable synergy.** Since the acquisition of resources takes place in a competitive market, full value is paid for the resources by the entrepreneur, and these resources synergies can be copied by other firms.[23] Rents from contestable synergy strategies are not long-lasting. In contrast, synergy that can produce long-lasting rents because the resources are one of a kind is called **idiosyncratic synergy.** However, acquiring the resources needed for idiosyncratic synergy forces the venture to negotiate within a bilateral monopoly (a market that consists of only one buyer and one seller). In a bilateral monopoly negotiation, the final price is indeterminate. The buyer can pay too much and never recoup, or the buyer can pay less than the full-value price and collect rents above these costs. So there is some risk pursuing this strategy.

QUALITY AS A STRATEGY

Considerable thought, energy, and money have been devoted to making quality a source of sustainable competitive advantage. Hundreds of articles and books have been written on the subject. A prestigious national contest, the Malcolm Baldrige National Quality Award, is promoted each year. Sixteen states now have programs to help companies develop and improve their products' quality.[24] Total Quality Management (TQM) programs that emphasize customer satisfaction (user-based quality discussed in Chapter 1) as the number one priority for the firm have entered the language and curriculum of top-rated business schools. Companies that promote TQM programs are themselves a fast-growing industry. Consultants sell "off-the-shelf" TQM programs based on some simple ideas that can be understood by the analogy with playing golf:

- **Continuous improvement.** This is the process of setting higher standards for performance with each iteration of the quality cycle. In golf terms, yesterday you shot a score of 112, so today you try to shoot 111.
- **Benchmarking.** This means identifying and imitating the best in the world at specific tasks and functions. If you believe that Ben Hogan had the best swing, you try to swing like Ben.
- **The quality cycle.** A loop of activities that include planning, doing, checking, and acting. Keep your head down, keep your eye on the ball, don't press. Now, where did it go?
- **Outsourcing.** This means procuring the top quality from outside the organization if the firm cannot produce it inside. If you can't hit this shot, will you hit it for me?[25]

TQM programs require a sure knowledge of the customer through highly developed market research. Once the knowledge base exists, the prescriptions often call for organizationwide commitment, top management involvement, training and team building, and empowering individual employees to be responsible for quality-related decisions.[26]

The resource-based approach calls into question the efficacy of these quality programs for long-term competitive advantage. If any firm can buy the principles of TQM off the street (so to speak), then they are not rare. Benchmarking, which is neither more nor less than copying, is by definition able to be copied. Outsourcing products from the best quality vendors is both substitutable by producing in-house or sourcing from other best quality vendors. Can TQM be an effective strategy for sustainable competitive advantage?

Research indicates that TQM programs are not magic formulas.[27] At best, they were termed a "partial success." Among the general conclusions were that:

- Copying other firms may expend time and money on the wrong things.
- Adoption of a TQM program, under certain conditions, can actually make things worse because the program is so disruptive.
- Companies often fail to link the TQM program with "bottom line" results.
- Benchmarking is not effective unless the company already has a comprehensive quality program.
- Lower-performing firms should adopt TQM programs gradually, middle performers are better able to begin full-scale adoption, and high performers benefit the most from TQM.

Because they are hard to implement and their contingencies are complex, TQM programs have value. Because successful quality programs depend on the firm's already having a well-developed resource base, the quality program enables the firm to add to that base. This means: *Quality can work as a strategy for sustainable competitive advantage because it is not easy to implement and everyone cannot master it.*

A successful TQM program has several requirements. First, it requires excellent market research. Market research is knowledge (one of those tacit, difficult-to-duplicate resources). Market research that is original and proprietary can be a source of sustainable competitive advantage. Next, TQM requires an organizational system capable of adapting to the new regime, incorporating its premises, and executing its policies. Organizational systems are incredibly complex because of social relationships, ambiguous cause and effect, and culture. This complexity can be a source of sustainable competitive advantage. Further, the highly capable human resources that the successful TQM program requires also possess the four attributes. Finally, the firm with a reputation for outstanding quality products and service is in a position to collect rent for the investment it has made.

E-NOTES 4–5   RESOURCE-BASED STRATEGIES

An entrepreneur can utilize strategies including:

- rent-seeking strategies,
- growth strategies,
- quality strategies.

Strategy and Industry Environments

But not all ventures enter the same industry. How much difference does the industry itself make in determining strategy? The answer is, "quite a lot." Entrepreneurs can significantly add to the success of their strategies by understanding the industry envi-

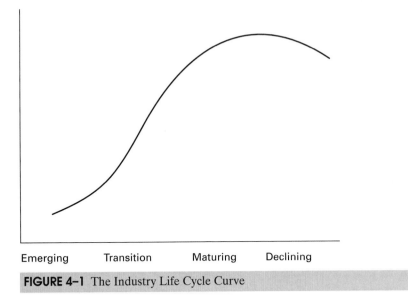

Emerging   Transition   Maturing   Declining

FIGURE 4-1 The Industry Life Cycle Curve

ronment they are entering. A static description of industry structure was presented in Chapter 3. However, industry environments are static only in the short term; over a longer period of time, they evolve. This evolution is called the **industry life cycle.** The industry life cycle progresses through four stages: emerging, transitional, maturing, and declining.

The industry life cycle progression is not the same for all industries. The length of each stage and the timing of the stages are highly variable and difficult to predict. The same is true for product and organizational life cycles. Entry and competition take on different forms, depending on which stage of the life cycle the industry is in.[28] Figure 4–1 presents a diagram of the industry life cycle. It follows the familiar S-curve of many economic phenomena.[29] The shape of the curve shows that emerging industries are characterized by increasing rates of growth. Transition occurs as growth continues at decreasing rates. In the mature stage, growth rates approach zero. A declining industry is characterized by no growth or negative growth rates, whether measured in total units of production or in dollars.

EMERGING INDUSTRIES

Emerging industries are the newly created networks of firms launched to exploit a new technology, a new market configuration or set of customer needs, or other changes in the macroenvironment.[30] Emerging industries experience high levels of uncertainty, rapid change, and a growing number of organizations (high rates of births). Recent examples of emerging industries are biotechnology, the electric automobile industry, cellular telephones, and the interactive television industry.

Individual firms and entrepreneurs can create or reconfigure entire industries through vision, creativity, and innovation. An innovation strategy can create a customer where none previously existed.[31] How can this be done?

- **By creating utility.** The entrepreneur can change something that is hard for people to do into something that is easy for people to do. For example, there had been "mail" since Roman times, but the industry arose with the creation of a postal service in Great Britain making it easier for people to pay for and send a letter.
- **By creating value.** The entrepreneur can change something that was expensive into something that is inexpensive, and thereby create value, through creative pricing. King Gilled did this when he unbundled the razor from the razor blade. Xerox did this when it realized it did not have sell copiers, just the use of the copiers. It changed a relatively large capital investment decision into a small operating expense to gain acceptance.
- **By changing the customer's reality.** The entrepreneur can help customers buy products through creative distribution and financing, and help customers use products by simplifying operation and providing training. Entrepreneurs help customers solve problems by selling systems instead of products.

Structural Uncertainties   Even for ventures on the verge of revolutionizing the market, however, entry into emerging industries imposes certain structural conditions and constraints. The most imposing structural condition is uncertainty. There are no "traditional ways of doing things," "rules of thumb," "standard operating procedures," or "usual and customary practices." There are only the unknown future and the entrepreneur's will to succeed. Technological uncertainty means that the final configuration of resources, especially technological resources, are still unsettled. Firms are, as laboratories, trying new combinations of technology, human resources, and organizational systems to discover what works. Successful combinations are adopted by other firms as fundamental, and further experiments are conducted to refine the concepts and practices. Usually a single standard emerges for all firms. Occasionally, two competing standards reach the public at the same time, as, for example, video technologies such as Beta and VHS. But only one survives.

Strategic Uncertainty   Emerging firms also face a great deal of strategic uncertainty. New ventures in emerging industries are often unaware of who the competition is (or will be), what types of products and processes the competition is working on, and what posture the government will take toward the new industry. Since birth rates are high, new firms are starting all the time, and it is difficult to keep up on who and what they are. Government regulatory agencies at all levels are slow and bureaucratic. They are unlikely to have existing rules to help guide the new ventures.

Resource Uncertainty   Additional uncertainty looms in the firm's input markets. It is often difficult for the new venture to raise capital, since financial sources are unfamiliar with the new industry's risk/reward profile. Although some venture capital firms specialize in supporting investments in emerging industries, most financial institutions shy away from them. Labor is another input that is difficult to procure, especially managerial talent. Managers and executives face a great deal of career risk and economic uncertainty when joining firms in emerging industries. Turnover may be high in an unstable and turbulent industry. Managers and executives may need to be as entrepreneurial as the founders in order to meet the challenge of a new venture in a new industry.

The procurement of raw materials, supplies, and parts may also be difficult during the industry's emergence. If these inputs are also employed by other industries, there may be shortages until the vendors can adjust their capacity. If the inputs are newly created, developed, or engineered, they may be of uneven quality *and* in short supply. In either event, input costs are likely to be at their highest during the emergence stage.

Customer Uncertainty   Uncertainty also plagues the output (customer) market. To a large extent, the customer market is only vaguely understood: buyer needs and wants, income levels, demographic characteristics, psychographic profiles, and buyer behavior characteristics (knowledge of these is complete). Prices and the points where customers will resist high prices are uncertain, and there may be quite a bit of instability as firms, producing widely diverse and nonstandard products, come to market with diverse, nonstandard prices. The customer is also confused by the variety of product offerings, the lack of standardization, the perception of rapid obsolescence, and the erratic quality of some competitors.

Controlling Uncertainty   In the face of difficult structural conditions and constraints, what must the new venture in an emerging industry do to be successful?

*Look toward developing, generating, acquiring, and controlling resources
that have the four attributes (rare, valuable, hard to copy, nonsubstitutable)
needed for sustainable competitive advantage.*

The first priority in an emerging industry is to acquire resources. Ventures that acquire resources early are more likely to set the rules and standards for industry competition, technological configuration, and product quality. Speeding up decision making, product development and introduction, and organizational systems and processes all have positive effects on firm survival and performance.[32] One industry that is attempting to speed itself up and that represents a typical emerging industry in its early stages is superconductive materials.

The next priority is to employ resources to gain a defendable foothold in the industry on which to build. The early acquisition of a core group of loyal customers is a major accomplishment. This enables the firm to develop experience in production and marketing, evaluate new products and alternative pricing schemes, and provide steady cash flow. From this base, expansion is possible.

Last, since knowledge and information can possess the four attributes of SCA, the new venture must move as quickly as possible to develop an intelligence network to forecast future environmental trends, competitive moves, and technological developments.[33] The initial turbulence and change that made the formation of a new industry possible are not likely to subside once a handful of early new entrants are formed. The turbulence continues unabated, often for years. While the new entrants sort out the standards, later entrants make their appearance and attempt to capitalize on the efforts of the first movers. Older and larger firms attempt to invigorate their operations by entering new markets or forming joint ventures. Regulators, organized labor, and the government conspire to appropriate and tax the "profits" of new ventures. These so-called profits are in reality the early excess returns and may be needed for reinvestment to recoup the up-front investment, encourage future investment, and maintain the firm's technological or marketing advantages. Taxes and other appropriations leave the firm and, in aggregate, the industry underinvested and therefore smaller than they otherwise might have been. The result, of course, is diminished output, innovation, and employment. When this problem is recognized by policy makers, protection can be authorized, such as patent rights, tax abatements and credits, and accelerated depreciation schedules. An intelligence system may not be able to stop these trends, but a forewarned firm is in better position to protect its assets.

TRANSITIONAL INDUSTRIES

Transitional industries—those moving from emergence to stability—have certain recognizable features. At some point there will be scarce resources, changes in customer tastes and values, and, finally, a shakeout. The shakeout period is crucial, for many firms go out of business at this time. The new venture can anticipate these developments, although their precise timing is always problematic.

Scarcity of Resources   As new firms enter the industry with an often dazzling array of products, strategies, and configurations, two powerful forces are at work. The first is that they bid up the prices of the resources they need to get started. Physical resources increase in price as they become more scarce. Scientific and managerial expertise costs more as people are lured away from current jobs with higher salaries and perquisites. Financial resources get more expensive as venture capitalists and investors demand higher yields from the later entrants. Overall industry costs rise as demand for industry inputs rises.

Customer Changes   The second force is the changing nature of the output market. Customers become more sophisticated and sure of what they want in terms of value, quality, and product characteristics. They become more powerful as they become more knowledgeable, they have more choices than they had earlier in the industry life cycle, and they are more likely to shop on price. The uncertainty of who the customer is and how large the market may be starts to fade as experience tells businesses who will buy and who will not. Competition for the existing customer base intensifies. Growth slows at the same time that shoppers become more price sensitive.

Survival Strategies in the Shakeout   What is the result of increasing production costs and decreasing selling prices? Smaller margins for everyone. Only the efficient survive. This is the transition phase, also known as the **shakeout.** Firms whose costs are too high will be forced out of business.[34] Firms that survive will be the ones that have resources with the four attributes of sustainable competitive advantage. When assets that are rare, valuable, hard to copy, and nonsubstitutable are deployed, the venture will be able to withstand price pressure and/or maintain lower costs than competitors.

The first priority in surviving the shakeout is to rationalize the resource base. This means pruning resources (of all six types) and the product/markets they serve if these resources are not earning rents and profits. During the emerging stage firms often acquire excess resources, or **slack.** They do this for two reasons: (1) Because they are uncertain which resources will be the most important, they seek to gain control over as many as possible; and (2) growth is difficult to absorb, and as resources build, it is not easy to reinvest or deploy them quickly enough. But during the shakeout period, as growth slows and margins are squeezed, slack must be wrung from the venture to restore it to an agile, lean, and flexible conditions.

The next priority is to get the most out of reputational and organizational resources. These are often the last to develop for the new venture. Reputation is slow to develop because it takes time for the market and other stakeholders to gain experience with the firm. The organization, with its systems, processes, and routines, is also often a late-developing resource. The organization tends to evolve as the business grows, experimenting along the way. The interaction between the people, work flow, and policies that compose the organization tends to evolve as the business grows, experimenting along the way. The interaction between the people, work flow, and policies that compose the organization are complex. It takes time for all these components to come together. Even after they have coalesced, it takes practice, and therefore time, before that system can be perfected.

Reputation and organization are two of the most difficult resources to copy. As technology becomes more diffuse, as financing becomes more available to entrants, and as physical resources evolve toward commodity-type inputs, reputation and organization (and, by implication, human resources) are the best defense against increased competition and rivalry. Another potent strategy during the shakeout period is to buy cheap assets from the losers in the competitive game. As firms go out of business and their investors look to recoup whatever they can by selling the company or liquidating its assets, these assets often come to market at prices below their rent-earning capacity. The surviving firms, with superior human resources and organizational skills, can employ the liquidated physical resources, patent rights, licenses, and newly unemployed workers, managers, and staffers more effectively than their previous owners could. This firm-specific talent enables the survivor to collect a quasi-rent on the loser's former assets.

The strategy of expanding within the same business line by acquiring (by whatever method) other businesses is also known as **horizontal integration.** For example, horizontal integration and resource rationalization are the hallmarks of the shakeout in the biotechnology industry. As Street Stories 4–2 illustrates, it is eat or be eaten in a transitional industry.

Shakeout Pitfalls   Firms must avoid pitfalls to survive this dangerous period. The most important of these is the "uniqueness paradox."[35] This is a blind spot that many companies have, especially those that are still relatively young. The "uniqueness paradox" occurs when people attribute unique characteristics to their own organization, characteristics that are, paradoxically, possessed by many other organizations. Although it may be good for internal cohesion for organizational members to differentiate themselves from their competitors by believing they are unique, it is bad for strategy. It is bad because it fools the firm into believing that some or all of its resources have the four attributes of SCA when, in fact, they do not. It makes the firm complacent and gives it a false sense of security. The firm is forced to react to outside pressures instead of generating its own proactive activities. This spells doom.

A second pitfall has already been mentioned, that is, keeping slack and excess capacity. The only thing worse than holding on to unused resources and facilities with too much capacity is acquiring new capacity that provides no rent-collecting possibilities. But firms do make the mistake of trying to "corner the market" on physical capacity even as growth slows.

A final pitfall is simply failing to recognize that the industry environment has changed. Sometimes the founders have difficulty adjusting to these new realities, and

Whole Lot of Shakeout Going On

CD-ROM—that imaginative software blend of text, audio, and video for your computer—is here to stay for a while. The number of CD-ROM players in the United States has exploded in recent years, and CD-ROM programs like Microsoft's "Encarta" and Broderbund's "Myst" helped to push CD-ROM software sales past 54 million units worldwide in 1994. Then why is it that an estimated 96 percent of the multimedia software developers never make a profit?

"There are more people pursuing this opportunity than can be sustained," flatly states Bill Gates, Microsoft's chairman and CEO. While there may be as many as 1,700 hot new developers churning out CD-ROM programs, many of those software firms are being zapped by the costs and risks of an immature industry.

A large part of the problem is the expense. The average CD-ROM costs $383,000 to create. With a wholesale revenue of $20 per disk, a software producer has to sell 19,000 copies to recoup expenses. A computer game with live actors like Id Software's "Doom" can cost as much as $3 million to produce, meaning that the publisher needs to sell 150,000 units to break even. However, PC Data Inc. says that nearly 20 percent of the CD titles it tracks sold less than ten copies each during the heavy retailing month of December.

Even creatively respected companies like Ebook Inc., which once had 25 employees and 40 titles, and longtime software producer Arnowitz Studios, have been forced to lay off employees, move into empty garages and lofts, and drastically reduce their produce line in an attempt to survive the industry shakeout. Many other companies have actually "gone virtual," meaning that they now exist only in cyberspace instead of reality. Just like business in the movie, record, and publishing industries, CD-ROM start-ups have found that you need a lot of financial resources and distribution power to stay in business.

The experience of RoundBook Publishing Group, Inc. is in some ways typical. The company was founded by two former Sony executives. In 1993 they made a deal to produce a multimedia-software version of the rock opera *Tommy* by combing film clips, rock concert segments, and 25 years of Who photos and memorabilia. By the fall of 1995 RoundBook had generated a lot of favorable publicity, but had gone through $1 million, including a small share invested by *Tommy* composer Pete Townsend, without completing the program. Then their distribution deal fell through. They made a last-ditch effort to raise additional funds from 30 venture capital firms, and almost closed on a $3 million dollar deal with Puerto Rican banks and venture capitalists, before losing the rights to *Tommy* and heading into bankruptcy.

Ironically, the *Tommy* CD-ROM title, which was never actually produced, was still voted one of the best titles of the year in a consumer survey. "Maybe this will make a funny book," jokes Mark Lediard, a former RoundBook executive.

Source: Adapted from Don Clark, "Multimedia's Hype Hides Virtual Reality: An Industry Shakeout," in *Wall Street Journal,* March 1, 1995.

the entrepreneur is forced out and succeeded by a less creative but more managerially efficient executive. This is more probable when outside investors control the firm and fear that failure to act will cost them their investments.

MATURING INDUSTRIES

It seems more appropriate to think of entrepreneurial strategies in the emerging and transitional environments because that is where the most visible and publicized entrepreneurial activity takes place. But entrepreneurs are not limited by law, economics, or customers to these two phases of the industry life cycle. Entry can take a place in **mature industries** as well. Some flatly reject the idea that there is such a thing as a mature industry—there are only mature (and poorly run) firms. The argument is over the direction of causation. Does a maturing industry lower firm profitability, or does low firm profitability bring on the mature condition?[36]

Mature industries are characterized by slower growth, little pure innovation, more product and process improvements, more sophisticated customers, and increasing concentration of producers.[37] The last characteristic means that a few firms may produce 40 to 80 percent of the goods and services in the industry. This increased concentration also means that one or two industry leaders have emerged. An industry leader is the one the others look to for price changes and strategic movements. Sometimes mature industries appear to be friendly "clubs" with minimum competition and a general understanding of how to compete. The U.S. auto industry, the beef packers, the television networks, and the beer brewers spend as much time cooperating with each other to fend off attacks from outsiders (the Japanese automakers, the pork lobby, cable TV operators, temperance societies) than they do competing against each other.

However, entry is possible in mature industries, although the barriers are high. The computer hardware business is an example.[38] Start-up and entry in this industry is increasingly rare. The business is saturated. Ben Rosen, the venture capitalist who bankrolled Compaq Computer in 1982, says, "In terms of main-line, hard-core computer companies, it's very hard to define an area where you can get to a critical mass of $50 million to $100 million" in sales. Short of that size, the chances of making big returns and taking the company public are slim. Veterans of the industry are sadly concluding that the heyday is over. "It may not be possible to start a new computer manufacturing company," laments Richard Shaffer, publisher of **Technologic Computer Newsletter.** There are other problems as well:

- Capital costs have soared. "It costs $50 million just to find out if anybody cares."
- Limits on technological innovation are being reached. Firms promising breakthroughs are often disappointed.
- Replacements are being ordered by customers slowly. Much of the computer machinery just doesn't wear out.
- The industry's move to standardized parts and operating systems limit the innovation small companies can provide.[39]

Attacking the Leader   One possible strategy is to attack the industry leader (an imposing task, but not impossible).[40] Industry leaders can become vulnerable when the business cycle is on the upswing and things look good. Leaders may become complacent. Those with unhappy customers can also be attacked; they have grown arrogant and are no longer providing value. And when leaders are under antitrust investigation, they are certainly less likely to retaliate. But never attack an industry leader with an imitative, me-too product or service. The challenger who does so has nothing to defend.

Three conditions must be present for the attacker. First, it must have some basis for sustainable competitive advantage. Some resources must possess the four-attribute qualities that would provide the entrant either a cost advantage or a sustainable difference. Second, the new entrant must neutralize the leader's advantage by at least matching the perceived quality of the leader's product. Last, there must be an impediment (more than one is even better) that prevents retaliation. These impediments are:

- Antitrust problems.
- A cash crunch caused by overextension.
- A blind spot such as the uniqueness paradox.
- An overdiversified portfolio causing neglect of key areas.
- A strategic bind (retaliation would jeopardize another business strategy).

If these three conditions are met, the entrant has a chance. One tactic is to **reconfigure** the ways of doing business. This means doing something startlingly different. For example, the makers of Grey Poupon mustard reconfigured the marketing of mustard by spending more on advertising than the mustard business ever had before. French's, Heinz, and others were forced to give up share to this upstart. A second tactic is to **redefine the scope of service.** A new entrant can focus on a particular niche, serve that customer exceedingly well, and gain a foothold in a mature industry. For example, La Quinta motels focused on the frequent business traveler on a small budget. There was little retaliation, lest the entrenched competitors ruin their own pricing structure and demean the reputation of their core brands. Last, the challenger can attempt to spend its way to success. It can attempt to buy market share through exceptionally low prices and heavy promotion and advertising. This is risky business and out of the reach of all but the best-financed entrepreneurs.

Specializing   One additional entrepreneurial strategy can be used to enter a mature market. This strategy calls for the new venture to do something for a mature business better than it could do it itself. New firms and small firms can thrive in a mature market if they can take over some specialized activities for a big concern.[41] It is not unusual for a highly specialized small firm to have lower operating costs than large firms. The larger, more mature firms carry more overhead, have older technology, and do not focus on the cost drivers the way a smaller firm can. For example, Ameriscribe operates mailrooms for National Steel and does it better and cheaper than the firm can do. The Wyatt Company, a consulting firm, did a survey and found that 86 percent of the nation's largest corporations had cut back on operations and contracted services to outsiders.

It should also be noted that there are costs to contracting out these services: legal contractual costs, monitoring costs, searching for contractors and proceeding bids, possible loss from opportunistic behavior, and recontracting costs. However, even after these transaction and agency costs are covered, it still may be cheaper to use an outside contractor. This is an example of the classic make-or-buy decision, and theo-

TABLE 4–3 Corporate Services Contracted Out to Smaller Firms		
Company	*Function and Service*	*Contractor*
DuPont	Product engineering and design	Morris Knudsen
AT&T	Credit-card processing	Total Systems Services
Northern Telecom	Electronic component manufacturing	Comptronix
Eastman Kodak	Computer support services	Businessland
Mobil	Refinery maintenance	Serv-Tech
Whirlpool	Distribution center management	Kenco Group
National Steel	Mail room operations and copying work	Ameriscribe
Security Pacific	Accounting and trust management	SunGard Data Systems
Texas Instruments	Packing and shipping materials	Harper Group

Source: Adapted from M. Selz, "Small Companies Thrive by Taking Over Some Specialized Tasks for Big Concerns," *The Wall Street Journal,* September 9, 1992, B1–2.

retical foundations of this problem are detailed in transaction cost theory and agency theory. Table 4–3 provides some additional examples of this phenomenon.

DECLINING INDUSTRIES

Declining industries are characterized by the end of unit growth and by flat constant-dollar sales (i.e., adjusted for inflation). Finally, both of these indicators decrease.[42] Current examples of consumer industries in decline in the United States are tobacco and hard liquor. Industrial sectors in decline include manufacturers of carburetors for automobiles, certain defense-related manufacturers and aerospace contractors, and producers of bias-ply tires for original equipment manufacturers (OEM). The primary causes of industry decline are technological substitution, shifts in the tastes and preferences of consumers, and demographic factors.

Technological Substitution   When an older technology is replaced by a newer one, the older technology goes into decline. However, it does not immediately disappear. Even after the invention and adoption of the transistor, which replaced vacuum tubes in radios, televisions, and other devices in the late 1950s and 1960s, producers of vacuum tubes continued to exist. They supplied replacement parts for existing sets and produced for the hobby and collector markets. Similarly, producers of vinyl long-playing records still exist, although these have been rapidly and overwhelmingly overtaken by producers of compact discs and cassette tapes.

Changes in Tastes and Preferences   Changes in tastes and preferences shift demand to alternatives but do not cause immediate extinction of the declining industry. The declining consumer industries noted previously reflect changing tastes. For example, the underlying trend today is for healthier lifestyles. However, millions of Americans each year have a steak for dinner, accompanied by a whisky, and light up a cigar after dessert. The volumes of all three products continue to be high, but they are decreasing a little each year.

Changes in Demographics   Changes in demographics are reflected in overall product demand (see Chapter 3). As the baby-boom generation makes its way through the population cycle, its members first produced a boom in children's clothing and furnishings, followed by a decline in these industries. Then they bought automobiles and residential real estate, which boomed; now each of these industries is in decline. The boomers are aging, as are their parents, and health care is the fastest-growing segment of GNP. Guess what will occur when the boomers start to die off? Health care will decline, and the mortuary business will boom.

Achieving Success   Under certain conditions, new entrants can establish successful niches in declining industries. The key for the new entrant is to find ways to help the incumbents leave the industry and then purchase their assets at low prices. This is an imposing task, however, since a number of factors increase the height of the **exit barriers** for firms in declining industries:

- Low liquidation value of specialized assets.
- Interrelationship of the business in decline with other businesses not in decline.
- Potentially negative effects of exiting on financial markets.
- Emotional and managerial effects of "calling it quits."

From the viewpoint of the entrepreneur, if the industry is still attractive and the entrepreneur has or can acquire resources with the four attributes of sustainable competitive advantage, opportunity still exists. Take the example of Donald J. "Jerry" Ehrlich, president of Wabash National, a manufacturer of truck trailers (a commodity product in a declining industry). In 1992, truck trailer production in the United States was 140,500, down from 214,300 in 1988. During the 1980s, many manufacturers had leveraged themselves to the hilt. Overloaded with debt, they were in poor shape to modernize their plants to meet the challenges of manufacturing in the 1990s. Jerry Ehrlich had seen this all happen from close-up. He used to be president of Monon Corporation, a $250 million maker of trailers. But Monon was a leveraged buyout victim of the 1980s and went into decline. So Ehrlich left Monon, went down the road about 30 miles to Lafayette, Indiana, and started Wabash.

Ehrlich's initial resource endowment included two Monon managers and 14 employees who went with him and his own 35 years of experience building trailers. He found cheap manufacturing space in an abandoned factory. His brother Rod joined him as chief of engineering. He had quite a few entry wedges to provide him momentum. One was a customer sponsorship. Sears, Roebuck & Co. had worked with Jerry for years, and it ordered ten trailers with a promise of 370 more if all went well. With this order in hand, Ehrlich employed underutilized resources and was able to buy equipment at fire-sale prices from other bankrupt rust-belt companies and start hiring workers. With government sponsorship, he was able to raise $3 million through industrial revenue bonds. His own reputation enabled him to raise another $2 million in outside equity.

How successful has Wabash become? In 1992, Wabash produced 100 trailers a day on its 58-acre, 700,000-square-foot facility, the largest site of its kind in the world. In 1992, revenue had grown to $300 million from $191 million in 1991. By 1996, revenue had reached $375 million. The company is now the largest manufacturer of truck trailers. Sales per employee were $180,000, easily the best in the industry. During the same period the two top competitors, Freuhauf and Great Dane, saw sales decline 64 percent and 25 percent, respectively, over the preceding five years. The current strategic keys? The know-how to manufacture and market trailers, build customer loyalty, produce the product at the lowest cost in the industry, and maintain a flexible workforce that can produce "15 different types of trailers for 15 different customers" on any given day.

FRAGMENTED INDUSTRIES

Figure 4–1 shows the life cycle curve for an industry that has, over time, consolidated. Consolidation means that the number of firms decreases, the birth rate of new firms diminishes considerably, and larger firms have advantages of scale and scope. But not all industries are dominated by large firms with megamarket shares. In other words, not all industries go through the life cycle of Figure 4–1. Industries that do not are called **fragmented industries.** Examples include professional services, retailing, distribution services, wood and metal fabrication, and personal care businesses, such as hairdressers and barbers.

The causes for fragmentation are diverse. Low-entry barriers can cause fragmentation because firms will always be faced with new challengers and therefore be unable to grow. An industry may not be able to generate economies of scale, since being larger brings no cost advantages. In these cases, firms do not get larger, and consolidation never takes place. Indeed, there may be diseconomies of scale; costs go up (on a per-unit basis) as the firms grow. High transportation and inventory costs may keep firms small and geographically limited.[44]

The effect of firm size on buyers and sellers also can keep an industry fragmented. If neither buyers nor sellers see advantages in dealing with larger firms, they will avoid such firms and negotiate with smaller, less powerful firms. Sometimes the market niches are too small to support larger firms because the needs of the market are so diverse. Any or all of these conditions can keep an industry from the path described in Figure 4–1 and, therefore, keep the firms in the industry small and relatively powerless.

Most of what we understand to be the small-business sector of the economy is actually the set of fragmented industries and the ventures within them. Businesses in fragmented industries can be profitable, and they can grow to be relatively large. But by definition, if they are large enough to have a market share that can influence conditions, then the industry is no longer fragmented.

Overcoming Fragmentation   New ventures in fragmented industries sometimes have the potential to introduce strategic, technological, or managerial innovations that may help the industry overcome fragmentation. If the new venture enters with technologies that introduce economies of scale, the venture will grow larger. For example, the brewery industry used to be fragmented, with thousands of local brewers. The technological breakthrough that overcame this fragmentation was the refrigerated freight car, which enabled brewers to ship their beer long distances without danger of it spoiling.

Fragmentation may also be overcome by strategies that reconstruct the way firms operate. The "sneaker" used to be a fragmented product in the sporting goods industry. With few exceptions it was sold as commodity footwear for kids (Keds, Converse). When it was reconstructed as an "athletic shoe," given technological developments, and promoted as a personal fashion statement, a highly profitable industry dominated by a few very large firms (Nike, Reebok, Adidas) emerged.

Another method of reconstructing an industry is to separate the assets responsible for fragmentation from other assets. This is known as "unbundling." Two classic examples are campgrounds and fast food.[45] These industries were characterized by thousands of small owners. Both require tight local control and supervision and must be located near their customers. But significant economies of scale in purchasing and marketing were achieved through franchising. Local control was maintained by the franchisee, and purchasing and marketing economies were obtained by the franchisor. The initial beneficiaries of these economies were McDonald's and KOA.

Investors, and especially venture capitalists, are increasingly targeting fragmented industries as neglected but high-potential opportunities. Why? Because a firm that overcomes fragmentation can become the industry leader, achieve enormous size and profitability, and provide rates of return in the thousands of percent range. The Chicago firm of Golder, Thoma & Cressy is often credited with originating this investment strategy. So far, it has applied its strategy to the nursing home, answering service, and bottled-water businesses. Other industries ripe for consolidation are small-niche food processors, small-town newspapers, security alarm companies, and (the ultimate local business) funeral homes.

The strategy is not easy to execute. First the investor identifies and acquires a company in a fragmented industry, one with no market leader. Then a new management team is recruited to run the business. Together the investors and new managers identify and negotiate to buy a few additional companies in the target industry. The hardest part is next: consolidating all the companies under a common name and set of operating practices. If it works, the payoffs are huge.[46]

Coping with Fragmentation   Quite often the new entrant lacks the resources, means, or imagination to overcome fragmentation. Excellent money can still be made, however, from high-quality implementation, and the firm that learns to cope with fragmentation can thrive. A solid and profitable small business can be built on the following foundations:

- *Regimented professional management.* The introduction of managerial techniques and professionalism into small-business operations can keep the firm profitable even under strong price pressure.
- *Formula facilities or franchising.* High degrees of standardization and efficient, low-cost operations provide protection against eroding margins.
- *Serving specialized, focus niches.* A business that is highly specialized by product type, customer type, order type, or geographic area can achieve minor economies of scale and add high value for buyers.

Warning! A firm can be so specialized that it may not have enough customers to be feasible. Do not plan to open a pen repair shop, a shoelace boutique, or a restaurant based on the concept of toast.

Global Industries

A **global industry** is one in which "the strategic positions of competitors in major geographic or national markets are fundamentally affected by their overall global position."[47] This means that the firm must compete worldwide or face major strategic disadvantages. For example, a firm may need the huge economies of scale generated by a world market or the marketing expertise developed in other parts of the world. The essential industry analysis techniques presented in Chapter 3 also apply to global industries. The major difference is that instead of considering each product and country separately, they must be considered jointly. This increases the complexity of the analysis.

Examples of global industries include television receivers, most computer hardware, sewing machines, capital equipment and machine tools, automobiles, aircraft, and athletic footwear. In each case the firm must account for all competitors around the world. Worldwide sourcing and manufacturing are requirements. A new venture in any of these industries is forced to consider some form of global operations as its best option. Given that it is unlikely there will be many (or any) new entries in these existing global industries, what is the point of this discussion in terms of entrepreneurship? The point is that entrepreneurs need to be able to recognize infant global industries to avoid being caught in a global squeeze. They also need to recognize pseudo-global industries to avoid overextension when it is not a requirement.

SOURCES OF GLOBAL MOMENTUM

Four major factors can lead an industry toward globalizations: (1) comparative advantage, (2) economies of scale, (3) global experience, and (4) global standards.[48] The most noteworthy of the global standards are the **ISO 9000 series rules,** promulgated by a Geneva-based organization and approved by over 60 countries. The rules spell out how companies should set up quality control and assurance programs.

These rules have produced opportunities for smaller firms, such as Rice aircraft of Hauppauge, New York, and Van Diest Supply Co. of Webster City, Iowa.[49] Rice Aircraft's compliance with these standards has set it apart from many of its competitors in aircraft-parts distribution. It rigorously keeps its inventory list current and demands that all shipments be logged into the computer as soon as they arrive. The company even fired an employee for failing to make the entries quickly enough. "People have to be much, much more accountable for what they do," says Paula Rice, executive vice-president.

The adoption of ISO 9000 standards has paid off. Rice won a $3 million contract with AMR Corporate's American Airlines, which was impressed with the small firm's quality systems. Rice created a quality assurance position at the vice-president level. Says the new vice-president, "My entire job is enforcing the system."

At Van Diest, a 400-employee supplier of chemicals and fertilizer, early conversion to the ISO 9000 standards strengthened supplier relations. The firm originally complied with the standards at the urging of Du Pont, a major customer. Workers at Van Diest spent over 500 hours documenting all the company's quality control procedures and rules. This assured continuity, since before ISO 9000 compliance, most of the rules were in the employees' heads. Now, "if somebody drops dead tomorrow, somebody else will be able to pick up the job," says Walt Sayer, Van Diest's senior vice-president.

However, conforming to the ISO 9000 standards can be expensive. It can cost $20,000 for a consultation, then thousands of employee-hours to document the procedures. In addition, independent certification is an annual event, with the registrars col-

---

Global Warning

In 1995 Bry-Air Inc., an Ohio manufacturer of industrial dehumidifiers, racked up more than $20 million in sales, and more than 60 percent of those sales came from overseas. "Nowadays, you don't really have much choice: You have to think globally," says Paul D. Griesse, company chairman.

"Companies are setting up connections overseas more than ever before," says J. David Richardson, an economist at Syracuse University. Analysts agree that many of the firms now starting to do business abroad are small companies. In the five years preceding 1992, the number of U.S. exporters climbed 20 percent to 127,000, and the bulk of those new firms are believed to be small entrepreneurs like Bry-Air. Many of these exporters eventually establish operations in foreign countries.

However, doing business abroad can be problematic, especially for small entrepreneurs. "The number of pitfalls is almost limitless," notes T. Quinn Spitzer Jr., chairman of a New Jersey consulting firm that helps multinationals set business strategies. Small companies often have trouble securing financing to cover their overseas start-up costs. Without the staff of international experts that large corporations have, small firms can encounter problems with foreign copyright or labor laws, or implement a marketing strategy designed for the United States which won't work in a foreign culture.

Computers and air transportation have made global trotting easier in the past decade, but time is still big cost. J.W. Kisling, chairman of Multiplex Co., a Missouri manufacturer of beverage-dispensing equipment with $9 million in annual overseas sales, estimates that he spends more than one third of his time abroad. "Going overseas in a real commitment," he says. "It's not conducive to improving your golf score."

In addition, many small business owners find that all that travel time translates into sacrificing control. Creating foreign operations, says D. DaWayne Flor of Laurel Engineering Inc., means that "You're placing a major new part of the company in the hands of other people, whom you have to trust." Some companies give up this control to foreign nationals because they may understand the market better than a transplanted American, and traditionally have a longer tenure on the job. But this can have mixed results. Azon USA Inc., a Michigan supplier of chemicals and machinery to aluminum window manufacturers, set up a sister operation in Wales and a company sales manager in Europe at roughly the same time. The autonomy they gave their Wales operation has paid off with expanded sales and profits. But they had to close their European office after racking up $705,000 in expenses with little results.

However, opportunities for profit keep Azon focused on overseas expansion, and they have retained a consultant to advise them on their next move. "You're a babe in the woods when you start out on these things," says James M. Dunstan, Azon's chairman. "If you're lucky, you don't get burned."

Source: Adapted from Jeffrey A. Tannenbaum, "Small Firms, Big Hurdles," in *Wall Street Journal,* September 26, 1996.

lecting fees for certification (up to $1,500 every six months and $3,000 for the complete three-year annual review).

IMPEDIMENTS TO GLOBALIZATION

Just as entrepreneurs need to understand which factors can lead to globalization, they also need to recognize the major impediments to globalization. The entrepreneur who behaves "locally" while the competition is behaving "globally" will be trapped in a narrow market. The entrepreneur who is behaving "globally" when "local" needs are prevailing will be overextended and spread too thin.

The five most important impediments to the formation of global industries are:

1. The lack of worldwide demand,
2. High transportation and storage costs,
3. Differing local product needs,
4. Managerial differences,
5. Governmental barriers.

For what are seen as political and economic advantages, governments protect their own national industries in ways that slow the development of global industries. Such barriers as tariffs, import duties, quotas, preferential procurement, local content requirements, "protected" research and development programs, and preferential tax treatment for local firms all give home-country businesses advantages relative to their international competitors. These impediments provoke retaliation by other national governments, which further globalization. As we can see in Street Story 4–3, entrepreneurs do encounter problems doing business overseas.

It takes strategic innovation and vision for the entrepreneur to exploit opportunities globally. Indeed, one of the major innovations a firm can make is to begin to think internationally. The increased information costs, complexity, and resource requirements of international competition often blind entrepreneurs to opportunities.[50] But even when exploiting global opportunity appears daunting, nation-to-nation international business may be feasible.

E-NOTES 4–6 INDUSTRY ENVIRONMENT

Six different types of industry environments, each with its own unique life-cycle, include:

- emerging industries,
- transitional industries,
- maturing industries,
- declining industries,
- fragmented industries,
- global industries.

Evaluating Strategy and Entrepreneurial Opportunities

Recognizing, assessing, and exploiting opportunities are among the keys to entrepreneurial success. Opportunity assessment can be broken into five stages (Figure 4–2). Each stage focuses on analysis and the actions that must be taken. Analysis rests on

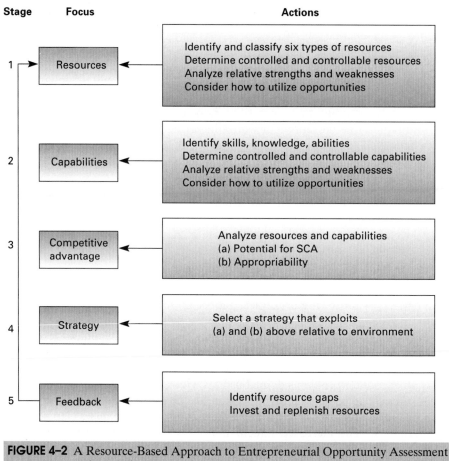

FIGURE 4–2 A Resource-Based Approach to Entrepreneurial Opportunity Assessment and Analysis

the entrepreneur's understanding of the nature of the business that he or she wishes to create. Traditionally, entrepreneurs must ask the question, "What is my business?" They then attempt to answer the question in terms of a target customer and the target's buying needs, tastes, and preferences. In a world with volatile markets and changing tastes and preferences, keeping up is a dicey proposition. So, in opportunity assessment, entrepreneurs should initially assess the ore stable set of *internal* capabilities rather than volatile external resources.

STAGE 1: IDENTIFICATION

The first stage requires entrepreneurs to identify and classify the resources they currently have and can obtain control over in their initial efforts to create a new venture. Identification and classification should be structured using the six categories previously described: financial, physical, human, technological, reputational, and organizational assets. A resource is currently controlled if the entrepreneur and the top management team have immediate and unimpeded access to it, legally and physically. An asset is controllable to the extent that it may be obtained sometime in the future. For a rigorous analysis, a probability distribution can indicate the likelihood of obtaining the resource. If extremely high or low, this probability can be factored into the next part of the stage one assessment.

The second part of stage one entails determining the relative strengths and weaknesses of the resource bundle and configuration. The entrepreneur should then examine how to use these resources and explore what business opportunities exist to make the most of them. What criteria should the entrepreneur use for this evaluation? The four attribute criteria: Is the resource under investigation

- Rare?
- Valuable?
- Hard to copy?
- Nonsubstitutable?

The entrepreneur also needs to ask, to what degree? To the extent that the entrepreneur can answer "yes" to the first question and "quite a bit" to the second, he or she has the basis for competitive advantage.

STAGE 2: CAPABILITIES

The capabilities of a firm are the skills, knowledge, and abilities needed to manage and configure resources.[51] The second stage, then, is similar to the first, except the analysis focuses on capabilities instead of resources. Few resources, as pure inputs, can form the basis for a successful business. Usually these resources must be employed in some way—a way defined by the capabilities of the entrepreneur and his or her team.[52] Capability makes the resources productive. The firm requires capabilities to coordinate resources and foster cooperation for efficiency. The hardest part of this analysis is maintaining objectivity. Entrepreneurs are tempted to overestimate abilities and skills or dwell on past accomplishments they may not be able to generalize.

- There is no one-to-one relationship between resources and capabilities. Each firm can create its own relationship to manage its resources. The most important outcome of this relationship, though, is the smooth coordination and cooperation among the members of the teams who perform the routines. The routines themselves become intangible resources that may have the four attributes.
- New firms have advantages over incumbents when developing routines and capabilities in industries undergoing great changes. Older firms will have trouble changing routines to adapt to the environment; while new firms can invent routines to fit the new realities. Of course, once the new venture has become established and its routines have been perfected, it is just as liable to assault from an even newer challenger. This highlights the trade-off between efficiency and flexibility.
- Some routines are widely distributed, while others reside in the skills and abilities of one person. For example, Walt Disney World is a complex amalgam of entertainment, art technology, traffic control, and highly motivated employees. In contrast, the junk bond underwriting at Drexel, Burnham, and Lambert in the 1980s was almost solely a function of the capabilities of Michael Milken.

STAGE 3: COMPETITIVE ADVANTAGE

Stage three focuses on competitive advantage. Here we try to determine whether the competitive advantages(s) identified in stages one and two may be sustained and if the profits and rents can be protected. Sustainable competitive advantage depends on the firm's ability to move first and create isolating mechanisms. First-mover advantages and isolating mechanisms prevent other firms from copying and crowding the firm's profit. The entrepreneur should ask:

- Do isolating mechanisms exist for the firm?
- Which ones should be employed to protect our resource advantages?

Any rent that the firm can collect may be eroded. Physical resources can be depleted, be depreciated, be replicated, or become obsolete. The probability of appropriation is high, too. The environment will seek to get a share of the rents through taxation (government), increased wage demands (employees), rising input costs (suppliers), or litigation (competitors and lawyers). The new venture's founders and leaders must be sensitive and alert to these pressures.

STAGE 4: STRATEGY

The next stage translates the assessment of competitive advantage into strategy. The firm requires two related strategies: one to protect and manage its resources, the other a product and market strategy. The first strategy has already been discussed in terms of isolating mechanisms and first-mover advantages. The second set of strategies entail dealing with the macroenvironment and the competitive environment described in Chapter 3.

STAGE 5: FEEDBACK

In stage five, the entrepreneur should focus on feedback, that is, evaluating and reassessing the continuous process of new venture creation. Through the first four stages, resource gaps may have appeared and requirements for resources that are neither controlled nor controllable may become apparent. Recycling through the process after having identified the gaps is recommended. Gap-reducing and gap-eliminating strategies can be the focus of the next round. Also, resource bases are inevitably depleted and depreciated. The next cycle must account for these erosions and make plans for investments to maintain resources and investments and to replenish stocks and assets.

E-NOTES 4–7   OPPORTUNITY ASSESSMENT
The five stages of assessing entrepreneurial opportunities include:

- identifying resources,
- analyzing capabilities,
- evaluating competition advantage,
- developing a strategy,
- reviewing feedback.

As we have seen throughout this chapter, no one strategy is best for all new ventures. Because choice is crucial and many paths can lead to success, we need a way to evaluate the strategy after it is chosen but before it is implemented. If we can do this, we can weigh various alternatives against one another and make a better choice without having to incur the consequences of a poor choice. The following four criteria may be used to evaluate proposals. [53] Each can be viewed as a test; if the strategy passes the tests, it is superior to strategies that fail the tests.

- *The goal consistence test.* Does the strategy help the firm to accomplish its goals? Are the strategy's outcomes predicted to be consistent with previous strategies and decisions? Will the strategy enable the firm to maintain its posture?
- *The frame test.* Is the firm working on the right issues? Does the strategy address resource issues and alignment with the environment? Does the strategy meet the requirements of the industry stage and help acquire and control resources possessing the four attributes of sustainable competitive advantage?
- *The competence test.* Does the firm have the ability to carry out the strategy? Can the strategy be broken down into problems that have solutions? Are these solutions that the firm can work out?
- *The workability test.* Will it work? Is it legal and ethical? Will it produce the desired end? Will the organization be willing to marshal its resources to carry out the strategy?

Summary

In this chapter we reviewed a combination of theory and practice from both the strategic management and the entrepreneurship literature. Entry wedges and momentum factors are the initial entrepreneurial strategies. The major wedges are innovation, parallel types of competition, and franchising, and the various forms of sponsorship compose the momentum factors. Resource-based strategies are geared toward rent-seeking behavior. The most prevalent of four rent-seeking behaviors is the entrepreneurial strategy. The resource-based model also accounts for the rate and direction of a venture's growth strategies. Firms grow in the direction of underutilized resources and toward areas where they have distinctive competencies.

Quality as a strategy was discussed in the resource-based framework. The choice of a strategy of Total Quality Management does not represent a sustainable competitive advantage for the firm. However, the implementation of such a program can provide advantages, since successful implementation requires superior market knowledge, complex service behavior from employees, and highly developed organizational systems. The best candidates for a successful TQM strategy are firms that already possess these resources.

We then looked at how industry conditions affect entry and strategy for a new venture. Six industry types were discussed: emerging industries, transitional industries, maturing industries, declining industries, fragmented industries, and global industries. Although new ventures can be successful in any of these environments, the emerging and fragmented environments provide the easiest entry and the most typical entrepreneurial case.

We concluded with a brief overview of the strategy evaluation process. Specifically, we identified four criteria for testing the appropriateness of a strategy before embarking on the market test itself. A strategy is appropriate if it is consistent with the goals of the organization, addresses the right issues, can be executed competently, and is workable both legally and ethically.

Key Terms

- Strategy
- Strategy formulation
- Strategy implementation
- Enterprise-level strategy
- Corporate strategy
- Business-level strategy
- Functional strategy
- Subfunctional strategy
- Entry wedge
- Franchisor
- Franchisee
- Geographic transfer
- Supply shortage
- Underutilized resource
- Customer contract
- Second source
- Licensing
- Joint venturing
- Market relinquishment
- Spin-off
- Ricardian rent
- Monopoly rent
- Entrepreneurial rent
- Quasi-rent
- Isolating mechanisms
- Property rights
- First-mover advantage
- Technological leadership

- Switching costs
- Focus effect
- Synergy effect
- Contestable synergy
- Idiosyncratic synergy
- Continuous improvement
- Benchmarking
- The quality circle
- Outsourcing
- Industry life cycle
- Emerging industry
- Transitional industry
- Shakeout
- Slack
- Horizontal integration
- Mature industry
- Reconfigure
- Redefine the scope of service
- Declining industry
- Fragmented industry
- Global industry
- ISO 9000 series rules
- Capability
- Goal consistency test
- Frame test
- Competence test
- Workability test

Discussion Questions

1. Why do new ventures need strategies?
2. How do the major entry wedges help create momentum for the new venture?
3. How do the minor wedges supplement the major ones?
4. Evaluate the pros and cons of the minor wedges. Which would be the most or least effective in the long run?
5. Describe the four different kinds of rents. Give examples of how an entrepreneur might attempt to collect these.
6. How will firms employ their resources for growth? Explain the focus effects and synergy effects.
7. Discuss "quality" as a strategy. How

can it be used to achieve sustainable competitive advantage?
8. What are the key elements affecting entrepreneurial strategy in these environments?
   a. Emerging industries
   b. Transitional industries
   c. Maturing industries
   d. Declining industries
   e. Fragmented industries
   f. Global industries
9. What are the five stages for assessing entrepreneurial opportunities?
10. What are the four tests of strategy? Why is it important to apply the tests before going into business?

Exercises

Develop a strategy for your new venture.

1. What entry wedges, major and minor, will you employ?
2. How will you attempt to collect and appropriate rents?
3. What industry environment are you entering? How will this influence your strategy?
4. Apply the four tests to your strategy. What questions do these raise? How would you answer these questions if posed by a banker or venture capitalist?

DISCUSSION CASE

Building the "Big Mac" of Health Care

Virtually every community in the United States today boasts an outpatient health center that can perform simple surgeries far cheaper than the local hospital.

HealthSouth Corporation of Birmingham, Alabama has capitalized on this trend, and taken it a few steps further, by transforming their health care delivery system care into a household name. Twelve years ago, HealthSouth founder Richard Scrushy spotted the federal government's growing concern for health care costs, and decided that providers who offered services at the lowest possible cost would gain an important competitive advantage. "I wanted to get on the side of government," the former respiratory specialist says. "I thought if I could bring down costs, I'd have a real hot product that Wall Street would want."

Careful pricing and an aggressive acquisition strategy has helped Health-South grow today to 700 outpatient rehabilitation centers and 135 outpatient surgery centers, in addition to a number of inpatient facilities, including 100 rehabilitation centers and six hospitals. The company has positioned many of its rehabilitation centers in prime locations, either adjacent or near acute-care hospitals. It also has contracts with about 2,000 self-insured corporation and managed-care companies to provide workers' compensation and rehabilitation services.

But attention to the bottom line isn't the only thing that has propelled HealthSouth into the largest provider of outpatient surgery in the United States, with facilities in 50 states and an estimated annual revenue of $2.5 billion. Richard Scrushy's real genius may be his observation that while chains with instantly recognizable names and products like McDonald's dominated restaurants, hotels, and other industries, no one was attempting to apply that same kind of marketing strategy to health care. "It's time health care standardized protocol and treatment," says Scrushy. "If people like to go to Holiday Inns because they like the quality, that's fine. That's what we're doing."

Scrushy has enlisted the marketing muscle of superstars like Michael Jordan, Bo Jackson, and Kristi Yamaguchi to give HealthSouth the name recognition he craves. One of his more aggressive marketing ploys is the HealthSouth Sports Medicine Council, a nonprofit organization which sponsors multimedia rock and laser shows that reach one million cheering children each year. The road shows feature live and videotaped pitches from athletic stars (HealthSouth clients include the U.S. Olympic Team and the Texas Rangers baseball team) to "stay in school and stay off drugs" in addition to promoting HealthSouth centers. The celebrities all appear free of charge. Scrushy and his Dallas County Line country-western band also promote HealthSouth by playing at events like Arthritis Foundation fund raisers, and distributing their "Honk If You Love to Honky Tonk" album and video. In the near future the company hopes to develop a children's television show and negotiate a HealthSouth athletic shoe and sports drink. They are already plastering their logo on gym bags, jogging suits, and other merchandise.

It's an exciting, if sometimes dangerous, time for entrepreneurs in health care. "What you're seeing is a transition from what is a trillion-dollar cottage industry into a professionally managed business," says James Hoover, general partner in the venture-capital firm of Welsh, Carson, Anderson & Stowe. While HealthSouth has prospered, other ventures in the largest industry in the United States have faltered. Medaphis Corp., a provider of management services for hospitals and doctors, saw its stock plummet more than 60 percent when it posted disappointment earnings. And the market value of Coastal Physician Group Inc., a pioneer in building networks of physician practices, dropped from $900 to $150 million during turmoil following aggressive expansion. "One thing that always amazes people is the health-care field doesn't always obey the laws of markets and commodities," notes Rick Wade of the American Hospital Association.

CASE QUESTIONS

1. What is HealthSouth's entrepreneurial strategy?
2. What were this company's entry wedges?
3. What are this company's resources?
4. Where would you place HealthSouth on the Industry Life Cycle (Figure 4–1)?
5. What might we predict about the company's future?

Source: Adapted from Anita Sharpe, "Medical Entrepreneur Aims to Turn Clinics into a National Brand," *Wall Street Journal,* December 4, 1996.

Notes

1. Quoted in A. Deutschman, "America's Fastest-Growing Companies," *Fortune,* October 5, 1992, 58–82.
2. There are a number of fine textbooks on the subject of strategic management. The following list is not meant to be complete or exclusive: G. Dess and A. Miller, *Strategic Management* (New York: McGraw-Hill, 1993); H. Mintzberg and J. Quinn, *The Strategy Process* (Englewood Cliffs, NJ: Prentice Hall, 1991); Pearce and R. Robinson, *Strategic Management: Formulation, Implementation and Control* (Homewood, IL: Irwin, 1992); A. Thompson and A. Strickland, *Strategic Management: Text and Cases* (Homewood, IL: Irwin, 1992).
3. D. Hambrick, "Some Tests of the Effectiveness of Functional Attributes of Miles and Snow's Strategic Types,"

Academy of Management Journal 26 (1983): 5–26.

4. The original concept and description of entry wedges was developed by Karl Vesper in *New Venture Strategies* (Englewood Cliffs, NJ: Prentice Hall, 1980). Revised 1990.

5. Vesper, 1980.

6. P. Drucker, *Innovation and Entrepreneurship* (New York: Harper and Row, 1985).

7. Drucker, 1985.

8. S. Winter, "Knowledge and Competence as Strategic Assets," in D. Teece, ed., *The Competitive Challenge* (Cambridge, MA: Ballinger, 1988), pp. 159–184.

9. Winter, 1988. Winter provides an example that some readers may relate to. A brain-damaged man may retain the ability to play golf and hit a one-iron a good distance and in the desired direction. This type of competency cannot be easily transferred by any known method of communication. However, if the damage is to the part of the brain that process declarative information, the man might not recall where the ball landed or be able to keep track of his score.

10. J. Emshwiller, "Federal Research Labs Can Help Small firms Compete," *Wall Street Journal,* December 9, 1992, B2.

11. J. Mahoney and J. Pandian, "The Resource-based View within the Conversation of Strategic Management," *Strategic Management Journal* 13 (1992): 363–380.

12. These rewards can rightly be characterized and defined as entrepreneurial rents, the difference between a venture's *ex ante* cost (or value) of the resources combined to form the venture. See R. Rumelt, "Theory, Strategy and Entrepreneurship," in D. Teece, ed., *The Competitive Challenge* (Cambridge, MA: Ballinger, 1988) pp. 137–158.

13. M. Lieberman and D. Montgomery, "First-Mover Advantages," *Strategic Management Journal* 9 (1988): 41–58.

14. Winter, 1987.

15. Winter, 1987.

16. Lieberman and Montgomery, 1988; R. Rumelt, "Theory, Strategy and Entre-preneurship," in D. Teece, ed., *Competitive Strategic Management,* (Englewood Cliffs, NJ: Prentice Hall, 1988), pp. 556–570.

17. This section follows Mahoney and Pandian, 1992.

18. Quoted in Mahoney and Pandian, 1992, from W. Starbuck, "Organizational Growth and Development," in *Handbook of Organization,* J. March, ed. (Chicago: Rand McNally, 1985), 451–533.

19. E. Penrose. *The Theory of the Growth of the Firm* (New York: John Wiley, 1959).

20. P. Rubin, "The Expansion of Firms," *Journal of Political Economy* 81 (1973): 936–949.

21. C. Montgomery and S. Hariharan, "Diversified entry by Established Firms," *Journal of Economic Behavior and Organization* 15 (1991): 71–89.

22. Economists have always debated whether any firm level strategy matters. The neoclassical economist has usually argued that industry effects overwhelm firm effects. If this is true, the only entrepreneurial decision that counts is the choice of industry.

23. J. Barney, "Strategic Factor Markets: Expectations, Luck and Business Strategy," *Management Science* 32 (1986): 1231–1241.

24. "Special Report: Quality," *Business Week,* November 30, 1992, 66–75.

25. W. Deming, "The Roots of Quality Control in Japan," *Pacific Basin Quarterly* (Spring 1985): 3–4.

26. D. Garvin, *Managing Quality* (New York: Free Press, 1988).

27. This study was conducted over a three-year period by Ernst & Young and the American Quality Foundation. Five hundred and eight firms participated. The findings reported here are taken from two secondary sources: *Business Week,* November 30, 1992, and *Wall Street Journal,* October 1, 1992.

28. S. Birley and P. Westhead, "Growth and Performance Contrasts between 'Types' of Small firms," *Strategic Management Journal* 11 (1990): 535–557.

29. For example, the production function or product life cycle curve.

30. M. Porter, *Competitive Strategy* (New York: Free Press, 1980). See Chapter 10.

31. Drucker, 1985. The following examples are from Chapter 19.

32. C. Schoonhoven, E. Eisenhardt, and K. Lyon, "Speeding Products to Market: Waiting Time and First Product Introductions in New Firms," *Administrative Science Quarterly* 35 (1990): 177–207; L. Bourgeois and K. Eisenhardt, "Strategic Decision Processes in High-Velocity Environment: Four Cases in the Microcomputer Industry," *Management Science* 34 (1988): 816–835.

33. M. Werner, "Planning for Uncertain Futures: Building Commitment through Scenario Planning," *Business Horizons* (May–June, 1990): 55–58.

34. In the short run firms can survive if price is less than average *variable* cost, but in the long run, negative contribution margins cannot be sustained. In the long run, price must be sufficient to cover average *total* costs.

35. J. Martin, M. Feldman, M. Hatch, and S. Sitkin, "the Uniqueness Paradox in Organizational Stories," *Administrative Science Quarterly* 28 (1983): 438–453.

36. C. Baden-Fuller and J. Stopford, *Rejuvenating the Mature Business* (London: Routledge, 1992).

37. Porter, 1980.

38. Adapted from W. Bulkeley, "Maturing Market: Computer Startups Grow Increasingly Rare," *Wall Street Journal,* September 8, 1989, 1, 16.

39. Bulkeley, 1989.

40. M. Porter, "How to Attack the Industry Leader," *Fortune,* April 29, 1985, 153–166.

41. M. Selz, "Small Companies thrive by Taking Over Some Specialized Tasks for Big Concerns," *Wall Street Journal,* September 11, 1992, B1–2.

42. Porter, 1980, Chapter 12.

43. E. Welles, "Least Likely to Succeed," *Inc.,* December 1992, 74–86.

44. Porter, 1980, Chapter 9.

45. These examples are from Porter, 1980.

46. S. Galante, "Venture Firms Are Foraying into Fragmented Industries," *Wall Street Journal,* October 6, 1986.

47. From Chapter 13 of Porter.

48. For an in-depth treatment of these four factors, see Chapter 13 of Porter, 1980.

49. J. Tannenbaum, "Small Companies are Finding It Pays to Think Globally," *Wall Street Journal,* November 19, 1992, B2. The examples that follow are also adapted from this article.

50. Mahoney and Pandian, 1992.

51. R. Grant, "The Resource-Based Theory of Competitive Advantage: Implications for Strategy Formulation," *California Management Review* 34 (Spring, 1991): 114–135.

52. These capabilities have, at various times, been described as "distinctive competencies" or "core competencies" by other authors. See C. Snow and L. Hrebiniak, "Strategy, Distinctive Competence and Organizational Performance," *Administrative Science Quarterly* 25 (1990): 317–336; C. Prahalad and G. Hamel, "the Core Competence of the Corporation," *Harvard Business Review,* May–June (1990): 79–91.

53. R. Rumelt, "Evaluation of Strategy," *Strategic Management,* D. Schendel and C. Hofer, ed. (Boston: Little, Brown, 1979), pp. 196–210.

CHAPTER 5

The Business Plan

Outline

Each plan, like a snowflake, must be different.
—JOSEPH MANCUSO

Learning Objectives

After reading this chapter you will understand:

- Why it is important to write a business plan.
- The elements of a business plan.
- How to write a business plan.
- What kinds of questions people will ask about your business plan.
- How to respond to critiques of your business plan.

How do we want to use all the analysis and evaluation we did in Chapters 2, 3, and 4? We want to write a business plan. The development and writing of the business plan marks the transition from strategy formulation to the implementation stage of new venture creation. The entrepreneur or entrepreneurial team members have thus far collected information and analyzed it. They have examined their own preferences and goals to determine why they want to go into business. They have evaluated the venture's resource base and determined what is rare, valuable, difficult to duplicate, and nonsubstitutable. They have sifted through mountains of product and market data, analyzing environmental variables, market trends, and the competition. They have performed innumerable mental experiments to visualize what the business will look like, how the products or services will be produced or delivered, and how quality will be continuously monitored and improved.[1]

Now it is time for action. The document produced is known as the business plan. The **business plan** is the formal written expression of the entrepreneurial vision, describing the strategy and operations of the proposed venture. The business plan also goes by other names, depending on its intended audience. Presented to a banker, it may be called a "loan proposal." A venture capital group might call it the "venture plan" or "investment prospectus." Other audiences might be potential partners or top managers, suppliers and distributors, lawyers, accountants, and consultants.

Many firms start without business plans, meaning that their implementation stage begins with no plan. Most of these firms find eventually that they have to recreate their beginnings and write a plan at some point down the road. In today's complex economic environment, only the most reluctant entrepreneur with the simplest business concept avoids writing a business plan.

This chapter is divided into four sections. The first section argues that every new venture should have a business plan and explores the benefits of developing one. The second section offers an extensive and detailed summary of the components of a business plan and explains how they combine to produce a comprehensive picture of the new firm. The third section explains what questions the entrepreneurs are likely to be asked by investors and others. The chapter concludes with suggestions for writing and presenting the plan. Business plans communicate more about the top management team than simply the scope of their entrepreneurial vision. Entrepreneurs are judged by the way they organize, write, and present the business plan. Therefore, it must be informative, concise, and complete.

Why Write a Business Plan?

Arguments can be made for and against writing a business plan. But if the new venture is looking for financing from an outside source, it must have a plan. Writing a plan is not without its costs and sacrifices, but overall, the benefits far outweigh the costs.

THE COSTS OF PLANNING

Entrepreneurs are often characterized as "doers," individuals who prefer action to planning and who let their deeds speak for themselves. One of the costs of writing a business plan is that the entrepreneurs must sit still long enough to do it. Hiring someone to write the plan is not an acceptable substitute; entrepreneurs should undertake the task personally. Although outsiders—consultants, accountants, and lawyers—should be tapped for their advice and expertise, the founder or the initial top management team should be responsible for the writing.[2] By personally writing the plan, the entrepreneurs ensure that they are familiar with all the details, for they will have to make decisions about the new venture and be responsible for those decisions. Moreover, investors expect the founders to be involved in and knowledgeable about the proposed enterprise.

Developing and writing the plan take time, money, and energy. In launching the new venture, the entrepreneurial team may believe that actually working in the business is the best use of these resources. For short periods of time that may be true. But over the long haul, the new venture team is the most valuable, rare, and unique resource the company has. The task of the entrepreneur is the task of the leader. The leader is the architect of organizational purpose.[3] The venture is created to achieve the vision of the entrepreneur. The best use of the entrepreneur's time and energy, therefore, is in creating, refining, and pursuing that vision.

Since every business plan must deal with economic uncertainty and the risks that the firm faces, one of the costs of writing a business plan is the psychological strain of admitting everything that can go wrong. Entrepreneurs are optimists, and they believe in the power of their own efforts.[4] They believe they will succeed. The serious business plan, however, exposes the possibilities that can lead to failure. To achieve full material disclosure for a potential investor, partner, or supplier,[5] the plan has to list the risks of the business, one by one. Recognizing these risks and facing an uncertain future can be psychologically uncomfortable for the entrepreneur. This is a cost, and it is one reason some business plans are never written.

THE BENEFITS OF BUSINESS PLANNING

The business plan can personally benefit the entrepreneurial team. Founding a new business can be enormously fulfilling and exhilarating, but it is also an anxiety-ridden and tense experience. Usually a great deal of money is at stake, and the consequences of poor decisions can affect many people for a long time. In developing and writing a business plan, the entrepreneurial team reduces these anxieties and tensions by confronting them. By projecting the risks of the new venture into the future, the team comes to grips with potential negative outcomes and the possibility of failure. The knowledge that comes from this experience can reduce the fear of facing an unknown future.

Conflicts   Also on a personal level, the entrepreneur is potentially in conflict with the new business demands that he or she may find imposing. The entrepreneur may desire wealth and increased income, high esteem, a period of stability once the venture is off the ground, or more time for leisure and recreation. Each of these motivations, however, is impeded by the demands of the organization.

First, the new firm requires reinvestment; the more successful it is, the more money it will need for growth. This reality is in conflict with the entrepreneur's desire for short-term income. Second, the organization demands that the entrepreneur be a leader and a manager. But these responsibilities often require tough personnel decisions. The individuals who are hurt by these decisions may not hold the entrepreneur in high esteem. There is always the risk of not being liked and even of making enemies.

The entrepreneur may also anticipate a period of stability once the business is launched. The process of starting the new venture can be exhausting, and entrepreneurs feel they deserve an interim period of consolidation and peace. But the organization may demand more risk-taking, additional crucial decisions may have to be made, and plans and strategies may have to be reformulated. Here again, the firm is in conflict with its creator. Last, once the business is off the ground, the founder may look forward to having more time for leisure or for family or community service. But the venture needs the entrepreneur's help with the daily tasks; he or she has to continue to make business decisions and lead the organization.

E-NOTES 5–1   BUSINESS PLAN

A business plan:

- explains entrepreneur's vision in writing,
- demonstrates implementation (strategy and operations),
- may function as financing proposal or investment prospectus.

Table 5–1 presents these naturally arising conflicts. The business plan helps the entrepreneur deal with these conflicts by recognizing the issues before they become serious problems. The entrepreneur decides which way the conflicts will be resolved. By anticipating these conflicting values and writing them into the plan, the entrepreneur can reduce the emotional strain that making these trade-offs entails. When the time comes for making a decision in a specific conflict, the entrepreneur can refer to the business plan as an objective standard for resolving it.

Planning and Performance   The firm also benefits from the planning process. Research shows there is a positive relationship between planning and performance in new and small firms.[6] *That is, firms that plan perform better and are more likely to succeed than firms that do not.*[7] There are four reasons why this is so.

1. *Comprehensiveness.* The business plan has to fully and completely treat all the major issues facing the new venture. It should leave nothing of importance out. This comprehensiveness enables the entrepreneur to see where trouble might

TABLE 5–1 Conflicts between the Entrepreneur and the Organization

Entrepreneur May Desire:		*New Venture May Require:*
Wealth and income	⟷	Reinvestment for growth
To be liked and esteemed	⟷	Leadership and management
Stability	⟷	Risk and action
Leisure and community service	⟷	Participation in the work

come from and to develop contingent strategies to reduce the effects of these problems.

2. *Communication.* The business plan is a document for communicating to various audiences the business's concept and potential. An effective plan succeeds in communicating the excitement and vision of the founders and can help to attract resources to the new venture.

3. *Guidance.* The business plan sets goals and milestones for the new venture. It lays out the intentions of the entrepreneurial team and the values the founders wish to preserve in their organization. Therefore, the plan can be referred to repeatedly to guide decisions of the firm's managers and employees. "When in doubt, consult the plan" could be the motto of a new venture. In the exciting and turbulent months and years after starting, it is easy for the individuals in the organization to lose sight of the venture's original purposes and intended strengths. A readily available written plan fosters cohesiveness because everyone can see what the firm's desired objectives are.

4. *The planning process.* The process of putting together a business plan, consulting it frequently, and reviewing and revising it periodically can improve the venture's performance even though some aspects of the plan may become obsolete before the ink is dry. This improvement is brought about by collecting information, sharing analysis, developing norms for decision making within the organization, publicly enunciating the values of the organization's leaders, reviewing objectives, and linking these with action—all elements of highly effective organizations. In other words, the planning process itself helps make the company a better organization.

Elements of the Business Plan

There are many variations on the theme of what goes into a successful business plan.[8] However, all these variations have the same essential elements:

PRELIMINARY SECTIONS

Cover page
Table of contents
Executive summary
1. The company
2. Management

3. Product/service and competition
4. Financial history
5. Use of proceeds and exit*

MAJOR SECTIONS

I. Background and purpose
   A. History
   B. Current situation
   C. The resource-based concept

II. Objectives
   A. Short term
   B. Long term

III. Market analysis
   A. Overall market
   B. Specific market
   C. Competitive factors
   D. Microenvironmental influences

IV. Development and production
   A. Production processes
   B. Resource requirements
   C. Quality assurance

V. Marketing
   A. Overall concept and orientation
   B. Marketing resources
   C. Marketing strategy
   D. Sales forecasts

VI. Financial plans
   A. Financial statements
   B. Financial resources
   C. Financial strategy

VII. Organization and management
   A. Key personnel resources
   B. Human resource management strategy

VIII. Ownership
   A. Form of business
   B. Equity positions
   C. Deal structure*

IX. Critical risks and contingencies

---

*Required primarily when the business plan is used as an investment proposal.

CONCLUDING SECTIONS

X. Summary and conclusions
XI. Scheduling and milestones

APPENDIXES

PRELIMINARY SECTIONS

The business plan has three preliminary sections, each of which is important. It has been reported that, on average, the reader will spend less than ten minutes evaluating the plan for a new venture.[9] To make the reader want to go on to the main body of the document and evaluate the details, these beginning sections must be both attractive and informative.

Cover Page Every business plan should have a cover page that includes the following information:

- The company name, address, telephone and fax numbers, and E-mail address, if it is available. The easier it is for the reader to contact the entrepreneur, the more likely the contact will occur.
- The name and position of the contact person, who should be one of the firm's top executives. The person designated as the contact person should be prepared to answer questions about the plan.
- The date the business was established (simply "established 1995," for example), and the date of this particular version of the business plan ("February 1997," for example).
- The name of the organization from which funding (or credit, or a supplier agreement, etc.) is being sought. The full name, correctly spelled, should be used.
- The copy number of the plan (for example, "copy 2 of 7 copies"). There are two reasons for this entry. The first is security. The entrepreneur must know how many of the plans are in circulation and who has them. Eventually, all of them should be returned. The business plan contains information that is sensitive and strategic. Unscrupulous competitors could put the firm at a disadvantage if the plan were to fall into their hands. The second reason for limiting circulation is exclusivity. It is not good practice to have dozens of copies of the plan circulating in the financial community. Financiers like to consider opportunities that are not being concurrently considered by others. If the plan is overcirculated, it could acquire the negative reputation of being "shopworn."
- The company's **logo**. Every firm should have a logo. A logo is a design, picture, or ideograph chosen to represent the company. The association of the company name with a pictorial design gives the reader (and eventually the customer) two ways of remembering your company and its products. A new venture can employ clip art or the latest computer technology to design its own logo, using a graphics or drawing program from a personal computer. A large firm with a substantial budget can have an advertising agency and a commercial artist to design its logo.

Table of Contents The first page after the cover page is the table of contents. The table should follow the format of the elements of the business plan shown above. Each major section should be numbered and divided into subsections, using two common numbering methods. The first is the Harvard outline method, which uses Roman numerals for the main headings, capital letters for the major sections, Arabic numbers for subsections, and the [number.letter] format for even smaller subsections. The second method is the decimal format. Each major heading is numbered, starting at [1.0], and subsections that follow are numbered as [1.10], [1.11] . . . [2.0], [2.10], [2.20]. The executive summary and the appendixes do not receive this form of numbering. The executive summary precedes the numbering and therefore has no number, and the appendix numbers are in Arabic preceded by "A" to indicate that they are appendixes (A.1, A.2, and so on).

If the plan has a significant number of tables, figures, drawings, and exhibits, a separate table can be prepared that lists these with their titles and page numbers. Any consistent and coherent method for organizing these may be used. However, since the purpose of the table of contents and the table of figures is to make it easier for the reader to extract pertinent information from the business plan, complicated and arcane systems of cataloging should be avoided.

Executive Summary   The executive summary is the most important part of the business plan because it is the first section of substance that the reader sees. Most readers of business plans, especially investors, never read beyond the summary. They have too many plans to read and too little time to read them all. Thus, if the summary is not convincing, the reader goes on to the next plan. It is estimated that only 10 percent of all business plans are read thoroughly, meaning that 90 percent are rejected after the summary.[10]

Although the summary is the first part of the business plan that is read, it should be the last part written. It should be one to three pages in length, with absolutely no padding or puffery. A sample summary is presented in Street Stories 5–1.

The company name and contact person should appear as they do on the cover page. Suggestions and recommendations for preparing the other sections of the executive summary are given below.[11]

Type of Business   About ten words are all that are necessary to describe the firm's industry or sector. Since particular investors will not invest in some industries, it is better to be clear up front and save time for everyone.

Company Summary   This summary should be a thumbnail sketch of your firm's history and background, and it should emphasize the positive. Be brief. More than half a page (150 words) is not a summary. State what your primary product or service is, but do not complicate matters by listing product extensions or auxiliary services. Stress the uniqueness of your product or service. If it is not unique, why will it succeed?

Management   Although who you are matters most, you do not have to provide much detail in the management description. List the top two or three people and emphasize their industry experience.

Describe Your Target Market   Mention the competition to illustrate the niche that your firm occupies. Again, this description should occupy no more than half a page (150 words).

STREET STORIES 5–1

Sample of an Executive Summary

Company: Luna SunCare, Inc.
400 South Adams Street
Bloomington, IN 47401
Telephone: (812) 555-1034

Contact: Steve Grover

Type of business: Luna SunCare markets and sells a line of premanufactured and prepackaged suntan lotions under its own label. The brand name of the line is Fritz SunTan Lotion.

Company summary: Fritz is available in a range of SPF levels, affording tanners a range of both sun protection and tan promotion. Fritz's specific tangible uniqueness is derived from its packaging form. The lotion is available in a two-chamber dispensing bottle, so the tanner can purchase two levels of suntan protection at one time. A tanner who desires sun protection for their face and tan promotion for their body will no longer need to purchase and keep track of two separate products: both levels of protection are available in one package.

Management: Steve Grover, President and CEO, will hold a MBA in Finance and Entrepreneurship from Columbia University. He also holds an AB in Engineering Sciences from Dartmouth College. Anne McCarthy, Vice President of Finance, will hold a MBA in Finance from Purdue University. She also holds a BS in Finance from Iowa State University. Chun Hui, Vice President of Marketing, received his MBA in Marketing from Illinois University. He also holds a BA in Industrial Design from the University of Notre Dame. Karyll Shaw, Vice President of Operations, received her MBA in Production Management from Michigan State University. She also holds a BA in Economics and History from Rice University.

Market and competition: Fritz targets its product at the 15–34 year old age group. This segment comprises a significant portion of the suntan lotion market, and possesses its own unique tastes and style. Most of the larger lotion producers do not specifically target this segment, leaving a significant niche unexploited. Luna SunCare's advertising campaign for Fritz will solely target this age group, and uniquely position Fritz as *the* suntan lotion for the young and active.

The competition in the overall market is led by Schering-Plough's Coppertone, which controls 31 percent of sales. The other major players are Playtex' Banana Boat with 11 percent, Warner-Lambert's Hawaiian Tropic with 10 percent, Bain de Soleil with 9 percent, and Vaseline Intensive Care with 6 percent. Of these products, however, only Hawaiian Tropic and Banana Boat seem to have strong appeal to young tanners. Coppertone, Bain de Soleil, and Vaseline have niche products aimed at young children (Waterbabies) and athletes (such as Coppertone Sport SPF 15, purchased by the 18–35 age group), but none of these companies specifically associate their brands solely to the young adult segment.

Funds requested: Luna seeks $485,000 raised via a preferred convertible security. The funds will be disbursed in three installments. Prior to each installment date, investors will have the option to either continue funding, or withdraw from the project. At the end of the third full year of operations, investors will have the opportunity to convert the preferred shares to common equity.

Collateral: None.

Use of proceeds: Luna SunCare will use its initial stipend of funds to conduct an approximately three-month concept test and refine the packaging, advertising, and formula for Fritz SunTan Lotion. The second infusion of funds will support a limited market test that will be confined to an isolated community representing a microcosm of the entire market. The test will afford Luna an opportunity to perfect its advertising, marketing, and sales strategies before the national launch of Fritz, without investing an inordinate amount of capital.

The proceeds from the third infusion of capital will be used for a nationwide launch of Fritz SunTan Lotion.

Financial History: None.

Financial Projection:

($000s)	First Full Year	Second Year	Third Year	Fourth Year	Fifth Year
Revenues	$3,759	$5,082	$7,135	$9,647	$11,577
Net Income	779	791	1,400	2,235	2,800
Assets	1,095	1,921	2,888	5,181	7,990
Liabilities	581	616	183	242	251

Exit: Luna SunCare intends to go public within five years of beginning operations. At that time, the founders will determine whether to retain or relinquish control of Luna SunCare, Inc.

Source: Adapted from a business plan prepared for a class project.

Funds Requested   Briefly state exactly how much money you need to raise. What is to be the investment vehicle: debt, equity, some hybrid? If you are flexible, state your preference and your willingness to consider alternatives. The investor may make a counterproposal, and the deal can be restructured.

Collateral   If you have offered a debt instrument, you should indicate whether collateral is available and what form it will take. If there is none, you should say so. The more collateral you have, the lower the interest rate and the less equity you may have to give up.

Use of Proceeds   The financial section in the main body of the business plan should be specific about the use of proceeds. Here you should simply indicate how the money will be used. Avoid overly broad terms like "pay expenses" and "increase working capital." More specific statements such as "pay salaries" and "build inventory" are preferred.

Financial History   In presenting the firm's financial history, show only these major categories: revenues, net income, assets, liabilities, and net worth. Figures for the last two or three years should be shown. Make sure that the figures presented in the history are exactly the same as those in the main body of the plan. If the venture is completely new and has no financial history, omit this section.

Financial Projections   Financial projections should follow the same format as the financial history. Three years are usually sufficient. Again, the figures must match those in the main body of the plan.

Exit   Investors expect to make money by selling their interest in the business to somebody else or back to the entrepreneur. This section of the executive summary indicates how and when the investor is most likely to accomplish this. A number of possible methods for investor exit will be discussed in Chapter 8.

Deal Structure   If complex combinations of investment instruments are being used to raise money, you should list them. For example, the deal structure might be:

Bank loan	$2,000,000
Subordinated debenture	1,000,000
Preferred stock	750,000
Common stock	250,000
Total	$4,000,000

MAJOR SECTIONS

The main body of the business plan contains the strategic and operating details of the new venture. Some redundancy among the sections is inevitable because the business is an integrated system and necessarily is self-referencing. This is not inherently bad. Some redundancy helps to focus the reader's attention. Where possible, a reference such as, "See Section III, Market Analysis" is preferable to repeating verbatim a long segment of the market analysis.

Background and Purpose

This section functions as an introduction to provide the reader with the context for understanding the business and its opportunity. Although history is not destiny in business, it is important for the reader to be able to gauge how far the firm has come and to comprehend where it is now in the new venture creation process. Suggestions and recommendations for preparing this material follow.

History   Briefly describe the history of your venture and its product or service. This section is especially important if the firm is offering a unique product or service. It tells the potential investor that you are a "first mover."

Current Situation   Briefly describe what your product is, to whom it will be marketed, and the technology necessary to make and deliver the product. This is known as the **product/market/technology configuration** (P/M/T). The P/M/T is the most concise statement of what your business is. You will have ample opportunity to expand on this statement later in the business plan. If the product or service is so technical that a nonexpert might not understand it, create an exhibit or appendix with a photograph or a drawing of the product, list its technical specifications, or present any available test results.

The Resource-based Concept   Briefly describe the key resources that contribute to the firm's success. Explain how the resources are translated into a product or service that is distinctive and has a competitive advantage. This is the first appearance of your strategy statement.

Objectives

Objectives are desired outcomes. The new venture has three broad objectives: creation, survival, and profitability. These objectives are relevant for all new ventures, although for firms with an operating history, of course, only survival and profitability are pertinent.

Objectives can be thought of in terms of their time frame and how they are measured. **Short-term objectives** are outcomes that can be achieved within one year. **Long-term objectives** are generally goals that require more than one year to achieve, often having a three- to five-year time frame.

The measurement of how well an objective has been achieved can be either quantitative or qualitative. **Quantitative measures** are stated as numbers, for example, return on sales, return on equity, or employee turnover. Quantitative measures usually signal the degree of the firm's **efficiency**. They tell how well the firm has deployed a given set of resources in terms of their output. For example, a quantitative objective that indicates efficiency is operating or gross margin, which shows cost of goods sold and direct labor charges as a percentage of sales. A high gross margin indicates an efficient ratio of cost to revenue, and a low gross margin indicates inefficiency.[12] Quantitative objectives tend to be concerned with operating issues and the short term.

Qualitative measures, on the other hand, resist reduction to numbers. For example, the objectives "to be a good corporate citizen" or "to have a reputation for integrity" or "to develop innovative products" are hard to quantify. Qualitative objectives are more concerned with the effectiveness of the new venture. **Effectiveness** is the extent to which the firm is able to maintain and expand its position in the competitive environment and in the macroenvironment. Qualitative objectives, therefore, tend to be concerned with external and environmental issues and with the long term. Table 5–2 lists possible objectives that a firm might have. The entrepreneur should try to make the firm's objectives both realistic and challenging and should ensure that they are consistent with the rest of the narrative and with the plan's financial projections.

TABLE 5-2 Specific Objectives

Objective	Measurement of Objectives		Time Frame for Objectives
	Efficiency	*Quantitative*	*Short term*
Sales	↑	↑	↑
Profitability			
Market share			
Market position			
Productivity			
Product/service quality			
Innovation			
Employee morale			
Management training and development			
Social concern and responsibility	↓	↓	↓
	Effectiveness	Qualitative	Long term

Market Analysis

The market analysis section should convince the reader or investor that the entrepreneur understands the competitive environment and the macroenvironment in detail. The purpose of this section is to demonstrate that (1) the market for the product or service is substantial and growing and (2) the entrepreneur can achieve a defendable competitive position. Suggestions and recommendations for the market analysis follow.

Overall Market   Describe the overall market for the firm's industry, its current conditions, and its projections for sales, profits, rates of growth, and other trends. Who are the leading competitors and why have they been successful? Where is the market located and what is its scope (international, national, regional, local)? Potential investors prefer industries with the potential for large sales volumes and high growth rates, so they should be given the big picture.

Specific Market   Narrow the focus to the specific target market, segment, or niche in which your firm will operate. Describe the present and projected conditions and the leading competitors. Describe the firm's customers—their needs, wants, incomes, and profits. How are purchasing decisions made, and by whom? If a market survey has been conducted, present the analysis in an appendix. What conclusions can be drawn from it? Present best-case, likely case, and worst-case sales projections for the total market segment. Who are the five largest buyers? What percentage of the firm's sales is projected to come from these customers? What are the trends for your customers' profits and incomes? How will the firm continue to assess its customer base and update information on its customers?

Competitive Factors   In this extremely important section, you should describe and explain how each of the factors covered in Chapter 3 affects the firm's sales and profitability. Analyze both the competitive nature of the firm's industry and the industry's attractiveness. Analyze the power of the buyers, the suppliers, substitute products and services, the height of entry barriers, and the nature of the current rivalry. Demonstrate how your resource base and strategy address these factors. For your most important competitors, evaluate their positions as well. Compare your strengths and weaknesses to those of the market leaders. Provide a summary statement of your firm's competitive position.

Macroenvironmental Influences   This is another vital section. Demonstrate your knowledge and competence by evaluating the impact of the macroenvironmental factors described in Chapter 3. Analyze the political, economic, technological, sociodemographic, and ecological factors that affect your firm. Develop scenarios for best, most likely, and worst cases. Draw a conclusion about the risks that each of these factors poses for your firm's survival and profitability.

Development and Production

This section emphasizes and describes the most important elements relating to the research, development, and production of your firm's basic product or service.

Production Processes   Outline the stages in the development and production of your product or service, briefly commenting on each stage. Detail how time and money are allocated at each stage in the production process or service delivery system. Discuss the difficulties and risks encountered in each stage. Create a flowchart to illustrate how the core function is accomplished. Evaluate each stage for its subcontracting potential. Where you face make-or-buy decisions, explain your choice. What resource-based competencies provide the firm with advantages during the production process?

Resource Requirements   Analyze each type of resource employed in the production process. These resources were described in Chapter 2 and include financial, physical, human, technological, reputational, and organizational resources. Where in the production process does the venture possess resources that are valuable, rare, imperfectly imitable, and nonsubstitutable? Present the cost/volume economics of the production process or service delivery system. Describe trends in the cost of resource procurement.

Quality Assurance   Discuss the quality dimensions (product, user, process, value) described in Chapter 1. What is the firm's perspective on quality? Specify how quality will be defined and measured for the firm's production process. Will the new venture employ the techniques and systems of Total Quality Management?[13]

Marketing

This section describes the actual marketing strategy of the firm or new venture. This strategy must be consistent with the objectives stated earlier. The marketing section explains how the firm will exploit its resource base to create a total marketing focus. It also describes how the new venture "connects" with its customers.

Overall Concept and Orientation   Return to the description of the venture's concept in the background section. Give it a marketing focus by transforming it into a statement of customer orientation. What benefits and positive outcomes will the customer derive from interaction with your firm? Evaluate the resources that the firm or new venture has or is capable of controlling in terms of their potential to create high levels of customer awareness and satisfaction. This introduction demonstrates your commitment to the marketing effort.

Marketing Strategy   Briefly restate a description of your primary product or service's P/M/T along with that of the firm's major competitors. How does your marketing strategy support your product's strengths? How will it exploit your competitors' weaknesses? Next, identify your target market and show evidence of market research. Why are you competing in this particular segment? Why and how does your product appeal to this segment? How does your marketing strategy communicate and activate this appeal?

Describe the image of the firm you wish to portray. Show how this image is consistent with your product or service. Why is it appealing from the customer's viewpoint? How will you communicate this image? Describe the packaging, branding, and labeling plans for the product. What advertising and promotional activities and campaigns will you initiate? Are you prepared to use a combination of techniques and media to get your message to customers? Prepare a budget and break down the costs of reaching customers by medium (usually in dollars per 1,000 people reached). If advertising materials (for example, copy, storyboards, photographs) are already available, present them in an appendix.

Discuss your pricing strategy. How do your prices compare with those of the competition? Is your pricing strategy consistent with the image you are trying to project?

Does it create value for customers? What is your profit margin per unit under various pricing schemes? Discuss your credit policy. Is it consistent with purchasing patterns within the industry? What is the firm's warranty policy? How will you continue to serve the customer after sales? Discuss your plans to create ongoing relationships with buyers and to encourage repeat business.

Explain how your product will be distributed. Describe the geographic scope of your distribution effort. What are the channels of distribution, and where is the power within these channels? Who will do your selling? What are the costs of reaching your market by using various channels?

Sales Forecasts   In the section on market analysis, you provided figures to indicate how many buyers there are for the firm's products, where they are located, and how purchasing decisions are made. In this section on marketing, describe your efforts and strategy to reach these customers, sell them your product, and serve them after the sales. The natural conclusion to these two sections is the sales forecast. The sales forecast is a function of three elements of market analysis: (1) the size of the market in units and dollars, (2) the fraction of that market that your firm will be able to capture as a result of its marketing effort and strategy (market penetration rate), and (3) the pricing strategy.

Present your sales forecasts in an exhibit or chart. Prepare the forecast in terms of units of products (or number of services delivered) as well as in dollars. Multiply the product units by the predicted average price. State the justification for this price. Use a five-year time frame. Present three sets of forecasts: a best-case, most likely case, and a worst-case scenario. What are the causes that separate the best, most likely, and worst cases? A graph might be used to illustrate sales trends and growth.

Financial Plans

The sales forecasts form the bridge between the marketing section and the rest of the firm's financial plans. The sales forecasts mark the end of the marketing portion of the business plan and the beginning of the financial analysis portion; they represent the "top line." The purpose of the financial analysis section is to illustrate the "bottom line." Bankers and potential investors evaluate this section to see whether enough profits will be generated to make the venture an attractive investment. It will also serve as the financial plan for the executives in the firm. This section is numbers oriented. Give the audience what it needs: rows and columns of figures carefully labeled and footnoted.

Financial Statements   If the firm has an operating history, summarize its past and present performance. Summarize past performance by calculating ratios that highlight its profitability, liquidity, leverage, and activity. Compare these ratios with the averages for your industry that you have collected from trade data.

If the firm is a new venture, you must present the following:

- Projected profit and loss statements (income statements) for five years. Prepare these monthly for the first year, quarterly for the next two years, and annually thereafter.
- Projected cash flow statements and analysis. Prepare these monthly for the first year and until the firm has positive cash flow, quarterly for the next two years, and annually thereafter.
- Projected balance sheets for the ends of the first three to five years.

Reference and discuss each of these statements, but place the actual statements in a financial appendix. If the statements and projections indicate seasonality and cyclicality, comment on this. Draw conclusions for the reader by stating what each statement means and what message the reader should take away.

Provide a break-even analysis for the business. If it is a service business, show how many hours of the service must be sold. If it is a product business, indicate how many units of the product must be sold to break even. Present a table of break-even points in the appendix.

Financial Resources   Discuss the start-up costs for the business. Prepare a detailed list of all the physical assets the firm needs to purchase or lease and a statement of organizational costs such as legal, architectural, and engineering. State how much money the business will need. If debt is being sought, what will you use for collateral? How will you repay the loan? Make sure the financial statements reflect this repayment. How will you use the money? Create a use-of-proceeds exhibit. Investors generally believe that initial proceeds that are expensed, such as research and development and training costs, are riskier than money spent on capital equipment, land, and buildings.

If you have established credit that you will not initially need, provide the details and the references. If the firm has receivables, provide a list and an aging statement. What are the probabilities of collecting these receivables? If you have existing debt, describe it. List delinquent accounts and their amounts. Describe any accounts payable the firm has and state how long these debts have been outstanding.

Financial Strategy   The firm's financial strategy consists of two components. The first comprises the sources and uses of funds. State your preferences for sources of new capital. Is it from continuing operations, new debt, or new equity? What combination is appropriate, and what debt/equity ratio and degree of financial leverage is the firm targeting? On the use side, what are the firm's priorities for using the excess cash generated by operations and by additional financing? Is expansion and growth the priority or are dividends? Both the managers of the firm and the investors will be guided by these strategic decisions.

The second component of financial strategy comprises the internal control and monitoring systems. What safeguards are being proposed to ensure the security of the funds generated by operations and by any additional borrowings or equity offerings? Describe any systems or procedures that help monitor and control cash disbursement. Briefly describe the firm's internal audit procedures. Who are the firm's external auditors?

Organization and Management

From beginning to end, the business plan is a document with a purpose. In the preliminary sections, the plan introduces the firm in a general way. In the main body of the plan, the firm reviews its objectives, its market, and the strategy for reaching its objectives. The financial portion indicates the funds that will be required to launch the venture and the size of sales, profits, and growth that are predicted. The question that recurs to the reader throughout is: "Why should I believe any of this?" The answer comes in the section on organization and management. This section describes the firm's people—the entrepreneurs and top management team—as well as the firm's technical, reputational, and human resources. Before proceeding to the next section on ownership, which presents the deal and actually makes the request for money, the reader will want to be assured that the people are of the highest quality. The saying goes, "Give us a B plan with an A team over an A plan with a B team . . . every time."

Key Personnel Resources Provide an organization chart with the names and titles of the key executives. Provide brief synopses of these individuals' previous experience, education, and related qualifications. The complete resumes of top managers and key executives may be placed in an appendix. State whether these people have worked together before and in what capacity.

What are these individuals' contributions to the company? Specify who will do what and why they were chosen for that role. What contractual relationships exist between the company and its principals, and between the principals? Are there employment contracts, severance packages, or noncompete agreements?

Describe the initial salaries, incentives, bonuses, pensions, and fringe benefits of the top people. Attempts should be made to keep initial salaries low to conserve cash and to keep deferred compensation (stock options and the like) high to produce long-term commitment. What key positions remain unfilled? Give the job descriptions of these positions and indicate the unique skills, abilities, and experience you will be looking for. Describe your plans to continue to attract, develop, and retain the firm's key personnel. Without such plans, growth will be inhibited by people problems.

List the members of the firm's board of directors; include their ages, their relevant experience, their other corporate affiliations, and their connection with your firm. Also provide the names of the legal, accounting, banking, and other pertinent organizations (marketing or advertising agencies, consulting firms, and the like) that will guide the firm. How will these people assist the firm?

Human Resource Management Strategy State the firm's basic philosophy concerning human resources and management. Does it favor close supervision or general supervision? Is unionization expected? What is the firm's approach to collective bargaining? Describe its strategy for employee compensation, profit sharing, and employee ownership. What is the rationale for such programs? How will the firm manage and control health-care and insurance costs? What are its strategies for employee and management development and training, for continuing education, and for hiring and promoting from within? What factors dictate criteria for promotion? How will performance be assessed?

How many employees does the firm currently have, or how many will be required to start the new venture? What are these employees' responsibilities, positions, and job descriptions? What percentages are skilled and unskilled? A pertinent analysis of the relevant labor markets by type of skill and geographic scope is required.

What equal opportunity employment regulations and other government requirements affect the firm and its work force? What strategies are in place to fulfill the firm's legal and regulatory obligations?

Ownership

In this section, the founders describe the legal form of the business, the contractual obligations of the owners to the firm and to each other, and, if the business plan is a proposal for financing, the nature of the deal. Note that only after the reader has become familiar with the experience, reputation, and character of the entrepreneurial team is it appropriate to ask for money.

Form of Business   Describe the legal form of the business—sole proprietorship, partnership, regular corporation, subchapter S corporation—and briefly explain why this is the best form for your firm. Discuss any special aspects of the ownership structure, for example, subsidiaries, holding companies, or cross-ownership agreements. If the firm is organized as a partnership, list the essentials of the partnership agreement, and include the actual agreement as an appendix.

Equity Positions   Prepare an exhibit to show the amounts that you and the other founders and executives of the company have invested in the business or will be investing in the near future. Also show the equity positions that these investments represent. Prepare another exhibit to show any rights to warrants and stock options, and indicate their nature (exercise price, expiration date). What proportion of equity would be controlled if these were exercised? If shares are held in beneficial trust, note this. Recent changes in the ownership of the firm should also be noted and explained. What percentage of stock is owned by the employees?

If these investments are debt, specify for each the coupon, maturity, and any special covenants in the loan agreement. What is the priority (seniority) of repayment?

Deal Structure   Briefly describe the financing required to start up the business or to fund the development or expansion of present business activities. A three- to five-year time horizon for financial plans is appropriate. Is the preference for new debt or new equity? What are the potential sources for these funds? For what purposes will the money be used? For equity financing, how much of the company are you willing to offer for the stock? Present a structured deal,[14] including the following information:

1. The number of shares of stock available for the offering, and the percentage of total ownership that this represents.
2. The price per share of each unit.[15]
3. The revised number of shares and each founder's percentage ownership after the proposed financing is completed.
4. The effect of dilution on new investors' shares.[16]
5. The potential returns per share to the investor. These need to be consistent with the previously reported financial plans. Avoid projecting something here that has not been presented and validated earlier in the plan.

Critical Risks and Contingencies

In this section, the new venture, following the rules of full disclosure, reveals all material and relevant information that a prudent investor needs before investing in the business. The nature of this information is inherently negative; the section lists every reason why someone would not want to consider an investment in the new venture. Having fully revealed this information, the entrepreneurs have performed their legal and moral obligation to be forthcoming and honest about the firm's prospects. Should the investors lose their investment, full disclosure may be a defense against claims of civil liability and criminal fraud. This section typically includes the following categories of information and the potential impact of each on the new venture:

1. Failure to produce the products and services promised.
2. Failure to meet production deadlines or sales forecasts.

3. Problems with suppliers and distributors.
4. Unforeseen industry trends.
5. Unforeseen events in the political, economic, social, technological, and ecological environments.
6. Failure to survive retaliation by competitors with significantly more resources.
7. The problems of unproven and inexperienced management.
8. The problems of unproven and undeveloped technology.
9. Difficulties in raising additional financing.
10. Other issues specific to the firm in question.

Unfortunately, sometimes some of the hypothetical critical risks come true. In Street Story 5–2, one entrepreneur explains how, even with a good detailed business plan, too many things went wrong, and the business did not survive.

E-NOTES 5–2 BUSINESS PLAN BODY
The major section or body of a business plan details the new venture's:

- background and purpose,
- objectives,
- market analysis,
- development and production,
- marketing,
- financial plans,
- organization and management,
- ownership,
- risks and contingencies.

CONCLUDING SECTIONS

There are still a few loose ends and details to report on in the concluding sections.

Summary and Conclusions

Briefly summarize the highlights and key features of your report. The most important elements to include are the firm's overall strategic direction, the reasons for believing the firm will be a success, a brief description of how the firm will be able to exploit its unique resources to advantage, the firm's sales and profit projections, its capital requirements, and the percentage ownership for the founders and for investors.

Since this is a summary, no new information should be reported here. You may even use the exact words you used in the earlier sections. Redundancy will reinforce your message and demonstrate that you are being consistent throughout the plan.

Scheduling and Milestones

The business plan outlines a number of actions that will be taken in the future. These actions are discussed in many different sections of the plan. To consolidate the timing of events, you should prepare a schedule, in chart form, of all of the important milestones that the firm expects to reach in the near and intermediate term. This helps the investor know when the firm will be needing additional capital

---

Six Rules We (Almost) Forgot to Tell You

The risks of starting your own business are real and entrepreneurs are aware of most of them. But even so, it is hard to focus on the downside when you think you have a great idea. Ken Elias thought he had one of those can't miss ideas. The Santa Monica, CA entrepreneur had support from prospective customers, a carefully prepared business plan, and financing, including $100,000 of Elias's own money and $500,000 from other investors.

Elias's new venture was called the "What's New" pavilion. It was a chain of kiosks located in shopping malls where consumers could taste, touch, and sample hot new products like Sony's MiniDisc, Pepsi's All-Sport drink or Toyota's new Tercel model. It was an innovation dedicated to innovation where the medium is the message. Revenue would come from manufacturers and advertising agencies would pay Elias to market their products directly into the impatient hands of mall shoppers. The proposal seemed like a winner; People Magazine signed on as a customer right away, and Toyota and Chrysler raved about the concept.

But Elias found that even with a super business plan, there was no guaranteed blueprint for success. After three years of continuous and difficult effort Elias's new venture folded, just like 80 to 90 percent of all new businesses. In the aftermath of his business failure, Elias developed a set of guidelines for budding entrepreneurs. They illustrate the limits of a plan, and the need for flexibility.

1. Be tough on your own budgets and forecasts. There is a certain beauty and elegance to the most optimistic set of sales forecasts and expense projections. They feel and look good, but that doesn't mean things will proceed as scheduled. But entrepreneurs should plan for the worst and be aware of the risks of faulty cash flow projections.

2. Hire qualified people and pay them appropriately. The first sales employee Elias hired was willing to work for a low base salary plus commissions, but he didn't make sales or even target the right kind of prospects. His replacement demanded a starting salary five times larger, but earned it by producing orders in excess of $1 million within six months.

3. Sell what you can deliver now. Toyota loved the "What's New" marketing approach, and was ready to close the deal as soon as Elias had 20 locations. The problem was, he never got that far. Now he notes that you can talk about the future, but should sell what you can deliver.

4. Match your strategy to the customer's needs. Elias's business plan called for slow market-by-market growth, allowing for good quality control and saturation of one market at a time. Unfortunately, most of his potential customers were more interested in national exposure, even if it meant only one location per market. By the time Elias's company realized this, it was too late.

5. Appoint a Board of Directors for perspective. A new venture entrepreneur may know everything about his business, but he lacks objectivity. Elias feels that an advisory board would have questioned his logic and been a sounding board for his ideas.

6. Make the sale, close the deal. Elias was excited when Chrysler executives met with him 15 times within the space of the six months. But even though they claimed that they all loved the "What's New" concept, Chrysler never signed on the dotted line.

Ken Elias is philosophical about his experience as an entrepreneur, and he may even try again. He found the experience rewarding and exciting and is intrigued that the elements for success are always within reach. But next time he'll keep these six rules handy.

Source: Ken Elias, "Why My Business Failed," in *The Wall Street Journal*, October 11, 1994, A 18.

infusions and allows the investor to track the firm's progress. Include the expected calendar dates for the following events that apply to the firm:

1. Seeking legal counsel and accounting services.
2. Filing the documents necessary to set up the desired legal form of business, and completing licensing requirements.
3. Completion of research and development efforts.
4. Completion of a working prototype.
5. Purchase or lease of production facilities, office and retail space.
6. Selection of personnel: management, skilled, semiskilled.
7. Ordering supplies, production materials, inventory.
8. Beginning production.
9. First order, sales, and payments.
10. Other critical dates and events.

Although it is usually desirable to speed up the timing of the new venture's launch, preparations will more likely take longer than expected. This is particularly true when the firm depends on some other organization or set of individuals for action before it can move on to the next scheduled task. Slack should be built into the schedule whenever possible.

Appendices

Throughout our discussion of the elements of the business plan, we have suggested items, exhibits, and documentation that belong in an appendix. The business plan will usually have a number of appendixes. A partial list of possible appendix sections is shown below.[17]

1. A photograph or a drawing of your product (if appropriate) including title and labels if necessary. If the product or process is highly technical, and it is believed that investors will have the technical section reviewed by a consulting engineer, the entire technical section should be under separate cover.
2. A photograph or drawing of your intended location and physical layout (if appropriate), annotated if necessary.
3. Sales and profitability forecasts in chart form.
4. Market surveys and documentation of size and nature of market.
5. Sample advertisements, brochures, and telemarketing protocols.
6. Sample press releases.

7. Price lists, catalogues, and mailing lists (just titles).
8. All detailed and footnoted financial statements, including income statements, cash flow statements, balance sheets, break-even calculations, and table of start-up costs.
9. Fixed-asset acquisition schedule.
10. Individual and corporate tax returns.
11. Resumes of founders, board members, and key individuals.
12. Letters of recommendation or character references from notable people.
13. Any additional information deemed appropriate.

Critiquing the Plan: Questions Likely To Be Asked

Although the entrepreneur has attempted in writing the business plan to answer all questions that might be raised, readers can still find problems. Professionals, like investors, will continue to ask questions and critique the proposal as they read it, and they need additional information when they meet the entrepreneur in person. It will be impossible to answer all the questions raised by the plan, or even anticipate what they may be. However, readers will have four major concerns, and the entrepreneur will have to address these in detail.[18]

MANAGEMENT

Repeatedly, entrepreneurs and the top management teams will be asked, "Who are you?" The reader must find a way to assess the entrepreneur's honesty. Although the business plan has been read and analyzed, no written document can answer doubts about the character and integrity of the entrepreneur. The entrepreneur's background will be researched and inconsistencies must be dealt with. (Everyone has inconsistencies in his or her background. No one is perfect. Even presidential candidates who have lived most of their lives in the public spotlight must refute these inconsistencies.)

If there is any doubt about the character of the entrepreneur, the financing will fall through. Entrepreneurs must be prepared to present their professional history, answer questions about their motivation, and discuss what they believe they can achieve.

Some entrepreneurs have been preparing for their new venture all their lives, and their previous careers are perfect matches for their intended new business. Street Story 5–3 gives us a prime example.

RESOURCES

Investors are continually reviewing proposals for financing, and one way of differentiating between businesses with high potential and all others is careful scrutiny of the resource base of the firm. What rare, valuable, hard to copy, and nonsubstitutable resources does the firm have, can it control, or will it produce? Uniqueness is crucial. Also, the firm will need to demonstrate how it will keep the profits and rents generated by these resources. The entrepreneur should be prepared for dozens of "what if" questions that describe scenarios in which the resource-based strategy of the firm is attacked or undermined.

Planning for the Passion

"It's almost like bungee-jumping," says John G. Simon, describing his experience as the founder of the UroMed Corp., a Needham, Massachusetts company that makes devices to manage urological disorders. "You might be scared, but if you watch six other people do it and they survive, you're able to do it."

John Simon represents a growing trend in this country; entrepreneurs who have systematically trained and prepared in anticipation of a business idea. Simon says that he knew almost from childhood that he wanted to do something entrepreneurial. The son of a physician, he worked for a venture-capital firm and spent one year as the marketing vice-president for another new venture, before founding UroMed at the age of 28. "With a more professional background, you can attract top-notch people," he says of his working and watching experience now. Those years of experience also helped him to pinpoint his product specialization; while he observed that many medical start-ups targeted the cardiovascular market, he also saw that the urology field was relatively free of competition.

Heartpoint, another medical firm located in Redwood City, California, was "10 years in the making," according to founder Wesley D. Sterman. Sterman earned simultaneous degrees in medicine and business from Stanford University in his deliberate quest to become an entrepreneur. He also worked for a venture capital firm for several years to learn more about small-company finance and writing business plans. "I had very specific ideas about how I wanted the business to be structured, based on my experiences," says Sterman. His business manufactures devices for minimally invasive cardiac surgery.

Many of the top business schools today have added or expanded their course offerings in entrepreneurship to accommodate a growing number of resume-building entrepreneurial students. Peter C. Wendell, general partner in the Sierra Ventures venture-capital firm who also teaches at Stanford, says that these students evolve into just the kind of investment risk his firm is looking for. "From their first job, they were thinking, 'I'm doing this so that 10 years from now, I can start a major opportunity company.'" While the typical new venture founder may have the fire of great ideas and technical expertise, investors know that the training and management experience of these so-called professional entrepreneurs makes them a safer bet.

But some experts question whether a methodical entrepreneur can ever achieve the success of a creative superstar like Bill Gates. "Accidental empires evolve because people have a passion for technology and for real problems that need to be solved," says Charles Federman, managing director of a New Jersey consulting firm that specializes in technology mergers and acquisitions. "If someone says they're going to start a company someday, but they don't know what the company is, it's like they're waiting for passion."

Source: Adapted from Stephanie N. Mehta, "As Ideas Beget Entrepreneurs, So Does a Plan," in *Wall Street Journal*, February 19, 1997, B1.

Most desirable ⟶

Level 4 Product/service fully developed. Many satisfied users. Market established.	4/1	4/2	4/3	4/4
Level 3 Product/service fully developed. Few (or no) users as yet. Market assumed.	3/1	3/2	3/3	3/4
Level 2 Product/service pilot operable. Not yet developed for production. Market assumed.	2/1	2/2	2/3	2/4
Level 1 A product or service idea, but not yet operable. Market assumed.	1/1	1/2	1/3	1/4
	Level 1 A single, would-be entrepreneur.	Level 2 Two founders. Additional slots, personnel not identified.	Level 3 Partly staffed management team. Absent members identified, to join when firm is funded.	Level 4 Fully staffed, experienced management team.

Product Service Level (left axis)

More desirable (right axis, pointing up)

Management Status

Source: From *Business Plans That Win $$$* by David Gumpert and Stanley Rich. Copyright © by David Gumpert and Stanley Rich. Reprinted by permission of Sterling Lord Literistic, Inc.

PROJECTIONS AND RETURNS

The firm's top management team will be asked to justify the assumptions underlying the sales forecasts, the cost estimates, the administrative costs, and the net profit figures. Because the entrepreneurial team will be required to defend these numbers, the data should have a concrete foundation in reality. At the same time, however, the projections need to be optimistic enough to indicate a solid return for the investors. This is a basic conflict in many new ventures, and inconsistencies will be examined thoroughly.

EXIT

Investors need to know how and when they will recoup their money. Investors can exit by means of many alternative mechanisms, and, in any case, the exit will take place in the future after many other uncertain and risky activities. Thus, the exit is fraught with peril. But this will not restrain investors from trying to pin down the exact details of the proposed exit. It is only natural for them to be concerned about their money, and the entrepreneur should expect the reader to pose many "what if" scenarios.

The overall evaluation of the plan may rest on the quality of the management team and the current status of the product or service. A useful tool to check the ranking an entrepreneur might receive is the Rich-Gumpert Evaluation System (Figure 5–1). The most desirable situation are the "4/4" firms.

E-NOTES 5–3   KEY BUSINESS PLAN QUESTIONS

- Management: who are you?
- Resources: are yours rare, valuable, hard-to-copy, and nonsubstitutable?
- Projections: can they be justified?
- Exit: how will investors recoup this money?

Format and Presentation

The format of the business plan and its physical presentation make the first impression on the reader. Deliberate care and attention are needed in preparing the plan to make this impression a positive one.

PHYSICAL APPEARANCE

Ideally the physical appearance of the plan is neither too fancy nor too plain. An extremely ornate binding and cover indicate a disregard for expense and a preoccupation with appearance over substance. Too plain an appearance may suggest a lack of respect for the reader and, ironically, not enough care for appearances. Rich and Gumpert recommend a plastic spiral binding and a pair of cover sheets of a single color.[19] They believe a stapled compilation of photocopied material will not be treated seriously.

The recommended length of the business plan is usually between 40 and 50 pages, plus appendixes. Because the appendixes and supporting documentation can be as long or longer than the plan itself, it is not unusual to bind these supplements separately.

The pages of the plan should be crisp and clean, with wide margins and easy-to-read type. Graphs and photographs should be of high quality, and all charts and exhibits should be labeled and referenced within the body of the plan.

WRITING AND EDITING

It is extremely important that the plan be well written and edited. Irrelevant information and self-adulation should be excised, and length for its own sake should be avoided.[20] Bad writing will kill a plan, and yet it is not recommended that the writing be jobbed out. It is up to the entrepreneur and the new venture's executives and advisers to write the plan together. A basic guideline for writing a business plan or any kind of business assignment would include:

PREWRITING

Begin by writing down your information and thoughts in an outline or organized way to find out what you know and need to know. At this stage you should also think about the audience for your writing, and arrange the material in a way that will suit the purpose of your piece and express your motivation.

WRITING AND REWRITING/REVISING

Ideally every writer should be able to transform their outline into a fully articulated rough draft, and then revise that initial piece for form, coherence, and style. Personal computers have made this process much easier. Clear and concise writing is always a goal, but don't get bogged down in the rewriting and revising part of the process. The best way to prepare for situations where you must write under a deadline is to practice writing every day.

EDITING

Editing should be the last thing you do with any piece of writing. Make use of all the tools available today, including the computer's spell checker and thesaurus. The word processing software on your computer may also include a grammar checker. If you have time, have a colleague or friend read and critique your writing piece before you review for a final time. Entrepreneurs should make sure that the plan says what they want it to say. Despite the availability of numerous published guides for writing business plans and general agreement on what the content should be, entrepreneurs continue to submit poorly written plans.[21] One researcher reviewed 20 business plans that were submitted to venture capitalists and found that:[22]

- Thirty percent failed to include a specific business strategy.
- Forty percent of the teams lacked marketing experience and the marketing sections of the plan were most weakly developed.
- Fifty-five percent failed to discuss technical idea protection.
- Seventy-five percent failed to identify the details of the competition.
- Ten percent had no financial projections at all, another 15 percent omitted balance sheets, and 80 percent failed to provide adequate details of the financial projections.
- The more plan deficiencies, the lower the odds of gaining support from venture capitalists.

Summary

Every new venture must have a business plan. The advantages of writing a business plan far outweigh the costs. The purpose of the plan is to enable the top executives of the established firm or new venture to think about their business in a comprehensive way, to communicate their objectives to individuals who may have a stake in the firm's future, to have a basis for making decisions, and to facilitate the planning process.

The essential elements of the plan are generally recognized. The preliminary sections set the stage for the reader. Make the first impression professional, concise, and informative because the reader may spend only a few minutes reviewing each plan. The major sections of the business plan describe the new venture's strategy, operations, marketing, and management, financial plan, and ownership structure. These sections need to be as detailed as possible and internally consistent. The concluding sections provide details on timing, schedules and milestones, and a summary. The appendix contains reference material for documentation.

Each plan must be well written and organized, and it must anticipate the many questions that the reader will have about the business. No plan, however, can answer all questions that may arise. It is important, therefore, that entrepreneurs be familiar with all the details so they can respond to potential unanswered questions and critiques.

Key Terms

- Business plan
- Logo
- Product/market/technology configuration
- Objectives
- Short-term objectives

- Long-term objectives
- Quantitative measures
- Efficiency
- Qualitative measures
- Effectiveness

Discussion Questions

1. Discuss the costs and benefits of writing a business plan.
2. Who should write a business plan? Who should not bother? Who must write a business plan?
3. Why are the preliminary sections so important?
4. What information should be conveyed in the executive summary?
5. Distinguish between short-term and long-term objectives. Between quantitative and qualitative objectives. Between efficiency and effectiveness. Give examples.
6. How is the market analysis section linked to the marketing section?

7. How is the marketing section linked to the financial sections?
8. How are the financial sections linked to the management organization sections?
9. How are the management and organization sections linked to the deal structure and ownership sections?
10. What questions are likely to be asked by investors reading your business plan? Why are these concerns important to the investor?
11. Discuss the benefits of careful presentation and effective writing style.

Exercises

1. Draft an outline of your (or your team's) business plan.
   a. What information do you already possess? Write it up in draft form.
   b. What information is still required? Prepare a plan to obtain this information.
2. Prepare as much of the executive summary of your business plan as you can. Be concise but informative. Follow the model given in the chapter.
3. Critique a business plan. Examples can be found in the case section of this

book or may be provided by your instructor.
   a. How well does the business plan address the key issues?
   b. What changes and improvements would you make to the plan?
   c. How well done is the presentation and writing? How has this influenced your impression?
   d. Would you be interested in investing in this business? Why or why not?

Just Like a Real Business

A. Robert Moog says all he wanted was to "learn how to run a bigger business by first doing this *little* business." Fred Gratzon says his plan was "to do this business to support my family while I decided what to do with the rest of my life." Rick Shangraw says he was only going to work at his business until he could accept a college faculty job and make some *real* money. But today the stop-gap companies these entrepreneurs founded are established stars on *Inc.* Magazine's list of the top 500 growth companies.

According to a survey done by the magazine, 10 percent of these company founders reported that mere survival was their initial business goal. A total of one third of them said that they never hoped for fast growth, believing instead that their company would stay small or grow slowly. *Inc.* conducted a special survey of those 175 "Cinderella" fast growth companies, and found that more than half of them thought they lacked the capital needed to place their start-up on the fast track. Almost as many (44%) wanted to limit growth as a means of keeping control. Some reported that they were fearful or cautious about fast growth (32%), or just didn't think that fast growth could happen in their situation (23%). Other founders said they underestimated the market demand (20%) or the economic conditions (20%), that they thought they lacked the business know-how to be truly successful (18%), or that they never intended to work hard enough to achieve fast growth (6%).

For A. Robert Moog, co-founder of University Games in Burlingame, California, fast growth was simply unintentional. After graduating from Stanford Graduate School of Business, Moog and a partner formed this company to produce a game called Murder Mystery Party. Their plan was to sell the company after three years to provide seed money for a more ambitious venture. But their ambitions were met when the game became a national best-seller overnight. University Games now grosses $30 million a year, and ranks #494 on the *Inc.* 1996 list.

Fred Gratzon was broke and out of work when he started Telegroup, Inc., a discount long-distance phone service provider. Six years later the Fairfield, Iowa company has $210 million in annual revenues, and ranks #151 on the *Inc.* list. The company's success has been a big surprise to Gratzon, who says that his whole idea for the new venture was accidental. He was inspired when he was trying to figure out a way to reduce his own phone bills, and he started investigating the package deals then being offered by AT&T.

Fifty-two percent of the Cinderella company founders responding to the *Inc.* survey said that their company has turned out "not even close" to what they expected. For many of them success was a personal affirmation. Rich Shangraw had been fired from his consulting firm job when he pooled the resources of four credit cards to start Project Performance Corp., the environmental management firm that ranks #272 on the *Inc.* list. His Sterling, Virginia start-up went from a one-man show to a company with eight employees almost immediately. "Within six months it became clear that there was a market, that there were clients, and that I had the ability to build something."

Shangraw's experience echoes the stories of many of the entrepreneurs surveyed. Forty percent traced their motivation to start their business to a desire to be their own boss. Twenty-three percent said they wanted to prove that they could do it. Twelve percent reported they went into business so they could leave a job or recover from being fired. Only 17 percent claimed that their primary reason was to make a lot of money.

Not surprisingly, 41 percent of the top growers report that their initial financial projections were "understated." More than one quarter said they didn't even have spreadsheets when they began. Thirteen percent said they were unprepared for fast growth when it occurred, and two thirds said they were just starting to gear up when growth took off.

Most fast trackers said what they needed most when growth exploded was more employees (33%). Others said they needed more money (27%) or a better operating structure and internal procedures (21%). Even though their growth wasn't planned, only ten percent said they need more experienced management. On the other hand, more than half of them reported that their personal lives have become "more complicated" since their company began to experience unanticipated fast growth.

Whether they planned for fast growth or not, many of these entrepreneurs have obviously enjoyed the surprise of success. Daniel W. Hunt started his Asphalt Specialties in Henderson, Colorado with a five-man crew and a dream of putting away enough money to retire in comfort. Two years later his company had 50 employees, annual sales of $8 million, was #367 on the *Inc.* top growth list.

Hunt can recall the moment when he was out on a job, and he realized that he was surrounded by his machinery and his employees working on his project, and he suddenly thought, "This is just like a real company!"

CASE QUESTIONS

1. Why do some entrepreneurs want their companies to grow slowly or not at all?
2. Why do many new ventures grow despite the entrepreneurs' lack of planning?
3. Why are there so many false assumptions about growing the business?
4. What is the relationship between growth and resources?

Source: Adapted from Robert A. Mamis, "Growth Happens," *Inc.*, March 1997, pp. 68–74.

Notes

1. Of course, the formulation of a new venture plan and the implementation of that plan frequently do not proceed consecutively. There usually is considerable overlap. Just the act of collecting information often puts the prospective entrepreneur in contact with other businesspeople, creating the network for the new venture, a process that could be considered implementation. Thus it is merely a simplifying convenience to divide analysis from action.

2. R. Hisrich and M. Peters, *Entrepreneurship* (Homewood, IL: Irwin, 1992). Chapter 5.

3. K. Andrews, *The Concept of Corporate Strategy* (Englewood Cliffs, NJ: Prentice Hall, 1980).

4. A. Cooper, C. Woo, and W. Dunkelberg, "Entrepreneur Perceived Chances for Success," *Journal of Business Venturing* 3 (Spring 1989): 97–108.

5. The concept of "full material disclosure" is a legal one. It means that, since others rely on the document for information regarding the business's prospects, these others are entitled to the full facts as they are known to the entrepreneur, or as they should be known to a reasonable person.

6. C. Schwenk and C. Shrader, "The Effects of Formal Strategic Planning on Financial Performance in Small Firms: A Meta-analysis," *Entrepreneurship: Theory and Practice* 17 (Spring 1993): 53–64. A meta-analysis is a statistical analysis of a group of other research reports. It is, therefore, a study of studies.

7. K. Vesper, *New Venture Mechanics* (Englewood Cliffs, NJ: Prentice Hall, 1993), 330.

8. For a book-length treatment of the essentials of the business plan, see S. Rich and D. Gumpert, Business Plans That Win $$$ (New York: Harper and Row, 1987); and David Gladstone, *Venture Capital Handbook* (Englewood Cliffs, NJ: Prentice Hall, 1988). For a detailed outline in article form, see W. K. Schilit, "How to Write a Winning Business Plan," *Business Horizons* (July-August, 1987): 13–22.

9. See Chapter 10 of Vesper, 1993.

10. Vesper, 1993.

11. The summary outline presented here is adapted from Gladstone, 1988, 26–27.

12. When talking about an accounting concept like gross margin, we need to remember that the terms *high* and *low* are relative to what is achieved (and achievable) by the other firms in the industry.

13. Total Quality Management is a system of organizing that emphasizes benchmarking (determining the ideal levels of achievable quality), teamwork and participation, and the dedication of the company to continuous and ceaseless improvement of product and service quality. It is embodied in the work of W. Edwards Deming, the American productivity expert who introduced the system to Japanese industry after World War II. See Chapter 4.

14. Some venture capitalists believe that the deal structure is their particular field of expertise and that the business plan should not contain a specific structure. If the venture capitalist is interested in the proposal, they will offer the deal they want. It can be argued that the entrepreneur is the one who has something to sell (equity in the new venture) and, as the seller, has the obligation to set the initial price.

15. The term *unit* is used because sometimes shares are combined with various other rights, such as warrants or options.

16. Dilution refers to the phenomenon that occurs immediately after the financing. The new investor's shares are diluted after the offering when the new investor has paid more than the average price paid by the founders. This is the usual case. Dilution will be covered in Chapter 8.

17. Adapted from Schilit, 1987, 13–22.

18. See Chapter 4 of Gladstone, 1988.

19. Rich and Gumpert, 1987.

20. Vesper, 1993.

21. Excerpted from E. Roberts, "Business Planning in the Start-up High-Tech Enterprise," in *Frontiers of Entrepreneurship Research*, ed. R. Hornaday (Wellesley, MA: Babson College, 1983), 107.

22. Roberts, 1983.

Marketing
the New Venture

Outline

Success is never final.
—WINSTON CHURCHILL

Learning Objectives

After reading this chapter you will understand:

■ The major *marketing activities* for an entrepreneur.

■ How *marketing research* is conducted for new ventures.

■ How the *diffusion process* can be used to introduce innovative products.

■ How a new venture's *marketing capabilities and plan* can be a strategic resource.

■ How a new venture can prepare a reasonable *sales forecast*.

161

The opening quote is a reminder that the entrepreneur still faces many challenges after the new venture is created and initial success is achieved. The completion of the business plan is only one milestone along the way. The next four chapters describe the ongoing requirements for the new enterprise. In these chapters we see that the marketing, finance, and organizational functions reflect continuous efforts to develop and maintain competitive advantage and to keep the firm entrepreneurial. There is no rest for those pursuing the entrepreneurial dream.

Effective marketing in today's competitive international environment requires constant vigilance and effort. "If you can't sell a top-quality product at the world's lowest price, you're going to be out of business," says Jack Welch, chief executive officer of the General Electric Company.[1] Just having a top-quality product is insufficient. Quality is becoming a commodity—even Americans can do it![2] Besides, there may be more than one standard for quality, and it may change over time. Without doubt, various top-quality products and services are available at any given time. Determining what represents top quality for a specific customer is often a marketing decision.

The opening quotation also implies that even if you succeed, there are no guarantees for the future. Although business is like a game, there is no clock, and the game never ends. Adding to the complexity, more than one game is going on at one time. Customers are not all the same: They have different preferences and standards, they are located in different parts of the world, and they belong to various demographic groups. The choices of which games to play are marketing choices. They are the result of the venture's marketing strategy.

Marketing contributes to a venture's success in two ways: (1) it defines the manner of communicating the firm's resource advantages, and (2) it can be a source of sustainable competitive advantage (SCA). The first role of marketing is fairly straightforward. Organizations are created to add value to resources for buyers, and the culmination of all this activity is the transaction between buyer and seller and their subsequent relationship. Because marketing activities focus directly on the nature of the transaction—the product, its price, the location and time of transaction, and communications related to the event—-marketing activities influence the success of the firm.

The second role of marketing is to be "its own resource." That is, marketing can be a source of SCA. Marketing capabilities and strategies can be rare, valuable, hard to copy, and nonsubstitutable. Aspects of the marketing strategy can exist across resource categories. Various elements may have technological components, human dimensions, and reputational characteristics, and the effective coordination of these elements also requires organizational resources. The development of marketing capability by the new venture is therefore a double imperative. The omission of a marketing plan by the entrepreneurial team is a red flag for investors and concerned stakeholders.

The Marketing and Entrepreneurship Interface

How are marketing and entrepreneurship similar? Marketing activities have much in common with entrepreneurial activities, and many entrepreneurs equate the ability to sell with entrepreneurial success.[3] Although selling remains an important element, marketing is more than selling. Marketing and entrepreneurship interface at four different points:

1. Both are concerned with customer needs. The marketer develops the customer's psychographic profile and documents buyer behavior patterns. The entrepreneur has seen or intuited an opportunity in the market—a gap between what current firms can deliver and what the customer wants or needs.
2. Both evaluate new product or new service ideas. The marketer conducts tests—concept, product, and market—to gather data concerning the prospects for an innovation. The entrepreneur envisions resource combinations and configurations (both existing and potential) and creates a venture to exploit them. Both need to understand the product and service diffusion and adoption process.
3. Marketing behavior and entrepreneurial behavior have other similarities. Both are continuously scanning the environment and evaluating information. Both are boundary spanning activities, going outside their own organization to build relationships with others. Both are aggressive representatives of their organizations and products to the community at large.
4. Both are growth-oriented. Marketers and entrepreneurs are interested in increasing the scope of their business: selling more to current customers, developing new customers, and finding additional products and services that meet the needs of the customer base.

Thus marketing and new venture creation share common interests. However, just as there are the positive interfaces, there are negative ones as well. These are traps for the entrepreneur and marketer. Four pitfalls marketers and entrepreneurs share are:

1. Both tend to believe that growth is assured by an ever-expanding number of people with wealth who will continue to purchase the product at increasing prices indefinitely.
2. Both tend to believe that there is no competitive substitute and that the product or service offered is unique.
3. Both have unwavering faith in the benefits of the experience curve—the notion that costs decrease over cumulative production. This leads to the strategic obsession with selling more and more of the same product.
4. Both tend to have a preoccupation with product issues; this is especially true of brand managers in marketing and engineer/inventor entrepreneurs.[4]

Marketers and entrepreneurs are therefore linked by common perceptions, goals, and behaviors. Yet many entrepreneurs underestimate the value of marketing and ignore many of marketing's key functions. A study of venture capitalists indicated that effective market analysis could reduce new venture failure rates by 60 percent. The same study found that 75 percent of entrepreneurs ignored negative marketing information.[5] In this chapter we will flesh out the significant marketing decisions and functions that the new venture must perform.[6] We will follow the format of the marketing section of the business plan presented in Chapter 5. By following the examples and illustrations in this chapter students can develop their own marketing plans.

We begin by considering the new venture's overall marketing concept and orientation. Then we examine the marketing resources controlled by and available to entrepreneurs and their firms. Next we review the key elements of a new venture's marketing strategy, with special emphasis on market research—potentially a source of

SCA. We conclude by describing various methods of sales forecasting. Sales forecasts (and, concurrently, actual sales) are the crucial outcome of the venture's marketing activities and provide the bridge between the entrepreneur's plans and aspirations and the organization's financial potential and performance.

E-NOTES 6–1   MARKETING AND ENTREPRENEURSHIP

Marketing and entrepreneurship both:

- cater to customer needs
- evaluate new product or new service ideas
- function as scanners, evaluators, boundary scanners and representatives for their venture
- are growth oriented
- often have misconceptions about consumers, competition, costs, and product

---

Marketing Concept and Orientation

Where does the entrepreneur begin thinking about marketing? The initial point is the marketing concept. The marketing concept is a managerial prescription (an "ought-to-do") for setting marketing goals and managing exchange transactions. It requires an understanding of potential and actual customer needs and of costs of meeting those needs. The venture then devises and implements a total system that integrates the marketing function with the other business functions. The single most important objective of marketing is **customer satisfaction**. Customer satisfaction is achieved when the firm has provided user-based quality and value (the quality/price ratio) to its buyers.

CUSTOMER ORIENTATION

The total marketing concept is fairly well established in most small businesses and new ventures.[7] But it is not the only point-of-view that ventures take. The marketing concept can be contrasted to other business postures, namely, a production orientation, a sales emphasis, or a social orientation.

A production orientation is preoccupied with manufacturing-based or product-based quality. It is internally directed at the activities of the firm and its functions. Production-oriented ventures are often founded by engineers, inventors, or high-tech wizards—people who are fascinated by the gadgets and gizmos they are attempting to bring to market.

A sales orientation is not a marketing orientation. Sales-oriented firms are interested in selling—that is their number one priority. Issues such as developing long-term relationships with customers, integrating business functions to provide maximum satisfaction, and working hard to deliver the product or service at the lowest possible price are not primary concerns. For sales-oriented ventures, moving product out the door is job number one.

Occasionally, firms that have a social orientation are successful. Examples such as Ben and Jerry's ice cream and The Body Shop prove that a social conscience is not necessarily in conflict with business effectiveness. Often customers purchase these firms' products to affirm their own social tendencies. The firms are able to charge a premium, which is a form of tax, that customers willingly pay knowing that a certain percentage goes to support the social causes espoused by the founding entrepreneurs.

Even experienced entrepreneurs can and do fail to employ the marketing concept when launching their businesses. Take the case of Minnesota Brewing Co., which almost lost it all by not knowing its market before introducing its products.[8] The firm was founded in 1991 and operated out of a closed Heileman Brewing plant. Investors ponied up $3.3 million to produce, distribute, and sell beer to a loyal blue-collar market. But along the way, the company forgot its customer. Laments lead investor Bruce Hendry, "Looking back, I've gotten a million-dollar education on how to sell beer—what to do and what not to do." The lesson: Know your market before you leap.

The venture had a number of important factors going for it: a landmark location, low-interest state-subsidized loans, and a highly reputed management team. It even had the good fortune of having the local St. Paul newspaper run a contest, called "Name the Beer," for the firm's first product. The winning name was Pig's Eye Pilsner (Pig's Eye was the city's name before it became St. Paul). But all the momentum was wasted as the venture's management made marketing mistake after mistake.

- *Mistake 1.* The firm did not name the beer "Pig's Eye." It chose "Landmark" as its first product's name. Hendry said it sounded more dignified. But it had no appeal and was considered boring. Beer drinkers were not impressed by dignity.
- *Mistake 2.* The beer was brewed to taste like old-style European beers—heavy and slightly bitter. Consumers, however, expected the beer to be a light lager like the typical American brew.
- *Mistake 3.* The venture's advertising campaign was misleading. It promised a lighter-tasting beer, like the Schmidt brand that used to be brewed in the old Heileman plant.
- *Mistake 4.* The price was wrong. Landmark was priced as a premium beer and cost as much as Budweiser. Competitors cut prices when Landmark was launched to make it seem even more expensive. Customers expected to pay $9.99 a case and were shocked when the price was $14.99.

Sales were disappointing and reached only one third of break-even. The investors, who prided themselves on their marketing expertise, had double-crossed themselves by moving away from what they knew to be the customer's needs. Before they lost it all, they needed a turnaround. Here's what they did: They developed a new, lighter beer and tested it on hundreds of drinkers at local bars, in focus groups, and in taste tests. They named the beer Pig's Eye Pilsner and priced it at $8.99 a case. The firm launched a new ad campaign that spoofed Stroh's "Swedish bikini team" ads. They developed a logo character named Pig's Eye Parrent (reputedly the founder of the city of Pig's Eye) whose grinning leer beneath his eye patch makes him appealing to men and women. The results have been impressive. Case sales are well over break-even and rising, intense brand loyalty is developing, and Pig's Eye Parrent's image will grace other products through a number of licensing deals. Says Hendry, "Pig's Eye saved our shirt."

MARKETING RESEARCH

Marketing research eventually put Minnesota Brewing back on track and turned the company around. The marketing concept requires that customer satisfaction be the primary objective, and understanding what customer satisfaction means in any particular business concept requires extensive knowledge of the potential purchasers. Marketing research is designed to provide that information.

Marketing research can be defined as "the systematic and objective process of gathering, coding, and analyzing data for aid in making marketing decisions."[9] In Chapter 3 we introduced a framework for analyzing customers, competitors, and industry forces, but the needed data came from marketing research. Effective marketing research can help the new venture answer such important questions as:

- *Who is the customer?* The customer profile includes demographic characteristics, values and attitudes, buyer and shopping behavior, and buyer location. Customers can be local, regional, national, or international. Understanding the customer is the basis for market segmentation.
- *Who are the players?* The competitive profile of existing competitors and potential competitors can indicate the likelihood of retaliation and the nature of the reaction. For example, Minnesota Brewing failed to realize that competitors would cut prices to impede its new product's introduction.
- *How can the customer be reached?* The distribution networks and channels represent the actual delivery of the product or service. Sometimes the answer to this question falls back on standard industry practices: "ship by common carrier," "retail channels," "in-house sales force." But other times the distribution system *is* the business—as at Avon, Domino's Pizza, and Amway.

Conducting Marketing Research   Many entrepreneurs conduct some sort of marketing research in the early stages of new venture creation.[10] Marketing research is also a common practice among small businesses. As many as 40 percent of smaller businesses do marketing research, and the vast majority are satisfied with the results.[11] Marketing research need not be an expensive and time-consuming exercise. Answers to the important marketing questions are frequently well within the grasp of the entrepreneur, and most marketing research can be done by the founders themselves.[12]

Conducting marketing research is a six-step process.

Step 1.   Marketing research begins with a definition of the purposes and objectives of the study. The entrepreneur must pinpoint the aspect of the product or market that requires the research: product features, design characteristics, packaging. Knowing what questions need answers will help save time and money and make the results easier to interpret. In this important preliminary stage, the researcher should be clear on the specific nature of the problem. The key for the researcher is to determine what facts, knowledge, and opinions would help the entrepreneurs make a better decision.[13]

Step 2.   The next step is to determine the data sources best suited to the objectives of the study. Data come from two types of sources: primary and secondary. Primary data are generated from scratch by the research team. Three common entrepreneurial primary-data projects are the concept test, the product test, and the market test.

Concept testing occurs very early in new venture planning, often before the final venture configuration is complete. The purpose of the concept test is to determine whether customers can envision how the product or service will work and whether they would purchase it. The customers respond to a *description* of the product or service; no physical representation yet exists. After reading the description, customers are asked if they understand the product and if they are likely to purchase.

Concept testing can also be used for potential investors, suppliers, or members of the managerial team. Each of these groups is in a position to evaluate the new venture concept, and the entrepreneur can gauge whether the concept is likely to be accepted by these important stakeholders. In addition, feedback from these people at the concept stage enables the entrepreneur to make the type of adjustments and alterations to the concept that can save time, money, and reputation down the road.

Product testing requires having potential customers or investors react to the actual use of a new product or service. The subjects may use the product briefly, even take it home for a more intensive test. Product testing is less abstract than concept testing, and therefore the responses are more reliable. However, some products are so expensive to manufacture, even as prototypes, that product testing becomes unrealistic, and concept testing must suffice.

Market testing is the most complex and expensive approach, but it is also the most realistic and most likely to produce reliable results. In a market test, the product or service is introduced using the full marketing strategy but in a limited area that is representative of the broader market. It is an attempt to duplicate the conditions of actually marketing the product, usually on a limited geographic scale. For ventures with a limited geographic reach anyway, the market test is the actual beginning of business operations. Small manufacturing operations that seek broad product distribution would be candidates for market test research.

Each of the three types of test has its costs and benefits, and proper selection requires a fit between the entrepreneur's needs and resources and the type of product or service under consideration. Table 6–1 summarizes each test and its appropriateness to a variety of situations.

Secondary sources consist of data, information, and studies that others have already completed and published. These sources are useful for planning original data collection activities because they provide in-depth background information on customers and markets. They can be extremely useful for the new venture's marketing research efforts because most are easily accessed and either free or inexpensive. A virtually unlimited volume of information is available from hundreds of sources. Sometimes already-published studies are examples of concept, product, and market

TABLE 6–1 Marketing Research: Appropriateness of Primary-Data Collection Methods

New Venture Characteristic	Concept Test	Product Test	Market Test
Single-product venture	High	High	High
Multi-product venture	Moderate to low	Low	Moderate
Importance of product performance	High	High	High
Importance of pricing strategy	High	High	High
Importance of promotion	Moderate to high	Low	Moderate to high
Importance of distribution	Moderate to high	Low	Moderate to high
Introduction of innovations, continuous	High	High	High
Introduction of innovations, occasional	Low	Moderate	High

Source: Adapted from G. Hills and R. LaForge, "Marketing and Entrepreneurship: The State of the Art," in *The State of the Art of Entrepreneurship*, eds. D. Sexton and J. Kasarda (Boston: PWS-Kent, 1992), 164–190.

tests similar to those the new venture might conduct itself. These are frequently available in public libraries and always available in the business library of major business schools. Additional resources can be located by searching the Internet.

Step 3. The third step in marketing research is to develop the data collection instrument or test. Marketing research data can come from a single source or multiple sources. If a variety of sources are employed, the results are more likely to be valid. For customer studies, personal and telephone interviews, focus groups, and direct observation might be appropriate. Mail studies and surveys are common data sources. Whichever method is chosen in step 2, a properly designed data collection instrument is required. This is self-evident for interviews and survey-type research, but it is also important for secondary data sources. These data sources have the potential to overwhelm the marketing researcher because there are so much data and the researcher will tend to believe that all of it is important. Too much data are as dangerous as too little because of the extra expense and the difficulty of coding and analyzing large data sets. The researcher should have a clear idea of the specific data required before investigating secondary sources.

Step 4. The fourth step is the design and choice of the sample. Occasionally the researcher will be able to speak to all of the firm's customers or collect data on all of the companies of interest. If this is the case, the researcher has not a sample but a census. Usually, however, there are too many people or companies to speak to, so it is necessary to choose a small proportion of them as representative of the total population. This is a sample. The key issues in sample design are representativeness and reliability. A sample does not have to be large to be representative of the whole population. National polls of voters may contain as few as 1,500 participants representing 60 million voters. Yet these polls are often very accurate. For statistically pure national samples, the venture probably should employ professional marketing researchers. For smaller, do-it-yourself efforts, the researchers simply need to ensure that the people they speak to have the information desired. Very small samples of one, two, and three respondents are seldom sufficient.

Step 5. The fifth step is data collection. This is the actual execution of the study. Data need to be collected in an unbiased and uniform manner. The correct design of the instrument and of the sample help to ensure this. Additional measures are also needed, such as training survey recorders and telephone interviewers, checking data records for errors, and scanning responses.

Step 6. The final stage of a marketing research project is the analysis of the data and the interpretation of the results. Often a final report is written, even when the project is relatively small and the goals of the study fairly narrow. This ensures that a record exists for the future and that others in the organization can refer to the study as necessary.

Many entrepreneurs must do their market research with limited funds. They face a "chicken or egg situation"—they cannot obtain financing without good market research, and they are unable to afford a large market research effort without financing. But the most expensive research is research conducted in a slovenly way. At best, it will lead to repeating the effort; at worst it will lead to erroneous conclusions. Still, the entrepreneur must conduct good market research "on the cheap." Cost-saving recommendations include:

1. Use the telephone instead of mail surveys and door-to-door interviewing.
2. Avoid research in high-cost cities; test more than one product at a time.
3. Avoid collecting unnecessary data.[14]

One source of good yet inexpensive research is a university. Professors, students, and staff are often involved in projects that enable them to piggyback their courses and assignments with the entrepreneur's market research needs. For example, the Small Business Institute (SBI) program of the U.S. Small Business Administration serves thousands of businesses each year on over 500 campuses. Donna Kane of Kane Manufacturing of Des Moines, Iowa, did not pay a penny for a 50-page market research study that was conducted by students at Drake University. Professor Robert Kemp supervised the students' market research report, which found a new market for Kane's livestock products in Germany. Kane expects exports to exceed 33 percent of sales. The next study will focus on Brazil.[15]

Market research is not only for new markets. Ongoing market research, the systematic analysis of sales trends for current customers, is part of the process. In Street Stories 6–1 we see how one company employs the latest technology to procure market information about its customers.

E-NOTES 6–2   MARKET RESEARCH

The six steps of market research are:

Define purpose and objectives;

Identify data sources, which may include date from primary sources such as:

- concept testing,
- product testing,
- market testing;

Design data collection instrument;

Conduct a sample data collection;

Actually collect data;

Analyze data.

Marketing Research on Innovation   Marketing research on innovations is particularly relevant for entrepreneurs, and considerable work has been done in this area of buyer behavior. The entrepreneur whose objective is to successfully introduce a new product or service has three intermediate goals: (1) to remove impediments to the purchase of the innovation, (2) to increase acceptance of the new product, and (3) to encourage repurchase over time. Impediments always confront an innovation, and they can take many forms. For example, existing channels of distribution may be difficult to enter, making it hard to present the product to the target market.

Next, the innovative entrepreneur must attempt to appeal to a wide audience and to gain broad market acceptance. Initial buyers may have special characteristics that make innovations appealing to them—for example, high levels of education, literacy, and income, an open attitude toward change, a sensitivity to external changes, and high social status. Age is negatively correlated with the propensity to adopt an innovation. However, the segment of buyers who immediately find the innovation desirable is usually too narrow to support the product and its organization. Wider appeal is therefore

---

No Belt-Tightening at Leegin

Jerry Kohl, 41, is the owner of Leegin Creative Leather Products of Industry, California. And he is a maniac. He is opinionated, passionate, and emotional about his business and his customers. Throughout most of the 1980s his company's sales had stagnated, staying at between $9 million and just short of $10 million. In an effort to escape the purgatory of flat sales and increasing foreign competition, Jerry attended Harvard's Owner/President Management program beginning in the summer of 1986 and for the next two summers.

Sales in 1987 pushed through to $10.8 million, $15 million in 1988, $20 million in 1989, and by the end of 1992 had reached $47 million. Jerry expected to do $65 million in 1993. Profits have increased, and there is less debt on the balance sheet. What's the secret for this little-known company that does no advertising? Leegin's reinvented itself to deliver total customer satisfaction.

In the 1980s the company resembled many small manufacturers. Leegin's had a limited line of belts and sold directly to mostly small stores. Salespeople were order takers, and when one quit, accounts were lost. Leegin's designers kept turning out new styles, but the proliferation threatened to choke the factory. The office was run like a feudal fiefdom, and office politics were normal. Leegin had no advantages and some serious disadvantages.

But Kohl came back from Harvard ready for change. Each salesperson is now a total marketer. They take the entire store inventory of belts. Then they record it on their portable PC. Stored in the PC is the customer's orders for the past year, current sales volume, and number of belts sold by style, color, or any other feature the store owner might want to see. The last job is selling. The salesperson can tell the customer which styles are selling at similar stores, what new styles fit with the rest of the inventory, and whether the depth and breadth of the line is appropriate for the rest of the product mix.

This information has changed the relationship between buyer and seller. First, the information is objective—the Leegin salesperson looks more like a belt consultant than a pitchman. Second, the information enables the customer to maximize returns on a small and often neglected product line.

All of Kohl's 60 outside salespeople use their portable PCs. No paper orders are required. Information flows both ways as orders are placed by modem and factory inventories are updated with production. Market information helps with the planning, and the database stays even if a salesperson leaves.

In order to support more productive salespeople, the office staff was reorganized and retrained as account specialists. They are now responsible for customer service, expedited shipping, solving problems, collections, and credit. Through training and computerization, an account specialist can handle roughly 1,000 accounts.

And marketing became a priority on the factory floor as well. Quality, empowerment, and teamwork programs were successfully established. Group incentives were established based on managing inventories and quality. Everyone on the shop floor can use the computer terminals to communicate with the salespeople.

Concludes Kohl: "We have 60 soldiers out there and each soldier calls on three customers a day. Unless you have the ability to call on 180 customers a day,"—not to mention the ability to provide them with up-to-the-minute sales information or the ability to produce and ship thousands of orders a week, including 250 for a single belt—"how are you going to compete with me?"

Source: Adapted from J. Case, "A Business Transformed," *Inc.*, June 1993, 84–91.

required. Also, if the product is to survive for any period of time, repurchase must be encouraged.

What is the diffusion process and why is it important? The marketer who understands the **diffusion process** is in the best position to meet the objectives outlined. *Diffusion* refers to the overall market understanding and acceptance of an innovation, whether it is a product, a service, or an idea. The most widely accepted model for the diffusion process has four stages.[16] The *knowledge stage* occurs as individuals become aware of the innovation. Information becomes available through various marketing communication media and techniques. People are repeatedly exposed to this information and to physical and social stimuli that reinforce awareness of the product. The earliest messages enable the consumer to recognize the innovation and recall its attributes.

The next stage of the process is the *persuasion stage,* which involves the transmission of favorable attitudes toward the product. These are more sophisticated messages. They describe operating and performance characteristics as well as buyer benefits. The consumer weighs the risks of purchase against the risks of nonpurchase and compares similar or competing products. The firm attempts to link positive images and personalities with the product at this time. This is known as the **halo effect.** Because consumers are actively engaged in searching for and processing information about the product at this stage, advertising and the various forms of marketing communication become powerful tools.

The *decision stage* follows. This is the crucial "make or break" time for the entrepreneur. The activities that lead to either acceptance or rejection occur now. Social and economic pressures can be brought to bear at this stage. The customer can be led through a series of smaller partial decisions that lead to the purchase of the product. At this point the entrepreneur must close the sale.

The final stage in the diffusion model leading to the adoption of an innovation is the *confirmation stage.* Here customers either reverse their decision (no repurchase) or are reinforced to repeat their decision. Between the decision to purchase and the confirmation is the trial period. This is another crucial time for the entrepreneur, since misuse of the product or unrealistic expectations during the trial period can cause the customer to reverse the purchase decision.

The entrepreneur who can successfully introduce innovations is able to communicate important facts and images during the knowledge stage. During the persuasion

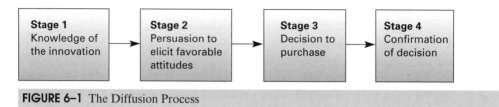

FIGURE 6-1 The Diffusion Process

stage the entrepreneur can demonstrate both the relative advantages of the product or service and the compatibility of the innovation with the buyer's values, needs, and behavior. Positive purchase decisions are encouraged by illustrating the ease of use of the innovation and its "try-ability." The probability that the customer will buy again is increased when the buyer can directly observe the benefits of the innovation.[17] Figure 6–1 illustrates the diffusion process.

Marketing Strategy

What is marketing strategy? **Marketing strategy** is the set of objectives and activities that enables the new venture to implement the total marketing concept. There are two keys. The first is to identify, develop, and control resources that are rare, valuable, hard to duplicate, and nonsubstitutable. Doing so provides the firm with its distinctive competence and competitive edge. The second key is to be creative and lucky. A recent study reported that among the 20 biggest outlets for the top American brands, the three primary sources of sustainable advantage were location, service, and luck (creativity).[18]

The study indicated that a venture's location, the primary aspect of a retailer's distribution strategy, is the key component of its overall marketing strategy. Good locations are always evaluated relative to the rents paid for them. The research indicated that the rent successful retailers pay is far below the true value of the property. Great service is also part of the product/service mix and another key component of the marketing strategy. For example, the leading Lexus dealer in the United States is located in south Florida. His service included a special washing of all of his customers' cars after Hurricane Andrew to rid them of acid created by burning debris. Finally, luck and creativity have roles to play because they are so difficult to imitate. According to Philip Kotler, international marketing guru at Northwestern University's Kellogg School of Management, successful outlets are likely to be "more creative. They may depart from some of the standard procedures—and perhaps even the principles in some cases. . . ."[19] Here we hear echoes of Sam Walton's Rule 10: "Break all the rules." Table 6–2 reports the results of a study of the biggest and best stores in the United States.

Our resource-based approach to marketing and the total marketing concept require that the marketing concept focus on the firm's distinctive competencies. Where the firm has advantages, these advantages should be pressed through marketing strategy. The first question to be addressed is: What is our distinctive competence? We have already explored this topic in Chapters 2 through 4. The second question is: Who values our competence? Although we addressed this question when we discussed re-source analysis, we include it here because it entails the selection of target markets and segments. The next questions are: What marketing activities enable us to interact most effectively with our markets? How will the marketing variables of price, promo-tion, product characteristics, and distribution be set to increase our market? Finally, given a set of marketing activities, how much can we expect to sell? Addressing these questions will complete this chapter.

E-NOTES 6–3   RESOURCE-BASED MARKETING APPROACH

A new venture's marketing plan in a resource-based approach should con-sider these questions:

- what is our unique competence?
- who values our competence?
- what marketing activities will help us reach our markets?
- how will marketing variables (price, promotion, etc.) affect our success?
- based on a specific marketing plan, what kind of sales can we project?

SELECTION OF MARKETS AND SEGMENTS

Not all customers are alike. Our analysis of buyer characteristics in Chapter 3 indi-cated that buyers differ, for example, in price sensitivity, brand loyalty, and require-ments for quality. **Market segmentation** identifies distinct buying groups and develops and implements marketing strategies to fit each group. Market segmentation is impor-tant for marketing strategy because it enables the venture to discriminate among buy-ers for its own advantage. For example, the venture can serve buyers who demand the latest technological innovations if that is where the venture has its distinctive compe-tence; or it can serve buyers who are most price sensitive if efficient operation is the core entrepreneurial competency. Since it is difficult, if not impossible, to be all things to all people (that is, to achieve world-class customer satisfaction levels across all classes of customers), effective market segmentation enables the firm to serve some segment of customers exceedingly well.

Bases for Segmentation   Sometimes it is possible to segment markets based on broad market types, for example, consumer end users versus commercial end users. Another basis for segmentation is the type of buying organization: manufacturing businesses, distribution organizations, wholesalers, retailers, service organizations, and not-for-profits. These represent different types of buyers, and each may have a distinguishable set of needs that can be the basis for segmentation. Also, it is possible to segment markets geographically by determining the scope of the venture's opera-tion: global, regional, domestic, or local.

Segmentation methods are widely used by new ventures and small businesses. One study reported that 62 percent of businesses employed some type of market segmentation strategy and that *effective segmentation strategies produced significant differences in return on invested capital.*[20] In other words, not only do segmentation strategies lead to higher customer satisfaction, but this satisfaction also translates

The 20 biggest and best stores in the United States owe their success to combinations of luck, service, and location. Because these are retail outlets, location does play a principal role in a way that might not be true in manufacturing businesses.

Parent Company	Biggest Outlet	Just How Big?
Amoco Oil	Station in Whiting, Indiana	Sold 5.2 million gallons of gas in 1992
Florsheim Shoes	Herald Square, New York City	Serves most customers; 28,000–30,000 per year
True Value Hardware	Kabelin True Value, LaPorte, Indiana	Over $7 million in purchases from supplier
Wal-Mart	Laredo, Texas	Most space, 151,915 square feet
Fanny Farmer Candy	Rockefeller Center, New York City	Sells most 1-pound boxes (62,000) in country
Chevrolet	Ed Morse Chevrolet, Lauderhill, Florida	More than 100,000 vehicles sold in 1992
H&R Block	Downtown Stamford, Connecticut	Most clients served, over 8,000
Federal Express	Center at 525 Seventh Avenue, New York City	Most volume; over 1,000 packages per day
FTD Floral Delivery	McShan Florist, Inc., Dallas, Texas	Most flowers-by-wire orders, over 1,100 per week
Goodyear Tires	Sullivan Tire, Rockland, Massachusetts	Biggest dealer, over 250,000 tires each year
Hertz Rent-A-Car	Los Angeles International Airport	Most rentals, daily average of 2,000
Hilton Hotels	Flamingo Hotel, Las Vegas, Nevada	Most rooms—3,530—with 90 percent occupancy
KFC	Fort Campbell, Kentucky, U.S. Army base	Biggest-grossing franchise, $2.4 million
Sears	Ala Moana Shopping Center, Honolulu, Hawaii	Highest revenue, over $50 million last year
Baskin-Robbins	Royal Hawaiian store, Honolulu, Hawaii	Top-grossing unit, estimated $925,000 in 1992
McDonald's	On turnpike, near Darien, Connecticut	Serves most customers (8,000/day) in chain
Domino's Pizza	U.S. Marine Corps base, near Twenty-Nine Palms, California	Sells most pizza, 4,000 per week
Midas Muffler	Wood's Car Care, Vienna, Virginia	Top-selling dealer, over $2 million
Radio Shack	Dadeland Mall, Miami, Florida	Largest gross sales
Lexus Automobiles	J.M. Lexus, Margate, Florida	Most sold, over 2,200 in 1992

Source: Adapted from R. Gibson, "Location, Luck, Service Can Make a Store Top Star," *The Wall Street Journal*, February 1, 1993, B1.

TABLE 6-2   (continued)

Key Resources

Location right across Illinois border saves motorists 13 cents per gallon in taxes. Open 24 hours. Automated credit card processing speeds service.

Location across from Macy's with three window facings. One-hundred-year reputation. Complete inventory, computerized ordering, open 70 hours per week.

Extensive service. Creative in-store promotions. Effective direct-mail advertising.

Location at the crossroads of Interstate 35 and the Pan-American Highway, the key route for trade under the North American Free Trade Agreement. Wal-Mart "associates'" outstanding service.

Location across from Radio City Music Hall in midtown Manhattan. Serves corporate customers. Open seven days a week.

Location in south Florida. Sells fleets to rental companies in this important tourist destination. Extensive inventory, sales force, and service.

"It's a mystery," says district manager Jack Marvill.

Location in center of garment district and near Penn Station. Large volume of tickets from travel agents. Open 6 days a week, 10 hours a day.

Reputation; literally grew up with Dallas. Large inventory, 24 phone lines, 50 delivery trucks.

Long-time reputation, associated with sports teams (Red Sox and Bruins). Family business. Specialized outlets for trucks and retreads.

Location. Open round the clock. Seventeen shuttle buses for quick service. Effective management of huge facilities.

Reputation. The hotel of Bugsy (Ben) Siegel. Location near the "Strip." Low prices appeal to tourists. Extensive services offered.

"Employees who don't smile end up working in the kitchen," says Terry Rogers, VP of operations. Open 20 hours each day. Home delivery. Competes with army food.

Location in Honolulu's biggest shopping mall. Sells gifts and beach clothes to tourists. Caters to Japanese visitors who expect high service levels.

Reputation. Year-round ice cream weather. Waikiki location. Staff speaks Japanese.

Location on busy Interstate 95. Open round the clock. Mammoth facility requires effective management.

Location. Isolated Mojave desert offers little competition. Returning marines need "pizza fix." Family business employs over 30 delivery drivers.

Location near high-density office buildings. Service—free pickup and delivery into D.C.

Reputation of chain. Location at tourist destination. Ships to Latin America and Puerto Rico. Commissions for sales force.

Location in high-income area. Elite advertising. Service department open 19 hours per day. Mechanics organized in teams trained to pamper customers.

TABLE 6–3   Bases For Market Segmentation Usage and Effectiveness

Basis	*Usage (%)[a]*	*Effectiveness[b]*
By geographic areas: such as state, county, census tracts.	13.6	3.9
By demographics: such as age, income, and gender.	15.5	3.6
By social class: high, middle, and low.	4.9	3.8
By lifestyle and opinions: such as hobbies, job type, political view.	4.4	2.7
By personality traits: such as masculinity-femininity, assertiveness.	4.1	2.6
By purchasing decisions: based on when customers get ideas.	2.4	3.7
By purchasing timing: based on when buyers buy.	3.1	4.2
By time of use: based on when customers use the product.	6.3	4.3
By benefits sought: based on what customers want.	11.8	4.6
By extent of usage: such as high users, ex-users, etc.	6.9	3.1
By buyer loyalty status: such as very loyal, ready switchers.	5.2	2.7
By buyer readiness: based on degree of awareness and intent.	3.8	3.9
By buyer attitudes: such as enthusiastic, hostile, etc.	5.6	4.1
By marketing attribute: product characteristic, price sensitivity, etc.	8.0	2.5

[a]Indicates primary method.
[b]Indicates satisfaction with technique on a scale of 1 to 5. Mean for all dimensions is 3.6.
Source: Adapted from R. Peterson, "Small Business Usage of Target Marketing," *Journal of Small Business Management,* October 1991, 79–85.

into profits. Table 6–3 presents a broad range of segmentation techniques, the percentage of small firms that employ them, and the reported effectiveness of each method.

MARKETING ACTIVITIES

Four major marketing activities need to be accomplished once the target markets are selected. These decisions are not made in isolation. They are all intertwined—with each other and with the venture's distinctive competencies, target market, and macro- and competitive environments. The four major activities are pricing decisions, product and service configurations, distribution strategies, and promotional campaigns.

Pricing   A price is the exchange value (usually denominated in money) of the venture's goods and services. Prices go by many names: fares, taxes, tuition, fees, tips, interest, and tolls. The pricing decision is probably the most important of the four major marketing activities because it directly affects the value relationship (quality divided by price). A mispriced product is a misplaced product—misplaced in relationship to the competition, misplaced in the perceptions of the buyers, and misplaced relative to other products and services the firm has to offer.

The entrepreneur must make fairly accurate price decisions, even before the product is introduced to the market, because the price of the product directly enters the sales forecast. If pricing is wrong, forecasts are wrong—and projected cash flow and profits are wrong as well. An incorrect pricing decision can cause the entrepreneur to get a "green light" on launching the business when more accurate forecasting would have produced a "red light" and saved everybody time and money.

Different pricing objectives require different pricing strategies. However, the primary objective of the pricing decision is to make profits. Entrepreneurs have five pricing subobjectives, each of which can help the venture achieve its primary objective.[21]

Skimming the Market   The **skimming the market** strategy identifies a segment that is price insensitive (inelastic demand) and charges the highest price the market can bear for short-term profits. It can be used when:

- No comparable products are available.
- There is uncertainty about costs.
- The product life cycle is extremely short.
- A drastic innovation or improvement has been made.
- There is a low probability that competitors will enter the market (due to high entry barriers, high promotion or R&D costs, or other isolating mechanisms).

After price-insensitive segments have been skimmed, prices are gradually reduced to include more sensitive segments. The primary advantages of this strategy are that it:

- Provides cash quickly for reinvestment in promotion or produce development.
- Allows for a market test before full-scale production.
- Suggests high quality in the mind of the customer.

The major disadvantages are that it:

- Assumes that a price-insensitive market segment exists.
- Can cause ill will in the market.
- Can attract potent competitors looking for similar high returns.

Exploiting the Experience Curve   As a manufacturer becomes more experienced in producing a product, or a service provider becomes more knowledgeable and efficient in delivering a service, variable costs may decrease. A firm can take advantage of these decreasing costs by "riding down the demand curve." This means that as costs decrease, prices are set to decrease proportionately. This effectively increases volume and expands the market. Thus, it is possible to maintain margins (price minus variable cost) with increasing market share. This strategy is most commonly employed by established companies that are launching innovations, in durable-goods industries (where the experience-curve effect has been most often noted), and in markets where the product life cycle is moderately long (long enough to ride down the curve). The advantages of this strategy are that:

- It enables the firm to exploit its low-cost position.
- The slow changes in price do not alienate customers.
- Profit objectives do not have to be sacrificed for market share.

The disadvantages are that:

- Some buyers may be discouraged by high initial prices.
- The experience-curve effect must be a documented reality.
- Price reductions could anger early buyers.

Meeting the Market Price   In this strategy, the venture prices its products at the same level as the competition. If this practice is generally accepted by competitors within a segment, then competition will not be based on price. Instead, firms will jockey for dominance based on distribution, promotion, and product improvements. These forms of competition help expand the market for everyone by making the product offerings more attractive, easier to buy, and better known. This type of pricing is most likely to prevail when competitors face each other in a number of markets (and wish to avoid devastating price wars), when costs are reasonably predictable over the entire product life cycle, and when the market is still growing. The major advantages of this strategy are that it:

- Requires less analysis and research.
- Treats all buyers, early and late, the same.
- Signals to other firms that there is no threat of a price war.

The disadvantages are that:

- Other marketing tools must be used to gain differentiation.
- Recovery of investment is slower.
- Errors in initial cost estimates are difficult to overcome.

Achieving Maximum Market Penetration   In this strategy the venture builds market share as quickly as possible by entering with low prices. It stimulates market growth. If successfully executed, the venture will be entrenched as the market-share leader and positioned for long-term profitability. The low price implies low margins, and this will deter some others from entering. It is best used in mass consumer markets when:

- The product has a long life span.
- Market entry is easy.
- Demand is highly price sensitive.
- There is no "top" of the market to skim.
- There is some experience-curve effect.

The primary advantages of this strategy are that it:

- Discourages entry.
- Focuses the customer on value.
- Enables maximum penetration and exposure in the shortest time period.

On the downside, penetration pricing:

- Assumes a degree of price inelasticity that may not be present.
- Stimulates high volumes that the venture may not be prepared to meet.
- Requires large initial capital investment to meet high volumes.
- Can lead to large losses if errors are made.

Establishing Preemptive Pricing   **Preemptive pricing** is a "lowball" pricing strategy designed to keep potential competitors out or to force existing competitors to exit the market. Prices are set as close to expected variable costs as possible, and cost savings are passed on to buyers. Because costs often decrease over time, initial prices will be below cost. Preemptive pricing is often employed in consumer markets and is sometimes combined with other product-pricing strategies that enable the firm to subsidize this potentially short-term money-losing policy. If this strategy is successful, its major advantage is that it limits competition and enables the firm to collect monopoly-type rents. If the strategy is not successful, however, and if competitors match the low prices, large losses can occur.

In addition to these five strategies, numerous other pricing tactics can be employed for various occasions and situations. Table 6–4 presents an entrepreneurial primer on creative pricing tactics.

Pricing policies also have legal implications and constraints. The **Sherman Act** prohibits conspiracy in restraint of trade. Such conspiracy includes collusive pricing tactics and attempts to fix prices. Although entrepreneurs are expected to make pricing decisions independently, market research on competitors' prices and signaling through price changes are legal.[22]

The Federal Trade Commission regulates pricing practices and prohibits deceptive pricing. Deceptive pricing occurs when it is difficult or impossible for the buyer to actually understand what the price of a product or service is. Some products, like insurance, are complicated and require simplified explanations of price policy. The **Truth in Lending Act** requires lenders to explain the true price of credit (interest and finance charges) to borrowers.

The **Robinson-Patman Act** and the **Clayton Act** prohibit discriminatory pricing. Illegal price discrimination exists when identical products or services are sold, under

TABLE 6–4   A Creative Pricing Primer: Approaches and Examples

Approach	*Description*	*Examples*
Bundling	Sell complementary products in a single package	Film and cameras
Unbundling	Separate products into distinct elements	Stereo components
Trial prices	Introductory sizes and short trial periods	Starter memberships; preview fees
Value-added pricing	Include "free" services to appeal to bargain hunters	Free service contract for durables
Two-fers	Buy one, get one free	Pizzas; theater tickets
Pay one price	Fixed-cost admissions or memberships	Amusement park rides; salad bars
Constant promotional price	List price is never charged	Consumer electronics; auto sticker price
Pricing tied to variable	Set a "price per" schedule	Steak by the ounce in restaurants
Captive pricing	Lock in the customer with a system, one inexpensive component, one expensive	Razors and razor blades.
Fixed, then variable	A "just to get started" charge followed by a different rate	Taxi fare; phone calls tied to usage
Price point breaks	Price just below psychological threshold	Charge $4.99 instead of $5.00

Source: Reprinted with permission of *Inc.* magazine, Goldhirsh Group, Inc., 38 Commercial Wharf, Boston MA 02110 (http://www.inc.com). "Naming Your Price," M. Modello, July 1992. Reproduced by permission of the publisher via Copyright Clearance Center, Inc.

similar circumstances, at different prices to different customers or to different market segments. What actually constitutes discrimination is the subject of many volumes of legal text, briefs, torts, and statutes. Basically, however, the following tenets of price discrimination are established:

1. Different prices cannot be charged based on buyers' membership in different social, ethnic, or religious groups.
2. Factors such as age, income, and gender may not be used as a basis for price discrimination.
3. However, sellers can charge different prices in different markets when the market is defined as the circumstances of location and cost.
4. If the costs of serving a market are variable, then the prices charged in those markets may also vary, for example, through trade discounts and volume discounts.
5. Lower prices are legal if they are necessary to meet the competition, for example, discounts for children and senior citizens and group rates on travel and insurance.

Setting prices in arbitrary and capricious ways is bad business and may be against the law. It is bad business because it affects the value relationship in unanticipated ways. When the customer receives a product or service with unpredictable value, the probability is high that you will have an unhappy customer.

Product and Service Configurations   Product decisions determine the bundle of physical and psychological attributes that form or are associated with the core benefit to be delivered. Physical products require decisions about the style of the product, its packaging, the colors it comes in, the sizes to be offered, and the extras that can be purchased separately. The product decision also includes the type of image the product will generate, the likelihood that the product can be branded, and the warranty and after-sale service that will be provided.

The product mix of a new venture may consist of a single product of a single design. However, because many companies are launched with more than one product, we may speak of a **product mix** with three attributes:

The **width** of the product mix refers to how many different product lines are found within the company. The **depth** of the product mix refers to the average number of items offered by the company within each product line. The **consistency** of the mix refers to how closely related the various products are in terms of end use, production and distribution requirements, target markets, or segment appeal.[23]

Service-related decisions parallel product-related decisions with a few important differences. Services usually incorporate some degree of customer involvement and participation. Part of the service design decision involves the extent of cooperation. For example, in the design and delivery of educational services, the customer's involvement can range from passive listener to active "hands-on" learner. Restaurant concepts can be designed with various levels of involvement, from traditional menu/table service, to self-service salad bars, to cafeteria self-service and table clearing—with many variations possible. The three major service-related decisions are:

- **Service Intensity.** The degree of depth and development that the customer experiences while receiving the service. Roller coasters provide an intense experience within a narrow (literally confined to the track) service range. Package delivery services are less intense, but they are more extensive.

- **Service Extensiveness.** The range or scope of services provided. The package-delivery service can handle a wide range of parcels and deliver them just about anywhere in the world. The more types of subservices or variations provided, the more extensive the service.
- **Time.** A pervasive decision for service design. When will the service be available and how long will it take? Will services be provided continuously or will interruptions be acceptable and appropriate? How frequently can the service be provided while maintaining server quality and customer interest?

Taken narrowly, product and service decisions include all the variables that make up the concept of product quality (see Chapter 1). Because these variables refer to the object produced or the service delivered *before* user-based quality and value are assessed, good product decisions are necessary but not sufficient to guarantee success. They must be made in the context of all the other marketing decisions within the marketing concept.

Distribution   Distribution decisions and activities relate to the location of the business and the choice and availability of distribution channels. These decisions are strongly affected, if not completely constrained, by the type of venture being considered. Businesses of certain forms and functions—retailers, wholesalers, warehousers, cataloguers, telemarketers, franchisers—are themselves types of distributors or channels. This reality limits the choices for entrepreneurs unless they are willing to reconfigure their venture in some nonobvious way. If they are, the decision is more strategic and less tactical and therefore is not a distribution decision at all. The major objective of a distribution or location decision is to get the venture's product or service to the target market. When the product or service is defined carefully and the target market is known, the distribution and location decisions should be clear. Effective distribution and channel activities match product to customer and complement these previous decisions.

Consumer Distribution Channels   Consumer distribution channels can employ as many as three intermediaries between producer and consumer. There are occasions, of course, when no intermediaries are used, such as the "factory-direct sales" system. In this case the venture manufactures a product and sells to the customer right from the factory. Since most manufacturers do not possess resources to do this well, they generally employ intermediaries. Figure 6–2 illustrates a consumer distribution chain. Any of the segments of the chain can be eliminated if industry practice, cost considerations, or venture resources dictate.

Industrial Distribution Channels   Industrial distribution channels are employed when the producer is selling to another organization, especially one that uses purchasing agents and has a specialized purchasing organization. The possibilities are diagrammed in Figure 6–3. Just as in consumer channels, certain nodes can be skipped or eliminated at various times, depending on circumstances. One of the major obstacles faced by an entrepreneur can be securing distribution. Street Story 6–2 shows how difficult placing a product in a store can be. But because the entrepreneurs were persistent, the story has a happy ending.

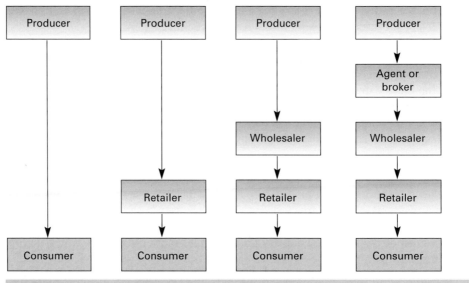

FIGURE 6–2 Distribution Channels for Consumer Goods

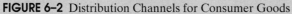

FIGURE 6–3 Channels of Distribution for Industrial Markets

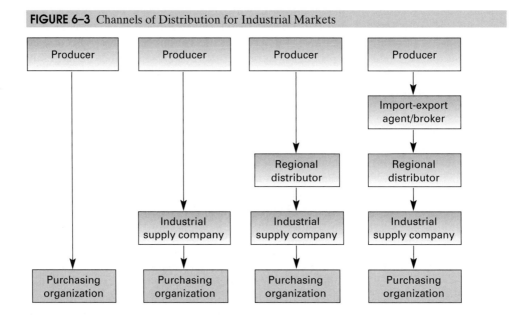

Working the Distribution Treadmill

The "Squirrel Mixer" may be a brilliant invention, but Ronn King can tell you that a good product just isn't enough to make a new venture successful.

King invented the Squirrel Mixer one day when his wife wanted to do some painting around the house. The paint cans they had were old and the paint separated, but King attached the kind of slotted cylinder that engineers call a "squirrel cage" (similar to the exercise wheel in a hamster's cage) to a power drill, lowered it into a gallon can of paint, and turned it on. In just a few seconds the paint was completely blended and ready to use.

Convinced that he had created the paint industry's next hot product, King formed the Site-b Corp. with an old high school buddy to market the invention. They hired an attorney to lock up the worldwide patents, found a job shop to manufacture the device, produced a demonstration video, and mounted a direct mail campaign to U.S. paint and hardware retailers from their Ridgecrest, California headquarters.

Nobody doubted the ingenuity of the Squirrel Mixer, but almost every retailer still said "No." Sears, Sherwin-Williams, and Menards all said that the Site-b Corp. was simply too small. They claimed the administrative cost of dealing with a vendor with just one product was too high. Wal-Mart said they liked the product, but in the end refused to carry it due to a company policy of not doing business with any vendor too dependent on Wal-Mart for sales.

With some research, King discovered that a small group of dealers and distributors act as wholesalers to the paint and hardware industry, creating a product line with items from many vendors. To reach those distributors, Site-b would have to hire independent sales representatives. They did that, and sales started to come in, although at a much lower volume than King expected. Sales picked up more when Site-b licensed the Squirrel Mixer to two paint tool companies who wanted to market the product under their own brand name, but the margin of profit was lower.

After a year of intensive promotion, Site-b sold less than 100,000 units at a couple of dollars each. "You've got to learn the industry," says the persistent King. "You've got to form relationships. And even with the best product in the world, you've got to take a lot of nos for a maybe."

It was a relationship formed by one of Site-b's sales representatives which may now pay off for Ronn King. Hardware industry giant Home Depot agreed to a Squirrel Mixer demonstration, and went on to negotiate a large sales contract with Site-b. "When we see people with new and cool and unique products, we take them seriously," said Kim Curtin, one of Home Depot's top buyers. That may be true, but Home Depot was one of the many retailers who repeatedly rejected King's earlier requests for a meeting. Just like the hamster in the cage, King now knows that you have to work the distribution treadmill over and over again to put some spin into your new venture.

Source: Adapted from Thomas Pitzinger, Jr., "Two Buddies Try To Get a New Product into the Retail Mix," in *Wall Street Journal*, January 31, 1997, B1.

Promotional Campaigns   Promotional activities encompass the methods and techniques that ventures use to communicate with their customers and with other stakeholders. The purposes of promotion are to inform and persuade. Included in the promotional mix are advertising, personal selling, sales promotion, publicity, and public relations. Each of these sets of activities has distinctive characteristics that make the design of the promotion strategy complex—complex enough to be a source of sustainable competitive advantage.

Advertising   Advertising can be defined as "any paid form of nonpersonal presentation and promotion of ideas, goods, or services by an identified sponsor."[24] There are many different forms of advertising, such as television, radio, newspaper and magazine, and yellow pages. Infomercials (commercials disguised as news and information shows), outdoor displays, direct mail, and novelties are also advertising media. Because of the complexity of their form and message, it is difficult to generalize about advertising activity and campaigns. However, the following attributes can be noted:

1. Advertising is a public presentation. Its very publicness confers credibility to the product and service. Because it is delivered anonymously to a large group, it implies a certain standardization of the product.
2. An advertising message can be repeated over and over to impress the message into the (sub)conscious of the buyer. The extent to which one brand's advertising is more embedded in the buyer's consciousness (top-of-the mind recall) is clearly an advantage for convenience goods and impulse shopping.
3. Advertising can be used not only to inform and persuade but also to associate other favorable images in the buyer's mind. Through copy, artwork, sound, and music, advertising can influence the buyer's mood.
4. The impersonality of advertising enables consumers to turn away, switch off, or ignore the venture's messages without cost or obligation.[25]

New ventures are usually operating on limited budgets and targeting niches that can be defined geographically or by consumer interest. This makes techniques such as use of local media or special-interest publications applicable. Yellow pages advertising is often effective. Direct mail, well designed and targeted, can be successful on a limited budget.

Today the Internet has also become an innovative tool for marketing new ventures. Fledgling novelist Nan McCarthy spent $5,000 to promote her self-published romance "Chat" with a Web page featuring excerpts and an order form. Sales were slow until McCarthy corresponded with humor columnist Dave Barry, and their letters were printed by several Internet news groups. Visits to McCarthy's web site skyrocketed overnight, and almost all the copies of her novel's first printing sold immediately. In addition to making her first book profitable, the web site enabled McCarthy and her Rainwater Press to compile a database of names to market her second novel.[26]

Obviously the Internet offers distinct advantages for some new ventures. The start-up costs for establishing a Web presence are low, and technologically astute companies can use the Internet to target particular niches and respond quickly to shifting demand. The Internet is an attractive advertising arena; market research indicates that the median household income for today's Web surfers is 65 percent higher than the national average. One computer consulting firm predicts that more than 50 million Americans will be on-line in the next few years.

Many analysts believe that companies who establish an Internet presence now may lead the pack during the next century. While the Web is currently dominated by male baby boomers, experts predict than nearly 33 percent of Internet users will be under 30 by the year 2001, and that more women will shop on-line. However, high-tech products such as computers and software will continue to dominate on-line sales as we enter the next century, followed by travel services and entertainment products such as books and compact disks.

On the down side, the sheer size of cyberspace makes it difficult for vendors and consumers to interact. Analysts also predict that the expected increase in Internet users may bring the median income down, and at the same time attract on-line competition from retailing giants such as Wal-Mart.[27]

Personal Selling   Personal selling is oral presentation, supplemented by other media (for example, overhead slides or computer graphic demonstrations), either in a formal setting or in informal conversation, for the purpose of making a sale to prospective buyers.[28] The decision to use personal selling is as much a management and human resource decision as a marketing one, because frequently a sales force is required to execute the strategy. (Exceptions are the use of manufacturers' reps or personal selling by the entrepreneur.)

The decisions required to develop a sales force strategy are complex and, as in advertising, contingent on product, distribution, and pricing decisions. The major issues are sales force size, sales force territory, recruitment and selection of salespersons, training, incentive schemes and promotions, and supervision and evaluation.[29] Because of the large number of variables, and particularly the social complexity of the relationship between salespeople and their customers, an effective sales force can be a source of SCA.

"Selling" is only one of the tasks of salespersons. Although the design of the sales job depends on the rest of the marketing mix and the characteristics of the market, salespeople perform as many as five additional functions:

1. *Prospecting* is the search for additional customers. Sometimes these have been previously identified by the company. These are known as "leads." At other times the salesperson makes "cold calls"—contacts with individuals and companies that have not expressed previous interest in the product or service.
2. *Communicating* information to existing buyers or potential buyers. The subject of the communication may be about price, product characteristics, new product developments, or competing product comparisons.
3. *Servicing* customers by consulting with them on their problems, providing technical or managerial assistance, or helping with financing or delivery schedules.
4. *Information collection* and the gathering of competitive intelligence is also a salesperson's job. The salesperson is a source of market research, passing on customer satisfaction information and data on how customers are receiving the competition's offerings.
5. *Allocating* scarce products at times when supply cannot keep up with demand.[30]

Personal selling is most appropriate when a relationship that goes beyond mere transaction is necessary. This relationship between salesperson and buyer is based on the salesperson's recognition, knowledge, and understanding of the buyer's problems and needs and the ability to help the buyer solve problems. Personal selling is one of the most expensive ways to reach customers, but because of the intensity of the salesperson's involvement with the buyer's situation, it can be the most appropriate method of marketing a product.

One of the keys to successful personal selling is the sales incentive scheme. At Electronic Systems Perspectives of Minneapolis, about 20 percent of the compensation package for new hires is based on personal-selling activity. The $2 million executive search firm tracks and rewards three basic activities: dally calls to potential job candidates, company visits, and "balls in the air," or contacts that could lead to sales. Meeting monthly goals earns a bonus of $400 a month. Averaging 30 calls a day is worth an extra $100 bonus. "Balls in the air" can earn another $100 a month. CEO Bob Hildreth understands that this bonus scheme is a risk, but a calculated one. His reps bill about 66 percent above the industry average.[31]

Publicity   Publicity can be defined as "nonpersonal stimulation of demand for a product, service, or business unit by planting commercially significant news about it in a published medium or obtaining favorable presentation of it on radio, television, or stage that is not paid for by the sponsor." Although by definition publicity is free, many firms allocate significant budgets to **public relations**—the activities that create a favorable image in the mind of the public. These are reputation-building tactics that, if successful, can be a source of SCA. For example, many recent start-ups have emphasized their "all natural" products and image. These companies are selling an altruistic image.

Publicity has three distinctive attributes:

1. *High level of legitimacy.* Many people believe almost everything they read, especially when it comes from a previously credible source such as the local newspaper or television station. Sometimes the media report publicity releases as if they were the efforts of objective news reporting.
2. *Elements of surprise.* It catches buyers at a time when they are not expecting a sales pitch. Publicity is packaged as news, not sales communication. A buyer who may not be receptive to an advertisement or sales call may listen intently to communication that is perceived as news.
3. *Attractiveness of message.* Like advertising, publicity can be dramatic and attention-getting. The context within which it is presented can connote other favorable images in the minds of the customers.

Because the media are inundated with requests for publicity, it is not always easy for a firm to stand out from the others. A well-organized event coupled with a well-written press release is needed. Good organizational citizenship may be a good source of publicity: Participation in civic events and clubs, members associations, philanthropic activities, and well-regarded political causes are examples.

Sales Promotions   Sales promotions are designed to stimulate customer purchasing and dealer effectiveness. Examples include point-of-purchase displays, trade shows and exhibitions, promotional events, and other non-routine selling efforts. Sales promotions attempt to provide inducements for buyers—reduced prices for items through coupon promotions, volume discounts, or attractive financing terms. By effectively reducing the price, the seller increases the value to the buyer.

Sales promotions are attention-getters. They often have an urgent quality, offering a once-in-a-lifetime opportunity, communicating to the buyer that quick action is needed. This has a certain appeal to the economy-minded, low-income, non-brand-loyal shopper. If the buyer is price sensitive, sales promotion can be effective. One of the most important sales promotions for the new venture is the grand opening sale. This represents a one-of-a-kind opportunity for the firm—to be followed by anniversary sales. For retail and service businesses, remote broadcasts by local media are popular. Introductory price discounts can attract customers to your location. Business can be generated by offering coupons or discounts for future dates.

Other sales promotions are event-based. Mother's Day, Father's Day, and Christmas are examples of events created or exploited by marketers' promotional campaigns. Some promotions are contests, like the magazine sweepstakes that offer $10 million for returning the direct-mail response cards. Sales promotions have become so ubiquitous that entrepreneurial opportunities exist for individuals who are particularly creative or experienced in these activities. Telemarketing firms, contest promoters and organizers, mailing list sellers, and event consulting firms have sprung up to serve these needs.

The persistent use of sales promotions can have negative effects on a business. The first is that the consumer will expect promotional discounts and not make purchases unless a discount is offered. This happened to auto manufacturers when they repeated factory-rebate sales promotions many times over the years. Car shoppers, expecting the sales promotion, would not buy until the rebate was offered. Manufacturers, seeing slow sales, then offered the rebates and reinforced customers' wait-and-see behaviors. The second negative of sales promotions is that they have a way of demeaning the image of the product or service. A sales promotion implies that without it people would not be interested in buying the product. To buyers who are concerned about brand image and status, frequently and carelessly used promotions raise doubts.

E-NOTES 6–4   MAJOR MARKETING ACTIVITIES
The four major marketing activities for an entrepreneur are:

- pricing decisions,
- product and service configurations,
- distribution strategies,
- promotional campaigns.

Sales Forecasting

Sales forecasting is the intersection of marketing research and marketing efforts. It is the first step in determining whether the new venture can and will be profitable. Thus, as we saw in Chapter 5, the sales forecast is the logical conclusion to the marketing analysis and the very first part of financial analysis.

Two broad techniques for forecasting sales are available data-based methods and judgmental methods. Examples of data-based methods are correlation analysis, multiple regression, time series analysis, and econometric models. Examples of judgmental models are sales force estimates, executive consensus, historical analogies, and "intention-to-buy" surveys. Most of these methods are appropriate for larger firms in well-established markets. The best guess at next year's sales is almost always last year's sales. But knowing this does not do the new venture much good.

A method that combines elements of both judgmental and data-based techniques, that is useful for new ventures, and that provides important insights into the financial consequences of the forecast is the **market-potential/sales-requirement (MP/SR) method**.[33] This method provides two different perspectives for the venture—likely sales and needed sales. The market-potential technique is a "top-down" method. It looks at the big-picture market. The sales-requirements technique is a "bottom-up" exercise. It starts with the firm's costs and expenses and builds up to the sales needed

FIGURE 6–4 Market-Potential/Sales-Requirement Approach

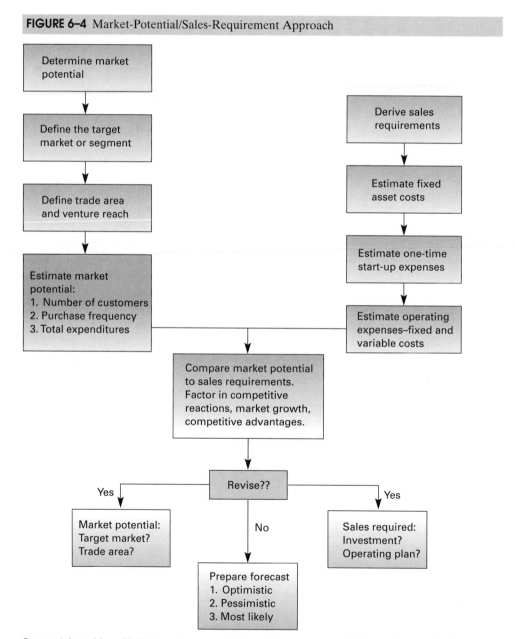

Source: Adapted from K. Marino, *Forecasting Sales and Planning Profits* (Chicago: Probus, 1984).

for profitability. These techniques can be conducted simultaneously. Figure 6–4 illustrates the two techniques diagrammatically. The emergency medical center (EMC) case in the appendix to this chapter provides a detailed example of how the MP/SR method works.

In the EMC case, the owner's first step was to determine the market potential for the emergency health-care facility. Trade association data and guidelines were used to help estimate the market targets and average incidents of usage. Census data provided the total population and number of households. The chamber of commerce was consulted to determine the direction of population trends. From this information the total number of patient visits per year was forecast. The second step in the process was to determine sales requirements and break-even for the EMC. Fixed-asset costs for the building and medical equipment were developed from quotes from local suppliers. One-time start-up expenses were estimated from the owner's previous experience. Estimates of operating expenses, both fixed and variable, were made from supplier data and from the owner's experience.

Since the essence of the sales-requirements approach is to develop a sales budget, the break-even number of patients was calculated. The third step was to forecast the likely market share. If the share were forecast above the break-even estimate of sales, the project was feasible. EMC estimated that a 25-percent market share was required. Determining whether this was realistic was a complex question incorporating analysis of competitive advantages and likely responses by competitors. At this point in the process the decision was made to raise the price per visit, thereby lowering the break-even point and the market share required.

Step 4 was to prepare the forecasts. Three forecasts were developed: an optimistic forecast showed the profitability with break-even at 6 months, a conservative but likely forecast had break-even within 10 months, and the pessimistic forecast delayed break-even market share until month 14.

Although the future is always uncertain, the forecasts did lead the owner to a hard look at the market and the firm's cost structure, and to a change in its pricing scheme. The forecasts provided a rational basis for negotiating credit and bank financing. And it gave the venture a set of performance standards that can be used to evaluate progress.

Summary

Marketing and entrepreneurship interface in a number of ways, with marketing being key to the success of any new venture. It is important for the new venture to take a total marketing approach to the customer and attempt to design a business system that ultimately can provide a high level of customer satisfaction.

Marketing research need not be extensive, sophisticated, or expensive, but it must determine what customer satisfaction means for the target market. Marketing research also provides other critical information about the target market that can be used to develop marketing strategies and activities. These activities—pricing, product/service decisions, promotion, and distribution—form the core of the venture's marketing effort. Because these activities are complex and the relationships between them ambiguous, the marketing strategy, organization, and resources can be a source of sustainable competitive advantage.

Sales forecasting is the bridge between the venture's marketing decisions and its financial decisions and outcomes. The sales forecast represents the "top line" of the venture's financial picture. Both a bottom-up and top-down approach to sales forecasting should be employed to produce a range of forecasts that indicate the prospects for venture success or failure.

Key Terms

- Customer satisfaction
- Marketing research
- Concept testing
- Product testing
- Market testing
- Secondary sources
- Diffusion process method
- Halo effect
- Marketing strategy
- Market segmentation
- Skimming the market
- Preemptive pricing
- Sherman Act

- Truth in Lending Act
- Robinson-Patman Act
- Clayton Act
- Product mix
- Product width
- Product depth
- Product consistency
- Service intensity
- Service extensiveness
- Public relations
- Market-potential/sales requirement (MP/SR)

Discussion Questions

1. In what two ways does marketing contribute to new venture success?
2. Discuss the marketing-entrepreneurship interface. What are the points of similarity, differences, and potential pitfalls?
3. What questions can marketing research help answer for the entrepreneur?
4. What are the steps in conducting market research?
5. Compare and contrast concept testing, product testing, and market testing.
6. Describe the diffusion process. How can the entrepreneur use this knowledge to design effective marketing campaigns?
7. What are the bases for market segmentation?
8. What are the pluses and minuses of the following pricing tactics?
   a. Skimming the market
   b. Exploiting the experience curve
   c. Meeting the market
   d. Achieving maximum penetration
   e. Establishing preemptive pricing
9. How do the product and service configurations influence the marketing strategy?
10. What are the key elements of promotional activities?
11. Describe the market-potential/sales-requirement forecasting method. What are its benefits and costs?

Exercises

1. Develop a list of questions that you would like answered regarding the marketing of your product or service described in your business plan. Prioritize the questions from "required to know" to "would be nice to know." Using the six-step process described in the chapter, conduct market research to answer these questions. Start with the highest-priority and work towards the lowest-priority question. If you run out of resources (time, money, cooperation), you may stop.

2. Develop the marketing section for your business plan. Discuss customer orientation, marketing strategy, and

tactical decisions such as price, product/services offered, distribution, and promotion.

3. Develop sales forecasts for your business plan. Develop three scenarios: pessimistic, optimistic, and most likely. What level of sales is required for break-even? Review your marketing strategy for consistency with the sales forecast.

A Serving of Aura, Well Done

In 1992, 29-year-old Tom Baron laughed when one of Pittsburgh's weekly newspapers named the fast-food chain Chi Chi's as the best Mexican restaurant in town. He couldn't resist calling his high school buddy Juno Yoon in Colorado to share a chuckle over the story. "That's pathetic," agreed Yoon. "We can do that."

Neither Baron nor Yoon had ever been to Mexico, and their joint business experience was a midtown Manhattan coffee shop that failed after eight months. But that didn't stop the two of them from raising $90,000 from family, charge cards, and bank loans to open Pittsburgh's Mad Max Mexican restaurant, or keep them from building a mini-empire of seven restaurants which has posted $6.8 million in sales after just 3 years of business.

Although technically they are in the food business, Baron and Yoon have made their success serving up image and attitude to customers who are tired of the cookie-cutter chains. Each of their restaurants serves an ethnic or exotic cuisine, and has a unique and funky decorative theme. "We're hoping to create an aura," explains Mr. Yoon. Mad Max's southwestern decor features wooden bar stools with carved cactuses and green lights inside the legs. The rock music blares, and the bar serves an assortment of microbrew beer not usually available in Pittsburgh. The first Mad Max (there are now two) opened at a prime location close to a university and major medical centers, so there's a steady stream of young image-conscious customers every night.

Baron and Yoon started out as real hands-on entrepreneurs. They helped tear down walls to build their first Mad Max, rolled burritos in the kitchen, and even drove the van to pick up their beer from a distributor four hours away. The hard work and long hours paid off when a student from the University of Pittsburgh brought her father and his business partner in for lunch one day. The two men, who comanaged a $4 million real-estate investment fund, liked the restaurant and its owners enough to pledge their assets as collateral for new financing, which led to the opening of the second Mad Max. Today Baron and Yoon's Big Burrito Inc. partnership has bank loans totaling $1.6 million, and hopes to secure financing of $5 to $7 million to enable future expansion.

The restaurant entrepreneurs toured trendy eateries in New York City before developing the concept for Soba, their newest pan-Asian restaurant, which features red-velvet couches along the walls, extra-large candles for lighting, and two-story windows. Their empire also includes the Caribbean-style Kaya, the eclectic Vertigo (where the menus are covered in fur), and the campy Mr. Jones, which specializes in home-cooked meatloaf and mashed potatoes.

Baron and Yoon are hands-on managers, too. They report that some of their best ideas come from informal market research over drinks with customers. They continue to read every customer comment card, and sometimes pick up the phone to personally respond to a complaint. They're still actively involved in planning the decor and advertising for their restaurants, and work to fine tune any concept that isn't working. When weeknight business at the Mr. Jones restaurant lagged, they revamped the menu, added kids' meals, and distributed discount coupons to local video, book, and appliance stores.

While all of Baron and Yoon's restaurants are currently making money, and attract long lines of customers every night, they're still aware that they're riding the crest of a risky business. "People wonder, 'Is the next (restaurant) going to fail and take down the whole house of cards?' " says Mark Riley, Big Burrito's controller. Start-up restaurants often experience high-volume sales and rapid expansion, but sometimes end up with no profits. Three out of ten new restaurants close in the first two years, and according to the Pennsylvania Restaurant Association, half of those who survive don't make it past three years.

But these unlikely restauranteurs appear to have beaten the statistics with their copy-what's-hot-in-New-York approach. Big Burrito, Inc. hopes to expand to both Philadelphia and Columbus, Ohio in the near future, and may even make an initial public offering of stock soon.

CASE QUESTIONS

1. What entry wedge (Chapter 4) are these entrepreneurs using?
2. What marketing strategies are used in this case?
   - segmentation
   - pricing
   - promotion
   - product
   - location

3. What strengths and weaknesses do you see in this strategy?
4. Would you invest in this business's expansion? Why or why not?

Adapted from Emily Nelson, "Two Neophytes Bring a Taste of New York to Hungry Pittsburgh," *Wall Street Journal*, February 18, 1997, A1, A10.

Notes

1. Quoted in *Fortune*, January 25, 1993.
2. W. Davidow, "Turning Devices into Products," in *Customer Driven Marketing*, ed. R. Smilor (Lexington, MA: Lexington Books, 1989), xiii–xxi.
3. G. Hills and R. LaForge, "Research at the Marketing Interface to Advance Entrepreneurship Theory," *Entrepreneurship: Theory and Practice* 16 (1992): 33–59.
4. The pitfalls are those described by T. Levitt, "Marketing Myopia," *Harvard Business Review*, 1960.
5. G. Hills and R. LaForge, "Marketing and Entrepreneurship: The State of the Art," in *The State of the Art of Entrepreneurship*, eds. D. Sexton and J. Kasarda (Boston: PWS-Kent, 1992), 164–190.
6. There are many fine marketing text-

books that provide detailed descriptions and models of much of what we will attempt to cover in this single chapter. Among the best for additional readings are: E. J. McCarthy and W. Perreault, Jr., *Basic Marketing*, 9th ed. (Homewood, IL: Irwin, 1987); K. Cravens, D. R. Hills, and C. Woodruff, *Marketing Management* (Homewood, IL: Irwin, 1986); P. Kotler, *Principles of Marketing* (Englewood Cliffs, NJ: Prentice Hall, 1980).

7. R. Peterson, "Small Business Adoption of the Marketing Concept versus Other Business Strategies, *Journal of Small Business Management* 27 (1989): 38–46.

8. B. Marsh, "Brewery Learns Expensive Lesson: Know Thy Market," *Wall Street Journal*, December 28, 1992, B2.

9. W. Zikmund, *Business Research Methods*, 3rd ed. (Hinsdale, IL: The Dryden Press, 1991). Other excellent resources include: P. Green, D. Tull, and G. Albaum, *Research for Marketing Decisions*, 5th ed. (Englewood Cliffs, NJ: Prentice Hall, 1988); A. Parasuraman, *Marketing Research* (Boston: Addison-Wesley, 1986).

10. However, there is evidence that entrepreneurs shy away from conducting detailed marketing research and that many do not have a detailed marketing plan. See D. Andrus, D. Norvell, P. McIntyre, and L. Milner, "Market Planning," *Inc. 500 Companies*, 163–171; reprinted in *Research at the Marketing/Entrepreneurship Interface*, ed. G. Hills (Chicago: University of Illinois at Chicago, 1987); D. Spitzer, G. Hills, and P. Alpar, "Marketing Planning and Research among High Technology Entrepreneurs," in *Research at the Marketing/Entrepreneurship Interface*, ed. G. Hills, R. LaForge, and B. Parker (Chicago: University of Illinois at Chicago, 1989), 411–422.

11. S. McDaniel and A. Parasuranam, "Practical Guidelines for Small Business Marketing Research," *Journal of Small Business Management* 24 (1986): 1–8.

12. One of the best guides is G. Breen and A. B. Blankenship, *Do-It-Yourself Marketing Research*, 2nd ed. (New York: McGraw-Hill, 1982). It covers almost every marketing research problem and offers practical advice on how to collect and analyze information. Especially appealing are the examples of surveys, telephone scripts, and cover letters for urging participant response. In addition, most marketing textbooks have some guidelines and describe techniques for marketing research. However, in the vast majority of cases, these guidelines and techniques are appropriate for large firms with established products.

13. Blankenship, 1982.

14. J. Pope, *Practical Market Research* (AMACOM: New York, 1981).

15. S. Greco, "First-Class Export Help," *Inc.*, October 30, 1993.

16. E. Rogers, *Diffusion of Innovations* (New York: Free Press, 1983).

17. Hills and LaForge, 1992.

18. R. Gibson, "Location, Luck, Service Can Make a Store Top Star," *Wall Street Journal*, February 1, 1993, B1.

19. Gibson, 1993.

20. R. Peterson, "Small Business Usage of Target Marketing," *Journal of Small Business Management*, October 1991, 79–85.

21. The following relies on R. Lindberg and T. Cohn, *The Marketing Book for Growing Companies that Want to Excel* (New York: Van Nostrand, 1986).

22. "Signaling" is discussed in more detail in M. Porter, *Competitive Analysis* (New York: Free Press, 1980).

23. The last two definitions are taken from *Marketing Definitions: A Glossary of Marketing Terms* (Chicago: American Marketing Association, 1960).

24. *Marketing Definitions*, 1960.

25. This presentation follows P. Kotler, *Marketing Management: Analysis, Planning, Implementation and Control*, 6th ed. (Englewood Cliffs, NJ: Prentice Hall, 1991).

26. K. Strassel, "Unknown novelist wins a following through website," *Wall Street Journal*, February 25, 1997, A9.

27. D. Kennedy, "Who's On-Line," *Inc. Technology*, March 18, 1997, 34–39.

28. *Marketing Definitions*, 1960.

29. See the following references for a more detailed discussion: G. Churchill, Jr., N. Ford, and O. Walker, *Sales Force Management*, 4th ed. (Homewood, IL: Irwin, 1993); W. Stanton, R. Buskirk, and R. Spiro, *Management of a Sales Force*, 8th ed. (Homewood, IL: Irwin, 1991).

30. This follows Kotler, 1991.

31. S. Greco, "Bonuses for the Right Moves," *Inc.*, October 1993.

32. *Marketing Definitions*, 1960.

33. K. Marino, *Forecasting Sales and Planning Profits* (Chicago: Probus, 1984).

Case Study: EMC Site Expansion

The Emergency Medical Center was founded by Dr. Anthony Petrillo as a free-standing emergency center (FEC). The FEC concept, which was relatively new at the time, is a cross between a physician's office and a hospital emergency room. The typical FEC offers extended hours (8:00 am to 11:00 pm), has lab and x-ray facilities, and will treat any non-life-threatening trauma or medical problem on a no-appointment basis.

The EMC opened in 1982 and grew rapidly its first year. When Dr. Petrillo was informed that a good location in another section of the same city had become available, he considered opening a second office. From a study of traffic patterns and population density in the area, proximity to area hospitals, and the sales experience in EMC #1, sales forecasts for EMC #2 were prepared. After leasehold improvements, equipment costs, and operating expenses were estimated, the decision was made to open EMC #2.

The facility was opened with a fanfare of advertising and press releases. Sales immediately exceeded the first month's forecast. After several months of continued growth, sales (that is, patient visits) leveled off at a point below break-even. Forecasted growth did not occur, and cumulative operating losses were mounting. Remedial action, in the form of intensified media advertising, was taken. A personal selling program directed at business establishments was started in an effort to treat more work-related injuries. Neither effort stimulated the necessary growth. Less than one year after opening, EMC #2 was determined to be a failure, and operations were consolidated with the original and still successful EMC #1.

Nonetheless, multiple sites offered important economic advantages in advertising, supply ordering, and management. Consequently, Dr. Petrillo continued to search out feasible locations for a second EMC facility.

A real estate developer contacted Dr. Petrillo concerning a site being developed in a small town about 22 miles outside the headquarters city of EMC. The site was at the intersection of an interstate and a state highway and offered excellent visibility. The town had one general hospital, a student health service on the campus of a university, and about 18 private physicians' offices. The developer and several of his financial backers felt that the growth of the community had created the need for addi-

EXHIBIT 1 Population Projections Based On Various Growth Rates		
Annual Growth = 1% *(pessimistic)*	*Annual Growth = 2.5%* *(likely)*	*Annual Growth = 4%* *(optimistic)*
1980 27,531	27,531	27,531
1981 27,806	28,219	28,632
1982 28,084	28,925	29,778
1983 28,365	29,648	30,969
1984 28,649	30,389	32,207
1985 28,935	31,149	33,496
1986 29,225	31,928	34,835
1987 29,517	32,726	36,229

tional medical facilities. They proposed the construction of a single-story building on the site and offered to finish a 2,000-square-foot section to Dr. Petrillo's specifications. A three-year lease with renewal options at an annual rental of $7.50 per square foot was available. Dr. Petrillo required a sales forecast for the venture in order to make a decision regarding the expansion and, if the decision was positive, to negotiate with a bank and an equipment leasing firm.

STEP 1: DETERMINING MARKET POTENTIAL

Target Market. The market for ambulatory health care includes the entire population. All people are subject to both minor injuries such as cuts, sprains, or fractures, and to minor illnesses such as colds and flu.

Consultants to the industry and the National Association of Free-Standing Emergency Centers (NAFEC), the industry trade association, focus on a more narrowly defined target market. They report that the primary targets for EMC services are families with young children, working women, and individuals with no regular physician. While these refinements will be of value in designing and placing advertising messages, it is best to consider the total population as the target market for feasibility purposes.

Trade Area. The city is a small community. The proposed site can be reached in 10 to 12 minutes driving time from anywhere within the city limits. The site is on the opposite side of town from the general hospital. Virtually none of the population would have to drive past a competitor to reach the EMC site. Hence, the trade area is defined as the entire city.

Market Potential. The 1980 census of population reports that the city and immediate residential areas were the homes of 27,531 people. The residents make up 8,924 households. The town has enjoyed substantial growth over the decade from 1970 to 1980. The number of housing units grew 55 percent over the decade. This is a positive sign, in that the people relocating to the area are less likely to have established physician relationships. Based on discussions with city officials and members of the Chamber of Commerce, growth is believed to have continued, but at a slower rate, during the 1980s.

In terms of market potential, NAFEC estimates that on the average, individuals experience between one and two incidents of minor trauma or illness per year. Based on assumed rates on population growth, estimates of total market potential in terms of patient visits can be developed.

EXHIBIT 2 Logan Total Patient Visits Based on Growth and Annual Incident Assumptions (1984)			
Population Growth	*Average Visits per Person-Year*		
	1	*1.5*	*2.0*
1.0% (pessimistic)	28,649	42,973	57,298
2.5% (likely)	30,389	45,584	60,778
4.0% (optimistic)	32,207	48,310	64,414

Total patient visits for 1984 are estimated to be somewhere between 28,649 and 64,414. This is a rather broad interval, perhaps too broad to be of use. The middle column of Exhibit 1 represents a more reasonable interval. Based on an average incident rate of 1.5 per person-year, total market potential for the area would be estimated at 43,000 to 48,000 patient visits per year (Exhibit 2).

STEP 2: DERIVING SALES REQUIREMENTS

Fixed-Asset Requirements.   Fixed assets required for the site are entirely equipment costs. Leasehold improvements such as plumbing modifications and remodeling will be avoided due to the developer's new construction. The required equipment includes both medical equipment and standard office furniture and equipment.

Local medical supply and office supply dealers were the source of price estimates presented in Exhibits 3 and 4. These dealers are familiar with the used equipment markets in the area. Price estimates reflect a mix of new and used equipment. Total fixed asset requirements are estimated at $64,500.

Deriving Sales Budgets.   The essence of the sales requirements approach is to develop a sales budget necessary to support the business. The break-even sales budget is easily calculated from Exhibit 5-6. Estimated monthly fixed operating expenses are $26,350. The average patient charge at the original EMC is $37.00. Assuming the charge would average the same amount at the new facility, each patient visit will contribute $31.63 to these expenses ($37.00 minus $5.37 variable expenses). Therefore, a total of 833 patient visits per month will be required to break even ($26,350/$31.63). The break-even point is graphically displayed in Exhibit 7.

The break-even computation ignores financing costs. Regardless of the sources of capital used, a rate of return must be earned. If Dr. Petrillo personally supplies all the capital, he will require a rate of return. If in fact the required capital is borrowed

---

EXHIBIT 3   Medical Equipment Requirements for Proposed EMC Facility

Medical Equipment ($51,000)

Laboratory ($6,000)	*X-ray ($30,000)*	*General ($15,000)*
Refrigerator	X-ray system	Trauma stretchers
Microscope	Processor	I.V. stands
Blood gas analyzer	Float table	EKG
Autoclave	Bucky table	Oxygen
Stain tray		Suction unit
Urinometer		Suture sets
Centrifuge		Ambu bag
Microcrit reader		Wheelchair
Incubator		Crash cart
		Head lamp
		Surgical table
		Cast cutter
		Defibrillator
		Woods lamp
		Laryngoscope

EXHIBIT 4 Office and Miscellaneous Furniture and Equipment Requirements for Proposed EMC Facility		
Office and Miscellaneous ($13,500)		
Office Equipment ($3,500)	*Exterior Signs ($6,000)*	*Miscellaneous Furniture ($4,000)*
Desks/chairs	Free-standing illuminated sign	Breakroom furniture
File cabinets	Building-mounted signs	Microwave/compact refrigerator
Typewriter		Waiting room furniture
Calculators		Window treatments/fixtures
Desktop copier		

from a commercial bank or an equipment leasing firm, the facility must generate revenues sufficient to cover interest expenses. The required capital investment includes medical equipment ($51,000—Exhibit 3); office equipment ($13,500—Exhibit 4) and nonrecurring start-up expenses ($17,729—Exhibit 5). In addition to these capital requirements, operating expenses in the early months will exceed revenue. If we establish, as a reserve, three months of operating expenses, approximately $80,000 in additional capital will be required. Total start-up capital is, therefore, estimated at $162,229. At a cost of capital of 18 percent, the facility will have to generate an additional $29,201 per year or $2,433 per month to cover its capital costs.

Break-even patient visits have been estimated at 833 patients per month. The sales budget to break even and cover anticipated capital costs would require 910 patients per month ($26,350 + $2,333)/$31.63).

STEP 3: JUDGING LIKELY MARKET SHARE

A comparison of the results of Steps 1 and 2 indicates that of an estimated 43,000 to 48,000 annual patient visits in the trade area, EMC must capture a 23 to 25 percent market share to break even and cover its cost of capital. This share represents substantial market penetration. The question facing Dr. Petrillo is, how likely is it that EMC could achieve such a market share? This is, of course, a complicated question. In order to formulate an answer, judgments regarding patient reactions and competitive reactions must be made.

EXHIBIT 5 Nonrecurring Start-Up Expenses	
Direct mail advertising (preopening)	$2,300
Legal/accounting	300
Rent/utilities deposits	4,226
Prepaid malpractice insurance	3,100
Housekeeping/security services	500
Initial medical supplies inventory	3,803
Nonphysician salaries (preopening)	1,500
Sundry	2,000
	$17,729

EXHIBIT 6 Estimated Monthly Operating Expenses for Proposed EMC Facility

Fixed Expenses

Advertising	$2,000
Rent/utilities[a]	1,500
Legal/accounting	200
Manager salary	1,600
Nonphysician salaries	8,050[b]
Physician salaries	10,000
Postage	200
Security/housekeeping	250
Telephone	250
Depreciation[c]	1,075
Sundry	1,225
Total Fixed Expenses	$26,350

Variable Expenses

Malpractice Insurance	$ .70 per patient
Supplies[d]	4.67 per patient
Total Variable Expense Per Patient	$5.37

[a]$1,250/month rent + $250/month average utility expenses.
[b]Estimated at 115 percent of salaries to cover FUTA, FICA, workmens' compensation, and state unemployment.
[c]Fixed assets of $64,000, straight line, 5-year life (60 months).
[d]Estimated from experience at EMC #1.

EXHIBIT 7 Break-Even Analysis for EMC Facility at Logan

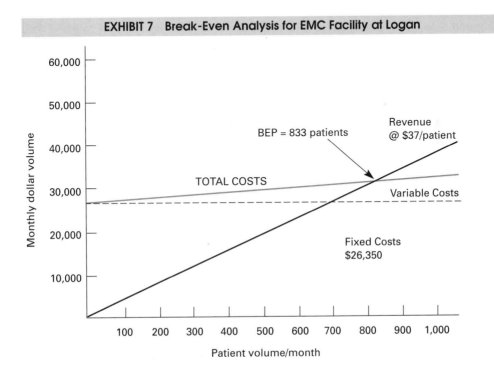

EMC Competitive Advantages.   EMC offers convenient service without the usual appointment necessary for a doctor's office, or the usual wait at a hospital emergency department. Due to lower overhead expenses, EMC is less expensive than a hospital on virtually all procedures. The combined advantages of economy and convenience have contributed to a favorable reception in the original EMC trade area and in other cities around the country where EMC-type facilities have been opened.

Competition.   The trade area is served by a general hospital with an emergency department and 18 physicians' offices. Several of the physicians' practice specialties, such as obstetrics, are not considered direct competitors of EMC. Nonetheless, 11 of the physicians either are general practitioners or practice family medicine. The EMC sales forecast will be affected by the behavior of these competitors. Faced with the entry of EMC into the market, how are these competitors likely to react?

In rapidly growing markets, the entry of a new competitor does not usually evoke a strong competitive response. The success of the new entrant is less a function of taking market share from existing competitors than it is of meeting a growing demand. Yet only under optimistic growth projections is it conceivable that EMC could prosper serving only new residents in the proposed site. EMC must attract patients from existing medical facilities. Physicians in private practice with established patient relationships are less likely to be injured by the entrance of EMC. However, because they generally view advertising and aggressive promotion allies as inappropriate, their likely response will be to "bad-mouth" EMC and raise questions regarding the quality of care offered. The hospital, as an institution with resources, and with the most to lose if EMC should enter, is expected to react more strongly. Hospitals have recently adopted advertising programs, modified fee schedules for minor emergencies, and changed staffing and triage activities to reduce waiting time in emergency departments. In short, the hospital, if forced, has the capabilities to negate EMC's competitive advantages.

In summary, EMC possesses some very real competitive advantages over traditional medical care providers. However, the hospital may react strongly to EMC's entrance into the market. Faced with high fixed costs of its own, the hospital administrators will be forced to do something if EMC approaches a 25-percent market share. Dr. Petrillo feels the operating plan of the facility must be changed in order to lower the break-even market share. A review of the estimated operating expenses indicates that expenses can't be reduced. Based on the historical costs incurred at EMC #1, Dr. Petrillo feels these estimates are accurate, and to expect lower expenses is unrealistic. This focuses attention on the fee structure. By raising the fees on certain routine procedures and lab tests, the revenue per patient visit can be raised to $41 from $37. This will lower the break-even market share to about 20 percent. This is considered an achievable level of penetration.

STEP 4: PREPARING THE FORECASTS

Due to the uncertainty surrounding the new facility, Dr. Petrillo and the EMC staff prepared three separate sales forecasts based on different assumptions of growth in the average number of patients treated per day. An optimistic forecast assumed that the break-even number of patients per day would be reached in the sixth month of op-

EXHIBIT 8   Emergency Medical Center Sales and Cash Flow Forecast Optimistic Case: Break-Even at Month 6

	Month 1	Month 2	Month 3	Month 4	Month 5	Month 6
Average patients/day	5	10	15	19	23	27
Revenue ($41/pt visit)	6,150	12,300	18,450	23,370	28,290	33,210
Cash received[a]	3,998	9,840	15,683	20,726	5,399	30,074
Cash expenses[b]	26,081	16,886	27,692	28,335	28,980	29,625
Cash gain (loss)	(22,083)	(17,046)	(12,009)	(7,609)	(3,581)	449
Cumulative cash position	(22,083)	(39,129)	(51,138)	(62,328)	(62,328)	(61,878)

	Month 7	Month 8	Month 9	Month 10	Month 11	Month 12
Average patients/day	30	33	35	37	38	39
Revenue ($41/pt visit)	36,900	40,590	43,050	45,510	46,740	47,970
Cash received	33,948	37,453	40,159	42,497	44,034	45,203
Cash expenses	30,108	30,591	30,913	31,236	31,397	31,558
Cash gain (loss)	3,840	6,862	9,245	11,261	12,637	13,645
Cumulative cash position	(58,038)	(51,176)	(41,931)	(30,670)	(18,033)	(4,388)

[a]Estimated as: 65% revenue received on 0–31 days
　　　　　　 35% revenue received in 31–61 days
　　　　　　 5% allowance for bad debts and adjustment
[b]Cash expenses = (Fixed expenses − Depreciation + $6.47 (Patient visits))
　　　　　　 = 25,275 + 5.37 per patient

eration. A pessimistic forecast assumed it would take 14 months to reach break-even patient flow, and a conservative but likely forecast assumed month 10 to be the break-even month.

Exhibit 8 is the sales forecast for the optimistic case. Once sales revenue is estimated, it is a fairly straightforward task to project the estimated cash flows. Similar forecasts were prepared for the pessimistic and likely break-even cases. By adding interest expenses into fixed costs, the same series of forecasts could be developed reflecting the costs of capital performance level as opposed to the break-even performance level. Having gone through this forecasting effort, Dr. Petrillo commented:

> The forecasting activity has provided us with a couple of advantages. First, it forced us to look hard at the market, the competition, and our costs structure. It also forced us to modify our fee schedule in light of those conditions. Second, it gave us a rational basis for negotiating a line of credit with our bankers. They can see where the money is to go, how much we will need, and at what rate we will be able to pay the line down. Finally, the forecasts set some standards by which we can evaluate our progress. If we're behind our forecast come month 4 or 5, I know I'll have to get our credit line raised, and intensify our promotion efforts. It also gives my managers some targets to shoot for regarding expenses. ■

This case was written by Kenneth E. Marino for his book, *Forecasting Sales and Planning Profits* (Chicago: Probus, 1984). It is reprinted here with the generous permission of its author.

Foundations of New Venture Finance

> *Anything for a friend, for a fee.*
> —FRED ALLEN, 1940S RADIO PERSONALITY

Learning Objectives

After reading this chapter you will understand:

- How to determine the amount of *capital* a new venture will need.

- The different types of *financing* available to the entrepreneur.

- The different elements involved in *cash and working capital management.*

- The pros and cons of different forms of financing—*debt versus equity.*

■ The major concerns of bankers and *how to approach them for a loan*.

■ The different methods for *valuing* a new venture.

As the quotation that opens this chapter indicates, it is now time to talk about money. New venture financing is about how much money the entrepreneur will need to start the business. However, it is more than that. It is also about creating value and wealth, allocating that value among the investors and founders, and determining financial risk for the business. This chapter and the next will explore and elaborate these matters.

The quotation has additional meaning for the financing of new businesses. It means that the parties to a transaction, especially an investment, should not take unfair advantage of each other; there should be consideration (a fee) for rights and privileges granted. Also, no matter how close a personal relationship the investors and founders have with each other, personal relationships should take a backseat to the overriding first priority—the successful launch of the new venture. The final inference to be drawn from the quotation is that money is important, and this importance must never be minimized. People can and will talk about their devotion to the business, their concern for the products and customers, their involvement with the "cause." All of these may be true, and they are valid intrinsic motivations. But dismissing the importance of money and the creation and the subsequent protection of wealth is naive and dangerous. People are concerned with financial issues, and some people care passionately about money. The entrepreneur may be one of these passionate people, and there are good reasons to believe that he or she is not alone.

Financing is one of the major hurdles that entrepreneurs must overcome. A Dun and Bradstreet survey reported that financial troubles (e.g., excessive debt and operating expenses, insufficient working capital) were responsible for 38.4 percent of business failures. Add in an additional 7.1 percent for inexperience (including financial inexperience), and it is clear that almost half of all ventures fail because of poor financial management.[1]

We begin the chapter by discussing the nature of financial resources. Next we turn to the crucial issue of determining how much money the new venture will need for a launch. The initial financing requirement will depend greatly on the enterprise's cash and working capital management. We summarize the elements of cash and working capital management, then return to the EMC case from Appendix 6 as an example.

The chapter continues with a discussion of the sources and types of debt and equity financing. It concludes by presenting a number of models for valuing new firms. The valuation process is crucial to both investors and entrepreneurs as a vehicle for determining how the profits of the firm will be allocated. It sets the stage for financial negotiation and deal structures.

Just one word of caution before beginning our financial analysis. Modern financial theory was developed in an attempt to understand the performance of the stock market, specifically the New York Stock Exchange. Many of the concepts and tools taught as the foundations of financial theory are best employed when analyzing the types of events and companies represented on major stock, bond, commodities, currency, options, and futures exchanges. Because the underlying theory and techniques were not built with the entrepreneur in mind, applying them to new venture financing is questionable. The entrepreneur and the individuals and firms who invest in new ventures need to be aware that applying financial theory developed for stocks and bonds may provide incorrect signals for firm value and risk.[2]

Determining Financial Needs

How much money does the entrepreneur need? One of the most important and difficult tasks for the start-up entrepreneur is to determine how much money is needed to start the business. It is important because if the entrepreneur raises too little money by underestimating the business's needs, the firm will be **undercapitalized**. Undercapitalized businesses may run out of cash, borrowing capacity, and the ability to raise additional equity just when a new infusion of funds could get the firm over some difficulty. The result is that the firm will go out of business at that point. It is often said that for new firms "cash is king," because when the entrepreneur runs out of cash, the king is dead, and the business is often lost. Street Stories 7–1 illustrates how difficult it can be for an undercapitalized entrepreneur to find enough cash to keep her business alive.

Although it may not seem possible to many entrepreneurs, being **overcapitalized** is a significant danger as well. An overcapitalized firm has raised too much money and has excessive cash. Having too much cash sends the wrong signals to all the new venture's stakeholders. For example, it may signal to employees that the firm is doing better than it is, causing them to press for wage and benefit increases. Customers may take longer to pay if they think the new venture has plenty of cash on hand. Suppliers could demand payment quicker using the same logic. If the cash is spent on unnecessary perquisites or office upgrades, investors will be concerned that the firm does not respect money and lacks a frugal attitude. Also, excess cash earns no or very low returns. This diminishes the total return to investors.

There must be a balance between raising too little money and not being prepared for a down cycle and raising too much. If the entrepreneurs have raised too much, then they have sold (or encumbered) too much of their business. Entrepreneurs who can resist the temptation to continue selling equity beyond the amount truly needed will be able to sell additional equity sometime down the road when it is both really needed and much more valuable. This is called **phased financing**, and we will discuss it in more detail in the next chapter.

WORKING CAPITAL AND CASH FLOW MANAGEMENT

The entrepreneur must focus on working capital and cash flow from the beginning of the financing process. Accounting profits do not pay the bills; only positive cash flow keeps the business solvent. It is estimated that over 60 percent of the average entrepreneur's total financing requirements are invested in working capital, 25 percent in accounts receivable alone.[3] Sufficient working capital is vital to the survival of the enterprise, and well-managed working capital and cash flow can significantly increase the profitability of the new venture.

Working Capital Concepts Working capital has two components. **Permanent working capital** is the amount needed to produce goods and services at the lowest point of demand.[4] Although it may change form over the course of the cash flow cycle

Clawing and Cutting Your Way to the Top

Sharon McCollick is ready to write her memoirs. "I've got a title," she says. "'Clawing Your Way to the Top Without Nails'." When McCollick says "clawing," she undoubtedly means the scratching at the doors of banks, venture capital firms, and other lenders she has had to do in order to secure financing for her now successful business.

McCollick makes business suits for women. Her suits are feminine with a unique power-look feeling reminiscent of fashions from the 1940s. Jackets that McCollick bought from thrift stores, and then re-cut and stitched to match her fashion sense, were in fact the precursors to the suits she now sells.

In 1992 McCollick left a $100,000-a-year marketing job with Intel Corp. to start her company in Bala Cynwyd, Pennsylvania. She wrote a business plan with the help of the Wharton Small Business Development Center, and cashed in $60,000 in Intel stock to get the business moving. She had orders for $50,000 of suits from women lawyers and accountants before she even started.

That's when she started clawing. She went to her local bank for additional financing, but the loan officer told her that without "nails"—in other words, collateral or some sort of track record—no bank would make her a loan. Unable to raise cash, McCollick finally found a manufacturer willing to produce her '92 fine of suits on credit. The garments sold well, but McCollick had to assign all her profits to pay interest to the manufacturer.

Her '93 season was almost identical. She sold a lot of suits, but had to pay 1% interest *per week* to the factoring company that provided the financing this time. Then McCollick managed to make a deal with a venture capital firm to finance her '94 season, but when that money fell through she had to pool her mother's nest egg, money borrowed from friends and her husband's salary as a computer consultant to meet her overhead. Once again her suits sold quickly, but McCollick missed mortgage and utility payments to keep her company afloat, and ending up owing the IRS $2,000.

Then the same bank loan officer who once turned her down contacted McCollick again. By this time the local bank had been taken over by the giant CoreStates Financial Corp., and armed with a new program for women borrowers from the Small Business Administration, the bank was actually looking for small businesses who wanted to borrow money. McCollick filed a loan application, only to be told the federal government doesn't lend money to people who owe the IRS. "I can't take no for an answer," McCollick told the bank loan officer. "You've got to do something to turn this around!"

Impressed by what she called McCollick's survival skills, the banker convinced the SBA to reconsider while the suit designer scraped together the money to pay the IRS. McCollick Enterprises Inc. finally raised about $250,000 in working capital, and was ready for its first New York fashion show, and the anticipation of its first million-dollar season.

Source: Adapted from Thomas Petzinger, Jr., "Sharon McCollick Got Mad and Tore Down a Bank's Barriers," *Wall Street Journal*, May 19, 1995, B1.

(for example, from inventory to receivables to cash), permanent working capital never leaves the business. As the firm grows and sales increase, the amount of permanent working capital increases as well. **Temporary working capital** is the amount needed to meet seasonal or cyclical demand. It is not a permanent part of the firm's financial structure. When these peak periods end, temporary working capital is returned to its source.

A firm that has too little permanent working capital runs the risk of losing business. If inventory levels are kept too low, stockouts occur and sales are lost. If the venture's accounts receivable policy is too restrictive, good customers who prefer to pay on credit may be turned away. If cash balances are too low, the venture runs the risk of not being able to procure supplies or pay its bills. This diminishes its ability to take advantage of short-term purchasing opportunities and damages its reputation.

An enterprise with too much working capital for a given level of sales is inefficient. Stocks and inventory levels will be much higher than necessary to fulfill customer orders. Receivables will represent too large a percentage of sales, and the venture will find it is providing inexpensive financing for its customers. Cash levels will be more than needed for transactions and precautionary uses. Each dollar invested in working capital must return at least the internal rate of return of the rest of the venture's investment to be "pulling its weight" in the financial structure.

The Cash Flow Cycle   The **cash flow cycle** and its importance to the profitability of the firm is illustrated in Figure 7–1.

The top portion of the figure shows the **production cycle** from material ordering to finished goods inventory. It shows, too, the cash cycle from payment for raw materials through the collection of receivables. The bottom half of Figure 7–1 illustrates the corresponding sources and uses of cash and the formula for calculating the length of the cash cycle.

Segment 1 represents the time period of the accounts payable for raw material. It is a source of cash financing. Here it is the time that materials are received until approximately half of the raw materials are used. Segment 2 represents the time period in which raw materials remain in inventory. This segment corresponds to the time when they enter raw materials inventory until they enter work-in-process (WIP) inventory.

Segment 3 represents the time interval the WIP goods are counted in inventory. Segment 4 represents the time goods spend in finished goods inventory, and segment 5 represents the time that goods that have been sold are in receivables.

Figure 7–1 gives the formulas for calculating each of these ratios. The figures used to calculate these ratios will be found on the pro forma balance sheet and income statement for the new venture, or on the actual financial statements for the existing business. The total length of the short-term cash cycle is given by the sum of 2 through 5 minus 1.

Figure 7–2 demonstrates the significance of these ratios. The top illustrates a typical cash flow cycle for a sample firm, and the bottom half depicts a "controlled" cash flow cycle with much of the slack and waste removed.[5]

The top half of Figure 7–2 indicates that the uncontrolled cash flow cycle is 120 days. This means that the firm, either through debt or equity, must finance every dollar of sales for 120 days. What does this mean in terms of firm profitability? If the

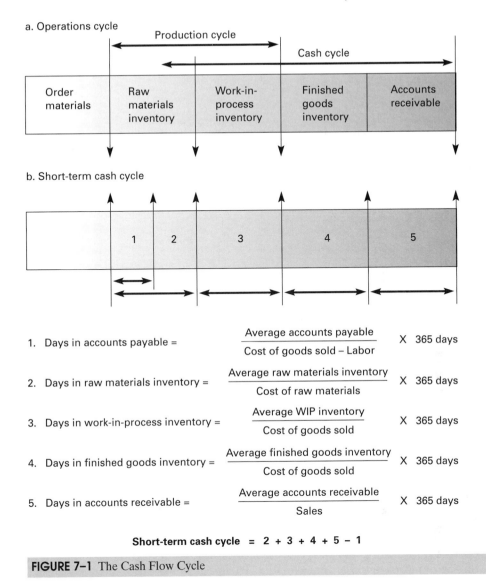

FIGURE 7–1 The Cash Flow Cycle

firm had $5 million in sales, before controlling the cash flow cycle, the net working capital required for 120 days of sales value would be approximately $1,643,836 [($5,000,000/365) × 120]. The bottom half of the figure shows a hypothetical "controlled" cash flow cycle. After control measures are introduced and the cash flow cycle is tightened, the required working capital is reduced to $616,438 [($5,000,000/365) × 45]. Where has the difference of over $1 million gone? Typically it goes to reduce debt or is invested in other assets that can increase sales. For example, Figure 7–2 shows a marked reduction in the time it takes to process WIP inventory (segment 3; 40 − 25 = 15, 15/45 = 37.5%). The reduction in working capital requirements could be used to retire the debt incurred to purchase the machine that made manufacturing so much

a. Hypothetical cash cycle before control

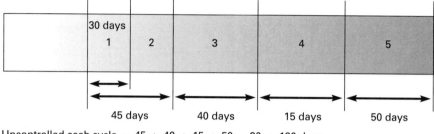

Uncontrolled cash cycle = 45 + 40 + 15 + 50 − 30 = 120 days

b. Hypothetical cash cycle after control

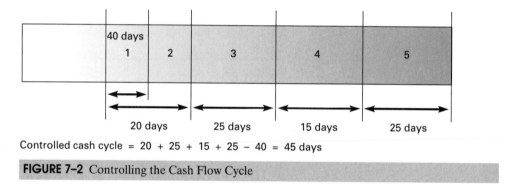

Controlled cash cycle = 20 + 25 + 15 + 25 − 40 = 45 days

FIGURE 7–2 Controlling the Cash Flow Cycle

more efficient. This illustrates one of the dramatic effects of tightly managing the venture's cash; investments can be made to pay for themselves very rapidly.

Another way of seeing the dramatic benefits of cash management is to imagine that the owner of this hypothetical company needs to raise $1 million from venture capitalists in order to expand the business. Venture capital often requires rates of return of between 30 and 50 percent. If the entrepreneur can raise the $1 million through improved cash management techniques, the firm has served between $300,000 and $500,000 per year in finance charges (dividends) paid to the venture capitalists. If the firm were netting 10 percent on sales of $5 million ($500,000), the cash control measures are the equivalent of increasing profitability between 60 percent and 100 percent.

Managing and Controlling the Cycle   Many excellent books detail the process of managing and controlling the cash flow cycle, so we will only summarize them briefly.[6] However, as the examples presented indicate, this is a subject that requires direct attention and tenacious control by top management.

Accounts payable.   The longer the average accounts payable for the firm, the shorter the cash flow cycle. Therefore, the entrepreneur should develop relationships with vendors that enable them to extend payments when needed. Accounts payable are part of the permanent working capital of the venture and should be managed, not reduced.

Raw materials inventory.   This is part of the permanent working capital of the firm, but look to keep it as low as possible. Just-in-time delivery systems, a good management information system, and accurate sales forecasting will help keep raw materials inventory down.

Work-in-process inventory.   The Japanese *kanban* system of tagging and monitoring all work in process will help. Also, the introduction of efficient operations, worker training and incentives, and capital investment are all possible investments.

Finished goods inventory.   Look to develop relationships with your buyers that enable you to deliver as soon as made. If your buyers can warehouse the goods, let them take delivery and thereby finance your finished goods inventory. Accurate sales forecasts and management information systems are vital.

Accounts receivable.   The key variables are payment terms, credit limits, and collection programs. Your customers should be encouraged to pay their bills on time and given incentives to pay them early if the discount does not hurt margins.

E-NOTES 7–1   FINANCING A NEW VENTURE

New business financial elements:

- Working Capital, including:
  - permanent working capital (to produce goods or services at lowest point of demand),
  - temporary working capital (to meet seasonal or cyclical demand);
- Cash Flow Cycle, including:
  - operations cycle,
  - production cycle,
  - cash cycle,
  - short-term cash cycle;
- Managing Capital and Cash, including:
  - accounts payable,
  - raw materials inventory,
  - work-in-process inventory,
  - finished goods inventory,
  - accounts receivable.

ACROSS THE VENTURE'S LIFE CYCLE

Will the financial needs of the business change as the business faces different challenges? Of course. Over the course of the venture's life, financing needs will change. Entrepreneurs must be able to recognize where their firm is in its life cycle and specify precisely the uses of these funds. By demonstrating to investors how the financing will further the venture's objectives, the entrepreneur significantly increases the probability of closing the deal.

Early-Stage Financing   There are two categories of early-stage financing: seed capital and start-up financing. **Seed capital** is the relatively small amount of money needed to prove that the concept is viable and to finance feasibility studies. Seed capital is not usually used to start the business, just to investigate its possibilities. **Start-up capital** is funding that actually gets the company organized and operational. It puts in place the basics of product development and the initial marketing effort. Start-up capital is invested in the business before there are any significant commercial sales; it is the financing required to achieve these sales. Start-up capital is also known as **first-stage financing**.

Expansion or Development Financing   There are three sequential categories of financing within the expansion stage. **Second-stage financing** is the initial working capital that supports the first commercial sales. It goes to support receivables, inventory, cash on hand, supplies, and expenses. At this point, the firm may not have achieved a positive cash flow. **Third-stage financing** is used to ramp up volumes to the break-even and positive-cash-flow levels. It is expansion financing. Throughout the third stage, the business is still private, a majority of the equity still in the hands of the founding top management team. **Fourth-stage financing**, sometimes known as mezzanine financing (because it is between the cheap balcony seats and the more expensive but desirable orchestra seats) is the bridge between the venture as a private firm and the prospect of its going public. Relatively few ventures are successful enough to make it to this stage. For a firm to be considered for this it must be attractive enough to lure professional investors and have the potential to be a public company (one traded on a stock exchange).

E-NOTES 7–2   LIFE CYCLE FINANCING

Early-stage financing:

- seed capital: to prove concept is viable;
- start-up capital: to make business operational.

Expansion or development financing:

- second-stage financing: to support first commercial sales;
- third-stage financing: to expand;
- fourth-stage financing: to make the leap from private company to public company.

START-UP FINANCING

Early-stage financing is a concern of most would-be entrepreneurs. How does the entrepreneur determine how much is needed to start the business? To answer this question, the entrepreneur must estimate how much will be needed for four types of uses: fixed assets, current assets, organizational costs, and cash flow requirements from continuing operations. No rule of thumb covers all business situations. Through experience, investigation, and estimation, the entrepreneurial team must make these calculations.

To illustrate start-up costs, we return to the EMC case found in Appendix 6. This case illustrates a sales-forecasting process for an emergency medical center (EMC). In addition to providing documentation and analysis for the sales forecast, the case also documents the venture's start-up costs. Appendix 7A of this chapter details the start-up cost calculations for EMC.

Sources of Financing

The initial financial objective of the entrepreneur is to obtain start-up capital at the least possible cost. Cost is measured in two ways. One is the return that will have to be paid to the investor for his or her commitment. The second is the transaction costs involved in securing, monitoring, and accounting for the investment. An investor may be satisfied with what appears to be a below-market return on investment, but if the cost of the transaction is significantly high, the entrepreneur may wish to consider an alternative source of financing.

The long-term sources of cash for the venture are debt and equity. In most cases equity financing is more expensive than debt financing. This is because pure debt has a fixed return over a period of time, while the potential gains to investors in equity financing are unlimited. Figure 7–3 illustrates how these two sources combine to build the liquidity level of the firm.

FIGURE 7–3 Permanent Sources of Venture Financing

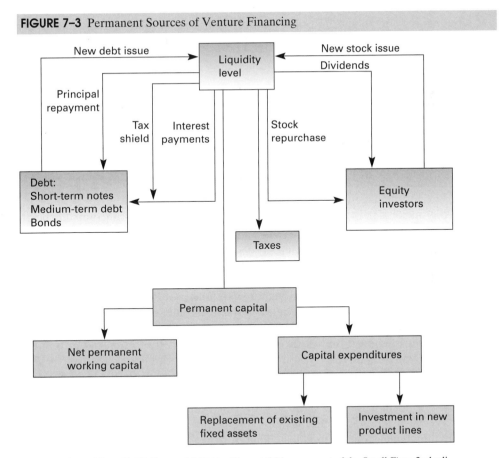

Source: Adapted from E. Walker and J. Petty, *Financial Management of the Small Firm*, 2nd edition, 144, Englewood Cliffs, NJ: Prentice-Hall, 1986.

The types and sources of financing available to the new venture depend on four factors:

1. The stage of business development.
2. The type of business and its potential for growth and profitability.
3. The type of asset being financed.
4. The specific condition of the financial environment within the economy.

The elements of the overall financial environment that should be considered are:

- Interest rates and their term structure.[7]
- The level and trend in the stock market.
- The health of various financial institutions, such as savings and loans, commercial banks, and international financial institutions.
- Level of confidence in the economy.
- Government monetary and fiscal policy.

The entrepreneur and the top management team need to be sensitive both to threats to successfully financing the venture (such as low consumer and producer confidence) and to special opportunities, such as government finance programs and subsidies.

EQUITY-BASED FINANCING

The liabilities and equity side of the balance sheet provides the general list of types of financing. On the balance sheet they are listed in ascending order of risk, and therefore cost, to the investor. We begin from the bottom of the balance sheet with equity capital and move up to the less risky and cheaper types of financing.

Inside Equity   **Equity** finance represents an ownership stake in the new venture. All businesses require equity. Initial equity most frequently comes from the founder and the top management team and from their friends and relatives. Founders traditionally make a personal equity investment commensurate with their financial level. They do this for a number of reasons: It is often the easiest money to obtain, it shows commitment to future outside investors, and it provides the right incentives for the business owners.

Family and friends are the natural next place to look for money. Take the case of Matthew Oristano, the CEO and major shareholder of People's Choice TV of Shelton Connecticut. This $25 million wireless-pay-tv company struggled for eight years to secure the financing it needed to make a big impact in the industry. So in the early days, family funds financed the future. Matthew offers this tip to other entrepreneurs employing family resources: "When you are dealing with family investors, it should be clearly defined which family members are actively involved in the business and which are involved only financially. To avoid confusion or misunderstandings, everything should be documented the same way any other financial relationship would be."[8]

At the beginning of the business, the risk is highest, and start-up equity carries with it the highest risk of total loss. Therefore, it also carries with it the highest returns if the business is successful later on. These initial investments are equity from the point of view of the firm, although the actual sums may have been borrowed. For example, an investor can borrow against the value of his home (and incur or increase the mortgage) to make an equity investment in the new venture. Equity from the owners, the top managers, friends, and relatives is called **inside equity** because it is generally believed that these investors will vote their stock in the best interests of the company "insiders."

Outside Equity   **Outside equity** comes from investors who have no personal relationship with the venture beyond their investment and their concern for its profitability and protection. Outside equity comes from three sources: private investors, venture capital, and public offerings.

Private investors.   **Private investors**, sometimes called "angels," are wealthy individuals interested in the high-risk/high-reward opportunities that new venture creation offers. A great deal of money is available from private investors, representing the largest single source of funds for new firms.[9] Wealthy investors exist in all communities and in all cities in the developed world. The best way to reach these people is through personal introduction by acquaintances or associates: lawyers, accountants, consultants, and others in the economic network of a community.

Wealthy investors will want to see the firm's business plan or offering memorandum. Obtaining expert legal counsel in this process is crucial. Many securities laws, both local (state) and federal, regulate the sale and distribution of stock.[10] Failure to comply with these laws and regulations may enable the investor to sue the entrepreneur for recovery of his or her investment if the company goes broke.

The main advantages of obtaining early financing from wealthy investors are its relative accessibility and the size of the investment pool. Also, these individuals may be in a position to lend their positive reputations to the venture to attract additional funds.

However, there are often disadvantages. Many wealthy people made their money in the professions or inherited it. They may lack the business expertise that would help the entrepreneur when advice is needed. Even when wealthy investors are businesspeople, they may have made their money in a different type of business or made it long ago when conditions were different.

A second disadvantage is the inability to invest more money sometime in the future (even rich people have limits). The most common range of investments from wealthy individuals is $10,000 to $500,000, with an average investment of about $50,000.[11] Although this may be enough in the early development stages of the firm, additional money will be needed later if the firm is successful. Additional sums may either be out of reach for the angel or represent too much risk in a single business for the wealthy investor.

A third problem concerns the relationship between the angel and the top management team. Private investors tend to be overprotective of their investment. They often call the entrepreneurs or complain when things are not going well. If the business is accessible and local, they may even personally visit, requiring extra time and creating headaches for the entrepreneur.[12]

Venture capital.   **Venture capital** is outside equity that comes from professionally managed pools of investor money. Instead of wealthy individuals making investments one at a time and on their own, they along with institutional investors pool their funds and hire professionals to make the investment and related decisions.

The venture capital industry has been long associated with new venture creation and has its own entrepreneurial history.[13] Also, like any industry, the factors that affect profitability within the industry are the power of the buyers (investors), the power of the suppliers (entrepreneurs who supply the deals), the threat of substitutes, the height of entry barriers, and rivalry between venture capital firms.[14] Also, macroenvironmental factors create both constraints and opportunities for these firms, just as they do for new ventures. These macro factors depend on the type of industry the venture capitalists specialize in. Because industry-specific knowledge is required for evaluating new-venture-financing proposals, venture capitalists tend to specialize in certain industries. For example, there are high-tech venture capitalists who prefer cutting-edge technological investments, distribution-type venture capitalists invest in ventures that provide logistical benefits, and restaurant specialists who look to invest in the next Domino's or McDonald's restaurant chain.

Thanks to strong returns in recent years, venture capital firms have raised record amounts of money, allowing them to make an increasing number of entrepreneurial investments. According to a Coopers & Lybrand study for the year 1996, venture capital firms invested an unprecedented $10.1 billion dollars in 2,136 small company finance deals, representing a 53 percent increase over the previous year. The average finance deal totaled $4.7 million. Most of the money was invested in communications (15.7%) and software (15.7%) firms, followed by health care (10.9%), electronics (7.1%), medical devices (7.0%), and biotechnology (6.4%) companies. Start-ups in California's Silicon Valley received the most venture capital funds, following by companies in Massachusetts, Texas, Colorado, and Florida.[15]

However, venture capital is risk capital. This means that the investors are aware of the high potential of receiving little or no return on their investment. To compensate the investors for this risk, venture capital looks for deals that can return at least 35 to 50 percent compounded over the life of the investment (typically a five-year planning horizon). To achieve such lofty return on investment goals, the business opportunity must be extremely attractive, with the potential for very strong growth, and the venture capitalist must be able to own a substantial portion of the firm.[16] However, venture capitalists are often able to bring additional money to the table when needed. And they can provide advice based on experience and important industry contacts for the firm. We will return to the subject of venture capital in the next chapter, when we discuss how investors evaluate proposals, structure the deal, and negotiate.

Public offerings. The ultimate source of outside equity and wealth creation is the public offering. When you own 100 percent of a company that earns $500,000 per year, you make a very good living. When you own 50 percent of a company that makes $500,000 per year, is publicly traded, and is valued at 25 times earnings (25 × $500,000 = $12.5 million × .50 = $6.25 million), you are a multimillionaire. Often, in order to go from well-off to rich, the founders of the venture must take their firm public. This type of financing creates significant wealth because it capitalizes earnings at a multiple (the price-earnings ratio). "Going public" is done through an investment vehicle known as the **initial public offering (IPO)** and with the aid of an investment banker.

The IPO enables a firm to raise a much larger amount of equity capital than was previously possible. It also enables the entrepreneur and the top management team,

---

Going Public: Pros and Cons

Although going public may appear to be an entrepreneur's dream, it has its costs and benefits.

ADVANTAGES OF GOING PUBLIC

For the business:

1. Cash for the company to expand.
2. Cash for the company for acquisitions or mergers.
3. Greater accessibility to long-term debt for the company.
4. Increased employee benefit plans and incentives with stock.
5. Increased public awareness of the company.

For entrepreneurs, top managers, and early investors:

1. Cash, enabling the entrepreneurs to diversify their personal portfolios.
2. The establishment of an ascertainable value of the company for estate purposes.
3. Equity available for executive incentives and compensation.
4. Personal satisfaction for the top managers.
5. Liquidity for the entrepreneurs.
6. Entrepreneurs can maintain effective control of the company.

Although there are clear advantages to going public, it can present some real obstacles. Several are detailed below.

DISADVANTAGES OF GOING PUBLIC

For the business:

1. Requirements to conform to standard accounting and tax practices.
2. Lack of operating confidentiality.
3. Lack of operating flexibility.
4. Increased accountability.
5. Demand for dividends from stockholders.
6. Initial cost of offering and ongoing regulatory costs.
7. Conflict between short-term and long-term goals.

For the entrepreneurs:

1. More stakeholders to please and coordinate.
2. Possible loss of control of the company in a takeover.
3. Increased visibility for job performance.

4. Increased accountability for earnings per share.

5. Restrictions on insider trading, conflicts of interest.

6. Focus on managing stock price.

7. Internal bickering and politics.

Sources: R. Saloman, "Second Thoughts on Going Public," *Harvard Business Review* 55 (September–October 1977): 126–131; S. Jones and B. Cohen, *The Emerging Business* (New York: Wiley, 1983).

as well as the earlier investors who still own shares of the firm, to sell some of their shares. This is an event that is often eagerly anticipated by founders and early investors, for it represents one of the most lucrative financial opportunities in a businessperson's career. It is estimated that the value of the firm increases by 30 percent at the completion of a public offering.[17] Appendix 7B offers a detailed look at the process of going public.

For many entrepreneurs and top managers of entrepreneurial companies, the process and event of going public mark the culmination of years of hard work, public recognition of success, and long-delayed financial rewards. However, there are disadvantages and real costs to going public. Entrepreneurs should consider all of the costs and benefits of going public; the pros and cons are detailed in Street Stories 7–2.

DEBT-BASED FINANCING

Debt is borrowed capital. It represents an agreement for repayment under a schedule at an interest rate. Both the repayment schedule and the interest rate may be fixed or variable or have both fixed and variable components. In most cases, debt costs the company less than equity. Interest rates on debt are historically less than rates of return on equity. Why would entrepreneurs ever seek anything but debt? Because debt often requires collateral and its repayment always requires discipline. Discipline is required to meet the regular interest and principal payments; otherwise, the company will be in default, putting the company in jeopardy of forced bankruptcy. If the loan is collateralized (has a specific physical asset encumbered as assurance of repayment of principal), default may cause the loss of that asset. Therefore, the entrepreneur often seeks higher-cost equity because the owner of shares has no legal right to the dividends of the company, and the equity holder is the owner of last resort. If the company is forced into bankruptcy or liquidated, the equity shareholders receive only the residual value of the firm after all other claims are settled.

Some entrepreneurs finance their businesses with equity instead of debt for a second reason: they often cannot get a loan. Banks and other lending institutions are conservators of their depositors' money and their shareholders' investments. In certain economic climates, they are extremely reluctant to lend money to risky ventures. In almost no circumstances are they in a position to lend money to start-ups. Thus, the entrepreneur is forced to raise equity capital in the initial forced to continue to raise equity even after passing the hurdles of the early stages. Because of the difficulty, new and small businesses have in procuring debt financing, various agencies and departments of the government offer special programs to help. One of the fastest growing and popular of these programs are the "micro lenders" that target women entrepreneurs and minority-owned firms.

E-NOTES 7–3   SOURCES OF START-UP FINANCING

Equity (ownership stake), including:

- inside equity: from founder, top management team, friends, family;
- outside equity;
- private investors;
- venture capital;
- public offerings;

Debt-based financing (borrowed capital):

- asset-based debt,
- cash-flow financing.

Micro loan Programs   Women and minority-owned businesses have had difficulties getting debt financing, partly because they start the wrong types of business and partly because of discrimination. Too often these small start-ups are in-service industries, have no collateral, have high failure rates, and contain no entry barriers to protect against competition. Yet the growth rates of start-ups by these individuals are high. For example, it is estimated that by the year 2000, 48 percent of all U.S. small businesses will be owned by women.

To address the gap between the need for debt financing and the availability of credit, the government has stepped in. In June 1992, the Small Business Administration announced a **Micro loan** program to help women and minorities get loans of up to $25,000 at market interest rates. This program's initial loan budget was $24 million. "I hope this program will give an opportunity to the small cottage industry; people who haven't had a chance before. There used to be a day when your friendly local banker would give you a small loan on your signature. That no longer occurs. This [program] restores some of that," said Patricia Saiki, SBA administrator.[18] Street Stories 7–3 profiles some of these Micro loan programs and their recipients.

The private sector is also trying to do more. Consider the case of the Earnings Resource Group, a $400,000 auditing firm owned and operated by Cynthia McGeever and Crisanne Buba. The firm is profitable, the owners are well educated, and both have been vice-presidents at major banks. When their Wayne, Pennsylvania, company needed expansion capital, they found their prestigious client list and 30-percent operating margins insufficient. "Some bankers didn't even give us a follow-up phone call," recalled Buba.

But Earnings Resource Group did eventually land a loan ($600,000) from Compass Rose Corporation, a financial services company dedicated to women's business. It is a division of a large insurance company, Capital Holding Corporation. Although the parent company expects Compass Rose to earn a 16-percent return on investment, the subsidiary is still intent on changing traditional lending criteria. "We feel our lending formula captures life experience, not just balance sheet equations," says President Rebecca Maddox.

In addition to the loan program, Compass Rose offers a Harvard-like MBA program for women entrepreneurs. At $1,100 for a week-long training course, the educa-

Micro Solutions for a Macro Problem

Government has once again provided the motivation for potentially thousands of new entrepreneurs. This time the push comes from the welfare reform bill signed by President Clinton in August 1996, which imposes a five-year limit on most welfare benefits and requires many beneficiaries to work, while at the same time giving states considerable latitude in redesigning their own public assistance programs.

While some social service agencies are scrambling to place welfare recipients in jobs, other programs are helping to set them up in micro businesses, defined as a company with one to five employees, including the owner. "This may not be the 100 percent solution, but it may be the 10 percent solution or the 5 percent solution," says Jeff Ashe, executive director of a Massachusetts non-profit micro business lending program. "A year or two from now it's going to be a major component of welfare policy," predicts John Hatch, founder of the non-profit Foundation for International Community Assistance (FINCA).

According to the Aspen Institute, a Washington, D.C. think tank, in 1996 there were about 248 micro enterprise programs in the United States, more than double the number of similar programs that were counted in 1992. The institute also estimates that more than 208,000 people received training, technical assistance, or loans from micro enterprise programs in 1994, the latest year for which this data is available. They believe the number of entrepreneurs helped by such programs is considerably larger today.

Diana P. Matson was on welfare for 23 years in Menahga, Minnesota before she went into business. She used a $500 loan from FINCA to buy the seeds and soil to start her greenhouse business. After two additional micro loans the business is now netting her $7,000 in annual income. "I'm more or less self-supporting," says Matson. "I'll make it on my own one way or another."

Charmaine Pascal decided to go off welfare and become an entrepreneur after taking a free course in day-care management offered by the Merchants Association in her Brooklyn, New York neighborhood. She and her partner Leighton Dixon started their venture with $1,000 in savings and a $500 grant from a micro financing group. To save money they operate the Caring Heart Center out of their two-bedroom apartment. The business is profitable and has flourished for three years, and they are now hoping to expand into a two-family house, utilizing one unit as the day-care facility.

In a poll of 405 randomly selected recipients of micro financing, the Aspen Institute found that 78 percent of the recipients of these small business loans were women, and 62 percent were members of minority groups. More than half of them said they now relied upon their micro business as their primary source of income, and 78 percent reported that their business had survived at least two years.

Jeff Ashe estimates that one out of every 10 or 20 micro businesses has the potential to grow into a bigger venture. But many micro entrepreneurs struggle to find financial and technical support, including larger loan packages, to do that. "It is not hard to provide tiny loans," says Peggy Clark, director of the economic opportunities program for the Aspen Institute. "What is much harder is helping small enterprises grow." Micro businesses like Caring Heart are still too small to attract bank loans. "It's like we're trying to break out of a box," says Leighton Dixon. Peggy Clark points out that micro business owners "really are not made to feel welcome at the banks and other traditional business services."

But some former welfare recipients remain optimistic about expanding their successful micro business. "(W)e will find a way" says Dixon. "That's the kind of people we are."

Source: Adapted from Michael M. Phillips, "More Poor People Launch Tiny Firms," *Wall Street Journal*, January 21, 1997, A2, and Stephanie N. Mehta, "Tiny Firms Find Growing Can Be as Hard as Surviving," *Wall Street Journal*, March 25, 1997, B2.

tion is not cheap, but it is valuable. Upon completion of the course, students have a business plan, one-on-one guidance, and guaranteed financing. Compass Rose hopes that the successful graduates will one day purchase insurance, Keogh plans, and other products from the company.

Says Cynthia McGeever, "If Compass Rose offers a product that I want, you can bet that I'll buy it from them because they've been there for us."[19] Anything for a friend, for a fee.

Positioning for a Loan   The time to establish a relationship with a banker, or lender, is *before* you need a loan. Because of their inherent conservatism, banks do not lend money in emergencies (unless they already have some money at risk) or on short notice. Call the president of the bank and introduce yourself. Ask to set up a meeting to tell the president about your business. Do not ask for a loan in this meeting. Ask the president who in the loan department might be a good match for your business-financing needs. When you call the person the president recommends, tell him or her that the president recommended that you speak directly with him or her. This is your referral.

The banker will be looking for the answer to four key questions when evaluating your business proposal. The answers to these questions should be clear and concisely communicated, both in writing and in discussion during the meetings the entrepreneur and the top management team will have with the lender.

1. *What will the money be used for?* Are there other sources of financing to help spread the risk?
2. *How much money is needed?* (Ask for too much, and you are paying for financing that you don't really need. Ask for too little, and you are unable to achieve your business purpose.)
3. *How will the money be paid back and when?* (Time is money, and the sooner the repayment, the higher the return and lower the risk for the bank.)
4. *When is the money needed?* Is it all going to be used now, or is it possible to draw down a balance over time?

Of primary importance to the lender is your ability to repay the loan. That is the first criterion. In considering the loan application, bankers will also be looking for five things (all beginning with the letter *C*).[20]

- *Character*. The banker's best estimate of whether you will be able (and willing) to repay your debt is your previous borrowing and business experience. If your reputation is worthy and your integrity is intact, you have passed the character test.
- *Capacity*. This is the numbers game. The banker wants to be sure that your business has the capacity (ability) to repay the loan, interest, and principal. Evidence of capacity is the cash flow of the business, the coverage ratio (earnings divided by debt service), and any personal guarantees that the banker may require.
- *Capital*. The lender is not interested in financing a business if the loan is the only source of long-term capital. This would mean 100 percent leverage. In case of default, the bank would be the owner of the business, and banks do not wish to be put in this situation. They are interested in situations in which there is sufficient equity to indicate that: (1) the owners of the firm are putting up their own money in good faith because they believe in the deal and (2) the debt/equity ratio of the venture is in line with comparable types of businesses.
- *Conditions*. These are the particulars of the industry, the firm, the general economy, and the current risk position of the bank that add complexity to the lending decision. The entrepreneur's business may be in good shape and the entrepreneur of fine character, but if the economy is taking a turn for the worse and the venture's industry is leading the way (for example, construction), then the banker may think twice and still deny the application. The banker is always in a position of asking: "What can go wrong here and what happens to my depositors' money when it does?" The fallout of the savings and loan debacle of the 1980s has been to make already risk-averse professionals even more deliberative.
- *Collateral*. If a loan has collateral, then the creditor can sell a specific asset to ensure that the principal and accrued interest obligations are met. Collateralized loans will generally have a slightly lower interest rate than unsecured loans. However, the quality of the collateral is important if the lower rate structure is to apply. Some assets may not be salable at anything approaching the value of the loan, and although these may be required as collateral, no lower rate will be extended. For businesses with short operating histories and service businesses with little tangible property, collateral often takes the form of personal guarantees and key-person life insurance.

Searching for a Lender Entrepreneurs often find themselves in a seller's market when it comes to searching for a loan. Sometimes it may appear that the chances of receiving a business loan approach zero. However, the entrepreneur can do a few things to improve the chances. First and foremost the entrepreneur needs to meet the requirements of the five Cs just described. Then the entrepreneur can begin to shop around as if the entrepreneur were hiring the bank to be its lender. Street Stories 7–4 describes some of the new places and new ways entrepreneurs are securing loans.

Small Businesses Score New Loan

Now that big corporations increasingly turn to Wall Street for low-cost financing, banks and other lenders have a new interest in providing money to small businesses that were once considered marginal risks. According to the Federal Deposit Insurance Corporation (FDIC), loans made by commercial banks to small business loans topped $310 billion dollars as of June 30, 1996. Commercial finance companies are being created or repositioned to also provide funds to small businesses in record numbers. General Electric Co.'s commercial finance unit created its small-business division in 1994, and now reports that it has $700 million in small-company loans on the books.

Many of these lenders are using credit-scoring, an automated loan-analysis method which evaluated an entrepreneur's personal credit history along with his or her business's financial condition. This method "allows us to make more loans to more owners for higher amounts at less cost and lower risk," says Lucille Reid, executive vice president at Wells Fargo & Co., which has been using a credit-scoring system for two years. The bank says the system accounted for $1.4 billion in new small-business loans during 1995 alone.

Kathleen Strakes is one entrepreneur who has benefited from the credit-scoring system. Her Paytime Inc. payroll-service company in Baltimore was so strapped for cash in 1995 that she couldn't afford an envelope stuffing machine, meaning her employees were forced to stuff hundreds of paychecks by hand. She was not optimistic when she received a one-page credit application from Wells Fargo in the mail. "I didn't expect to be approved," she says now. "I was just so used to being turned down."

But in less than one month Paytime had a $25,000 credit line, and was able to buy new equipment, including a machine which stuffs 50 envelopes a minute. Now the company is making money, and expects to report 1996 sales in of almost $1 million dollars for 1996, representing a four-time increase over company sales for the year 1994.

Robert Doyle was nervous, too, when he started looking for financing to take over Managed Medical Specialties Inc., in Bensalem, Pennsylvania, the company Doyle originally formed as a division of another firm. A bank promised him $200,000 but needed six weeks to make the final approval, which pushed Doyle past his takeover deadline. Instead, Doyle secured the cash in less than two weeks from Business Alliance Capital Corp., a newly formed commercial finance company. Business Alliance was created by two former commercial bankers to lend money to start-ups, money-losing companies, and even firms that have filed for bankruptcy. In less than two years they have placing $15 million in financing with 30 small companies.

Some of this easy-to-access financing can be expensive for small businesses. Interest rates can exceed 30 percent a year, and some analysts are concerned about the implications. "When we go through a real recession and expose the full extent of these loans, a lot of lenders rushing into this market will awaken to deep losses," says Hoyt Wilkinson, a managing vice president of the First Manhattan Consulting Group in New York. But many entrepreneurs are now delighted to be able to get credit after having the door slammed in their face so many times before.

Source: Adapted from Michael Selz, "Struggling Entrepreneurs Find Banks More Willing to Lend," *Wall Street Journal*, January 13, 1997, B1.

As in any hiring situation, the entrepreneur should check the bank's references. Other people who do business with the bank will be able to tell the entrepreneur whether the bank is a friendly institution, one that is willing and able to work with the venture in good times and bad. Some banks have reputations for foreclosing early or calling in loans when the bank's balance sheet needs cleaning up. The bank's reputation is one of its most important assets, and a poor reputation should not be rewarded with the account.

Find a bank that has experience lending within your industry. Banks have different experiences, and their loan officers and lending committees have their own knowledge resources. If the lenders have experience, they will be more likely to understand the particulars of your loan application. Also, look for a bank that is the right size for your firm. A bank that is too small for your firm will not be able to finance follow-up loans. (Banks have regulations about how much they can loan to any single client.) A bank that is too big considers your account trivial, and you might feel lost among the megadeals being made. If your business is international, and you will be importing, exporting, or carrying on a banking relationship outside the home country, look for a bank that has both experience with these issues and correspondent relationships in your host countries.

Personal chemistry is important in choosing a banker. Do business with people you like and people who like you. Look for a bank that has someone who will be your "champion." A champion will try to present your firm and its prospects in a positive light within the bank itself, even when you are not personally there. Here are some other criteria you can consider when looking for a banker:[21]

Does it see you through adversity? The Milwaukee architecture firm of Engberg Anderson geared up for a major construction project, and then ran into contract problems. The negotiations went on four months, and the company was hard pressed to meet their payroll, but their bank expanded their credit with good faith as their only collateral. "They understood the nature of the business," says founder Charles M. Engberg, "and saw us as a company they were willing to take a risk for."

Does it save you time? The Mississippi Blending Co. may be located in Norwalk, Connecticut, but they bank in Keokuk, Iowa. Why? Because the bank there knows cornstarch, and Mississippi Blending blends food products made from cornstarch. When the company needed $2 million to cover a market bid, their bank got it for them in less than 24 hours without paperwork.

Does it treat you as an individual? The loan officer at a local bank practically overwhelmed Reynolds, a Lynnwood, Washington retail-store-fixture manufacturer, with detailed questions about his business. The company got the loan, and then the bank got the rest of the company's business. "I decided that if they were smart enough to ask these intricate questions, they must be worth banking with," explains Paul A. Abodeely, Reynolds CEO.

Does it teach and advise? The Tampa Bay Vending Company "couldn't believe it" when their banker volunteered to spend a day riding a company truck so he could learn about their business. But the inside knowledge he gained that day transformed that banker into an expert consultant when Tampa Bay took over another company, started exporting their machines, and set up a retirement fund for their employees. As an added bonus, the banker even showed the owner's young son how to become a gumball machine entrepreneur.

Does it do something special for you? By 10 a.m. every morning, there's a report sitting on the desk of Jack Greenman, financial officer of the Sterling Healthcare Group, Inc., in Coral Gables, Florida, from his local bank. The report shows all the deposits and disbursements from the previous day, including the deposits from lockboxes in 19 states that the bank has swept into its central account. The service doesn't cost Sterling Healthcare a dime.

Does it accept responsibility for you? Garden-tool maker DeJay Corp. of Palm Beach, Florida, was upset when a bank posting error caused some of their checks to bounce. But they were smiling when the bank not only apologized, but also called every customer and vendor who might have received an unpaid check and explained that it was the bank's mistake.

Does it let you borrow against the future? The TPL technology-equipment manufacturer of Albuquerque won a big U. S. Army contract, and then were upset when they discovered their bank wouldn't increase their existing $250,000 line of credit. Another bank 100 miles away heard the TPL story through the grapevine, and extended them the half million dollars they needed, saying "You're the kind of company we need to encourage in New Mexico."

Does it find customers for you? A bank in Southern California played matchmaker for two of its customers, garment manufacturer Flap Happy and the local science museum. When the museum expanded its gift shop, Flap Happy hats were included in the retail mix.

These stories demonstrate that some commercial banks are willing to "go the extra distance" to attract small business customers, and that entrepreneurs need to shop around and communicate with their banking staff to find a lender who can be a true partner in their success.

Types of Debt Financing There are two basic types of debt financing: asset-based financing and cash flow financing. **Asset-based financing** is collateralized. The most common form of asset-based financing is trade credit. Trade credit is extended for the period between product or service delivery to the new venture and when payment is due. It is not uncommon to have a 25- to 30-day "grace period" before payment without penalty is expected. A discount is sometimes offered for early payment.

Asset-based debt. A business usually borrows money to finance an asset. The asset may be short term—for example, seasonal accounts receivables—or long term—for

TABLE 7–1 Asset-Based Financing and Borrowing Limits	
Type	*Borrowing Limits*
Accounts receivable	For short-term receivables: 70%–80% For longer-term receivables: 60%–80%*
Inventory	Depending on risk of obsolescence: 40%–60%
Equipment	If equipment is of general use: 70%–80% If highly specialized: 40%–60%
Conditional sales contract	As a percentage of purchase price: 60%–70%
Plant improvement loan	Lower of cost or market appraisal: 60%–80%
Leasehold improvement	Depending on general reusability: 70%–80%
Real estate	Depending on appraisal value: 80%–90%
First mortgage on building	Depending on appraisal value: 80%–90%

*This is from a factor, a business that specializes in collecting accounts receivable and overdue debts for firms and lending them money against the total invoice amounts.

example, equipment or property. When a specific asset is identifiable with the borrowing need, asset-based financing is appropriate. Table 7–1 illustrates some types of assets that are "bankable" and the typical maximum percentage of debt financing the firm can count on.

For example, a new venture with a positive cash flow conversion cycle (they spend before they receive) could borrow 70 percent of the money needed to finance accounts receivable, with the receivables themselves serving as collateral. Up to 60 percent debt financing is possible for inventory, with the inventory as collateral. Note that the more stable, long-term, and tangible resources have higher debt ceilings, while the short-term, high-turnover assets have lower ceilings.

Smaller banks have traditionally turned away from asset-based financing because they lacked the ability to evaluate and dispose of collateral. However, increasingly, these banks are moving toward developing special expertise in asset-based financing. In 1989, it was estimated that over $100 billion would be borrowed by small businesses with asset-based financing.[22]

Cash flow financing. **Cash flow financing** refers to unsecured financing based on the underlying operations of the business and its ability to generate enough cash to cover the debt. Short-term (under one year) unsecured financing is usually for temporary working capital. A line of credit is an intermediate level of unsecured financing. Long-term unsecured financing takes the form of a note, bond, or debenture.

Because the debt is unsecured, banks may take other precautions to try to protect their asset (the loan). These protections, or **covenants**, are agreements between the lender and borrower concerning the manner in which the funds are disbursed, employed, managed, and accounted. For example, an unsecured loan covenant might require the borrower to maintain a certain minimum balance in an account at the lending institution. In this way the bank can restrict a portion of its funds from general use, raise the cost of the loan to the borrower, and potentially attach the balance in the account in case of default. Further details on this type of financing and its limits are discussed in the next chapter.

New Venture Valuation

What is the new venture worth? How can it be valued? Determining its value is a problem that cannot be avoided, even though the methods for calculating value are uncertain and risky. When a new business is created by purchasing another business or its assets, a valuation is required to ensure a fair purchase price and to determine taxes.

A valuation is also needed when a new venture is created and the entrepreneurs are looking for equity investors. In this case the valuation tells investors approximately what their investment might be worth in the future.[23] Investors need this information so that they can calculate their expected return on investment and bargain for the share (proportion of stock) in the venture that enables them to achieve this return.[24]

Because of lack of historical data, the valuation of new ventures and small businesses is difficult and uncertain. There is no efficient market to determine value, these ventures do not trade their equity on a stock exchange and thus have no market value in this sense, and they have no record of accomplishment to indicate potential future earnings. Unproven companies need to raise equity without being able to point to historical returns to investors.[25]

Despite these problems, valuations must be made. Three basic approaches to valuation include asset-based valuations, earnings-based valuations, and the use of discounted cash flow techniques.

ASSET-BASED VALUATIONS

Asset-based valuations reveal the maximum exposure that investors face. The purpose of these valuations is to determine how much the venture would be worth if it were forced to cease operation and be sold for its tangible and intangible parts. Asset-based valuations can also be used to determine the cost of assets for types of asset-based valuations are book value, adjusted book and replacement value, and replacement value.

Book Value   The book value of an asset is the historical cost of the asset less accumulated depreciation. An asset that was originally purchased for $10,000 and has been depreciated on a straight-line basis for half its useful life will have a book value of $5,000. A fully depreciated asset will have a book value of zero, even though it may still have some economic value. Because accelerated depreciation schedules and techniques are employed primarily as tax shields, during the early life of an asset, the book value may understate the economic value of the asset. Frequently, the book value of an asset is completely an artifact of accounting practice and bears little relationship to its actual economic value.

Adjusted Book Value   Sometimes an asset's book value and its actual economic value are so at variance that it is necessary to adjust the book value to give a better picture of what the asset is worth. This adjusted book value can be higher or lower, depending on the circumstances. A frequent reason for an upward adjustment is to account for land values. Adjusted book valuations increase the value of real estate, which often rises over time, but because of accounting rules is always left on the books at historical cost. Many types of businesses are undervalued on the books because the land they own and control is worth many times the value of the business as an ongoing operation. Examples of this phenomenon include land-based businesses such as hotels, parking lots, and golf courses.

Land value can be adjusted downward if, for example, a parcel of property has major environmental problems and incurs cleanup costs. Also, sometimes neighborhoods and areas deteriorate for a variety of reasons, and property that was once valuable falls in value.

Inventory valuations are sometimes adjusted downward because the parts, supplies, or stock has become obsolete. A computer store retailer that maintained a stock of machines produced by out-of-business manufacturers might have to write down the value of the inventory. A clothing retailer who overordered and has a large stock of last year's fashions would be in a similar position. On the other hand, if held long enough, obsolete inventory and out-of-fashion stock can be a source of *increased* value. Eventually, this merchandise becomes rare. If a market in historical goods or collectibles develops, long-held "worthless" goods can become a source of revenue for the owner.

Liquidation Value   This is the value of the assets if they had to be sold under pressure. Sometimes firms face extreme cash shortages and must liquidate assets to raise cash to pay their creditors. At other times, courts order liquidation under bankruptcy proceedings. When buyers know that the venture is being forced to raise cash by liquidating, they can negotiate to pay below-market prices. Often liquidation is done at auction, and the prices paid might be only 10 to 20 percent of the market value of the assets. The liquidation value of the assets represents their absolute floor value. From the investor's point of view, the difference between the value of the investment and the liquidation value of the assets (after priority claims are met) represents the maximum risk or exposure for the investment.[26]

Replacement Value   Replacement value is the amount it would cost to duplicate the firm's current physical asset base at today's prices. When valuation is used for buying or selling a business, the replacement value of the assets can be a point of reference in the negotiation between buyer and seller. Because inflation is the historical trend in developed Western economies, the replacement cost of an asset is frequently higher than the original cost. However, because of technological and productive improvements, the replacement cost of computers and computing power is an example of an historical downward trend in replacement costs.

EARNINGS-BASED VALUATIONS

Earnings valuations entail multiplying the earnings of the venture by a price-earnings ratio or dividing the earnings by some capitalization factor (these are mathematically equivalent techniques). Two problems are inherent in this technique. The evaluator must determine which "earnings" should be used for the calculation and which "factor" is most appropriate for capitalization. The resolution of these issues is not trivial; differences in valuation provide arbitrage opportunities that can be practically riskless and very lucrative.[27]

Which Earnings?   Three possible earnings figures can be used in calculating an earnings valuation.[28]

Historical earnings. **Historical earnings** are the record of past performance. Past performance is no guarantee of future achievement, but it is sometimes an indication. In cases of valuation for the purpose of buying or selling a business, sellers rely on past performance for their valuation; after all, it was their management that was responsible for that performance. However, since in most cases the sellers will no longer be part of management, the context within which the historical performance has occurred no longer exists. Therefore, historical earnings should not be used to value future performance.

Future earnings (historical resource base). Calculations based on **future earnings** and the historical resource base represent a middle-of-the-road approach. They correctly identify the important earnings stream for the future out of which dividends will be paid. Also, the firm's future earning capacity will determine a market value. However, the use of the historical resource base assumes that the relationship between the firm's capabilities and its environment will remain unchanged. This calculation would represent the value to the current owner who anticipated no major changes in the assets of the firm, its strategy, or its competitive or macro situation. In a buy-sell situation, the buyer should not rely on this estimate, since the probability is high that the underlying resource base will indeed be modified under new ownership.

Future earnings (present and future resource base). This is the most appropriate measure of earnings in both the buy-sell and new venture valuations. Future earnings are the basis for future returns. And these future returns flow directly as a result of whatever new resources and capabilities are developed by the firm's founders and top managers. Therefore, valuation is always a forward-looking process, and its calculation requires estimates of future performance.

In addition to the problem of determining which earnings to include and under what circumstances to include them, valuation also must grapple with the problem of comparable earnings. Earnings can be stated and calculated in a number of ways: earnings before interest, depreciation and taxes (EBIDT), earnings after taxes (EAT), and earnings before and after extraordinary items. Extraordinary items should be omitted from earnings calculations because they represent "non-normal" operating situations and one-of-a-kind events. Because we are interested in valuation of an ongoing business, special situations should be factored out of the calculations.

Both EBIDT and EAT are legitimate earnings to use in the valuation process. The advantage of EBIDT is that it measures the earning power and value of the business fundamentals and underlying resources *before the effects of financing and legal (tax) organization.* From the viewpoint of a new venture in search of financing, as well as in a buy-sell situation, EBIDT is preferred, since future financial and legal structures may be altered according to the tax preferences of the owners. However, EAT is a reasonable and workable figure to examine. The important consideration is to be consistent in valuation methods. The entrepreneur should not employ EAT for one scenario and EBIDT for another.

Which Capitalization Factor? Determining the capitalization factor is no less an exercise in estimation and judgment. The **capitalization factor** or **price-earnings (P-E) ratio** is the multiple that represents the consensus among investors concerning the growth and reliability of the firm's earnings over time. The P-E ratio is the price that an investor is willing to pay to buy a claim on $1 worth of current earnings. Higher P-E ratios mean that investors believe that earnings will be much higher in the future, while lower P-E ratios indicate that investors do not believe earnings will increase very much.[29]

For example, large, stable, slow-growth businesses are often capitalized at five to ten times earnings. Firms that are expected to grow as well as or slightly better than the economy as a whole might have price-earnings ratios in the teens to low twenties. Small firms with high-growth potential often come to market at IPO at multiples of 30, 40, and 50 times earnings. Their earnings are valued at higher ratios because certain investors look for the high-risk/high-reward stock that could be the next Intel, Microsoft, Cisco Systems, or Genentech.

No method of determining the correct price-earnings ratio for any specific new venture valuation is exact. The best process generates a range of potential values and evaluates outcomes within the range. In determining the P-E ratio, there are a number of reference points to check:

1. Look for similar or comparable firms that have recently been valued and employ that capitalization rate as a base. This is not easy, since there are few "pure plays" available for comparison.[30] Sometimes private valuations have been made by buyers or sellers, but these are not public information and may be difficult to access.

2. Estimate the range for the stock market's overall P-E ratio for the period under evaluation. If the market is expected to be a bull market, P-E ratios will be above the historical average. In this case, adjust the new venture ratio upward. In a bear market, ratios are down, and the new venture rate should reflect this.

3. What are the industry's prospects? Those under heavy regulation or competitive pressures will be valued lower than those that are considered "sunrise" industries—that is, industries just beginning their development under government protection and with little competition.

The earnings methods are commonly used because they are relatively efficient (you need only two reliable numbers) and easy to use for comparisons. They are volatile because any change in future earnings estimates produces a valuation change that is multiplied by what is sometimes a very large number. In addition, earnings from an accounting viewpoint are designed to minimize tax liability. They seldom represent the amount of cash actually available for returns to investors and owners. To examine these, we need a cash flow model of firm value.

E-NOTES 7–4   NEW VENTURE VALUATIONS

Asset-based valuations:

- book value,
- adjusted book value,
- liquidation value,
- replacement value.

Earnings-based valuations:

- historical earnings,
- future (historical resource base) earnings,
- future (present and future resource base) earnings.

DISCOUNTED CASH FLOW MODELS

The value of a firm can also be estimated using discounted cash flow (DCF) models. DCF models were originally developed to estimate returns on specific projects over limited time horizons in the context of capital budgeting. They were then expanded for use in valuing publicly held firms traded on major stock exchanges. The application of DCF models to entrepreneurial opportunities is relatively new and must be applied with some caution.

Advantages of DCF Valuation   The DCF model of valuation can provide valuation estimates that are superior to asset-based and earnings-based methods if used appropriately. One advantage of the DCF model is that the valuation is based on the cash-generating capacity of the firm, not its accounting earnings. For new ventures, "cash is king"; when you are out of cash, you are out of business. An earnings model may depict the business as healthy, although it cannot pay its bills or open its doors to customers. A cash-based model is more sensitive to that issue.

Another advantage of the cash model is its inclusion of cash flows that can be appropriated by the founder/owner and the top management team. Cash payments to the entrepreneurs, such as contributions to Keogh plans and other retirement schemes, returns from debt repayments, interest payments, salaries, tax shields and advantages, dividends, and cash replacement perquisites (e.g., automobile insurance), can all be included in calculating the value of the firm to its owners. When a firm is "owned' by hundreds of thousands of small shareholders, these items are irrelevant. (Indeed, these decrease the value of the firm to the stockholders.) For a closely held firm, they are quite relevant.

Disadvantages of DCF Valuation   One of the most important disadvantages of the DCF model is that there are usually few other choices for the entrepreneurs to evaluate. Recall that DCF analysis was originally used for capital budgeting. In capital budgeting, the DCF model can provide a reliable ordering of alternatives. For the entrepreneur, there are few alternatives to the single new venture under consideration. Therefore, the benefit of reliable ordering is lost. If the other essential numeric inputs into the DCF calculation are also unreliable, the valuation will be a prime example of "garbage in, garbage out."

A second problem arises from estimating the numerical inputs into the DCF equation. Three major ones include the estimation of the period cash flows (usually annual), the estimation of the weighted cost of capital (discount rate), and the estimation of the terminal (or horizon) value of the firm. If these calculations are off, the valuation will be wide of the mark, too.

Discounted Cash Flow Example   To calculate the value of the firm with the DCF model, the following equation is used:

$$V = C_0 + C_1/(1 + k) + C_2/(1 + k)^2 + C_3/(1 + k)^3 + C_n/(1 + k)^n = \Sigma \, C_t/(1 + k)^t$$

where:

V is the value of the firm.
C is the cash flow in each period t.
k is the firm's cost of capital.

For example, suppose the entrepreneur had projected that a business could be started for $1 million and generate the cash flows listed in the following table. If an entrepreneur has a weighted cost of capital of 15 percent, and the firm's capitalization rate is .20 (its terminal value, or TV, then is $1,000,000/.20) = $5,000,000, then the value of the venture is $3,557,720.

Cash Flows in $000

Yr. 0	Yr. 1	Yr. 2	Yr. 3	Yr. 4	Yr. 5	TV 5
−1,000	200	400	800	1,000	1,000	5,000

Method: discount these flows by $(1 + k)^n$

The internal rate of return on this stream of cash flows is 68.15 percent. This is calculated by setting the initial investment ($1,000) equal to the five-year stream plus the terminal value and solving for k. As long as the entrepreneur can finance this project at rates less than 68.15 percent, value is being created and appropriated by the firm. At rates above 68.15 percent, the value is appropriated solely by the investor.

Residual pricing model. The brief example above illustrates how an entrepreneur might use the DCF model to value the firm from his or her point of view. But it is also important to consider how an investor would value a new venture. One common method that investors employ is called the **residual pricing method**. It is called this because it is used to determine how much of the firm must be sold to the investor in order to raise start-up funds, with the "residual" left for the entrepreneurs.

From the investor's point of view, the pretax annual cash flows generated for years one through five are not important, since they generally will not be available to the investor. These will be paid out as perquisites to the entrepreneur and reinvested in the firm to keep it growing. The investor is interested in the after-tax profits at a point in time (let's say year five). If the pretax cash flow were estimated at $1,000,000, let's say that the after tax profits were $500,000. At a multiple (P-E ratio) of 10 times earnings, the firm is valued at $5,000,000 at the end of year five.

Instead of using a weighted-cost-of-capital figure, say, 15 percent, the investor would use a "required-rate-of-return" figure. This is because the investor needs to see if the firm will be able to cover all the risk exposure, expenses, and the cost of no- and low-return investments the investor has made. The investor's required rate of return is invariably higher than the entrepreneur's weighted cost of capital (because the entrepreneur will also use low-cost debt when possible).

Let's say that the entrepreneur wants to approach the investor with a proposition: The entrepreneur wants to raise $500,000 from the investor for an equity share in the business. How much equity (i.e., what percentage ownership of the business) should the entrepreneur offer in exchange for a half-million-dollar stake?

To achieve a 40 percent return on investment, the investor would have to have $2,689,120 worth of stock at the end of year five. This was calculated by taking the $500,000 initial figure and compounding it at 40 percent for five years $(1.4)^5$. The future-value factor of this term is 5.378. If the investor's stock must be worth $2,689,120 in five years and the total value of the stock will be $5,000,000 in five years (10 × $500,000), then the investor must own 53.78 percent of the company ($2,689,120/$5,000,000).[31]

Anytime the entrepreneur knows:

- The investor's required rate of return,
- The amount of the investment,
- The number of years the investment is to be held,
- The after-tax profits for the horizon year,
- The expected price-earnings multiple, the amount of equity ownership the investor will require can be calculated.

As we will see in the next chapter, the investor may or may not actually require a 53.78 percent stake in the new firm. Elements such as potential dilution and management control need to be factored into a negotiation. No formula can fully express the complexity of a negotiation process or alleviate the desire of all parties to achieve the highest returns for the least amount of risk.

Summary

Entrepreneurial finance builds on traditional financial theory yet goes beyond it in certain ways that recognize that the entrepreneurial problem is unique and multifaceted. Financial resources are required, although seldom are they a source of competitive advantage. Yet they are a formidable hurdle for the entrepreneur.

The entrepreneur must be able to accurately determine the venture's financial needs, not only at the beginning of the venture but throughout the venture's life cycle. Determining start-up costs, predicting cash flows, managing working capital, identifying sources of financing, and accessing this money are key activities. Equity must be raised both inside and outside the firm; debt, both asset-based and cash flow-based, will lower the overall cost of capital for the new venture.

In the process of raising the money, the entrepreneur will have to confront and solve the valuation question. Three types of valuations are possible: asset-based valuations, earnings-based valuations, and discounted cash flow models. All have their strengths and weaknesses. The use of a specific technique depends on the purpose of the valuation.

In the next chapter we will examine more comprehensive and complex models of valuation and discuss the elements and structure of new venture financial deals.

Key Terms

- Management of financial resources
- Undercapitalized
- Overcapitalized
- Phased financing
- Permanent working capital
- Temporary working capital
- Cash flow cycle
- Production cycle
- Seed capital
- Start-up capital
- First-stage financing
- Second-stage financing
- Third-stage financing
- Fourth-stage financing
- Equity

- Inside equity
- Outside equity
- Private investors
- Venture capital
- Initial public offering (IPO)
- Micro loan
- Asset-based financing
- Cash flow financing
- Covenants
- Historical earnings
- Future earnings
- Capitalization factor
- Price-earnings (P-E) ratio
- Residual pricing method
- Prospectus

Discussion Questions

1. Why are financial resources not a source of competitive advantage even though they are a continuing hurdle for the new venture? (See Chapter 2 for review).
2. Why is undercapitalization dangerous for a new venture? How can overcapitalization pose a problem?
3. What are the elements of the cash flow cycle?
4. How can managing and controlling the cash flow cycle save the entrepreneur money?
5. How do the financing needs of the enterprise change over its life cycle?
6. What variables affect the choice of financing sources for the entrepreneur?
7. What are the pros and cons of raising start-up capital from private investors?
8. What are the pros and cons of going public?
9. What steps should the entrepreneur take to position the new venture for a loan?
10. Discuss the models and methods of new venture valuation. What are the pros and cons of each method?

Exercises

1. Calculate the start-up capital needed to finance the new venture described in your business plan.
2. Analyze the cash flow cycle from your business plan pro forma statements.
3. Develop a plan to control your firm's cash flow cycle. Recalculate question 1. How much money did you save?
4. Calculate the prospective value of your new venture at the end of five years by adjusted book value or replacement value, by using the appropriate earnings method, and by using the discounted cash flow method.
5. Match your financing needs to the appropriate sources of capital.
6. Using the residual pricing method, how much equity would you have to sell in order to raise money from a venture capitalist?

DISCUSSION CASE

The Pressures and Payoffs of Going Public

Frank Ingari remembers the day he became a multimillionaire, because he spent a lot of it trembling in a men's bathroom at the Shiva Corporation. "I was ready to throw up," the 45-year-old CEO recalls. "I was sweating badly, and I could barely stand up. When I looked in the mirror, I had blood coming out of my nose."

But it was worth it, because that was the day that Shiva, a highly regarded Massachusetts software maker, became one of the hottest initial public offerings of 1994. More than 3.7 million shares of Shiva were traded on the Nasdaq exchange that day, including 66,000 shares owned by top executive Mr. Ingari, at a price that ranged between $30.50 and $31.50. The IPO also raised $28 million dollars for the corporation.

Shiva was founded in the early 1980s by Daniel Schwinn and Frank Slaughter after they graduated from MIT. The company produces innovative software and hardware, which permit desktop and laptop computers to connect directly to a corporate system from outside the office. The founders claim it's only a coincidence that the network-promoting company shares the same name as the multi-armed Hindu goddess. Shiva's sales totaled $42 million in 1994, which was a 41 percent jump over sales for the previous year, but the company chose to go public because it was hard-pressed for the cash it needed to expand.

Schwinn and Slaughter began the preparations for their public offering more than a year in advance. First they hired Mr. Ingari to stabilize company management. A former rock guitarist, Ingari headed the marketing efforts for the Lotus Corporation's popular Notes software, and was a respected software industry veteran. Ingari in turn hired Goldman, Sachs and Company to head a syndicate of 29 underwriters to bring the IPO to market.

Shiva filed with the Securities and Exchange Commission, and submitted to an onslaught from lawyers, accountants and bankers, spending $900,000 on audits and other expenses in preparation for the IPO. Lawton W. Fitt, a Goldman Sachs partner, then coached Frank Ingari and Frank Slaughter for a grueling two-week "road show," where they made presentations to influential traders such as Fidelity Investments, Janus, and Alliance Capital in 16 cities. "We felt like door-to-door salesmen," Mr. Ingari recalls.

During those presentations it became obvious that Shiva was a hot prospect. Potential orders for the stock were 30 times larger than the actual offering, and while Goldman Sachs had originally set the price at $12, they now suggested raising the opener to $15. Both Shiva and Goldman Sachs executives say they were stunned when the first "buy" order on November 18 was accepted at $30.50.

While both Shiva and insiders like Ingari, Slaughter and Schwinn made lots of money from the IPO, fortunes were also made by early subscribers who bought shares at $15 and then "flipped" them quickly on opening day. 'It's not an embarrassment to see a stock gap of up to 100 percent in a case like this," says Charles Ronson, publisher of the IPO Value Monitor and an analyst at Balestra Capital. "You don't know what the real interest is." The year 1994 was a relatively soft year for IPOs, with just $5 billion raised in 116 offerings verses $8.5 billion raised in 156 offerings during 1993.

"Pricing an IPO is not just about what the market will bear at that time," notes Lawton Fitt. "We're trying to get the company launched for the long term and build a good investor base." Three months after the IPO Shiva was holding its own, trading at $36.25. In contrast, General Magic, one of the other highly anticipated IPOs of 1994, had dropped to $19.75 after its initial offering of $32.

Frank Ingari says that Shiva is happy, but he and the company founders admit that their anxiety over the IPO was simply about money. "We all realized how much additional pressure there was on us," says Frank Slaughter, referring to the scrutiny from investors and analysts that shadows every move made by a publicly traded company. Frank Ingari echoes this by talking about his renewed sense of responsibility to Shiva employees. "I've got 200 people with their dreams, relying on me. The dream hasn't happened—it is happening now."

QUESTIONS

1. What are the benefits Shiva Corporation and its founders received by going public?
2. What were the negatives of the IPO?
3. Describe the steps Shiva went through in the process of going public.
4. Why is setting the price for the IPO so difficult? So important?

Source: Adapted from Glenn Rifkin, "Anatomy of a Highflying IPO, Nosebleeds and All," *New York Times*, February 19, 1995, F7.

Notes

1. *Wall Street Journal*, October 16, 1992, R7.
2. For example, the lessons of portfolio theory require a portfolio to exist. For many entrepreneurs, their business is their major, if not only, asset. Similarly, many of the assumptions of the capital asset pricing model do not hold for small, new, privately held firms.
3. This is for firms with total investments under $10 million. U.S. Bureau of the Census, *Quarterly Financial Report: Manufacturing, Mining and Trade Corporations, 4th Quarter, 1983*, 65, 130, 135 (Washington, DC: Government Printing Office, 1984).
4. This section follows Chapter 6 of E. Walker and J. Petty, *Financial Management of the Small Firm*, 2nd ed. (Englewood Cliffs, NJ: Prentice Hall, 1986).
5. Adapted from R. Owen, D. Garner, and D. Bonder, *Arthur Young Guide to Financing for Growth* (New York: John Wiley, 1986), 231–233.
6. In addition to the previously mentioned books by Walker and Petty, 1986; and Owen, Garner, and Bonder, 1986; see B. Mavrovitis, *Cashflow, Credit and Collection* (Chicago: Probus, 1990); L. Masonson, *Cash, Cash, Cash* (New York: Harper, 1990); and Chapter 5 of B. Blechman and J. Levinson, *Guerrilla Financing* (New York: Houghton-Mifflin, 1991).
7. This refers to the relationship of short-term rates to long-term rates. A "normal" structure has short-term rates lower than long-term rates to account for the extra risk of distant time. Some-

times short-term rates are higher than long-term, indicating a severe contraction in the money supply in the economy. In this case, borrowers will prefer long-term money. Sometimes the gap between the long-term and short-term rates is too large. In this case no one will want to borrow long-term money, preferring a series of short-term loans.
8. Jill Andresky Fraser, "Capital Steps," *Inc.*, February, 1996, 42–47.
9. J. Timmons and H. Sapienza, "Venture Capital: The Decade Ahead," in *The State of the Art of Entrepreneurship*, eds. D. Sexton and J. Kasarda (Boston: PWS-Kent, 1992), pp. 402–437.
10. The state laws are known as blue sky laws. The federal laws are primarily those of the U.S. Securities and Exchange Commission (SEC) that regulate private offerings. It is imperative that any entrepreneur navigate these waters with the aid of experienced legal counsel.
11. Freear and Wetzel, 1992.
12. H. Stevenson, M. Roberts, and I. Grousbeck, *New Business Ventures and the Entrepreneur* (Homewood, IL: Irwin, 1989).
13. W. Bygrave, "Venture Capital Returns in the 1980s," in *The State of the Art of Entrepreneurship*, eds. D. Sexton and J. Kasarda (Boston: PWS-Kent, 1992), pp. 438–461.
14. Timmons and Sapienza, 1992. An excellent analysis of the venture capital industry.
15. S. Mehta, "Venture Capital Raised by Companies Was a Record $10.1 Billion

in 1996," *Wall Street Journal*, February 5, 1997, B2.

16. Thus the epithet "vulture capitalist" when the investors leave only bare bones of the firm for the original entrepreneurs.

17. J. Emory, "The Value of Marketability as Illustrated in Initial Public Offerings of Common Stock," *Business Valuation Review* (December 1990), 114–116.

18. E. Carlson, "SBA Introduces Its 'Micro loan' Program," *Wall Street Journal,* June 6, 1992, B2.

19. L. Touby, "The New Bankrolls behind Women's Businesses," *Business Week*, September 21, 1992.

20. Adapted from J. Timmons, *New Venture Creation*, 3rd ed. (Homewood, IL: Irwin, 1990).

21. Adapted from Robert A. Mamis, "Can Your Bank Do This?", *Inc.*, March 1996, p. 29–38.

22. L. Berton, "Asset-backed Loans Aid Cash-strapped Entrepreneurs," *Wall Street Journal*, November 28, 1989, B2.

23. In Chapter 5 we suggested that unless there were good business reasons, a valuation could be calculated at the end of a five-year period of projections.

24. They may also be bargaining over a host of other issues. These will be discussed in the next chapter.

25. Of course, historical returns are no indication of future returns. This is boilerplate language that all who solicit investments must use. However, statistically, the best prediction of future returns is past returns. This may be a misuse of statistics, however.

26. The government (taxes) is paid first, then employees. Creditors are paid next, followed by equity investors, first preferred stockholders, then common stockholders.

27. Arbitrage Occurs when an asset (or business) has different prices in different markets. For example, a stock can be selling, for a very short period of time because of the speed of information, more in Tokyo than in London. Why? Because news affecting earnings (in this case positively) is released in Tokyo first (because of the time difference). An arbitrageur can profit briefly by buying the stock in London and selling it in Tokyo. Because the price difference will be small and the window of opportunity brief, in order to make money only very large transactions make sense.

28. This discussion follows Stevenson, Roberts, Grousbeck, 1989.

29. This is how Thomas Parkinson of Northwestern University's entrepreneurship program describes it to his students.

30. A "pure play" is a firm that is undiversified and operates in a single line of business. Since most new ventures operate as pure plays, but few ongoing larger firms do, it is difficult to get comparable capitalization rates.

31. Of course, the actual amount of equity the investor will own is subject to negotiation and many other variables. These will be discussed in the next chapter. This example is simplified for computation purposes.

Appendix 7A

Financing Requirements for EMC

In Appendix 6 we presented the start-up case of EMC, the Emergency Medical Center. Detailed below are the calculations for the financing requirements for this enterprise. All of the exhibits referred to can be found in Appendix 6.

Fixed-Asset Costs Fixed-asset financing is needed for resources such as property and land, office buildings and leasehold improvements, factory plant, productive equipment and machinery, office equipment, and the like. The EMC case, Exhibit 3, provides a list of the medical equipment requirements for the proposed facility. Every new venture will have a list of equipment with estimates of costs. In this case it is $51,000. Exhibit 4 details the costs of office equipment, miscellaneous furniture, and exterior signs. These costs are estimated at $13,500. Because the EMC will be renting space in a building that is being designed for the EMC, there are no start-up costs for property, land, or improvements.

Current Assets and Organizational Costs Current-asset financing (working capital) includes receivables, inventories, prepaid expenses, and cash on hand. Exhibit 5 presents a list of the estimates for current assets and other nonrecurring organizational costs. Although these are combined in the exhibit, this practice is not recommended for two reasons. First, when there are a significant number of these costs, they are easier to understand when separate lists are provided. Second, investment in current assets is not a tax-deductible expense; it is a capitalized expense. It represents part of the permanent capital of the firm (see "Working Capital Concepts.") Investments in organizational costs may be tax deductible in the period in which they are paid. Other types of organizational costs include feasibility studies, engineering studies and designs, architectural designs, and research and development costs. The total costs for these are $17,729.

Cash Flow from Operations It is not uncommon for a new venture to "burn" cash in the early months of operation. This means that its cash receipts do not cover its cash outlays. The extent to which the venture burns cash and the cumulative amount of additional cash needed to survive are calculated through the cash flow statement. The cash flow statement tells the entrepreneur how much additional financing is needed and when it is needed. Exhibit 8 illustrates this. The venture uses more cash than it generates for the first five months of operation. Here it reaches a total cumulative cash deficit of $65,809. After the fifth month case flow is positive, and the firm begins to recollect this cash advance that the owners have made. The founder knows from his cash flow statement that in addition to the fixed-asset financing, the current assets, and organizational costs, he will need $65,809 (and actually Dr. Petrillo estimates somewhat more, $80,000, as precautionary cash balances just to be safe) until the firm begins to cover all its expenses.

Therefore, the total start-up capital needed for the emergency medical center is:

Equipment assets	$51,000
Other fixed assets	13,500
Current assets and organizational costs	17,729
Cash flow requirements	80,000
Total financing requirements	$162,229

Appendix 7B

The Initial Public Offering Process

A public offering in the United States takes between six and nine months to plan and execute. Administrative costs, printing, and legal fees may run from $500,000 to $1,000,000. The underwriters typically receive fees of 7.5 percent of the total proceeds as well as options to purchase additional stock at reduced prices.

The underwriter(s) are the investment bankers and brokerage houses that sell the stock to the public, generally through their retail distribution network. There are three types of selling efforts: best effort, best effort (all or none), and firm commitment. In the simple best-effort case, the underwriter agrees to sell as much as possible of the stock that is authorized, and the public issue goes into effect even if all the authorized stock is not sold. The best-effort scenario arises when the company is relatively small, the investment banker is regional, and the company's prospects are somewhat in doubt.

The best-effort (all or nothing) scenario requires the investment banker to sell all of the authorized issue or cancel the offering. This means that the company will not be public unless it can sell all its stock and raise all the money that it requires for financing its future. The advantage here is that the firm will not become public and undercapitalized. The disadvantage is that fees and costs associated with this strategy are not recovered if the offering is canceled.

The firm-commitment selling effort is the safest and most prestigious for the new venture's IPO. The underwriters guarantee that the entire issue will be sold by buying most of it themselves. Then they resell it to their customers. This selling effort is for companies that have the most solid backgrounds, products, and management. The underwriters share some of the risk of the offering by purchasing shares for their own accounts.

The process of going public begins long before the venture actually sells shares. The preliminary stages require the venture to meet the criteria of a public firm: a demonstrated record of growth in sales and earnings, a record of raising capital from other outside investors, a product that is visible in the market and of interest to investors, audited financial statements, clear title to the technology, an estimable board of directors, and a management team that is sufficiently seasoned to run the company and manage the IPO process simultaneously.[1]

If these criteria are met and the venture's managers have determined that the next step for the firm's financial strategy is a public offering, the process may formally begin. At this point management will solicit proposals from underwriters for the IPO. Underwriters will respond with their philosophy, strategy, and tactics—as well as with the estimated costs of their services. Management must then select among the proposals and has the option of suggesting joint and cooperative efforts if that seems reasonable. Once the underwriter is hired, the offering begins.

1. Organization Conference   This is the first meeting that brings together the three major parties to the IPO process: management, the underwriter, and the independent accounting firm that will prepare the financial statements. All parties bring their lawyers. They discuss the timing of the IPO, the nature of the offering in terms of amounts to be raised, the selling strategy, and the allocation of tasks. The lawyers inform all parties, but especially management, of the legal constraints of trading and disclosure that are now in effect.

2. Initial Registration Statement   There are three major parts to the paperwork that need to be done for the regulating authorities (the SEC). The first is the registration statement, a lengthy form that must be completed. Because of the detail and comprehensiveness of the registration statement, a significant number of appendixes are usually attached.

The second component is the prospectus. The **prospectus** is the document that is used to "sell" the new stock of the company. Although in some areas it must conform to certain regulatory standards, in other respects it is a great deal like the business plan. It describes the business, its product/market technology configuration, the competition and operations, and includes full audited financial statements. It is prepared under the rule of "full disclosure." This means that the company must reveal all information known to the company that might materially affect the decision of the investor to invest. From a practical standpoint, this means the company must reveal all risks, conflicts of interest (real and potential), and transactions that the top managers have had with the business that might be construed to be self-interest. This provides the firm some legal protection against claims of fraud.

The third component consists of supplemental data. This material is the equivalent of a huge appendix with such information as copies of leases the firm has entered into, the employment contracts of the top managers, sales and distribution contracts, and loan agreements. These can run to several hundred pages.

3. SEC Review and Comment   The package is then sent to the SEC for review and comment. In its review, the SEC staff looks for internal consistency of business plans and use of proceeds. It reviews the description of the issuer's unique risks that avoid the simple "boilerplate" disclaimers.[2] The SEC looks for areas in which the investor might be misled—for example, overoptimism concerning new-product development, overstatement of the actual size of the firm, overoptimism concerning contracts for work in hand and signed, and understatement of projected expenses for the use of proceeds. The SEC does not comment on whether the business will be a success; instead it looks for areas in which the investor should be protected against malfeasance and fraud.

4. Preparation of the Revised Statement   No IPO review is approved on the first submission. The SEC's review letter will request revisions and resubmission. Amendments are added to the application statement, deficiencies are corrected, and language is modified.

5. Preliminary Prospectus   Once the approval letter is issued, the preliminary prospectus can be prepared (it has been in process during this time) and then circulated. This prospectus is sometimes called a "red herring" because the border of the cover page is red and because of the speculative nature of IPOs in general. The number of shares and the price are not included in this document. The purpose of the preliminary prospectus is to gain visibility for the new issue within the investment community. It represents the beginning of the organization of the underwriting group or syndicate. The lead underwriter organizes a larger group of investment houses to help sell the issue and spread the risk.

6. Due Diligence   This is the process the underwriter must perform to ensure that the stock to be sold is a legitimate investment. If the underwriter were to sell stock without completing an investigation of the company, it, too, might be liable for fraud and damages (both from investors who lost money and from other brokers who lost money and reputation). Independent accountants review the company's financial picture, policies, and prospects and issue a letter to the underwriters explaining what they found. All the lawyers also write letters to each other describing the company's legal situation (current lawsuits as well as potential liability). All this investigative diligence is designed to weed out legal problems before they occur and to protect the underwriters, lawyers, and accountants from liability if they are "fooled" by the top managers.

7. Pricing the Issue   As the company gets closer to the time of actually declaring the date of the offering, negotiations begin to determine the price of the issue. Many factors are involved: the current state of the stock market, the earnings of the company, the total dollars the company is attempting to raise, the prices and performance record of other recent IPOs, and so on. There is a natural conflict of interest between the underwriters and the current owners of the company. The underwriters have the most to gain by slightly underpricing the issue: If the new issue comes to market at a discount, the underwriters' customers will be happy because the price will soon rise to its "market" level. Also, the underwriters will make additional profit, since they often take an option (called the "shoe") on as much as 10 percent of the issue. The current owners, on the other hand, want the issue to come to market at a premium. If the issue is slightly overpriced, they will receive more money for the shares they sell (personally), and the company will receive more money for whatever percentage of shares are offered. As it gets closer to the time of the offering, the underwriter generally assumes control.[3]

8. Market Timing and Closing   The last step is the actual closing of the deal. The date of offering is set, and the underwriters and managers closely monitor the stock market in the weeks and days leading up to the offering. If the stock market starts to fall precipitously, the offering can be canceled up to the last minute. If the market is steady or rising, the night before the offering the final price is set, and a financial printer works all night to produce the prospectus for the IPO with the price on the front page.

Notes

1. L. Orlanski, "Positioning for the Public Offering," *Bio/technology* 3 (1985): 882–885; and S. Jones and B. Cohen, *The Emerging Business* (New York: John Wiley, 1983).
2. L. Orlanski, "SEC Comments on the Offering Prospectus," *Review of Securities Regulation*, 17, no. 11 (1984): 887–896.
3. There is a good deal of evidence that new issues, on average, come to market underpriced. Quality new issues then rise quickly and the underwriters and those favored customers that were given the option of making early purchases then sell and make a quick profit. With 6 to 18 months the shares are earning "normal" returns and no excess profits remain for investors. Low-quality new issues decline even quicker.

CHAPTER

8

Securing Investors and Structuring the Deal

Outline

> *Things may come to those who wait,*
> *but only the things left by those who hustle.*
> —ABE LINCOLN

Learning Objectives

After reading this chapter you will understand:

- What constitutes a *good investor*, and a *good investment*.

- The nature of the *investment process*.

- The *financial factors* that are involved in making a deal.

- How the entrepreneur can *create value* with a well-structured deal.

- The *legal forms of organizing* a business in the United States.

- The special conditions involving *taxes*, *private placements*, and *bankruptcy*.

How does the entrepreneur obtain the money to launch the new venture? The chapter's opening quote implies that securing investors is an active process. If the era ever existed when investors beat a path to the door of the entrepreneur with a better mousetrap, it is gone. The entrepreneur cannot be passive and assume that financing will follow automatically from a well-designed business plan. There are many more entrepreneurs searching for financing than there are investors and money available to launch them all. The best deal will result from an aggressive, confident, and realistic approach.

What is a deal? It is usually much more complicated than a simple "Give me money, and sometime in the future, I will return it with gain." A **deal** is the structure and terms of a transaction between two or more parties.[1] For the entrepreneur this definition has important implications. The first is that a deal has a structure. The structure indicates sets of preferences for risk and reward. These preferences depend on the personal characteristics of the bargainers, the current financial situation of the industries involved as well as custom and tradition. The second implication is that terms must be negotiated—terms such as the rights and duties of the parties to the deal, the timing of the activities of the financiers and the entrepreneurs, and the constraints and covenants that establish the rules the entrepreneur and investors will follow. These are most often written so that the investors are assured, insured, and reassured that their money will be secure.

The final implication of the definition is that there may be more than two parties to the deal. It is unusual (and most of the time not preferred) for the entrepreneur to obtain all the financing from a single source. This may mean having debt from one source and equity from another. In reality, there are often layers of debt with different risk/return characteristics, and there are distinct layers of equity as well. A deal is always a team effort, and many roles are available for the players.

The entrepreneur's key task is to create value. This is accomplished by making the whole greater than the sum of its parts. This process involves using the marketing concept of segmentation to raise financial backing. In essence, the entrepreneur is selling equity in the firm, ensuring cash flow, and guaranteeing return and repayment.

Just as products and services have different characteristics that appeal to different people, financial instruments in a new venture financial deal also are differentiated, creating opportunities for market segmentation.

To be successful, the entrepreneur must demonstrate understanding and insight in three areas.[2] First, the entrepreneur and the top management team must understand their business. Without a clear understanding of the business and its environment, the entrepreneur and the investors will never be able to reach a consensus on the fundamentals, let alone the financing. Entrepreneurs must know the business well enough to understand the absolute amount of money they will need and when they will need it. They must understand the risks involved and the cause-and-effect factors because they will need to explain and defend their actions to potential investors. And they need to understand the nature of the returns the business can offer—the sources of these returns, their magnitude, and their timing.

Next, entrepreneurs need to understand financiers and the context in which they make their decisions. Investors are interested not only in the amount of money they may make but also in the risk of the investment, the timing of the returns, the controls to protect their money, and the mechanisms needed to (1) reinvest, if necessary; (2), abandon, if prudent; and (3) harvest, when appropriate.

Perhaps most important, entrepreneurs need to understand themselves. What are their preferences for ownership, control, wealth, and risk? Without self-knowledge, entrepreneurs may make a deal that will not have long-term positive benefits for the founders and, indeed, can sow the seeds for a lifetime of discontent and bitterness.

This chapter explores the issues of structuring deals and financing new ventures. We review the process by which entrepreneurs approach investors and examine the criteria investors use to make investment decisions. Then we build two models to illustrate the issues of deal structure. A simple discounted cash flow example was illustrated in Chapter 7, and understanding this basic model is necessary to understand the more elaborate models presented in this chapter. The chapter continues with a discussion of the negotiation process. Experience and common sense provide many of the guidelines for the "dos and don'ts" on deal negotiation. Last, we review legal and tax-related issues. Legal forms of organization, private placements, and the tax code all affect the final deal structure.

E-NOTES 8–1   A DEAL

A deal is the structure and terms of a transaction between two or more parties.

Approaching Investors

What do you need to know in order to meet with investors? Approaching investors requires knowledge of investing patterns and traditions. At its most basic it is a selling job; the entrepreneur is selling a part ownership of the new venture (equity), a percentage of the anticipated cash flow (debt), or both. And every selling job requires knowledge of the customers, their purchasing habits, their sensitivity to price, and the substitutes and alternatives they face. In Chapter 3 we discussed selling products. A review of the concepts of "buyer power" applied to financiers provides some of the insight needed to plan an effective strategy to attract investors.

THE IDEAL INVESTOR

Every entrepreneur has his or her vision of a dream investor. However, the ideal seldom exists in real life. What are the characteristics of the ideal investor? The ideal investor is one who:

- *Is actually considering making an investment.* An investor who is not liquid or has no desire to make an investment, no matter how rich, is unapproachable.
- *Has the right amount of money to invest.* An investor with too little money cannot buy into the deal. An investor with too much money may think your deal is trivial.
- *Is interested in the business.* Investors should have some, if not all, of the same enthusiasm and optimism about the business's prospects as the founders.
- *Has knowledge that can help the new venture.* Counseling from an investor who has experience, expertise, or network resources is ideal. The investor may be savvy about the business or industry or the geographic area where the business will operate. If the investor knows another individual who is interested in investing, this is important knowledge, too.
- *Is reputable and ethical.* The investor's reputation is part of the new venture's reputational capital. Ethical standards are important because investors could take advantage of inside information or manipulate their investment to the entrepreneur's disadvantage in a potential conflict of interest.
- *Has a good rapport with the top managers and founders.* The ability to communicate freely, to get along and see the situation from the founder's point of view, can go a long way to easing strain between management and investors.
- *Has experience in this type of investing.* Because of the wide swings in performance and emotions that are part of the entrepreneurial process, investors who know what to expect and can hang on for the duration are most desirable.[3]

Investors with all these characteristics are human resources that are rare, valuable, hard to duplicate, and nonsubstitutable. Therefore, they can provide sustainable advantage for the firm.

The ideal investor can exist within any of three primary investor groups.

1. Friendly investors such as family, friends, business associates, potential customers or suppliers, prospective employees, and managers.
2. Informal investors such as wealthy individuals (e.g., doctors, lawyers, businesspersons) and angels.
3. Formal or professional investors in the venture capital industry.

For example, professional investors were a source of outside finds and expertise for Software Artistry, Inc., a fledgling developer of artificial-intelligence software packages. The Indianapolis venture capital firm CID Equity Partners invested a total of $2.2 million in nine separate deals with Software Artistry over a period of five years. More importantly, CID encouraged the company to concentrate its efforts into developing Expert Advisor, a program that centralizes information from a business' internal experts at a central help desk. This unique and successful software has enabled businesses like Sony Electronics Inc., General Mills Inc., and the U.S. Senate to reduce the number of employees who handle customer inquiries, cut phone time, and slash the number of transferred calls within the organization. CID also recruited a new CEO for Software Artistry before the company went public in 1995. During the initial public offering, CID sold enough of its Software Artistry shares to recoup their cash investment, but retained shares which still gave them a $40 million interest in the venture.[4]

The amount of money being committed by venture capital firms to individual start-ups is now on the rise. According to a study produced by Coopers & Lybrand and the VentureOne Corp. Research firm, the average company which receives venture capital today needs $16 million during its first five years, versus the $7 million a similar start-up needed in 1980. After surveying 464 venture-backed firms, the study concluded that successful, fast-growth start-ups are spending more on research and development in their early years to achieve a shortened product-development cycle, and also allocating more money for skilled workers and managers.[5]

E-NOTES 8–2   IDEAL INVESTOR

From the entrepreneur's viewpoint, a potential investor should have:

- liquid and sufficient capital
- knowledge of the business or knowledge which will help the new venture
- reputable and ethical standards
- good communication with management
- investment experience

THE IDEAL ENTREPRENEUR AND NEW VENTURE

Investors also have their "dream" investment. It has little risk, a big payoff, and takes place overnight. More realistic investment opportunities require careful study and evaluation. The five most important investment criteria are:[6]

1. *Market attractiveness.* There are four major elements of market attractiveness: size of market, growth rate of market, access to market, and need for the product. All enable a firm to build volume while sustaining selling margins.

2. *Product differentiation.* Product uniqueness and patentability are two dimensions of product differentiation. Both make the product hard to copy and are bases of sustainable competitive advantage. These result in higher profit margins. Value added through the employment of technical skills is also a component (part of the human and technical resource base of the venture).

3. *Management capabilities.* The skill levels of management and their implementation abilities are also key components. The development of organizational resources is the result of management capabilities. Also, the employment of inert resources, such as financial and physical assets, is enhanced by management and organization.[7]

4. *Environmental threats.* Research indicates the investors do not separate the industry environment from the macroenvironment, as we did in Chapter 3. The major threats indicated by investors are lack of protection from competitive entry, resistance to economic cycles (economics), protection from obsolescence (technology), and protection from downside risk.

5. *Cash-out potential.* This was the least important factor among all the evaluation criteria, not because money was not important, but because profitability and

wealth are the result of all the other factors falling in place. The key items of this criterion were the potential for merger with another firm and other opportunities for exit. These factors are summarized in Figure 8–1.

An investor looks for the fatal flaw in an entrepreneur's plan, perhaps an inconsistency that negates all other positives. The investor attempts to view the new venture proposal as a business system, a set of interconnected parts. If the parts do not fit together, this is a red flag for investors—perhaps even a deal breaker, a "can't be negotiated demand," that catches the investor's eye and causes him or her to reject the proposal.[8]

Timmons sums up investor criteria in three broad strokes.[9] He says that the investment must be forgiving, rewarding, and enduring. A *forgiving* opportunity is one that has some allowance for variation. In other words, everything does not have to go perfectly for the venture to be a success. Since events seldom turn out perfectly, this is important. If the venture must be launched with the precision and perfection of a

FIGURE 8–1 Venture Capital Investment Decision Process

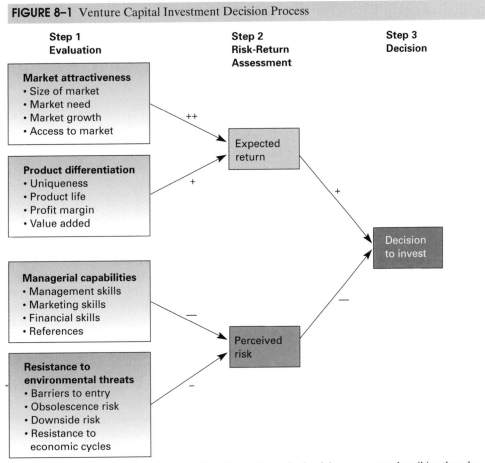

Note: ++, +, −, −− symbols indicate the direction and magnitude of the parameters describing the relationships of the variables.

NASA space shuttle, investors will steer clear. A *rewarding* opportunity is one that makes money. Returns do not have to be 100 percent compounded annually to be considered rewarding (although it helps). But if early projections show returns in the 10 to 15 percent range, and the investors know that early projections are optimistic, then the project is not rewarding enough. Finally, the investment should be enduring. An *enduring* venture has a semblance of sustainable competitive advantage and is able to resist economic and competitive pressures. It must endure long enough to provide a clear exit for early investors as they pass the reward and risk to the next level of investors.

One of the characteristics of an idea entrepreneur is track record. In Street Story 8–1, we see how entrepreneurs who have a history of accomplishment do not have problems finding money—money finds them.

E-NOTES 8–3   IDEAL INVESTMENT

For an investor, a potential new venture must be:

- *forgiving*—meaning that it must have enough market attractiveness and product differentiation to allow it to survive even if some things go wrong;
- *rewarding*—meaning that it must have sufficient managerial capabilities and resistance to environmental threats to allow it to make an attractive profit;
- *enduring*—meaning that it must have or generate enough sustainable competitive advantage so the investor can foresee the cash-out potential.

INVESTOR PROCESSES

From the point of view of the investor, the investment process is a seven-phase cycle.[10] Each phase is designed to maximize the potential gain for the investor (or minimize the potential loss) at the least possible cost in terms of time spent evaluating proposals. Investors view the world as having many more proposals and entrepreneurs than they can afford to finance or even to review. So their emphasis is on getting the most likely proposals through their doors and eliminating others that waste time and human resources.

The Search   Investors scan and monitor their environment just as entrepreneurs do. When investors find an opportunity that appeals to them, they make the first contact through a reference or introduction from a mutual acquaintance or business associate. Cold calls are rare. The entrepreneur should attempt to emulate this behavior. There are, however, directories of venture capitalists for entrepreneurs who cannot arrange a personal introduction or reference.[11] The entrepreneur can save time and money by pre-screening investors by size and investment preference. Once suitable investors have been identified, a letter of introduction (with a personal reference, if possible) followed by a phone call is customary.

Only a few investors should be contacted at a time. Whereas one-at-a-time contacts are too slow and deliberate, a shotgun approach should also be avoided. The investment company is small enough that soon everyone would know that everyone received your business proposal. It is estimated that 60 to 80 percent of the initial contacts made by phone result in rejection or at least a statement of noninterest.[12] For the 20 to 40 percent who are encouraged to follow up, the next step is to send the business plan or proposal to the investor for screening.

Ideal Investors for Ideal Entrepreneurs

While most entrepreneurs go begging at the door of venture capital firms, sometimes it works the other way around. In 1996 when Judith Estrin and William Carrico founded Precept Software Inc. and planned to finance the venture out of their own pockets, the venture capital firm which had funded their two previous projects came pounding on their door. "I said, 'You guys can't do that,'" recalls Philip Greer, managing partner in Weiss, Peck & Greer Venture Partners of San Francisco. "I told them, 'We've been in business together since 1981. We've been damn helpful and you know it; we deserve to be a part of your venture.'"

Weiss Peck has good reason to want to be included in Estrin and Carrico's projects. Their investment of $5.1 million in Bridge Communications, the computer-network product firm that Estrin and Carrico formed in 1981, netted the venture capital firm $26 million when it was sold six years later to 3Com. The firm's $4.1 million investment in Computing Devices, the computer-hardware manufacturer that Estrin and Carrico started next, produced a gain of more than $31 million when the company went public in 1992. "I can't imagine them doing a venture without us," says Philip Greer. The entrepreneurial duo finally accepted a $1.6 million investment from Weiss Peck for Precept, but gave up less equity to the venture capital firm then they had in the past.

Analysts say that as the venture capital market has matured, long-term and repeat alliances between investors and entrepreneurs have become more common. Timothy Barrows, a partner in the venture group Matrix Partners, says that the annual meeting of entrepreneurs which his firm repeatedly funds has started to look like a Christmas reunion. "We're more likely to back a guy we've backed before or give him the benefit of the doubt because we know him," notes Barrows. These close knit relationships have helped the group produce a seven to eight hundred percent return on investments. "Matrix has done an outstanding job of keeping entrepreneurs in the fold," notes Gary Bridge, who manages venture investments in companies like Matrix for pension funds and other institutions.

Sometimes venture capital firms make their repeat investment directly in personnel. Morganthaler Ventures recruited Allan Wallack as CEO for a new software start-up it was funding because it had funded two other companies that Wallack had managed. Wallack explains that the Morganthaler partners "know my philosophy and I know theirs. That saves a lot of time." Since joining the Chrysalis Symbolic Design Inc. venture, Wallack has hired new senior managers, strengthened marketing teams, engineering groups and customer relations, and raised additional venture financing. He expects that stock options he received from the deal will earn him twice the reward than his earlier Morganthaler-financed ventures.

Strong track records, familiarity, and shared philosophy may not be the only triggers for repeat investments. Precept's Phil Carrico identifies one additional factor in his decision to make another finance deal with Weiss Peck. "Phil persuaded us that it would be bad luck to do a start-up without him," he says.

Source: Michael Selz, "For Start-Up Stars, Coming Up With Seed Capital Is No Problem," *Wall Street Journal,* October 21, 1996, B2.

The Screen   Once in the hands of the investor, the business plan is screened for further interest. In a large investment company, initial screening might be handled by junior staff people. (The criteria for investor screening were discussed in the previous section.) As the plan passes various tests, it may be moved along to more senior people for serious review. Timmons estimates that only one in five business plans or proposals are deemed interesting enough to invite the entrepreneurs in for a meeting and presentation. (A little arithmetic shows that if 20 percent of the proposals pass the search and 20 percent of those pass the screen, only 4 percent of total proposals have progressed this far.) A presentation by the entrepreneur to an investor committee follows. It enables personal factors and chemistry to enter the equation. The question-and-answer session that follows (or interrupts) the presentation will demonstrate the entrepreneur's mental agility. If the meeting goes well, the evaluation phase begins.

The Evaluation   In this phase, the plan is dissected and evaluated from every conceivable angle as the investors perform what is known legally as "due diligence." Since professional investors are employing money that is not their own, they are legally obligated to protect their customers' finances by thoroughly investigating the potential of the proposed business. Legal opinions and certified accounting expertise are required. The process of due diligence has precisely the same intent as it does for the initial public offering described in Chapter 7. It is a time-consuming process lasting six to eight weeks. It is also expensive, consuming hundreds of professional hours. The time and expense help explain why only 4 percent of proposals make it this far.

The Decision   After the due diligence phase is completed, the investors are able to make a decision. If the decision is "no," the investors should be pressed for their reasons. The entrepreneur needs this feedback before beginning this long and frustrating process again. Common reasons for rejection include:

- *Technological myopia.* Technological myopia occurs when entrepreneurs are so caught up in the excitement of their technology, processes, or product that they have not analyzed the market or developed a marketing system.
- *Failure to make full disclosure.* The entrepreneurs may have failed to divulge pertinent facts to the investors that were later discovered. This stains the reputation of the team and makes them less trustworthy in the investors' eyes.
- *Unrealistic assumptions.* The entrepreneurs have exaggerated certain claims about the product or the market and used those exaggerated figures to produce highly optimistic and improbable forecasts and scenarios.
- *Management.* The investors do not believe in the capabilities of the top management team. Investors often say they prefer a B proposal with an A team to an A proposal with a B team.

If the proposal has been rejected and the entrepreneur has received feedback, he or she should respect the input and attempt to adjust to investor requirements. If the proposal is accepted, the negotiation phase begins, and the actual details of the deal will be hammered out.

The Negotiations   The objective of the negotiation phase is to come to an agreement concerning the rights, duties, contingencies, and constraints that will bind the parties to the deal. These results are later codified in a formal investment contract known as the investment agreement. An outline of a typical investment agreement appears in Table 8–1.

An entrepreneur who has created a venture that possesses many of the four attributes of sustainable competitive advantage has negotiating power. But if the business is already using up cash faster than it can generate sales, the power may reside with the investors. The investors and the entrepreneurs must come to agreement on three crucial issues: the deal structure, protecting the investment, and exit.[13]

The Deal Structure   The two issues that need to be resolved here are (1) how is the venture to be valued? and (2) what investment instruments will be employed? We discussed valuation issues in Chapter 7. The entrepreneur will want to be able to justify the highest valuation possible, thereby requiring him or her to sell less equity and relinquish less ownership. For example, if the entrepreneur can reasonably negotiate a value of $2 million for the business, and a $1 million investment is required, the post-investment value of the firm is $3 million. The $1 million investment represents 33.3 percent of the postinvestment ownership. If the original valuation had been only $1 million, the postinvestment equity ownership position of the investor would have been 50 percent.

The investment instruments are also an issue of negotiation. Investors prefer capital structures that maximize their return and minimize their risk. They try to negotiate deals in which their investment is preferred stock or some form of senior debt (with collateral, interest payments, and guaranteed return of principal) *unless* the business is a success, in which case they want their debt to be convertible into equity! Once converted, investors can share proportionately in the venture's profits. The entrepreneur, on the other hand, prefers a simple capital structure of common equity. It is simple and clean and does not require any cash payout unless and until the company can afford them.

Many other provisions and covenants are often included in the deal structure. Definitions, descriptions, and examples of these negotiable terms are provided in Appendix 8A.

The Harvest   For many investors, the primary source of returns occurs at the end of the investment's life—when the investor "cashes out" and **harvests** the profits. The details of the harvesting process can be negotiated and spelled out in the investment agreement. **Registration rights** enable the investor to register stock, at company expense, for sale to someone else. Because of restrictive regulation on the sale of private placement investments, investors are required to register their shares (an expensive and time-consuming process) before they may resell them. The two most common registration rights are **piggyback rights** and **demand rights**. Piggyback rights give the investor the right to sell shares on any registration statement that the company makes with the Securities and Exchange Commission for sale of shares to the public. Demand rights require the company to register the investor's shares for sale (at company expense) on demand whenever the investor wants. Demand rights are the more onerous to entrepreneurs because they can force the company to go public before it wants to. A demand registration exposes the venture to the high costs and external pressures of public ownership (see Chapter 7).

Other forms of investor exit may be negotiated. The entrepreneurs can negotiate a "put" contract, in which they agree to repurchase the investors' shares at a certain

TABLE 8–1 Investment Agreement Outline

Following are the general contents of an investment agreement. The major sections are typical; details can be added or deleted depending on practice, tradition, and the negotiating skills of the participants.

I. Description of the Investment
This section identifies the parties, defines the basic terms, and includes descriptions of the amount of the investment, the securities issues, any guarantees, collateral, and subordinations. When the agreement includes warrants and options, the schedules and timing of exercise are included here. Registration rights, transferability provisions, and dilution effects are all essential parts of the investment and are described in this section.

II. Conditions of Closing
The closing of the deal is the actual transfer and execution of documents and funds. Typically, documents need to be submitted to close the deal. These are corporate documents and articles of incorporation, audited financial statements, contracts with related parties that could be construed to represent conflicts of interest, and important business documents, such as leases, supplier agreements, and employment contracts.

III. Representations and Warranties by the Venture
This section describes in full legal disclosure terms the material facts of the new venture's condition. Typical statements include the following:

- That the business is duly incorporated.
- That the officers' decisions legally bind the company.
- That the offering is exempt from SEC registration (if indeed it is).
- That all material facts have been disclosed.

IV. Representations and Warranties of the Investors
These are the legally binding statements by the investors that they are indeed who they say they are and that

- They are organized and in good standing.
- That the investors' decisions legally bind their corporation (or organization).
- That they will perform all of their obligations if all conditions are met (usually this means that they come up with the money if conditions are met).

V. Affirmative Covenants
These are all the things that the entrepreneurs agree to do under the terms of the investment agreement and in the operation of their business. Typical covenants are:

- Pay taxes, file reports, obey regulations.
- Pay principal and interest on debts.
- Maintain corporate existence.
- Keep books, have statements audited, allow investors access.
- Maintain insurance.
- Maintain minimum net worth, working capital, and asset levels.
- Hold director's meetings.

VI. Negative Covenants
These are all the things that the entrepreneurs agree not to do in the course of operating their business. Negative covenants may be abrogated with investor approval. Typical covenants are:

- Not to merge, consolidate, or acquire another business.
- Not to change the corporate charter or bylaws.
- Not to sell additional stock unless specified in the agreement.
- Not to pay dividends unless specified.
- Not to violate any of the affirmative covenants.
- Not to liquidate the business or declare bankruptcy.

TABLE 8–1 (continued)

VII. Conditions of Default
This section spells out the circumstances under which entrepreneurs are considered to have violated the agreement. These include:

- Failure to comply with affirmative or negative covenants.
- Misrepresentations of fact.
- Insolvency or reorganization.
- Failure to pay interest and principal.

VIII. Remedies
The specific remedies available to the investors if violation should occur, include:

- Forfeiture to the investor of voting control.
- Forfeiture of stock held in escrow for this purpose.
- The right of the investor to sell his stock back to the company at a predetermined price.
- Demands for payment of principal and interest.
- The payment of legal costs to ensure compliance.

IX. Other Conditions
Anything not covered elsewhere.

Source: Adapted from J. Timmons, *New Venture Creation* (Homewood, IL: Richard D. Irwin, 1994), pp. 774–777.

date for a certain price. If the put contract has a scale of dates and payment amounts, it can be considered a warrant held by the investors. Exit scenarios in case of merger or liquidation are possible, too. The entrepreneur must be careful not to be trapped in a situation where the investor can call for the liquidation of the business or an immediate cash payout when a merger/acquisition occurs.

Because the investment agreement cannot anticipate all contingencies, both sides will want to negotiate the process by which their rights under the contract can be modified. This may be done with a two-thirds vote of the board, for example.

Negotiations between investor and entrepreneur are paradoxical. While they are being carried out, the two parties are in conflict; one's gain is often the other's loss. The investor should be expected to do everything possible to secure his or her investment and increase the potential for return. The wise entrepreneur should also negotiate hard for economic rights and provisions favorable to keeping control of the company. Once the agreement has been reached, the two parties are partners, and their gains are often mutual and shared. After the investment is made and the proceeds employed to grow the venture, the relationship between investor and entrepreneur is more like a marriage and less like a haggle over the price of beans. It would be extremely shortsighted for any party to the investment to pollute the atmosphere of the courtship and have that carry over into the marriage.

E-NOTES 8–4 A SEVEN-STEP PROCESS	
1. Search	5. Negotiations
2. Screen	6. Deal Structure
3. Evaluation	7. Harvest
4. Decision	

Structuring the Deal

At its most basic level, a **deal structure** organizes a set of cash inflows and outflows. It describes what monies are coming into the business as investment and what monies are going out of the business as payments in the form of dividends, interest, and return of principal. At another level, the deal structure indicates levels of risk and reward and addresses the questions of who gets what and when. By breaking the outflows down by type according to risk level, the entrepreneur is able to segment the investor market and sell the investor the level of reward and risk that best matches the investor's own profile.

SEGMENTING THE INVESTOR MARKET

A simplified deal structure is presented in Figure 8–2.[14] To understand the figure, imagine that the cash flows shown represent an investment and subsequent returns in a biotech company that does genetic engineering. The entrepreneurs have calculated that they need to raise $2 million to found the venture at year = 0. Figure 8–2 shows their final estimation of cash flows for the project for each year through year five.

The internal rate of return on the cash flows in Figure 8–2 is 59.46 percent. This can be deemed sufficient to proceed with the analysis. The projection of five years is also sufficient and typical. However, the example shows only the aggregated bottom line numbers on the deal. To segment the investor market, we need to break down these numbers into their original component parts. In this way, we can view the risk/reward attributes of each part of the cash flow.

Table 8–2 does this and indicates that for a $2 million investment, the project generates cash flows from three sources:

1. **Tax incentives** are positive in the first three years of the project but then become negative (tax payments) in years four and five.
2. **Free cash flow** (CF) from operations is positive throughout the five-year horizon, beginning at $200,000 in year one and rising to $1.2 million in year five.
3. There is the projected **terminal value** of the business. In this example, it is predicted to be $10,000,000. This was derived (hypothetically) by taking the free

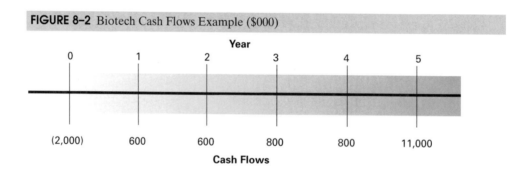

FIGURE 8–2 Biotech Cash Flows Example ($000)

Year

| 0 | 1 | 2 | 3 | 4 | 5 |

(2,000)   600   600   800   800   11,000

Cash Flows

TABLE 8–2 Segmented Cash Flow Structure ($000)						
Source of Flow	*Year 0*	*Year 1*	*Year 2*	*Year 3*	*Year 4*	*Year 5*
Investment	($2,000)					
Tax incentive		$400	$400	$100	($200)	($200)
Free CF		200	200	700	1,000	1,200
Terminal value						10,000
Total CF	($2,000)	$600	$600	$800	$800	$11,000

Source: Adapted from J. Timmons, *New Venture Creation*, (Homewood, IL: Richard D. Irwin, 1994), pp. 774–777.

cash flow for year five and subtracting the tax liability for year five ($1,200 – $200) and applying a price-earnings multiple of 10 to the result (10 × $1,000,000 = $10,000,000). Note that the "Total CF" figure is the same as the one at the start of the example in Figure 8–2.

We can also calculate the net present value of each of the sources of cash flow by discounting the cash flows on any given line of Figure 8–2 by the internal rate of return on the whole project (about 59.5 percent). The net present value (NPV) of the investment component is (−$2,000,000), since it is in year zero. The other NPVs are calculated as follows ($000):

$$\text{NPV (Tax)} = \frac{400}{(1 + .595)^1} + \frac{400}{(1 + .595)^2} + \frac{100}{(1 + .595)^3} + \frac{-200}{(1 + .595)^4} + \frac{-200}{(1 + .595)^5}$$

$$\text{NPV (CF)} = \frac{200}{(1 + .595)^1} + \frac{200}{(1 + .595)^2} + \frac{700}{(1 + .595)^3} + \frac{1,000}{(1 + .595)^4} + \frac{1,200}{(1 + .595)^5}$$

$$\text{NPV (TV)} = \frac{10,000}{(1 + .595)^5}$$

The results are as follows:

> NPV(Tax) = $383,383, which is 19.1% of the returns
> NPV(CF) = $647,272, which is 32.4% of the returns
> NPV(TV) = $968,716, which is 48.5% of the returns
> Total   = $2,000,000 (rounded off)

In this example we see that most of the returns from this deal come from the terminal value of the company. This is the riskiest figure in the example, since it depends on a great many things turning out right five years from now. Deals like this are appropriate for venture capital firm investments.

Other Investor Segments   But the entrepreneur would not want to go directly to a venture capitalist to finance this deal. There are two places the entrepreneur should go to before approaching venture capitalist. By finding a business angel (wealthy investor) and then a bank willing to lend money, the cash flows can be "sold" to investors who are less risk averse and accept lower returns than do venture capitalists. Table 8–3 suggests how these other flows might be partitioned.

TABLE 8–3 Partitioned Cash Flow Structure by Investor ($000)						
Source of Investment	*Year 0*	*Year 1*	*Year 2*	*Year 3*	*Year 4*	*Year 5*
Total CF	$600	$600	$800	$800	$11,000	
− Wealthy investor	400	400	100	(200)	(200)	
− Lending institution	100	100	100	100	1,100	
= Remaining	$100	$100	$600	$900	$10,100	

The goal of our Figure 8–2 example is to raise $2 million. The investment's tax benefits might appeal to a wealthy investor looking for a tax write-off. People in high marginal tax brackets can often protect their incomes or cash flows by investing in businesses that may have high early losses. Let's assume that the entrepreneurs have been able to convince a wealthy individual with a required rate of return of 20 percent that the tax benefit cash flow projection is accurate and reliable.

How much would the wealthy investor be willing to pay for this cash stream? This can be determined by discounting the tax cash flow by the investor's required rate of return. In this case, we arrive at a present value of $492,155. This means that the individual should be indifferent to a choice between an investment of $492,155 and the cash flows from the tax benefits. After a modest amount of convincing, the entrepreneurs are able to receive a commitment from the investor for the money in exchange for the tax benefits (which could be larger if the firm loses more money in the early years).

With some money now in hand, the entrepreneurs are ready to approach a lending institution such as a commercial bank. Banks are not interested in tax benefits; few of them make enough money to pay very much in taxes anyway. They are interested in the ability of the firm to generate cash for interest payments and the repayment of principal. Although the free cash flows of the firm are relatively risky, some portion of them should be considered safe by conservative lending officers. For our example, assume that $100,000 (see Table 8–2) is considered fairly safe in any given year. If the entrepreneurs could find a bank inclined to accept an interest payment of $100,000 each year and a repayment of principal in year 5 with an interest rate of 10 percent, they could borrow $1 million.[15] Added to the $492,000 from the wealthy investor, the entrepreneurs need only $508,000 to complete the deal.

Selling Equity   But there are not many alternatives for the remaining $508,000. So, the entrepreneurs are forced to sell equity in their business to a venture capital firm. Venture capitalists are interested in the riskiest portion of the deal, the terminal value. In exchange for this risk, they demand the highest returns (upwards of 50 percent). We can use the residual pricing method (see p. 230) to determine just how much equity in the firm must be sold to the venture capitalists to raise $508,000 at a required rate of return. To calculate this, we discount the remaining cash flows not previously committed to the wealthy individual or bank (see Table 8–3) by the venture capitalist's 50 percent required rate of return. This gives a residual value of $1,796,707. The amount of the proposed venture capital investment is $508,000, which is 28.3 percent of $1,796,707. So the entrepreneurs offer the venture capitalists 28.3 percent of the common equity in their business for the $508,000. If the venture capitalists accept the offer, the entrepreneurs have completed their $2 million financing and have kept 71.7 percent of the firm for themselves. In fact, the entrepreneurs would be creating value for themselves at any point where they were able to raise money at less than the total IRR for the project (59.5 percent).

RISK SHARING

The previous example was intentionally simplified to show that investors have different risk/reward preferences and that entrepreneurs who can identify these needs have an advantage in securing financing for their ventures. If the entrepreneurs in the example had gone directly to the venture capitalists (with their 50 percent required rate of return), they would have had to part with 79.9 percent of the equity to secure the entire $2 million.[16]

An additional assumption in the example was that the venture capitalists would take common stock and provide all of their investment up front, at the beginning of the initial period. These assumptions are relaxed in the example that follows.

Risk Sharing: Some Examples   Table 8–4 presents a simplified set of cash flows for a deal.[17] If we require this to be an all-equity deal with a required rate of return for the venture capitalist of 40 percent, then the NPV of the set of flows is $1,204. (The reader is encouraged to calculate this for themselves). The venture capitalist will demand 83 percent of the equity ($1,000/$1,204) for this investment, leaving 17 percent of the equity for the entrepreneurs. The net present value for the investors is $0, since 83 percent of this set of cash flows exactly equals the investment of $1,000, and the NPV for the entrepreneurs is $204.

However, the real world is not quite so neat. In a more likely scenario, both future cash flows and the appropriate discount rate are unknown. The parties to the deal will disagree about the amount and timing of the cash flows and the appropriate discount rate. The investors and entrepreneurs will disagree about interpretation of laws and regulations and the tax treatment of certain events. There will be conflicts of interest between the investors and founders; when one acts to protect his or her interest, it is at the expense of the other.

So let us relax just one assumption and say that instead of a certain $500-per-year cash flow, the amount is "expected" to be $500 per year, but the actual amount will be known only over time. How does this change the rewards and risks of the deal? The top portion of Table 8–5 shows the effects of this change on a common stock deal of proportional sharing.

If the probability is equal that the returns will be $450 or $550 (with the expected value still at $500), then the investor will receive $373 (.83 × $450) in the bad year and

TABLE 8-4 A Series of Cash Flows						
	Period 0	*1*	*2*	*3*	*4*	*5*
Investment	($1,000)					
Cash flow		$500	$500	$500	$500	$500
Terminal value						1,000
Net cash flow	($1,000)	$500	$500	$500	$500	$1,500

Source: From "Aspects of Financial Contracting," *Journal of Applied Corporate Finance,* 1988, pp. 25–36. Reprinted by permission of Stern Stewart Co.

TABLE 8–5 Sharing the Risk						
Common Stock (Proportional Sharing)	*Venture Capitalist*		*Entrepreneur*		*Total*	
Share of total stock		83%		17%		100%
Annual cash received: Bad scenario	$373	83	$77	17	$450	100
Annual cash received: Good scenario	456	83	94	17	550	100
Expected annual cash received	415	83	85	17	500	100
PV of cash received (incl. TV)	1,000	83	204	17	1,204	100
Net PV (incl. investment)	0		204		204	
Standard deviation of PV (and of NPV)	85	83	18	17	102	100
Preferred Stock	*Venture Capitalist*		*Entrepreneur*		*Total*	
Share of total stock		83%		17%		100%
Annual cash received: Bad scenario	$415	93	$35	7	$450	100
Annual cash received: Good scenario	415	73	135	27	550	100
Expected annual cash received	415	83	85	17	500	100
PV of cash received (incl. TV)	1,000	83	204	17	1,204	100
Net PV (incl. investment)	0		204		204	
Standard deviation of PV (and of NPV)	0	0	102	100	102	100

Source: From "Aspects of Financial Contracting," *Journal of Applied Corporate Finance,* 1988, pp. 25–36. Reprinted by permission of Stern Stewart Co.

$456 (.83 × $550) in a good year. The expected annual return is the average of the two ($415), and the standard deviation (a measure of risk) of the PV to the investor is 83 percent of the total deal's NPV standard deviation of $102, or $85. The investor in this scenario receives 83 percent of the rewards and assumes 83 percent of the risk.

However, the venture capitalist will desire a different deal structure and, owing to the "golden rule" (whoever has the gold, makes the rule), will be able to bargain for it. The investor will negotiate for preferred stock with a fixed dividend and some liquidation preference. The sophisticated investor will probably want the preferred stock to be cumulative as well, meaning that any missed dividend payments accumulate and must be paid before any dividends on common stock are declared and paid. The bottom half of Table 8–5 shows how preferred stock changes the risk/reward ratio in favor of the investors.

In this scenario, the investors receive their $415 expected cash flow dividend regardless of whether the actual cash flow is $450 or $550. In the bad year, the investors receive 93 percent of the cash flow, in the good year, 73 percent. All the risk of a bad year (and extra reward for the good year) is borne by the entrepreneurs. The standard deviation of the investors' returns is zero because there is no variation. The investors bear no risk (unless we include the risk of bankruptcy, which accounts for the 40 percent discount rate) because of the use of preferred stock instead of common stock.

So the investor will want preferred stock. There are two reasons for this preference in addition to minimizing risk. First, by enabling the entrepreneurs to achieve maximal gain under the "good year" scenario, the investors provide incentives for the entrepreneurs to work hard and smart to produce a good year. Second, if the entrepreneurs' forecasts are too rosy, and the entrepreneurs themselves do not think they can achieve these forecasts, they will have to admit to this before agreeing to this deal. Why? Because they know they will not be able to achieve the cash flows necessary for them to see any of the profits of the business. In essence, they will be working for the investors without hope of personal gain. This process is known as "smoking them out."

STAGED FINANCING

Few deals require all the money up front. Most new venture development occurs in stages, and therefore most deals should allow for **staged (or phased) financing** as well. Let's say that the entrepreneurs need $20 million and are willing to sell 75 percent of the firm for this capital investment. Table 8–6 illustrates one possible way of staging or phasing, the financing. Often, first-stage financing is used for market studies, development of prototypes, and early organizational costs. The amounts are small relative to the entire financing plan and serve to prove the venture viable. In this scenario, $1 million goes to pay for these development and start-up costs and buys 50 percent of the venture. The implied valuation, therefore, is $2 million.

As the venture succeeds in its initial efforts, it becomes more valuable. Let's say that the second-stage money is needed to purchase plant and equipment for a small manufacturing facility that will enable the firm to test engineering concepts and design and to produce for a test market. Four million dollars are needed for this stage. The $4 million buys 33.3 percent of the firm. Since the investors already own 50 percent, this share is diluted, and they end up owning 66.7 percent at the end of this round. The company is more valuable at this point. Its implied valuation is now $12 million ($4 million × 3).

If the venture is on track and succeeding as planned, third-stage financing will be for a full production ramp-up. If this will require $15 million, the investor can be brought up to the originally determined 75 percent ownership by purchasing another 25 percent of the company. The postinvestment valuation of the firm is now $60 million. At each stage the investor was willing to purchase less of the firm at a higher price.

Why was the investor willing to do this? Because the continued success of the entrepreneurs as they met their goals and milestones made the venture more valuable (and less risky).

THE OPTION TO ABANDON

Not all staged-financing deals proceed as smoothly as the one depicted in Table 8–6. If things go wrong and the deal turns sour, the investors will not want to put additional money in, especially at the $4 million and $15 million dollar levels. That is, they want the **option to abandon**. The earlier example (Tables 8–4 and 8–5) shows what happens

TABLE 8–6   Phased Investment Scheme

Round of Financing	Amount Invested This Round	Percent Received This Round	VC's Share	Founder's Share	Implied Valuation (Post Money)
First round	$1,000,000	50.0%	50.0%	50.0%	$2,000,000
Second round	4,000,000	33.3	66.7	33.3	12,000,000
Third round	15,000,000	25.0	75.0	25.0	60,000,000

Formula for the second round: 50% + (33.3% × (1 − .50)) = 66.7 %
Formula for the third round: 66.7% + (25% × (1 − 66.7)) = 75.0%

Source: From "Aspects of Financial Contracting," *Journal of Applied Corporate Finance,* 1988, pp. 25–36. Reprinted by permission of Stern Stewart Co.

if staged financing is used and the entrepreneurs predict small variance in the expected cash flow of their venture. What happens if we increase the variance? If we increase the variance of outcomes to $50 cash flow in a bad year and $950 in a good year (the expected value is still $500), we increase the importance of being able to reevaluate the investment decision. In Table 8–5, with the spread only between $450 and $550, the investor was going to get paid in either case. With the wider spread, however, the investor will not get paid at all in the bad scenario.

Suppose the venture needs $500 in two stages. For this example, we need to compare two sets of rules for the investor. The first rule is that the venture capitalist has no choice but to invest in the second round, even if the cash flow is only $50. The second rule is that the investor may choose not to invest the $500 in the second round and thereby abandon the project. If the investor abandons the project, he or she forfeits any claims to an annual cash flow and receives a reduced share of the terminal value, $750. Table 8–7 illustrates the possibilities of these cash flow scenarios and rules.

The top portion of Table 8–7 illustrates a situation in which the investor is required to invest in both years. Because the discount rate is still 40 percent and the ex-

TABLE 8-7 The Option to Abandon the Project

	0	1	2	3	4	5	PV@ 40%
Rule I: VC Invest in Both Years							
Good scenario		$950	$950	$950	$950	$950	$1,933
Bad scenario		50	50	50	50	50	102
Expected annual cash		500	500	500	500	500	1,018
Terminal value						1,000	186
Expected cash inflow		500	500	500	500	1,500	1,204
Investment	($500)	(500)					(857)
Expected net cash	($500)	$0	$500	$500	$500	$1,500	$346

	0	1	2	3	4	5	PV@ 40%
Rule II: VC Has Option to Abandon in Year 1							
Good scenario							
Annual cash flow		$950	$950	$950	$950	$950	$1,933
Terminal value						1,000	186
Investment	($500)	(500)					(857)
Net cash flow	(500)	450	950	950	950	1,950	1,262
Bad scenario							
Annual cash flow		0	0	0	0	0	0
Terminal value						750	139
Investment	(500)						500
Net cash flow	(500)	0	0	0	0	750	(361)
Expected (or average) value of scenarios							
Expected net cash	($500)	$225	$475	$475	$475	$1,225	$451
Expected value of option to abandon (Rule I—Rule II): $105							

Source: From "Aspects of Financial Contracting," *Journal of Applied Corporate Finance*, 1988, pp. 25–36. Reprinted by permission of Stern Stewart Co.

pected value of the annual cash flows have not changed from the original example (Table 8–5), the PV of the venture is still $1,204. But because $500 of the investment is delayed one period, the NPV for the entire project rises to $346 from $204.

The bottom portion of Table 8–7 is more complex and requires us to calculate the average of expected values of a good year and a bad year when the investor may abandon the project after the first period. The good scenario shows a periodic cash flow of $950 and a NPV of $1,262. The bad scenario shows an initial investment of $500, no cash flow, and a terminal value of $750. The NPV of this is (-$361). The average of a positive $1,262 and a negative $361 is $451. So, the value of the difference between the expected NPV of the first situation (top of table) and the expected NPV of the second situation (bottom of table) is $105 ($451 minus $346). Therefore, the investor can gain up to $105 in expected value by operating under the option to abandon. If the option is granted for "free," the investor gains the full $105. Clearly, the investor would be willing to pay up to $105 at the outset for the right to abandon. By changing the structure of the deal, the entrepreneur has created value and can sell that value in the form of an option to the investor.

Of course, this was a simplified example, and calculating options such as this is generally more complicated because there are more than just two possible cash flows ($50 and $950) and more than two possible investing stages ($500 in the first period and $500 in the second period). But the principle is illustrated—**the deal structure can create value**.

Other option types exist as well. For example, the option to revalue the project helps to determine at what price new capital will come into the deal if it is needed. A fixed-price option for future financing is also a possibility. If the value of the firm is above the exercise price, the investor will invest. If the value is below the exercise price, the investor will allow the option to expire or sell it to another investor who might find the option more rewarding because of a different risk/reward profile and preference.

WARRANTS

A **warrant** is the right to purchase equity and is usually attached to another financial instrument, such as a bond or debenture. Ordinarily, debt holders' returns are limited to interest and principal. The purpose of a warrant is to enable debt holders to add to their total return in case the venture turns out to be quite profitable. In this case the warrant is sometimes called an "equity kicker" and in fact represents equity that, if the warrant is exercised, is off the balance sheet.

A callable warrant enables the entrepreneurs to pay the creditor off, thereby retiring the debt and recovering the equity according to a fixed schedule. The price of the warrant can be calculated for each period outstanding. Table 8–8 provides an example of the calculation of the price of a callable warrant.[18]

Let's assume that the investor has a subordinated debenture with a face value of $1 million, a coupon of 10 percent, and a warrant that guarantees the investor a total return of 15 percent. Calculating the call price (or value) of the warrant requires two preliminary steps. First, the analyst must determine the present value and cumulative present values of the interest payments. In Table 8–8 the third column shows the present value of the cash flow from the interest payments, discounted at 15 percent. Next, the analyst must calculate the future payment that makes the entire cumulative pre-

TABLE 8–8   Calculating the Value of a Warrant

Perion n	Cash Flow Interest Payments	Present Value @ 15%	Cumulative Present Value to Date	Value of the Warrant
0	−$1,000	−$1,000	−$1,000	
1	100	87	−913	
2	100	77	−836	
3	100	66	−770	
4	100	57	−713	
5	100	50	−663	$333

Assumptions: 1. $1,000,000 subordinated debenture with a 10% coupon.
2. Warrants attached guarantee debt holder total return of 15%.

1. Calculate the future payment in period *n* that will provide for a positive present value equal to the cumulative negative present value to date. This makes the entire present value equal to zero at the guaranteed 15% rate.

$$\text{For period 5: } \$663 = \frac{X}{(1.15)^5} = \$1,333$$

2. The warrant price is the difference between this value ($1,333) and the return of principal ($1,000) = $333.

3. This calculation can be made for any year, thus producing a schedule of warrant prices or values.

sent value equal to zero at the guaranteed (in this case 15 percent) rate. The fourth column in the table shows the cumulative present value.

The actual calculation of the warrant's value, however, requires two additional steps. These are also described in Table 8–8. The first step calculates the total future payment, discounted (for *n* periods, in this case 5) at the required rate of return (15 percent in this case) that brings the cumulative present value (column 4; −$663) to zero. In this example, the amount is $1,333. The warrant price is the difference between this amount ($1,333) and the return of principal ($1,000), in this case $333.

PITFALLS AND PROBLEMS TO AVOID

There is only 100 percent of anything. This is true of the equity in a new venture and the cash flow from a start-up. Attempts to sell more than 100 percent of the equity and cash flow will come to grief (and prison). So each time the entrepreneur raises money, the future is somewhat constrained by the acts of the past. Each deal limits future options. In addition, each deal comes with covenants and legal restrictions that further bind the entrepreneur within a net of obligations. Unless the business is self-financing from the start, these constraints are inevitable, and the entrepreneur should focus on the controllable factors and not the uncontrollable ones.

First, the entrepreneur should avoid choosing investors and, especially, investment houses for their size or prestige alone. The choice should be made based on the needs of the business and not the egos of the founders. Conflicts of interest between the financiers, investment houses, and entrepreneurs are inevitable. The conflicts should be resolved in favor of what is best for the business. Bad advice abounds in these situations. Some of it results from ignorance, but much from self-interest. Although the entrepreneur is probably new to this game, the lawyers, brokers, and investors are not. Caution is advised.

The entrepreneur also needs to guard against his or her own greed. If he or she offers to give up too little—too little equity, too little control, too little authority—the investors will walk away. However, the entrepreneur must also guard against the appearance of giving up too much. This appears as either naivete or a lack of commitment to the new venture's future.

Last, the entrepreneur should prepare for the reality that future financing is always a possibility. The initial and early deals should not foreclose on this need. Incentives for the current investors to invest more should be built into each contract. Incentives for others to invest and not be crowded out or preempted by the initial investors should also remain. And everyone involved in the deal should have some latitude in their decisions and the ability to exit after a reasonable time period with their integrity intact (and maybe some money, too).

Legal and Tax Issues

Obtaining experienced legal assistance is critical to financing the new venture and resolving the legal and tax issues confronting it. Failing to obtain a good lawyer and accountant is worse than the trouble of choosing one.[19] Legal and tax assistance is needed for:

- The formation of business entities.
- Setting up books and records for tax purposes.
- Negotiating leases and financing.
- Writing contracts with partners and employees.
- Advising about insurance needs and requirements.
- All litigation procedures.
- Regulation and compliance.
- Patents, trademarks, and copyright protections.

Not all attorneys will be competent in all of the areas listed, but competent legal counsel knows its limitations, and experts can be brought in when required. As with many other aspects of business, there is no substitute for experience.

The best way to find competent legal service is word of mouth. The entrepreneur should then follow up by checking with legal referral services and interviewing lawyers personally to determine the rapport and the lawyer's understanding of the entrepreneur's business needs. Good legal counsel is not cheap; rates can run from $90 to $350 per hour. Some lawyers who specialize in getting new ventures up and running are willing to take equity in lieu of cash as payment for services.

There is an old saying that "a person who represents himself in a legal matter has a fool for a client." But if an entrepreneur insists on self-representation, he or she should be conversant with the content and the process of the law. A course in contracts and real estate law is recommended.

LEGAL FORMS OF ORGANIZATION IN THE UNITED STATES

In the United States there are five major types of legal organization: sole proprietorships, partnerships, corporations, S corporations and limited liability companies (LLC). Each has its own characteristics in terms of legal identity and continuity, liability, taxation, and financing regulations.

Sole Proprietorships   **Sole proprietorships** are the easiest to form and represent the majority of small businesses and self-employed persons. The company is simply an extension of the owner. For tax purposes, the sole proprietor completes an income statement (Schedule C). The sole proprietorship is taxed at the individual's rate, and earnings are subject to self-employment tax. A proprietorship ceases to exist when the owner dies, retires, or goes out of business; it cannot be transferred to another as a going concern. The owner is personally liable for all business activities (legal and financial).

Partnership   A **partnership** is defined as a voluntary association of two or more persons to carry on as co-owners of a business for profit. All partnerships should be regulated with partnership agreements conforming to the Uniform Partnership Act. This agreement should cover such issues as:

- The contribution and participation requirements of each partner.
- The allocation of profits and losses.
- Responsibilities and duties.
- Salaries and compensation contracts.
- Consequences of withdrawal, retirements, or deaths.
- The manner and means by which the partnership will be dissolved.

Partnerships are not considered separate tax entities for tax purposes. The partners are taxed only at one level, that of the partner. Earnings flow proportionately to each individual, and the tax treatment is then similar to that of the sole proprietor. A partnership ceases to exist on the death, retirement, or insanity of any of the partners, unless a provision for continuation has been made in the partnership agreement.

There are two types of partnerships. A **general partnership** has only general partners and conforms to the description and limitations just listed. A **limited partnership** has both general and limited partners. The general partners assume responsibility for management and have unlimited liability for business activity. They must have at least a 1 percent interest in the profits and losses of the firm. The limited partners have no voice in management and are limited in liability up to their capital contribution and any specified additional debts. A limited partnership is limited to 35 owners.

One of the dangers of partnerships that is often unanticipated is that partners are agents for each other. The actions of one partner can cause unlimited personal liability for all the other partners. This is referred to as joint and several liability.

In Street Story 8–2 we see how partners' skills can be complementary, how their partner relationship can help their company to survive and the problems partners can have.

Corporation   A corporation (also called a regular **C corporation** for the section of the law that describes it) is a separate legal person under the laws of the state within which it is incorporated. Its life continues even after the founders or managers die or retire. The central authority resides with the board of directors, and ownership resides with the stockholders. Shares may be bought and sold freely. No investor is liable beyond his or her proportionate capital contributions except for "insiders" in cases of securities fraud or violations of the tax code.

Playing the Partnership Game

James Cameron, CEO and one of the five founders of Equipe Technologies of Sunnyvale, California, knows the down side and the up side of partnership agreements. "In the last year, I've gotten into screaming matches with all four of my partners," recounts Cameron. "But within a day that's over, and we've moved on. We recognize that we're all in this for the long haul, and frankly, it's quite lucrative for us to stay together."

According to *Inc.* magazine, 44.8 percent of the start-ups on their list of the fastest-growing private companies were created by partnership agreements. Equipe, which designs and builds robots for the semiconductor industry, ranked number nine on that list in 1996. Each of the five entrepreneurs who formed this firm had a specific expertise to contribute to the venture. They included a mechanical engineer, an electrical engineer, and software engineer (representing the three domains that are integrated in robot design), a former Big Six CPA, and Cameron, whose strength is sales and marketing.

Equipe's partners faced a serious challenge almost as soon as they set-up shop. The company they had all previously worked for decided to sue them in federal court for breach of fiduciary duty and "misappropriation" of trade secrets. During the next 18 months almost all the income generated by the fledgling venture went towards their legal expenses. This meant the partners had to make sacrifices. Strapped for cash, two of the partners were forced to move into the office, using a hibachi outside the back door in lieu of a kitchen. "I'd come in for an early meeting, and I'd have to rouse those guys out of bed and jam their stuff into a closet before the customer arrived," remembers Cameron. Cameron himself moved into a communal home, while another partner rode a bike eight miles to work each day after he crashed his car.

Today Cameron credits the company's success to its unusually large and diverse partnership. "In a more conventional approach, Paul (the partner with the CPA who functions as president and chief financial officer) and I would have raised more money and hired the three engineers," says Cameron, "But I'm glad we didn't. We'd have had to pay them somewhere near market wages, and with the lawsuit that would have been unachievable."

After a six-week trial, Equipe lost the lawsuit when the jury awarded $75,000 to the former employer. But the company and its five partners went on to become a winner, chalking up more than $28 million in sales during 1995.

Source: Adapted from Jay Finegan, "Party of Five," *Inc. 500 Special Issue*, 1995, p. 89.

A corporation is taxed as a separate entity according to the corporate tax code and rates. Dividends declared by the corporation are "after-tax" from the firm's point of view, then taxed again at the shareholder level. This is known as the "double taxation" problem. To get around the double taxation problem, entrepreneurs often resort to tactics that are regulated by the Internal Revenue Service under the Federal Tax Code. These tactics usually revolve around issues of salary and interest expense.

For example, an entrepreneur could arrange to pay himself or herself a salary so high that it wipes out all profits of the corporation. Since the corporation has no profits, it pays no taxes, and the entrepreneur pays taxes just on the salary at individual tax rates. Under Section 162 of the Federal Tax Code, the Internal Revenue Service can reclassify as dividends portions of salary that are unreasonably high. This creates a corporate tax liability in addition to the personal tax liability.

Interest expense is deductible from a corporation's pretax profits and therefore reduces its tax liability. This may tempt an entrepreneur to lend the new venture money for start-up and expansion capital instead of taking an equity position. This practice is considered legitimate, but only to a point. Under section 385 of the Federal Tax Code, a thinly capitalized company (one with a debt/equity ratio over 10:1) can have its debt reclassified as equity. Also, if the debt does not look like debt because, for example, it has conditional payment schedules instead of fixed coupon rates, it may be reclassified as equity. This means that what were tax-deductible interest payments are now double-taxed dividends.

The losses of regular corporations accumulate and can be used as tax shields in future years. The losses of proprietorships and partnerships are passed along to the principals in the year they are incurred. One exception to this involves "section 1244 stock." If this type of stock is selected in the firm's initial legal and tax organization, the owners of the firm would be able to deduct their losses from their regular income if the business goes bankrupt. If they had selected a regular corporation, their losses would be treated as capital losses at tax time.

S Corporation   An **S corporation** is a special vehicle for small and new businesses that enables them to avoid the double taxation of regular corporations. To qualify for S corporation status, the firm must:

- Have only one class of stock (although differences in voting rights are allowable).
- Be wholly owned by U.S. citizens and derive no more than 80 percent of its income from non-U.S. sources.
- Have 35 or fewer stockholders, all of whom agree to the S corporation status.
- Obtain no more than 25 percent of its revenue through passive (investment) sources.

Although S corporations are incorporated under state law, for federal tax purposes they resemble partnerships. Usually, stockholders receive proportionally the profits or losses of the firm. This percentage is deemed to be a dividend. The monies paid to shareholders are considered self-employment income, but they are *not* subject to self-employment tax.

Limited Liability Company (LLC)   The **limited liability company** is a relatively new type of business organization that shares characteristics with both corporations and partnerships. Like a corporation, an LLC is legally a separate entity that provides liability protection for its owners. But when it comes to taxes LLCs are treated like a partnership, meaning that the LLC does not pay taxes itself, and that all profits and losses *flow through* directly to LLC owners and are reported on their tax returns.

While a corporation can be described by four basic characteristics (limited liability, continuity of life, centralized management, and free transferability of interests), an LLC maintains its tax status by selecting two and only two of these traits when it drafts its operating agreement. In other words, if an LLC decides that it will offer limited liability and be organized under a centralized Board of Directors, then it cannot legally continue as an entity after its owners die, or freely sell and trade its shares. So, an LLC receives some of the benefits of a partnership and some of the advantages of a corporation, but not all of them. For many firms, this means that either the partnership or the corporation remains the preferred choice.

LLC owners are called "members" and may be individuals, corporations, trusts, pension plans, other LLCs, or almost any other entity. The organization is required to file Articles of Organization with the Secretary of State in the state where it operates, and is also required to file some sort of annual report in most states, but an LLC still spends less time producing legal and tax reports than most corporations.[20]

Table 8–9 compares the different forms of legal organization on a number of important dimensions.

TABLE 8–9 Legal Forms of Organization Compared

Characteristic	Sole Proprietor	General Partnership	Limited Partnership	C Corporation	S Corporation	LLC
Limited Liability for ALL Owners	No	Yes	Yes	Yes	Yes	Yes
Owners can participate in management w/o losing liability protection	n/a	No	Partially	Yes	Yes	Yes
Easy to form w/o maintaining extensive record keeping	Yes	Yes	Yes	Yes	No	Yes
Number of owners	1	1 or more	1–35	2 or more	1–35	2 or more
Restrictions on ownership	No	No	Yes	No	Yes	No
Double tax	No	No	No	Yes	No	No
Able to deduct business loss on individual return	Yes	No	Yes	No	Yes	Yes

Source: Adapted from "LLC vs. Corporation vs. Sole Proprietorship; What are they and how do they differ?" http://www.hia.com//llcwed-struc.html, April 3, 1997.

> **E-NOTES 8–5 LEGAL ORGANIZATION**
> There are five major ways to organize businesses in the United States:
> - Sole proprietorships,
> - Partnerships,
> - Corporations,
> - S corporations,
> - Limited liability companies (LLC).

PRIVATE PLACEMENTS UNDER U.S. SECURITIES LAWS

Whenever one party supplies money or some item of value expecting that it will be used to generate a profit or return for the investor from the efforts of others, a security is created.[21] All national governments regulate the issuance and redemption of securities, and all U.S. states do so as well. In the United States, the regulatory agency that oversees this function is the Securities and Exchange Commission (SEC). Because compliance with SEC regulations is always expensive and time-consuming, small firms and new firms have found it burdensome to comply. In response, regulations providing "safe harbors" for small and new businesses have been enacted. These safe harbors enable the smaller firm to issue securities (with constraints and limits) without conforming to the high level of effort necessary for large public offerings (see Chapter 7 on the IPO). These are called **private placements**. The specific regulations should be consulted directly for complete details. Experienced legal counsel should always be retained when interpreting these rules. Minor rule infractions and small deviations from the regulations can cause the firm selling unregistered securities to lose its safe harbor and leave it without any protections. These private financing regulations (found in regulations D and A of the SEC rules) include:

- **Rule 504.** Rule 504 is most useful when a venture is raising small amounts from many investors. A venture can raise up to $1 million during any 12-month period with up to $500,000 free from state registration as well. There is no limit on the number or nature of the investors, no advertising is permitted, and there are qualified limits on resale of these securities. Issuers cannot be investment companies.
- **Rule 505.** Permits sale of up to $5 million to up to 35 investors and an unlimited number of "accredited" investors. No general solicitation or advertising is permitted, and there are limits on resale. Issuers cannot be investment companies. Disclosure is required to unsophisticated investors but not to "accredited" investors.
- **Rule 506.** Permits the sale of an unlimited amount of investors and an unlimited number of qualified "accredited" investors. No solicitation or advertising is permitted. There is no limit on the nature of the issuer. Unsophisticated investors may be represented by purchasing representatives who can evaluate the prospectus.
- **Rule 147 (Intrastate).** For issues that meet the 80 percent rule for assets, income, and the use of proceeds. Investors must be residents of the same state. There are no limits on the nature of the issuer, the number of purchasers, or the amount of the issue. There is a nine-month holding period before resale.
- **Regulation A.** Securities sold under this regulation must be less than $1.5 million in any 12-month period and sold only to "accredited" investors. Advertising is restricted, but there are no limits on the nature of the issuer or the number of in-

vestors. There are no limits on resale, but an offering circular must be filed and distributed. A "mini-registration" filing in the SEC regional office is required.

- **Rule 144.** If shares are sold and not covered by Regulation A, then there are problems with resale (because the securities are not registered) unless they can be sold under Rule 144. Rule 144 requires a holding period and a filing registration before the shares can be resold.

These regulations refer to "accredited" investors. The term **accredited investor** has a very specific legal meaning.[22] Generally, accredited investors are investment companies, individuals with wealth and income above certain floors, and the officers of the issuer of the securities. The language of the regulation indicates the importance of having experienced legal counsel guide the process of issuing and selling private security offerings.

In addition, all the exemptions listed are subject to **integration principles**. This means that the securities should conform to a single plan of financing, for the same general corporate purpose, be paid for with the same consideration, and be the same class of securities. They should also be offered or sold at or about the same time; under Rule 147 or Regulation D, any offering made six months prior or six months after will be integrated into the exempt offering. Violation of any of these principles violates the regulation, and the entire offering will be considered nonexempt and therefore in violation of the securities laws.

Last, in addition to compliance with all laws requiring securities registration, entrepreneurs must recognize the importance of providing potential investors with full and complete disclosure about the security, the use of funds, and any other consideration affecting the decision to invest. Both federal and state law make it unlawful to make any untrue statement of a material fact or to omit any material fact. A "material fact" is one that a reasonable investor would consider substantial in making an investment decision.

If an investor can show that the issuer misstated or omitted a material fact in connection with the sale of securities, the investor would be entitled to recover the amount paid from either the firm or possibly the individual directors and officers of the venture. Liability may also be imposed on the entrepreneur as the "controlling person" of the actual issuer. Actions such as these must begin within one year of the discovery of the misstatement and no later than three years after the sale of the security.

Cases such as these are complex and expensive. The court has the benefit of hindsight, which can lead to second-guessing the original issuer. The outcomes frequently depend on who can prove what was a "fact" at the time of the issue. A carefully prepared offering document can be invaluable in legal proceedings.[23]

U.S. BANKRUPTCY LAWS

We have stressed the risky nature of entrepreneurial activity but have not directly confronted the ultimate negative consequences of risky behavior—bankruptcy. Bankruptcy is an option for dealing with financial troubles, primarily an impossible debt burden. The declaration of bankruptcy by a firm is an attempt to wipe the slate clean, equitably pay off creditors, and start again. Because of the potential rejuvenating effect of bankruptcy and the forgiveness of a portion of debts, a person or a corporation can declare bankruptcy only once every six years.

The prospect of bankruptcy is always with the entrepreneur and the firm's financiers. It partially accounts for the high required rates of return needed by equity investors. Because equity investors understand that in case of bankruptcy they are likely to receive no gains and even lose all their capital investment, they need high returns from the "winners." And our repeated discussions about the resources that provide sustainable competitive advantage for the venture have implicitly included the prospect of bankruptcy. Ventures created with resources that are rare, valuable, imperfectly imitable, and nonsubstitutable are more resistant to environmental threats, competitive attacks, and internal implementation errors than forms without these resources. Therefore, firms with a solid resource based strategy are more resistant to bankruptcy.

Warning Signs/Predictive Models Bankruptcy seldom sneaks up on a firm. There are usually warning signs, and these signs can appear as early as a year to 18 months before the crisis actually occurs. Financial problems, specifically the inability to make interest and principal payments, are the usual precipitating event. However, any time the business has liabilities greater than its assets, it may file a bankruptcy petition. Because of the accounting rule that requires the acknowledgment of liabilities as soon as they are known, firms that may have cash to pay debts often find themselves with negative net worth. This can happen when a firm must recognize future liabilities for employee health costs or pensions. But the signals are evident earlier, and the longer-term cause is poor management. The early signs include unhappy customers, a faulty production or service delivery process, bad relations with investors or the bank, employee unrest and work stoppages, and, ultimately, poor financial management.

There are telltale signs of impending crisis. For example, when the firm changes management, its advisers, and especially its accountants and auditors, this is an indication that problems are mounting. These changes often result in late financial statements. Other indicators are:

- Qualified and uncertified accountants' opinions.
- Refusal to provide access to key executives.
- Sudden searching for an alliance partner.
- New interest in a merger or acquisition without strategic reasons.
- Writing off assets.
- Restrictions in credit terms and availability.

Because creditors can either save their investment or attempt to save the firm if they can become aware of the crisis early enough, research has been conducted to provide an early warning system for bankruptcy. The most famous of these predictive models uses information commonly available in financial documents.[24] There are two models, one for private companies, the other for public firms. The models are equations that calculate Z-scores from a discriminate analysis of the data. The models are shown in Table 8–10.

By plugging in the venture's actual financial ratios, multiplying these ratios by their weights (coefficients), and calculating the total, an analyst can determine whether the firm is in danger of bankruptcy or is above the safe range. Ventures with Z-scores in the intermediate range need watching.

TABLE 8–10   Predictive Model of Bankruptcy

Model 1: The Public firm

Z-score = 0.012 (WC/TA) + 0.014 (RE/TA) + 0.033 (EBIT/TA) + 0.006 (MVE/TL) + 0.999 (Sales/TA)

If the Z-score is less than 1.81, the firm is in danger of bankruptcy.
If the Z-score is greater than 2.99, the firm is considered safe.
Values between 1.81 and 2.99 are considered cautionary.

Model 2: The Private firm

Z-score = 0.717 (WC/TA) + 0.847 (RE/TA) + 3.107 (EBIT/T) + 0.998 (Sales/TA)

If the Z-score is less than 1.23, the firm is in danger of bankruptcy.
If the Z-score is greater than 2.90, the firm is considered safe.
Values between 1.23 and 2.90 are considered cautionary.

where:

$$
\begin{aligned}
WC &= \text{Working capital} \\
RE &= \text{Retained earnings} \\
EBIT &= \text{Earnings before interest and taxes} \\
MVE &= \text{Market value of the equity} \\
Sales &= \text{Sales} \\
NW &= \text{Net worth} \\
TA &= \text{Total assets} \\
TL &= \text{Total liabilities}
\end{aligned}
$$

Source: E. Altman, R. Haldeman, and P. Narayanan, "ZETA-Analysis: A New Model to Identify Bankruptcy Risk," *Journal of Banking and Finance* (June 1977): 29–54.

The Bankruptcy Reform Act of 1978   The Bankruptcy Reform Act of 1978 codifies three specific types of voluntary bankruptcy. These are known by their chapter designations: Chapter 7, Chapter 11, and Chapter 13. Each of these chapters details a separate manner by which the firm and its creditors can seek protection. A venture can be forced into bankruptcy (involuntary) by its creditors under the following conditions:

- When three or more creditors have aggregate claims that total $5,000 more than the value of their collateral.
- When there is one or more of such creditors and the total number of creditors and claim holders is under 12.
- When any one general partner in a limited partnership begins legal proceedings.

The failure to pay on time is sufficient criteria for a filing of involuntary bankruptcy, even if the firm has the ability to pay. One way to avoid involuntary bankruptcy is to make sure that no three creditors are owed more than $5,000 in the aggregate and that the firm has more than 12 claim holders.

Chapter 7 Bankruptcy.   A **Chapter 7 bankruptcy** provides for the voluntary or involuntary liquidation of the firm. The process provides for an accounting of all of the assets of the debtor, the identification of all creditors and claim holders, the appointment of a trustee to supervise the process, and a meeting of the creditors' committee to work out a plan of liquidation and distribution.

Portions of the debtor's assets are exempt from liquidation. The debtor is allowed to keep, among other things, a $7,500 interest in a principal residence, up to $1,200 interest in a motor vehicle, up to $200-per-item interest in personal household goods, and the continued rights to receive Social Security benefits, unemployment compensation, public assistance, and disability benefits.

The remainder of the estate will be liquidated and claims paid on a priority basis. First priority is the administrative expenses of discharging the petition for bankruptcy. Also at the top is the government for the payment of taxes in arrears. Employees are usually next in line. These are followed by secured creditors, unsecured creditors, preferred shareholders, and, last, common shareholders. If there is not enough money to pay a class of creditors in full, the money is distributed on a prorated basis.

After all the funds are distributed, the business is "wound up" and ceases to exist. If the debtor is an individual, the court will issue a discharge, and the person is free of all debts except those arising from alimony, child support, and, of course, back taxes.

Chapter 11 Bankruptcy. A **Chapter 11 bankruptcy** is filed for the purpose of reorganizing the firm's debts so it can continue to operate. The goal is to keep the business running and eventually emerge from Chapter 11 as a healthier, albeit smaller, company. Creditors and claim holders may prefer this form of bankruptcy if they believe that there is a probability that they will receive more of their money than under Chapter 7.

Chapter 11 proceedings are often entered into voluntarily by the owners of the business because once the filing is made, all payments of debts and obligations are stopped until a settlement can be worked out. The process calls for the appointment of a trustee, the formation of a committee of general unsecured creditors, and meetings between the committee and the owners to work out a plan for reorganization. The debtor has 120 days to file the reorganization plan and 60 more days to obtain acceptance by the committee. The plan shows how the different classes of creditors will be treated and how the business will be operated until all the classes have had their reorganized claims satisfied. The court must approve the final plan. If the court approves the plan, the debtor is discharged of the old debts and obligated to the new debts as described in the plan.

However, many times firms do not emerge from Chapter 11. Then they are forced to liquidate anyway under Chapter 7. Evidence suggests that instead of forestalling liquidation and protecting the venture, Chapter 11 hastens the end. The chances of a small firm emerging from Chapter 11 are estimated at between 10 and 30 percent. The primary reasons for this are:

- The high costs of legal proceedings to discharge the debts.
- The diversion of often shallow management to legal proceedings instead of business management.
- Weakened bargaining power when creditors come face-to-face.
- Market disruption because of negative publicity. Customers and suppliers jump ship at the announcement of a bankruptcy filing.

Sometimes it is recommended that the use of personal persuasion and negotiation be employed before the owner takes the precipitous and risky move of a Chapter 11 filing.

Chapter 13 Bankruptcy.   A **Chapter 13 bankruptcy** covers individuals, primarily sole proprietorships, with regular incomes of less than $100,000 and secured debts of less than $350,000. Its purpose is to discharge the debts of the person and protect the person from harassment by creditors. The plan can call for an extension of credit, paid in full over time, or a reduction in outstanding debt with a payment schedule over three years.

Options and Bargaining Power   Although debtors and owners in bankruptcy feel stigmatized and powerless, they often have a great deal of latitude and bargaining power. This is because the courts protect them from the full payment of debts. Creditors are usually loathe to see anything less than full payment. Therefore, in many cases, creditors will cooperate with the owners to avoid bankruptcy proceedings. The power of the owners derives from the conflicts of interest among the creditors. Since creditors are paid off according to the class to which they belong, they have different interests. Lower-priority creditors will be more hesitant to put the firm in bankruptcy because they will receive less. *Therefore, these lower-priority, or unsecured, creditors may even be a source of additional credit to prevent an involuntary bankruptcy filing!* It is often possible for the debtor to arrange postponement of payments, extended payment schedules, moratoriums on interest and principal payments, renegotiated leases, and the forgiveness of accrued interest under these circumstances. Of course, creditors do not have to be so understanding and can move legally against the firm. Good financial relationships and good personal relationships are extra insurance for the troubled business.

Summary

This chapter elaborated and expanded the ideas in Chapter 7. The entrepreneur must understand the criteria that investors use to evaluate the decision to invest in the new venture. Because different investors possess different criteria, the entrepreneur has opportunities to segment the financing market and sell investment vehicles that match the risk/reward preferences of the market.

Investors will use a seven-stage process in the investment cycle. They will search, screen, and evaluate proposals. After evaluation they will make the decision, negotiate the details, structure the deal, and, last, harvest the investment. The elements of the deal structure (risks, rewards, and timing) help provide important positive incentives for both the investor and entrepreneur to make the new venture work. The types of investments offered, the manner in which they spread risk and reward, and the use of phased financing and options all combine to make the deal structure one of the more interesting, and potentially lucrative, aspects of entrepreneurship.

Last, the chapter covered some of the basic legal issues regarding new venture financing and start-up. The choice of organizational form affects business and personal liability, cash flow, and tax assessments. Careful consideration of securities laws can enable entrepreneurs and investors to avoid some of the more burdensome regulations. Bankruptcy, although always a negative from someone's point of view, can also be a bargaining tool for the new venture that needs a little more time and patience from its creditors. Expert legal advice is a must for all these issues.

Key Terms

- Deal
- Technological myopia
- Harvest
- Registration rights
- Piggyback rights
- Demand rights
- Deal structure
- Staged financing
- Option to abandon
- Warrant
- Sole proprietorship
- Partnership
- C corporation
- S corporation
- Limited Liability Corporation
- Private placement
- Rule 504
- Rule 505
- Rule 506
- Rule 147
- Regulation A
- Rule 144
- Accredited investor
- Integration principles
- Chapter 7 bankruptcy
- Chapter 11 bankruptcy
- Chapter 13 bankruptcy
- Anti-dilution provisions
- Performance and forfeiture provisions
- Employment contracts
- Control issues
- Shareholder agreements
- Disclosure

Discussion Questions

1. What are the components of a deal?
2. In the financing process, what three things must the entrepreneur understand in order to successfully complete the process?
3. What are the characteristics of the ideal investor?
4. What are the characteristics of the ideal entrepreneur and new venture?
5. Describe the investor process. What are the barriers and major pitfalls for the entrepreneur?
6. Why is the negotiation over the "harvest" so important?
7. How do risk preferences and risk sharing enter into the deal structure and the negotiation?
8. How do options and warrants add value to the deal?
9. Discuss the pros and cons of the various legal forms of organization.
10. How do U.S. securities laws aid in promoting entrepreneurship through private placements?

Exercises

1. Calculate the cash flows for your proposed venture if you have not already done so.
2. Partition these flows and segment your investor market.
3. Calculate the amounts you need to raise from each source.
4. Calculate the returns that each investor will make.
5. Develop a risk-sharing financing proposal. Include an option to reinvest.
6. Revise your financing plan to incorporate staged financing at the appropriate times.
7. Add a warrant for your debt investors to raise their return. Calculate the price of the warrant in a five-year schedule.
8. Choose a legal form of organization for your proposed venture.

Scoring a Financing Goal

Bank financing, venture capital investments, and IPOs aren't the only financing options available to small businesses. In 1995 street-savvy entrepreneurs benefited from more than $134 billion in private placement finance deals from pensions funds, private investment pools, large insurance companies, "angel" individuals, and other investors, according to a study made by the Securities Data Co. research firm from Newark, New Jersey. Analysts say that these private placement investors tend to be more flexible, more open to risky or small scale investments, and less volatile than other funding options.

Gary Russell is one of the fortunate ones who tapped into this vast but often overlooked market. Russell, a former teacher, is the founder and chief executive of the North American Sports Camps or Norwich, Connecticut. The company has successfully focused on organizing soccer camps throughout the United States for more than 20 years. NASC is fueled by Russell's unique dedication, his approach to motivating youngsters and building self-esteem through sports, and his mission of "lifting people beyond their vision of capability." In 1995 NASC enrolled 40,000 campers in 600 camps in 34 states, and produced revenues of almost $3.5 million.

But former NASC camper Paul Garofolo showed Russell that he had the capability to lift the vision to even more people. Garofolo, now president of a sports-marketing firm, suggested that Russell could duplicate his soccer program with golf, tennis, football, and other sports camps. He recommended that Russell pursue agreements with professional sports organizations to discourage competitors, and that NASC build on these agreements by marketing more sports products to its campers, which would also increase revenue. Garofolo introduced Russell to Jack Nicklaus, Jimmy Connors, and other big-name athletes. He also set up a meeting between Russell and Bill Vogelgesang, the senior vice-president of the regional investment firm of Brown, Gibbons, Lang & Co., who secured the private placement finance deal that made NASC expansion possible.

Before they began the search for a private placement investor, Brown, Gibbons conducted an extensive investigation into NASC. They spent six weeks pouring over the company's past financial statements, corporate minutes, and other records to make sure that they understood the company they were about to pitch. Russell and Garofolo wanted to raise NASC expansion, and Brown, Gibbons agreed to accept the assignment in exchange for 10 percent of the money raised plus 5 percent of NASC stock.

Then Brown, Gibbons prepared a 24-page offering memorandum, which included NASC financial statements and projections, job descriptions, and other key information. They faxed a condensed version of this to 100 firms and individuals that they had identified as potential investors. About ten of these targeted investors responded. The most promising response came from Sirrom Capital, a Nashville, Tennessee specialty finance firm with a $197-million-loan portfolio.

Sirrom vice-president John Scott says he receives 150 similar proposals every month. He analyzes the proposals that appeal to him, and then conducts an initial 60- to 90-minute interview over the phone. Scott explains, "In one of those conversations, I'll ask a lot of questions to try to identify where the real risks are in a business. But in the end, what I'm trying to do is get a real sense of the business owner." Scott and Sirrom decided that they liked Gary Russell, and that therefore they were willing to invest in NASC.

A few weeks after receiving the offering memorandum, Sirrom faxed its initial financing proposal to NASC. They offered a five-year loan of $1.5 million, with the possibility of an additional $1 million if certain performance objectives were met. They wanted 13.5 percent in interest, with an additional 2.5 percent fee. While the cost was a little high, Sirrom did not demand seats on NASC's Board of Directors, and only wanted warrants for 16 percent of NASC stock, while a venture capital investor probably would have demanded a majority stake.

Scott visited NASC headquarters a few weeks after that, and made his final offer. The closing date was just two years after Paul Garofolo had first contacted his former coach with his ideas for NASC expansion. For Gary Russell the closing was traumatic. "If you've ever closed on a house, multiply that awful experience by 10," he says. "I had more faxes and more papers to sign than Jack Nicklaus has golf clubs."

It now looks like everyone scored with the NASC deal. Sirrom expects to net a 20 percent to 30 percent return on their investment. Gary Russell has the money he needs to help his program grow. He has also developed a pilot football camp with the NFL and a pilot golf camp with Jack Nicklaus's Golden Bear, and is negotiating a Major League Soccer affiliation. NASC's projected revenues for 1997 are $5.7 million, and $10.6 million in 1998. And just like the great coach that he is, Russell says he is proud of Paul Garofolo, Bill Vogelgesang, and all the other "team players" that made his deal happen. "There are a lot of people who worked very hard to help our company find an operational way to make our dream happen," Russell says. "They earned fees, true, but they also accomplished a tremendous amount."

CASE QUESTIONS

1. If you were Gary Russell, what would you be looking for from your ideal investor?

2. If you were a potential investor in North American Sports Camps, what would you be looking for from the company?

3. What were the pros and cons of the deal eventually struck by Sirrom Capital and NASC? From the entrepreneur's point of view? From the investor's point of view?

Source: Adapted from Jill Andresky Fraser, "The Deal," *Inc.*, October 1996, pp. 56–64.

Notes

1. H. Stevenson, M. Roberts, and I. Grosbeck, *New Business Ventures and the Entrepreneur*, 3rd ed. (Homewood, IL: Irwin, 1989). See Chapter 6.

2. This follows Stevenson et al., 1989.

3. This follows J. Timmons, *New Venture Creation* (Homewood, IL: Irwin, 1990).

4. N. Heikens, "Software firm bets future on artificial intelligence," *Indianapolis Business Journal*, October 11–18, 1993 and A. J. Schneider, "CID cashes in again; new firm goes public," *Indianapolis Business Journal*, March 27–April 2, 1995.

5. S. Mehta, "Firms Are Raising More Venture Capital," *The Wall Street Journal*, April 16, 1997, B2.

6. These are based on the research of T. Tyebjee and A. Bruno, "A Model of Venture Capitalist Investment Activity," *Management Science* 30, no. 9 (1984): 1051–1066. Others have confirmed these findings, most notably: 1. Macmillan, R. Siegal, and P. N. SubbaNarasimha, "Criteria Used by Venture Capitalists to Evaluate New Venture Proposals," *Journal of Business Venturing* 1 (1985): 119–128; W. Sandberg, D. Schweiger, and C. Hofer, "The Use of Verbal Protocols in Determining Venture Capitalists' Decision Processes,' *Entrepreneurship: Theory and Practice* 13, no. 2 (1988): 8–20; R. Hisrich and A. Jankowicz, "Intuition in Venture Capital Decisions: An Exploratory Study," *Journal of Business Venturing* 5 (1990): 49–62.

7. R. Hisrich and A. Jankowicz, 1990. In a study employing a small sample, it was found that management was the most important of three factors. The others were opportunity and return.

8. See Chapter 3 of R. Alterowitz and J. Zonderman, *New Corporate Ventures* (New York: John Wiley, 1988).

9. Timmons, 1990.

10. Adapted from V. Fried and R. Hisrich, "Venture Capital Research: Past, Present and Future," *Entrepreneurship: Theory and Practice* 13, no. 1 (1988): 15–28.

11. The most comprehensive directory is *Pratt's Guide to Venture Capital Sources* 13th ed., J. Morris and S. Isenstein, eds. (Needham, MA: Venture Economics, 1989).

12. Timmons, 1990.

13. This section follows H. Hoffman and J. Blakey, "You Can Negotiate with Venture Capitalists," *Harvard Business Review* 65, no. 2 (1987): 7–11.

14. This example was suggested by Stevenson et al., 1989.

15. Bank lending on cash flow is improbably without collateral, a guarantor, or a relative on the bank's board of directors. Therefore, this example should be considered hypothetical.

16. To see this, discount the total cash flow line by 50 percent. This figure is approximately $2,510,000. Divide the $2 million needed by this figure for 79.9 percent.

17. The source of this example is W. Sahlman, "Aspects of Financial Contracting," *Journal of Applied Corporate Finance* (1988): 25–36.

18. This example follows the one provided in the Duncan Field case (9-392-137) by R. O. von Werssosetz and H. I. Grosbeck, and accompanying Teaching Note (5-385-074) by M. Roberts, 1982 (Cambridge, MA: Harvard Business School).

19. R. Hisrich and M. Peters, *Entrepreneurship*, 2nd ed., (Homewood, IL: Irwin, 1992).

20. Adapted from http://www.hia.com/llcweb/ll-struc.html. "LLC vs. Corporation vs. Partnership vs. Sole Proprietorship; what are they and how do they differ?" April 3, 1997.

21. Stevenson, et al., 1989.

22. As used in Section 2(15)(ii) of the Securities Act of 1933 shall include the following persons:

(a) Any savings and loan association or other institution specified in Section 3(a)(5)(A) of the Act whether acting in its individual or fiduciary capacity; any broker or dealer registered pursuant to Section 15 of the Securities and Exchange Act of 1934; any plan established and maintained by a state or its political subdivisions, or any agency or instrumentality of a state or its political subdivisions, for the benefit of its employees, if such plan has total assets in excess of $5 million; any employee benefit plan within the meaning of Title I of the Employee Retirement Income Security Act of 1974, if the investment decision is made by a plan fiduciary, as defined in Section 3(21) of such Act, which is a savings and loan association, or if the employee benefit plan has assets in excess of $5 million or, if a self-directed plan, with investment decisions made solely by persons that are accredited investors;

(b) Any private business development company as defined in Section 202(a)(22) of the Investment Advisers Act of 1940;

(c) Any organization described in Section 501(c)(3) of the Internal Revenue Code, corporation, Massachusetts or similar business trust, or partnership not formed for the specific purpose of acquiring the securities offered, with total assets in excess of $5 million;

(d) Any director, executive officer, or general partner if the issuer of the securities being offered or sold, or any director, executive officer, or general partner of the issuer;

(e) Any natural person whose individual net worth, or joint net worth with that person's spouse, at the time of the purchase exceeds $1 million;

(f) Any natural person who had an individual income in excess of $200,000 in each of the two most recent years or joint income with that person's spouse in excess of $300,000 in each of those years and has a reasonable expectation of reaching the same income level on the current year;

(g) Any trust, with total assets in excess of $5 million, not formed for the specific purpose of acquiring the securities offered, whose purchase is directed by a sophisticated person as described in Rule 506(b)(2)(ii); and

(h) Any entity in which all of the equity owners are accredited investors.

23. These observations are from comments made by Stephen J. Hackman, Esq. in a talk entitled, "Financing Entrepreneurial Ventures," at the Indiana Entrepreneurial Educational Conference, Indianapolis, Indiana, March 1, 1991.

24. See E. Altman, R. Haldeman, and P. Narayanan, "ZETA-Analysis: A New Model to Identify Bankruptcy Risk," *Journal of Banking and Finance* (June 1977): 29–54.

Appendix 8A

Negotiable Terms to a Financial Agreement

COVENANTS AND PROVISIONS PROTECTING THE INVESTMENT

Investors have a legitimate interest in protecting their investment. They seek to do this in the following ways:

Anti-dilution provisions protect investors from having their investment's value diminish if the entrepreneur is forced to seek additional financing. It does not mean that the investors will never suffer a shrinkage of ownership percentage. As long as any new stock is sold at a price equal to or higher than the original investor's conversion price, the original investor will not suffer dilution. If the new stock is sold below the conversion price, the original investor loses economic value, and to prevent this, an anti-dilution provision, or "ratchet," is included.

There are two types of ratchets: full and weighted. A full ratchet is onerous for the entrepreneur because it requires the original investor to be able to convert all shares at the lower price. In our example (page 257), the investor purchased 33.3 percent of the company for $1 million. If shares were issued at $1 each, the investor would own 1 million shares. Let's say that a full ratchet is in effect and the company needs additional financing. Subsequently it sells shares at 50 cents per share. The conversion rate for the original investor will drop to 50 cents. The 1 million shares becomes 2 million shares. If 250,000 fifty-cent shares have been sold, the total value of the shares outstanding is now $4.125 million (the entrepreneur's $2 million, the original investor's $2 million, and the new investor's $125,000). But the original investor's percentage of ownership has risen to 48 percent (2 million shares divided by 4.125 million shares). Over time and in case of financial crises, full ratchets severely reduce the share of ownership and value of the firm to the founders.

The weighted ratchet is fairer to the entrepreneurs. The conversion price is adjusted down by the weighted average price per share outstanding. The formula is:

$$X = (A \times B) + C/(A + D)$$

where

X = New conversion price
A = Outstanding shares prior to the sale
B = Current conversion price
C = Amount received on sale of new stock
D = Number of new shares sold

To illustrate from our example, if:

A = 3,000,000 shares
B = $1.00

$C = \$125,000$
$D = 250,000$

then the new conversion price for the original investors is $0.9615, not the fully ratcheted $0.50:

$$\frac{(3,000,000 \times \$1.00) + \$125,000}{3,000,000 + 250,00} = 0.9615$$

This becomes a critical area of negotiation for the entrepreneur, especially when cheap shares of common stock are offered to officers, directors, employees, and consultants, as is common in start-up situations. A provision should be negotiated that these sales not trigger the anti-dilution provisions.

Performance and forfeiture provisions call for the entrepreneurs to forfeit a portion (or all) of their stock if the company does not achieve a specified level of performance. It protects the investor from paying too much for the company in the event the entrepreneur's original projections were too rosy. If the entrepreneur fails to meet the rosy projections, the entrepreneur pays the price of reduced ownership in the company. Also, the forfeited stock can be resold to new executives brought in to improve the firm's performance. This provision serves to motivate the entrepreneur and protect the investor.

In a new start-up, a significant portion of the founder's equity may be at risk due to the performance/forfeiture provision. As the company achieves its early goals, the entrepreneur should negotiate less severe penalties and can legitimately negotiate an end to this clause because the firm's performance has shown that the initial valuation was reasonable. If the investors are reluctant to give in on this, the entrepreneur should insist on bonus clauses for beating the projections. In short, for each downside risk, the entrepreneur should negotiate for an upside reward.

Employment contracts serve to motivate and discipline the top management team. They often protect the investors from competing with the founders of the company if the founders are forced to leave. All terms of the founders' and top executives' employment contract (salary, bonuses, fringe benefits, stock options, stock buy back provisions, noncompetition clauses, conditions of termination, and severance compensation) are negotiable. The investors will want an employment contract that protects their investment in the venture. Especially if investors are buying a controlling interest in the company, the founder will want to negotiate a multi-year deal. The drawback to multi-year contracts is that if the entrepreneur wishes to leave early to do other things, investors can sue for breach of contract and/or prevent the entrepreneur from engaging in a competing business.

Control issues are negotiable and not solely dependent on the proportion of stock the investors have purchased. All minority stockholders have rights. A nationally recognized accounting firm will be hired to audit the financial statements, and important managerial positions may be filled with people recommended by the investors. All important business transactions (mergers, acquisitions, asset liquidations, and additional stock sales) will require consultation and consent. The entrepreneur who accepts a minority interest after the investment should negotiate for all the rights and options that the investor would.

Shareholder agreements are favored by investors to protect their stake in the company. Shareholder agreements can bind the company when offering new shares, forcing the firm to offer new shares to the original investors by giving them rights of first refusal. Sometimes agreements will call for the management to support the investor's choices when electing board members. Although these agreements are usually made at the insistence of the investor, entrepreneurs should ask for equal power as they negotiate for their stake in the new venture.

Disclosure is the process by which entrepreneurs provide investors with the full and complete details of the information and relationships under which the investor makes his or her decision. The investor requires audited financial statements, tax returns, and assurance that the company is in compliance with the laws and regulations. Investors are especially concerned about contingent liabilities. Contingent liabilities occur when the company has future liability based on some prior event or action. For example, when producing a product, the firm has contingent liability if the product ultimately is dangerous, mislabeled, or causes harm, even if the company has no reason to believe in the present that this may happen. Because of the changing nature of U.S. environmental laws, contingent liability often resides in past decisions concerning waste management, the disposal of hazardous materials, or the use of building materials that prove to be dangerous or poisonous.

The entrepreneur should attempt to negotiate a cushion that will protect the founders and the new venture in case of an omission during the disclosure process. For example, if an omission is honestly made and results in company costs under a certain dollar amount, entrepreneurs will not be considered to be in breach of disclosure representations. This is also known as a "hold harmless" clause. The representations that the entrepreneurs make should also have a time limit attached, so that there is not liability for misrepresentation forever.

Creating
the Organization

Outline

> *Good fences make good neighbors.*
> —ROBERT FROST

Learning Objectives

After reading this chapter you will understand:

- Some of the issues involved in creating and maintaining a *top management team* (TMT),

- The composition and responsibilities of a *Board of Directors*,

■ The concept of a *virtual organization*,

■ How different strategies create different *organizational structures*,

■ Some *ethical issues* facing entrepreneurs, and

■ Some successful strategies from the *entrepreneurial workplace*.

When the entrepreneur creates the organization for the new venture, he or she is building fences. As the opening quote indicates, setting and determining boundaries—what is "in" versus what is "out"—has important effects on the venture's neighbors: its suppliers, customers, competitors, and stakeholders. "In" refers to the things the organization decides to do itself through its own people, administration, and hierarchy. "Out" refers to the things the organization lets other firms do by acquiring goods and services through the market at a price.

"Good fences" are boundaries that make sense for the venture's strategies, its transactions with its neighbors, and the resources that provide it with sustainable competitive advantage (SCA). When good fences are built, relationships with other organizations—with neighbors—will also be good—that is, profitable and sustainable for both vendors and customers. In setting boundaries, the entrepreneur makes choices about issues such as what to make versus what to buy, what to own versus what to let other firms control, how to grow, and what kinds of growth are sensible. These are all decisions relating to the creation of the organization and its boundaries.

Usually, before these boundaries are set and these difficult issues are addressed, the entrepreneur looks for help. Among the many tasks the entrepreneur has to perform is assembling the top management team. Members of the team help the entrepreneur determine organizational boundaries in two ways. First, by providing advice, they add input to the decision. Second, depending on their unique skills and experience either as individuals or collectively, they serve as human resources with the four attributes of SCA: rare, valuable, hard to copy, and nonsubstitutable. These people can help to determine the best places to draw the lines around the organization's activities.

We start by looking at the creation and development of the top management team from the viewpoint of the founding entrepreneur. We examine the characteristics of top managers and the process and dynamics of how teams are formed and maintained. Because research has shown that some teams produce at higher levels than others, we review the nature of high-performing teams.

Next we examine the factors that affect the boundaries of entrepreneurial organizations. We describe an unusual but highly effective form of organization called the "virtual organization." From this follows a discussion of organizational design and structure. Given a set of boundaries and activities, each organization faces choices on how to delegate authority and responsibility and how to make use of the productive power of specialization. These are the key elements of organizational structure.

The chapter concludes with a discussion of the major issues in creating and maintaining an entrepreneurial workplace. The ethical climate and culture should be consistent with high standards and the aggressive nature of the business. Entrepreneurs want the people who work for them to be as motivated, innovative, and productive as themselves. Examples of how entrepreneurs create an exciting environment for their workers are presented at the end of the chapter.

The Top Management Team

There is little doubt that the top management team (TMT) is a key component in the success or failure of the new venture.[1] The team is crucial to attracting investors, for investors look for experience and integrity in management.[2] The team is also a key element in new venture growth.[3] Without a team to plan, manage, and control the activities of the growing firm, the firm's growth will be limited to what the founder can personally supervise and manage.[4]

The general manager of any enterprise—here, the entrepreneur—has three leadership roles to play: organizational leader, architect of the organizational purpose, and personal leader. When the entrepreneur is putting the TMT together, all these roles are in action at once. Since the characteristics of the team will help determine the venture's performance,[5] creating and maintaining the TMT is one of the major responsibilities of the founding entrepreneur. As the **organizational leader** the entrepreneur selects the members of the TMT, and also works to blend their skills and expertise together to ensure that the top management team will be highly productive. As the **architect of organizational purpose**, the entrepreneur serves as an analyst and strategist, helping the TNT determine what goals, objectives, and directions the business will pursue. Finally, as the **personal leader** the entrepreneur serves as a model for behavior in the organization.[6] This is the individual to whom people look for leadership about what is right and wrong for the organization. The entrepreneurial leader creates the climate and the culture of the workplace, and models the ethical standards of the venture for all to see. The roles of the entrepreneur are summarized in Figure 9–1.

FIGURE 9–1 Roles of the Entrepreneur As General Manager

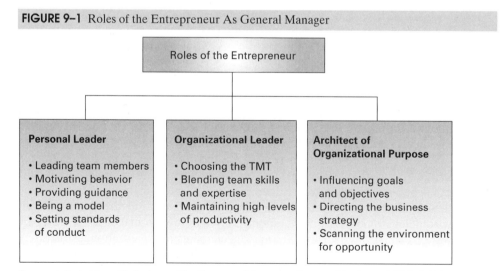

Source: Adapted from K. Andrews, *The Concept of Corporate Strategy* (Englewood Cliffs, NJ: Prentice Hall, 1980).

CREATING THE TOP MANAGEMENT TEAM

A **team** can be defined as "a small number of people with complementary skills who are committed to a common purpose, set of performance goals, and approach for which they hold themselves mutually accountable." How many is "a small number"? Some experts say it can be anywhere between 2 and 25.[7] However, boards with more than 12 to 15 members generally must form subgroups to facilitate communication and decision making. Subgroups begin to form hierarchies. The pace of group activity slows down, time is lost, and the logistics of meeting face-to-face becomes a problem.[8]

A useful distinction to make at this point is that between a team and a working group. A **working group** is a collection of individuals whose jobs are related to each other but who are not interdependent. The members are individually, as opposed to collectively, accountable. They do not really work together; they simply work for the same organization and are placed at about the same level in the hierarchy.

In contrast, a team is connected by the joint products of its work. Members of a team produce things together and are jointly accountable for their combined work. And in the case of the TMT of a new venture, their joint output consists of the enterprise's managerial systems and processes. Team members value listening and constructive feedback, and they encourage each other in a supportive spirit. In a team, the whole is greater than the sum of the parts. Why? Because in addition to the individual's efforts, the venture receives the benefits of relationships. And these relationships often transcend and overshadow individual contributions. When people are working on effective teams, they are sparked, motivated, and inspired by their interactions with the other team members. John Rau, president and CEO of Chicago Title and Trust, and former Dean of the Indiana University School of Business, studied high-performance top management teams while at McKinsey and Co. Street Story 9–1 summarizes the conclusions of this research.

The process of TMT formation should begin with an evaluation of the talents, experience, and personal characteristics that are required for the new venture's operating environment. This evaluation provides the entrepreneur with a map of the ideal team. This map guides the entrepreneur through the process of putting the TMT together and of answering the three fundamental TMT recruitment questions: From what sources will TMT members be recruited? What criteria for selection will be used? What inducements will be offered to potential members?[9]

Sources of TMT Members   TMT members are recruited either from people with whom the entrepreneur is already familiar or from "unfamiliars." **Familiars** may include family, friends, and current and former business associates. The advantages of choosing members of the TMT from among these groups are that the entrepreneur already has established trustworthy personal relationships with them, is acquainted with each person's capabilities, and may already have established working relationships with them. This prior knowledge and experience can help speed up team formation and decision making in the early stages of new venture creation. Recruiting familiars, however, can have disadvantages, and these come from the same sources as the positive factors. Familiars may come with the psychological baggage of former relationships when status and circumstances were different. Also, it is likely that familiars have much the same background, work experience, education, and world view. By du-

---

STREET STORIES 9–1

The Winning Traits of Companies and Leaders

Twenty years of corporate experience has convinced John Rau that there are two types of corporations: the "companies you never worry about—the ones that adjust to change on their own, (and) are out ahead of the curve," and the companies that are losers.

Rau should know, because his own career reads like a road map of business triumphs. Currently President and CEO of Chicago Title and Trust, the 47-year-old Rau has also served as CEO of both the Exchange Bank and the LaSalle National Bank in Chicago, Chairman of the Illinois Economic Development Board, special counsel to the consulting firm of McKinsey & Co., and professor at Northwestern University, in addition to presiding as Dean for four years at Indiana University's School of Business.

Rau says a McKinsey & Co. study helped him to identify seven basic traits that describe the top management teams of successful corporations. These characteristics include:

High-performing companies are driven by leaders.   Rau notes that good leaders don't just authorize and direct. Effective leaders have also learned "the skills of getting groups to work together by sharing vision and enthusiasm."

High-performing companies relentlessly pursue a vision.   He says that successful companies have developed broad goals and simple performance measures to achieve market dominance. Using Whirlpool as an example, Rau believes that this vision must include a clear understanding of the company and its markets, its competitors, what its consumers want, the role the company wants to play, and what factors can keep the company on top.

High-performance companies are intense, performance driven and demanding.   Rau cites a McKinsey observation that these companies are "good, but not nice places to work."

High-performing companies develop simple structures.   Using Bank One Inc. as an example, Rau notes that successful companies have a "strong spine of structure" with clear reporting lines and unambiguous accountability.

High-performing companies provide world-class training.   Rau says that companies like Motorola, which has its own university, know that education can be a critical competitive weapon. He points out that these companies also challenge business schools to keep their research and teaching relevant and up-to-date.

High-performing companies value "people skills."   Leaders must be sure that their best team members are being utilized at their full potential, and that they have a good grasp of top employee turnover, attrition, promotions, reassignments, and performance.

High-performing companies are entrepreneurial.   Rau explains this by quoting McKinsey's Mike Murray: "What this says is that the best big companies behave like small companies." Drawing on his own experience, Rau says that when his bank lent to small firms, he usually had a good grasp of each company's business, the reliability of its structures, the strength of its leadership, and the depth of its talent. In contrast, when they lend to big businesses, the bank tended to focus too heavily on financial and industry analyses, and therefore couldn't always predict problems a particular business would encounter.

For those entrepreneurs who aspire to join successful top management teams, Rau has also outlined some basic advice in a book called *Secrets from the Search Firm Files*, based on his study of executive searches conducted by the headhunter firm of Ray & Bemdtson. These tactics include:

Attach yourself to the right people,

Learn to manage people who know more than you do,

Look for positions where you can make a difference,

Don't hire managers to run the organization you have; hire those who can run the organization you want to create,

Some time off can help you define what you really want out of life, and

Learn the defining issues of your time.

Rau explains, "There are issues that define every generation, and companies will select as leaders the people who can best handle those issues."

Source: Adapted from John Rau, "Nothing Succeeds Like Training for Success," *Wall Street Journal*, September 12, 1994, A 11; and Hal Lancaster, "John Rau Learns From His Staff, Then Finds a Way to Guide," *Wall Street Journal*, May 6, 1997, B1.

plicating the entrepreneur's own personal profile, they do not add complementary skills to the team.

Unfamiliars are people who are not known to the entrepreneur at the start of the new venture. They are individuals who have the potential for top management and may have had previous start-up experience. The entrepreneur can find these people through personal connections, business associates, or traditional personnel recruitment techniques: employment agencies, executive search agencies (headhunters), and classified advertising. Unfamiliars are a potential source of diversity for the TMT. They bring in new views, skills, and experiences that can complement the entrepreneur's. The most important potential negative factor is the lack of a prior working relationship with the founder.

Criteria for Selection   If the TMT is to be a highly effective group and an important contributor to enterprise performance, it should be composed of individuals with either of two primary characteristics. The TMT members should either personally possess resources that are rare, valuable, hard to duplicate, and not easily substituted, or they should be able to help the firm acquire and employ other strategic resources that do have these qualities.

Good personal chemistry and attraction to the entrepreneur can be a factor in selecting an individual for the TMT. It may be reassuring for the entrepreneur to work with people who have a mutual affinity. Such individuals put the entrepreneur at ease and help provide a comfortable working situation in which the entrepreneur can employ all of his or her talents and creativity.

More frequently, members of the top management teams are chosen for direct instrumental reasons. Entrepreneurs look for people who in some manner—perhaps through technical knowledge or functional expertise—complement existing human resources and add to the resource base. Other criteria include age, education, and tenure. For example, it has been found that when TMTs are composed of younger, better-educated, and more functionally diverse individuals, they are more likely to promote innovations and changes in the firm's strategy.[10] On the other hand, TMTs made up of older, longer-tenured people who are accorded high levels of discretion by the CEO tend to follow strategies that conform to the central tendency of the industry. They are able to achieve performance levels that are close to industry averages but not above average.[11]

Money is frequently a reason for recruiting TMT members. The entrepreneur in search of financial partners usually allows the partners to be either members of the board of directors (discussed later) or working participants on the TMT. Connections (business, social, and technological) are also a good basis for choosing members of the TMT. These people help the new venture acquire or have access to new resources that would otherwise be beyond reach for the emerging business.[12]

Cultural Diversity   A final set of criteria address the potential need for demographic and **cultural diversity**. Because background and environment are major influences on individual perceptions and orientations, people from different demographic and cultural groups have different viewpoints. These differences, when expressed and processed by an effective group, can form the basis for a wider understanding of the firm's own environment. Each separate contribution adds to the firm's knowledge of its customers, employees, markets, and competitors, and to its awareness of factors in the remote environment. It has even been suggested that TMTs should be composed to match the conditions of environmental complexity and change. Recent research has suggested that homogeneous TMTs tend to perform better in stable environments, while heterogeneous TMTs perform better in rapidly changing environments.[13] Therefore, since entrepreneurs most frequently operate in rapidly changing environments, a heterogeneous team should be most effective.

However, achieving the benefits of diversity is not easy. Some cultural groups, like the Japanese, fret about having to work with people of different cultures. They often attribute their success to cultural and racial uniformity. American managers, on the other hand, have more experience in diverse situations. Recent integration of European markets has made Europeans more sensitive to the power of diversity. European firms are now looking for people who are Euro-managers—people who can work well within any of the different cultures and ethnic communities in the European Union (EU).[14]

A recent study shows how diversity works.[15] Groups of students were formed to do case analyses in a principles of management course. About half the groups were composed of white males, and the other half were racially diverse. The groups had to do four case studies over the semester. The results showed that the homogeneous groups performed better at first, but that the diverse groups just about caught up by the end of the semester. The diverse groups took longer to learn how to work effectively with each other, but their rate of improvement was higher, and "by the end of the experiment, the diverse teams were clearly more creative than the homogeneous ones, examining perspectives and probing more alternatives in solving the final case study."[16] The study's senior author said that he believes that if the experiment had lasted longer, the diverse groups would have passed the others in overall performance.[17] In the real world of new venture creation, TMTs are expected to last significantly longer than one semester. Therefore, the long-term benefits of a diverse TMT can be achieved.

Inducements   The final issue concerning team composition is the range of inducements offered to people to join the team. These take the form of material and nonmaterial rewards. **Material rewards** include equity (stock in the company), salary, perquisites, and benefits. It is vital that most of the rewards of TMT membership be contingent on performance. This is true even in the early stages of new venture creation, when performance and profits may still be in the future. Moreover, the entrepreneur should consider the total rewards offered to the potential TMT member over the life of the opportunity. This will obviate giving too much too soon and will lead to the team member's commitment to the long term.[18]

Nonmaterial rewards can be equally important. A person may relish learning about the new venture creation process. People who someday will be entrepreneurs themselves may agree to participate in a start-up experience the process as preparation for their own endeavors. Being a TMT member is also a sign of upward mobility, distinction, prestige, and power—an additional inducement for many.

In the final analysis, the TMT will probably consist of some people whom the entrepreneur already knows and some unfamiliars. Some will be recruited for the team because they are strategic resources. For example, in the biotech industry where genome research is so highly specialized, companies are competing in the recruitment of biotech personnel for their TMTs. "All of the top-level scientists have probably been locked up [by companies]," reports Stanford University Nobel laureate Paul Berg.[19] The scientists themselves are the key resources in such companies. Firms cannot enter unless they have acquired this scientific expertise.

People can also be added to the TMT in a "just-in-time" fashion, that is, as they are needed.[20] This would argue for familiars in the early stages of a start-up, when there is the most uncertainty and the entrepreneur most needs trustworthy people for support. Later, team members can be recruited specifically for their money, connections, skills, and experience, as those resources are required.

E-NOTES 9–1   CREATING THE TOP MANAGEMENT TEAM

The TMT can be defined as a small group of people with complementary skills who are committed to a venture's purpose and goals, and dedicated to an approach for which they hold themselves mutually accountable. Issues relating to the formation of the TMT include:

- sources,
- familiars,
- unfamiliars,
- criteria for selection,
- cultural and demographic diversity,

- inducements,
- material rewards,
- nonmaterial rewards.

MAINTAINING TOP MANAGEMENT TEAMS

The recruitment of the top management team is only the beginning. Teams must learn to work together, and this takes time, especially if the group is composed of individuals from diverse backgrounds and cultures. A great deal of research has been conducted to determine the properties of highly effective work groups.[21] In this section we will simply provide an overview of the properties as they relate to new venture TMTs.

Goals   It is essential that the goals of the TMT be the goals of the new venture. Research has shown that agreement within a TMT on what the goals of the firm should be is positively related to firm performance.[22] However, over time the TMT will develop its own goals and objectives, subject to the overriding vision of the entrepreneur. These subgoals are essential if the team is to create its own identity and sense of mission. The accomplishment of these subgoals represents the joint work product of the team. Sometimes these goals are quite distinct; for example, the development and implementation of a management accounting system. Other goals might be fuzzy, as with becoming a leader in innovation. Fuzzy goals are acceptable, since they provide increased discretion and flexibility for the team.[23]

Norms and Values   Norms represent the team's shared standards for behavior, and values represent its desired outcomes. The most important of these norms and values are:

Cohesion. The understanding that when the team gains, each individual member gains.

Teamwork. The acknowledgment that collective activities and accomplishments can surpass what any individual can achieve on his or her own.

Fairness. Acceptance that rewards and recognition are based on the contributions of individuals to the team's efforts and its success. This implies an "equal inequality," because the rule is applied equally but the outcomes may be unequal.[24]

Integrity. Honesty and the highest standards of ethical behavior within the framework of the top manager's fiduciary relationship with the enterprise's owners and investors.

Tolerance for risk. The willingness to be innovative and to accept ambiguous situations.

Tolerance for failure. The willingness to accept that innovation and ambiguous situations sometimes lead to failures.

Long-term commitment. The obligation to promote the interests of the organization, its customers, employees, investors, and other stakeholders.

Commitment to value creation. The recognition that personal wealth will become a function of how valuable the new venture becomes as an ongoing, growing, and profitable entity.

Roles   Within every group certain people play certain roles. Sometimes people play multiple roles and can change roles as the situation warrants. **Contributors** are task-oriented and initiators. They are usually individuals with special knowledge or expertise in the area to which they are contributing. **Collaborators** are joiners. They align themselves with those making the contribution of the moment. The presence of allies adds to the likely acceptance of the contributor's initiative. **Communicators** aid in the process of defining that task, passing information from contributors to other members of the group, and restating positions held by potentially conflicting members. **Challengers** play the devil's advocate. They offer constructive criticism and attempt to portray the downside of the contributor's recommendations. Their role is to ensure that no course of action is taken or decision is made without considering what can go wrong or whether alternative courses might be more effective.[25] Over the course of a single meeting or day and certainly over the life of the group, any TMT member can play all of these roles successfully.

Communications   Highly developed interpersonal and communication skills are essential to the success of the TMT. Communications have three types of content: task, process, and self-serving. **Task-oriented communication** addresses directly the subject under discussion. Its purpose is to provide substantive information that helps the group make a decision. **Process-oriented communication** is concerned with how the group is operating and how people are behaving. It is reflective and attempts to make the group members aware of what is happening in the discussion. Both task and process communication are necessary for effective decision making. **Self-serving communication** contributes neither to task nor process but instead tries to put the speaker at the center of the discussion. The content of self-serving communications can vary, but frequently it can be identified as attempts to take credit, assess blame, or self-righteously accuse another of not adhering to the group's norms for behavior.

Effective communicators concentrate on task and process communication. Effective group members attempt to minimize self-serving communications.

Leadership   The founding entrepreneur is both a member of the team and the team leader. In effective teams, however, leadership is often shared, depending on what the problem at hand is. If a particular individual possesses superior knowledge, experience, skill, or insight, that person takes the temporary leadership of the group.

THE ENTREPRENEUR AS PERSONAL LEADER[26]

Entrepreneurs would benefit from learning the effective use of three approaches to leadership, and equally important, what conditions call for which of these three approaches. Leadership of people is concerned with how to influence them to do what is good for the enterprise, especially when it may not be in their short-term self-interest.[27] The problem is to motivate people to high performance even when they have little short-term interest in high performance. Some people can be influenced by a paycheck, others by the security of an employment contract. However, most people require more from the entrepreneur—they require leadership, a special relationship over and above the employment relationship. In fact, the test of leadership is whether or not people perform when they are really needed: in an emergency, in volatile and uncertain conditions, when sacrifice is required. Unfortunately, this is not the best time to discover any lack of leadership!

Managership Is Not Leadership   **Managership** is performing the role of supervisor strictly according to the employment contract. Under the contract, people are required to subordinate themselves to their supervisor as a condition of employment.

Managers do not really influence people directly but instead use the employment contract as a tool. In this case, people have a relationship with the company (the employment contract) but not with their supervisor. Managers are not leaders: Managers try to do things right, while leaders try to do the right things. Unfortunately, some people refuse leadership of any kind. Such people respond only to managership under the contract. These people should receive only managership. Others can be convinced to go beyond the impersonal relationship of the contract and accept the social exchange of leadership.

THREE APPROACHES TO LEADERSHIP

Leader-based Leadership   Table 9–1 summarizes the three approaches to leadership. The approach that most people think of first is **leader-based leadership**. In this approach the focus is on appropriate behavior of the person in the leader role. This behavior is concerned with establishing and communicating a vision for the company, inspiring commitment to its welfare, and instilling pride in the enterprise. The advan-

TABLE 9–1   Entrepreneur's Approaches to Leadership

	Leader-Based	*Relationship-Based*	*Follower-Based*
What is leadership?	Appropriate behavior of the person in the leader role.	Trust, respect, and mutual obligation that generates influence between parties.	Ability and motivation to manage one's own performance.
What behaviors constitute leadership?	Establishing and communicating vision; inspiring and instilling pride.	Building strong relationships with followers; mutual learning and accommodation.	Empowering, coaching, facilitating, and giving up control.
What are the advantages?	Leader as rallying point for organization; common understanding of mission and values; can initiate wholesale change.	Accommodates differing needs of subordinates; can elicit superior work from different types of people.	Makes the most of follower capabilities; frees leaders for other responsibilities.
What are the disadvantages?	Highly dependent on leader; problems if leader changes or is pursuing inappropriate vision.	Time-consuming; relies on long-term relationships between specific leaders and members.	Highly dependent on follower initiative and ability.
When appropriate?	Fundamental change; charismatic leader in place; limited diversity among followers.	Continuous improvement teamwork; substantial diversity and stability among followers; network building.	Highly capable and task-committed followers.
Where most effective?	Structured tasks; strong leader position power; member acceptance of leader.	Situation favorable for leader between two extremes.	Unstructured tasks; weak position power; member non-acceptance of leader.

Source: Adapted from G. Graen, M. Ulh-Bien, and J. Dean, "Relationship-based approach to leadership: Development of Leader-Member Exchange (LMX) theory of leadership over 25 years," *Leadership Quarterly,* 6 (2): 219–247.

tages are that the leader serves as a rallying point for the company, communicates a common mission and values, and can initiate wholesale change.

In contrast, the disadvantages to this approach are that people are highly dependent on the leader and may follow inappropriate vision without question. It is most effective when conditions are most favorable for the leader. Conditions are most favorable when there are ample money, resources, and time to do the job. This approach can work when there is a need for fundamental change requiring uniform direction by a charismatic leader and limited diversity among followers. This is the approach favored by military academics.[28] This approach may be most appropriate when the entrepreneur is in the role of organizational leader or architect of organizational purpose.

Relationship-based Leadership   When people will not accept the leader-based approach because they feel it subordinates them too much, they often will accept **relationship-based leadership.** This approach is based on developing mutual trust, respect, and obligation between leader and follower, which generates influence between the parties. This is more of a partnership between leader and follower. It is focused on building strong relationships with followers and on mutual learning and accommodation.

Its major advantages are that it accommodates differing needs of subordinates and can elicit superior work from different types of people. Its major disadvantages are that it can be time-consuming and relies on long-term relationships between particular leaders and followers. It is appropriate when one seeks continuous improvement teamwork, when substantial diversity and stability among followers exists, and when network building is desired. It is most appropriate for grooming key people, including successors.

Follower-based Leadership   When conditions for the leader are unfavorable, the approach of choice is **follower-based leadership.** In this approach, ability and motivation to manage one's own performance is critical. Leadership here involves empowering, coaching, facilitating followers, and generally giving up control to followers.

The advantages of this approach are that it makes the most of follower capabilities and frees up leaders for other responsibilities. Its major disadvantage is that it is highly dependent on follower initiative and ability. It is appropriate when one has highly capable and task-committed followers.

In this approach leaders cannot direct, but they can support the followers' proper actions. This is closely related to the subcontractor model of supplier relations—cut the most positive deal with your self-managing people and support their actions.

Entrepreneurs must learn to control their natural preference for the leader-based approach and to use the other two approaches when they are more appropriate to existing conditions. These other approaches to leadership, follower-based and relationship-based, are most appropriate when conditions facing the entrepreneur and new venture are not ideal. The difficulty for the entrepreneur is that the spotlight is not focused on him or her. In the follower-based approach the emphasis is on the follower. In the relationship-based approach, the focus is on the relationship between the leader and the follower.

Once an entrepreneur learns the three basic approaches to leadership, they can be used in combinations at the same time with different followers. Moreover, an approach employed with a particular follower may change if conditions change over time. Effective leadership requires that entrepreneurs be flexible and employ all three approaches in an honest and open manner. Clearly, to be followed with confidence, a leader must foster trust, respect, and mutual obligation. People do not follow blindly along risky paths, but they do follow people they consider their partners. Therefore, leadership of people is a necessary condition for successful entrepreneurship.

E-NOTES 9–2   MAINTAINING THE TMT

Important issues include:

- goals
- norms and values
- roles: who are the
     contributors?
     collaborators?
     communicators?
     challengers?
- communications
- leadership.

BENEFITS AND PITFALLS OF TMTs

The creation of a new venture top management team offers the benefits of team decision making.[29] These include breadth of knowledge, diversity, acceptance of decisions, and legitimacy.[30] The team approach to top management offers a balance of skills and attracts vital human resources to the emerging organization. It is also a test of the venture's viability—if no one will join the team, this raises questions about the venture's potential for market acceptance. A well-developed initial team will minimize the disruption caused by the loss of a single member and may save the time and energy needed for later recruitment. Such a team also demonstrates to external stakeholders that the founder has a willingness to be a people person and share authority and responsibility.[31]

However, the team approach to top management is not without potential problems and pitfalls. Timmons notes several possible problems in the process of forming a TMT for a new venture. For example, the TMT members may lack start-up experience, or they may be recruited too quickly, without careful attention to their commitment to the long term. Also, the team may be too democratic, in an effort to recruit, the entrepreneur may exaggerate the amount of decision-making discretion the team will have. Later discovery of such exaggeration is bound to be disappointing and demotivating, since in reality the new venture remains under the control of the founder and majority stockholders. Last, the TMT may make decisions too rapidly under the mistaken impression that everything must be settled on day one.[32]

There are also the problems that can afflict any team, such as inefficiencies of time, groupthink, groupshift, and poor interpersonal skills.[33] Good group processes take time. People need a chance to discuss, communicate, revise their views, and develop new options. Sometimes time is of the essence, and the entrepreneur cannot wait for group discussion and consensus. Under these circumstances the team must act quickly and forgo the "group process" it has carefully nurtured.

Groupthink prevents the team from critically evaluating and appraising ideas and views. It hinders the performance of groups by putting conformity ahead of group effectiveness as the priority. The principal symptoms are rejection of evidence that seems to contradict assumptions, direct pressure on doubters and nonconformists to drop their objections, self-editing by group members who are reluctant to present opposing points of view, and the illusion of unanimity. The best ways to avoid group-think are to have the leader remain impartial until the end of the discussion and to develop norms that enable all members to express dissent without retribution.[34]

Groupshift is the phenomenon in which the collective decision of a team is either more risky or less risky than the disaggregated decisions of the team members. This means that sometimes people take larger or smaller chances in a group than they would on their own.[35] To make their point, people tend to exaggerate their initial positions in group discussions. As agreement is reached, the exaggerated positions become the ones adopted by the group. Moreover, when teams make decisions, the team is accountable. Sometimes this translates into "no one is accountable." This sense of diffused responsibility causes members to be less careful about what they approve.

Group effectiveness can also be ruined by the domination of a single member or a subgroup of members. If the discussions are so dominated, the advantages of diversity and breadth of knowledge are lost. Additionally, people are demotivated if they cannot contribute. Last, sometimes the person dominating the discussion may not be highly skilled or knowledgeable. When the mediocre control events, mediocre outcomes can be expected.

THE BOARD OF DIRECTORS

The top management team may be augmented by a board of directors. However, while the board and TMT members may overlap, the board is not the top management team and should not attempt to micro manage the venture.

There are two types of boards: an advisory board and a fiduciary board. The primary task of the **advisory board** is to provide advice and contacts. It is usually composed of experienced professionals who have critical skills important to the success of the business. For example, if the business is primarily a retail establishment, merchandising, purchasing, and marketing experience would be important resources. Also, people who have good contacts and are open-minded, innovative, and good team players are prime candidates for an advisory board.[36] A **fiduciary board** is the legally constituted group whose primary responsibility is to represent the new venture's stockholders. It is usually made up of insiders (the managing founder and senior TMT members) and outsiders (investors and their representatives, community members, and other business persons). In firms that are still very closely held—that is, those whose founder has not yet gone to the professional investment community for expansion funds—insiders tend to dominate. When venture capital has been used to support growth, venture capitalists often dominate the board.[37]

Members of the board, as trustees of the shareholders' interests, are the broad policy-setting body of the company. They also advise and mentor the founders and the TMT in the execution of their strategy. Specifically the board exercises its power in seven areas, as follows.

Shareholder Interests   In representing shareholders, the board is accountable for the new venture's performance. It must approve the audited financial statements and all reports to the shareholders. The board must approve any changes in the venture's bylaws and then get shareholder approval for these changes. The board is also responsible for all proposals made to shareholders and approves the annual report prepared by top management.

Financial Management and Control   The board sets and declares all dividends. It sets all policies regarding the issue, transfer, and registration of company securities. It must also approve any financing programs; the TMT cannot seek financing that changes the status of current shareholders without board approval. The board must also approve the selection of the outside auditors top management has recommended. Then the shareholders, too, must approve the auditors.

Long-Range Plans   The board advises top management on its long-term strategy. The board does not make strategy, but it can help mold the venture's future from the recommendations of the top managers. The board establishes broad policies regarding the direction and means of growth. It must approve all acquisitions and mergers, subject to further approval by the shareholders.

Organizational Issues   The board elects its chairperson, the firm's president, and, usually with the president's recommendation, the other officers and top managers of the company. It writes and approves the chairperson's and president's job descriptions. It establishes their compensation levels, stock options, and bonuses, and it subsequently reviews their performance. From recommendations of the president, the board also approves the appointment, termination, promotion, and compensation of the other managers who report directly to the president.

Operational Controls   The board approves the annual operating and capital budgets. It reviews forecasts and makes inquiries about variances from forecasted amounts. It can request information and special reports from top management, which it may then use to carry out its other fiduciary duties. If performance falters, the board may recommend a reorganization, restructuring, or even voluntary bankruptcy to protect the shareholders.

Employee Relations   The board approves the firm's compensation policies, pensions, retirement plans, and employee benefit options. It also reviews the behavior of employees and top managers to ensure that they act in accordance with the highest ethical, professional, and legal standards.

Board Internal Operations   The board is responsible for its own internal operations. Based on the recommendation of the CEO and president, the board members approve their own compensation and expense accounts. They appoint subcommittees to study special issues, such as, for example, the protection of minority shareholder rights. They must attend board meetings at the request of the chairperson.

E-NOTES 9–3   BOARDS OF DIRECTORS

There are two types of boards:

- Advisory Board—
  - provides advice and contacts,
  - composed of experienced professionals;
- Fiduciary Board—
  - legal group which represents stockholders,
  - composed of insiders (founder and key TMT members) and outsiders (investors, venture capitalists, community members, etc.).

GUIDELINES FOR SUCCESSFUL BOARDS

Information and research about top management teams and group processes can provide a set of guidelines for successfully selecting and employing advisory and fiduciary boards. These key factors should be part of the creation of the new venture's board of directors:

Keep the board to a manageable size, 12 to 15 members at most.

Board members should represent different capabilities and resource bases. For example, the board should have a balance of people with financial backgrounds, operational and industry experience, and local community knowledge.

Since the board's primary responsibility is to the shareholders, both majority and minority shareholders should be directly represented.

People with good communications skills and the ability to voice an independent opinion are needed. If everyone agrees about everything all the time, there is not enough diversity on the board.

In Street Story 9–2, Harry Edelson reports his experiences with small company boards of directors. It's not a pretty picture, indicating that there is sometimes much room for improvement.

E-NOTES 9–4   BOARD RESPONSIBILITIES

A Board of Directors exercises power in seven areas:

- shareholder interests,
- financial management and control,
- long-range plans,
- organizational issues,
- operational controls,
- employee relations,
- board internal operations.

STREET STORIES 9–2

Enough Room for Fist Fights

Harry Edelson still remembers the board meeting where he watched a dispute between the chairman and the president disintegrate into a fist fight that knocked over the table and chairs. Edelson, managing partner of the New Jersey venture capital firm Edelson Technology Partners, thinks that when antagonism between two members is so strong one or both of them should be removed from the board—or that the company should at least provide a meeting place with enough room so other board members can observe fights without fear of personal injury.

Edelson and his partners have served on the boards of dozens of companies where they have placed investments. They describe a third of these boards as excellent, another third as mediocre, and a final third as terrible. Their experience has enabled Edelson to identify specific problems with inept boards of directors, and to prescribe solutions.

Topping his list of ineffectual boards is the **Do-Nothing Board**. This passive group comes to meetings to listen to the management report, and then goes home without providing any guidance or direction. Edelson suggests that this can be combated by distributing each meeting's agenda and background reports to board members well in advance of the meeting, and by making sure that important issues are placed on the agenda for discussion. If that isn't enough, Edelson recommends replacing feeble board members with energetic and talented ones.

In fact, substituting new members is Edelson's solution for many problem boards. For an **Ignorant Board**, where members are using board meetings for self-expression or self-education, Edelson says that tactful persuasion or an outright vote may be the only way to get these individuals off the board. For the **Gutless Board**, where some members are intimidated by their responsibility or perhaps reluctant to remove a bad CEO, Edelson recommends recruiting new members, and then introducing the potential board candidates to the current members with the most fortitude so you can see if they'll feel comfortable flexing their muscles together. Edelson believes that small companies with revenues of $50 million or less have a particular need for talented, experienced board members who are willing to go beyond simple monitoring. He says that some boards become **Furtive Boards** because management is either too afraid or too embarrassed to deliver bad news about the company. Other firms seem to be run by **Gullible Boards** who are eager to hear rosy and optimistic reports from management instead of realistic future projections. Edelson's prescription for both scenarios is basically the same. Board members need to ask tough questions, establish a relationship with at least one management member other than the CEO, suggest intermediate goals or milestones for long-term projects, and demand hard-nosed budgets.

Sometimes a board can be soured by just one or two members. Edelson's examples of this include the **Panicky Director** who lives in fear of being sued, and the **Information Freak** who is obsessed with data and details to the point where he fails to see the big picture. Even more dangerous is the **Stacked Board** where some members' loyalty has been bought by the CEO with a consulting or contract fee.

While he describes more than half of the boards where he's served as less than perfect, Edelson recognizes that it's difficult for small companies to recruit good directors. He points out that small firms can't pay their directors very much, and that their board slots are often filled by people picked by investors as a condition of their financing deal. Edelson also suggests that the most serious problems with bad boards of directors stem not from the people elected to serve, but from the one hired to lead. In his experience, 25 percent of small company CEOs have stayed past their time, 15 percent are incompetent, and another 10 percent are just plain crooks.

Source: Adapted from Harry Edelson, "Dispatch from the Boardroom Trenches," *Wall Street Journal*, February 6, 1995, A 14.

The Organization's Boundaries

The previous discussion concerning the creation and maintenance of a top management team assumed that there was sufficient justification for building an organization. That is, the entrepreneur needed help and found that the best way to secure this help was to form a TMT and hire people to work in the company. But is it possible to be an entrepreneur without a TMT and, implicitly, without building an organization? The founder could conceivably rely solely on outside contracting and a network of independent suppliers and distributors to produce, deliver, and market the product or service. To understand the choice the entrepreneur faces when determining whether to use the market or build an organization, we need to understand the forces that determine the organization's boundaries.

THE VIRTUAL ORGANIZATION

In Chapter 2 we defined entrepreneurship as "the creation of an innovative economic organization (or network) for the purpose of gain or growth under conditions of risk and uncertainty." At that time we suggested that it was possible for an entrepreneur to develop a **virtual organization**. The virtual organization could be the model for the global business organization in the years ahead. It consists of a network of independent companies—suppliers, customers, and even rivals—linked by common goals and information technology to share skills, costs, and access to one another's markets. This new, evolving corporate model is fluid and flexible—a group of collaborators who quickly unite to exploit a specific opportunity.

For example, Kingston Technology Corporation of Fountain Valley, California, is a virtual corporation that has grown to over $500 million in sales. It is a world leader in computer upgrades, and it operates within a network of related firms that lead complementary corporate lives. This is not simply subcontracting. These companies share know-how, markets, and capital. Here's a typical example:

> On a recent Tuesday, a Los Angeles branch of ComputerLand received a call from Bank of America. It wanted 100 IBM PCs pronto. The problem: They needed lots of extra memory and other upgrades, the better to run Windows, Microsoft's ubiquitous operating system, and link into the bank's computer network. ComputerLand called Kingston, which snapped into action. Within hours it had designed a sophisticated upgrade system—its particular specialty—and relayed "specs" to a key partner, Express Manufacturing. Express, which specializes in assembling electronic parts, cleared its manufacturing lines, filled Kingston's order, and sent the finished systems back that very afternoon. By evening, Kingston had tested all the components and returned them, via FedEx, to ComputerLand. By the weekend, Bank of America's computers were up and running. "You've heard of just-in-time inventory?" asks VP David Sun, referring to Japan's vaunted principle of cost-effective management. "This is just-in-time manufacturing."[38]

In the concept's purest form, each company that links up with others to create a virtual corporation contributes only what it regards as its core competencies. Each firm is organized around the specific resources that are rare, valuable, hard to copy, and nonsubstitutable. All other resources are provided by other firms, which also possess the four attributes of sustainable competitive advantage. These advantages, however, remain protected within these other firms.

Technology plays a central role in the development of virtual corporations. Entrepreneurs in different companies can work together concurrently rather than sequentially on computer networks in real time.[39] To participate in a virtual corporation, an enterprise must focus on the things it does best and then forge alliances with other companies, each bringing its own special capability. Such an organization would be a world-class competitor, with the speed, power, and leading-edge technology, to take advantage of market opportunities.[40] One such virtual corporation is Walden Paddlers. Its story is related in Street Stories 9–3.

E-NOTES 9–5   VIRTUAL ORGANIZATION

A virtual organization is an alliance of independent companies:

- linked by common goals and information technology,
- which share skills, costs, and access to each other's markets.

TRADITIONAL ORGANIZATIONAL STRUCTURE

Virtual organizations can and do exist, but the question is, for how long? Kingston Technology may be long-lived because it has design capabilities that serve as its source of sustainable competitive advantage. In the case of Walden Paddlers, the alliances are built on trust, a much shakier foundation in a low-trust society such as the United States.[41] The more traditional view of organizational boundaries is based on the strategy-structure hypothesis.[42] The strategy-structure hypothesis states that "**structure follows strategy**." This means that the boundaries of the organization are adjusted periodically to meet the requirements of the firm's strategy.

Stage One: Simple Structure   A historical analysis of firm behavior provides the template for this hypothesis.[43] In the earliest stages of firm creation, an organization's boundaries began and ended with the entrepreneur and a few close associates. The strategy pursued by the top management team of such a new business was to increase sales volume. This simple structure, depicted in Figure 9–2, is the first stage of the organizational structure life cycle.

Even though the structure in Figure 9–2 is simple (there is no TMT, just a single entrepreneur), it nevertheless illustrates the two basic characteristics of all organizational structures: differentiation and integration. **Differentiation** is the way an enterprise divides authority and tasks. **Integration** is the way the venture pulls its different parts together into a cohesive whole. Authority is allocated on a hierarchical basis (sometimes called the hierarchy of authority), with a small number of individuals or groups at the top of the organization generally having authority to control the tasks and behavior of a larger number of people lower in the hierarchy. The differentiation of tasks within an organization is the result of division of labor—deciding who does what and how specialized the various jobs will be. In Figure 9–2 the hierarchy of authority is very flat; only two levels exist in this organization. Yet there is a hierarchy. And although there is not a great deal of specialization in how the tasks are divided among the employees, each person is assigned a specific job as his or her priority.

A Virtual Success Story

Paul Farrow started Walden Paddlers of Acton, Massachusetts, with the goal of designing, producing, and marketing a "technically sophisticated kayak fashioned from recycled plastic." He wanted it to undercut the competition on price and outperform the competition in handling. It looks like he may have succeeded. And he did it with only one employee, himself.

Because Walden Paddlers is a virtual corporation, outsourcing just about everything, it has some distinct advantages: flexibility, low overhead, and the best contributions that each of his suppliers can make. His alliances with a manufacturer, a designer, and a network of dealers give him all the advantages of a fully integrated company with few of the costs.

The opportunity to start the business came when Farrow's previous job and career were the victim of "corporate restructuring." He knew he wanted to start a business, one that would be good for people, healthful, and related to the outdoors. He got the idea for Walden Paddlers watching his son struggle with an entry-level kayak. He knew that a better boat could be built, and he knew that at $0.40/pound for plastic, there was profit to be made in a boat that retails for over $400.

He did his market research and found what he was looking for—a niche at the bottom of the market and a chance to expand the market with an easy-handling product. There were only three other manufacturers and only a small number of dealers—75 sold 80 percent of all the units.

His first alliance was with a manufacturer that would mold the plastic boat to Farrow's specifications. They negotiated an agreement where the manufacturer offered a low price by amortizing the start-up costs over the life of the project. The manufacturer had considered going into this business itself, but thought that its strength was in manufacturing and that it did not have enough marketing know-how to make it work.

The next alliance was with a designer. Farrow searched engineering schools for the high-level design expertise he would need. He connected with the partner of a friend of his brother-in-law—a top-flight engineer and a self-described "river rat." The designer agreed to be compensated based on design milestones achieved and on a percentage of the gross. He went along with Farrow because, he said, "I feel real good about his marketing skills."

Last there was the dealer network to attract. During his market research Farrow had visited key dealers and explained his product to them. He offered them good marketing support, a product that completed their lines, and most of all a free demo kayak. They could do anything they wanted with the demo, and they did. They loved the product, became loyal sales reps for the company, and offered advice about improving the product. Through word of mouth, the product's reputation continues to grow.

There are some potential hazards in the future, and Farrow is considering his options. He does not know how long he will be able to continue as a virtual corporation. Rapid growth puts pressure on him and his alliances. But for now, his strategy is to continue outsourcing everything.

He also does not know the value of what he has created. How can he sell it, in whole or part, and how can he pass it on to his sons? All he has are alliances. The company has no real assets to call its own, other than the glue Farrow provides to hold it together.

And what if one of his alliance partners turns competitor? Although at present the partners say they are not interested, it could happen. The future for Walden Paddlers is virtually unpredictable.

Source: Adapted from F. Welles, "Virtual Realities," *Inc.*, August 1993, 50–58.

Stage Two: Departmentalization   Historically, as the firm grew larger, entrepreneurs found themselves engaged in more and more administration and fewer and fewer entrepreneurial tasks, such as allocating resources to various activities. This was detrimental to firm performance. In Chandler's words,

> Whenever entrepreneurs act like managers, whenever they concentrate on short-term activities to the exclusion and detriment of long-term planning, appraisal, and coordination, they have failed to carry out effectively their role in the economy as well as in their enterprise.[44]

FIGURE 9–2 Simple Structure for a Hypothetical Retail Store

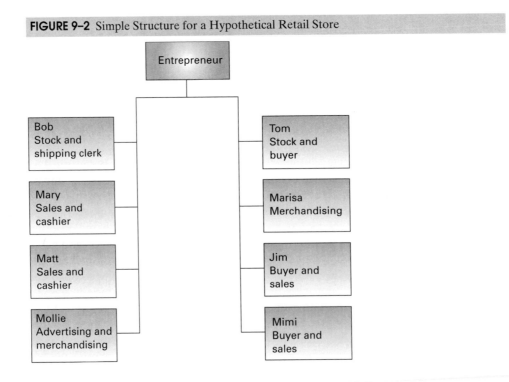

And so, when the volume of the business grew so large that the entrepreneurs themselves could no longer make the top executive decisions that needed to be made, they hired managers: production managers, marketing managers, sales managers, engineering and design managers, and personnel managers. These managers supervised groups of similar activities that were combined together into departments. The firm now consisted of a main core, a center, that produced a product, and surrounding this core was a set of functionally differentiated managers. **Departmentalization** is the second stage of organizational structure. An example of a functional structure is provided in Figure 9–3.

Stage Three: Divisional Structure   Volume can grow only so large in a single location. Constraints such as plant capacity, transportation costs, logistical problems, and the limits of the market itself meant that if a firm were to continue to grow, it had to expand to other locations. So the next strategy that entrepreneurs undertook was geographic expansion. Initially, the firm continued to attempt to manage both the original location and the new geographic location from the origin. But as the number of expansion sites increased and the number of branches and outlets proliferated, this became impossible. Thus, the structure of the firm had to change to meet the demands

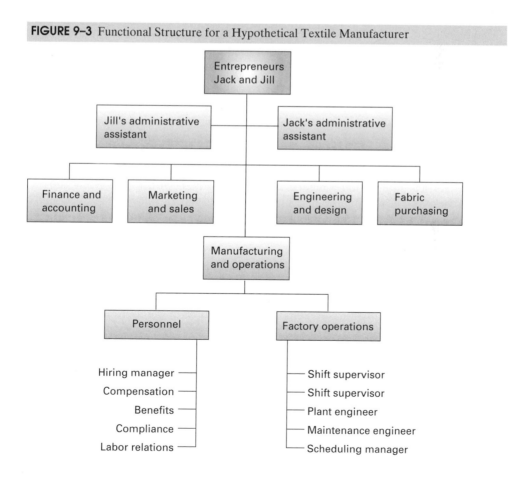

FIGURE 9–3 Functional Structure for a Hypothetical Textile Manufacturer

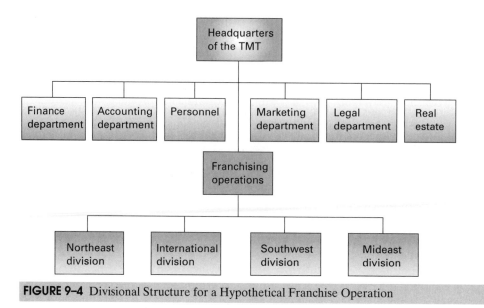

FIGURE 9–4 Divisional Structure for a Hypothetical Franchise Operation

of the new strategy. The new structure called for the grouping of units within a geographic region to form geographic divisions. This new structure was added to the functionally differentiated structure that was now clearly delineated as departments. Both reported to the firm's headquarters. This third stage of structural development, called the **divisional structure**, is illustrated in Figure 9–4.

Stage Four: Multidivisional Structure   Future growth in a single product, like the single location, was also a limiting strategy; there was satiated demand for the product and missed opportunities from related products and related markets. As the firm continued to pursue growth, it changed its strategy to one of related diversification and vertical integration. General Motors integrated with Fisher Body. Jersey Standard expanded its refining and marketing. DuPont developed new product groups based on its chemical research and development. Sears took on the insurance business and merged with Allstate Insurance. This diversification put new demands on the old divisional structure. Stress and strain were created. Inefficiencies occurred and finally a new structure was developed. This was the **multidivisional structure**, the fourth stage of development. Again, it grouped similar products and activities together so employees could achieve their highest productivity without the negative influences of other products or activities. An example of the multidivisional structure is given in Figure 9–5.

Stage Five: The Conglomerate   The fifth and final structure resulted from a change in strategy from related diversification to unrelated diversification. When firms began to enter businesses that were completely unlike any business in which they had previously engaged, the old structure again began to break down. The executives in the older divisions did not understand the new businesses, and they did not share the perspectives of the newer managers. There was no reason for these unrelated divisions to

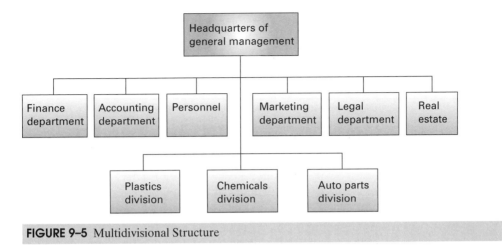

FIGURE 9–5 Multidivisional Structure

be grouped together, since they did not share markets, products, or technologies. In fact, it was better to keep them separate so that the performance of each could be measured independently. From this change in strategy came the **conglomerate**, also known as the **holding company**. A hypothetical holding company structure is shown in Figure 9–6.

In summary, the "structure follows strategy" hypothesis says that an organization's boundaries are a result of the pursuit of different strategies. The boundaries are fixed for periods of time, but as the strategy changes and stress is put on the organization's structure, eventually a new structure arises. Each time a new structure comes into being, the enterprise's boundaries expand, and it takes on more activities within those boundaries.

FIGURE 9–6 Holding Company Structure

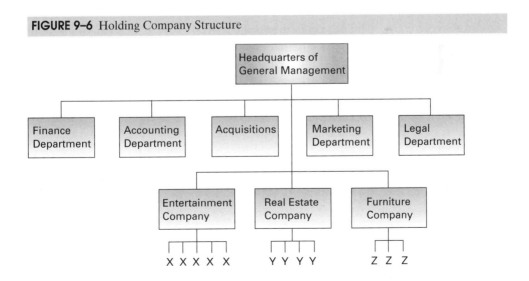

E-NOTES 9–6 ORGANIZATIONAL STRUCTURE

Based on the "structure follows strategy" thesis, the organization of a business venture evolves according to the complexity of its product(s) and production.

Simple Structure
- structure designed to increase sales for new or small venture,
- flat hierarchy of authority (two levels),
- employees not very specialized;

Departmentalization
- structure for a growing company,
- management hierarchy differentiated by function;

Divisional Structure
- structure for a company with more than one location,
- management hierarchy differentiated by location and function;

Multidivisional Structure
- structure for a company with more than one product,
- management hierarchy differentiated by product, location, and function;

Conglomerate
- structure for a company with unrelated products,
- management hierarchy differentiated by type of products, product, location, and function.

The Entrepreneurial Workplace

The new venture is not only a vehicle for the entrepreneur and the top management team to realize their dreams and ambitions; it is also the place where people work. The challenge of the entrepreneurial workplace is to enable employees to feel the same excitement, motivation, commitment, and satisfaction that the founders feel. Otherwise, they will fail to carry out their tasks and responsibilities energetically and effectively. Part of the responsibility of the entrepreneur is to create an organization where the culture, the ethics, and the human resource management system are consistent with the goals and ambitions of the enterprise.

THE ENTREPRENEURIAL CULTURE

The **culture** of the organization is reflected in its philosophies, rules, norms, and values. It defines "how we do things around here" for employees and consequently for customers. A strong entrepreneurial culture mirrors the entrepreneurial values of the founders. Entrepreneurs often start their business because they want to do things "their own way," and creating the entrepreneurial culture is their opportunity to see that everyone does it "their own way." Therefore, it is imperative that the entrepreneurs communicate what they believe is important for the organization to be doing. This communication can be face to face, or it can take place in meetings, employee newsletters, or in other written forms. But often the culture is communicated in rituals, rites, and the folklore of the company.[45] Entrepreneurial companies can do things their own way. For example:

Amy Miller, president of Amy's Icecreams Inc., of Austin, Texas, is a self-described "hyperactive," so she wants her stores to be hyperactive, too. She encourages her employees to toss ice cream from scoop to bowl, and she allows and encourages employees to dance on the freezer tops. To recruit people as uninhibited as herself she gives potential applicants a paper bag and ask them to do something creative with it.[46]

At Tweezerman Corp. in Port Washington, New York, the slogan is "We aim to tweeze" and the goal is 24-hour service. Working for the tweezer and body-care products company can be frenetic and tense. Because the owner, Dal La Magna, does not employ secretaries, all the employees are constantly in a mad rush to answer phones, letters, and customer demands. The pace creates tensions and fights, so the company has "Fight Day" when all the stored-up steam can be let off once each month. Postponing the arguments gives most people a chance to cool off and get down to work. Also, the company has space set aside for employees to meditate when it gets to be too wacky.[47]

Frank Meeks has 45 Dominos Pizza units in his Washington, D.C., franchise area. Every week he and his managers do a no-nonsense 10-kilometer run before their meeting. "The company believes in integrating health and fitness," Meeks says. Recruits are told about the requirement before they are hired, and the only excuse not to run is a death bed plea. Meeks does not want any lazy people on the team. The competitive atmosphere created makes the meetings more like pep rallies than sales reports.[48]

The entrepreneurial culture is clearly different from the culture of traditional large organizations. It is future-oriented and emphasizes new ideas, creativity, risk taking, and opportunity identification. People feel empowered to manage their own jobs and time. Everyone can make a contribution to the firm's success, and the common worker is a hero. Communication is frequently horizontal and bottom up—while the worker serves the customer, the manager serves the worker. Table 9–2 compares the organizational culture of the traditional firm with that of the entrepreneurial organization.

TABLE 9–2 Organizational Culture: A Comparison

Dimension	*Traditional Organization*	*Entrepreneurial Organization*
Strategy	Status quo, conservative	Evolving, futuristic
Productivity	Short-term focus, profitability	Short and long term, multiple criteria
Risk	Averse, punished	Emphasized and rewarded
Opportunity	Absent	Integral
Leadership	Top-down, autocratic	Culture of empowerment
Power	Hoarded	Given away
Failure	Costly	OK; teaches a lesson
Decision making	Centralized	Decentralized
Communication	By the book, chain of command	Flexible, facilitates innovation
Structure	Hierarchical	Organic
Creativity	Tolerated	Prized and worshiped
Efficiency	Valued, accountants are heroes	Valued if it helps realize overall goals

Source: Adapted from J. Cornwall and B. Perlman, *Organizational Entrepreneurship* (Homewood, IL: Irwin, 1990).

ENTREPRENEURIAL ETHICS

An important part of the culture in the new venture is its ethical climate. The ethics of the organization are never clear enough. They are frequently ambiguous and shifting. Stereotypically, entrepreneurs are seen as having low ethical standards. The great robber barons of the American industrial revolution—the Rockefellers, Fords, Mellons, and Carnegies—were all seen in their time as ruthless and unethical.[49] In today's Chinese economic revolution, the use of public office for private gain, the lack of a "rule of law," and the endemic use of bribes contribute to the belief that the entrepreneur is an unethical, selfish economic animal. In fact, entrepreneurs and small business owners are neither more nor less ethical than managers and other people, but they have different tolerances for different types of unethical behavior. Table 9–3 reports the results of a large study of the ethical differences between managers of small and large businesses.

Entrepreneurs repeatedly face some ethical dilemmas. These all involve the meaning of honesty. At times the entrepreneur may feel that to be "completely honest" does a disservice to the new venture and his or her efforts to create it. Yet to be less than completely honest puts the credibility and reputation of the entrepreneur and the new venture in question. These are the dilemmas of the promoter, the innovator, and the transacter.[50]

Promoter Dilemmas   When the entrepreneur is in the early stages of promoting the business to financial supporters, customers, potential partners, and employees, a certain euphoria is associated with the effort. The entrepreneur is in a very positive state of mind and trying to see the new venture in the best light possible. The entrepreneur gives positive impressions about the new venture even though the entrepreneur is quite aware of the dangers, risks, potential pitfalls, and barriers to success the firm faces. The entrepreneur weighs the pragmatic costs of revealing all this negative information against the benefits of being completely honest—the **promoter dilemma**. It is not clear at what point in the process and to what degree the promoter is obligated to communicate his or her most dire fears about the new venture.

Innovator Dilemmas   The creation of new businesses often means the creation of new technologies, products, and combinations. The **innovator**/entrepreneur frequently has the **dilemma** of expediting production and distribution or engaging in a long process of product testing for safety. Even if there is no reason to believe the product is unsafe, there is always the risk of the "Frankenstein" effect. If the unwitting entrepreneur creates a monster, a product that does harm or is perceived to do

TABLE 9–3   Ethical Issues: Comparison Between Managers of Small and Large Firms

Small Firm Manager More Tolerant of:	*Large Firm Manager More Tolerant of:*
1. Padded expense accounts	1. Faulty investment advice
2. Tax evasion	2. Favoritism in promotion
3. Collusion in bidding	3. Living with a dangerous design flaw
4. Insider trading	4. Misleading financial reporting
5. Discrimination against women	5. Misleading advertising
6. Copying computer software	

Source: J. Longnecker, J. McKinney, and C. Moore, "Do Smaller Firms Have Higher Ethics?" *Business and Society Review* (Fall 1989): 19–21.

harm, the new venture will never recover. If the entrepreneur waits until the risk and uncertainty has been eliminated, someone else may be first to market.

Relational Dilemmas   Over the course of new venture creation, the entrepreneur becomes a member of a number of different networks, or groups of individuals and firms. Frequently, conflicts of interest exist. The ethical demands of membership in one group may conflict with those of another, creating a **relationship dilemma**. For example, the scientist/entrepreneur belongs to academic societies that insist that studies be reviewed by peers and published in professional journals to ensure that the science is valid. But by doing so the scientist may be revealing important proprietary information that is a source of SCA for the new enterprise.

A different type of relationship dilemma is a function of transactions that the entrepreneur engages in. An example often concerns investor relationships. One investor's commitment may depend heavily on the commitment of another investor, and vice versa. The entrepreneur may attempt to "ham and egg" it: tell the first investor that the second investor has made a commitment, and tell the second investor that the first investor has done so as well. From the point of view of the new venture, complete honesty would mean that there would be no investor commitment. From the point of view of the relationship between the entrepreneur and the investors, there is less than complete honesty.

The entrepreneur faces additional tests of his or her ethical character. The "finders keepers" problem can occur when value is created by the collective efforts of many firms and individuals, but the entrepreneur has the ability to appropriate all of the gain for the new venture. Should the entrepreneur take all the gains, or should these gains be distributed among all the deserving parties? A second problem occurs when the goals of the firm and of the entrepreneur diverge. If the entrepreneur wants to live in a high style and spend more money than the business can afford, who is to say no? Often there is no one to control the entrepreneur in this situation. Last, the entrepreneur occasionally has to decide whether to engage in unsavory business practices, such as paying bribes, or forgo business opportunities. In some industries and cultures, such practices are commonplace. Refusing to pay the bribe simply means that someone else will and they will get the contract or sale. Should the entrepreneur go along or refuse to deal?

These are all difficult issues, and their resolution depends on the criterion used by the decision maker. A **utilitarian rule** would resolve the issue by asking, "Which choice produces the most good for the most people?" An **absolute rule** would decide the dilemma by consistently appealing to a moral or religious code—which almost invariably forbids lying, cheating, stealing, and taking advantage of less powerful people. A **relativist approach** to making these types of decisions looks at what everyone else is doing in the same situation and goes along with the crowd. To further complicate the ethics issues, it is not unusual to find a single individual using all three criteria at one time or another, depending on the situation.

E-NOTES 9–7   ENTREPRENEURIAL ETHICS
Ethical issues facing an entrepreneur may include:

- promoter dilemmas,
- innovator dilemmas,
- relational dilemmas.

MOST SUCCESSFUL HUMAN RESOURCE PRACTICES

There are few rules for successful human resource practices, since each company is different and human resource management is complex. Although standard practices and guidelines are easy to come by, these provide little insight into how to make the venture's human resource management a source of sustainable competitive advantage.[51]

Each business needs to identify its own managerial strengths and develop a system around them. That is what the companies described later have done, and it has earned them the reputation as some of the best entrepreneurial companies in the United States to work for.[52] These practices can be used by others as benchmarks, but the real challenge is to customize them to the special context of each enterprise.

Best Compensation Practices   The level of pay alone does not motivate workers, but it is an essential component. Pay fairness is equally important, as well as a transparent process that enables people to see how pay issues are determined. And rewards must be directly related to what the company wants its people to accomplish. It is fallacy to hope that people do A while their rewards come from B.

> Empower employees to determine what skills are needed to do the job and then reward them for proficiency and the ability to teach others. They grade themselves. (Ashton Photo, Salem, Oregon, photo-image printer, 110 employees, sales of $5 million.)
>
> Set compensation for each employee to the level of customer satisfaction. An annual customer survey and a measure of product service and reliability are used. (Aspect Telecommunications, San Jose, California, communications equipment maker, 400 employees, sales of $71 million.)
>
> Offer customized pay packages with cafeteria-style benefits. A menu of annual salary, hourly salary, or a blend can foster mutual risk sharing between employer and employee. (ESP Software Services, Minneapolis, Minnesota, computer consultants, 72 employees, sales of $4.9 million.)
>
> Institute a **gain-sharing** program that rewards employees with a percentage of the savings or profits from their suggestions and innovations. Encourage ideas with a "Gainsharing News" newsletter. (Rogan, Northbrook, Illinois, manufacturer of plastic knobs, 107 employees, sales of $9.6 million.)[53]

Best Training Practices   Training is an investment in human resources, and exceptional training can be a source of SCA for the enterprise. Skill-intensive training improves the current level of employee productivity. Training can anticipate changes in the nature of work so that when job requirements change, there is no decline in productivity. Management training serves three purposes: It enables workers to better understand their managers' roles, it helps employees manage themselves, and it prepares people for promotion to management ranks.

> Enable employees to mentor each other. An expert employee spreads both skill and management knowledge to peers. (Datatec Industries, Fairfield, New Jersey, computer systems installer, 325 employees, sales of $40 million.)
>
> Focus training on "learning to learn" with Saturday sessions of exercises and role-playing where people can break down barriers to communication and improve teamwork. (Dettmers Industries, Stuart, Florida, airplane furniture maker, 25 employees, sales of $1.5 million.)

Tie training to business strategy by formally building employees' identification with the company. In class, stress everything from basic product knowledge to interpersonal relationships. (Starbucks Coffee, Seattle, Washington, coffee retailer and wholesaler, 2,800 employees, sales of $93 million.)[54]

Street Story 9–4 illustrates how training employees insures quality products and service.

Best Job Autonomy   Employees who have authority and responsibility to do their jobs often display stronger motivation, better work quality, higher job satisfaction, and lower turnover. Job autonomy is one of the key components in making a company a great place to work. Not all employees can handle the freedom, but for those who can, it is the best way to manage people.

Urge employees to "make it happen," to solve problems, to motivate themselves. Set loose boundaries so everyone feels responsible for everything. (Action Instruments, San Diego, California, instrument manufacturer, 200 employees, sales of $25 million.)

Hire rigorously, train intensively, and then turn people loose to perform. Little supervision is needed for most people. Review monthly or weekly progress reports. (Advanced Network Design, phone service reseller, La Mirada, California, 20 employees, sales of $3.7 million.)

Empower sales people to cut deals on their own. Urge service department teams to boost customer satisfaction. Actively solicit and implement employee ideas. (Childress Buick, Phoenix, Arizona, automobile dealer, 105 employees, sales of $30 million.)[55]

Best Career Advancement   Employee advancement does not always mean a promotion up the ladder in the bureaucracy. Indeed, with increasing emphasis on flatter organizations, many businesses would be better off not having much bureaucracy at all. Then how are employees to advance and consider their jobs career opportunities?

Home-grow managers and hire from within. Hire for one or two levels up from the position available so that the employee can grow into the job as the company grows in its demand for managers. (Creative Staffing, Miami, Florida, temporary placement agency, 30 employees, sales of $9.2 million.)

Map out career tracks up to 15 years in advance with the expectation that the new hire will retire with the company. (Phoenix Textile, St. Louis, Missouri, linen distributor, 95 employees, sales of $35 million.)

Clearly communicate career growth opportunities to all employees. Promote competent learners. (Stonyfield Farm, Londonderry, New Hampshire, 87 employees, sales of $12 million.)

Enable staff members to market their own ideas by developing personal interests that can create new businesses. Promote lateral job moves if beneficial to all. (Prospect Associates, Rockville, Maryland, health communication policy consultant, 150 employees, sales of $11.2 million.)[56]

Best Quality of Life   Increasingly people are merging their work with their family life. Outside concerns about things such as child care, working spouses, and parental leave all influence job performance. People are concerned about the quality of their

---

The College of Barbecue Knowledge

In most restaurant chains the training for new employees consists of watching a short video, followed by a few hours of "on the job" experience. But at Gates Bar-B-Q in Kansas City, Missouri, perspective employees are required to sit in a classroom for one of seven basic two-hour training courses, and then pass a written exam, before they can report for work. Even veteran employees are required to attend classes to maintain their position, qualify for promotion, and earn raises.

"There is no other way to train my employees fast enough to meet my standards," explains Ollie Gates, owner of the restaurant chain. Gates created his "Rib Tech, the College of Barbecue Knowledge" in the late 1970s with the assistance of a local community college. He says that his training program has helped him to combat one of the most serious problems in the restaurant industry: how to maintain consistent quality in multiple locations.

Mr. Gates has high quality standards indeed. "If (a dish) has barbecue sauce splattered on the sides of the plate, send it back," instructed one of his trainers during a recent course. "If it has little puddles of pickle juice leaving a trail across the plate, send it back." During training Gates' employees, or "barbecue artists," learn the best way to massage seasoning into meat, cut ribs quickly, paint on the barbecue sauce, and slice one of the restaurant's signature triple-decker sandwiches without leaving fingerprints on the bread. They also learn the Gates' pledge of allegiance, which is recited while holding your hand over your heart: "I pledge allegiance to the product at Gates Bar-B-Q and to the quality for which is stands."

Training programs are not entirely unique in the restaurant industry; McDonald's Hamburger University is famous. But the Gates program is unusual because the chain is relatively small. Gates Bar-B-Q has just seven locations and 300 employees. The company was founded by 1946 by Ollie Gates' father, a railroad waiter who became an entrepreneur when he believed he was passed over for a supervisory position because he was black. The company doesn't release its sales figures, but the business today has been described as "substantial." Ollie Gates believes future growth will depend on keeping Gates Bar-B-Q quality high.

That commitment to quality has earned Gates a loyal following. Long lines of tourists and local diners often wait hungrily outside their Kansas City eateries, and their special barbecue sauce is sold nationwide. Past patrons have included Lena Horne, Sarah Vaughan, and Count Basie. When Bill Clinton visited in 1994, Gates created a $48.95 "Presidential Platter" loaded with ribs, chicken, ham, turkey, beef, and sausage in his honor.

Training has improved Gates' employee retention, too. While it hasn't really enabled the company to hold onto most entry-level employees, who rotate every few months throughout the industry, it has helped them to retain their most ambitious employees. Gary Cooper, who now runs one of the largest restaurants in the chain, earned his promotion by spending a few hours every week for 22 weeks in a Gates management training class. "It was challenging, because I was going through both on-the-job training and classroom instruction at the same time," he says six years later. Even entry level employees earn an immediate 10 cents per hour raise for every training course they complete. Thomas Little, director of training and professional services at Baltimore City Community College in Maryland, thinks that other service businesses could benefit from the Gates model. "Employees are more likely to stay with a company that they feel has a vested interest in their advancing and succeeding," notes Little.

Source: Adapted from Kia Shant'e Breaux, "In Ribs 101, Star Pupils Win Promotion," *Wall Street Journal*, September 10, 1996, B2.

total life, not just the on-the-job part. The best companies to work for recognize this and make it possible for people to realistically combine their personal values and job requirements.

Provide on-site school and child care before and after office hours. Offer financial support for adoptions. Offer benefits to part-time employees. (G.T. Water Products, Moorpark, California, plumbing products manufacturer, 28 employees, sales of $3.5 million.)

Give extended family leave at two thirds pay plus six months unpaid leave. Use flexible scheduling, offer dependent-care assistance. (Hemmings Motor News, Bennington, Vermont, old-car magazine publisher, 90 employees, sales of $19 million.)

Establish on-site adult day care and child care, employee fitness center, emergency counseling program. (Lancaster Laboratories, Lancaster, Pennsylvania, research and analysis lab, 475 employees, sales of $25 million.)

Make available on-site laundry facilities, English and high school equivalency classes, door-to-door transport, and a children's clothing swap center. (Wilton Conner Packaging, Charlotte, North Carolina, commercial packaging maker, 200 employees, sales of $8.6 million.)[57]

These small businesses and new firms have been creative and enterprising in developing human resource systems that integrate the needs of both the business and workers. When the venture's human resources are working to full capabilities, they are saving the company money, adding value for customers, adapting to the changing marketplace, taking responsibility, and managing themselves. The entrepreneur must consider the creation and development of the organization as an opportunity to achieve a sustainable competitive advantage.

Summary

This chapter has provided an overview of the theoretical and practical aspects of creating an organization. One of the top priorities for most entrepreneurs is the recruitment, selection, and organization of a top management team. The team serves as both the basis of sustainable competitive advantage by virtue of the uniqueness of its members and as the protector of the venture's resources.

Although some ventures can survive as virtual organizations, primarily using the market and alliances as support, most ventures create an organization that is hierarchical and divides authority and task responsibility among its members. As the firm's strategy changes and its industry develops, the entrepreneur must reappraise the earlier choices of which things to do internally and which to leave to the market.

The entrepreneur and the TMT are responsible for the business's culture and ethical climate. Creating an exciting and motivating environment for employees is a challenge that must be met. The entrepreneur should employ innovative methods in compensation, training, promotion and advancement, job autonomy, and total quality of life. Attention paid to human resources can have long-term benefits for the firm and be a continuing source of advantage.

Key Terms

- Personal leader
- Organizational leader
- Architect of organizational purpose
- Team
- Working group
- Familiars
- Unfamiliars
- Cultural diversity
- Material rewards
- Nonmaterial rewards
- Contributors
- Collaborators
- Communicators
- Challengers
- Task-oriented communication
- Process-oriented communication
- Self-serving communication
- Groupthink
- Groupshift
- Advisory board

- Fiduciary board
- Virtual organization
- "Structure follows strategy"
- Simple structure
- Differentiation
- Integration
- Departmentalization
- Divisional structure
- Multidivisional structure
- Conglomerate
- Holding company
- Culture
- Promoter dilemma
- Innovator dilemma
- Relationship dilemma
- Utilitarian rule
- Absolute rule
- Relativist approach
- Gain-sharing

Discussion Questions

1. What are the three leadership roles of the entrepreneur? Give examples of each.
2. How is a team different than a working group? Give examples.
3. Where do the venture's TMT members come from? What are the pros and cons of recruiting familiars versus unfamiliars?
4. What are the arguments for and against a TMT that is culturally diverse?

5. What types of efforts must be made to maintain a TMT as a high-performing group?
6. What is the role of the board of directors? How can the board and the entrepreneur cooperate to make the venture a success?
7. What is a virtual organization? How can it exist and survive? When is a virtual organization an effective way of organizing the new venture?
8. Describe the changes in organizational

structure that a firm might go through as it grows.

9. How do entrepreneurial organizations create and maintain culture?

10. What are some of the major ethical issues for the entrepreneur? Give examples. How should these be resolved?

11. How can the management of human resources reinforce the culture, the ethics, and the values of the entrepreneur? Give examples.

Exercises

1. Construct an "ideal" TMT for a new venture or for your business plan project.

2. Role-playing exercise: Recruit a potential TMT member away from a large corporation and convince this person to join your team.

3. Decide which activities your business plan project venture should do for itself and which it should rely on the market for.

4. Create an organization chart for your business plan project. What are the duties, responsibilities, and reporting relationships of the people represented in the chart?

5. What are the entrepreneurial values you wish to create and sustain in your business plan project organization? How will you do this?

DISCUSSION CASE

Calculating Risk

"Many people think of entrepreneurs as plungers and gamblers," says Howard H. Stevenson, professor at Harvard Business School. "But most successful entrepreneurs, if they take any risk at all, are very calculating about it."

Robert S. Reiss, whose trivia-game business is portrayed in one of the entrepreneurship cases studied at Harvard, may be one of the most calculating risk takers of all time. In the early 1980s Reiss saw that the game Trivial Pursuit was becoming popular. Reiss approached the U.S. magazine TV Guide about developing a TV Guide version of the Game. He thought the magazine's name recognition would reduce the risk of marketing the game, and also hoped to convince the publisher to provide advertising space.

Reiss's hunches proved right. He was able to parlay his TV Guide Trivia Game idea into $7 million in sales. What's unusual is that he did it without investing any funds of his own, and without incurring much personal risk. The $50,000 investment Reiss needed to get the game started was provided by a wealthy partner. He then used his partner's line of credit to arrange for manufacturing, after contracting with a game specialist to design the game in exchange for a royalty instead of paying a fee in advance. Splitting the profits and structuring the deal this way were more expensive in the long run, but Reiss says it was worth it because it reduced his risks.

Reiss has started 16 small businesses since he left his job as a pencil company executive in 1959. In all his ventures he keeps overhead to a minimum, brings in partners to share the investment, and avoids building factories or warehouses. Reiss says that laying off risk has enabled him to avoid losing money even when his ideas aren't right. In 1988 Reiss created R & R Recreation Products to produce a Time Magazine "Man of the Year" photo frame along with other novelty magazine cover frames. "All I could lose on a deal like the picture frames is time," says Reiss. He recruited a picture frame company in Massachusetts as his partner, and arranged to pay only royalties to Time and the other magazines. The company garnered $3 million in initial orders, but the frames weren't popular with consumers, and they stopped production after two years. Reiss says he made a small profit, and the only investment he lost was the six months he spent setting up the business.

Reiss's current project is Valdawn, Inc., a New Jersey company that markets Asian-made novelty watches. Reiss selected a cat motif for the first Valdawn watch after a buyer told him that particular design would be popular. (Once again Reiss's hunch provided correct.) True to form, Valdawn owns neither a manufacturing facility or a warehouse, and places watch orders with its suppliers only when it has firm orders from its own customers. The company chalked up $20 million in sales in its fourth year of business. Even though he's been a successful entrepreneur, Reiss calls Valdawn "my first chance to build a long-term, large-volume company, something that isn't just a fad."

Reiss, who has a Harvard MBA, credits some of his success to sales techniques. He believes that the fundamentals of making a sale are as important as anything else taught in business programs, even though sales is an area overlooked by most schools. "The most effective thing is learning how to listen," he notes. He says salespeople need to learn how to listen patiently while their customers talk about their needs, then ask the customer for the order, instead of making a feverish pitch. Listening instead of speaking is almost an obsession with Reiss. "I have no idea what people at big companies do in meetings all day," he says. "They talk things to death."

CASE QUESTIONS

1. What are some additional ways a business might reduce risk?

2. In his quest to reduce risk Robert Reiss has not only diminished profits but also given up significant control. What are the pros and cons of doing this? Do you think most entrepreneurs would be willing to take that gamble?

3. Now that you understand that Reiss recruits partners to reduce his risk, and invests little or none of his own money in his ventures, would you be willing to become his partner?

4. Do you agree with Reiss's criticism that business schools don't adequately teach selling techniques? How much emphasis should salesmanship have in a business school curriculum?

Source: Adapted from Jeffrey A. Tannenbaum, "Entrepreneur Succeeds by Avoiding Risk," *Asian Wall Street Journal,* January 13, 1994, 8.

Notes

1. B. Virany and M. Tushman, "Top Management Teams and Corporate Success in an Emerging Industry," *Journal of Business Venturing* 1 (1986): 261–274.

2. T. Tyebjee and A. Bruno, "A Model of Venture Capitalist Investment Activity," *Management Science* 30, no. 9 (September 1984): 1051–1066.

3. B. Bird, *Entrepreneurial Behavior* (Glenview, IL: Scott, Foresman, 1989).

4. A. McCarthy, D. Krueger, and T. Schoenecker, "Changes in Time Allocation Patterns of Entrepreneurs," *Entrepreneurship: Theory and Practice* 15 (1990): 7–18.

5. D. Norburn and S. Birley, "The Top Management Team and Corporate Performance," *Strategic Management Journal* 9 (1988): 225–237.

6. K. Andrews. *The Concept of Corporate Strategy* (Englewood Cliffs, NJ: Prentice Hall, 1980).

7. J. Katzenbach and D. Smith, "The Discipline of Teams," *Harvard Business Review* (March–April 1993): 111–120.

8. Katzenbach and Smith, 1993.

9. J. Kamm and A. Nurick, "The Stages of Team Venture Formation: A Decision-Making Model," *Entrepreneurship: Theory and Practice* 17 (1993): 17–27.

10. See M. Wiersema and K. Bantel, "Top Management Team Demography and Corporate Strategic Change," *Academy of Management Journal* 35 (1992): 91–121; and K. Bantel and S. Jackson, "Top Management and Innovations in Banking: Does Composition of the Top Team Make a Difference?" *Strategic Management Journal* 10 (1989): 107–124.

11. S. Finkelstein and D. Hambrick, "Top Management Team Tenure and Organizational Outcomes: The Moderating Role of Managerial Discretion," *Administrative Science Quarterly* 35 (1990): 484–503.

12. Kamm and Nurick, 1993.

13. A. Murray, "Top Management Group Heterogeneity and Firm Performance," *Strategic Management Journal* 10 (1989): 125–141.

14. "The Melting Pot Bubbles Less," *The Economist*, August 7, 1993, 69.

15. W. Watson, K. Kumar, and L. Michaelsen, "Cultural Diversity's Impact on Interaction Process and Performance Comparing Homogeneous and Diverse Task Groups," *Academy of Management Journal* 36 (1993): 590–602.

16. "The Melting Pot Bubbles Less," *The Economist*.

17. Ibid.

18. J. Timmons, *New Venture Creation*, 3rd ed. (Homewood, IL: Irwin, 1990).

19. J. Carey and J. Hamilton, "Gene Hunters Go for the Big Score," *Business Week*, August 16, 1993, 44.

20. Timmons, 1990.

21. For in-depth treatments of the research on groups in general and work groups in particular, see: J. R. Hackman, ed., *Groups That Work (and Those That Don't)* (San Francisco: Jossey-Bass, 1990); M. Shaw, *Group Dynamics: The Psychology of Small Group Behavior*, 3rd ed. (New York: McGraw-Hill, 1981); S. Worchel, W. Wood, and J. Simpson, eds., *Group Processes and Productivity* (Newbury Park, CA: Sage, 1991).

22. G. Dees, "Consensus on Strategy Formulation and Organizational Performance: Competitors in a Fragmented Industry," *Strategic Management Journal* 8 (1987): 259–277.

23. D. Slevin and J. Covin, "Creating and Maintaining High Performance Teams," in *The State of the Art of Entrepreneurship*, ed. D. Sexton and J. Kasarda (Boston: PWS-Kent, 1992): 358–386.

24. Timmons, 1990.

25. G. Parker, *Team Players and Teamwork: The New Competitive Business Strategy* (San Francisco: Jossey-Bass, 1990).

26. This material was contributed by Professor George Graen, director of the Center for International Competitiveness of the University of Cincinnati. Professor Graen is well known for his leadership research. Professor Chun Hui of Hong Kong University of Science and Technology also contributed to the writing of this section.

27. G. Graen and M. Wakabayashi, "Cross-cultural Leadership Making," in *Hand-*

book of Industrial and Organizational Psychology 2nd ed., ed. H. Triandis, M. Dunnette, and L. Hough (Consulting Psychologists Press: Palo Alto, California, 1994): 4: 415–446.

28. In fact, the military spends a great deal of effort and resources to maintain these favorable conditions for their leaders.

29. L. Michaelson, W. Watson, and R. Black, "A Realistic Test of Individual versus Group Consensus Decision Making," *Journal of Applied Psychology* 74 (1989): 834–839.

30. See S. Robbins, *Organizational Behavior*, 6th ed. (Englewood Cliffs, NJ: Prentice Hall, 1993), Chapter 10.

31. Bird, 1989.

32. Timmons, 1990.

33. Robbins, 1993.

34. See C. Leanea, "A Partial Test of Janis' Groupthink Model: Effects of Group Cohesiveness and Leader Behaviour on Defective Decision Making," *Journal of Management,* Spring 1985, 5–17; and G. Morehead and J. Montanari, "An Empirical Investigation into the Groupthink Phenomenon," *Human Relations*, May 1986, 339–410.

35. See N. Kogen and M. Wallach, "Risk Taking as a Function of the Situation, the Person and the Group," *New Directions in Psychology*, vol. 3 (New York: Holt, Reinhart and Winston, 1967).

36. C. McCabe, "Entrepreneur's Notebook: The Value of Expert Advice," *Nation's Business*, November 1992, 9.

37. J. Rothstein, A. Bruno, W. Bygrave, and N. Taylor, "The CEO, Venture Capitalists and the Board," *Journal of Business Venturing*, March 1993, 99–113.

38. M. Meyer, "Here's a 'Virtual' Model for America's Industrial Giants," *Newsweek*, August 23, 1993, 32.

39. John A. Byrne, "The Virtual Corporation," *Business Week*, February 8, 1993, 98–102.

40. "Virtual Corporations: Fast and Focused," *Business Week*, February 8, 1993, 134.

41. M. Casson, *Enterprise and Competitiveness* (Oxford, UK: Clarendon Press, 1990).

42. A. Chandler, *Strategy and Structure: Chapters in the History of American Industrial Enterprise* (Cambridge, MA: MIT Press, 1962.)

43. Chandler, 1962.

44. Chandler, 1962, 8–21.

45. J. Cornwall and B. Perlman, *Organizational Entrepreneurship* (Homewood, IL: Irwin). See Chapter 5.

46. B. Marsh, "Dance, Damn It," *Wall Street Journal*, special small business report, November 22, 1991, R4.

47. B. Bowers, "Ommmmmmmmmmmm," *Wall Street Journal*, special small business report, November 22, 1991, R4.

48. E. Carlson, "What if You Just Ate a Pizza?" *Wall Street Journal*, special small business report, November 22, 1991, R4.

49. It is only with the passing of history and the noticeable philanthropy of these families that we think positively about their wealth and fortunes.

50. J. Dees and J. Starr, "Entrepreneurship through an Ethical Lens: Dilemmas and Issues for Research and Practice," in *The State of the Art of Entrepreneurship*, D. Sexton and J. Kasarda, eds. (Boston: PWS-Kent, 1992), 89–116.

51. For standard treatments of human resource theory and personnel practice, see the following texts: G. Milkovitch and J. Boudreau, *Human Resource Management*, 6th ed. (Homewood, IL: Irwin, 1991); W. Cascio, *Applied Psychology and Personnel Management*, 4th ed. (Englewood Cliffs, N.J.: Prentice Hall, 1991); W. Werther and K. Davis, *Human Resources and Personnel Management*, 4th ed (New York: McGraw-Hill, 1993).

52. These examples are drawn from *Inc.* magazine's July 1993 issue on the best small businesses to work for.

53. T. Ehrenfeld, "Cashing In," *Inc.*, July 1993, 69–70.

54. T. Ehrenfeld, "School's In," *Inc.*, July 1993, 65–66.

55. J. Finegan, "People Power," *Inc.*, July 1993, 62–63.

56. D. Fenn, "Bottoms Up," *Inc.*, July 1993, 58–60.

57. M. Cronin, "One Life to Live," *Inc.*, July 1993, 56–57.

CHAPTER **10**

Corporate Venturing, Networking, and Franchising

Outline

Nothing is so firmly believed as what we least know.
—MICHEL DE MONTAIGNE

317

Learning Objectives

After reading this chapter you will understand:

- What intrapreneurship is, and why some corporations adopt it,
- The differences between intrapreneurship and entrepreneurship,
- The obstacles to intrapreneurship,
- The motivation for a business to form a joint venture,
- The kinds of business alliances and alliance behaviors, and franchising.

Our previous discussions of entrepreneurship have focused almost exclusively on the creation of independently owned and operated enterprises. Part of this focus was a function of our definition of entrepreneurship in Chapter 2: "the creation of an innovative economic organization (or network or organizations) for the purpose of gain or growth under conditions of risk and uncertainty." This limiting definition helped simplify much of the analysis, allowing us to examine the foundations of entrepreneurship that are common to all new ventures. In fact, the constraints of this definition do apply to a large proportion of entrepreneurial events. In this chapter, however, we will ease the constraints on this simplification and describe and analyze new venture creation in other contexts and environments.

First, we will relax the requirement that all entrepreneurship exists through the formation of independent firms. Large corporations create ventures too. This phenomenon is called "intrapreneurship," with the prefix *intra* denoting "inside" the organization.[1] Intrapreneurship is different from entrepreneurship in a number of significant ways: the motivation for developing new ventures, the consequences and rewards to the individuals and teams involved, the process of new venture creation, and the barriers and opportunities along the way. Because intrapreneurship has become such an important aspect of the restructuring of U.S. businesses, guidelines for successful efforts in this area have been developed from a number of sources. These guidelines will be presented in this chapter.

The second part of this chapter deals with networking and alliances. Just as corporate venturing is one way for a large organization to expand its scope and still maintain control, networking and alliance formation enable the entrepreneur to control and leverage more resources. By joining with other organizations, both smaller and larger, our new venture can extend its reach and the scope of its activity.

The last part of the chapter examines franchising. Franchising has provided hundreds of thousands of people the opportunity to own and operate their own businesses. It is an important organizational form for both domestic and international business, and it has been the source of many entrepreneurial fortunes. Franchising is a hybrid form of organization in that it combines the entrepreneur's venture and resources in a unique way with other entrepreneurs' human and financial assets. The chapter concludes with a set of guidelines that can be used to evaluate a franchise opportunity.

Intrapreneurship

In all sectors of today's global economy, large corporations are developing new products and services and creating innovative technologies and systems. When these creations are closely related to existing products or services, they take the form of line extensions, brand extensions, and related-product development. This is *not* what we mean when we identify intrapreneurship in the corporate setting. Brand proliferation and "line extensions can make a lot of money, but Honey Nut Cheerios and Diet Cherry Coke are probably not the path to world economic leadership."[2]

Similarly, if the technological innovations are natural extensions of contemporary scientific development, and if they are used to solve old problems in a more effective or efficient manner, this, too, is *not* what intrapreneurship is about. Although innovations and incremental changes are important to corporate success, they are not directly part of the intrapreneurship phenomenon.[3]

Intrapreneurship, rather, is the development, within a large corporation, of internal markets and relatively small autonomous or semiautonomous business units, producing products, services, or technologies that employ the firm's resources in a unique way.[4] It is something new for the corporation and represents, in its fullest manifestations, a complete break with the past. Intrapreneurship gives the managers of a corporation the freedom to take initiative and try new ideas. It is entrepreneurship within an existing business.

E-NOTES 10–1   INTRAPRENEURSHIP

Intrapreneurship can be defined as:

- entrepreneurship within an existing business;
- the development within a corporation of internal markets or autonomous or semi-autonomous business units which produce products, services, or technologies in a unique way;
- an opportunity for corporate managers to take initiative and try new ideas;
- an internal corporate venture (ICV).

THE NEED FOR INTRAPRENEURSHIP

Why do existing businesses allow this internal entrepreneurship and encourage intrapreneurial efforts?[5] They do so because top executives in the corporate world generally recognize that the macroenvironment and the marketplace change much faster than a corporate bureaucracy can. Intrapreneurship provides large corporations the opportunity to adapt to the increasingly dynamic, hostile, and heterogeneous environment businesses face today.[6]

It also enables the corporation to diversify from its core business through internal processes. Many companies have an aversion to trying new technologies and products that were "not invented here." Diversification by acquisition and merger is often a risky business, with the corporation overpaying for an acquisition (known as Winner's Curse) or merging with a partner that does not share the goals and values of the company. Internal development is often preferred because it allows the corporation to manage the process and control its costs.

Intrapreneurship gives the corporation the ability and opportunity to conduct market experiments. These experiments can be compared to the evolutionary biological process of natural selection. Each intrapreneurial venture is a form of mutation of current corporate resources. These mutations provide diversity. If the corporate and economic environment is receptive to the mutation, it is "selected" and may grow into a large and profitable division or company. Other corporations may imitate the success, and a whole population of these types of businesses may emerge. Just as entrepreneurship can help to create entire new industries, so can intrapreneurship.

E-NOTES 10–2   REASONS FOR INTRAPRENEURSHIP

Intrapreneurship provides a corporation with the opportunity:

- to adapt quickly to changes in the macroenvironment,
- to diversify from core business internally,
- to conduct market experiments.

A few U.S. companies are noted for their sustained ability to be intrapreneurial. Among these are Proctor and Gamble, Johnson and Johnson, and the 3M company of Minneapolis, Minnesota.[7] 3M has created over 100 new businesses or major product lines in its history. Four out of five of these have been successful. At 3M any young engineer can pitch a new business or product idea to top management and be appointed head of the project if it is approved. The project or new venture is then set up as a separate business. The innovative product is assigned a project manager, who remains in charge of the venture until it is successful or abandoned. The project manager can mobilize all the skills and resources necessary for the product's development. The incentives for the new business team are aligned with the project's success—members of the team are rewarded and promoted as the business grows.

COMPARISON WITH ENTREPRENEURSHIP

Compared to external markets and processes, the internal market for ideas, the resource evaluation process, and the individuals who champion intrapreneurship are different. Figure 10–1 illustrates many of these differences, as well as some important similarities.[8] Both intrapreneurs and entrepreneurs seek autonomy and freedom and have fairly long-term perspectives. Intrapreneurs, however, must be much more sensitive to the corporate hierarchy and way of doing things. This means that intrapreneurs still respond to traditional corporate rewards and must be politically astute. Although intrapreneurs must deal with a bureaucracy and corporate culture, they also have a support system to help with their projects. While intrapreneurs must gather approval, entrepreneurs must gather nerve.[9]

Both intrapreneurs and entrepreneurs disdain status symbols in the short term, preferring to get the venture off the ground. Entrepreneurs can maintain more independence in decision making, but they pay a higher price by putting financial resources at risk. Corporate intrapreneurs are just as likely as independents to have a technical background. And while independents have to rely on their own market research, intrapreneurs have to sell their ideas to their own organization before worrying about the outside market.[10]

FIGURE 10–1 Comparison Between Entrepreneurial and Intrapreneurial Contexts

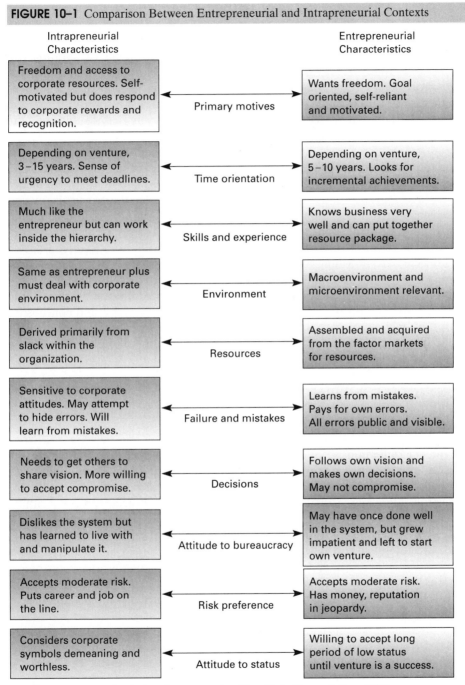

Intrapreneurial
Characteristics

Entrepreneurial
Characteristics

Intrapreneurial Characteristics		Entrepreneurial Characteristics
Freedom and access to corporate resources. Self-motivated but does respond to corporate rewards and recognition.	Primary motives	Wants freedom. Goal oriented, self-reliant and motivated.
Depending on venture, 3–15 years. Sense of urgency to meet deadlines.	Time orientation	Depending on venture, 5–10 years. Looks for incremental achievements.
Much like the entrepreneur but can work inside the hierarchy.	Skills and experience	Knows business very well and can put together resource package.
Same as entrepreneur plus must deal with corporate environment.	Environment	Macroenvironment and microenvironment relevant.
Derived primarily from slack within the organization.	Resources	Assembled and acquired from the factor markets for resources.
Sensitive to corporate attitudes. May attempt to hide errors. Will learn from mistakes.	Failure and mistakes	Learns from mistakes. Pays for own errors. All errors public and visible.
Needs to get others to share vision. More willing to accept compromise.	Decisions	Follows own vision and makes own decisions. May not compromise.
Dislikes the system but has learned to live with and manipulate it.	Attitude to bureaucracy	May have once done well in the system, but grew impatient and left to start own venture.
Accepts moderate risk. Puts career and job on the line.	Risk preference	Accepts moderate risk. Has money, reputation in jeopardy.
Considers corporate symbols demeaning and worthless.	Attitude to status	Willing to accept long period of low status until venture is a success.

Source: Adapted from G. Pinchot, *Intrapreneuring* (New York: Harper & Row, 1985).

Although entrepreneurs search markets to acquire resources for new ventures, intrapreneurs typically look inside the organization for resources that are not currently being used or employed efficiently. The intrapreneur can pry these resources for some current business operation, they probably closely resemble the corporation's core resources. In other words, the machines and physical plant the corporation is not using are probably not too different from the same resources actually being employed. The same can be said for human, technical, and organizational resources. The trick, then, for the intrapreneur is to employ these resources in a way that is sufficiently different from their traditional use.

There is also a basic difference between intrapreneurs and entrepreneurs regarding the separation of ownership and control.[11] Entrepreneurs own and control their businesses, so ownership and control are not separated and there are no inconsistencies. In a large corporation, however, the shareholders are the principals (owners) and the managers are the agents. But when a manager wants to undertake an intrapreneurial venture, the manager needs to be able to act as a principal and have the same incentives as a principal. The owners of the corporation tend to discourage this because they are unwilling to trust managers and give them these types of incentives. Frequently, this means that intrapreneurs are forced to leave the company. Although this resolves the agency problem, it often leaves the corporation worse off, for managers leave with resources that are valuable, rare, hard to copy, and nonsubstitutable. Most often these resources are technical information, expertise, and the manager himself (the human resource). The corporation is left with less intrapreneurship than it needs to be successful.

THE PROCESS OF INTRAPRENEURSHIP

Figure 10–2 displays five recognizable stages in the process of intrapreneurship or corporate venturing.[12]

Problem Definition   State 1 begins with problem definition. Problems–or alternatively, opportunities–may come from sources within the company or industry. The key to recognizing intrapreneurial opportunities is to be sensitive to change and open to surprise. One source of ideas comes from unexpected occurrences[13]—either unexpected successes or unexpected failures. If customers are demanding a product or service into which the corporation did not put much effort or thought, this success can be a source of an entirely new business once enough resources are invested. Similarly, if a product is a failure, understanding why and determining what the customer really wants can also launch an intrapreneurial venture. For example, 3M developed an adhesive that no industrial user seemed to want and was ready to abandon the product. The engineer who led the project took the samples home and let his family use them. He discovered that his teenage daughters used the tape to hold their curls overnight. He recognized that there might be household and personal uses for the adhesive, later renamed Scotch tape.[14]

Incongruities—things that stick out as not being consistent—can also be the source of ideas.[15] That is, disparities between the assumption of an industry or business and economic realities give rise to ideas for intrapreneurial opportunity. Questioning the conventional wisdom ("everybody knows") or the perceived practice

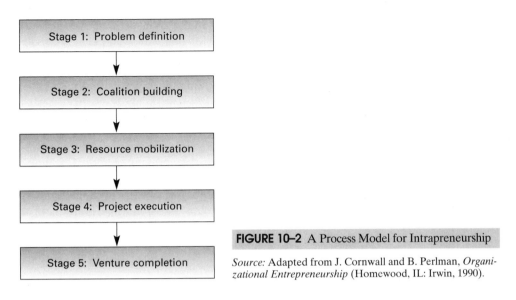

FIGURE 10–2 A Process Model for Intrapreneurship

Source: Adapted from J. Cornwall and B. Perlman, *Organizational Entrepreneurship* (Homewood, IL: Irwin, 1990).

("it's the way things are done") can point up these incongruities. When what "everybody knows" is no longer known and accepted by everyone, and when the way things are done doesn't work anymore, resources can potentially be redeployed to exploit an opportunity.

Coalition Building   Stage 2 requires coalition building. The intrapreneur must develop relationships within the corporate bureaucracy that help support the innovative project throughout its early development. This parallels the entrepreneur's search for legitimate partners and supporters. For an idea to attract support, it must in some way "fit" with the company and be congruent with company goals. This is a paradox of sorts, since if the innovation is too congruent, it is not innovative. But to sell the idea, the intrapreneur does need to make this case. In addition to personal persuasion, the best vehicle for drumming up support and building a coalition is the business plan. We described the business plan for an entrepreneur in Chapter 5. The major difference between an intrapreneurial business plan and an entrepreneurial one are:

1. The intrapreneurial plan does not have an ownership section that details the conditions and requirements for selling shares. The corporation "owns" the venture.
2. The intrapreneurial plan does not seek outside financing. However, it does need to meet the requirements of the corporation's internal financing and capital-budgeting criteria.
3. The intrapreneurial plan needs a section to describe the relationship (strategic, operational, financial, and marketing) between the corporation and the internal corporate venture.

The business plan helps the intrapreneur find a sponsor or set of sponsors, who can then help get resources and pave the way for political acceptance. This is crucial, since corporate managers and the bureaucracy often see these **internal corporate ventures (ICVs)** as threats to the current power structure and resource allocation process. Also, the sponsor will help the intrapreneur remain objective about the prospects for success and failure. It is easy to lose objectivity when caught up in the excitement of creative innovation.

Resource Mobilization   Stage 3 calls for resource mobilization. The intrapreneur is looking for the same types of resources as the entrepreneur: physical, technological, financial, organizational, human, and reputational. To make the internal corporate venture a success: They must be rare, valuable, imperfectly imitable, and have no good substitutes. In the early stages of resource acquisition, the intrapreneur may be "borrowing" resources that are officially assigned to others in the corporation. As the project gains momentum and resource needs mount, official and formal recognition of the ICV is needed. This will occur when the ICV passes the test of the corporation's internal capital market and receives its official budget.

Project Execution   Stage 4 is the actual execution of the ICV. It is parallel to an entrepreneur's official launch of a new venture, except that there are multiple levels of managers with different degrees of experience and learning to work with.[16] Otherwise, a similar set of conditions now surround the execution of the intrapreneurial strategy (see Chapter 4). The ICV must develop its entry strategy and determine its entry wedges. If it has first-mover advantage, it must employ isolating mechanisms to protect its advantage for as long as possible. It must assess the industry environment, both static and dynamic, and make appropriate operating and tactical decisions. It may be necessary to open up the ICV to influences from external sources and to recruit personnel and technology from outside.[17] Finally, the venture must adopt a strategic posture and put criteria for evaluating performance and strategy in place.

Venture Completion   Stage 5 is the venture-completion phase. If the ICV has been less than a success, it can be dismantled and its resources reabsorbed by the corporation. If it has been successful, it can be continued and additional investment can be made. The more or less permanent position of the ICV in the organizational structure (see Chapter 9) should be established at this time. If the agency problem has proved too difficult to overcome for any reason (uncertainty, incentive alignment, opportunism), the ICV may become a spin-off—a completely independent company.[18] In such a case, the intrapreneurial managers can buy the assets from the corporation and then sell stock to the investment community or the public.

Even though they understand the process, recognize an ICV's potential benefits, and have extensive knowledge of the impediments to intrapreneurship, corporations nevertheless find the task daunting. They need to recognize, however, that intrapreneurs and a viable intrapreneuring process are two resources that are rare, valuable, imperfectly imitable, and nonsubstitutable. Thus, intrapreneurship is a source of sustainable competitive advantage. One example of a company that has tried intrapreneurship and continues the effort with mixed success is DuPont, reviewed in Street Stories 10–1.

Intrapreneurship and Innovation at DuPont

In American industry, the DuPont Company, has long been a leader in science. But great science doesn't lead to generous margins and significant returns unless it also produces great products that can be marketed at a profit. The list of potential home runs hit by DuPont scientists is long, including such spectacular "big busts" as:

- *Kevlar*, a synthetic fiber stronger than steel. But tire makers preferred cheaper steel-belted radials, and Kevlar lost its key market. After an investment of $600 million, the company just breaks even on Kevlar bulletproof vests and army helmets.
- *Quina*, a synthetic silk that cost over $200 million to develop. After a brief success, it was abandoned as designers turned to natural fibers.
- *Electronic imaging* has cost the company over $600 million. Although the technology is dazzling, it has never come close to producing a profitable product.

In response to these disappointments, DuPont started to encourage its salespeople to create informal "skunk works" and to work with in-house researchers who were frustrated by the company's bureaucracy. The skunk works were encouraged to go outside normal channels to push their projects. But again, these projects often failed to produce products that generated much profit.

A "skunk works antidote" is being tried by several DuPont departments. Cross-functional, interdisciplinary teams were formed. These small teams try to field all new product ideas. The teams get just two weeks to make a decision, and if they get approval to move ahead with the idea, they get two more weeks to form another team to implement the project.

The problems associated with in-house development and intrapreneurship can be overcome by forming separate stand-alone ventures, often with other companies. DuPont has recently created such a venture, InterMountain Canola Co., with a much smaller firm, DNA Plant Technology. The joint venture developed canola oil and has a supply contract with Anheuser-Busch's Eagle Snacks Inc. unit. The oil will be used to make potato chips.

The new oil has great potential. It is lower in saturated fat than either sunflower oil, corn oil, or soybean oil. But the venture doesn't have access to consumer markets directly, so it must sell to companies like Proctor & Gamble and Anheuser-Busch for the oil to be used in branded, consumer products.

So successful intrapreneurship still proves elusive for DuPont. But, with its tremendous scientific resources and strong financial standing, it continues to experiment with the intrapreneurial process.

Sources: Adapted from S. McMurray, "DuPont Tries to Make Its Research Wizardry Serve the Bottom Line." *Wall Street Journal*, March 27, 1992; R. Blumenthal, "DuPont Venture with DNA Will Supply New Canola Oil to Anheuser-Busch Unit." *Wall Street Journal*, January 9, 1992.

OPPORTUNITIES AND BARRIERS TO INTRAPRENEURSHIP

Large companies have certain advantages in creating and exploiting intrapreneurial ideas. Some of these advantages relate directly to the intrapreneurs. Intrapreneurs are somewhat more secure operating from a position within an large organization. They already have a job and a steady income with benefits. They benefit from being part of a social network within the firm, a group of friends, colleagues, and knowledgeable individuals who can provide encouragement, resources, and technical aid.

Intrapreneurial Resources   The financial resources for the internal corporate venture come from the corporation. Although no corporation has unlimited financial resources, it must have resources well beyond the capabilities of private individuals and their friends and relatives. This source of financing lowers the personal financial risk for intrapreneurs. Of course, there is an element of career risk if an intrapreneur is unable to make the new venture a success. However, a supportive environment for intrapreneurship is more forgiving of failure than the external environment facing independent entrepreneurs.

Moreover, the corporation has all or most of the necessary resources that will make up the resource base of the new venture. It already has a set of organizational systems—marketing, engineering, personnel, legal, and accounting—that have many of the attributes that support its sustainable competitive advantage. Finally, most large corporations have a visibility and a reputation that can be extended to the new venture. These can provide early credibility and legitimacy for the intrapreneurial effort and act as strategic momentum factors.

Intrapreneurial Barriers   However, there are also barriers to corporate venturing and impediments to successful execution.[19] The major barrier is the corporate bureaucracy. Large corporations have many levels of management, and often all levels must approve the use of company resources for the intrapreneurial venture. Rules, procedures, and processes slow down decision making at the very time it should be expedited.

Sometimes the new venture threatens another product that the company produces, and incumbent product managers put up resistance. Frequently, there are opposing requests for resources in the corporation, and resources devoted to the new venture cannot be used to support established products and markets. Often people do not wish to change their orientations, goals, and behaviors to do the things necessary to implement change. The paradox here is that the very security the large corporation provides that enables a manager to take a risk also discourages people from taking any risks.

There are structural impediments as well. Internal capital markets lack venture capitalists. Venture capitalists can be very important contributors to the success of new ventures: They have technical expertise, contacts, and experience initiating new ventures that most corporate executives lack. Without venture capitalists the investment process resembles a capital-budgeting exercise and may fail to capture all the subtleties of entrepreneurship. This can lead to the corporation's managing resources for efficiency and return on investment rather than for long-term advantages.[20]

In the same vein, intrapreneurs do not own the ICV. The incentives and risks are therefore different from those of independent entrepreneurship. Uniformly compensating everyone involved—a bureaucratic procedure—removes an important motivating force for the ICV. The result is that the corporation either abandons projects prematurely or escalates commitment to projects that have little chance of success.[21]

Some people doubt whether true entrepreneurship can ever exist inside a corporation.[22] Many companies that began as entrepreneurial ventures lose their fervor and excitement as they become investment-grade corporations. It is difficult to pay the rewards of intrapreneurship without incurring the resentment of other employees and managers. Shifting the major reward mechanism from status and rank to contribution to earnings is a challenge for the corporation.[23] Some companies may succeed for a while in motivating their brightest people to start ICVs, but since most of the rewards accrue to the corporation, these people are almost always destined to leave the confines of the larger corporation to start their own businesses.

E-NOTES 10–3 BARRIERS TO INTRAPRENEURSHIP

- corporate bureaucracy,
- internal product competition,
- competing demands for resources,
- resistance to change,
- absence of "internal venture capitalists" for guidance,
- employees' lack of ownership reduces commitment,
- corporate environment not as free to creative as entrepreneurial environment.

GUIDELINES FOR SUCCESS

Intrapreneurship does not work without radical changes in the thinking of corporate managers and their stockholders.[24] And even when these changes have been implemented, successful intrapreneurship may develop only after the corporation has gained some experience and learned some lessons from the market.[25] Top corporate executives must nurture the atmosphere and supply the vision necessary to encourage their people to intrapreneurial activity.[26] Intrapreneurs practically need a bill of rights to set them free and enable them to simulate the external entrepreneurial environment within the organization. These "freedom factors," developed by Pinchot, are as follows:

1. The right to appoint oneself as an intrapreneur. Intrapreneurs cannot wait for the corporation to discover them and then promote them to an intrapreneurial position. People must have the right to take initiative themselves.
2. The right to stay with the venture. Corporations often force the originators of ideas and projects to hand off their creations as they require additional resources, expertise, and become better developed and bigger. Intrapreneurs need the right to continue with the project and see it through.
3. The right to make decisions. Intrapreneurs need the right to make the important decisions that affect the future of the venture. Pushing decision-making up the hierarchy moves it from people who know and care to people who don't.
4. The right to appropriate corporate slack. In large bureaucracies, managers control resources so tightly it is often impossible to redeploy them to more productive uses. Intrapreneurs need discretion to use a percentage of their budgets, time, and physical resources to develop new ideas.

5. **The right to start small.** Large corporations have a home-run philosophy. They prefer to have a few well-planned large projects going. Intrapreneurs need permission to create many smaller, experimental ventures and let natural selection processes produce the winners.

6. **The right to fail.** Intrapreneurship cannot be successful without risk, trial and error, mistakes, and failures. False starts are part of the process. If intrapreneurs are punished for failure, they will leave the organization, and others will be reluctant ever to take chances again.

7. **The right to cross borders.** Intrapreneurs often must cross organizational boundaries to put together the resources and people needed for the project. Corporate managers resist incursions on their turf. Intrapreneurs need passports and the freedom to travel.

8. **The right to cross borders.** Intrapreneurs often must cross organizational boundaries to put together the resources and people needed for the project. Corporate managers resist incursions on their turf. Intrapreneurs need passports and the freedom to travel.

9. **The right to recruit team members.** Intrapreneurs need the freedom to recruit for the cross-functional teams they must assemble for the project. The team must be autonomous, and members should have first allegiance to the team, not their former department.

10. **The right to choose.** Independent entrepreneurs can choose among many suppliers, financial sources, customer groups, and personnel. The intrapreneur must not face internal corporate monopolists who constrain the choices for procuring resources. The intrapreneur needs the freedom to choose from external sources when they are superior.[27]

Networking and Alliances

According to Peter Drucker, large corporations which do not or cannot learn to innovate and intrapreneur will not survive. He says for some companies that means reinventing themselves. Increasingly, large companies are growing through alliances and joint ventures. Yet very few of the big boys know how to manage an alliance. They're used to giving orders, not to working with a partner, and it's totally different. In an alliance or a joint venture, you have to begin by asking, "What do our partners want? What are our shared values and goals?" Those aren't easy questions for somebody who grew up at GE or Citibank and is now at the top or near the top of a huge worldwide enterprise.[28]

Today's entrepreneurs are deeply embedded in networks, partnerships, alliances, and collectives.[29] **Networking**, the process of enlarging the entrepreneur's circle of trust, is a negotiation process.[30] How entrepreneurs access networks and how those help them succeed are the subjects of this section.

BENEFITS AND MOTIVATIONS FOR NETWORKING

Entrepreneurs usually have a wide range of friends, acquaintances, and business associates. They are able to make use of these **informal network** relationships to obtain resources and opportunities for their firms. These networks provide them with information about their environment, and they enable entrepreneurs to build reputation and credibility for themselves and their firms. Networks of people (and of other firms) are socially complex, casually ambiguous, and usually very idiosyncratic. They depend on that particular entrepreneur. So the networks themselves can be sources of sustainable competitive advantage as well as a means of procuring other resources that can be a source of sustainable competitive advantage.

We have already touched on many of the opportunities that entrepreneurs have for various forms of networking. We talked about the pros and cons of taking in a partner in Chapter 8 when we discussed legal forms of organization. We illustrated the benefits of alliances called "virtual organizations" in Chapter 9. And we talked briefly about joint ventures in Chapter 4 when we discussed momentum factors and entrepreneurial strategy. We saw how networks are important in finding sources of financing (Chapter 7). The modern "well-connected" entrepreneur has distinct advantages over the "rugged individual" of previous generations.

We can also distinguish four basic motivations for **formal network** participation or joint-venture formation.[31] (1) joint ventures increase the internal capabilities of the venture and protect its resources, (2) joint ventures have competitive uses that strengthen the current strategic position, (3) joint ventures have longer-term strategic advantages that augment the venture's resource flexibility for the future, and (4) joint ventures further the social concerns and promote the values of entrepreneurs.[32]

E-NOTES 10–4 JOINT VENTURES

A joint venture is an organization:

- created by two or more independent organizations,
- for a specific purpose,
- over a set period of time.

Internal Motivations   **Internal uses** of alliances are motivated by various cost and risk-sharing arrangements. These help reduce uncertainty for the venture. For example, sharing the outputs of minimum-efficient-scale plants avoids wasteful duplication of resources, utilize by-products and processes, and maybe even allow the partners to share brands and distribution channels. Joint ventures can also be used to obtain intelligence and to open a window on new technologies and customers. These relationships can help a firm copy and imitate innovative managerial practices, superior management systems, and improved communications patterns.

According to a survey on resource sharing conducted by an entrepreneurial assistance firm, Kessler Exchange of Northridge, California, over one third of the respondents engage in resource sharing for internal economies. They share operating space, office and manufacturing equipment, information, and personnel. Sharing is also becoming more common for start-up ventures. The number of business incubators, where ventures share overhead and expertise, has doubled to more than 500, according to the National Business Incubation Association of Athens, Ohio.[33]

Sometimes businesses cooperate to save time. For example, Richard Kauflin, president of Supersign Inc., of Boulder, Colorado, which makes and installs signs, has an agreement with two other local companies. He can borrow supplies from them if he runs out, and he lends them his company's hydraulic-lift truck when they need it. In explaining the motivations for the cooperation, he says, "It's expedient. We'd have to wait a week to get some of these things delivered or go all the way to Denver to pick them up."

External Motivations   **External motivations** for alliance behavior lead to improved current strategic positions. A set of firms is more likely to be able to influence the structure of an industry's evolution than a single firm. Sometimes a joint venture can serve to preempt possible entrants and thereby give the partnership a first-mover advantage that is unlikely to be challenged. This first-mover advantage can be extended to gaining rapid access to the most desirable customers and obtaining their loyalty, expanding capacity to serve the entire market niche, and acquiring resources on advantageous terms before they become fully valued. Also, it is quite common to take on a foreign partner when entering that partner's domestic market.

Strategic Motivations   The third motivation concerns the future position and resources of the venture. Joint ventures can be undertaken for creative reasons, to exploit synergies, to develop new technologies, or to extend old technologies to new problems. Joint ventures can be a mechanism to give the firm a toehold in a market that is not completely ready for the product or service but needs long-term credibility. For example, many entrepreneurs are currently engaged in joint ventures in China and Russia. Most of these have no current payoff possibilities. But the entrepreneurs recognize that in the longer term, the relationships created and the knowledge developed will serve them well.

Social Motivations   A final motivation for entrepreneurs to engage in networking is to promote their own values and social agenda. One such network is the Social Venture Network (SVN). The primary goal of the members of the SVN is simple: They get to meet other entrepreneurs who are committed to social change through business. The network is a loose collection of entrepreneurs, social activists, corporate executives, and philanthropists. It has attracted some high-visibility entrepreneurs: Mitch Kapor of Lotus Development Corp.; Joe LaBonte, president of Reebok International Co.; Mel Ziegler, founder of Banana Republic and Republic of Tea; Anita Roddick, founder of The Body Shop International Inc., the British skin and hair-care firm; and, of course, Ben Cohen, cofounder of the ice cream maker, Ben & Jerry's Homemade Inc.

The network brings individuals of common purpose together. But not just any individuals. "The idea is not just to get people interested in social action, but in social action by successfully growing companies," says Joshua Mailman, the cofounder of SVN. "We provide a peer network for people that's based on values, not just on business. We are the YPO [Young President's Organization] for the 90s."[34]

E-NOTES 10–5   REASONS FOR JOINT VENTURES

Businesses are motivated to participate in formal networks or joint-venture formation in order to:

- increase internal capabilities and protect resources (internal motivation),
- strengthen strategic position and competitiveness (external motivation),
- develop long-term strategic advantages which increase future flexibility (strategic motivation),
- further social concerns and values of entrepreneurs (social motivation).

TYPES OF NETWORKS

One type of network is known as the **personal network**. This is an informal network that consists of all the direct, face-to-face-contacts the entrepreneur has.[35] These include friends, family, close business associates, former teachers, and professors, among others. The ongoing relationships in a personal network are based on three benefits: trust, predictability, and "voice."[36]

Trust enables the entrepreneur to forgo all of the activities and legal formalities that guard against opportunism. The entrepreneur can negotiate within a personal network without worrying about monitoring and controlling the other side. Trust can replace contracts and save the need to incur legal costs. Trust can enable the parties to enter into agreements without having to specify the details of who will do what, and when, and for how much. It means that the entrepreneur has the flexibility to call on resources and people very quickly.

Predictability reduces uncertainty. People within the personal network behave the same way time and time again. Their patterns of behavior are well known, as are their values and beliefs. Their consistent behavior enables the entrepreneur to have a mental map of the personal network—to know who will be where and when. Thus, he or she can navigate through the personal network rapidly when resources and information are needed for business purposes.

The third benefit of the personal network is **voice**—the permission to argue, negotiate, complain, and verbally dispute any problem within the network and still maintain good relations with the person on the receiving end. This permission, or norm, can be contrasted with the norm of **exit**. In some relationships characterized by less trust, once reciprocity is broken, displeasure is communicated, or a verbal argument takes place, the parties feel pressure not to do business anymore, and they "exit" from the network.[37]

Personal networks have **strong ties**.[38] Such ties are formed because the relationship may have a long history, there may be a family relationship, or people may share a common culture, common values, or common associations. Strong ties are especially important in the early stages of business formation, particularly in financing and securing the initial resources for new venture creations.[39]

The second type of network is the **extended network**.[40] Extended networks are formal, firm-to-firm relationships. The entrepreneur develops these by means of boundary-spanning activities with other owners and managers of enterprises, customers and vendors, and other constituents in the operating environment. These are the normal cross-organizational activities that are required for the operation as an "open system."[41] Extended networks become more important to the firm as it moves beyond the initial founding stage.

Extended networks contain more diversity than personal networks and, consequently, more information. The relationships are more instrumental and based less on trust. There is also more uncertainty and less predictability in these relationships. The customer of a customer may be included, as well as the supplier of a supplier. There may be many indirect associations in an extended network. As a result, these are **weak ties**.

But there is "strength in weak ties."[42] Weak ties enable the network to be much larger. As such, it will contain more diverse information, people, resources, and channels for the entrepreneur to use. Whereas strong ties produce trust but redundancy, weak ties provide unique information about opportunities, locations, potential markets for goods and services, potential investors, and the like. In addition, the extended network adds to the credibility and legitimacy of the firm and expands its reputational capital.

Outside directors who are involved in the enterprise and make a contribution provide a good example of the benefits of weak ties. These outside directors provide an invaluable check on the entrepreneur's decisions, and possible mistakes, by complementing the entrepreneur's information base and offering an objective outside viewpoint. Their fresh perspective can change the course of the venture's strategy. For example, Kurtz Bros. Inc, a landscape materials business in Cuyahoga Falls, Ohio, is a family business that decided to diversify a few years ago. It was ready to make a move into industrial materials, and initially its management forgot to consult the firm's three outside directors. When these directors heard of the plan, "They were pretty tough on us," concedes Lisa Kurtz, company president. "They told us we were fracturing our organization, and that we should stick to our knitting." The outsiders' views made a deep impression. The family owners quickly reconsidered their decision and liquidated the new unit.[43]

One technological example of the extended network is the proliferation of electronic bulletin boards that are designed and used by entrepreneurs to share and receive information. Take the case of Bill Vick, owner of a Dallas-based executive recruiting firm. When he needed some new ideas for getting clients and building his visibility and reputation, he put out a call for ideas on a bulletin board used by thousands of entrepreneurs. He received many suggestions, including one that proved to be a bonanza: Vick started mailing boxes of Vick's Cough Drops to sales executives with a postcard saying that his firm could "cure sick sales." A few days later at an industry conference Vick was shaking hands and handing out more cough drops. "That one idea must have gotten me $25,000 worth of business," he says.[44]

Networking takes considerable time and money for the entrepreneur.[45] If the networking does not improve firm performance, it could prove detrimental to the enterprise and frustrating to the entrepreneur. Entrepreneurs should have both strong-tie personal relationships and weak-tie extended relationships. The ideal situation is for them to develop strong-tie extended relationships. By doing this, entrepreneurs can have the speed and flexibility of strong ties as well as the informational and resource advantages of the extended network.

ALLIANCE BEHAVIORS

Entrepreneurs engage in four basic types of alliances: (1) confederations, (2) conjugate alliances, (3) agglomerations, and (4) organic networks. These types are distinguished by two characteristics: (1) whether the relationship is direct or indirect (entrepreneur's business to alliance partner) and (2) whether the relationship is with competing or noncompeting firms.[46] The integration of these two dimensions produces the two-by-two matrix shown in Figure 10–3.

Confederate Alliances   Direct contact with competitors is called a **confederate alliance**, or simply a **confederation**. In concentrated industries, where a few firms have most of the market to themselves, confederate alliances are usually motivated by an

	Direct contact	Indirect contact
Competing organizations	Confederate alliance	Agglomerate network
Noncompeting organizations	Conjugate alliance	Organic network

FIGURE 10–3 A Typology of Alliances

Source: Adapted from G. Astley and C. Fombrun, "Collective Strategy: Social Ecology of Organizational Environments," *Academy of Management Review* 8 (1983): 576–587.

attempt to avoid competition through techniques such as point pricing, uniform price lists, standard costing, and product standardization.[47] Because the alliance resembles a cartel, the firms may find themselves engaged in collusion that violates U.S. antitrust law.

But smaller firms in fragmented industries—and this applies particularly to new ventures in emerging industries—have many opportunities for cooperation and alliances that are not illegally collusive. For example, firms can share transportation costs by ordering enough for a full-truckload shipment. Or they can engage in bilateral hiring practices. By hiring each other's workers on a regular basis, the firms can share expertise, information, and intelligence about the market, and they can upgrade each other's operational procedures by imitating the best of what the other has to offer. Two other examples show how manufacturing capability and capacity can be shared by competitors:

> Michigan's Flint River Project is a network of 15 or so auto parts suppliers each of which individually is too small to bid on work offered by the Big Three U.S. automakers. They have come together in a confederation to share manufacturing, marketing, and engineering experience while continuing to operate as separate legal entities. As a collective they are big enough for Big Three contracts.[48]

> The Northern Flathead Manufacturing Network is a collective of small firms that design and manufacture cabinetry and other wood products in Montana. But in addition to helping each other with manufacturing, their alliance is pursuing a common regional strategy: to lure resources to the underpopulated and underinvested state of Montana.[49]

Entrepreneurs must use good judgment in entering into confederate relationships. There is always the possibility of an unscrupulous competitor taking advantage of the trust inherent in such relationships. Another risk is that former rivals may be tempted to collude to raise profits by restraining production, raising prices, and holding back threatening new technologies. The lack of free-for-all competition can lead to complacency and the stifling of creativity and new ideas.[50]

Conjugate Alliances   Direct contact with noncompeting firms is called a **conjugate alliance**. Examples include long-term purchasing contracts with suppliers and customers and joint research and development projects. Companies that keep their separate identities and engage in conjugate relationships are mimicking the vertical-integration strategies of larger firms and attempting to obtain those benefits without incurring the inherent risks. An example would be a joint R&D effort that enables a manufacturer to test the operating characteristics of a supplier's materials (for a fee) and that reports back to the supplier how the material holds up under various real world operating conditions (an advantage for the supplier). Similar to the confederate form, the conjugate form is a task-oriented, tightly coupled, voluntary relationship within a weak-tie network.

By working together, conjugate networks can do things that no individual firm could accomplish. For example, in Indiana a network called the FlexCell Group combines makers of metalworking patterns and tools with mechanical engineers, producers of plastic injection molding, a prototype machine shop, and a contract machine shop. All the members are independent companies with sales of less than $10 million each. But the result is a vertically integrated, "virtual" single-source supplier. Tom Brummett, the owner of the Columbus, Indiana, firm that supplies the network with marketing and management services, says that FlexCell "can offer its existing customer base more capabilities and quicker turnaround time, usually with more cost effectiveness. This is a way small and medium-size companies can leverage their re-

---

TABLE 10–1   Confederate and Conjugate Alliances: Examples

Confederate Activities: Direct Contact with Competing Firms
Joint purchase agreements
Joint sales agreements
Sharing information with competitors
Contractual joint ventures
Contractual joint research
Joint advertising
Sharing transportation costs
Hiring competitors' workers
Joint training exercises
Licensing agreements
Conjugate Activities: Direct Contact with Noncompeting Firms
Joint ventures with suppliers and customers
Joint research with suppliers and customers
Joint advertising with suppliers and customers
Hiring suppliers' and buyers' workers
Sharing transportation costs
Sharing information about competitors
Joint training
Licensing agreements

Source: Adapted from M. Dollinger, "The Evolution of Collective Strategies in Fragmented Industries," *Academy of Management Review* 15 (1990): 266–285.

sources to compete in a global economy." Recently, FlexCell beat out two large multinational corporations from Europe and South America in its bid to produce engine components for a U.S. customer.[51]

Table 10–1 provides a list of the most frequently employed confederate and conjugate alliances.

Agglomerate Networks   An **agglomerate network**, or an agglomeration, is a set of indirect relationships between firms that are competitors. It serves as an information network that enables the firms to secure information about the capabilities and competencies that are regarded as necessary but not sufficient for success. Control of the network is maintained by dues and membership rules. An example of this type of network is a trade association. Such a network usually exists in highly fragmented and geographically dispersed environments that are populated by very small, homogeneous ventures, such as retailing and small farms. They are loosely coupled, voluntary, and have a low-task structure—no single member of the agglomeration can influence another member to do anything.

Organic Networks   An **organic network** is an indirect relationship (indirect in terms of the business, not the individual entrepreneur who represents the firm) between noncompeting organizations. These relationships are not task-oriented and may consist of strong-tie linkages such as friends and close business associates or weak-tie links such as might be found at the chamber of commerce or within a United Way campaign. Table 10–2 provides examples of the agglomerate and organic networks.

TABLE 10–2 Agglomerate and Organic Alliances: Examples

Agglomerate Alliances: Indirect Contact with Competing Firms
Members of trade associations
Members of professional associations
Employing standard costing from publicly available manuals
Employing standard pricing from publicly available manuals
Manufacturing industrywide standard items
Organic Networks: Indirect Contact with Noncompeting Firms
Member of the chamber of commerce
Member of an executive roundtable
National Federation of Independent Business member
Networking through a religious organization
Networking through a community-based voluntary organization
Active in the United Way campaigns
Participating in government-sponsored training programs at the Small Business
    Administration and Small Business Development Centers
Participating in university-sponsored programs for management assistance, technical
    assistance, or technology transfer
Serving on any boards of directors

Source: Adapted from M. Dollinger, "The Evolution of Collective Strategies in Fragmented Industries," *Academy of Management Review,* 15 (1990): 266–285.

> **E-NOTES 10–6 ALLIANCES**
> There are four types of alliances:
> - confederations,
> - conjugate alliances,
> - agglomerations,
> - organic networks.

PARTNER SELECTION CRITERIA

Choosing a partner for a joint venture, for an alliance, or even for one of the shorter-term relationships just discussed becomes a crucial issue for the entrepreneur.[52] A poor choice can doom not only the joint venture but also the entire enterprise the entrepreneur has worked to build. Two primary criteria must be met:

1. The potential partner must have a strong commitment to the joint venture.
2. The top managements of both firms must be compatible.

The first criterion must be met so that the firms have a mutual sense of responsibility and project ownership. If one side believes the venture is unimportant, it will devote less time and resources to the undertaking and be tempted to behave opportunistically. It may let the other side do all the work and take all the risks, while it enjoys the benefits of cooperation.

The second criterion must be met in order to join the two enterprises' cultures and to develop a strong sense of trust. The top managements of the two firms not only must be able to work together but also must be able to model cooperative behavior for their subordinates. When subordinates see that it is acceptable and even desirable for the two firms to work together and share resources and information, they will be much more likely to cooperate, too. The commitment and leadership of top management are essential.

After these two criteria are met, the other criteria for partner selection are typically contingent on the goals of the joint venture and its nature: product orientation, service delivery, technology sharing, or the like. Partners look attractive when they have complementary skills with little duplication and when the relationship creates a mutual dependency that makes cooperative behavior in everyone's self-interest. Good communications, similar cultures and values, compatible operating policies, and compatible goals—all make partners attractive for selection. A partner with a strong reputation is valuable because it enables the other firm to enhance its legitimacy.[53]

One additional issue for the entrepreneur is the size of the venture partner. Usually firms that meet the criteria listed are of approximately equal size. Many times, however, entrepreneurial firms are still quite small. There are some dangers when a small firm attempts to join forces with another enterprise that is considerably larger. Although sometimes this is justified—for example, when the smaller firm has a technology that is needed by the larger company—problems can be anticipated.

One problem is the distinct possibility that the larger firm will not be as dependent on the relationship for its survival or profitability as the smaller firm. Another is that the larger firm is more likely to have a bureaucratic culture in which decision making can be inflexible and slow. Smaller entrepreneurial firms are likely to feel paralyzed by the snail's pace at which the bureaucracy moves. The larger firm and its em-

---

When Teaming with a Big Partner, Watch Where You Step

In January 1990 two companies, Reebok International Ltd. of Stoughton, Massachusetts, and Sports Step Inc. of Atlanta, joined forces to promote the newest hot idea in exercising: step aerobics. Reebok, whose sales of athletic footwear totaled over $500 million at wholesale (1989) teamed up with Sports Step (1989 sales, $7.8 million; 1990, $19.8 million; 1991 estimate, $40 million) in an agreement that was expected to be a big winner but that later turned sour for Sports Step. Sports Step is now in danger of being an also-ran in a field it pioneered.

The sporting-goods industry is volatile, with fashions and fads changing rapidly. Small companies with hot products, like Sports Step, can succeed by filling these niches before the larger firms can get started. The big firms, on the other hand, need these innovations and have the cash and name recognition to support them. This is the scenario for the Sports Step and Reebok partnership. Sports Step was founded in 1989 to exploit the new fitness trend in step aerobics. It sold three versions of the step device (a plastic step) and videotapes. Reebok figured that it could sell more footwear and apparel with a product tie-in. So in exchange for putting the Reebok name on its products sold to health clubs, Sports Step received promotions and advertising ($7 million worth) from Reebok. And the alliance appeared to work well for both, with Sports Step's sales rising over 500 percent.

But the success in saturating the health club market with the product sowed the seeds of disagreement. Future sales would have to come from the home exercise market. Sports Step expected to capitalize on its success and capture this market. It expected Reebok to stick to its strengths—apparel and footwear. But its expectations were shattered when Reebok initiated plans to offer its own step exercise unit for the home market—in direct competition with its partner's plans.

Sports Step sued in U.S. district court both to remove itself from the original agreement and to prevent Reebok from selling its own step exercise unit. Reebok denied the charge that it had violated its agreement and countersued when Sports Step stopped putting the Reebok name on its products. Although the firms had discussed a Reebok takeover a few months before this conflict, they could not negotiate mutually agreeable terms.

Experts in the industry say that Reebok's entry into the market may not kill Sports Step if the smaller firm can continue to innovate and promote its product creatively. But clearly this is a major threat and will limit the smaller firm's potential. Without Reebok, Sports Step may return to the minor leagues.

Source: Adapted from L. Grossman, "Teaming Up with a Big Player May Not Assure a Win," *Wall Street Journal*, March 18, 1992.

ployees might feel that they should dominate the venture, since they are the older and historically the more successful of the two companies. This may make the personnel of the smaller firm feel resentful, since they, no doubt, believe that their contribution is just as significant as the larger firm's.[54]

One "elephant and mouse" joint venture that did not work as predicted was that between athletic footwear giant Reebok International Ltd. and Sports Step Inc., a new venture with big plans. Their story is told in Street Stories 10–2.

Differences in decision making, flexibility, degree of dependence, and management style all decrease the trust and rapport of the two partners. This need not be fatal. A special operating environment, in which both sides have a free hand and consider themselves equal, can be created. This can reduce red tape and enable the larger firm's employees to feel as if they, too, are part of a smaller unit. Even when one partner is much larger than the other, the larger partner can find a smaller operating unit within its structure to be the counterpart of the small entrepreneurial venture.[55]

E-NOTES 10–7   PARTNER SELECTION

Both partners in a joint venture, alliance, or business relationship should have:

- strong commitment to joint venture,
- compatible top management,
- shared goals (product orientation, etc.),
- complementary skills,
- good communications,
- strong reputations.

PROCESSES OF RECIPROCITY

How do entrepreneurs position themselves and their firms to enter into these alliances, networks, and cooperative partnerships? Why do people allow entrepreneurs to do this? From the business viewpoint, the primary reason is that the entrepreneurial firm has something to offer the partner—a skill, a process, a technology, a system for administration, access to a customer, or a desirable location.

But it is the entrepreneur who on a personal level initiates the contact and maintains the relationships so that they may be turned into contracts and formal arrangements. People allow entrepreneurs to approach them with these cooperative and collective strategies for four reasons:

1. *Friendship.* The entrepreneur has developed a nurturing and caring relationship with the people at the target organization.
2. *Liking.* There is pleasure and comfort in reciprocity and finding someone with an affinity and a liking for you.
3. *Gratitude.* The entrepreneur has put a member of the target's firm in his or her personal debt through a personal favor, and the discharge of that debt (reciprocity) is the mechanism for the cooperation.
4. *Obligation.* The target firm must repay some obligation it owes to the entrepreneur.[56]

In each of these cases, the entrepreneur has established a positive environment for cooperation by "being nice" and by doing it first. What kinds of things can entrepreneurs do to encourage cooperative behavior?

1. Share information with the target firm.
2. Help the target firm solve a problem and be open to receiving help with a problem of its own.
3. Give and receive favors, both business and personal.
4. Create opportunities for others to receive recognition and achievement.
5. Build and use networks and allow others access to these networks. The entrepreneur's strong ties can be another's weak ties.
6. Ask others to make their networks available and piggyback on the reputation and credibility of the partner.

E-NOTES 10–8 FORMS OF RECIPROCAL AGREEMENTS

alliance: an informal agreement between two or more businesses for a specific purpose

partnership: a formal bilateral agreement with pooled assets between two or more businesses for a specific purpose

network: an loose amalgamation for the sharing of information

collective: a group of businesses or individuals organized to work together as one unit

---

The Franchising Alternative

Another way to expand the organization's boundaries and the reach of its activities is through franchising. **Franchising** is a marketing system by which the owner of a service, trademarked product, or business format grants exclusive rights to an individual for the local distribution and/or sale of the service or product, and in turn receives payment of a franchise fee, royalties, and the promise of conformance to quality standards.[57] The **franchisor** is the seller of the franchise and the **franchisee** is the buyer.

To what extent is the franchise an entrepreneur? Any distinction between the two must focus on the concept of innovation. The franchisee creates an economic organization, perhaps a network of organizations. Gain and growth are clearly goals, and risk and uncertainty are ever-present. But because the franchisee is contractually obligated to operate the business in a prescribed manner, he or she has little apparent room for innovation. Also, the franchisee does not usually have total control of the disposal of the business; franchisors usually reserve the right to choose or approve the next franchisee. However, franchisees frequently do make innovations that are either tolerated by the franchisor or adopted by the franchisor and incorporated into the system. For example, as we say in Chapter 9, Childress Buick, an automobile dealer, gives salespersons the autonomy to cut the best deal they can. And some of McDonald's best new product ideas originated with franchisees eager to improve their sales.

Franchising is one of the fastest-growing forms of business and now represents a major share of all business in areas such as fast-food restaurants, auto parts dealers, and quick-print copy shops. Also included in the vast array of franchise opportunities are automobile dealerships, major league sports teams, national and international real estate brokers, child-care centers, and accounting and tax services. Franchising accounted for more than $246 billion in sales in 1993.[58] It is estimated that total franchise sales could reach $1 trillion by the year 2000.[59]

The reason for franchising's popularity is clear. Over one third of all independently owned and operated retail and service businesses fail within their first year, and two thirds fail within five years. But less than 5 percent of franchise businesses fail in any given year.[60] A 1991 Gallup poll reported that:

- 94 percent of franchise owners say they are successful.
- 75 percent of franchise owners would repeat their franchise again. Only 39 percent of Americans would repeat their job or business.
- the average gross income before taxes of franchisees is $124,000; 49 percent reported gross incomes less than $100,000 while 37 percent reported gross incomes of more than $100,000.[61]

The fantastic success of franchising is one of the fundamental changes in business in the post-World War II era. But why is franchising so successful for both franchisor and franchisee, and how does it work?

E-NOTES 10–9   FRANCHISING

A marketing system where the owner of a service, trademarked product, or business format:

- grants exclusive rights to an individual for local distribution or sale,
- receives in return:
  franchise fee,
  royalties,
  promise of conformance to quality standards.

THEORETICAL FOUNDATIONS

Franchising is a method of implementing the growth strategy of the franchisor's venture. The successful franchisor possesses resources that are rare, valuable, imperfectly imitable, and nonsubstitutable. Usually these resources are a business concept, an operating system, a brand name, and an actual or potential national reputation. Franchising enables the franchisor to multiply the rents collected on the four-attribute resource through the franchise agreement. Each franchisee becomes an outlet for the value added by the special resource configuration. Franchising enables the franchisor's venture to grow using the franchisee's money, knowledge of the specific locale, and human resources. It also allows the franchisor to enjoy increasing economies of scale in purchasing, building development and improvements, and advertising and promotions. Finally, it enables the firm to enjoy two traditional strategic advantages at once: local control of costs through close supervision of the franchisee, and effective product and service differentiation nationally (or internationally) through the marketing efforts of the franchisor.[62]

Organizational Boundaries   Franchising is a way of setting the boundaries of the organization. Businesses that can expand by opening individual units always have the choice of establishing a chain through company-owned units or franchising. In fact, most franchising systems do contain a significant number of company-owned units in addition to the franchised ones. This enables the franchisor to conduct market experiments, gain knowledge of customer trends and changes, and maintain a solid understanding of procurement and operating costs. Frequently, the franchisor attempts to keep the best locations as part of the company-owned chain, even repurchasing these locations from franchisees who have made them a success.

Franchising is a hybrid form of organization and employs a hybrid mixture of capital and resources. The franchising agreement defines those boundaries by delimiting the organizational and financial constraints on the franchisor.[63] Therefore, it expands the organization's boundaries, which would otherwise be smaller because of limits on resources and money.

Additionally, franchising is a way of balancing the bureaucratic transaction costs of owning, monitoring, and controlling all the outlets or units of the venture (as a chain operation) with the market transaction costs of contracting with the franchisee.

The Agency Problem   The agency problem occurs when ownership and control are separated and the agent (or manager) substitutes his or her own goals and objectives for those of the owner. But because the franchisee is the owner/manager of the unit, the problems arising from the separation of ownership and control are greatly diminished. Since it would be difficult for the franchisor to monitor the quality and behavior of all the venture's outlets spread over the globe, the franchisor instead trusts that owners need much less monitoring than managers. Therefore, franchising is a partial solution to the agency problem.[64] A study using data from the U.S. Census on the food and motel industries found that franchising enables the franchisor to better control the most physically dispersed outlets and to protect the system's brand-name capital. The same study also indicated that franchising permits larger local outlets than using nonfranchised operations.[65]

However, franchising is only a partial solution because sometimes the owner of a franchise outlet also hires managers to run the business. Therefore, the agency problem still exists. Also, when franchisees serve a transient customer base, such as travelers on highways or in airports, they often let quality slip because they know there is little repeat business.[66] In summary, franchising enables the owner of a resource that is rare, valuable, imperfectly imitable (by the outsiders) and nonsubstitutable to make perfect copies of the resource without lessening its rarity. To do this, the franchisor must grant exclusive *local* operating rights to the franchisee so that, from the point of view of the final customer, the product or service is locally rare and somewhat hard to get.[67] And the franchisor must build a national reputation. As we saw in Chapter 2, a reputation is one of the resources that can possess the four attributes of sustainable competitive advantage. So what franchisors give up in the complexity of local organization and the proprietary nature of technology or physical resources, they attempt to overcome with reputation, high visibility, and a systemwide culture of high performance.

FRANCHISOR CONSIDERATIONS

The primary form of franchising is the **business format franchise**. The franchisor grants the right to the franchisee to operate the business in a prescribed way. The franchisor can sell these rights one unit at a time or for a geographic territory. The one-at-a-time approach enables the franchisor to maintain close control over locations and the speed of growth. The geographic area approach actually speeds growth, since it is usually in the interest of the franchisee to saturate the territory as quickly as possible. But it enables some franchisees to become very large and powerful. This might be undesirable and risky from the franchisor's point of view because powerful franchisees can sometimes demand contractual concessions and resist royalty increases.

In the business concept format, the franchisor is selling the business or marketing system, not the hamburger or the quick-copy service. It is estimated that before the first franchisee is operating, the total costs for a franchisor of setting up these systems can run between $110,000 and $950,000. Table 10–3 shows the different cost drivers for the franchisor.

Franchising takes other forms in addition to the popular business format mode. A franchisor can grant an **exclusive right to trade**. For example, an airport or highway authority grants to specific companies the exclusive right to sell food and beverages in the airport or along the highway. A **distributorship** is also a form of franchise. An example would be a franchise to sell a particular make of automobile or computer. A **registered trademark franchise** enables the franchisee to use a name with the expectation that it is recognizable to the customer and that quality will be maintained. An example of this is the Best Western Hotel system. Each unit is independently owned and operated, but each uses the name Best Western and meets certain minimum standards.

The Franchiseable Business   Certain types of businesses are appropriate for franchising. The first and primary requirement is a successful series of **pilot stores**, locations, or operating units. The franchisor bears the cost of developing the formula during the pilot period. The franchisor must learn enough about how to make the business a success to be able to train others to be successful, too. This means learning the key elements of accurate site selection, efficient operations, internal and external financial keys and ratios, operating cost control, a consistent and workable pricing policy, and training procedures for both potential franchisees and their employees. In

---

TABLE 10–3   Estimated Costs of Franchising

Research and Development Costs
Associated with the creation of the initial product, market research for the product and the franchise system, and the franchising blueprint.

Creation of the Franchise Package
Requires the hiring of a legal team to prepare the Uniform Franchise Offering Circular (UFOC) for the U.S. Federal Trade Commission. Franchisors are highly regulated by state authorities as well.

Marketing the Franchise
Will cost money for advertising the franchise's availability, recruiting and selecting franchises, further product and service development, and additional operational expenses.

Working Capital
For ongoing operations such as training franchisees, continued promotions, further development and refinement, and possible financial capital to help franchises get started. Plus some extra in reserve.

Source: Adapted from R. Justis and R. Judd, *Franchising* (Cincinnati, OH: South-Western Publishing, 1989).

addition to systematically perfecting each of these areas, the potential franchisor must be sure that after all costs are met, enough is left over for the franchisee to earn a respectable return and pay the royalty to the franchisor.

Businesses suitable for franchising often have a number of common elements. They have a product or service that is able to satisfy a continuing demand. Because it will take two to three years for both the franchisor and franchisee to see a return on their money, the franchise idea cannot be based on a fad or a quick "make-a-buck" opportunity.

The format of the franchiseable business needs to be simple and mechanical. A high degree of customized personal service or individual flair and skill may prove difficult for the franchisee to duplicate. Uniform standards of quality and appearance for the stores or outlets are important. This means that the franchisor must give serious thought to what quality means to the customer and be able to define and measure it accurately.

The franchisor looks for a simple and easy-to-remember name for the business. Strong advertising and promotional support are needed. The franchisee locations must be good enough to support the business but not so expensive that they absorb all the profits. This is why developing accurate site selection criteria is vital.

The administration of the franchise system should be kept simple. The franchisor needs a method to ensure that sales and profits of the franchisee are accurately reported and royalty payments are correct and timely. If possible, the franchisor should arrange for a bank or financial syndicate to provide financial assistance to prospective franchisees.

But even the best business format franchise system cannot long endure if the original pilot operations do not have the resources to obtain sustainable competitive advantage.

Competitive Issues   The franchise system engages in two simultaneous sets of competitions: The franchisor competes to sell franchises, and the franchisee competes locally to sell the product or service. These are interrelated problems. If the franchisee is facing stiff competition and losses are accumulating, the franchisor will find it more difficult to sell franchises. Conversely, if the franchisor is having trouble selling franchises, this decreases the brand value, name recognition, advertising support, and purchasing economies of scale that the franchisee relies on for marketing and operations.

The dependency of franchisees on the franchisor is illustrated by the case of Checkers Drive-In Restaurants, Inc., of Clearwater, Florida. Checkers was started in 1986 and looked like it had found a niche that the giants of the fast-food burger industry had missed. It offered quick service, low prices, and a limited menu of burgers, fries, and cola. This was the original strategy of McDonald's and Burger King, but over time, these large, multinational corporations had abandoned this focus. A Checkers unit was simple: 99-cent burgers, two drive-through windows, walk-up service, and no inside seating.

With this strategy came success. Revenues topped $50 million in 1991, the year Checkers went public, and climbed to almost $190 million in 1993. Profits also rose rapidly as the company grew to 277 company-owned stores and 177 franchised outlets. But some doubted that the firm could sustain its success. Checkers founder James Mattei answered critics when the stock began to fall in early 1994 by saying, "We're not a flash in the pan. The newness is off who we are, but we have so many opportunities."

But the skeptics were right. In March 1994 Mattei resigned and retired at the age of 45. Later that month the company announced it was scaling back expansion plans, posting its first quarterly loss since going public and swapping some restaurants with other companies to gain concentration and clout. What had happened?

"Someone woke the elephants," said Robert Morrison of Checker's former advertising agency. McDonald's and Wendy's had begun to return to their roots with value pricing. Burger King introduced its own 99-cent Whopper in a back-to-basics campaign. Checker's same-store sales—a key industry barometer—fell 5.9 percent. Franchisees suffered the most because of somewhat out-of-the-way locations, advertising that was spread too thin, and operations that were too inflexible to introduce new products when the majors attacked the core product.[68] The story indicates that the franchisor's competitive strategy must be sound for the continued success of the franchisee.

The dependency can run in the other direction, too. Franchisors depend on their franchisees for cooperation. A franchisee rebellion can be a serious problem for the franchisor. Although a franchisor can discipline individual franchisees who fail to live up to quality standards of contractual agreements, when the entire franchisee system rebels, the franchisor may have little choice but to negotiate or capitulate. Franchisee rebellions have occurred at some of the most famous and popular fast-food organizations, including Taco Bell, KFC, Holiday Inns, and Burger King. But for the most part, power is held by the franchisor, who screens and selects the franchisee, draws up the contracts, and collects the royalties.

Because of the preponderance of power on the franchisor side, the government regulates the franchise industry, primarily to protect franchisees. The franchising business is regulated both by the individual states and by the Federal Trade Commission (FTC). Much of the regulation has to do with ensuring that the franchisor provides the franchisee with the information necessary to make informed decisions. Franchisees contend that these rules are widely abused.

Under the current franchise rule, the franchisor must disclose all financial terms and obligations of the franchisee. Franchisors do not have to state how much money franchisees can expect to make, but if they voluntarily do so, they must document their claims. Civil penalties of $10,000 can be levied for each violation. However, individual franchises cannot sue the franchisor under the FTC rule; only the FTC can bring action in federal court.[69]

But despite regulation and potential problems with franchises, franchising remains popular because it enables businesses to expand quickly with other people's money and to have a self-motivated owner/manager control the operation. For franchisors to take advantage of these two benefits, they must be able to deliver a franchiseable product and business system. One example of a franchisor who has expanded quickly and profitably is Subway Sandwich Shops of Milford, Connecticut. Its current situation is summarized in Street Stories 10–3.

FRANCHISEE CONSIDERATIONS

Franchisees must be careful in evaluating franchise opportunities and choosing the franchising option best for them. Potential franchisees are urged to examine their personal preferences for risk, autonomy, and hard work. They should consider how their talents and experience will contribute to making the franchise a success. Because of the constrained nature of the franchise agreement, franchising is not for every entrepreneur "wannabe."

Spectacular Growth But at a Price

No one can argue that Subway Sandwich Shops has become the fastest-growing franchisor in the world and in all of history. Started in 1965 by 17-year-old Fred DeLuca with a $1,000 loan from partner Peter Buck, the company struggled at first. But by 1982 it had set a goal for itself of "5,000 units by 1994" and had actually exceeded that number by 1990! Today, it approaches 8,000 units and is opening new ones at the rate of 100 per month. Expansion is taking place all over the world, with new locations in Canada, Australia, Japan, Ireland, Israel, Mexico, and other countries.

The pursuit of growth has made both DeLuca and Buck very rich, with personal fortunes estimated at over $100 million each. How did they do it? First, operations are kept simple. A typical Subway shop is about 1,000 square feet of simple decor, a few booths, and food preparation counters and equipment. The staff make submarine sandwiches to order, slicing breads and filling them with meats, hot and cold, and condiments and fixings. Soft drinks, chips, and cookies complete the menu.

Second, the buy-in price for a franchisee is quite low. A new Subway costs between $45,000 and $70,000 up front. This means that on the low end, a Subway franchise is cheaper than 70 percent of all the franchises listed in **Entrepreneur** magazine and cheaper than 50 percent on the high end. Moreover, Subway will help finance the equipment up to $32,000.

Something must be working well. Subway claims that there is a mere 2 percent annual closing rate and that 50 percent of all new franchises are purchased by existing franchisees. Franchisees are active in regional and national boards of directors that control marketing and advertising policies. An advisory council of franchisees also oversees quality control and attempts to improve purchasing power. Apparently they are pleased with the product the franchisor is selling.

But there has been criticism of how Subway operates by former and current franchisees. Franchisees have claimed that the constant push for new store development cannibalizes current store sales. Sales and new store development are farmed out to agents. These agents are often selected from the ranks of current francisees. They are paid on a commission basis and they help pick locations, negotiate leases, and train the new franchisees. In all three areas—site selection, leases, and training—problems have been reported.

And individual franchises often find that instead of a profitable business, they have bought themselves low-paying, long-hour jobs. If a store falls below break even, estimated to be about $4,000 per week before debt expense, the franchisees face bankruptcy. DeLuca estimates that about 50 percent of the time they have to sell their franchises at cost or below.

There is also the complaint that Subway will grant a franchise to anyone who can pay the fee. Some say that this includes people who can barely read, write, or do simple arithmetic. DeLuca does not deny it and says, "Very few of our people were voted most likely to succeed in high school. And I wasn't either."

Source: Adapted from S. Barlow, "Sub-stantial Success," *Entrepreneur,* January 1993, 125–126; B. Marsh, "Sandwich Shop Surges, But to Run One Can Take Heroic Effort," *Wall Street Journal,* September 16, 1992, A 1, A 6.

Franchisee Requirements   What are the most important things for franchises to look for?

1. *Proven operating locations* serve as a prototype for the franchisee. This demonstrates do-ability to the customer. These stores have been tested and their operations refined. They are profitable, and the books should be open for qualified franchisees. The operation must be transparent enough so that the franchisee can believe that he or she can manage it.

2. *A credible top management team* demonstrates to franchisees that they will not be alone and that there is sufficient expertise at the franchisor level to handle any emergency or contingency.

3. *Skilled field support staff* are the people who will train the franchisee and communicate the franchisor's message to the units in the field. They help the franchisee attain his or her goals.

4. *A trade identity* that is distinctive and protected will enable the franchisee to use the trademarks, signage, slogans, trade dress, and overall image. The franchisee should be concerned that quality, perceived or real, is similar throughout the system.

5. *A proprietary operations manual* comprehensively explains the proven methods of operation and management. It should be easy to read and understand.

6. *Training programs*, both on-site as well as at headquarters, should be regularly updated, and franchisee staff and management should be trained as well.

7. *Disclosure and offering documents* that meet all federal and state regulations are needed. In addition, a franchise agreement that balances the needs of the franchisor and franchisee should be prepared. Table 10–4 summarizes the types of issues that need to be resolved in the contract.[70] Franchisees should retain competent counsel to advise them on all matters.

8. *Advertising, marketing, public relations, and promotion* plans should be prepared and available. The franchisor should be ready to show how a national and regional product reputation will be developed for the benefit of the franchisee.

9. *A communications system* establishes the ongoing dialogue that takes place between franchisor, franchisee, and the entire network of units. This includes meetings, schedules of visiting, and attendance at association conferences, as well as random calls and inspections.

10. *Sufficient capital* is needed to get the franchise system off the ground. These are substantial costs to the franchisor. These were described in Table 10–3. The franchisee is responsible for due diligence before investing in any franchise operation. Many horror stories can be told of franchisees caught unaware and unprepared either by unscrupulous franchisors or simply by difficult economic times. Despite regulation, unprincipled dealers and susceptible buyers abound.

TABLE 10-4	Issues to be Addressed in a Franchising Agreement
Issue	*Questions to Resolve*
1. Franchise fee	Amount? One time or per unit?
2. Royalties	Amount? As a percentage of net or gross? Sliding scale?
3. Quality control	Quality specifications? Inspections and monitoring? Rewards and sanctions?
4. Advertising	Fee? Local budget? National? Extensiveness and intensiveness? Messages and campaigns?
5. Offerings	Product line? Product mix? Required offerings? Alternatives? Franchisee generated offerings?
6. Equipment	Required? Additional? Financing?
7. Location	Site selection requirements? Franchisor aid? Financing?
8. Operations	Signs? Hours? Maintenance? Decor? Personnel policies?
9. Reporting	Types of reports? Frequency? Auditing? Sanctions?
10. Dispute resolution	Methods? Equity?
11. Termination	Timing? Causes? Sanctions?

Source: Adapted from R. Justis and R. Judd, *Franchising* (Cincinnati, OH: South-Western Publishing, 1989).

Take the case of all the would-be entrepreneurs who have been the alleged victims of such franchise opportunities as Juice Time, Cola Time, Lotto Time, Water Time, and Tater Time.[71] In each of these cases a slick sales franchisor convinced hundreds of people to sink upwards of $40 million in these schemes. People were duped by the apparent connection of these business opportunities with such famous corporate giants as Coca-Cola and American Telephone and Telegraph. But there were no opportunities here, only unfulfilled promises, nonexistent products and equipment, and training programs that never occurred. The results were millions of dollars lost and thousands of hours in court.

Even once-reputable franchisors fall on tough times, and the franchisees must bear the burden. In the mid-1980s, Nutri/System was a franchisor of diet centers with a bright future and optimistic prospects. But because of increased competition, negative publicity resulting from lawsuits from customers, and the heavy debt burden of a leveraged buyout, Nutri/Systems was in trouble. A severe financial crisis hit the firm in early 1993.[72] When the franchisor suffers, so does the reputation of its units, its advertising campaigns, and its field support and training. In the case of Nutri/System, the franchisees also depended on the franchisor to supply its exclusive line of diet foods for sale to customers. With no support, a failing reputation, and no product to sell, where were the franchisees to turn?

Franchisee Guidelines The potential franchisee should investigate a franchise opportunity by doing the following:[73]

1. *Perform a self-evaluation.* Is franchising really for you? If you are very entrepreneurial, franchising may not be for you, since it requires discipline to operate under someone else's concept. But if you are just getting started with the idea of owning your own business, franchising can give you some low-risk experience.
2. *Investigate the franchisor.* Visit other company stores and talk to other franchisees. Question earnings. Find out how the franchisor treats the franchisees, in

good times and bad. Pay particular attention to the extent the franchisor respects the franchisee territory. You do not want to be in competition with your own franchisor.

3. *Study the industry and competition.* There are no sure things, and overall industry conditions and the nature of the competition will affect the individual franchisee. Also look at the degree of regulation in the industry. Many convenience store/gas station franchisees were stunned in the 1980s when they had to replace their underground gas storage tanks after the government mandated tighter environmental controls. Few were prepared for the expense.

4. *Study the Uniform Franchise Offering Circular (UFOC).* The UFOC is the document required by the FTC of every franchisor. It contains some 20 items, including the history of the franchise, the background of the franchisors, a description of the franchise, the financial obligations of the parties, territories and sales restrictions, and matters related to copyrights, trademarks, logos, and patents.

5. *Investigate the franchisor's disclosures.* The franchisor is obligated to report any "fact, circumstance, or set of conditions which has a substantial likelihood of influencing a reasonable franchisee or a reasonable prospective franchisee in the making of a significant decision related to a named franchise business or which has any significant financial impact on a franchisee or prospective franchisee."[74]

6. *Know your legal rights and retain counsel.*

Summary

Typically, the entrepreneur has practically unlimited freedom to do business where and how he or she chooses. This chapter, however, has presented two types of business environments that are special cases of entrepreneurship because they limit this freedom of action. Both intrapreneurship and franchising raise organizational and contractual constraints to consider.

Intrapreneurship is entrepreneurship that takes place within a corporate setting. It is difficult to master and has many barriers to its success, most notably the corporate bureaucracy. For a corporation to be successful at intrapreneurship, it needs to give the intrapreneurs many of the same types of freedom that entrepreneurs enjoy, thereby mimicking the external market system within the organization. But the intrapreneur must still conform to some, if not all, of the organization's values, goals, and processes. Political considerations within the organization are necessary hurdles for the intrapreneur to surmount.

Networking skills and alliance formation is vital to both new ventures and growing firms. Networking is actually a series of methods of securing resources without taking ownership. These include various forms of partnerships, alliances, and informal agreements. The ability to convince others of the desirability of an alliance and to negotiate favorable terms for the venture is a fundamental skill for today's entrepreneur.

Franchising presents the entrepreneur with the opportunity to expand the boundaries of the organization and, potentially, to retain control of the strategic resources that provide the basis of SCA. The franchisor contributes the key resource of the business system and the product or service's reputation. The franchisee contributes knowledge of the specific location, human resources, and a highly motivated owner/manager to maintain quality. The combination has led to tremendous growth in franchising systems.

But the parties to the franchising agreement are also constrained. The franchisor must continue to support the franchisees through training, product development, advertising and promotion, and procurement assistance. The franchisee lives by the letter of the agreement and must operate the franchise as designed by the franchisor. Neither has the complete unlimited freedom of action of the entrepreneur. But the franchisee is particularly constrained and holds little power relative to the franchisor.

Key Terms

- Intrapreneurship
- Internal corporate venture (ICV)
- Networking
- Informal network
- Formal network
- Personal network
- Voice
- Exit
- Strong ties
- Extended network
- Weak ties
- Confederate alliance
- Conjugate alliance
- Agglomerate network
- Organic network
- Franchising
- Franchisor
- Franchisee
- Business format franchise
- Exclusive right to trade
- Distributorship
- Registered trademark franchise
- Pilot store
- Uniform Franchise Offering Circular (UFOC)

Discussion Questions

1. What benefits can corporations gain through successful intrapreneurship?
2. What are the important similarities and differences between entrepreneurship and intrapreneurship?
3. How is the intrapreneurial business plan different from the entrepreneurial business plan? Why is this so?
4. What impediments do large corporations impose on intrapreneurial efforts?
5. Why is networking important for the entrepreneur?
6. What is meant by the "strength of weak ties?"
7. Are franchisors entrepreneurs? Are franchisees entrepreneurs? Give reasons for your answers.
8. Why has franchising been so successful in the United States? Does it have the same potential worldwide?
9. Why is the pilot store so important for the potential franchisor?
10. What are the characteristics of a franchiseable business?
11. What is the nature of the dependency between franchisor and franchisee?
12. What should a franchisee look for in evaluating a franchise opportunity?

Exercises

1. Interview a local franchisee. Ask the franchisee about the relationship between the franchisee and franchisor. What are the problem areas and the positive points, and what does the future hold? Find out whether the franchisee is satisfied with the franchise and if he or she would do it again.

2. Send away for a package of material from a franchisor. Advertisements for these can usually be found in *Inc.* or *Entrepreneur* magazine, among other places. Evaluate the material you are sent. Does it answer the questions that a potential franchisee will have? Follow up by calling the franchisor. What

additional information can you obtain this way?

3. Evaluate your own business plan for

its franchiseability. Does it meet the criteria for franchising? If so, develop a franchise plan.

Networking Exercises

1. Identify a trade or professional organization that serves the type of business that you are writing your business plan for. Call or write this association and request materials. What does this organization do for its members? How can members get the most out of belonging to this group?

2. Attend a meeting of a professional organization or group. What types of activities go on? What kinds of behavior can you observe? Interview attendees.

What reasons do they give for attending these meetings? What successes have they experienced?

3. Join a student club or group (if you do not already belong). Go to meetings and participate in a few activities. Make new friends. What kinds of things did you do to become friends with these people? What is the extent of the relationship? If you were going into business, how could these new friends help?

DISCUSSION CASE

Oniisan Is Watching

"We stopped learning from U.S. retailers long ago," declares Toshifumi Suzuki, chief executive of Ito-Yokado, the Japanese company which operates 6,875 7-Eleven convenience stores in Japan. "Now *we* have the world's most advanced retailing system."

7-Eleven franchisees in the United States will soon have a chance to see if that's true. Ito-Yokado also has a majority interest in the Southland Corporation, parent company of the 5,634 7-Eleven stores in the United States and Canada, and is now in the process of exporting their management methods and philosophy to this side of the Pacific. Suzuki is unequivocal about the impact this will have. "American 7-Elevens don't have a choice: It's either adopt our plans or die," he explains.

The key component in the Ito-Yokado Co.'s retail operation is a point-of-sale (POS) computer cash register that transmits data to corporate headquarters every time a sale is made. Store managers in Japan can use their computer to order food deliveries an unprecedented three times a day. Suzuki says the POS register has enabled him to implement the same "just-in-time" inventory control that has made Japanese auto makers so successful, and to slash a store's average inventory turnover from 25 to 7 days.

Cash registers that track sales and inventory aren't really unusual in either the United States or Japan today. But this register does more. It allows managers to track and predict product sales by analyzing sales data, demographic trends, and even local weather forecasts. It also allows Ito-Yokado to play *oniisan* or "big brother" by monitoring how much time each store manager spends analyzing that data and those trends. *Oniisan* is watching every time a 7-Eleven manager touches the register keyboard.

"Sometimes I don't know who's really running the store," complains Michiharu Endo, who operates a 7-Eleven franchise in Tokyo. An Ito-Yokado inspector warned Endo last year that he was researching only 600 inventory items each week, and that he needed to "shape up and use the computer more." Ironically Endo quit his marketing job three years ago to purchase this 7-Eleven franchise because he wanted to be his own boss. Now he's not certain whether he's in control or not. "It's like being under 24-hour surveillance; it's like being enslaved."

A pilot program last year, which placed an Ito-Yokado register in 300 7-Eleven stores in New Jersey and Oregon, produced mixed reviews. Some managers were amazed to discover that as much as 40 percent of their inventory had sales of less than one unit per month. But some managers echoed the negative sentiments of Ted Poggi, owner of a 7-Eleven store in Newark, New Jersey and chairman of the National Coalition of Associations of 7-Eleven Franchisees. Poggi asserts that there is a deep "philosophical difference" between American and Japanese retailers, and that the *oniisan* electronic system is in direct conflict with American entrepreneurs' desire for independence. He also contends that Ito-Yokado's electronic register is inferior to the less invasive computer system his own store has been using to track inventory for several years. Jim Keyes, Southland's chief financial officer, points out that American 7-Eleven stores have a higher tolerance for slow-moving items because their stores are much larger than their counterparts in Japan.

But Ito-Yokado hasn't become one of the world's largest retailers, with annual revenues of $30.3 billion, by listening to excuses. Suzuki says that Southland has allowed a culture of dependence to spread among its franchisees. "They think it's the corporation's job to find hot-selling products and take care of distribution and inventory," he says. "They just want to sit behind the cash register."

While Ito-Yokado's methods may not be popular with everyone, the results certainly are. Sales have doubled at Japanese 7-Eleven stores. In this country Southland's operating revenues were up 29 percent in 1996 thanks to chainwide refurbishing, including the addition of gas stations to many stores. Revenue per store is still 67 percent higher in Japan, but that equation may change now that *oniisan* will be watching in the United States.

CASE QUESTIONS

1. Do you think electronic controls represent the "most advanced" retailing methods in the world today? What other methods typify successful retailers now?

2. How do you think most 7-Eleven franchisees in the United States will respond to Ito-Yokado's methods? How much will they be swayed by the prospect of doubling their sales?

3. What could Ito-Yokado do to promote their methods and electronic management to U.S. operators?

4. What message does the Ito-Yokado model send to other franchisors?

Source: Adapted from Norihiko Shirouzu and Jon Bigness, "7-Eleven Operators Resist System to Monitor Managers," *Wall Street Journal*, June 16, 1997, B1; and Marcia Vickers, "In Japan's Rebound, Exporters May Be the Stars," *New York Times*, June 29, 1997, F 4.

Notes

1. The word was coined by G. Pinchot in his book, *Intrapreneurship* (New York: Harper & Row, 1985).
2. B. Dumaine, "Closing the Innovation Gap," *Fortune*, December 2, 1991, 56–62.
3. J. Pierce and A. Delbecq, "Organizational Structure, Individual Attitudes and Innovation," *Academy of Management Review* 2 (1976): 27–37.
4. Adapted from R. Nielsen, M. Peters, and R. Hisrich, "Intrapreneurship Strategy for Internal Markets: Corporate, Nonprofit and Government Institution Cases," *Strategic Management Journal* 6 (April/June 1985): 181–189.
5. R. Burgelman, "Corporate Entrepreneurship and Strategic Management: Insights from a Process Study," *Management Science* 29 (December 1983): 1349–1364.
6. S. Zahra, "Predictors and Financial Outcomes of Corporate Entrepreneurship: An Exploratory Study," *Journal of Business Venturing* 6 (July 1991): 259–285.
7. The information on 3M is extracted from P. Drucker, *Innovation and Entrepreneurship* (New York: Harper & Row, 1985).
8. This discussion follows G. Pinchot, 1985.
9. I. Hill, "In Intrapreneur-Turned-Entrepreneur Compares Both Worlds," *Research Management* 30 (May/June 1987): 33–37.
10. R. Knight, "Technological Innovation in Canada: A Comparison of Independent Entrepreneurs and Corporate Innovators," *Journal of Business Venturing* 4 (1989): 281–288.
11. G. Jones and J. Butler, "Managing Internal Corporate Entrepreneurship: An Agency Theory Perspective," *Journal of Management* 18 (1992): 733–749.
12. J. Cornwall and B. Perlman, *Organizational Entrepreneurship* (Homewood, IL: Irwin, 1990).
13. These sources are suggested in P. Drucker, *Innovation and Entrepreneurship*.
14. Ibid.
15. Ibid.
16. R. Burgelman, "Strategy Making as a Social Learning Process: The Case of Internal Corporate Venturing," *Interfaces* 18 (May/June 1988): 74–85.
17. R. Garud and A. Van de Ven, "An Empirical Evaluation of the Internal Corporate Venturing Process," *Strategic Management Journal* 13 (Summer 1992): 93–109.
18. D. Garvin, "Spinoffs and the New Firm Formulation Process," *California Management Review* 25 (1983): 3–20.
19. This discussion follows Pinchot, 1985.
20. H. Sykes and Z. Block, "Corporate Venturing Obstacles: Sources and Solutions," *Journal of Business Venturing* 4 (May 1989): 159–167.
21. Ibid.
22. H. Geneen, "Why Intrapreneurship Doesn't Work," *Venture* 7 (January 1985): 46–52.
23. R. Kanter, "The New Workforce Meets the Changing Workplace: Strains, Dilemmas, and the Contradictions in Attempts to Implement Participative and Entrepreneurial Management," *Human Resource Management* 25 (Winter 1986): 515–537.
24. J. Duncan, P. Ginter, A. Rucks, and T. Jacobs, "Intrapreneurship and the Reinvention of the Corporation," *Business Horizons* 31 (May/June 1988): 16–21.
25. I. MacMillan, Z. Block, and P. Narasimha, "Corporate Venturing: Alternatives, Obstacles Encountered and Experienced Effects," *Journal of Business Venturing* 1 (Spring 1986): 177–191.
26. J. Quinn, "Managing Innovation: Controlled Chaos," Reprinted in *Entrepreneurship: Creativity at Work* (Cambridge, MA: Harvard Business Press, 1985).
27. Adapted from G. Pinchot, *Intrapreneurship*, pp. 198–199.
28. "Q & A: The *Inc.* Interview—Flashes of Genius" (George Gendron interviews Peter Drucker). The State of Small Business, 1996. *Inc.* Special Issue, p. 38.

29. M. Granovetter, "Economic Action and Social Structure: The Problem of Embeddedness," *American Journal of Sociology* 91 (1985): 481–510.

30. P. Dubini and H. Aldrich, "Personal and Extended Networks Are Central to the Entrepreneurial Process," *Journal of Business Venturing* 6 (1991): 305–313.

31. We use the terms *networking, partnering, joint ventures*, and *alliances* interchangeably to make the text more readable. Sometimes distinctions are made between these different forms based on ownership, control, number of participants, and other factors.

32. K. Harrigan, *Managing for Joint Venture Success* (Lexington, MA: Lexington Books, 1986).

33. M. Selz, "Everybody in the Pool! Sharing Resources Makes a Splash," *Wall Street Journal*, October 16, 1992, B2.

34. Quoted in U. Gupta, "A Shared Commitment," *Wall Street Journal*, November 22, 1991, B2.

35. Dubini and Aldrich, 1991.

36. Ibid.

37. A. Hirschman, *Exit, Voice, and Loyalty* (Cambridge, MA: Harvard University Press, 1972).

38. M. Granovetter, "The Strength of Weak Ties," *American Journal of Sociology* 78 (1973): 1360–1380.

39. S. Birley, "The Role of Networks in the Entrepreneurial Process," *Journal of Business Venturing* 1 (1985): 107–117; B. Johannison, "New Venture Creation: A Network Approach," *Frontiers of Entrepreneurial Research* (Wellesley, MA: Babson College, 1986).

40. Dubini and Aldrich, 1991.

41. M. Dollinger, "Environmental Boundary Spanning and Information Processing Effects on Organizational Performance," *Academy of Management Journal* 27 (1984): 351–368.

42. Granovetter, 1973.

43. From E. Carlson, "Outside Directors Are an Asset Inside Small Companies," *Wall Street Journal*, October 30, 1992.

44. Quoted in J. Saddler, "Electronic Bulletin Boards Help Businesses Post Suc-

cess," *Wall Street Journal*, October 29, 1992.

45. A. McCarthy, D. Krueger, and T. Schoenecker, "Changes in the Time Allocation Patterns of Entrepreneurs," *Entrepreneurship: Theory and Practice* 15 (1990): 7–18.

46. G. Astley and C. Fombrun, "Collective Strategy: Social Ecology of Organizational Environments," *Academy of Management Review* 8 (1983): 576–587.

47. M. Dollinger, "The Evolution of Collective Strategies in Fragmented Industries," *Academy of Management Review* 15 (1990): 266–285.

48. Ibid.

49. Ibid.

50. P. Coy, "Two Cheers for Corporate Collaboration," *Business Week*, May 3, 1993, 34.

51. M. Selz, "Networks Help Small Companies Think and Act Big," *Wall Street Journal*, November 12, 1992, B2.

52. M. Geringer, *Joint Venture Partner Selection* (New York: Quorum Books, 1988).

53. J. Starr and I. Macmillan, "Resource Cooption via Social Contracting: Resource Acquisition Strategies for New Ventures," *Strategic Management Journal* 11 (1990): 79–92.

54. Geringer, 1988.

55. Ibid.

56. Starr and Macmillan, 1990.

57. F. Fry, *Entrepreneurship: A Planning Approach* (Minneapolis/St. Paul: West, 1993).

58. "Understanding the Franchise 500," *Entrepreneur*, January 1993, 130–131.

59. International Franchising Association, Fact Sheet, August 20, 1993.

60. Remarks based on U.S. Small Business Administration and U.S. Commerce Department figures by William B. Cherlasky, president of the International Franchise Association. Published in R. Justis and R. Judd, *Franchising* (Cincinnati, OH: South-Western Publishing, 1989), iii.

61. Reported by the International Franchising Association, August 20, 1993.

62. C. Hill and G. Jones, *Strategic Management: An Integrated Approach* (Boston: Houghton-Mifflin, 1992).

63. M. Carney and E. Gedajlovic, "Vertical Integration in Franchise Systems: Agency Theory and Resource Explanations," *Strategic Management Journal* 12 (1991): 607–629.

64. M. Jensen and W. Meckling, "Theory of the Firm: Managerial Behavior, Agency Costs, and Ownership Structure," *Journal of Financial Economics* 3 (1976): 305–360.

65. S. Norton, "Franchising, Brand Name Capital, and the Entrepreneurial Capacity Problem," *Strategic Management Journal* 9 (1988): 105–114.

66. J. Brickley and F. Dark, "The Choice of Organizational Form: The Case of Franchising," *Journal of Financial Economics* 18 (1987): 401–420.

67. This is somewhat problematic when a company like McDonald's considers the trading area for one of its locations to be a four-minute drive.

68. G. DeGeorge, "Someone Woke the Elephants," *Business Week*, April 4, 1994, 55.

69. J. Tannenbaum, "Angry Franchisees Turn Spotlight to FTC Enforcement," *Wall Street Journal*, October 13, 1992, B2.

70. A. Sherman, "Franchiser Checklist," *Inc.*, January 1992, 89–90.

71. J. Emshwiller, "Investors Claim Ventures Meant No Opportunity," *Wall Street Journal*, June 8, 1992, B1.

72. J. Tannenbaum and L. Valeriano. "Nutri/System Franchisees Live Franchiser's Nightmare," *Wall Street Journal*, May 3, 1993, B1.

73. U.S. Department of Commerce, *Franchise Opportunity Handbook* (Washington, DC: Government Printing Office, 1984).

74. FTC Rule at 436.2(n).

:X:X:X:X:CASES:X:X:X:X:

Case 1 Prolingua

In early April 1990, Jennifer Malott faced a critical decision. In her MBA entrepreneurship course the previous semester, she had researched the market for a language translation service, Prolingua. What she believed she had discovered in the process was a market opportunity that pleaded for a professionally managed organization to fill it. In addition, the project whetted her appetite for the independence that creating a new venture could provide.

But to keep her options open, and because all of the other students were doing it, she went through the placement office and interview process as well. And she was successful—her best offer was with Ameritech Publishing in Michigan. Ameritech was pressing her for a decision when she received a phone call from Samuel Eberts, an attorney with whom Jennifer had discussed her proposed business and plan. Attorney Eberts was ready to hire Prolingua, and he told her on the phone that he was prepared to offer a $1,000 per month retainer against billables to get her started (see Exhibit 1).

She spoke to friends and family and solicited their opinions. To her professor, she said,

> As an "army brat" I never lived in the same place for more than two years until I went to college. I attended countless schools and made numerous friends, all of whom were left behind when we made the next move. In a lot of ways, I missed having a conventional childhood—living in the same house for years, having a best friend, and graduating from the same school you entered as a freshman.
>
> But, being an "army brat" did have its advantages. By the time I was 18, I'd lived in more countries than most people visit in a lifetime and found myself fascinated with the diversity and the similarities of people throughout the world. While it's not necessary for military families to learn native languages, when you're immersed in a society and cannot understand your environment, some people develop a real sense of urgency to communicate. I was one of those people. I was fortunate that I had a good ear for language, because I became fascinated with learning all I could about the countries where we lived, and that included the languages.
>
> Unfortunately, we never stayed long enough that I could develop fluency in all of them, but I am fluent in French and have excellent reading skills in Italian, Spanish, and German.
>
> After finishing my MBA, I intended to work for a large, multinational company so that I could indulge my taste for world travel, maintain my skills in languages, and develop my skills in management. But I also want to be pre-

pared to create my own company and design my own life after I have enough experience. With more and more companies pursuing international business ventures, the opportunity exists to fulfill my basic requirements—make a living and be involved with languages. I've spent the last six months developing a business plan that will allow me to capitalize on my previous experience, be my own boss, and do the work I love!

Jennifer scheduled a meeting for the first of May with Eberts. Ameritech said it would wait at least that long for her decision. Did she have the resources to start her own business? Was now the right time? It was becoming harder and harder to fall asleep at night as she reviewed the pros and cons of each side.

BACKGROUND AND PURPOSE

Translation has occurred ever since there have been different written languages and a concurrent need for communication. Multinational communication and translation are more developed in areas where cross-national trade has become essential for economic and biological survival. The Europeans in particular are masters in multilingual communication because of the economic and geographic proximities to other countries.

Sensitivity to the problems of multilingual communication has not been strong in the United States because of America's historic economic independence. Today, U.S. corporations recognize the need to compete effectively in multinational markets. Foreign companies have also recognized the need to more closely integrate their distribution through American subsidiaries. Both American and foreign corporations are learning that their corporate survival is dependent on capturing expanding international markets. Translation services will become an ever-increasing part of corporate America until everyone is multilingual or only one universal language exists.

CURRENT CONDITIONS

Prolingua's core business will be to provide translation services to/from any major Eastern or Western language. Additional services, such as international marketing consultation, page layout, and foreign language typesetting, will also be offered. Potential areas that require translation services include law, marketing and sales, and various technical reports and plans. Potential clients are primarily corporate, including large multinationals, small and medium import-export companies, government agencies, and legal and patent firms.

THE CONCEPT

The competitive strengths of Prolingua include (1) the use of only accredited translators to ensure a quality product, (2) the ability to exploit the new desktop publishing and laser-printing capabilities of minicomputers, and (3) aggressive, yet personal, marketing techniques.

Accredited translators are persons who have successfully passed language-specific and field-specific tests (i.e., Spanish to English, medical) administered by the American Translators Association. Prolingua will hire only accredited translators, thus reducing the chance of translation error. A country-specific computer network for native-land proofreading will also be set up, further enhancing quality translation assurance (see Exhibit 2).

Prolingua will also offer foreign language desktop publishing and laser printing, eliminating the client's need for typesetting. Desktop publishing, combined with laser printing, provides camera-ready print at a fraction of the cost of traditional typesetting. For many smaller companies, the cost of foreign language typesetting is prohibitive. Desktop publishing will allow Prolingua to offer translation services to this sector, opening an entirely new market.

The increasing international focus of midwestern U.S. business will present unique growth opportunities in the next five to ten years. For example, during a recent session of the Indiana legislature, four bills were passed to promote Indiana as a trade state. The governor's office has established an office to promote international growth. Attracting foreign investment is expected to become an even more important issue in the future. As foreign investment in the Midwest increases and local companies increase their own transnational business, demand for translation services will increase. Prolingua believes that the time is right to capture a new and exciting market—that of multilingual communication and translation.

MARKET ANALYSIS

The overall market for translation services is international in scope, since the need for translation services spans all countries; Prolingua has considerable potential for expansion. The demand for translation services is growing and is likely to continue to grow in light of the increasing trend toward international trade.

The translation industry has grown rapidly in recent years as American producers have increasingly expanded into foreign markets. While the Fortune 500 companies have always been relatively sophisticated about language, recent growth in the translation industry is largely attributable to small and medium-sized firms that do not have the resources to prepare translations in-house. The industry is highly fragmented and very competitive. Berlitz, an industry leader, recently reported about $30 million from translation income. Alphnet, another industry leader, had $22.5 million in revenues in 1990. With many small and privately held firms, there are few reliable estimates of the size of the industry. One expert, Michael J. Mulligan of Berlitz, notes that if corporate and government translations are included, "the total industry could be as high as $10 billion."[1] Since the industry is highly fragmented, small and large firms compete for the same contracts. The largest firms such as Berlitz and Alphnet with offices around the world ensure high-quality translations by providing translations prepared by native speakers in the country where the item is to be read. To remain competitive, smaller firms keep costs low by employing freelance staffs.

The future for the translation industry remains bright. As Richard Huarte, executive director of operations for U.S. operations of Inlingua, a Swiss firm, observed, "The United States is really in its infancy in this area. We've come a long way, but we're still quite behind."[2]

---

[1] C. Levy, "The Growing Gelt in Others' Words," *New York Times*, October 20, 1991.
[2] Ibid.

The company's strategy will initially be to segment the overall translation services market on the basis of geographic region, beginning operations in the Indianapolis area and then later expanding to regional, national, and international levels. Within a given region, three market segments will be targeted: large corporate clients, small business clients, and government. The company will need to target all three of these segments to ensure sufficient sales volume levels.

Based on Malott's experience as a consultant to a small translation service firm, Prolingua estimates that within a given region, the breakdown of sales among the three major customer categories being targeted is likely to be 60 percent corporate clients, 30 percent small business clients, and 10 percent government work. The small firm where Malott worked was generating $50,000 in annual sales with little or no marketing effort, therefore making a projection of $200,000 a reasonable one in light of this firm's more aggressive marketing plans. Based on the experience of the small firm, a growth rate of 10 percent per year seems to be a reasonable assumption, with no growth and 20 percent growth being the worst- and best-case scenarios. Based on these figures, sales projections by customer segment are shown in Exhibit 3.

The Indianapolis area is a good choice for the company's first regional target for several reasons. First, several large corporations currently operating in the Indianapolis area are likely to require translation services, including Eli Lilly (a pharmaceutical firm with overseas branches and a considerable amount of international trade), Cummins Engine (a producer of diesel engines for domestic and international customers), Detroit Diesel-Allison (a division of General Motors, which also produces diesel engines), Boehringer-Mannheim (a German manufacturer of medical equipment), and Barnes and Thornburg (a law firm that represents many foreign companies). Second, in addition to these large companies, other promising potential customers in this area include patent law firms doing international business and small firms seeking export business. Third, there is currently a lack of organized competitors providing translation services. The lack of competition will provide the company with a relatively insulated environment in which to gain initial experience in providing translation services with virtually no threat from competitors. Later, this experience will be invaluable in expanding into regions where more substantial competition already exists.

COMPETITIVE FACTORS

The key features of the competitive environment for this company will be:

1. *Current Competitors.* The translation services industry is fragmented, with much of the translation business being conducted by independent translators. Universities are often contacted with requests for assistance; customers are entrusting the translation of important documents to people with whom they have had no prior contact and whose translating skills may lie anywhere along a rather broad continuum, creating the potential for poor translations. Since inaccurate translations of important documents can create costly errors for the customer, the customer is likely to respond favorably to a company that features accredited translators and that eliminates the need to seek a translator on an ad hoc basis.

The firm should also be able to protect itself from new competitors in several ways. The "first mover" advantage can allow a firm to establish a strong reputation. After having established some goodwill and built on contracts with some of the key clients in the region, the firm can then market itself against new competitors by stressing to customers the risks of going with a new firm rather than one of known quality. The firm will also be better able to protect itself as it expands to other regions and becomes successful enough to reap the advantages of broader-based advertising as well as word-of-mouth advertising based on its outstanding reputation.

2. *Clients.* The purchasers of translation services are not likely to be price sensitive because of the importance of accurate translations. Firms are likely to prefer to pay a higher price for a translation by an accredited translator with a high probability of being accurate. Those with a slightly lower price, but whose accuracy may be in doubt, will be at a large disadvantage. This is true particularly in light of the potential costs of basing business decisions on inaccurate translations. This lack of price sensitivity gives the firm flexibility in its marketing program.

3. *Potential "Substitute" Services.* There are two potential "substitutes" for the services offered by this firm. One is in-house translators hired by clients who would have otherwise used our services; the other is increasingly sophisticated computer software for translation purposes. Eventually it may be possible to use optical scanners for translation purposes. The firm can protect itself against these threats in several ways. First, the firm will be able to provide translation services at cost-effective rates that decrease the likelihood of potential clients hiring in-house translators or purchasing translation technology. Second, the firm will adopt new technology as it becomes cost-effective, offering clients the benefits of that technology and thereby maintaining its customer base.

MARKETING

Marketing is a key to the success of this company. Since the venture is essentially a service business, marketing will be one of the major ways in which the company can establish barriers to entry and create a competitive advantage with its distinguished service and excellent reputation. The overall marketing effort will be based on a customer orientation; marketing will center on the needs of translation service clients, and a marketing mix will be designed with those needs in mind.

Essentially, the firm's marketing strategy will be to use the components of the marketing mix to establish a strong reputation for the firm as a professional provider of accurate and dependable translation services and services ancillary to translation.

Product

The firm's "product" will really be a service—the translation of documents, audiotapes, videotapes, or other media for our clients. The firm will offer ancillary services to the translation itself, such as typesetting and laser printing of the completed translations.

Pricing

Establishing a quality image for the firm through promotion and referrals from satisfied customers will enable us to charge a higher price for translation services relative to competing firms and individuals. Currently, individual translators working on an ad hoc basis charge $10 to $18 per hour for their services. This business intends to charge small business customers $20 per hour and large corporate clients $30 per hour.

In service businesses, pricing is often based on the value of the service to the customer. By stressing through advertising the importance and value of accurate and timely translations, the firm will increase customers' perceptions of the value of our services and make them more willing to pay our prices.

Promotion

Aggressive promotion efforts will be a critical factor for Prolingua's success. Currently, competitors in the translation services industry make little, if any, effort to market their services. While some competitors do have a phone listing in the yellow pages, they are not taking advantage of the opportunity to use display ads in that medium. This lack of marketing effort by competitors is a weakness that Prolingua can exploit.

Prolingua will use a four-pronged promotion strategy. First, direct calls will be made to potential customers identified by informal research by Malott. Second, brochures and mailings will be sent to especially promising customers. Third, the firm will place a display ad in the yellow pages. Finally, the firm will advertise in selected business and trade journals read by potential clients, such as the *Indianapolis Business Journal.*

The promotion budget for Prolingua for the first five years in business is:

Year 1	$4,200
Year 2	6,000
Year 3	8,000
Year 4	11,000
Year 5	11,000

FINANCIAL SUMMARY

See Exhibits 4, 5, and 6.

KEY EXECUTIVES

As president of Prolingua, Jennifer Malott will provide direction for the strategic growth for the company. Initially, her duties will be as general administrator and coordinator for all projects. Malott will market Prolingua's services, act as liaison between customers and translators, and provide layout and international marketing consultation. Her responsibilities will also include supervision of all general business activities, including financing and accounting.

Malott's personal background has led her in the direction of language and the international marketplace. She is fluent in French and can read Italian, Spanish, and German. She has worked and studied overseas in Paris and Vienna, doing market research and translation. Her U.S. translation experience has been as a consultant for an Indianapolis competitor, the International Translation Consortium (ITC). At ITC, Malott gained direct experience with the growing Indianapolis international market.

Malott's marketing background is extensive; although primarily in the retail arena, her most recent experience has been with Merrill Lynch. The cold-calling and consulting experience she gained at Merrill Lynch has evolved into Prolingua's general marketing philosophy. Exhibit 7 lists her varied work experiences.

Board Members

Gert and Monica Kool   Ages: 69 and 70. Nationality: Dutch and Austrian. Corporate affiliation: Cemalta, Oss, The Netherlands. Owners and operators of an import-export business that deals primarily with chemical adhesives and vibratory deburring machines. Annual sales are approximately $15 million. Both have master's degrees in chemical engineering and have extensive international marketing backgrounds.

Thomas I. Malott   BA, Mechanical Engineering, Purdue University, 1962; MBA, Western Michigan University, 1965. Age: 50. Nationality: American. Corporate affiliation: Siemens AG, Atlanta, Georgia. Senior vice-president for a division of the German multinational with sales of $700 million annually. Worked extensively in the import-export markets and within other cultures.

Other Working Affiliations

Legal   Patrick C. Flynn, associate, Cotteleer and Flynn. Experienced attorneys in international litigation and corporate law.

Accountant   Steve Taylor, partner, Taylor and Murphy, a CPA firm specializing in small and medium-sized business. Initial fee approximately $600.

Banking   Joan E. Brown, financial consultant, Merrill Lynch. Offers combined checking and brokerage account with opportunity to apply for line of credit. Merrill Lynch also offers seminars for small business persons. Having a specific consultant as opposed to a bank allows for more personalized service.

Advertising   Greg Dixon, Laser Communications. Local direct mail advertiser with good contacts and innovative ideas.

Video Production   Diana Falk, Final Cut Video. Complete dubbing facilities with experience in foreign videos. Quality product with good prices.

Other Personnel

Translators   Translators will be kept on retainer for each language until volume in any given language increases to a level that can support a full-time salary. Until that time, the translator pool will consist of a network of people connected electronically (modem, fax, telephone) with the office. This pool will be built from the *Directory of Accredited Translators* from the American Translators Association (ATA). We will contact each prospective translator via direct mail solicitation and follow up with a brief telephone interview. Prospective translators will then be asked to do a test translation and have a more extensive telephone interview. Translators will be treated as subcontractors, receiving no additional benefits above their hourly wage.

The labor market for translators is sufficiently large to allow for rapid expansion; currently there are over 700 active translators in the ATA. If necessary, a worldwide translator pool can be accessed through similar translation associations in Europe and Asia. Prolingua will hire only accredited translators to ensure quality. They will be compensated on an hourly basis to ensure adequate compensation of more difficult work.

Every document needs translation and proofreading. If excessive mistakes are routinely found as part of ongoing quality control, the translator will be dropped from the pool. Consistently superior work by a translator will generate more subcontracted work. Possibilities for promotion to production assistant or sales representative also exist for a translator who demonstrates management capabilities, strong interpersonal skills, and computer knowledge. Promotion opportunities will be limited principally by the sales volume within a particular language or language group.

Stylists   Stylists format a translation from rough form to final form for laser printing. They will work closely with the translators to ensure a linguistically proper layout and with the sales representatives to ensure overall client satisfaction. Prerequisites for this position include a general knowledge of several languages and excellent desktop publishing skills.

OWNERSHIP

The legal form of the business will be an S corporation. We have chosen this type of close corporation because the three partners want to maintain a partnershiplike relationship for federal tax purposes. Therefore, the three shareholders will be able to report earnings or losses of the business venture on their individual federal income tax returns.

Equity contributions will be as follows:

Jennifer Malott	$5,000
Thomas J. Malott	$10,000
Gert and Monica Kool	$15,000

Debt will be in the amount of $20,000, a 12 percent loan from a local bank. The money will be used for capital expenditures and for operating expenses during the first five years of the S corporation's life. All retained earnings will be reinvested to enhance the ability of the company to capitalize on expansion opportunities.

Jennifer Malott will own 50 percent of the firm, Thomas Malott will own 20 percent, and the Kools will own 30 percent.

CRITICAL RISKS AND PROBLEMS

Some of the critical risks facing this business venture include:

1. Failure to meet translation deadlines.
2. Failure to attain sales and financial goals.
3. Unforeseen industry trends.
4. Management inexperience.
5. Competitive price cutting.

Each of these risks has been considered, and the business plan has incorporated preventive elements where possible. For example, in order to ensure timely translations, we will hire only accredited translators, which will provide the greatest likelihood of professional behavior. Although there are no guarantees of success for this venture, risks have been minimized, and we anticipate the achievement of our goals. ■

EXHIBIT 1   Letter from Eberts to Malott

BARNES & THORNBURG

Samuel F. Eberts III
(317) 555-7269

April 23, 1990

Ms. Jennifer L. Malott
Indiana University
Eigenmann Hall, Room 203
Bloomington, Indiana 47405

Dear Ms. Malott:

It was a pleasure to discuss your proposed business venture and review your written business plan with you last week. As you know, my practice centers almost exclusively upon representing foreign manufacturers in product liability actions in this country. This litigation necessarily involves a high volume of documents such as engineering reports, interoffice memos, etc. Most of my clients' documents are in their native language.

Although clients often provide me with some rough translation of the documents, I have found their unfamiliarity with the English language results in poor translations that we would not want to use at trial. Often, the plaintiff's counsel also obtains translations that, of course, are different from mine. Thus, not only do I have the need for translation services for various documents, but I often require a competent, certified translator to be available as an expert witness at trial. Unfortunately, there is no company in Indianapolis that can provide these services. Your business proposal will fill an obvious need for the Indiana legal community. I can already anticipate several projects for which I would want to retain your company.

More generally, I would note that many of our clients have begun to recognize the need to compete in a global market and extend both their material purchasing and product distribution internationally. Indiana is also attempting to attract foreign investment to this area. I would expect that your company's services will be in great demand as we enter the next decade.

Please let me know when you begin to implement your business plan. I look forward to a rewarding professional exchange.

Regards,

F. Samuel Eberts III

FSF/bed
7637n(28)

EXHIBIT 2 Accreditation and the American Translators Association

The American Translators Association (ATA) administers a program in which translators may take a written examination in one or more of 14 language pairs (from English into French, German, Italian, Polish, Portuguese, Russian and Spanish or from those languages into English). This book lists ATA members who have passed those examinations.

The program operates on the principle that translation requires more than simply a knowledge of two languages. Problem solving and writing skills are two obvious examples. Since a small number of errors is allowed on the examination, accreditation certifies only basic competence as judged by the professional translators who serve as graders.

An additional program currently in development will test subject knowledge and the ability to produce translations of superior quality.

Accreditation is only one part of the program ATA offers its members. Founded in 1959 in New York City, ATA has spread throughout the United States and beyond and has grown to nearly 2,500 members. Annual conferences and the associated proceedings provide a forum that reflects the interests of its members. Academic studies, computer-aided translation, academic training, lexicography, and intercultural communication are all legitimate concerns of the professional translator. Eight ATA chapters and two divisions (literature and science and technology) serve geographical and specialized-interest groups.

ATA has a publications program that includes this *Translation Services Directory* edited by Justus Ernst, the monthly newsletter *ATA Chronicle* edited by Dr. Leland D. Wright, Jr., proceedings of the annual conference, and a *Survey of Schools Offering Translators and Interpreter Training*, last published in 1983 under the direction of Dr. Marilyn Gaddis Rose. Dr. Rose is also the editor of the forthcoming *ATA Journal*, a thematic annual to be published in collaboration with the State University of New York at Binghamton.

Membership in ATA is open to active translators and interpreters and to anyone with an interest in the profession, including corporations and institutions. Its affairs are governed by an elected Board of Directors. Further information about ATA and its activities can be obtained from Staff Administrator Rosemary Malia at ATA headquarters.

Patricia Newman
ATA President

Source: From the sixth edition of the *Translation Services Directory*.

EXHIBIT 3 Prolingua: Sales Forecast

	0 Percent Growth	*15 Percent Growth*	*25 Percent Growth*
Year 1	$200,000	$200,000	$200,000
Year 2	200,000	230,000	250,000
Year 3	200,000	264,500	312,500
Year 4	200,000	304,175	390,625
Year 5	200,000	349,801	488,281

EXHIBIT 4 Prolingua: Five-Year Cash Flow

	Year				
	1	2	3	4	5
Beginning Cash Balance	22,718	22,607	32,187	49,277	60,564
Sales (a)	200,000	230,000	264,500	304,175	349,801
Agency Fees from Translators:	*12,000*	*13,800*	*15,870*	*18,251*	*20,988*
Operating Expenses:					
Rent (b)	7,800	7,800	7,800	8,580	8,580
Salaries: (c)					
Executive	30,000	36,000	37,000	38,000	39,000
Production Assistant	—	—	—	—	28,000
Stylist	—	—	—	18,000	18,900
Secretary	15,000	15,750	16,538	17,364	18,233
Accounting	1,800	1,200	1,200	1,200	1,200
Advertising (d)	*10,200*	*12,900*	*15,935*	*20,125*	*21,494*
Hiring	300	300	300	300	300
Office Supplies (e)	3,710	2,400	2,400	2,400	2,400
Legal	2,000	2,000	2,000	2,000	2,000
Travel (f)	1,000	1,000	1,000	1,000	1,000
Insurance (g)	500	500	500	500	500
Operating Total:	**72,310**	**79,850**	**84,673**	**109,469**	**141,607**
Translating Expense (h)	120,000	138,000	158,700	182,505	209,881
Trans. Expense/Sales	*60%*	*60%*	*60%*	*60%*	*60%*
Interest Expense (i)	2,400	2,400	2,400	2,400	2,400
Incorporation Fee	1,500	—	—	—	—
Operating Cash Flow	**$ 15,790**	**$ 23,550**	**$ 34,597**	**$ 28,051**	**$ 16,901**

(a) Sales: Based on "most likely" growth rate of 15 percent.
(b) Rent: Indianapolis; north side; three-year lease with increase capped at 10 percent. Office of 600 square feet at $13 per square foot; includes janitorial services, utilities, and parking.
(c) Salary: Executive—initial salary $3,000 per month for first two years; modest increase until firm financially stable.
Production Assistant—initial salary of $28,000 per annum; will add to staff prior to year 5, if possible.
Stylist—initial salary of $18,000 per annum; cost-of-living increase estimated at 5 percent; will add to staff prior to year 4, if possible.
Secretary—initial salary of $15,000 per annum; cost-of-living increase estimated at 5 percent.
(d) Advertising: Initial marketing program includes listing in the yellow pages for $1,200; 5,000 brochures for $2,500; 1,000 mailings for $500. Subsequent year expansion for additional mailings to potential clients, follow-up mailings to existing clients, and advertising in trade journals.

EXHIBIT 4 (continued)

(e) Initial office supplies:

PageMaker	$595		Rolodex	$18
Trash cans	120		Scissors	16
Telephone (2 line)	100		Paper punch	15
Refrigerator	100		Hanging folders	14
Desk accessory	75		Paper tablets	13
Computer paper	60		Dictionary	10
Clock	50		Postal scale	10
Staplers	40		Desk blotter	10
Disks	30		Tape	10
Manila envelopes	30		Invoices	8
Coffeepot	30		Copier paper	8
Surge suppressors	25		Purchase orders	7
Pencil sharpener	25		Misc. small items	31
File folders	25			
Clock	25		Total	$1,500

(f) Travel: Gasoline expense.

(g) Insurance: Property.

(h) Translating expense: estimated at 60 percent of sales; includes translating fees, mailings, notary public, printing, and typesetting fees.

(i) Bank Loan: Five-year note at 12 percent interest, no principal retired.

(j) Equity:

J. L. Malott	$5,000
T. J. Malott	10,000
G. and M. Kool	15,000
Total	$30,000

(k) Furniture:

Workstation (secretary)	$970
Desk	695
Lateral file	530
Credenza	395
Desk chair	295
Arm chairs (2@185)	370
Conference table	250
Chairs (6@185)	1,110
Chairs (2@225)	450
Bookcases	258
Lamps	240
Storage cabinet	109
Total	$5,672

(l) Equipment:

Desktop computers (2)	$7,000
Laptop computer	3,500
Laser printer	2,500
Dot matrix printer	2,500
Photocopier	2,000
Telefax	2,000
TV	300
VCR	300
Total	$20,100

EXHIBIT 5   Prolingua: Income Statement

	Year 1	Year 2	Year 3	Year 4	Year 5
Sales	200,000	230,000	264,500	304,175	349,801
Agency Fees from Translators:	*12,000*	*13,800*	*15,870*	*18,251*	*20,988*
Operating Expenses	72,310	79,850	84,673	109,469	141,607
Translating Expense	120,000	138,000	158,700	182,505	209,881
Incorporation Fee	1,500	—	—	—	—
Depreciation	10,309	6,185	3,711	2,784	2,783
EBIT	7,881	19,765	33,286	27,667	16,518
Interest Expense	2,400	2,400	2,400	2,400	2,400
Distributable Income/Loss	**5,481**	**17,365**	**30,886**	**25,267**	**14,118**

EXHIBIT 6   Prolingua: Balance Sheet (At End of Period)

	Year 0	1	2	3	4	5
Assets						
Cash	$22,718	$22,607	$32,187	$49,277	$60,564	$62,463
Accounts receivable	0	7,535	10,729	16,426	20,188	20,821
Office supplies	1,500	1,500	1,500	1,500	1,500	1,500
Furniture and equipment	25,772	25,772	25,772	25,772	25,772	25,772
Less depreciation	0	10,309	6,185	3,711	2,784	2,783
cumulative		10,309	16,494	20,205	22,989	
Total assets	50,000	47,105	53,694	72,770	85,035	84,784
Liabilities						
Accounts payable	0	1,500	2,488	5,350	7,231	7,232
Debt	20,000	20,000	20,000	20,000	20,000	20,000
Equity	30,000	30,000	30,000	30,000	30,000	30,000
Retained earnings	0	(4,395)	1,206	17,420	27,804	27,552
Total liabilities	$50,000	$47,105	$53,694	$72,770	$85,035	$84,784

EXHIBIT 7   Curriculum Vitae Jennifer L. Malott

EDUCATION: MBA, FINANCE. Indiana University, May 1988.
B.A., ECONOMICS. College of Wooster, May 1984.
Dean's Honor List, Omnicron Delta Epsilon. Thesis: "A Study on the Motivations of Merger Activity."

EXPERIENCE: Business Intern. Merrill Lynch, Indianapolis, IN. General exposure to all facets of full-service brokerage operations. Received training in market presentations, brokerage productions, and retail financial marketing. Analyzed selected growth stocks and prepared financial forecasts and recommendations. Worked with existing client groups and developed new accounts. June 1987 to present.

Consultant. International Translation Consortium, Indianapolis, IN. Introduced computer-based account management system. Managed and promoted corporate translation accounts for Fortune 500 companies. Responsible for developing new accounts with domestic and foreign corporations. Generated 10 percent of new corporate billings for 1986. August 1986 to present.

EXHIBIT 7 (continued)

Accessory Coordinator. L. S. Ayres and Co., Indianapolis, IN. Increased sales by 40 percent in one classification during fall season by creating and implementing effective strategies to educate store personnel in visual presentation, product knowledge, fashion trend lines. Expanded customer service through direct customer contact. Promoted to Senior Assistant Buyer, January 1986. Administered merchandising program in department with annual volume of $2.9 million. Responsible for contract negotiations with vendors and distributors. August 1985 to August 1986.

Executive Trainee/Assistant Buyer. The M. O'Neil Co., Akron, OH. Established and administered strategies in merchandising, advertising, promotion, and personnel relations in a department with an annual volume of $2 million. Increased gross margin of one classification by 11 percent. Acted as a liaison between merchandising management and vendors. August 1984 to August 1985.

Business Intern. Renault Corp., Boulogne-Billancourt, France. Translated machine tool specifications and contract proposals from Renault-Caterpillar negotiations. Performed and interpreted a quantitative and qualitative market analysis of investment opportunities for foreign firms in the United States by state. April 1983 to June 1983, June 1984 to July 1984.

Market Analyst Assistant. Parker Hannifan Corp., Cleveland, OH. Executed and interpreted quantitative regional market share studies on seal products. June 1982 to August 1982.

Trustee, Student Investment Club. College of Wooster, Wooster, OH. Managed a $100,000 portfolio yielding over 16 percent annually. September 1981 to May 1984.

This case was written by Karen Byers and Alan Ellstrand under the supervision of Marc Dollinger. The events and data in this case are real. Some of the names and places have been disguised.

Case 2   Fumero Artfabrics, Inc.

Margaret Helms was not the typical business school student. Her speech was not typical; she spoke of art, literature, and history instead of target markets, cash flows, and power lunches. She dressed in jeans and a work shirt and was never observed in a tailored suit on her way to an interview. And although it was true that she was a little intimidated by some of her fellow students' capacities to quantify any analysis, she also knew that when the time came, she would be able to hire a number cruncher to work for her. She had returned to school to set the stage for creating a new venture—Fumero Artfabrics, Inc.

MR. FUMERO

"Fumero" referred to José Fumero, the famed fabric designer. In the 1940s, José Fumero started his career as a fabric designer with the firm of Chenie & Greeff, which at the time specialized in reproducing and adapting historic document textiles for appeal to the general public. Previously, he had worked at the Cooper Hewitt Museum in New York, cataloging its historic textile collection while still a full scholarship student at the prestigious Cooper Union School of Art. While he was a designer at Chenie & Greeff, Fumero "inherited" a collection of approximately 1,500 interior fabric samples from the elderly textile designer under whom he had trained.

After leaving Chenie & Greeff, Fumero joined the automotive division of the major textile producer Collins & Aikmann. Here he designed contemporary jacquard upholstery fabrics for the automobile and airline industries for 25 years. His designs met with great success, and he became a design executive for C&A, running its design department within a few years. Toward the end of his career at C&A, he designed the first commercially accepted velour automobile upholstery fabrics in both a woven-structure and knit-structure version. These products were so successful that after Fumero's retirement, C&A went on to build two separate plants individually dedicated to each of these structures.

Fumero was trained in designing jacquard fabrics before the use of computers in the industry. He can visually analyze the structure of any fabric. Many of the designs in his collection contain weave structures no longer familiar to textile designers trained in modern computer-aided design. He is uniquely qualified to recognize when a weave structure is no longer producible and to suggest an appropriate adaptation.

Margaret had met and worked with Fumero in 1984. She had been hired by the Columbia Museum of Art (South Carolina) to catalog, prepare, and evaluate part of Fumero's personal collection of 185 historic textiles. The museum had scheduled an exhibition of art nouveau and art deco interior textiles, and Fumero's collection was prominently displayed. Margaret had done the only historical research on the fabrics that had been done at that time and provided the only positive historical identifications (artist, materials, dates) that existed. Margaret was uniquely suited for these tasks. She had studied textile and furniture design as an undergraduate and had previous experience in design, business, and research (see Exhibit 1).

THE CONCEPT

Margaret's concept was to launch Fumero Artfabrics, Inc., as a historic textile reproduction venture. She planned to locate the business in Asheville, North Carolina, close to the furniture manufacturers and textile mills of that area. Fumero would license, produce, and market reproductions and adaptations of art nouveau and art deco interior fabric samples from the José Fumero collection. The production of fabric yardage would be subcontracted out to textile mills specializing in producing fabrics to custom specifications. This was the "high-price, high-quality" segment of decorative textiles. Marketing and distribution would be accomplished by mail order, direct mail advertising, trade magazine advertising, and trade show participation. The target was the historic preservation industry. Margaret and José would split 70 percent of the equity for their organizational contributions and the rights to José's collection. The remaining 30 percent of equity would be sold to investors. A $100,000 bank loan would also be needed. Margaret estimated the venture would require $270,000 of start-up capital and offer investors about a 20 percent return for a five-year commitment.

GETTING READY

Margaret had used her classwork as a vehicle to put together the business plan for Fumero Artfabrics. In her operations management class, she completed a project on the jacquard weaving process, the primary manufacturing technology for producing historic textiles. In marketing, her project was titled "Strategic Marketing Management: A Proposed Historic Textile Reproduction Firm." In her entrepreneurship class she attempted to tie it all together with a business plan.

Margaret's methodology for developing her plan was to find a firm that appeared similar in concept and execution and attempt to duplicate (with minor adjustments where necessary) its strategy and tactics. She identified several successful and expanding historic interior reproduction firms that marketed similar products: Bradbury & Bradbury, J. R. Burroughs, Schumacher, Scalamandre, and Brunschwig. This suggested to Margaret that there would be an opportunity for another firm in the historic reproduction niche if the firm could produce a product sufficiently differentiated from those currently available. She even sent a draft of her plan to the owners of Bradbury & Bradbury and asked for feedback. Indeed, Bruce Bradbury responded, and his letter is reproduced in Exhibit 2.

THE PLAN

As she approached graduation, she put the finishing touches on her plan for Fumero Artfabrics. Her major concerns were raising the money, choosing subcontractors for production, and Fumero's advancing age. He would be in his seventies by the time the venture could get off the ground. But in any case, she was determined to succeed. Table 1 shows the table of contents for the business plan.

Introduction

Each pattern/design has three possible applications: drapery, upholstery, or wall coverings. In addition, five different interior contexts exist for any historic fabric, which aid in defining targetable market segments. These segments can be divided into two groups. The first group comprises historic properties built between 1870 and 1935 in public or private hands and museum roomsets striving to re-create rooms of the period. The second group is less sensitive to questions of historical authenticity and integrity and consists of modern "revival" homes built to resemble those of the period,

---

TABLE 1   Abridged Business Plan for Fumero Artfabrics, Inc. December 1988

Table of Contents

Introduction
Goals and Objectives
Market Opportunity
Environmental Analysis
Competitive Advantage and Disadvantage
Risks and Critical Assumptions
Deal Structure
Exhibit 1
Exhibit 2
Exhibit 3
Appendix A
Appendix B

commercial establishments such as restaurants and office buildings, and thoroughly contemporary homes deliberately decorated in a historically eclectic style.

The initial plan is to subcontract the production of six different patterns, each in four colorways, with production runs of 100 yards per colorway. This would require a single warp of 2,400 yards, which is the minimum a textile manufacturer will consider running on a subcontract basis. The lead time required from start-up to product introduction will be approximately one year. Fabric prices for 54-inch widths will be from $60 per yard up to $400, depending on the historical accuracy of the reproduction and fiber content. Average price will be $100 per yard for purposes of sales projections, and sales of 1,700 yards are anticipated for the first year of business. Cost of goods sold will be approximately $19 per yard based on industry estimates, finishing costs, and royalty fees. Initial equipment costs will be $6,000, and the first production run of 2,400 yards will cost $45,056.

Our marketing strategy is largely one of a demand/pull nature, based on the experiences of similar firms. The major marketing thrust will be direct mail, and likewise, the distribution strategy will be largely geared to mail-order sales with minimum "middleman" incentives provided to interior design professionals.

Goals and Objectives

The major objective of Fumero Artfabrics, Inc., is to bring the beauty and enjoyment of these fabrics to fabric and decorative art connoisseurs, whether professional or amateur, everywhere.

Additionally, Fumero Artfabrics plans to establish the company's reputation for quality reproduction interior fabrics to suit any need. Once this reputation is established, we will broaden the product line to include other patterns from the same "master" collection of 1,500 antique fabric samples from which the 185 art nouveau and art deco samples in the Museum of Art's collection were originally culled. This expansion will allow us to develop and target additional market segments and create a sustainable commercial enterprise, as opposed to one tied to the look of one time period. Ultimately, the founders plan to launch a line of contemporary fabrics of their own design.

Finally, this enterprise plans not only to exploit a market opportunity that at this time has only been addressed in a minimal way but also to educate our target markets about the reproduction and adaptation process so that they value the effort put into the product and our attempts to maintain the maximum degree of historical integrity suitable for each design's intended market.

Market Opportunity

Five different interior contexts exist for any historic interior fabric, which aid in defining five targetable market segments:

1. Historic properties built between 1870 and 1935 in public or private hands.
2. Museum roomsets or "re-created" rooms.
3. Victorian revival homes (modern homes built to look like Victorian or Edwardian homes, such as those with building plans available in *Victorian Homes*).
4. Commercial buildings such as restaurants, architects' offices, interior designers' offices.
5. Contemporary homes decorated in the "eclectic" interior design tradition.

The first two contexts require designs that can be documented as belonging to the period of interest in their original or near-original form (no scale adaptations, limited color adaptations, limited fiber adaptations). The last three contexts allow much more latitude—in fact, they can even be said to depend on adapting the design in question in terms of colorways, scale, fiber, and weave structure. The ideal situation is to plan for both of these markets by dividing the collection into two groups—those that are most suitable for producing in a historically accurate form and those that will be more commercially successful if adapted for use in contexts 3, 4, and 5.

The textile and apparel industries utilize very inefficient distribution networks (the interior fabrics industry is no exception), which tend to cannibalize what could otherwise be a very generous profit margin. In the "contract" textile industry, defined as the sector of the interior fabric industry providing furniture manufacturers and building contractors with upholstery and wall fabrics, it is not uncommon to find six tiers in the distribution chain: (1) textile mill, (2) textile convertor, (3) contract textile firm, (4) furniture manufacturer showroom or sales representative showroom, (5) interior designer or architect, and (6) ultimate consumer. The phenomenal success of a firm like Bradbury & Bradbury, producer of hand-printed nineteenth-century reproduction wallpapers, can largely be attributed to the fact that this firm is manufacturer, interior designer, and ultimate distributor to the consumer via largely mail-order sales (see Appendix A for a strategic market study based on the firm of Bradbury & Bradbury). To the extent that Fumero Artfabrics, Inc., can duplicate B&B's demand/pull environment, the firm will be able to realize the market opportunity that critically depends on bypassing the traditional distribution institutions.

Environmental Analysis

In the general upholstery fabric industry, there has been a recent surge in demand for leather upholstery fabrics. Leather's market share has climbed to 10 percent in the residential furniture market. Cited as the fastest-growing upholstery fabric by over one third of all retailers polled in a survey released December 5 by *Furniture Today* (Exhibit 3), leather beat out jacquards (with a 25 percent market share), which were only cited as the fastest-growing segment by 22 percent of the retailers polled. Leather's recent gains in market share can be said to have largely occurred at the expense of printed upholstery fabrics. Although no longer cited as often as the fastest-growing segment, jacquards are still considered the best-selling upholstery fabric by 33 percent of respondents, down only 1 percent from last year.

In addition to competitors such as Scalamandre, Brunschwig & Fils, and Schumacher discussed in the strategic market study (Appendix A), some additional competitors must be addressed. Although no company is producing a significant line of historic jacquard fabrics of the same period as the wallpapers produced (largely to stock, rarely custom) by Bruce Bradbury, a few companies produce printed fabric designs of the same period as B&B's papers. Although wallpapers certainly could never be used as upholstery fabrics, wallpapers are suitable substitutes for wall fabrics. In addition, printed historic fabric patterns can substitute for both historic wallpapers and woven-patterned fabrics, although woven-patterned upholstery fabrics are usually much more durable than printed ones. Obviously, these products interact as *both* substitutes and complements.

With the exception of Classic Revivals, Inc., which mainly produces historic textiles on a custom basis only (they act merely as middlemen on the fabrics they stock), the remaining potential competitors each specialize in a particular artist or period. B&B specializes in late Victorian and early Arts and Crafts wallpapers (William Morris, Aesthetic Movement, Christopher Dresser, Neo-Grec, Fenway, and Japonais). J. R. Burroughs Historical Design Merchants will soon be launching its first interior fabrics with the patterns of turn-of-the-century Arts and Crafts designer Candace Wheeler. The Scottish firm of Hidden Road (outside Glasgow) hand-screen-prints historic textiles reproduced from Scottish architect Charles Rennie Mackintosh's textile works, which apparently have been quite a commercial success in the British Isles, even at £60 per yard. In the United States again, Sanderson sells the printed fabric designs of William Morris. DesignTex does not manufacture woven-pattern fabrics itself but sells under its label adaptations of print works by the graphic artist Max C. Escher, one of its most successful lines, in addition to fabrics by Joséf Hoffmann. Ian Wall carries some of the same fabric reproductions of Hoffmann's work as DesignTex plus some additional fabric reproduction/adaptations from the same period. Scalamandre, Schumacher, and Brunschwig & Fils have at times carried reproductions of Charles Voysey's printed fabrics. To date, no one seems to be producing the luxuriously patterned jacquard and dobby fabrics designed by Morris or Voysey. (Fumero Artfabrics has two positively identified Charles Voysey designs.)

Competitive Advantage and Disadvantage

The major competitive vulnerability that threatens Fumero Artfabrics concerns the lack of direct control over quality, which any firm that subcontracts production of its product faces. Adding to this vulnerability is the founders' lack of experience in negotiation directly with mill owners, although Fumero possesses a formidable technical vocabulary based on his past experience working with textile engineers while at Collins & Aikmann. In this sense, because he learned to design jacquard fabrics before the advent of the computer into this industry, he possesses more knowledge of the weave structures than many mill owners may. However, negotiation skills are still a critical requirement.

Competitive advantages would include access to the historic collection itself and licensing of the name of the Columbia Museum of Art. In addition, the ability to largely bypass middlemen (convertors, showrooms, and interior designers and architects) will, along with low capital intensity, provide for the success of this venture.

Risks and Critical Assumptions

Besides the fundamental assumption that a clear demand exists for the products of Fumero Artfabrics, Inc., a few other key assumptions have been made. The most obvious of these concerns the estimates of sales figures for the first five years of this venture. The estimate of 1,700 yards sold for the second year of operation was obtained during discussions with J. R. Burroughs Historical Design Merchants regarding its plans to launch a line of reproductions of Candace Wheeler fabrics in the upcoming year. Before beginning a venture of this sort, the firm apparently calculates breakeven yardage required and then decides if it thinks there is a minimum market for that amount of product. For the Candace Wheeler fabrics, it estimates that it must sell a minimum of 2,400 yards for the venture to deliver approximately a 20 percent rate of return (considered average for this industry). Although it has never offered printed interior fabrics before, it anticipates selling the majority of this yardage in the first year. It also stated that the required lead time for a project of this sort, from preparation of artwork to introduction of the product, is approximately one year.

Other critical assumptions involve production costs and are footnoted below the production plan provided in Appendix B. Finally, assumptions regarding the direct-mail volumes required to produce the projected sales figures are largely based on the direct-mail marketing practices of the firm Bradbury & Bradbury and are examined in detail in the strategic market study provided in Appendix A.

Deal Structure

This venture requires raising a total of $270,000, of which $100,000 will be bank loans at 10 percent annual interest with a balloon payment in year 5 of the principal. Another $150,000 will be from outside investors for 30 percent equity, and the final $20,000 will largely come from one of the founders, Margaret Helms, for 35 percent equity in the company. The other founder, José Fumero, will contribute, in exchange for a 35 percent equity position in the company, the reproduction rights of his historic textile collection.

Fumero Artfabrics, Inc., will offer 30,000 shares out of an outstanding 100,000 shares at $5 per share. Projected sales of the business in year 5 at 10 times earnings will give investors an 18.8 percent IRR, which approaches an acceptable level of return in this industry. Because of the specialized nature of the product, we think that regardless of rate of return, there is a limited pool of potential investors from which we can draw. We believe that only interested investors who are familiar with the textile and historic preservation industries will actually invest. For this reason, the business has been structured to require no more than a $150,000 contribution from outside investors. Initial plans to invest heavily during the start-up phase in sophisticated computeraided jacquard design equipment have been postponed until the company has established both positive cash flows. As a result, it will be necessary for us to subcontract out all but the design reproduction/adaptation function, the marketing and financial functions, and the distribution function. In order to establish maximum credibility with mill owners, with whom we will be continually required to negotiate, our first priority is to attract investors who have worked firsthand with mill owners in producing fabrics and yarns to custom.

APPENDIX A

Strategic Market Study: Bradbury & Bradbury

Bruce Bradbury founded his firm in 1979 after having decided in 1976 to pursue the historic reproduction of Victorian and Arts and Crafts movement wallpapers as a vocation. Previous experience as a fine-art printer and three years of working for two wallpaper manufacturers in San Francisco had given him the necessary expertise and confidence to begin small-scale production in the home of a fellow printer. The interior design industry initially showed little interest in his first efforts, but when articles about his work reached the public, he was inundated with direct inquiries (bypassing interior designers and decorators as most wallpaper sales are executed) about his product and its pricing from private homeowners, museum professionals, and historic preservation architects. From the beginning the level of interest in his highly specialized product has allowed him to largely ignore both advertising expenses and issues of a demand/push nature.

Bradbury wallpapers are entirely handprinted on the premises of the large studio in Benicia, California, and the majority of sales to date have been done on a mail-order basis. Bradbury wallpapers are not currently available through any "interior paint and paper" stores, nor does B&B even produce the traditional wallpaper collection "books" on display at such stores. Interior professionals who wish to promote B&B wallpapers are free to buy small quantities of each of the 100-plus designs and put together their own sample books, but B&B, unlike other wallpaper companies, has no interest in or need for providing these. It does make an exquisite brochure available to interested parties at a price of $8 each. This brochure comes out twice a year. Its arrival is advertised through direct mail to a list of 21,000 people who have contacted B&B at one time or another. Three thousand of the people on the computerized mailing list hold paid yearly subscriptions to the brochure. This subscription base illustrates the high level of demand for B&B products, which allows it to pursue a demand/pull marketing strategy.

Word-of-mouth referrals make up a large part of B&B's advertising. To encourage direct contact from private homeowners (bypassing interior professionals) B&B places small ads in every issue of *Old House Journal*, which comes out an average of four times a year and is a highly specialized technical historic preservation publication enjoying wide support among professional and nonprofessional historic preservation buffs. *Victorian Homes*, which appears six times a year, also carries one of its small ads in every issue. This magazine attracts a readership with slightly less purist tendencies than that of *Old House Journal. Victorian Homes* undoubtedly has a much larger subscription base, since it is available in bookstores, drugstores, and grocery stores on a per-issue basis, whereas *Old House Journal* is available only on a per-issue basis in art and architectural or museum bookstores.

In addition to these small print ads and its brochure publication, B&B has rented a booth for the past four years at the Rehabitat exhibition held annually by the National Trust for Historic Preservation. Rehabitat is basically a historic preservation trade show where manufacturers and vendors (most being characterized as small businesses) of period architectural and interior products such as stained glass, woodwork, tiles, wallpapers, and interior fabrics can promote, but not sell, their product lines. All new applicants to the Rehabitat exhibition must have their products judged by a National Trust architect to see that they meet the National Trust's standards for quality and authenticity. Once a vendor has qualified for exhibition, its work is reviewed yearly on an informal basis. The cost of a 10-foot by 10-foot booth is $685, whereas a 10-foot by 20-foot booth costs $1,050. Bradbury & Bradbury has always reserved a small booth. The exhibition lasts three days and is open to the general public at a cost of $3 per person. It is held in conjunction with the annual National Trust for Historic Preservation Convention, which is open only to convention attendees who are usually history professionals of some sort. Convention attendees see Rehabitat free of charge. Between the general public and convention attendees, the Rehabitat exhibition draws an average yearly audience of 3,000. During the 1987 Rehabitat, held in Washington, D.C., Bradbury & Bradbury gave a "how-to" workshop that was attended by 450 people.

At one time B&B's line was displayed in a showroom of the Chicago Merchandise Mart with the lines of other small wallpaper manufacturers. This proved to be an unsatisfactory arrangement in its view because the sales representative was not knowledgeable about historic wallpapers and the handprinting process. It felt that its product required the attention of someone trained in its specialized business, and yet its production volumes and cost structure could not justify the dedication of one employee to representing its line exclusively. In April 1988, B&B opened a small showroom in San Francisco as a joint venture with an already well-established antique dealer in an upscale neighborhood. (San Francisco in general has a profusion of Victorian-era houses, which led Bruce Bradbury to locate his business there.) Its showroom is above the antique dealer's store and will be staffed by a full-time surface design professional and two part-time draftspeople (the entire art department staff excluding the director, who is currently still located at the studio). These individuals provide, for a small fee, an in-home "room design" service advertised in the brochure. An interested customer provides a floor plan of the rooms in question (noting any unusual design features such as bay windows, fireplace mantels, etc.) and choice of wallpaper pattern for each room. B&B's in-house surface designer will then plan the layout of the pattern repeat for the entire room, providing detailed working drawings, in color, for the buyer's use or the use of whomever the buyer is paying to actually hang the wallpaper on-site.

The provision of such a service allows the customer (and therefore B&B) to bypass the expensive services of a local interior designer or decorator and ensures proper use of the pattern in a historical context. Detailed plans also eliminate possible pattern layout errors of homeowners doing their own hanging. Bradbury & Bradbury maintains that it cannot afford to sell its line through showrooms or middlemen, nor can it afford to provide sample wallpaper books. The lack of sample books and the fact that it only gives decorators and designers with a retail number a 33 percent discount effectively discourages design professionals from placing unusual demands on the firm. Direct contact with historic homeowners and museum/preservation professionals ensures the high margins a labor-intensive business like B&B requires.

In summation, the nichemanship strategy of B&B has allowed it to effectively compete with much, much larger firms like F. Schumacher & Co., Scalamandre, Waverly, and Brunschwig & Fils. These firms all offer a similar product, with many of them providing individual patterns in both wallpaper and matching interior fabric in addition to custom-order papers, which B&B also provides. How does such a small firm using such antiquated production practices compete with the automated giants in the industry having names that have been established for decades?

Bradbury & Bradbury has differentiated its products in a manner subtle enough to be largely missed by those not familiar with either historic interiors or the commercial design process. The difference between F. Schumacher & Co.'s adaptation of period wallpapers in the Victoria & Albert Museum, promoted as Schumacher's "Victoria & Albert collection," and both B&B's period reproduction patterns and contemporary "knockoff" of period patterns, is obvious to a trained eye. Most observers would not realize the extent to which the Schumacher patterns represent contemporary popularized versions of the Victorian aesthetic ideal. The real clincher is that, even in Victorian times and indeed in any time, commercialized versions of the most "modern" and "pure" designs of the period existed side by side with the designs they "bastardized." B&B is reproducing unadulterated designs of the Victorian era. F. Schumacher is taking the unadulterated designs and adulterating them much like a conventional commercial enterprise of the period would have. B&B targets the purist, the big companies target the masses, and both target the wealthy.

The niche in which B&B has positioned itself also allows the firm to avoid distribution channel expenses that the bigger firms, with their pattern proliferation (relative to B&B's 100 patterns), cannot avoid. B&B has an infinitesimal share of the wallpaper market, but the segment they have targeted is virtually 100 percent theirs. That and the inherent flexibility of their labor-intensive process make up their differential advantage. This strategic positioning and targeting of the "purist" segment make it possible for the firm to get away with handprinting of papers and the mixing of color-printing pigments by eye. These practices are an element of showmanship even if one's customers never actually witness them. They go over big with purists.

COMPARE AND CONTRAST

The first factor that must be taken into account concerns the differences in the role of wallpaper and interior fabrics throughout history. Historically, interior fabrics have been used to cover both furniture and walls. Needless to say, wallpapers did not become available until the latter half of the nineteenth century when wood-pulp paper technology was developed. When wallpapers per se appeared, they were intended to serve as the poor man's substitute for the luxurious wall fabrics in use at the time. To this day, comparable patterns will be cheaper in wallpaper than in fabric. Of the two types of interior fabrics that were available prior to the development of wallpaper, those with printed patterns and those with woven-in patterns, the former had been developed to imitate the look of the latter at a price more accessible to homeowners. Interior wall and upholstery fabrics with woven-in designs, the type of fabrics the proposed business intends to manufacture, have always been associated with higher status and higher price. Higher price is entirely due to the different technology and amount of materials used.

Obviously, printed wallpapers (or printed fabrics for that matter) are produced when pigments conforming to particular design patterns are simply laid onto a paper surface. Even though printing designs by hand is naturally more labor intensive than machine-printing them, the basic concept is the same. With woven-in textile patterns, a much more complicated process is involved wherein both the pattern and the surface are created simultaneously. We will not go into the principles of weaving here. It suffices to say that a large portion of the designs being considered for reproduction represent some of the most complicated weave structures in existence, although simpler structures make up a portion of the collection.

The difference in technology has several implications. Producing this collection of fabrics will mean higher materials costs and higher setup costs. Roughly equivalent yardage can be produced in the same time periods at a slightly less labor-intensive level for textiles. What is lost in setup time might be compensated for by the lower labor content of the actual production process once it is started. Bradbury & Bradbury's most expensive paper, having 17 colors, wholesales for $150 per yard for a 27-inch-wide roll. Interior fabrics come in a 54-inch width so the same pattern in a woven-in fabric could wholesale for a minimum of approximately $300 per yard, depending on type of fiber used. If the end consumer recognizes the higher value of both wall fabrics as opposed to wallpapers, and woven-in designs versus printed designs, a higher price would be justified. Generally, in the historic preservation market, a skimming strategy prevails.

The choice of whether to subcontract manufacture of the textiles would have to be made on a design-by-design basis, since no contract textile manufacturer will quote a price for a particular fabric's production without examining the piece closely. Again, this is attributable to the wide range of individual complexity that textiles can exhibit. Generally, 100 percent cotton jacquard fabrics of average complexity are sold to distributors at approximately $10 per yard by their manufacturers. The distributor then sells them for $20 per yard to a retailer. The retailer sells them for $40 per yard to the end user. A search of interior fabric samples currently available revealed a 100 percent cotton jacquard fabric by Brunschwig & Fils similar in complexity to one Charles Voysey design in our collection that retailed for $72 per yard at a 54-inch width. Being the possessors of sophisticated computer equipment, jacquard houses can reproduce the fabrics in question in considerably less time than can an individual setting up a jacquard loom in the old way. This is what would allow jacquard houses to reproduce these fabrics at very low cost (excluding materials costs, which vary tremendously by fiber). The disadvantage with subcontracting manufacture of these textiles would concern the degree of control one would have over the quality of the final product.

Regarding in-house reproduction, the Joel S. Perkins Co. of Gloucester City, New Jersey, salvages used textile equipment from manufacturers, restores the equipment to some sort of minimal running condition, and then sells it "as is." If the proposed business chose to manufacture the fabrics in-house, the purchase of a minimum of three looms would be required. Joel S. Perkins Co. estimates that acquisition costs of these looms would be as follows:

1. Jacquard loom @ $2,000
2. S-6 Stobbly-head loom @ $1,000
3. Jim-head loom @ $1,000

Costs of moving the equipment to the production site, the services of a consultant to set up the equipment on-site, and the acquisition of pre-wound warp beams would be additional expenses along with the more obvious expenses such as materials, personnel, administrative, and setup time for each production run. Initial investment would be much higher than that of Bruce Bradbury when he started his business in 1979. Nevertheless, equipment costs are much less than expected.

The areas in which a historic textile reproduction firm and B&B would overlap suggest the possibility of a joint venture between the two if the textile business became successful. Marketing and distribution practices could be the same with the exception of pricing and the supplying of sample books. In an interior fabric business, sample books are a must because the great appeal of textiles lies in many of their qualities that cannot be captured through photographs. Sample books are not generally provided free of charge, but neither is B&B's brochure.

Differential advantage would also contain elements of "pure" design considerations, quality control, avoidance of distribution channel expenses by choosing mail order over conventional channels for interior fabrics, and the highly specialized nature of the product (nichemanship). In addition, the ability to require lower minimum yardage for custom work than firms like Schumacher, Scalamandre, and Brunschwig & Fils stipulate would also provide competitive advantage. Finally, the proposed venture would have a differential advantage to the extent that it would not have to purchase or obtain licenses to reproduce the fabrics in question. Bradbury & Bradbury currently purchases its historical documents to reproduce from the English firm of E. K. Burroughs. Similarly, the giants of the industry, Scalamandre, Brunschwig & Fils, Schumacher, and Waverly, have all had to purchase their designs at one time or another (they all have extensive archives they have purchased over the years).

After discussing the proposed business with a variety of professionals in the historic preservation, historic reproduction, and contract textile industry, particularly owners of small textile mills reproducing historic fabrics of earlier periods, the question of starting this business is not only more tempting but also more promising. A small "support network" of minimill owners, who provide services to each other on a consultant basis, was found to exist. In contrast, the large manufacturers were very hostile to inquiries about the historic fabric reproduction industry. The completely unanticipated discovery of this minimill network and the encouragement received by the owners of these businesses lead me to conclude that the dream of establishing a historic textile reproduction firm is more accessible than expected.

Even before discovering Bradbury & Bradbury, my plan for establishing such a business was similar to Bruce Bradbury's. I intend to work in the home furnishings industry, specifically either the furniture industry or the upholstery fabric industry. Once I have acquired some general industry experience, I hope to transfer to the contract textile industry. Exposure to this sector of the furnishings industry would give me both the credibility and expertise to subcontract the manufacture of a small subset of these designs and test market them to determine whether there is a significant enough demand to consider full-scale production of these designs under my own label. ∎

Bibliography

Burke, Robin. National Trust for Historic Preservation. Dept. of Conferences. Washington, D.C. Phone conversation, 7 March 1988.

Craig, Tracy Linton. "Packaging the Past." *History News*, July 1983, pp. 6–11.

Fumero, José Augustin. Studios II. Blowing Rock, NC. Phone conversation, 28 February 1988.

Griswald, Alice. Griswald Co. East Lansing, MI. Phone conversation, 9 March 1988.

Harmon, Robert. Old Abingdon Weavers. Abingdon, VA. Phone conversation, 8 March 1988.

Hartmann, Robert. Joel S. Perkins, Inc. Gloucester City, NJ. Phone conversation, 8 March 1988.

Kingsley, Robert. Mill Rive Textiles. Mill Rive, MA. Phone conversation, 2 March 1988.

McHargue, Janet. Bradbury & Bradbury. Benicia, CA. Phone conversation, 2 March 1988.

Nylander, Jane C. *Fabrics for Historic Buildings*. Washington, DC: National Trust for Historic Preservation, 1983.

———. "Using Fabrics to Capture the Past." *Historic Preservation*, 1983.

Read, Rochelle. "Fine Work." *House & Garden*, January 1988, pp. 18–24.

Slaton, Deborah. Wiss, Janey, Elstner Associates. Northbrook, IL. Phone conversation, 16 February 1988.

Wagoner, Richard. Knoll Textiles, Inc., Division of Knoll International. Phone conversation, 2 March 1988.

Appendix B

Fumero Artfabrics: Financial Statements and Production Plan

	Year				
	1	*2*	*3*	*4*	*5*
Production Plan					
Number of patterns available	0	6	12	18	24
Price/yard	0	100	105	110	116
Beginning inventory	0	2,400	3,100	3,000	4,300
Production	2,400	2,400	2,400	4,800	4,800
Sales	0	1,700	2,500	3,500	5,000
Ending inventory	2,400	3,100	3,000	4,300	4,100
Discount yardage	0	510	750	1,050	1,500
Dollar discount/yard		20	21	22	23.20
Total discounts		10,200	15,750	23,100	34,800
Production Expenses					
Number of patterns produced	6	6	6	12	12
Number of new patterns produced	6	6	6	6	6
Prototypes	5,000	5,000	5,250	5,500	5,725
Scan/cardcut[a]	5,724	5,724	6,019	6,310	6,626
Fiber to cloth[b]	24,000	24,000	25,200	52,920	55,566
Finishing @ $2.70/yd.	6,480	6,480	6,804	14,288	15,003
Tests: ASTM standards					
Lightfast @ $32/pattern[c]	192	192	202	424	444
Abrasion @ $535/pattern[c]	3,210	3,210	3,371	7,078	7,432
Flammable @ $75/pattern[c]	450	450	473	980	1,042
Total	45,056	45,056	47,319	87,500	91,838
Production	2,400	2,400	2,400	4,800	4,800
COGS/yard	18.77	18.77	19.71	18.23	19.13

Assumptions:
[a]Scan to Cardcut: Baxter Corporation
Assumes average repeat of 8″ width average set of 75 picks per inch, or 600 picks per repeat. $79.50/per 100 cards, so

$477 for first repeat
477 for second repeat
954 per new pattern
× 6
$5,724

[b]Weaving: Burrwich Weaving @ 10/yd. maximum per John Burwede
[c]Testing: U.S. Testing

Light fastness—40 hrs. per sample @ $0.80/hr. for 6 samples
Abrasion—3,900 cycles @ $55/3,000 cycles for first 3,000 then $40/3,000 cycles for subsequent cycles
Flammability—$75/sample

			Year		
	1	*2*	*3*	*4*	*5*
Income Statements—Fumero Artfabrics					
Sales	0	170,000	262,500	385,000	580,000
Discounts		10,200	15,750	23,100	34,800
COGS		31,909	46,925	68,985	91,150
Gross margin	0	127,891	199,825	292,915	454,050
Selling					
Expositions		6,000	6,300	6,600	6,900
Mailing lists	1,625	1,625	1,706	1,791	1,881
Prebrochure mail	2,500	2,500	2,625	2,756	2,894
Brochures @ $1.00		5,000	5,250	5,513	5,789
Brochure design[d]	1,500	1,500	1,575	1,654	1,737
Six $\frac{1}{3}$ page HP ad	7,890	8,285	8,699	9,134	9,591
Six $\frac{1}{6}$ page OHJ[e]	4,740	4,977	5,226	5,487	5,761
Swatches @ $.10		1,000	1,050	1,103	2,316
Swatch fabric		450	450	473	875
Freight out @ $1/yd	1,700	2,625	3,859	5,788	
Royalty @ $1/yd		1,700	2,500	3,500	5,000
Total	18,255	34,737	38,006	41,870	48,532
Administrative					
Incorporation	5,000				
Travel to mills	2,000	2,100	2,205	2,315	3,000
Personnel/benefits	70,000	70,000	75,000	75,000	80,000
Consultants fees	5,000	5,000	5,250	5,513	5,789
Shipping	1,000	2,500	2,625	2,756	2,894
Rent	1,200	1,200	1,500	1,500	1,500
Phone	1,000	2,500	2,625	2,756	2,894
Utilities	250	250	263	276	290
Insurance	500	1,000	1,000	1,100	1,100
Legal/audit	1,000	1,000	1,100	1,100	1,100
Postage/office	250	250	263	276	290
Amortization	1,000	1,000	1,000	1,000	1,000
Depreciation	1,200	1,920	1,152	691	2,691
Total	89,400	88,720	93,983	94,283	102,548
EBIT	−107,655	4,434	67,836	156,762	302,970
Interest	10,000	10,000	10,000	12,200	112,200
EBT	−117,655	−5,566	57,836	144,562	190,770
Tax loss carryover	0	0	57,836	65,385	0
Taxable income	0	0	0	79,177	190,770
Taxes	0	0	0	30,087	72,493
Net income	−117,655	−5,566	57,836	114,475	118,277

[d]*Historic Preservation Magazine.*
[e]*Old House Journal* magazine.

EXHIBIT 1 Résumé

MARGARET HELMS
123 E. 8th Street
Bloomington, Indiana 47401
(812) 331–0552

EDUCATION:	INDIANA UNIVERSITY, Graduate School of Business, Bloomington, IN Degree Program: Masters of Business Administration, December 1988. Concentration: Marketing.
	APPALACHIAN STATE UNIVERSITY, Interdisciplinary Studies Program, Boone, NC Degree Program: Bachelor of Arts, May 1985. Concentration: Textile Design & History. Minor: Industrial Education and Technology [Furniture Design, Technical Drawing].
	INDIANA UNIVERSITY, Graduate School of Business, Bloomington, IN. 1987—present. Business Editor: *Indiana Review*, a nationally recognized literary review. Conduct all business-related activities, including budgeting, preparation of financial statements, marketing, grant writing, planning.
WORK EXPERIENCE:	APPALACHIAN CULTURAL CENTER, Appalachian State University, Boone, NC. June 1985–Dec. 1986. Adjunct Curator, Textiles: Evaluated collections for historic and artistic merit. Developed grant application materials for Director related to textile holdings. Researched, designed textile component of permanent exhibit. Coordinated project between designers and fabricators to develop custom storage system for textile holdings. Museum store planning.
	RICKER ARCHITECTURE LIBRARY, School of Architecture, University of Illinois, Urbana, IL. 1979–1981. Acquisitions Clerk: Worked with Technical Services to update hard and soft computerized bibliographic records. Supervised, trained graduate assistants, staff in serials, circulation duties. Ordered, accessioned rare books of considerable artistic value. Liaison between faculty and librarian. Collection development, reference and public service duties.
	ETHAN ALLEN CARRIAGE HOUSE, Champaign, IL. 1978–1979. Service Representative: Customer service including housecalls to provide damage estimates for insurance claims, determined remedial action in customer grievance settlements, made replace/return policy decisions. In-house repair of dealership's freight-damaged furniture.
	THE WOODWORKS. Saybrook, IL. 1977–1978. Apprentice: Turned rough-cut, unsurfaced lumber into refined components to owners' specifications. Stained, refinished and repaired furniture. Assisted owner in final assembly of custom pieces.
OTHER PROFESSIONAL ACTIVITIES:	H&R Block Basic Tax Course. Bloomington, IN office. Fall 1988.
	American Production and Inventory Control Society, student member, Columbus, IN chapter. 1988.
	American Red Cross, Bloomington Chapter, Bloomington, IN. 1988. Market Research intern, volunteer.
	Blue Ridge Fibers Guild, Boone, NC. 1983–1986. Founding member, Vice-President, Newsletter Committee member.

EXHIBIT 1 (continued)

	Columbia Museum of Art, Columbia, SC. 1984–1985. Catalogued, evaluated personal collection of 185 historic textiles belonging to textile designer José Augustin Fuméro for an exhibition of Art Nouveau and Art Deco interior textiles. Fall 1985.
SCHOLARSHIPS AND AWARDS:	Merit Fellowship, Graduate School of Business, Indiana University. Graduate Assistantship, Graduate School of Business, Indiana University. Academic Scholarship, Indiana University. Graduated Magna Cum Laude. Appalachian State University. Academic Scholarship, Appalachian State University.
REFERENCES:	Available upon request.

EXHIBIT 2 Letter From Bruce Bradbury

Dear Margaret:

1. Marketing Strategy: We really had none, except that we wanted to produce the best Victorian wallpaper in the world, and get it to the people who wanted it. In the end we have created a niche for ourselves, but it was never the original driving force.

2. High return on investment: One would wish! As I started alone and with no capital at all, it took about six years to build the business up to where I could take a normal working wage. Perhaps in the future it will bring a high return, but again, it really wasn't the idea behind the business.

3. Competition: I suppose anyone else making 19th century wallpaper—there are quite a few firms, but as the head of Scalamandre said to me when I started—there's room enough for everybody. We try to keep our mind on what to do best rather than what someone else may be doing. The more good wallpaper that is produced, the more good wallpaper will be used—we all win in the end if we make beautiful things.

4. About copyrights and licenses—they're a matter for lawyers, really, as the law is simultaneously simple and complex in regards to copyrights. Right or wrong, you can be sued by a larger company, just because they can crush you with legal fees. It's called a "business tactic." Yuk!

5. We attend the National Trust exhibition yearly. We actually advertise very little—we try to put our energy into the product and rely very heavily on word of mouth. It's a little old-fashioned, but in our case it seems to work.

P.S. 99% of everything written on marketing is unnecessary.
It's the same as it was 1,000 years ago:
1. Make something you believe in.
2. Sell it at a fair price.
3. Treat your customers kindly.
4. Don't take your success seriously (pride before the fall).

Hope this is of some help. Fan's busy so I hope you'll forgive me sending this untyped.

Best Wishes,

Bruce Bradbury

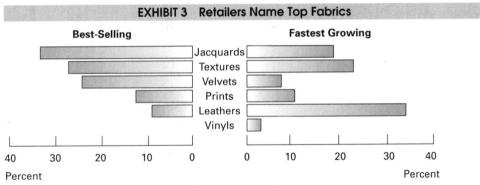

EXHIBIT 3   Retailers Name Top Fabrics

Best-Selling

Fastest Growing

Jacquards
Textures
Velvets
Prints
Leathers
Vinyls

40 30 20 10 0   0 10 20 30 40

Percent   Percent

Source: Furniture/Today's Study. December 1988, pp. 24–31.

This case was written by Marc J. Dollinger. Portions of this case were researched and written by Margaret Helms under the supervision of Professor Hans Thorelli and Marc Dollinger.

Case 3   e-station

Ravi Lal had just stepped out of the shower, and was beginning to dress for his date that night with his girlfriend, when the phone rang. "You'd better get over here right away," he heard a familiar voice say into the phone. "I think this could be the end."

Fortunately it wasn't his girlfriend on the phone. Instead Ravi recognized the nasal tones of Paul Robins, the maintenance supervisor at the Indianapolis International Airport. Lately Ravi had been receiving phone calls from Paul at least once a day, and the calls seldom contained good news. Two weeks ago Ravi and his **e-station** company had installed five computer terminals in the United Airlines corridor of the Indianapolis Airport. The terminals, with the name **e-station** painted boldly in red letters on each side, were actually "ATM" style computer kiosks which travelers could use to access the Internet, and thereby send or receive e-mail or log-on to the world wide web for entertainment or information while they were waiting for their flights. Now Paul was saying that the fifth and last terminal was no longer operational, because an irate customer had apparently hurled a cup of hot coffee at the computer's keyboard.

Ravi told Paul he would come to the airport as soon as he could. He called his girlfriend to cancel their date, and then he called Jim Foster, **e-station**'s VP of Operations. Jim was an electrical engineer with six years of experience with both the hardware and software systems that made **e-station** possible. Jim had designed and produced the five prototype terminals that had been installed at the airport. Just as Ravi had hoped, Jim said he thought this unit could be easily repaired by replacing the keyboard. He said he would grab the keyboard from the third unit, now lying in pieces in Jim's dining room, and pick Ravi up in twenty minutes so they could go to the airport together.

While he waited for Jim, Ravi reflected upon their **e-station** experience. Ravi, Jim and a third friend named Jake Moser had decided to form their **e-station** new venture about a year ago. The three partners had met when a sudden snow storm stranded them overnight in the Denver Airport. They spent a long night together in the airport lounge, bored because they had nothing to do, and frustrated because they couldn't send e-mail messages to their offices and clients explaining why they would have to miss work appointments the next day. If only there was way to log-on to the Internet directly from the airport, they kept saying to themselves. Even Jake, who traveled everywhere with his laptop computer, couldn't connect to the Web because the pay phones wouldn't accept his long calling card number when he entered it from the laptop modem. By the time the dawn broke the next morning in Denver the three men had convinced themselves that there was a way to offer convenient, dependable, and inexpensive Internet access from public places like airports and restaurants, and that they had the expertise to design that product. Ravi, who had a background in marketing and industrial engineering, agreed to serve as President and CEO of their **e-station** venture. Jake, who had commercial banking experience, signed on as VP of Finance.

The three new partners started to work on their business plan right away. First, they tested the concept. Research showed that there were more than 37 million people currently using the Internet in North America, and that statistics showed that these people had the same high demographic profile (more wealth and more education) as many of the 444 million passengers which use the USA's 100 largest airports in a single year. They spoke to several airport managers, who were very enthusiastic about the **e-station** concept and explained that the computer terminals could be placed in airports for a relatively small percentage of sales. The Indianapolis Airport manager even offered to let them install their prototype **e-station** units for a three-month trial at no charge. The partners also evaluated the portable electronic devices that were just coming onto the market, and concluded that like the laptops, they did not offer serious competition because they were expensive to buy, expensive to operate, and also not convenient in an airport setting. In contrast, they projected they could offer Internet access through **e-station** terminals for a flat fee of $0.99 plus $.39 a minute, making their service cheaper than pay phones.

Next the partners tested the product. After months of tinkering Jim Foster had developed what they all thought was an excellent prototype. The shell was engineered from reinforced steel similar to that which is used in an ATM machine. The engine was a single board, industrial grade Pentium based microcomputer, manufactured to withstand many hours of continuous operation and harsh environmental conditions. A scratch resistant Plexiglas shield covered the monitor. Jim had purposely not included any flat horizontal surfaces to discourage a user from resting drinks on the **e-station** unit, and had devised what he thought was a spill-proof keyboard, although experience now showed that wasn't enough to protect Unit #3. They had tested prototypes in the MBA lounge at a local university for a month with no problems.

But now Ravi had to admit there had been serious problems with their market test of the five units in the Indianapolis Airport. The first two units had vanished without a trace the first night after they were installed. Ravi and an airport security guard had spent the next night in sleeping bags behind the remaining three units while Jim figured out a way to bolt them more securely to the floor. Then passengers who were using the machines began to complain to airport personnel about computer malfunctions. All three partners made repeated trips to the airport to check the software on the machines. Unit #3 went dead after just 10 days of operation, when either a virus or a malfunction erased all its hard memory, and Unit #4 succumbed to the same problem a few days later. Jim had removed both of those units after Ravi insisted that he didn't want customers to see e-stations with "out of order" signs taped across their screens. While today's problem with Unit #5 could be relatively minor, Ravi had just received another serious blow from an unexpected source. His girlfriend told him that she had seen a row of GTE Sprint computer kiosks similar to his **e-station** in the Dallas airport when she flew to a business meeting there two days before. This meant that Ravi and his partners had lost the "first-mover advantage" they thought was so important to their success. When he heard Jim honk his car horn in the driveway Ravi was asking himself if this might indeed be the end of their **e-station** dream.

Excerpts from the initial business plan that Ravi, Jim, and Jake developed were as follows:

OVERVIEW

Product Description

The **e-station** is an Internet connected computer kiosk that delivers entertainment, communications, shopping, news, and other services using the Internet and the world wide web. It delivers this content to its users in public places.

It enables its customers to surf the Internet with a browser program and read and write personal e-mail. The service will have the Netscape Navigator preloaded into the terminal and users will be able to access the Internet through the Netscape browser. In addition, customers will be able to use the Netscape mail client as an e-mail interface.

The machines will also come preloaded with a variety of different programs such as Pegasus, America Online, or CompuServe so that users will be able to access the Internet with a product they are familiar with.

The method of payment will make it extremely easy for customers to pay for the service. Users will pay with an ATM card, Visa, or MasterCard credit card by swiping the card through a reader attached to the unit. After the user's card is approved, the machine will let them into the system and they will be able to start accessing the world wide web, and other services. The terminal will charge the customer a flat fee of $.99 to log on to the system plus a per-minute charge of $.39, and then provide the customer with a summary of charges on screen after the session with the machine is finished.

The technology for delivering this information is based on the TCP/IP network standard, the same network standard that all servers use to connect to the Internet. Each machine will be connected to the internet via conventional phone lines, and all of the technology required to construct and operate this device is well established and accessible. Since all of the equipment to set up the machine is already available, the outlays for research and development will be low.

Company Vision

The core vision of the company is to:

1. Deliver entertainment, information, and communications services using the Internet
2. in areas it is not currently available
3. at an *affordable* price.

We believe this is a very unique market position which is currently not being served by other competitive offerings. Currently, the players in this market are attempting to place portable electronic devices in the hands of consumers to access the Internet. This scheme, though, relies on a vastly different billing scheme which will involve very steep one-time costs for the hardware and high monthly charges for the service.

Our market research has shown that there will be a significant part of the market that does not want to pay these high one-time and monthly charges. Instead, we are offering consumers Internet access with a single transaction. Our customers will only pay for exactly the amount of service they desire. The ability of the customer to precisely control his telecommunications spending is one of the key characteristics of the **e-station** that we feel creates value for the consumer.

The **e-station** will also offer much better usability than portable electronic devices because it will have a full-size keyboard and full-color monitor as opposed to the small LCD grayscale screens typically found on a portable device.

Company Status

E-station is a corporation that has been formed to produce, distribute, and manage the **e-station** terminals. The three employees at the company all have ownership in the company and they possess backgrounds and skills that complement the venture. **E-station** is in the developmental stage of its life cycle and is currently conducting marketing and product research. By introducing a working prototype into a nearby airport, the management team hopes to gain the support needed for widespread introduction of the terminals. The company is currently in negotiations with the Indianapolis Airport for the initial placement of **e-station** terminals and is optimistic about the outcome of placement of the stations. This plan is written on the assumption that the data returned from this test will warrant a full-scale introduction of the product as described in the plan below.

OBJECTIVES

The strategic objective of the company is to become the preferred communications tool among price-conscious Internet users. The management team's vision is to build a service that consumers will readily accept as the best medium to utilize the services of the Internet when away from the home or office. Since usage will be inexpensive, the terminal will be cost competitive and not susceptible to high-priced substitutes. In addition, **e-station** will pursue a strategy of very aggressive growth into new locations. The generous cash flow provided by the operating nature and cost characteristics of the terminals will be used to secure additional financing to quickly distribute additional machines.

The quick introduction of additional machines and growth of installed base will not only help the company achieve aggressive revenue growth, but also fulfill its operational strategy of securing distribution channels quickly and completely. Since the company is aware that others will likely attempt to enter the market and introduce a similar product, the strategy is to lock up preferred locations. By negotiating exclusive contracts with airport, hotel, and restaurant locations where the **e-station** will be located, the company will make it difficult for competitors to effectively compete against the **e-station**. Once the **e-station** is placed in a location, the company will have an agreement that bars any other competitor's terminal or station from being placed in that establishment for the length of the contract.

The financial objectives of the company are to attain aggressive growth in cash flow, net income, and revenue. The financial goals for years 1, 3, and 5 are as follows:

($000)	Year 1	Year 3	Year 5
Revenue	1,893	14,345	37,749
Net Income	(112)	3,779	12,609
Assets	1,750	6,778	26,968
Liabilities	200	147	147
Net Worth	1,550	6,631	26,821

MARKET ANALYSIS

Within the last few years, the Internet has quickly emerged as a fundamental medium of communications and entertainment. In addition to the early technical users, many mainstream users are now using its services on a daily basis and consider it an acceptable substitute for the telephone, conventional print media, and increasingly television. This broad acceptance of the Internet will make the **e-station** a service that consumers will quickly demand for two reasons: long blackout periods where Internet access is not available, and low cost.

Overall Market

The overall market for the **e-station** is the estimated 37 million people currently connected to the Internet in North America. These users currently connect to the Internet through a wide variety of sources, including Internet service providers, educational and business accounts, and the large on-line service providers (i.e., America Online). Each one of these sources will be accessible through the **e-station**, enabling all consumers easy access.

As a group, Internet users make up a desirable demographic group with higher income and education levels than the general population. This consumer group will compose the broad target market of the **e-station** product. The list below highlights some of the key characteristics of this target group:

Basic Demographic Information (May 1996):

- The median income of Internet users is between $50,000 and $60,000, with an estimated average income of $69,000.
- 25 percent of Internet users earn household incomes of more than $80,000.
- 50 percent of WWW users consider themselves to be in professional or managerial occupations.
- 66 percent of Internet users last used the Internet at work.
- 89 percent of Internet users are either in college or have graduated; 36 percent have post-graduate degrees.
- The mean age of Internet users is 35 years old.

As statistics show, this group is wealthier and more highly educated than the average consumer. Also important is the fact that these demographics match those of consumers that visit the locations where the terminals will be located.

For example, higher income individuals in professional and managerial occupations often have to travel on business, causing them to frequent airports and larger hotels. These are the same group of consumers who also heavily rely on e-mail and other Internet services.

By placing this product in the locations discussed under Specific Markets below, the company will deliver a new and unique service to this consumer group. As Internet usage rises, consumers will come to demand e-mail and Internet service in public areas in the same way they now expect public telephone service to be available, and this product will deliver it.

Competitive Factors

The competition for the **e-station** will come from a wide variety of sources. Although the product is not particularly high-tech, the industry that it participates in changes very rapidly as technology advances and consumers' tastes change. The company will be faced with challenges from new entrants into the same business and from the introduction of products that allow people to have wireless Internet access. The **e-station** will be well-positioned to face these threats, though, because of its unique positioning and product offering.

Product Substitutes   In a general sense, the company will be challenged by two types of products: portable electronic devices that allow wireless Internet access, and copies of the actual terminal idea.

A) Wireless internet access products.   As technology advances, many new wireless devices are coming onto the market. These devices were originally designed to be electronic calendars or to store phone lists, and are called Personal Digital Assistants (PDAs). Later on, connectivity elements were added to them. These devices do not pose a credible threat to the **e-station**, because their product offering and pricing are both very different from this company's product.

Currently these devices are *not* capable of delivering wireless Internet service. They connect to the Internet with a conventional phone line that plugs into a wall jack. It is anticipated that wireless service will take anywhere from 12 to 18 months at the very least to become available. However, the product descriptions below are written on the assumptions that these services will eventually be available.

1) *Apple Newton MessagePad 2000.* Perhaps the most widely known PDA is the Newton built by Apple Co. The MessagePad 2000, which is not yet commercially available, is currently Apple's most advanced offering. It has no keyboard, a small grayscale screen, a limited battery life, and is too big to fit in a typical person's coat pocket. If the users wants wireless connectivity, she must purchase a separate modem unit and subscribe to a monthly Internet service provider. The MessagePad will probably list for around $1,000, but this price will not include the added cost of the wireless modem card.

2) *Nokia 2000 Communicator.* The Nokia 2000 Communicator is a cross between a Newton and an ordinary cellular phone. It is also bulky, has a very small keyboard,

and only comes with an eight-line LCD screen. Therefore, users will only be able to read and write e-mail and not surf the web in the graphic-rich environment they are accustomed to. This cumbersome product costs in the neighborhood of $700, requires an account with an Internet service provider, and has only 3 hours of battery life.

3) *Casio Cassiopeia.* The Casio product is a cross between a traditional hand-held electronic calendar and a laptop. Although this device has a larger keyboard and uses a Microsoft-developed operating system, it is too large to be truly portable. Again, battery life is short, an Internet access account is required, and additional hardware must be purchased to make the unit wireless (although this feature is not currently available).

4) *PDA Analysis.* As can be seen from the descriptions above, the PDA concept does not really fulfill the identified needs of the **e-station** user. The initial investment is high, the monthly charges are high, the actual functionality is cumbersome, each device has a steep learning curve, the product will become obsolete as new innovations are introduced, and the actual portability is questionable when size and battery life are considered.

These products are trying to do too many tasks at once and are considered curious gadgets by many. That is not to say that some consumers will not adapt to them, but these devices have yet to show a credible market presence.

The required monthly charge is a source of major product differentiation. Internet service providers and telecommunications companies try to sign up customers for long periods of time at approximately $20/month. This is an annual fee of $240. Even if prices go down, many consumers will not want to make this type of investment. The **e-station** only charges users for exactly what they use. This allows consumers more opportunities for impulse buying and it also allows them to tailor their communications spending.

Copycat Terminal Products   New entrants into this business represent the largest threat to the **e-station**. The high-tech electronics industry has always been very competitive and exhibited a high degree of innovation and change. Although the **e-station** will not compete for the same price segments targeted by the major telecommunications companies, other firms may decide to enter the business and introduce their own **e-station** terminals.

The company will attempt to construct barriers to entry against other companies trying to enter the Internet terminal business. The standard procedure for introducing the **e-station** in a new location will include the negotiation of an exclusive contract for the location. No other Internet terminals of any kind will be allowed in that location. By ensuring exclusive use of locations, competitors will be locked out of the best locations and the company will be entrenched. **E-station**'s corporate strategy is to expand quickly so that the company gains a foothold in prime locations.

In addition, the company will benefit from first-mover advantage. New locations that are up for grabs will be more likely to go to the company that has more experience and knowledge about the business. The company has formulated excellent strategies and contingencies that will keep new entrants from invading and taking away market share.

Supplier Analysis   The **e-station**'s parts suppliers will have little influence or power over the company. All of the parts in the **e-station** are relatively standard and widely available, with industry-standard pricing and quality. Even after the production process has been refined, the company will be able to switch suppliers when needed to meet production. In addition to parts, the company will use a qualified Internet service provider to connect each terminal to the Internet. These vendors offer a commodity product and prices for their services are expected to fall in the long-term. These factors will all lead to low switching costs for the company if it needs to change suppliers.

However, as a key link in the company's strategy, airport retail management may have a small degree of short-term leverage over the company because they control the areas where the company wants to place its product. An action plan to address this is discussed later in section 4.2 of the plan.

Buyer Analysis   Consumers that use the **e-station** will not have much influence over this market and their power will be relatively low. The reason for this is that the **e-station** will be positioned as a unique product that will be the only product of its kind in a particular airport, hotel, or restaurant. As a broad group, the consumers are disorganized and will not be able to collectively bargain for lower prices. Since price for this service is already low and does not represent a large percentage of income for most buyers, consumers will not exert downward pressure on the price. In fact, this service will be priced so low that it could be an impulse purchase in many situations.

In addition, the switching costs will be high. Consumers that wish to switch to a personal communications device or wireless e-mail will have to step up to billing and payment schemes that are out of reach for most consumers. Rather than using **e-station** e-mail only when they need it, consumers will lock themselves into a subscription agreement by switching to wireless e-mail. Switching entrails high prices and fixed monthly fees for the consumer. Both of these will make abandonment of the **e-station** costly for the customer.

For the airports, hotels, and restaurants that carry the **e-station**, the switching costs will also be high. If new entrants start introducing similar Internet terminals, locations will have to remove and reinstall equipment and then re-educate customers about the new system. In addition, the amount of information to the consumer will be limited. As more companies seek to compete in this market, the general level of complexity will go up. E-mail systems will change and improve as time passes, but will also become more sophisticated. Even though **e-station** will evolve, it will still maintain an interface familiar to the customer. This familiarity will retain consumers who use the **e-station** because of ease of use.

Specific Market

The company has segmented its customer base into the three specific market niches of airport travelers, hotel guests, and restaurant patrons. All three of these groups cannot easily access their Internet services or e-mail while they are away from home or the office while at these locations.

Customer Motivation   The **e-station** will satisfy this group of Internet users by offering:

1. Low cost.
2. Ease of use.

3. Widespread distribution in the correct locations.

4. Full-screen color graphics.

5. Full-size keyboard.

We believe that this unique bundle of services is not currently available in the marketplace, and will not be served by the PDA devices described above.

The major advantage of the **e-station** versus a conventional PDA is the life cycle cost of use. The **e-station** will cost much less. The life cycle PDA cost is composed of the initial price of the unit and the required accessories, the monthly phone line service charge, and the monthly Internet access charge. This can come to an annualized yearly cost of $200.

Alternatively, the **e-station** offers users the flexibility to pay for exactly as much service as they want. They will not be subjected to the long-term billing practices of the telecommunications industry which often forces cellular phone users to sign up for one or two year contracts to get the most attractive rates. Potential users will not have to pay the steep up-front charge of these devices either, which are projected to be above $500 when the wireless modem attachments are included.

Ease of usability will also be a major benefit. No matter how advanced PDA technology becomes, these devices will never be able to offer full-size screens or keyboards because they have to stay portable. It will be interesting to see how many users will decide to surf the net on these small screens regardless of resolution.

Airport Customers. The potential airport market for the **e-station** product is enormous. Literally hundreds of thousands of airport customers pass through the nation's airports every day. According to the Department of Transportation, approximately 444 million passengers passed through the country's 100 largest airports in 1993. The top 10 airports accounted for 164 million of these passengers.

Airport travelers have a unique need that the **e-station** is well-positioned to fill. Airports are plagued by long waiting times and a poor choice of activities. When travelers enter an airport, they typically arrive early and do not immediately board their flight. In addition, many travelers must wait in the airport for a connecting flight. In the Indianapolis airport, for example, travelers spend an average of 94 minutes in the terminal and presecurity areas before boarding their flights.

During this time, they often search for activities to do, or they attempt to catch up on work, and the **e-station** is a perfect tool for either. Consumers in the airport are a captive audience for this product, and will use it for entertainment or online shopping. The business traveler can surf to his company's or a vendor's intranet, or check his e-mail if it is available. The **e-station** offers value by increasing the potential use of this blackout time.

In addition, airport travelers will have easy access to the **e-station** because of its convenient location. The company plans to place the units in terminals, lobbies, and baggage claim areas where crowds gather. These are high traffic areas where the machines will have superior visibility and high potential for use. The **e-station** kiosks will be placed in groups of four or five in airports to create greater visibility and to minimize the chance that a customer will have to wait to use the terminal. Airport customers will use the product often because it will be easy to see and easy to access.

The airport market is the most attractive location for the **e-station** terminal, and the company will seek to aggressively grow in these locations first and foremost. Since there are a large number of airports and many of them have vast areas of terminal and lobby space, this is where the majority of the **e-stations** introduced in the first five years will be placed.

The Indianapolis Airport Authority has indicated a strong interest in the product and believes that an Internet terminal will soon become a baseline service that travelers expect and demand. After speaking to the Indianapolis retailing manager in charge of vendors, it became apparent that this airport authority had a strong interest in the concept of an Internet terminal.

The Louisville Airport Authority, a public entity, shares the same sentiment. Although set up differently, the retail manager in charge of new vendors for the airport expressed interest. She indicated that typical airport authorities would require a share of anywhere from 8 percent to 20 percent of such a business. This would cover all expenses like rent and utilities. Also, any contract written that lasted at least five years would have to be bid out to the public. Therefore, the **e-station** contract would only be negotiated for periods of less than five years. The retail manager also relayed that she had not received any other inquiries to locate an Internet terminal in the airport.

Hotel customers.   Hotel guests are another group that are cut off from cheap Internet and e-mail access, and would benefit from using the **e-station**. Business travelers need to stay in touch with the office, and casual vacationers desire an enjoyable and inexpensive way to use excess leisure time. When a guest stays in a hotel for a night or more they have the ability to check voice-mail and messages, but lack an inexpensive and convenient way to communicate via the Internet. The **e-station** will capture this market by placing units in lobbies and other high traffic areas of larger business-class hotels. Business travelers will be able to use the terminals to stay in touch with events at the office, and vacationers and people on personal business will be able to use the product for communication with friends and family, or entertainment. The company has identified this group as another niche which has excess leisure time but not quick, efficient, and inexpensive Internet access.

Even though many hotels provide data jacks for guests to plug in personal computers in their rooms, the **e-station** will not be hurt by laptop computers that customers bring with them to the hotel.

Again, the **e-station** will have much lower life cycle costs. Laptop communications require making a phone call from the data jack within a customer's hotel room, and it is extremely difficult to enter a calling card number into the laptop while trying to dial out. If guests need to make a long-distance call from the laptop's modem, the hotel's charge for the call will be very costly as hotels routinely charge high rates for this service.

In addition, laptops are very expensive, complicated, and many Internet users simply do not own them. Those that do own laptops must go through the trouble of unpacking, connecting, booting up, and then reconfiguring the laptop to dial out of the room's line. Consumers will find it more convenient to walk up to an **e-station** and log on.

The company considers the hotel market to be its second most attractive opportunity to market to e-mail users.

Restaurants.   People visiting restaurants represent another unique group of captive customers. The "waiting experience" in a restaurant is particularly unpleasant, and customers will be happy to use a product like the **e-station** while they are waiting to be seated. Although the individuals in restaurants are not cut off from the Internet for as long a period as airport travelers and hotel guests, they are still captive to an area where they do not have access.

Large restaurants are high traffic areas where consumers must wait and spend idle time. If the entertainment value and convenience of being able to easily access the Internet is provided to these consumers, enough will use the product to make its placement in restaurants profitable. An individual **e-station** only needs an average of 15 users per day to be profitable, and large restaurants that cater to a younger crowd (age 18–40) would be able to generate this amount of usage.

MARKETING

The **e-station** is an Internet-connected terminal that delivers world wide web services to its users through an easy-to-use graphical interface. It will allow people to stay in touch with their office, get information and entertainment service, or even do electronic shopping.

The main product attributes of the **e-station** will be simplicity and low cost. The terminals will be targeted at locations where likely Internet and e-mail users spend a lot of idle time. By being highly visible in an area where consumers must spend time away from their home or office, the **e-station** will be a convenient and unique way to access desired Internet services.

The product will be marketed to both consumers and airport/hotel/restaurant (AHR) management. Consumers will use the actual product, but the company will also need to convince the managers of airports, hotels, and restaurants to place the **e-stations** in their facilities.

Marketing Strategy

The primary objective of the marketing strategy will be to create demand among consumers, raise barriers to entry for competitors, and create a large installed base. This will be accomplished through product positioning and other marketing activities outlined below.

The **e-station** concept will be marketed to AHR management through a sales presentation that shows how the product enhances the productivity and service provided to customers. In fact, company sales efforts will stress that the **e-station** be considered a "baseline" service by most customers in the same way that pay phones are now considered a "baseline" service in many public places. In addition, AHR management will be offered a share in the revenue of the **e-station**'s at their site. In exchange for choice locations inside the facility and exclusive rights to the location, AHR will be given a concession of 16 percent of their location's revenue. This offer will be well-considered among the AHR management, since payphones have a much costlier arrangement. An installed pay phone is the closest analogy to a newly installed terminal, and locations *pay the phone company* $100 to install a pay phone in addition to $33 a month to maintain the phone on site. Obviously, **e-station** will not be able to charge locations for installing machines, but the company will be able to negotiate favorable treatment from the locations.

The cosmetic appearance and location of the terminals inside airports will be vital to generating business for the **e-station**. The banks of four to five **e-stations** will be lined up against the wall in terminal areas where passengers sit and wait for their planes. The housing for the terminals' monitors and the kiosks will come in bright colors such as yellow, red, or orange. It will be extremely important to have a product that will catch the eye of passer-by's, and the appearance of the **e-stations** will be designed to achieve this.

At the same time, the company will create entry barriers against potential competitors in four ways: (1) prevent competitors from entering sites already occupied by the **e-station**, (2) partner with the major airlines to help create demand for the product in airport terminals, (3) create a frequent user plan to make switching for customers high, and (4) build market share as fast as possible to prevent entry.

The cumulative effect of these strategies will be to create a sustainable and loyal customer base, create a large installed base of **e-station** units, and raise barriers to entry against other potential competitors.

Competitive Blocking Strategies

Exclusive Contracts   The company will set up exclusive contracts with the airports, hotels, and restaurants that it operates in. This means that potential competitors that try to set up Internet terminals will be blocked out by this agreement. Once the **e-station** has penetrated a particular airport, other competitors will not be allowed to enter.

The airport management in Indianapolis and Louisville reacted favorably to this idea. In general, airport management does not want competing Internet terminal products in their airports because this will cause customer confusion and hinder acceptance.

In addition, airport management will be offered a bundled set of incentives to persuade them into signing these contracts. All contracts will be negotiated on a case-by-case basis. As mentioned above, locations will be offered a share in a portion of the revenue on each machine in exchange for exclusive rights to the location.

Growth   The objective of the company is to grow as fast as possible because this will enable the **e-station** to build a brand awareness and block competitors from entering. The vision is to have **e-stations** as common as ordinary pay phones.

On the business-to-business side, major penetration is required to block competitors from occupying spaces already taken by the **e-station**. There will only be a limited number of favorable sites for an Internet connected terminal, and once the **e-station** occupies them other competitors will not be able to move in. For example, the waiting area for many restaurants may be limited and only have enough space for one or two **e-stations**. Once these spaces are occupied by the company's product, other terminal companies will be locked out.

Airports represents the most desirable location for the company's product. It will be a very high priority to enter these areas first.

Airline Partnerships   Over the longer term, the company is planning on initiating partnerships with the major airlines. These airlines now exercise considerable control over their respective terminals. The company will leverage this control by forming partnerships with the airlines for the purpose of becoming the exclusive world wide web access providers for a particular airline's terminals. This partnership could jointly target airport management with a much larger degree of leverage.

This plan will be marketed to airline companies as a way of attracting business travelers, their most desirable customers.

Frequent Usage Benefits Plan   Over the longer term, the company will attempt to develop a frequent usage plan to make switching to a competitor's e-mail terminal more expensive for the consumer. If they switch, they will lose their accrued benefits. In keeping with the overall theme of simplicity, the plan will simply discount the fee of a particular usage occasion after the customer has built up enough time. There will be no complex schemes that involve points or coupons to confuse customers and create administrative work for the company. The financial plan budgets 2 percent of gross sales per year for this expense.

Operation Issues

Pricing   Pricing for the **e-station** will be broken into two segments. In the first segment, customers will be charged a flat fee of $0.99 to log on to the **e-station**. After that, consumers will pay $.39/minute for the total time they use. Consumers pay far more to use pay phone services in airports, and will be able to easily afford long and frequent usage with this pricing scheme. In addition, there will be few substitutes for immediate and convenient Internet access in the airport.

Pricing for this product compares very favorably with wireless e-mail products currently being offered. Ordinary Internet access currently costs between $15 and $20 per month, but to receive wireless e-mail, a customer must also sign up for a paging type service which costs between $225 and $275 per year. Although these costs will decline in the future, many customers will never prefer to use them on a regular basis. This is analogous to cellular customers today who prefer to use a convenient public pay phone even if they have their portable phones with them. This behavior is common because a pay phone costs $.35 for three minutes versus A cellular phone charge of between $.70 and $1.00 per minute.

Distribution   The company will control all distribution of the **e-station**. This includes storage, transportation, and setup of the device.

Customer Communications

Advertising and Selling   The company will do very targeted advertising to potential users to make sure the return on these dollars is appropriate. Potential media buys include airport billboards and terminal TV networks like CNN airport. These ads will stress the simplicity, low cost, and enhanced productivity that consumers will get from the **e-station**. The goal will be to raise product awareness and acceptance.

Most of the direct marketing effort will consist of personal selling to airport, restaurant, and hotel management. The company will target airport management first and will educate them on the operation and benefits of the product. The sales presentation will include a demonstration of how the **e-station** works and how it will directly benefit airport travelers. For instance, the presentation will demonstrate how business travelers will benefit by saving time. In addition, restaurant owners will be convinced that the **e-station** will make waiting for a table less unpleasant and thus enhance the overall dining experience. Hotel management will be sold on how the product delivers enhanced services to its customers.

The selling effort will be conducted by a dedicated **e-station** sales force. Their job function will be to conduct primary sales activities and manage the installation and initiation of new airports as they come on-line. The sales force will be selected from qualified applicants who have previous hospitality and technology selling experience.

Company Image and Branding   All marketing communications will strive to portray the product as simple, convenient, and economical to use. It will be billed as a "low-tech" high-tech product. In other words, the **e-station** will be marketed as a high-tech product that is very simple to use. The marketing strategy will center on building a brand image in the consumers' mind that focuses on these attributes.

DEVELOPMENT AND PRODUCTION

Product Overview

The **e-station** is a credit card-operated microcomputer that will allow users to connect to the Internet. From there they can find entertainment, games, shopping, information, and access to their e-mail account. Because there is a lack of activities for people to do while waiting in airport terminals, the **e-station** will be an excellent way for people to entertain themselves and use the terminals for work.

The external construction of the **e-station** is engineered to withstand the harsh environments expected for the units. A scratch resistant Plexiglas shield will cover the monitor, and the shell will be formed from aluminum or steel, not unlike the typical public telephone. A touch pad that is commonly found on laptops will act as the mouse. Because beverage spills are a concern, there will be no flat surfaces for a user to rest cups, cans, or bottles. A swipe reader is used to accept smart card, credit card, and phone card payments. The keyboard will be ruggedized and spill-proof.

The internal components of the **e-station** are appropriate for the demands of full-time operation. The engine of the **e-station** is a single-board, industrial-grade, Pentium-based microcomputer. The single-board computer and its peripherals were originally designed for manufacturing control applications and are built to withstand many hours of continuous operation and harsh environmental conditions. A diskless (EEPROM) hard card is used in the unit as opposed to a hard drive to avoid hard drive crashes resulting from hardware failures. Thermocouples, built into each of the cards, can be used to monitor the unit for thermal problems.

Each machine will have a variety of widely used Internet software loaded so that consumers will be able to use the program most familiar to them. The Netscape browser, which includes a mail client, will be the predominant software on the machine, but users will also be able to use programs such as Pegasus, Microsoft Mail, or Explorer. Customers will also be able to access the large online service providers through the **e-station**, since each machine will also have America Online's, CompuServe's, and Prodigy's software loaded. Some companies have firewalls, which prevent accessing e-mail accounts from outside company terminals. Over time we anticipate the extra productivity available through external access will cause firms to rethink this extra security.

Ease of installation, maintenance, and upgrades of both hardware and software are aided by using modular, off-the-shelf components. The unit simply requires two telephone lines, typical 120 Volt AC Power, and an appropriate location to be bolted down. No special tools or training will be required to install the unit. Software upgrades are downloaded remotely from a central server. Hardware upgrades require only standard tools, minimal training, and no special skills. Each terminal will phone in daily utilization to a central server.

Product Stages

The **e-station** will go through three product development phases: research and development, production, and maintenance.

Research and Development

Two months and $150 thousand are required to have five working prototypes built and operational. Minimal implementation risks exist as all technology required is low-tech, proven, and readily available. The prototype stage will prove the concept and help iron out unexpected problems. The prototypes will later serve sales and demonstration functions.

All electrical design, system design, and software development will be done by Jim Foster. Jim is an electrical engineer with six years' experience in hardware and software systems development. His background includes development of products not unlike the **e-station**. His knowledge of the technology involved and contacts in the industry are sufficient for developing this product.

Production

Two hundred units will be built in the first year with a cost of $2,450 per unit. Minimal software expense is expected as most software will be provided by the software providers as a promotional OEM product.

Materials are provided by outsourcing some production and buying off-the-shelf components from electronics vendors. The panels will be outsourced to a machine shop. The components will be bought either directly from the manufacturers or through vendors, whichever is more economical. The advantage of using these sources is that it would be too expensive to build the components in-house. In the future it may be more sensible to have all production outsourced to a local manufacturer with excess capacity. Outsourcing will be controlled by Jim Foster, who has experience buying from both machine shops and electronics vendors.

Production of the unit involves first building the case, the computer chassis and the video units in parallel, followed by inspection as separate assemblies. After inspection, the components will be brought together and the **e-station** will be tested and burned-in as a complete unit. The external case will be built in-house by a technician and inspected for quality. The computer chassis creation involves the chassis build, software installation, and test. The video unit will also be built and tested independently. The video unit and computer chassis is then installed into the case and the unit is burnt-in. Burn-in involves running test routines for a 48-hour period to test for infant mortality. Infant mortality refers to the tendency of electrical components to either fail very early in their lifetime or not at all.

The production facility will be a job shop with three full-time electrical technicians performing various tasks. The facility will be a rented office that will contain ample space for production, storage, and an administrative office area. We expect to pay $56,000 yearly for office space initially with the rent increasing proportionally as demand increases and more space is required. No special tools and minimal training will be required by the technicians to build the units. The technicians will be paid $28,000 per year either directly or through a contracting agency.

Installation and Maintenance   Installation requires either man hours, two phone lines, one 120 VAC power outlet, and a location for bolting the unit down. Installation will be done by technicians directly employed by **e-station**. The reason for having these technicians as direct employees is due to their direct contact with the owners of the locations of the units. The performance of the units at the various location must be of the highest quality, and we feel direct employees will have higher motivation. Each **e-station** unit will be either picked up by the technician, shipped to his site, or shipped to the location of the installation. The company has allocated a cost of $300 per machine for installation costs. This cost may seem low, but travel costs will be kept low because many installation jobs will be comprised of placing up to 50 machines in a single airport (for example, Chicago's O'Hare Airport would not be adequately served by a handful of terminals). Installation will cover lodging for the installation crew, travel, and other miscellaneous costs.

The units will be built as to require minimal maintenance. Maintenance will be outsourced and allowed an allocation of $500 per station per year. Since a typical service call from an outsourced provider would run $250, every machine has been allowed two service calls per year. The machines are rugged and are designed to never need serving, so it is likely that this cost is very conservative. Software maintenance and upgrades will be done over phone lines, and will not require technician intervention. The units will phone in a daily usage status including any unit hardware problems. Technician intervention will be required under three conditions: when the unit reports a hardware problem, when the unit fails to report, and for hardware upgrades. Again, the units are of rugged construction with high-quality parts, and very few hardware problems are expected.

FINANCIAL PLAN

The deal structure will take the form of paid in equity from the three founders, ongoing debt financing, and phased-in venture capital. The founders will each invest $33.3 thousand in the business for a total of $100 thousand paid in capital. The first-year debt will be a $200 thousand nine-month bank note, secured by personal assets of the founders and all of the assets belonging to **e-station**. Additional start-up capital will come from investors in the form of $1.45 million equity financing in the first year. The majority of this start-up capital will be used to construct the first 200 terminals with the remaining funds going toward salaries, rent, and other expenses. The company plans to rapidly expand the number of stations in service from 200 at the end of the first year to a total of 2,490 in the fifth year.

Sales Forecasts

For our revenue stream, we are assuming that consumers will use each terminal about 6 percent of the available time in a 24-hour day. This comes to approximately 90 minutes per day during the first year of operations. The charge for use of the station will be 39 cents per minute with a flat log-on fee of 99 cents. Our assumption is that 15 consumers will use an individual station per day and each will use the machine an average of five minutes. This results in an average machine revenue of $49.95 per day. With a revenue producing usage of 86 minutes per day on each of the terminals installed in the first year, the total revenue for the company comes to an estimated

$1.75 million for the first year. Financials are calculated by assuming that the company will manufacture and install 17 terminals per month in the first year. So in February of 1998, the company will have 33 terminals in service. Production will increase in subsequent years so that by year five the company will be producing 60 terminals per month. Given the extremely large amount of traffic in airports in the United States, **e-station** will only need to achieve a small market penetration with consumers to be extremely profitable. If only 1 percent of travelers in the top 100 airports utilized the service of **e-station**, that would amount to approximately 4.4 million customers.

Scenario Analysis

To do a scenario analysis, the @Risk statistical software for Microsoft Excel was utilized. This software gives the ability to assign pessimistic, most likely, and optimistic variables for a variety of financial inputs. Using these inputs, the software has the ability to run thousands of simulations and assign the probability that a company will have negative net income or run out of cash. In the case of **e-station**'s financials, the price per minute and the percentage of utilization per day per terminal were used as the input variables. For the pessimistic scenario, it was estimated that prices could drop to $.25 per minute and that utilization could fall from 6% of a 24 hour day to 4%. That is a drop in utilization from approximately 90 minutes of usage to 60 minutes of usage. The most likely scenario was assigned values of $.39 per minute and a utilization rate of 6 percent. Finally, the optimistic scenario was assigned values of $.45 per minute (if the company could raise its price) and a utilization rate of 8 percent (approximately 120 minutes of use per machine per day). With these inputs, there is less than a 10 percent chance that the company will have negative net income in the second year of operations. In addition, there is less than a 30 percent probability that the company will run out of cash in the second year. If the company does run out of cash, an additional infusion from a line of credit or additional financing will be necessary.

Cost Assumptions

The cost for producing and manufacturing the **e-station** is broken down into raw materials and salaries for manufacturing staff. Every **e-station** that is manufactured is assumed to take a total of 20 labor hours to assemble. For the first 200 machines manufactured in the first year, this amounts to a total of 4,000 manufacturing hours. The raw materials and parts for an individual station has been estimated at a cost of $2,450 by Jim Foster (exhibit 2, omitted). **E-station** will initially hire three technicians at a cost of $28,000 per assembler for a total manufacturing salary cost of $84 thousand. This salary level is projected to increase by 10 percent per year for all five years, and the number of technical and administrative staff is budgeted to increase from three in the first year to 26 in year five.

Phone lines are estimated at a cost of $100 per month for an individual machine, and the cost of an Internet service provider is $20 per month per machine. This amounts to a first-year cost of $144 thousand and a second-year cost of $396 thousand for phone and Internet service. The salaries for technicians, staff, and salespeople are allocated for personnel who will be responsible for aiding in the day-to-day management of the firm. Technicians will be needed to work on software upgrades and hardware problems that can be handled remotely. The company will hire five salespeople at the start of operations to place **e-station** with airport authorities, restaurants, and hotels. Salary, commission, and benefits is estimated at $85,000 per year for each salesperson. This figure increases 10 percent per year through year five, and the number of salespeople is expected to increase from five in year one to 20 in year five.

ORGANIZATION AND MANAGEMENT

The key personnel will include a three-person management team, technicians, production technicians, and a sales force.

The top management team will include the founders of **e-station**: Jim Foster, Ravi Lal, and Jake Moser. Jim Foster has an electrical engineering degree and six years' experience in the field, and has designed products similar to the **e-station**. Ravi Lal has an industrial engineering degree and four years experience, while Jake Moser has three years experience in banking and finance. All three founders have also recently received MBA degrees from a top university. Compensation for the three founders will be modest in the first several years until the company shows a positive cash flow.

Jim Foster will take the position of VP of operations, with responsibilities including oversight of production and hiring maintenance and production personnel. His knowledge of both hardware and software systems will play a key role in design, development, and production of the **e-station**. He has worked in the industry for six years developing systems similar to the **e-station**. His MBA in operations will contribute to the efficient production and maintenance of the **e-station**. In addition, his experience with machine shops and electronics vendors will aid in the procurement process.

Ravi Lal, the originator of the **e-station** concept, will take the position of President and CEO of **e-station**. His responsibilities will include leading the **e-station** management team, managing any internal staff members, and controlling all marketing functions. His knowledge of information systems and an MBA in Marketing will be key to executing the marketing plan. His background in industrial engineering will aid in supporting the production function. The breadth of his experience is sufficient for overseeing all aspects of **e-station**.

Jake Moser will take the position if VP of Finance and Controller of **e-station**. His responsibilities will include managing company financing, cost accounting, relevant staff, and soliciting accounting and legal counsel. His background in commercial banking will aid in working with investors and lending institutions. His experience and education is sufficient to perform financial analysis and planning functions. In addition, he will provide a key input in applying cost accounting methods to the production, maintenance, and marketing functions.

Human Resource Management Strategy

Staffing requirements are anticipated in four primary areas: professional office staff, nonprofessional office staff, technical staff, and a sales force. Professional staff includes accountants, lawyers, finance and marketing personnel, while nonprofessional staff includes administrative and clerical. The company's technical staff will include production and inspection personnel.

To recruit and staff employees for **e-station**, the company will use a variety of headhunters, placement agencies, and its own recruiting. To recruit technicians, the company will search for qualified applicants who have experience in either job shop or production line electrical manufacturing. Since most of the assembly will be simple repetition with supplied components, engineering or design skills will not be a prerequisite. Hiring and recruiting a team of salespeople will require the aid of a headhunter. The company will need experienced and seasoned sales professionals who are adept at selling either high-technology items or have experience working with hospitality customers. Finding and maintaining an effective sales force is neither inexpensive nor easy. The company has allocated $85,000 in salary, commission, and benefits per salesperson in the first year. The compensation plan will be constructed so that 50 percent of pay comes from salary and 50 percent from commission.

A profit-sharing plan commensurate with employee salaries will be instituted to promote optimal performance. Promotion from within will be favored to help motivate and retain valuable employees. Employees will be hired and compensated according to all laws relevant to such a corporation.

OWNERSHIP AND FORM OF BUSINESS

When the company is formed, it will be incorporated as a subchapter S corporation, with each founder owning 18 percent of the business after the first year of financing. It is proposed that the financial institution lend funds in the form of a $200 thousand, 10 percent, nine-month secured credit line. Cash flow will be adequate to repay this debt if financial projections are accurate. The credit line will be secured by all of the personal property of the three founders, and all property belonging to **e-station**. Each of the founders has a legal duty to the firm, and will have a contractual noncompete agreement.

Equity Positions

The founders will have an equal share of the business and will hold 1,000 shares of stock in **e-station**. In exchange for these shares, the founders will each contribute $33,333 of start-up capital for a total contribution of $100,000. No rights, warrants, or stock options will exist. Venture capitalists will be offered 45 percent of the Firm's equity in exchange for $1,450,000 of start-up capital in the first year. The founders will collectively retain the remaining 55 percent of equity in the firm.

Deal Structure

The firm will require $1.75 million of financing in start-up capital in the form of 17 percent debt and 83 percent equity for the first year. Two-hundred thousand will be provided by a bank, $100 thousand by the founders, and $4.45 million from venture capitalists in the first year. The company will need this much in financing because negative cash flow does not end until July of 1999, when the company's cash reserve dips below a safety margin of $100 thousand. After that time, the company will reach positive cash flows and will not need any additional financing to grow its installed base.

E-station will use the short-term debt for the initial procurement of start-up parts and inventory, and will replay after a period of nine months. The venture capitalists will be given one of three seats on the board of directors, with Ravi Lal occupying one of the other seats. An additional board member will be elected by agreement between the venture capitalists and the founders.

Exit Strategy

The planned exit strategy is to sell the company to a large communications company after a period of not less than five years. It is highly likely that large firms such as AT&T and MCI will decide to enter and compete in this market against **e-station**, and a buyout would be a logical alternative for an exit strategy. A company such as AT&T would have good strategic fit in this business, and would be able to integrate **e-station** into their business line. For the investors, the terminal value of their share of the company would be approximately $68 million dollars at the end of year five. This assumes a P/E ratio of 12, and multiplies that against year five estimated net income. With an initial investment of $1.45 million, investors will realize a return on investment of 117 percent (Exhibit 1).

CRITICAL RISKS AND CONTINGENCIES

Prior to making an investment decision, prospective investors should carefully consider the following special factors among other matters in this business plan:

1. The potential that the product will not perform as expected does exist and would jeopardize the venture. Maintenance expenses would increase dramatically if the product proves to be unreliable and fails more than anticipated.
2. Sales figures may be too high or too low depending on customer acceptance. Moderately lower sales will not cripple expansion as each individual unit ultimately produces a positive cash stream. In this case, growth will just be slower. A low level of acceptance that does not cover initial fixed costs would prevent growth and profitability.
3. Problems with suppliers are not perceived because trends in the industry show increasing demand for their products while costs are shrinking. However, losing a supplier would force re-engineering of the product that would incur significant unforeseen expenses.
4. Substitutes such as cellular technologies and other unforeseen technologies would render the **e-station** useless.
5. Barriers to entry are small and as such competitive threats cannot be ignored. A competitor with a superior product at a more competitive price would jeopardize the venture.
6. The founders of **e-station** are inexperienced at running such a business, and failure to perform effectively could jeopardize the company.
7. In the event that sufficient funds cannot be raised, the venture would be jeopardized. ∎

EXHIBIT 1 Return on Investment			
	Founders	*Investors*	*Total*
% of Equity Owned	55.0%	45.0%	100.0%
Assumed P/E Ratio		12	12
Net Income		$5,674,420	$12,609,821
Initial Investment	$(100,000)	$(1,450,000)	$(1,550,000)
Total Market Value of Firm			$151,317,854
Investors' Share of Market Value		$68,093,034	
Annualized Return on Investment		117.0%	

The original research for this case was provided by Ravi Lal, Jake Moser, and Jim Foster. The case was prepared under the supervision of Marc Dollinger. Some of the names and places have been disguised.

Case 4   TV Answer: An Interactive Video Data Service

PART I: BIRTH OF AN INDUSTRY

Early on the morning of March 4, 1992, Mike Carter was reading The *Wall Street Journal* in his usual spot in the School of Business library. First, he checked the stock tables and noted that AT&T, his former employer, was down an eighth to 40 ½. Overall the stock was up about five points since Mike had returned to school, making him a couple of thousand dollars richer. Then he scanned the headlines on the first page. "Nothing exceptional to note for the day," he thought. Finally, he began to turn the pages of the front section. The full-page advertisement on page A5 caught his attention immediately, and he read it with great interest. A portion of the advertisement (without graphics) is reproduced in Exhibit 1.

The advertisement went on to say that TV Answer had formed an alliance with Hewlett-Packard and that it planned to market over 1.5 million interactive television home units in the first year of service and millions more in the following years.

Due to regulatory changes made earlier in the year by the Federal Communications Commission, individuals and firms would have the opportunity to participate in a lottery for local FCC licenses for 2-Way Interactive Video and Data Services.

The ad continued, "The implications are immense; for consumers it means a whole new way to interact with the world. For advertisers . . . including retailers . . . it means a whole new way to generate immediate direct response. For TV producers it means achieving levels of viewer interest and involvement never before possible. For educators it means turning the television into a classroom. For banks it means a branch office in every home with a TV set. And for potential local FCC licensees, it could mean the opportunity of a lifetime."

The advertisement closed with the following offer: "If you're interested in participating with TV Answer as a potential FCC licensee, network service provider, or strategic partner, write: TV Answer, Inc., P.O. Box 3900, Merrifield, VA 22116-3900. Or call us today at 1-800-222-3584 (fax 1-800-988-7733)."

Mike found the ad exciting. It described an opportunity to start a new business in the field of interactive television. The opportunity was apparently open to anyone. And as the ad said, the "implications were immense." Interactive TV was one of a number of revolutionary technological innovations that were predicted to change the way people were entertained, the way they shopped, and their patterns of communication.

Mike anxiously awaited his afternoon entrepreneurship class so that he could see what the professor and his classmates thought of this potential opportunity. In class they were always talking about "getting in on the ground floor of a business," and this appeared to be, as the advertisement said, the "birth of an industry."

PART II

Mike made enough copies of the ad for distribution in class that day. The students had a lively discussion over the pros and cons of TV Answer and the advertisement. Was it really the "birth of an industry"? What kind of "participation" with TV Answer was being suggested here? Was this really an opportunity open to everybody, or only very wealthy "anybodies"? Finally, at the end of class, the professor asked Mike to call the toll-free number in the ad and request additional information. Mike said he would do it, and he did.

It took about two weeks, but a large package of information from TV Answer finally arrived. There was quite a bit of information to sift through, but Mike began to read the material immediately. The documents were enclosed inside a glossy folder that depicted a schematic drawing of how the TV Answer Network would work.

The first document was a press release dated September 9, 1991, announcing a contract between TV Answer and Hughes Network Systems, Inc., to build personal satellite earth stations for TV Answer's interactive television system (Exhibit 2).

This was followed by a corporate fact sheet and some details about TV Answer's potential products and services (Exhibit 3). The more Mike read, the more fascinated he became. During his seven years at AT&T, he had worked on various projects that were closely related to the TV Answer concept: satellite transmission and communication, network software, cellular telephones, and expanded telephone applications. And although TV Answer was designed to be independent of telephone hookup, he was aware of its myriad uses and commercial potential.

Exhibit 4 offers a technical history of TV Answer and describes the network configuration, the hardware and software requirements, and the estimated cost of building a network (hub and cells). This would require close examination. Although the engineering feasibility was documented as reliable, the business aspects were still a bit fuzzy to Mike.

The final part of the package contained a series of press releases about the TV Answer system and the concept of interactive TV. Exhibit 5 presents the news release from the Federal Communications Commission announcing the allocation of a part of the broadcast spectrum for Interactive Video and Data Service (IVDS). According to the FCC, the awarding of two IVDS licenses for each of the nation's 734 cellular service areas would be made by lottery. The filing fee was $1,400. The FCC said that more information would be released later in the year.

Exhibit 6 contains two press releases (January 16 and February 27) issued by TV Answer. January 16's release announced a joint venture between Hewlett-Packard and TV Answer to build and market a two-way television system. As Mike read on, he was impressed with the speed of TV Answer's action and the reputation of its alliance partners. These people seemed to know what they were doing.

But Mike was not satisfied with company press releases and documents. He began his own research into the TV Answer company and concept. He went to the library and did a computer search of a database of business periodicals. Using keywords such as "interactive television," "Hewlett-Packard," and "TV Answer," he found some important additional information.

In an article in *Investor's Business Daily*, dated February 28, 1992, Mike found a description of Hewlett-Packard's plans to form an alliance with TV Answer. According to John Young, president of H-P, interactive television is one of the "areas we have been active in, interested in, and think we have something to contribute." Young went on to say that H-P planned to make some 1.5 million interactive TV appliances next year and that he believed demand for the devices would be healthy, if the television content is strong. He specifically mentioned such innovative programs as an interactive "Sesame Street" or other educational and entertainment programs.

In *Time* magazine (January 27, 1992), Mike found a small article with a slightly negative slant. It was entitled, "A coup for couch potatoes," and it announced that the TV Answer systems would be available in 25 major cities by the end of the year. But it went on to add that "while the concept may be a boon for exhausted nine-to-fivers too weary to dial Domino's, it may be a bane for parents of the always hungry twelve-something set."

Next he found a story by Jennie Aversa in *Multichannel News* dated January 20, 1992. It described the boost that the FCC had given to interactive television by adopting a new set of rules. The article described how anyone who could afford the $1,400 filing fee could apply for a license in this new interactive band. The licenses would be awarded on a market-by-market basis through a lottery at the FCC. The only restriction seemed to be that no one group can own two licenses in the same market. The article also quoted TV Answer officials as being confident that they will be able to compete against fiber optic technology.

An article in *Broadcasting*, dated January 20, 1992, by Joe Flint and Peter Lambert gave some of the industry reaction to the FCC rule change. Not all of the reaction was positive. Even some FCC commissioners were not so enthusiastic about IVDS's long-term viability. Said Commissioner Andrew Barrett: "I question the longevity of the service: it seems to me that fiber optics or a very basic or plain cable can provide the service seemingly more efficiently." Barrett questioned why TV Answer would "spend the massive amount of time (and money) lobbying as they have done for a service that for all practical purposes can be provided now."

In the same article, a competitor, David Lockton, criticized TVA's months-long media blitz. Lockton is the president of Interactive Network Inc. (part owned by

NBC), which delivers interactive services via public TV stations, FM subcarriers, and telephone. He said TVA ads in major newspapers have implied "that the FCC is making TVA technology the U.S. standard for interactive services." Wireless IVDS is "one of many, not the only" way to deliver interactive video-data.

Mike's computer-aided search also turned up an article by Michael Langberg of the San Jose Mercury News dated February 27, 1992. This article focused on Hewlett-Packard's attempt to recapture some of the consumer electronics market it had lost to Asian competitors over the years. It described H-P's plan to manufacture a device called an "interactive television appliance" or ITA, that would be sold under the Hewlett-Packard name and should reach electronics stores early next year at $400 to $500.

Langberg went on to report on how many Silicon Valley firms had been "virtually shut out of consumer electronics as competitors in Japan and other Far Eastern nations dominated the market." But H-P was making a bold but risky bid to recapture market share with a new generation of products combining computers with television, touted as one of the world economy's biggest growth areas in the 1990s and beyond. The article noted that consumer electronics is viciously competitive, marked by cutthroat pricing and constant battles for space on store shelves. Additionally, consumers are less familiar with the Hewlett-Packard name than established Asian brands such as Sony and Panasonic. H-P faces over obstacles to persuade the public to adopt its vision. Among them:

- *Other futuristic systems.* At least 10 companies are seriously pursuing interactive television projects that compete at least partly with TV Answer. Interactive Network Inc. of Mountain View started selling a $200 ITA in Sacramento last summer that allows TV viewers to play along with quiz shows and baseball games. The company says it will enter the Bay Area market in April.
- *Learning a new business.* "I just think they're kidding themselves that they're bringing anything to the party besides their manufacturing ability," said Robert Herwick, an electronics industry analyst with the investment firm Hambrecht & Quist in San Francisco.
- *Consumer reluctance.* Numerous attempts in the past decade to develop interactive electronic systems for the home have failed, apparently because no one has yet found the right combination of services and cost.

A *Wall Street Journal* article by G. Pascal Zachary dated February 27, 1992, also commented on the Hewlett-Packard and TV Answer alliance. The article suggested that consumers might not find interactive TV compelling. Potential problems are that the initial price for the equipment may be too high, and that programmers are likely to resist tailoring their broadcasts to take advantage of the technology.

Zachary found numerous examples of failures. Commodore International Ltd. introduced a novel product called CDTV, which skillfully blended features of TV, compact disk players, and PCs. It hasn't been a hit with shoppers. And interactive broadcasting, which was once called two-way TV, has its own dismal past. One of the most spectacular failures occurred in the early 1980s in Columbus, Ohio, and other cities, where a joint venture between American Express Co. and Warner Communications launched an ambitious test of interactivity.

But in an article by E. Andrews in the *New York Times* dated January 17, 1992, Mike found an optimistic slant provided by TV Answer President Fernando Morales. "I feel very enthusiastic," Mr. Morales said. "The F.C.C. decision is really a critical step to build this industry." To be successful, TV Answer must first recruit licensees, who would operate its interactive services in each city. The plan called for the F.C.C. to begin handing out licenses for cities and towns in the next three to six months, awarding them through a lottery.

Morales said the networks of local antennas for each city could be mounted on the rooftops of buildings and be installed within a few months at a cost of several hundred thousand dollars. To reach most residents of New York City, for example, about 20 radio repeater stations would have to be built at a total cost of roughly $6,000,000.

By the time he had finished reading the material, Mike was extremely excited, and his mind was racing with questions. What was his next step? Where could he get additional information? How should he evaluate the business and technical aspects of this opportunity? How much would it cost to get in? Was a TV Answer franchise in his future? ■

EXHIBIT 1 Advertisement

NEVER BEFORE SEEN ON TELEVISION!
ON JANUARY 16TH,
THANKS TO A LANDMARK FCC DECISION AND TV ANSWER,
TELEVISION BECAME A 2-WAY MEDIUM
• Soon you'll be able to . . . play along with live sporting events and game shows
• . . . preview a whole day's worth of programming and automatically set up your VCR
• . . . check bank balances, transfer funds, and pay bills
• . . . order a pizza
• . . . instantly request product information or coupons
• . . . even order direct response merchandise without using your phone!

Source: Wall Street Journal, March 4, 1992, p. A5.

EXHIBIT 2   **Press Release**

TV Answer, Inc.
1941 Roland Clarke Place
Reston, Virginia 22091
(703)715-8600
Contact: Sallie Omsted

EMBARGOED UNTIL
SEPTEMBER 9
    703-715-8856
    Paul Sturiale
    703-715-8606

TV ANSWER, HUGHES NETWORK SYSTEMS
SIGN MULTIMILLION DOLLAR SATELLITE CONTRACT

Reston, VA, Sept. 9, 1991—TV Answer has signed a multimillion-dollar contract with Hughes Network Systems, Inc. (HNS) to install personal satellite earth stations for TV Answer's interactive television system. Total value of the contract could reach $120 million as TV Answer technology spreads across the nation.

TV Answer, the pioneer in real-time, wireless Interactive Video Data Service (IVDS) technology, and HNS, the leader in interactive Very Small Aperture Terminals (VSATs), announced the contract today at TV Answer headquarters in Reston, VA.

Under the initial phase of the contract, HNS will build and install 1,000 VSAT units for use at the TV Answer cell sites. The units will allow TV Answer to introduce its technology to areas around the country if the Federal Communications Commission (FCC) issues licenses permitting companies to operate IVDS systems. The initial phase of the contract is valued at approximately $13.5 million and includes a $2.1 million hub-and-network control center that will be located at TV Answer headquarters.

The FCC is expected to determine whether to authorize IVDS usage of airwaves after it studies public comments received on the issue. If approved, the FCC could issue IVDS licenses by mid-1992, and the technology could be offered to consumers by the end of the year.

"This contract is an important part of our commitment to the Interactive Video Data Service industry," said Fernando Morales, president of TV Answer. "Though the FCC has not yet approved the use of airwaves for this purpose, we are anticipating that the commissioners will allocate a portion of the spectrum to IVDS use, and allow the industry to offer its services to the public. By starting the process now, we will be prepared to meet the initial needs of those who win IVDS license when the FCC begins holding lotteries."

The Hughes Integrated Satellite Business Network system will provide direct transmission paths between all remote VSATs and the TV Answer Hub Earth Station. The VSATs could collect information and instructions from local cell sites, then uplink the data via Ku-band geostationary satellite to TV Answer's headquarters and designated service providers. The FCC spectrum allocation in process now will create the technical rules for use of the two-way radio link between cell sites and subscribers' homes.

TV Answer estimates that 1,000 VSATs will be needed to meet projected build-out requirements for the system in the first year. The estimate is based on tentative and expected FCC guidelines requiring licenses to be able to provide service to at least 10 percent of the television households in their designated service areas within a year of receiving their license. TV Answer estimates that this will allow service to be offered to some 10 million households across the nation.

The FCC also tentatively said it will require licensees to increase their service capabilities to cover 60 percent of their market area within the first five years after the licenses are issued. This will require TV Answer to provide an additional 5,000 VSATs to meet FCC guidelines. The remainder of the VSATs will be phased in based on market demand.

EXHIBIT 2   (continued)

TV Answer estimates that a minimum of 10,000 VSAT units will be needed to provide nationwide coverage for its technology. When completely installed, the TV Answer System will be available to almost all of the estimated 98 million television households in the United States.

The TV Answer System is similar in structure to a cellular telephone network. Each cell site can service a radius up to four miles. The VSAT technology provides high-volume, simultaneous transmissions from multiple cell sites to the TV Answer hub.

EXHIBIT 3   TV Answer Corporate Fact Sheet

Name of Company:	TV Answer, Inc.
Ownership:	Privately-held corporation
Leadership:	Fernando Morales, President
	Richard Miller, Chief Operating Officer
Year Incorporated:	1986
Corporate Description:	The pioneer company in the field of wireless, real-time, interactive television. TV Answer is heavily involved in the development and marketing of technology and services to promote and support the interactive Video Data Service industry (IVDS), commonly known as interactive television.
The TV Answer System:	TV Answer provides technology and services that transform the average television into a two-way communications tool that viewers can use to accomplish daily tasks like shopping, banking, and ordering prepared food delivered to their home. The system may also include the ability to vote in polls, interact with educational programming, respond to interactive game shows, advertising, and interactive news programming.
	TV Answer technology is similar in structure to a cellular telephone network. It uses radio waves to transmit signals between users' home units and central cell sites to create interactive television services. The cell sites bounce the signals to satellites, which relay the signals to TV Answer headquarters and designated destinations.
Corporate Offices:	Two buildings comprising 73,000 square feet in Reston, Virginia.
Number of Employees:	170

Benefits of TV Answer

Consumers:
- Consumers will be able to integrate all of their remote controlled audio/visual equipment into one easy-to-operate remote that will also easily program their VCRs.
- Consumers will have access to a TV listing service customized to their needs, which will allow them more control over their children's viewing.
- Consumers will have access to information, products or services that they might not otherwise have time to request, plus access to an exclusive new generation of pay-per-view and home shopping catalog television services.
- Consumers will be able to shop at home, with instantaneous billing and shipping—all by remote control!

EXHIBIT 3   (continued)

- Consumers will have the opportunity to become instantaneously involved in their communities' opinion polls, using in-home technology that can be installed without modification to their existing equipment.

Broadcasters:

- Conduct opinion polls instantly for all types of programming, as well as provide "true" ratings data, at rates much less costly than interactive cable.
- Use advertising as "point of purchase" direct response medium to increase the broadcaster sales effectiveness for goods and services.
- Increase audience size and attention while decreasing channel "zapping" by actively involving them. Increase program effectiveness, especially for educational and children's programming.
- TV Answer is a proven broadcast technology, independent of telephone and cable hookup. The technology can be deployed in any broadcast environment.

TV Answer: More than "Just" Interactive Television

Imagine a device that transforms the average television set from a mere entertainment device into an essential household communications tool. Such a device would enable you to accomplish daily tasks such as shopping for groceries, banking, paying your bills, or ordering a delivered meal from your favorite restaurant all by using your television. Responding to game shows, advertisements, interactive news programs, educational programs, and television polls would be possible—and your response would be instantly received.

This new television accessory is more than the workings of an active imagination; it's a reality called TV ANSWER—the first perfected system that allows viewers to interact directly with on-screen television programming as it happens. TV ANSWER is not tied to any one type of broadcast technology. This revolutionary system works equally well with cable, satellite, and rooftop antenna systems.

There is more to TV ANSWER than interactivity, however. TV Answer also functions as a universal remote control. Viewers can operate their televisions, VCRs, satellite or cable converters, and stereo equipment easily using TV ANSWER's unique remote control. In an age where two or three remote controls sit in front of the television and the average universal remote costs $100, TV ANSWER will transform the marketplace.

In many markets the quantity of channel selections is vast. With over 120 program sources available, including premium channels, the networks, pay-per-view services, and myriad other viewing opportunities, the viewer is often faced with the irritating process of matching cable system numbers with familiar channels. Through a simple, menu-driven process, TV ANSWER streamlines this information and simplifies channel selection.

All of the possible channel choices are organized in menus by categories including Networks, News and Information, Sports, Premium Channels, Music, Education, Religion, and Home Shopping. Using the TV ANSWER remote control joystick, the viewer finds the program he wants by positioning the on-screen curser on the desired channel logo and pulling the remote control trigger. TV ANSWER also displays TV listing information automatically using this simple process.

With TV ANSWER, programming your VCR is as easy as changing channels. Spending hours with your VCR owner's manual is no longer necessary. Once TV ANSWER is installed using the menu-driven setup progress, your VCR is controlled by the TV ANSWER unit. The viewer simply makes on-screen program selections from a regularly updated TV MENU service. TV Answer activates the VCR to record automatically.

To increase viewer control, this technology has the ability to memorize passwords for channels or credit cards and to lock out access to certain channels. These features are an aid to parents who need to prevent young children from purchasing items or watching inappropriate programming.

TV Answer offers the definitive standard for interactive television. This product will not only provide the vehicle for literally hundreds of new interactive television services, it will also redefine the way TV viewers use their televisions.

EXHIBIT 4   TV Answer: History

THE BIRTH OF AN INDUSTRY: INTERACTIVE VIDEO DATA SERVICE

When the Federal Communications Commission voted unanimously on January 10, 1991, to issue a Notice of Proposed Rulemaking, proposing the allocation of .5 megahertz of radio spectrum for an Interactive Video Data Service, they began the formation of what is rapidly becoming the IVDS industry. To see what prompted the FCC action and to gain a historical perspective, we must look back on the development of TV Answer.

When TV Answer, Inc., was formed in 1986, the company centered around a technology and its inventor, Fernando Morales. Mr. Morales developed a system that uses the radio spectrum to transport viewer responses and orders from the home to a mainframe computer for processing. Convinced of the technology's potential applications in the cable and broadcast industries, Mr. Morales formed a Delaware corporation and raised the capital needed to develop and test the system for a group of Mexican industrialists. Mr. Morales applied for two U.S. patents in 1987, which were subsequently granted.

TV Answer, Inc., then applied to the FCC for experimental authorization to broadcast in the Washington, D.C. metropolitan area. This test, conducted over the Media General Cable System, in Fairfax, Virginia, used digital data, encoded in the cable broadcast, to load the viewer's home box with questions. The radio frequency then served as a return path for the responses. The test utilized the patented transmitters that are an integral part of today's TV Answer system. This test demonstrated a viewer appetite for interactive television and the efficient use of the radio spectrum between 218.00 megahertz and 220.00 megahertz.

After the conclusion of the Fairfax test in 1989, the system was further refined and improved. The company then began developing a more ambitious system that used radio to load home units with questions for polling, interactive commercial offerings, home banking information, and consumer databases. The return path was also further refined to share the radio frequency in a "duplex" model, making two-way use of the spectrum possible. The other major innovation in this period was the incorporation of send/recieve satellite dishes (Hughes VSAT personal earth stations) to connect a national network of receiver-transmitter sites. The VSAT technology, developed by Hughes Network Systems and in use throughout the world, provides extremely fast transfer of data to and from a central source and local cell stations located throughout the country.

With the successful test in Fairfax, Virginia, and the technology improvement of VSATs and two-way digital radio transmission, the company petitioned the FCC to permanently allocate .5 megahertz for an interactive service.

On January 16, 1992, the FCC authorized 1 megahertz of spectrum for Interactive Video Data Service Technologies. This action was an official recognition of the potential value to consumers of "talking back" to their televisions. The Commission will issue two local operating licenses per market by lottery. It is expected that construction of a national IVDS network will begin by the fourth quarter of 1992.

EXHIBIT 4 (continued)

TV Answer has taken a strong leadership role in the development of the IVDS industry. We have continued perfecting the technical operating system, designing business models, negotiating with manufacturers and software developers, and have begun national marketing efforts to the business sectors that will become the primary users of the viewer response system. While the FCC finalizes its action, TV Answer will continue to improve its technology and develop the infrastructure to guarantee the success of this new industry.

THE TRANSMISSION/RECEPTION PATH

The TV Answer network is similar in structure to the cellular phone network. To provide service to a market area, individual cell sites are installed. Each cell site has a maximum service capacity of 2,800 home units. At the heart of each cell site is a VSAT (Very Small Aperture Terminal) two-way satellite dish earth station, which communicates with a Hughes satellite; and a TV Answer radio receiver/transmitter, which communicates with TV Answer home units.

There are two communication "loops" involved in the TV Answer system. The first loop carries data between TV Answer headquarters and the individual cell sites. Using its VSAT/satellite uplink and downloading capabilities, TV Answer headquarters sends TV program listings, interactive commercials, order forms for goods and services, news about TV Answer, updated memory card information, and order confirmations to each cell site. This information travels as digital data from TV Answer headquarters to the cell sites via the Hughes satellite.

The VSAT and radio transmitter/receiver at the cell site provides the link between the first and second communications loops. At the cell site, the data received via satellite is transformed into a radio signal (218–219 Mhz). Using this signal, the second communications loop carries digital data transmissions between the VSAT earth station, which is the nucleus of each cell site, and the TV Answer units in the home. This same loop relays viewer responses from the home units to each cell site. In this way viewers' orders are placed, and other information, such as downloaded TV listing information, memory updates, and order confirmation information, are exchanged between the cell site and the home TV Answer units.

Viewer responses to commercials, service offers, or product orders are collected by the cell site transmitter/receiver and are similarly relayed to TV Answer headquarters by the cell site VSAT via the Hughes satellite. These responses are processed; appropriate collection, ordering, and billing activities are performed by TV Answer and other parties related to the viewers' responses. The same downlink information received by TV Answer headquarters is also available to program originators. Using their own VSAT earth stations, interactive service providers such as television networks, shopping services, food sellers, or pay-per-view providers can receive viewer responses at the same time as TV Answer.

EXHIBIT 4   (continued)

TECHNICAL PROFILE

Description: The TV Answer System is a wireless, instantaneous transmission system that transforms televisions from one-way entertainment and information vehicles into two-way communications tools that allow viewers to perform routine tasks such as shopping, bill paying, banking, polling, and organizing program data directly through their television sets, with no telephone or personal computer hookups. The system involves four components: the Home Unit, Cell Site, Satellite, and HUB site. Consumers access the TV Answer system by transmitting instructions to their Home Unit by using a joystick. The Home Unit then relays the signal via radio wave to a local Cell Site, which translates and transmits it to a satellite. The satellite then transmits it to a national HUB site at TV Answer headquarters. The signal is relayed through TV Answer's Transaction Switching Center to goods and services providers around the nation for fulfillment. Responses to consumers' instructions are sent back to consumers' televisions along the same transmission path.

Consumer Hardware/Software:

Home Unit
Function: The Home Unit attaches to consumers' television sets with two easy-to-install cables. It programs the set to provide service options and collects instructions from users. It then transmits the instructions/information via VHF radio frequency wave to a local cell site. It also receives response transmissions from TV Answer to consumers.

Dimensions:	15 in. × 8 ¾ in. × 2 1.2 in.
Weight:	8 lbs.
Memory Card Capacity	16 MB
Internal Memory Capacity:	Static RAM: 64 K, ROM: 128 K
Radio Transmission Frequency:	218–219 Mhz.
Power Source:	A/C Power

Software/Memory Cards
Function: Memory cards are the medium that carries the software to the Home Unit. The Cards perform several functions, including: activating the system; storing updatable information; providing an additional memory capacity; and providing specific services to users. Each memory card provides one or more user services, i.e., banking, shopping, bill paying, TV Search, ordering home deliveries, etc.

Card Dimensions:	3 ¼ in. × 2 in. × ⅛ in.
Memory Storage System:	Random Access Memory (RAM) & Read Only Memory (ROM) cards
Memory Capacity:	RAM: 128 K and 512 K, ROM: 1 Megabyte
Card Type:	Single-side, 60-pin, battery-backed, Custom Format Complementary Metal Oxide Semiconductor (CMOS) chip

EXHIBIT 4 (continued)

Power Source:	3 Volt, Mercury-Oxide Battery with a maximum life of 5 years
Applications:	Banking, Shopping, Bill Paying, Program Data Organizing, Ordering Home-Delivered Items
Software:	Proprietary

Joystick

Function: The joystick is the handheld unit through which consumers indicate their choices to the TV Answer Home Unit software. Consumers use a thumb-operated joystick located at the thumb port to direct a cursor on the television screen. When the cursor reaches the proper symbol on the screen, consumers squeeze a trigger on the joystick to indicate their choice. The Home Unit then reads the selection to begin processing or acting upon the instruction or information.

Dimensions:	8 in. × 2 in. × 3 in.
Weight:	6 ounces
Features:	• Cursor Control
	• Trigger
	• Infrared (IR) Transmitter
Link Type:	Infrared Light

Network Components:

Cell Site

Function: The cell site is a self-contained structure that houses the hardware and software needed to collect, process, and transmit information and instructions between the Home Units and TV Answer headquarters. It receives and routes responses from TV Answer to system users.

Equipment Housing Dimensions (excluding antenna):	3 ft. × 2 ft. × ft. (12 cu.ft.)
Components:	• Radio Frequency (RF) Transceiver
	• Uninterruptible Power Supply
	• Radio Frequency Antenna
	• Very Small Aperture Terminal (VSAT) Hughes Personal Earth Station 8000 (1.8 meter diameter)
RF Transceiver Maximum Signal Strength:	20 Watts
Power Source:	A/C power with an uninterruptible backup energy source using plate batteries with a service life up to 5 hours.
Service Area:	2–8 miles, depending upon terrain
RF Transceiver Link Speed:	120,000 bits per minute
Radio Frequency:	Very High Frequency (VHF), 218–219 Mhz
Average Per Unit Cost:	$30,000
Software:	Proprietary

EXHIBIT 4   (continued)

HUB Site
Function: The HUB site is a central location that houses the technology needed to collect, process, and transmit information and instructions between TV Answer corporate headquarters and two receivers: goods/services providers and local cell sites.

Dimensions:	• Total HUB site area: 1,900 sq. ft. • Satellite Dish: 6.1 meters • Radio Frequency Terminal: 800 cu. ft., fiberglass shelter
Components:	• 6.1 meter satellite antenna with Low Noise Amplifiers and natural gas deicing system • Radio Frequency Terminal (RFT) containing high-power amplifiers, up converters, down converters, uplink power control system • Network Control Center containing Baseband and Intermediate Frequency (IF) subsystems, VAX mini computer, Hughes IllumiNET console and system, and even printers
Power Source:	• A/C power with an uninterruptible backup energy system using plate batteries with a service life of up to 15 minutes to stabilize the system while it switches onto an emergency power system using a diesel generator.
Service Capacity:	Each network connected to the RFT has the capability of one 512 kilobit-per-second (KSPS) outroute for sending data to remote dishes and cell sites, and up to thirty-one 128 KBPS inroutes for receiving data.
Microwave Frequency:	KU-band, 11–14 GHz.
Cost:	$2.1 million

Corporate Data Center
Function: TV Answer's Corporate Data processes all transactions received at the HUB, applies industry standards in encryption and decryption techniques to every transaction to assure confidentiality, and switches the transaction to the proper provider of goods and services via the HUB.

Components:	To be determined
Location:	TV Answer corporate headquarters in Reston, Virginia

Satellite
Function: The cell site is the central routing point in the transmission system. The satellite collects signals from the cell site, then relays them to the HUB site at TV Answer corporate headquarters.

Type:	Geostationary
Transponder:	To be determined

EXHIBIT 5   News Release

NEWS: FEDERAL COMMUNICATIONS COMMISSION

Report No.   **ACTION IN DOCKET CASE**   January 16, 1992

INTERACTIVE VIDEO DATA SERVICE ESTABLISHED
(GEN. DOCKET 91-2)

The Commission has established the Interactive Video and Data Service (IVDS) and allocated spectrum for its use.

IVDS is expected to be a convenient, low-cost system that will allow two-way interaction with commercial and educational programming, along with informational and data services that may be delivered by or coordinated with broadcast television, cable television, wireless cable, direct broadcast satellites, or future television delivery methods. IVDS will be regulated as a personal radio service under Part 95 of the Commission's rules.

This action comes as a result of a petition by TV Answer, Inc., which asked the Commission to allocate spectrum in the 218–219 Mhz range for IVDS using technology that TV Answer had developed. It also asked for promulgation of technical rules consistent with its proposed system design to minimize interference to TV channel 13, which occupies a nearby band.

... The Commission will issue two IVDS licenses per service area. Service areas will coincide with the 734 cellular service areas. These cellular service areas are well known to the communications industry and cover the entire country.

Selection of licensees will be by lottery. The Commission adopted an abbreviated filing procedure for the lottery. It will require applicants to file only FCC Form 155 specifying the applicant's name and address, the service area and the fee code along with a filing fee of $1,400.00 for each application. Lottery selectees will be required to timely file a complete license application package consisting of FCC Form 574 and required showings. A Public Notice will be released later detailing specific instructions for filing lottery applications and the deadline for each market.

The Commission also adopted regulations to ensure than an applicant that obtains a license through the lottery process actually builds the IVDS system. These include construction benchmarks and a prohibition on sale or transfer of IVDS licenses before 50 percent of the IVDS market is covered.

News Media contact: Rosemary Kimball at (202) 632-5050. Office of Engineering and Technology contact: Damon C. Ladson at (202) 653-8106.

EXHIBIT 6   TV Answer: Press Releases

1941 Roland Clarke Place
Reston, VA 22091

PRESS RELEASE

FOR IMMEDIATE RELEASE
**FCC LAUNCHES WIRELESS INTERACTIVE TELEVISION INDUSTRY
RESTON, VA, JANUARY 16, 1992**—The Federal Communications Commission (FCC) today launched America's wireless interactive television industry by unanimously allocating a portion of the radio spectrum for Interactive Video and Data Services (IVDS) use. IVDS is commonly known as interactive television.

The FCC decision effectively creates a completely new, wireless broadcast industry. The FCC's action now allows these companies to provide technology that turns consumers' televisions from one-way information/entertainment vehicles to two-way communications tools. Interactive television will allow consumers to perform services like shopping, polling, banking, and bill paying directly through their television, without using computers or telephones. Previously, companies in the interactive field had been unable to provide interactive wireless services because they could not use the airwaves to transmit their service.

The FCC announced that it would allocate one megahertz in the 218–219 Mhz range of the spectrum for use by companies to provide IVDS to consumers. The FCC is expected to begin accepting applications for IVDS licenses within three to six months using an expedited lottery procedure. The agency is expected to begin issuing the licenses before the end of 1992, with the first service expected to reach consumers soon thereafter.

The FCC announced that the initial licenses will cover service areas based on Metropolitan Statistical Areas (MSA)/Rural Service Areas (RSA).

The ruling followed a year-long evaluation period by the agency which began in January 1991, when the FCC unanimously voted to issue a Notice of Proposed Rule Making (NPRM). Following that ruling, the FCC received public comments on the proposed allocation until June 10, 1991. The FCC then received replies on the initial comments until mid-July. Since then, the FCC has been evaluating the comments and establishing licensing procedures, guidelines and timetables.

The FCC action was the result of a petition filed by TV Answer—the leader in wireless interactive television—in December 1987. At that time TV Answer requested that the FCC allocate a portion of the radio spectrum for use as an interactive viewer response system.

TV Answer has been an active participant throughout the process. In addition to offering suggestions and proposals through the public comment process, TV Answer has also been actively involved in developing and testing interactive television technology. TV Answer has been granted three patents by the U.S. Patent and Trademark Office for its state-of-the-art wireless interactive system. TV Answer also has been granted international patents by Canada, Spain, South Africa, and has a European patent pending.

TV Answer is believed to be the only company in the wireless interactive field that has technology capable of serving as a wide-scale platform for wireless interactive television services.

EXHIBIT 6 (continued)

TV Answer also conducted a two-year test of interactive television under an experimental license issued by the FCC. The test involved over 600 volunteers in Fairfax County, VA, that were provided with technology that allowed viewers to participate in interactive programming 24 hours per day. Programming included public opinion questions, news polls and entertainment programming. Using sender/receiver units, participants could respond to questions, rate music videos, and participate in contests.

TV Answer President Fernando Morales lauded the Commission's decision as "a great step in establishing the interactive television industry. The fact that the FCC vote was unanimous indicates that the commissioners recognize that interactivity is the next logical generation of advanced television and that they fully support the industry's growth and prosperity."

"Now our challenge becomes to help the industry get firmly established in its initial service areas. TV Answer will do everything possible to educate consumers about this medium and to help business understand how it can be a valuable tool in their marketing and service programs," Mr. Morales added.

In preparation for the industry launch, TV Answer has been busy during the past year preparing the technology, satellite network, and business alliances needed to establish the interactive television industry.
TV ANSWER

PRESS RELEASE

FOR RELEASE
FEBRUARY 27, 1992

TV ANSWER AND HP TO SPEED DEVELOPMENT OF FIRST, NATIONAL INTERACTIVE TV SYSTEM

NEW YORK, Feb. 27, 1992—TV Answer, Inc., and Hewlett-Packard Company today announced a manufacturing and marketing agreement designed to speed acceptance of interactive television by U.S. consumers and the development of the first national interactive, or two-way, television system.

The agreement authorizes HP to use TV Answer's patented wireless interactive technology to manufacture and market affordable interactive television home units used to activate and control a two-way TV system in the home. HP said it plans to make more than 1.5 million home units available in the first year of service through consumer-electronics stores and other retail outlets.

The compact plug-and-play home unit is about the size of a VCR and attaches to cable-ready or standard-broadcast TV set with two easy-to-install cables. A wireless, handheld joystick activates and controls the system. Unlike many personal computers (PCs), the home unit is easy to set up and requires no special training to use. The suggested list price for the home unit is expected to be less than $700, significantly below the original entry point for consumer electronics such as VCRs or CD players. TV Answer intends to establish, operate, and maintain the national interactive television network.

... "HP's participation will greatly accelerate the development of a national, wireless interactive television industry," said Fernando Morales, Presi-

EXHIBIT 6   (continued)

dent of TV Answer. "HP's experience of turning advanced technologies into high-quality consumer electronics makes HP ideal for bringing interactive television technology to market."

... Robert J. Frankenberg, HP Vice-President and General Manager of the Personal Information Products Group, said, "With TV Answer we are at the threshold of bringing together the two most powerful information tools available to consumers—the television and the computer. TV Answer has successfully moved interactive television from an exciting concept to an emerging market, and HP is committed to driving the hardware standard by being the first company to deliver high-quality home units at really attractive prices."

Last month's decision by the Federal Communications Commission (FCC) to allocate 1 Mhz of radio spectrum for interactive television use now allows companies to provide technology to consumers that could change television from a one-way information/entertainment vehicle to a two-way wireless-communications tool. Television programming companies are interested in interactive television for its potential to increase viewers and revenue, according to TV Answer. Unlike telephone-based interactive systems, TV Answer technology employs an open-systems architecture enabling a wide range of service providers to participate.

The FCC decision was the result of a petition filed by TV Answer in December 1987. TV Answer believes it is currently the only company with the technology and hardware designed to operate within the bandwidth allocated by the FCC for interactive-TV use.

Availability of the first HP home units will be determined by the licensing schedule for cell sites established by the FCC. The FCC will issue two licenses per market by lottery—covering service areas based on Metropolitan Statistical Areas (MSA)/Rural Service Areas (RSA)—following a process similar to the rollout of cellular telephone service in the United States. The FCC is expected to begin issuing licenses before the end of 1992.

In September 1991, TV Answer announced that Hughes Network Systems, Inc., would install satellite personal earth stations called VSATs (very-small-aperture terminals) for use in TV Answer cell sites across the nation. Information is transmitted from the home unit to local cell sites' VSATs, then onward to TV Answer's satellite network hub site in Reston, VA. From there, the signal is rerouted via satellite to service providers who satisfy customer requests.

"The development of interactive television will help redefine the playing field in consumer electronics by taking the best of what the U.S. computer industry has pioneered in digital electronics and making it pervasive and easily accessible," said HP's Frankenberg.

This case was prepared by Marc Dollinger from original company documents and public secondary sources. It is not meant to be construed as an endorsement or a critique of the TV Answer concept. TV Answer is now called the Eon Corporation.

Case 5   Blitz

Tom Kinney and his three partners think they have a practical business idea and a do-able business plan, but no one wants to give them any money. Encouraging words have been easier to come by than financing. But they are not giving up and the search continues.

Tom and his partners—Eric Olson, Pat Dunne, and Kurt Moeller—all share a love for beach volleyball. Tom, in fact, was actively involved in the creation of the Professional Beach Volleyball League. It seemed like a natural for these four beach-loving friends to form Zuma Sun Care, Inc. to market a new kind of suntan lotion to the consumer group they know so well; highly active men and women between the ages of 15 and 34. While other suntan lotion companies target children or athletes in their marketing plan, Zuma will be the first to gear their product specifically to the young adult market.

Zuma has developed a unique product to reach those consumers. Known as Blitz, their suntan product is actually two different lotions packaged in a dual-cham-ber dispensing bottle. Blitz will allow sun worshippers to apply lotions with different SPFs to different parts of their body (a higher SPF for the face and sensitive areas, a lower SPF for areas where they want to tan quickly) without forcing consumers to purchase two separate products.

Zuma has a unique marketing plan for Blitz, too. Instead of selling the product in drugstores and supermarkets, Zuma wants to sell Blitz exclusively to gift stores and independent shops at resorts, hotels, cruise lines, and beaches. They feel that these outlets will be more receptive to a new brand, and that consumers will be more likely to appreciate the unique appeal of Blitz without the rows of competing products you find at a mass merchandiser.

Armed with multiple college degrees and lots of enthusiasm, Tom Kinney and his partners spent more than a year preparing their business plan. They produced re-search on the $620 million U.S. annual retail market for suntan and sunscreen prod-ucts, which demonstrated that it was a growing market where other small companies with a special niche had succeeded. Their review of demographic statistics revealed that 64 percent of their target market of age 15–24 young adults currently use sun care products. A professional market survey by a reputable firm indicated that 60 percent of females and 29 percent of males in their target group expressed a strong interest in a dual-chamber bottle with multiple SPF suntan lotions. As long as the sun keeps shining, Blitz is sure to be a winner.

Now Zuma needs $485,000 to perfect the product, conduct additional market tests, refine packaging and advertising, and launch Blitz nationwide. But despite their well-documented research and carefully prepared financial projections, they can't seem to find an investor. They believe that the problem is that while all four partners have good credentials, none of them actually has any experience launching a new business, which makes potential investors leery.

Recently Tom had an inquiry from a regional venture capital firm that might be willing to invest in Zuma. However, they would require Zuma to completely restructure their financial offer and to hire Steven Smith, an experienced entrepreneur they have worked with before, to be President and CEO of Zuma as a condition of their investment.

Tom just returned from lunch with Steven. This new venture veteran was impressed by Zuma's business plan, but he had two serious problems. First, he thought the name "Blitz" was a negative factor because it sounded too much like the word "blister." He suggested they needed a new name which would suggest the dual SPF concept. Steven also thought a marketing plan geared exclusively to small independent stores was inadequate, and that they should instead concentrate on nationwide mass marketers like Target and WalMart.

Tom Kinney liked Steven, but his instincts told him that both the Blitz name and the exclusive marketing plan are 100 percent right for this product. He thought that 50-something Smith simply did not understand their target market. Tom was uncertain whether he or his original partners were willing to change their plans after they've put so much time and energy into developing the concept, even if it means losing their investment.

Zuma's Executive Summary appears in Street Stories 5–1 in Chapter 5 of this book. Here is the rest of the business plan that Tom shared with Steven Smith and the venture capital firm.

BACKGROUND AND PURPOSE

The market now has a preponderance of health and beauty aid products targeted at consumers with youthful, active life styles. The founders of Zuma SunCare realized, however, that one product, perhaps more readily identified with "fun" and "youth" than any other, had not found a home with these consumers: suntan lotion. Thus, Blitz SunTan Lotion, the sun protection product of the young and active, came into being.

Current Situation

Blitz SunTan Lotion is a line of tanning and sun protection products, with varying degrees of SPF levels for varying degrees of tan promotion and sun protection. Blitz will be marketed to the 15–35-year-old age group, those with active, youthful lifestyles. The technology needed to make the product is the specialty of the manufacturers and packagers to whom we will subcontract orders for the product. The product will be delivered to market through direct sales of our own, the sales efforts of brokers in the industry, and through established channels of experienced health care and beauty aid distributors.

Our Resources

This section describes the key resources that the founders bring to Zuma SunCare, as well as other important factors that contribute to Zuma SunCare's success.

Human Resources

The founders of Zuma SunCare are unique in the levels of vision, drive, creativity, and intelligence. The insight that enabled the founders to recognize an unexploited market niche, and the creativity behind the inception of the dual-chamber dispensing bottle, were not one-time only phenomena. The founders possess unique skills which will enable them to continually perceive opportunities where others do not, and thus ensure that Zuma SunCare will remain at the forefront of suntan lotion marketing innovation.

President and CEO Tom Kinney brings with him an enormous amount of relationship capital. Having grown up playing volleyball on the beaches of Southern California, Mr. Kinney is intimately familiar with the driving forces behind the burgeoning sport of Professional Beach Volleyball. The marketing appeal of Professional Beach Volleyball to young and active consumers is strong, and Mr. Kinney's contacts in the sport promise unique access to an excellent source of promotional capital.

Reputational Resources

Because Blitz SunTan Lotion will be the first brand name sun care product exclusively aimed at the young and active, it will garner enormous first mover brand loyalty. With continued high profile marketing to the young and active, Blitz's name will be inextricably linked to the concepts of "fun" and "youth." Blitz will be able to retain a firm hold on market share in its niche, even in the face of competition from "me too" imitators.

Organizational Resources

Zuma SunCare's organizational structure will be lean, tight, and flat. Consequently, Zuma SunCare's decision making will be fast and responsive to perceived market opportunities. In combination with the strong Human Resources of the firm, Zuma SunCare's organizational resources promises to help make it a success.

OBJECTIVES

Short Term

The short-term, one-year goals of Zuma SunCare are as follows:

From October 1996 through January 1997 Zuma's goals are to perfect the formula, packaging, and advertising of Blitz SunTan Lotion by conducting concepts tests in a college/beach community such as Gainesville, Florida. Through a series of participative panels, screenings, and tests Zuma will be able to determine the ideal Blitz formulation (scent, consistency, color, etc.), which packaging provides the greatest appeal, and which advertising schemes generate the greatest response.

Beginning in February 1997 Zuma SunCare will begin promoting and selling the perfected Blitz product in a limited test market representing a microcosm of Blitz's eventual national market. Again, Gainesville, Florida might represent a community selected for the test. The market test will enable Zuma to gain valuable experience establishing distribution channels and implementing its marketing and advertising strategy, but will not require large financial losses.

The concept and market tests will assist Zuma SunCare in realizing its short term goals: creating the optimal product, crafting highly effective marketing and advertising strategies, honing the implementation of those strategies, and perfecting the establishment of sales and distribution channels.

Long Term

The long-term, two to five year goals of Zuma SunCare are as follows:

Using the knowledge and skills gained from its concept and marketing tests the previous year, Zuma will ramp up its advertising and sales strategies for a national launch of Blitz SunTan Lotion in 1998. Zuma will attempt to maximize market share as early as possible with intense media and trade promotions. This strategy will be important to defend competitive threats. The company will minimize direct competition from mass-market brands (Coppertone, etc.) by targeting regional convenience stores, surf shops, and beach and ski resorts. The national brands have less impact on these channels since their sales are concentrated on national supermarket and drugstore chains. By the end of this first year of national operations, Zuma SunCare projects that Blitz will achieve approximately 1 percent share of the total sun care market, and earn $779,007.

By the end of its fourth year of national operations, Zuma projects a 2.5 percent market share for Blitz, earnings of $2.8 million, and the ability to tender a successful initial public equity offering if desired.

An additional goal of Zuma during years 2 through 5, is to exploit the high brand name recognition that Blitz SunTan Lotion will have established with consumers. Zuma wishes to cash in on the intangible value of the Blitz name by branding out into other product lines bearing the Blitz name, such as apparel and gift items.

MARKET ANALYSIS

Overall Market

Zuma SunCare will compete in the $620 million U.S. retail market for suntan and suncreen products. This market has averaged a 5 percent annual growth (Exhibit 1), representing a trend that is expected to continue with the growing concern for the harmful effects of the sun's rays. The entire skin-care industry is one of the fastest growing segments of the personal products category. The distribution channels that have shown the most growth have been mass merchandisers and alternative markets such as direct sale ("The Body Shop") and informercial/cable TV. Specific high-growth niches are expected to be ethnic and men's markets, as well as all-natural products. The European market will also be important since sales there are about twice as those in the United States.

There has been a strong proliferation of health and beauty products developed over the past ten years, particularly among sunscreens and sunblocks. Seventy percent of the suncreen market has gone to products with an SPF of 15 or higher, as consumers become more concerned about the harmful effects of the sun's ultraviolet rays. Also, recent segmentation efforts have prompted manufacturers to develop brands that fit consumers' lifestyles, not just an SPF factor. The high growth of products specifically for children is a result of studies that indicate regular use of sunscreen before the age of 18 reduces the likelihood of melanoma skin cancer by 78 percent. Likewise, sunless tanning products have boomed, currently comprising 15 percent of the sun care market. A deluge of new sunless tanning products is expected to be introduced in both mass market and prestige channels.

Leading Competitors

The market is divided between a half dozen major manufacturers and a multitude of small, independent and private label brands (Exhibit 1). Currently, the strongest player in this market is Schering-Plough with its brands Coppertone, Coppertone Kids, Coppertone Sport, Water Babies, and Shade. These lines comprise 33 percent of the market, and have achieved this by having a long brand history, heavy marketing expenditures (over $30 million annually), and the resources of a large pharmaceutical and packaged goods corporation. Their closest competitors, Banana Boat and Hawaiian Tropic, have less than half Coppertone's market share, yet have aggressively expanded their lines and sharply increased media spending. Other firms sell prestige market sunscreens in department stores, aimed at high end users, with cosmetic oriented brands toward women. The major brands sell products across the United States as well as overseas, while the smaller companies concentrate sales in regions with heaviest use, such as the Southeast and West coast.

Despite the strength of the major brand names, numerous start-ups have successfully entered the market with niche positioning. About 30 percent of the market is divided among numerous smaller companies which stress ties to a particular region or a reputation gained by word of mouth at beaches and resorts. This segment, rather than the mass-merchandised segment dominated by the major brands, is the one in which Zuma will directly compete in the early years.

Specific Market

Target Market

The Blitz brand will be specifically marketed to the segment of young men and women between the ages of 15 and 34 who live highly active lifestyles. Particular emphasis will be placed on college students between ages 18 and 24. Both the 15 to 19 and the 20 to 24 age groups are expected to grow significantly faster than the general population (Exhibit 2), and they have traditionally been among the highest users of sun care products. About 38 percent of this segment uses sun care products on a regular basis, which creates a base of 28.9 million users. Given this, it is estimated that the "young adult" portion of the retail market is $318 million retail.

Based on preliminary market surveys, this market purchases according to price, product efficacy, and brands that appeal to this lifestyle. Sixty-four percent of respondents use sun care products "to achieve a good tan without burning," while 27 percent want complete protection from UV rays. This agrees with secondary research that indicates a growing trend for many young adults to limit exposure to the sun altogether.

A significant number of respondents tend to use more than one product at a time, using higher SPF products on their face, neck, and shoulders. Eighty percent of females and 29 percent of males expressed a strong interest in a dual-chamber bottle with multiple SPFs. They saw value in being able to carry multiple suncreen types in one company package. It is very inconvenient to carry two or three separate bottles. One hundred percent of females and 43 percent of males would also like smaller packaging when going to the beach or sporting events. The lower response rate from males is consistent with the fact that men in general use less suncreen, are less involved in sun care purchases, and often borrow lotion from others.

Most purchasing is "on the go" at supermarkets or convenience stores, as active people enjoy outdoor activities. Since 70 percent of all sun care sales are the result of impulse buying, countertop displays of Blitz will be incorporated in the retailing plan. Zuma SunCare's marketing efforts will concentrate initially on the 15-million college students enrolled in the United States, particularly during summer and spring break vacations (see marketing strategy).

Direct Competitors

Direct competition consists of other manufacturers that sell to our market segment and carry the beach promotional theme. This includes two national brands, Banana Boat (Playtex) and Hawaiian Tropic, as well as several lesser known regional brands (BioTropic, Sunbrella, Malibu Tropic, etc.).

Competitive Factors

Below the top four or five manufacturers, the sun care market is highly fragmented in terms of both product offerings and target markets. Generally, a new firm has three options in which to carve a niche:

Create a superior formulation: This is difficult to achieve. R&D costs are high, development takes a long time, and manufacturers must meet guidelines for FDA over the counter drugs.

Have a "me-too" product at a lower price point: Although it is possible to earn some market share, profits are limited. Retailers and distributors will be less likely to carry the product for similar reasons. They will not see much differentiation between a new brand and the ones they already carry.

A hook. With new packaging or marketing angle, a generic formulation can gain shelf space, as evidenced by successful start-up brands from BioTropic and Sunbrella. Distributors, retailers, and consumers are intrigued by a unique *looking* product since many assume the lotion inside is about the same. This requires minimal capital with little or no R&D costs since all manufacturing and packaging can by outsourced. This is the approach Zuma SunCare will follow.

With the success of Zuma's positioning strategy for Blitz, major competitors may target the 18–35 market in retaliation. However, Schering-Plough will not enter the fray with the total commitment and zeal of Zuma for fear of jeopardizing its appeal to the overall market, securing Blitz's position. Start-up imitators will also not be able to supplant Blitz from its position.

Industry Analysis

Buyer Power

Several factors indicate consumer buyer power: low switching costs, several competitive products, and a trend toward higher retail prices. As prices rise, and as consumers begin to use sunscreen as an everyday product, buyers will become more price sensitive. On the other hand, buyer power is limited since they do not threaten to integrate and they do not always possess full market information. In many cases consumers will buy whatever product is readily available, particularly at resorts and surf shops.

The heaviest buyer power lies with the distributors and retailers. Just like consumers, they have many sun care products from which to choose. Selling the distributors on the unique positioning of the product will be critical to ensure penetration at the retail level. However, retailer interest in sun care products is expected to grow for several reasons:

- Sun care products offer retailers high margins, between 30 percent and 50 percent off list price.
- More retailers are stocking the products during non-summer months, hoping that consumers will purchase before traveling to vacation spots.
- Many retailers are advertising earlier in the season to impress consumers that the products are already available in stores.

Supplier Power

Due to the great number of suppliers for blow-molded plastic bottles, injection molded caps, and labels of comparable quality, they do not possess as much power as individual suppliers. Although fewer in number, there are several contract fillers of sun care formulas as well.

Substitute Products

Direct substitutes include products with sunscreen additives, such as moisturizing lotion, insect repellent, and anti-aging cream. These categories have shown recent growth, although most of these substitutes are aimed at older consumers outside our target segment.

Rivalry among Firms

Although rivalry is substantial, it mainly exists between brands that share common distribution channels. Based on that, the whole market can be subdivided into three segments:

- High-end cosmetics sold in department and drugstores (Clinique, Estee Lauder, Neutragena),
- Mass-market national brands sold in national chain drug and supermarket stores (Coppertone, Hawaiian Tropic, Banana Boat);
- Small independent brand, sold primarily through independent surf shops, beach and ski resorts, and local convenience stores (Body Drench, BioTropic, etc.).

Zuma SunCare will focus on the third segment, earning shelf space at the independent shops and resorts where the strength of the national brands is diminished. The resorts, hotels, and cruise lines are more receptive to carrying new brands because of closer sales relationships and slightly higher retailer margins. These are ideal outlets for Blitz because the consumers are captive, without the opportunity to purchase at a mass-merchandiser.

Macroenvironmental Influences

Demographics

As mentioned above, the target age groups of 15–19 and 20–24 are both expected to rise over the next ten years. Much of this is attributed to the "baby boomlet," or the children of baby boomers who will demand the bulk of the household spending for the rest of the decade (Exhibit 2).

The sun care market is affected more by annual weather than by the business cycle. Although sun exposure is relatively constant, consumers have tended to purchase more in years of warmer temperatures.

Social Trends and Values

Perhaps the strongest factor for this industry's macroenvironment is a general trend toward healthier lifestyle, particularly as consumers value health over vanity. Concern about melanoma, skin cancer, and the harmful effects of the sun's UV rays has risen dramatically. About a million cases of non-melanoma skin cancer are diagnosed each year, equal to all other kinds of cancer combined. Since one in six people can expect to develop skin cancer, the American Academy of Dermatology (AAD) recommends that people use sunscreen with an SPF of 15 or higher on a daily basis. SPFs of 15 and above continue to drive the category, currently accounting for more than 50 percent of sales. Also, the UV Index, which describes the level of UV hitting the ground, will become part of daily weather forecasts, advising people to wear a sunscreen with an SPF of 15. After this index was introduced three years ago in Canada, sunscreen sales increased, and American manufacturers are expecting a similar trend here. The pale look is becoming "in," yet that has not stopped people from enjoying outdoor activities. Due to marketing efforts by the largest manufacturers, people are beginning to think about sunscreen 365 days a year. The popularity of sunless tanning products has already made sun care a year-round category.

Government Regulation

In recent years FDA rulings have actually stimulated the sun care market by allowing manufacturers to use SPF numbering and cancer-prevention claims as marketing tools. In the near future, the FDA Monograph on sunscreens is expected to be modified, which will regulate labeling and product claims. Some of the expected changes include:

- No SPFs greater than 30, since the FDA does not believe that they provide significant added benefit.
- Suncreens would also have to carry a static and water-resistant SPF.
- Must show a Sun Alert Warning stating the damage of the sun's rays on the skin.
- A Tanning Products Warning for products without a sunscreen, stating that fact.
- Any product that claims to inhibit exposure from UV rays and declare an SPF must be regulated as a drug.

Zuma SunCare plans to follow each of these when necessary, even welcoming the change. We predict that stricter labeling rules will weed out competitors that sell low-quality products that claim sun protection yet do not have UV-inhibiting active ingredients. The new regulation will be more of a challenge to makers of cosmetic products with "added sunscreens," which have been stealing a piece of the overall market.

DEVELOPMENT AND PRODUCTION

Production Processes

Zuma SunCare Inc. plans to contract the manufacture of its lotions, bottle caps, and labels. This is the most cost-effective way of entering the market. It avoids upfront capital costs in research and development and manufacturing. It allows Zuma to take advantage of contract manufacturers' expertise and economies of scale in manufacturing these products. Our long-term plan (more than five years into operations) is to bring these steps in-house, beginning with development of new lotion formulas.

Zuma will contract for the manufacture of two-chambered bottles with two openings. The bottles can contain sunscreens of two SPF factors, or a sunscreen and an after-sun product. The sunscreen manufacturer will receive the two-chambered bottles, plus the caps and labels. The manufacturer will fill the bottle, cap the bottle and add the label. The manufacturer will ship the filled bottles to Zuma's warehouse. Then Zuma will send the sunscreen to distributors, brokers, and retailers (Exhibit 3).

We have talked with a contract manufacturer to determine costs. The costs will range from $1.35 for a bottle with sunscreens of SPF4 and 8 to $2.63 for a bottle with sunscreen of SPF 30 and aloe (Exhibit 4).

Resource Requirements

Zuma SunCare Inc. believes that subcontracting production to those companies with the resources to produce sunscreen and the experience in manufacturing sunscreen will be helpful in several ways.

- It will lower capital required. Zuma will not need to spend money to buy or lease land, buildings, and manufacturing equipment.

- It will allow Zuma to focus on its competency, marketing. Companies are increasingly specializing in areas where they excel and subcontracting other parts of their operations. Companies are only concerned with working on areas where they can add value. Zuma is not a manufacturer; it is a marketer. Companies with whom Zuma subcontracts will have expertise in making bottles, caps, labels, and sunscreen.

As Zuma's sales grow and its finances become more stable, Zuma will examine the benefits of bringing product development and production in-house. Doing so would require many new facilities and personnel:

- A laboratory to research and develop new formulas and sunscreens;
- A factory to produce the sunscreen;
- Trained scientists to invest and thoroughly test new sunscreens;
- Experienced manufacturing managers to start, refine, and monitor the production processes;
- Employees to work in the manufacturing plant.

Product Differentiation

The biggest factors differentiating Zuma's product will be its bottle and label. The two-chambered bottle is something no other sunscreen manufacturer offers. It will enhance profit margins and be more convenient for consumers. As discussed in the "Target Market" section, survey results indicate that many consumers carry more than one bottle of sunscreen, for such reasons as wanting varying degrees of sun protection on different body areas, or wanting an after-sun product.

The label will be designed by Zuma's marketing department. We will aim for a unique, flashy label that will grab consumers' attention. It will be designed to appeal to the 15–34 age bracket, not the wide range of consumers most sunscreens target.

Quality

Zuma will ensure quality by carefully selecting contractors. We will choose only firms that have consistently delivered excellent products to small companies in the past. Zuma will diligently monitor the products suppliers deliver, and randomly test them to confirm that the products meet the standards specified.

MARKETING

Overall Concept and Orientation

Blitz will combine tanning safety with a fun-youthful, high-energy, and stylish image. The "MTV Generation" of 15-to-24-year-olds use sun care products on special occasions, either at the local beach or on a spring break vacation. For them, getting a safe tan is important, yet they do not want to feel they need a medicinal product to do so. Brand image particularly influences their purchase intentions, even more so than product efficacy claims. Blitz will appeal to these attitudes with high-impact, fresh graphics, radical promotional images, and sponsorship of popular events such as volleyball tournaments, swimwear contests, and outdoor concerts.

Marketing Strategy

Based on preliminary market research, we view the young adults to be an untapped segment in the sun care industry. Based on the competitive map in Figure 1, most products appeal to a slightly older crowd of 30-to-44-year-olds, predominated by female users. Zuma SunCare will aim for the hole in this map of 18-to-24-year-olds with a stronger appeal toward male users. The secondary target group will be males and females flanking this age group, down to 15-year-olds and up through 34-year-olds.

Communication of the Image

The critical elements and costs required to execute the marketing plan are outlined in Table 1, followed by detailed descriptions of each. (Other annual costs are included in Exhibits 5, 6, and 10.)

Packaging

Beyond the image of the Blitz brand, Zuma SunCare will appeal to another consumer need—convenience. This will be accomplished with a unique dual-chamber bottle that allows users to carry a high and low SPF in one package. Our consumer research has indicated a strong tendency to use multiple SPFs, such as SPF 8 or 15 on the body and SPF 30 on the face. A combined sunscreen and after-sun aloe vera gel will also be available (see Exhibit 4 for product line). All of the sunscreens will be PABA free, waterproof, and moisturizing.

Advertising

Zuma SunCare will communicate Blitz's cool image with a three-pronged advertising strategy:

- *Print advertising*: Bold images and attention-getting slogans (i.e., "Hey, don't get fried, Get Blitzed!") will be used in ads placed in college newspapers, youth-oriented magazines (*Wired*, *Spin*, etc.), and alternative urban newspapers.

FIGURE 1 Demographic Map of Competing Brands

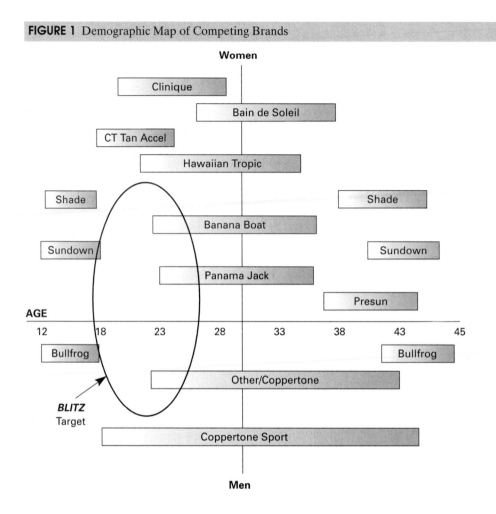

- *Radio spots*: Initially with low-cost college radio stations and stations in "spring break" locales.
- *Billboards*: Initial use will be bus billboards.

Promotions and Sponsorship

Once Blitz establishes sufficient brand recognition, Zuma SunCare will sponsor local volleyball tournaments and other beach-oriented events. Free samples will also be important to induce early trial and raise brand awareness. These promotions will occur at college campuses, spring break parties, and sponsored events. Other sales promotions directed at retailers will include point-of-purchase countertop displays and discounted initial orders to earn shelf space.

Zuma SunCare will aggressively market the Blitz brand at industry trade shows. The purpose is not only to expand brand exposure but to line up key distributors, brokers, and retailers.

	TABLE 1 **Summary of Marketing Costs**					
	Year 0 *(Market test)*	*Year 1*	*Year 2*	*Year 3*	*Year 4*	*Year 5*
Package design	15,000					
Logo and art work	10,000					
Advertising development	75,000					
Other R&D	20,000					
Media spending						
Television	0	0	524,333	545,307	562,432	584,929
Radio	5,000	100,833	104,867	109,061	112,486	116,986
Print	7,000	25,208	26,217	27,265	28,122	29,246
Billboard	8,000	25,208	26,217	27,265	28,122	29,246
Trade shows	0	50,000	52,000	56,243	63,266	74,012
Promotion						
Sponsorships	0	75,000	78,000	84,365	94,899	111,018
In-store promos	0	35,500	36,920	39,933	44,919	52,549
Free samples	5,000	5,000	5,200	5,624	6,327	7,401

Pricing Strategy

An 8-ounce, dual chamber bottle of Blitz SPF 15/30 will retail for $8.95. This price point is high enough to reflect the quality ingredients and provide a significant profit, yet slightly lower than competitive brands in order to meet the target market's need for value. Lower SPF products will have a slightly lower price due to the lower cost of the active sunscreen ingredient, which is typically the highest cost item per ounce. Single application packets will cost $1.25 for 0.75 ounces.

Distribution

In order to maximize penetration in retail channels, Zuma SunCare will need to established strong relationships with distribution partners. This will be done in three ways:

- *Health and beauty aid distributors/wholesalers*: their margin ranges from 5 to 15 percent depending on the level of extra services they provide to retailers. Retailers earn between 40 percent and 50 percent of the retail price.
- *Sales brokers* will act as Zuma SunCare's agents, selling to smaller surf shops and resort stores. They will make additional sales to distributors as well. Commissions range from 5 percent to 7 percent.
- *Direct sales* calls made by Zuma's owners: These efforts will concentrate on resorts and surf shops in vacation spots throughout Florida and Mexico. Additionally, the owners will begin to establish contractual agreements with beach resorts, ski resorts, cruise lines, and collegiate football stadiums to become preferred suppliers of sun care products with direct sale, discounted price. These arrangements may allow dual branding of the product with each venue, such as "Club Med Sunscreen, *from the makers of Blitz.*" The single-application packets show particular promise for concession sales at warm weather football stadiums.

Based on the above estimates, average revenue is calculated as a 55 percent margin of total retail dollar sales.

Marketing Time Line

Concept Testing

During the first year Zuma SunCare will conduct concept tests in a representative market in order to finalize the details of product form, pricing, advertising, and distribution. Two to three variations of the product will be shown to consumers, each with a different mix of product ingredients (moisturizers, fragrances, etc.) and label graphics. We will also test different advertising mock-ups to determine which elicits the best consumer response. Estimated cost of this testing period is $172,000. During this time the founders will establish relationships with distributors of health and beauty items, as well as brokers specializing in sales to independent retailers.

Market Testing

Once the product concept is finalized, production will ramp up for sales to a specific region selected as a representative sample of our total market (i.e., Gainesville, Florida). We will launch an intense promotional campaign of local radio advertising, print media in youth-oriented magazines, and moving billboard (bus) advertising. Direct sales efforts will be made to retailers within this test market, particularly hotels, resorts, surf shops, party stores, and convenience stores. The purpose of the market testing is to forecast future sales, fine-tune promotional strategy, and strengthen our distribution network.

Full-Scale Production

If the market test indicates that Blitz will reach a target 2 percent share of the Gainesville young adult market, Zuma SunCare will initiate full-scale marketing and production. Zuma will attempt to maximize market share as early as possible with intense media and trade promotions. Once a foothold is achieved, this strong marketing effort will continue in order to defend against competitive threats.

Although the long-term goal is to achieve national distribution, Blitz will initially be launched in the coastal resort communities in California and Florida. Subsequent regions (every 6 to 8 months) will be added, including Cancun, Mexico, Texas, South Carolina, and the southeastern seaboard. In addition to these regional targets, marketing promotions will continue at major universities throughout the country, anticipating student travel to our target regions.

Sales Forecasts

Based on the market-potential/sales-requirement (MP/SR) method, estimated sales for the first full year of production (after the concept and market tests) are $3.76 million. Beginning with the market potential technique, sales were forecasted with the following assumptions:

- The target market of 15–34-year-olds has a population of 77.2 million; of those people 28.9 million are regular users of sun care products (Exhibit 2).
- Average retail dollars spent per person is $11.00 annually, which was calculated by dividing total retail market over total sun care users. This amount averages those that buy more and those that buy less.

- Total dollar market of the segment is therefore $318 million.
- Successful independent sun care start-ups have been able to achieve 1 to 2 percent of the *total* $620 million retail market.
- With concentrated marketing efforts to the youth segment, Zuma SunCare could expect to earn 1.1 percent of the overall segment or 2.15 percent of the young adult segment.
- 2.15 percent × $318 = $6.84 million retail, 1.1 percent × $620 = $6.20 million.
- With an average gross margin of 55 percent of retail, this translates into company revenues of **$3.76 million**.

With the sales requirement technique, the break-even point for the first year of full production is 330,547 bottles of lotion. This requires a 0.45 percent share of the overall retail market, which is feasible with Zuma SunCare's strong marketing push.

Detailed sales forecasts appear in Exhibits 8–10. Monthly sales for the first year are adjusted to account for seasonality, with more shipments expected in the early spring and summer months.

FINANCIAL PLANS

Financial Statements

Projected profit and loss statements for Zuma SunCare appear in Exhibits 8–10. The statements report monthly data for the first year of full operations, 1997, quarterly data for the first three years and annual data for the first five years. Sales for the first year average 67,943 bottles per month over the period. Because sales of suntan lotion is subject to seasonal trends, the number of bottles sold in each month is multiplied by a seasonality factor (see Exhibit 7). Over the first year of production, sales are projected to grow by 5 percent each month, and net income is projected to be $779,007. Sales grow in the following four years by 30 percent, 35 percent, 30 percent and 20 percent, respectively, and net income grows to $2,799,612.

Quarterly balance sheets for the first three years of full operations, and annual balance sheets for the first five years, appear in Exhibits 13–14. The growth in sales of Blitz leads to a growth in Zuma SunCare's assets from $1,095,538 at the end of year one, to 7,989,813 at the end of year five. Accounts payable are assumed to be paid on a net 90-day basis. All sales are made through accounts receivable, and allowance for doubtful accounts is 5 percent. Accounts receivable will also be paid on a net 90-day basis, insuring that Zuma will have adequate working capital.

Statement of Cash Flows for Zuma appear in Exhibits 11–12 on a quarterly basis for the first three years, and on an annual basis for the first five years. Due to the contracting out of manufacturing and bottling, Zuma makes no cash investment in property, plant and equipment. Accumulated depreciation pertains to office equipment and computers purchased in 1996. Zuma will receive its third and final cash infusion from investors just prior to the beginning of operations in 1997. Consequently, the Statement of Cash Flows show no cash from financing activities, and a beginning cash balance of $200,000. The founders of Zuma project a growth in cash flow from operations from $770,926 in 1997 to $2,723,325 in 2001.

Financial Resources

Zuma's start up costs appear in Exhibits 5–6. The concept test will require approximately $172,700, of which $30,000 will come from the owner's initial investment, leaving a need for $142,700 in outside funding. Because Blitz's image is the key to its success, much of these funds, $50,000, will be needed for advertising development. The rest of the funds will go towards the basics of conducting the test, the majority being earmarked for salary and living expenses. Zuma is contracting out all manufacturing and bottling, so other than the cost of desks and computers, no funds will be needed for physical equipment.

The market test will require an additional $172,700, which will be comprised of another $30,000 investment from the founders, and $142,700 in outside funding. The primary use of these funds will be for salary and living expenses, and the remainder used to conduct the test. Just prior to the beginning of full operations in 1997, a final infusion of $200,000 in outside resources will be required to fund initial production and marketing costs. Following this last infusion, the business will be funded internally from operations. The total outside funds required will be $485,400.

The incurred debt will require interest payment of 15 percent paid at the end of each fiscal year, beginning in 1997. At the end of Zuma's third full year of operations, investors will have the option of converting the debt to an equity ownership position equaling 20 percent of the company's outstanding shares. Should investors choose not to convert, Zuma will have the right to call the loan, and repay the debt in full. The entries in the income statement, statement of cash flows, and balance sheet reflect the scenario of Zuma repaying the loan in full at the end of the third year.

Financial Strategy

After the final installment of funds from its investors, Zuma will be able to fund all necessary expenditures out of cash flow from operations. At the end of its fifth year of full operations, Zuma will tender an initial public offering. At that time, we will examine ways to use that money to help Zuma grow, such as purchasing a competitor and achieving economies of scale, or vertically integrating by beginning our own manufacturing and bottling operations.

MANAGEMENT AND ORGANIZATION

Key Personnel Resources

Zuma SunCare's four founders will take crucial roles within the company. They have varied backgrounds and skills which will allow Zuma to function well as a firm.

Tom Kinney, the company's President and CEO, has extensive knowledge and contacts in the Professional Beach Volleyball tour. He grew up playing volleyball on the beaches of Southern California. Mr. Kinney understands and can anticipate consumers' needs in the area of sun and beach products.

Eric Olson, the company's Vice President of Finance, was previously an Officer in the United States Marine Corps. While in the service, he developed numerous leadership and communications skills, a keen ability to plan and coordinate the actions of others, and an acute sense of attention to detail. This experience enables him to view the business from a strategic angle with long-term growth as an objective. Other experience includes a position with the Internal Audit department of a Fortune 500 firm. Specific projects included capital projects audits, bench marking studies, and due diligence analysis. Furthermore, Mr. Olson has extensive experience creating and refining complex financial models that allow accurate sensitivity and scenario analysis in dynamic circumstances.

Pat Dunne, the company's vice president of marketing, has five years' experience in product design and marketing communications. He has extensive project management experience at a multimillion dollar entrepreneurial firm that specialized in custom trade show programs and displays. Mr. Dunne's responsibilities included helping clients position their products in the marketplace, plan and design their displays, and effectively market those products.

Kurt Moeller, the company's vice president of production, has experience working in just-in-time manufacturing environments. He has identified and maximized opportunities in new areas for previous employers. Mr. Moeller can quickly learn about new topics and pinpoint the most important questions.

The founders will receive salaries of $40,000 per year, payable in equal, biweekly checks.

Zuma's founders will have significant ownership stakes in the company. Their shares in the company will provide incentive for them to continue working toward Zuma's success. However, the founders will have to forfeit all of their shares if they leave the company before it has completed three years of operations. Founders will have to relinquish 8,000 shares if they leave the company during its fourth year of operations. They will have to forfeit 4,000 shares if they leave the company during its fifth year of operations.

Founders will sign noncompete contracts with Zuma. They will be prohibited from working for another sun care products company during the first five years Zuma conducts operations and for 12 months after they leave Zuma.

Human Resource Management Strategy

Zuma will have few employees. The founders will have the vast majority of responsibility for such tasks as marketing, distributor and manufacturer relations, and financial controls and performance measures. Zuma's main need will be for employees to take orders, serve customers, and help coordinate logistics between Zuma, its suppliers, and its distributors.

Zuma will not incur future liabilities on behalf of its employees. The company will not sponsor a defined-benefit or a defined-contribution pension plan. Zuma will try to pool with other small businesses and receive discounted health insurance rates.

Zuma does not anticipate that any employees will be covered by a collective bargaining agreement.

OWNERSHIP

Form of Business

Zuma Inc. will be formed as a limited liability corporation (LLC). Nearly every state in the United States permits LLCs. These allow corporate profits to be passed to owners as dividends, without being taxed twice. LLCs limit investors' liability to only the money they have put into the company. They do not have restrictions on investors in the company, such as a maximum of 35 investors and no foreign owners, that "S" corporations have.

Equity Positions

Zuma Inc. will begin with 100,000 shares. Each founder will own 20,000 shares. The remaining 20,000 shares will be reserved for investors who can convert their debt into equity.

Founders will have the first right to purchase shares sold by other founders. Founders will also be able to vote the shares of any founder who has relinquished his shares, which have been returned to the corporate treasury.

Deal Structure

Each founder will make an initial investment of $15,000 in cash, plus $5,000 in physical capital. That investment will purchase 20,000 shares apiece.

Zuma plans to raise the rest of the money Zuma needs by issuing debt which can be converted into equity. We recognize that start-up ventures are risky, and investors need appropriate assurances and rewards to compensate for those risks. By holding debt, investors will have first claim on the firm's cash flow. But the debt's convertibility will allow investors to enjoy great rewards if Zuma succeeds.

Zuma will ask investors for money at three points. Zuma wants to minimize losses that founders and other investors might suffer if Zuma is unsuccessful. Zuma will conduct two separate tests to be as certain as possible that Blitz Sun Tan Lotion will be a success. We will ask for funding to conduct a concept test, and we will ask for additional funding if a concept test is successful and if a market test is successful.

Zuma's founders will invest $30,000 in cash before the first test, the concept test. Zuma will ask outside investors for $142,700 before the concept test. This test is designed to determine formulation, packaging, and advertising likely to appeal to Zuma's largest market. It will begin in October 1996 (See Exhibit 5 for more details).

Zuma's founders will invest $30,000 in cash before beginning the second test, the market test. Zuma will ask outside investors for an additional $142,700. This test will occur only if the concept test is successful. The market test will begin in February 1997, in a limited market representing a microcosm of Zuma's eventual national market. This test is expected to help Zuma develop distribution channels and refine and implement its marketing strategy. (See Exhibit 6 for more details.)

If both tests are successful, Zuma will ask outside investors for $200,000. That money will be used to fund the beginning of operations. Those will begin in October 1997.

Investors will receive quarterly interest payments, starting in the first quarter Zuma begins nationwide operations. These payments will be at an annual interest rate of 15 percent per year. During the first 30 days of fiscal year 2000 (Zuma's fourth full year of operations), investors will have the option of converting their debt into equity. Their ownership stake will be worth 20 percent of the company. If the outside investors choose not to convert their debt into equity, Zuma will have the option of converting the debt to equity and buying out investors by paying them the value of their equity.

Zuma hopes to obtain all venture capital funding from the same source and to line up commitments for that funding before beginning the concept test. That will allow Zuma's founders to focus their efforts on successfully developing and marketing Blitz SunTan Lotion, instead of needing to devote their time and efforts to raising more capital.

Zuma realizes that the investment in the concept test is the riskiest. But since Zuma is receiving all its funding from the same source, Zuma will pay investors the same interest rate and allow them to convert their principal to equity.

Summary of Funds Needed

Date	Amount	Use	Int. rate
Sept. 1996	$142,000	Concept test	15%
Feb. 1997	$142,700	Market test	15%
Sept. 1997	$200,000	Nationwide launch	15%

Value of the Company ($000s)

	1997	1998	1999	2000	2001
Revenues	3,759	5,082	7,136	9,648	11,577
Net Income	779	791	1,400	2,235	2,800
P/E ratio	22	22	22	22	22
Total value of equity	17,138	17,402	30,800	49,170	61,600
Value of equity offered				6,160	

Zuma has valued itself at a P/E ratio of 22. This is the value the stock market has typically assigned comparable consumer products companies: Schering-Plough, Johnson & Johnson, and Proctor & Gamble. These companies are more stable and have a long track record of consistent growth. However, Zuma's small size the entrepreneurial culture will give it the ability to grow more quickly than those large companies, which already sell many products over large geographical areas.

POTENTIAL RETURNS TO INVESTORS ($000s)

If conversion occurs:

	Year 0	Year 1	Year 2	Year 3	Year 4	Year 5
Investment	(485.4)					
Interest		72.8	72.8	72.8		
Equity received				6,160		
% of equity owned				20%		
Value of company				30,800	49,170	61,600
Terminal value						12,320

If conversion does not occur:

	Year 0	Year 1	Year 2	Year 3	Year 4	Year 5
Investment	(485.4)					
Interest		72.8	72.8	72.8	72.8	72.8
Principal						485.4

Corporate Governance

Zuma will have a nine-person board of directors. Each founder will sit on the board. Entrepreneurs with experience in consumer product development and marketing will be asked to sit on the board; Zuma hopes to find two such entrepreneurs. The remaining three directors will be chosen by investors. Investors from each of the three issues of convertible debt will choose one director.

Each share of stock will be worth one vote. Convertible debt offering will allow outside investors one vote for every two shares of stock they would hold if they converted their debt into equity.

Zuma plans to obtain legal, accounting, and promotional services from companies with experience helping entrepreneurial firms grow quickly.

CRITICAL RISKS AND CONTINGENCIES

Any new business venture poses significant risks to investors. There can be no guarantee that investors will receive the principal they have invested. Below are some of the larger risks which will face Zuma SunCare Inc.

Failure to Produce the Product as Required

This could result from the inability of Zuma to reach of viable agreement with manufacturers of bottles, caps, labels, or sunscreen. This could also arise from the inability of the manufacturer to deliver a suitable product or to refund Zuma's payments once an agreement is reached.

Failure to Meet Production Deadlines

If products are not produced or shipped quickly enough, Zuma could miss the peak selling season for sunscreen. This could also hurt Zuma's efforts to coordinate its marketing for Blitz SunTan Lotion with the product's introduction; customers could seek the brand but be unable to buy it. This would give competitors a greater chance to imitate Zuma's plans and build the awareness of their brands.

Inability to Convince Distributors and Retailers to Carry the Product

Manufacturers introduce many new products, only a small fraction of which succeed. Zuma will have to persuade distributors to haul an unproven product from a new company. Zuma will also have to convince retailers to use their finite shelf space to stock Blitz SunTan Lotion.

As mentioned earlier, Zuma will do several things to persuade distributors to carry its products. We will give distributors, brokers, and retailers a full refund for any products unsold after four months. Zuma will offer its middlemen a similar margin as other leading regional sunscreens. However, Zuma will still be able to retail for about 20 percent less than those brands. Zuma will stress the benefits of having a sun care product targeted to a specific age group which frequently spends time in the sun.

Failure of the Market to Embrace the Product

Simply put, Blitz SunTan Lotion may not appeal to the consuming public. Or it may appeal to the public, but it may not be appealing enough to convince consumers to buy the product. This would result in lower revenues, because of lower prices per unit and/or lower unit sales. The subsequent revenue decrease could result in Zuma being unprofitable and unable to repay its investors.

Difficulty Raising Additional Financing

Zuma has to raise funds three times. By doing this, Zuma hopes to prevent investors from unnecessarily risking capital. However, this could cause Zuma to not have enough funding to launch its products nationwide, even if both preliminary tests are successful. That would leave Zuma unable to fully recover its investors' initial investments.

A Large Sun Care Product Manufacturer Invading Zuma's Niche

One of the large sunscreen manufacturers may see what Zuma is doing and try to copy it. Zuma will trademark its name, logos, and advertising tag lines. But Zuma's product and two-chambered bottle will not enjoy patent protection. A larger competitor would have the ability to do more product promotions and advertising. It could sustain deeper short-term losses than could Zuma and try to underprice Zuma.

Zuma will combat this in several ways. In the contract with our bottle manufacturer, we will prohibit that company from selling two-chambered bottles for use by other sun care product manufacturers. We will also suggest that Zuma's retail price be about 20 percent below the retail price of our nearest competitors, other regional sunscreen makers. Those companies will have larger overhead and advertising budgets, which should deter self-destructive price competition.

Management Is Unproven

This is the first entrepreneurial venture Zuma's managers will have launched. There will be setbacks and challenges which may surprise Zuma's founders. Zuma's founders may be at a disadvantage with potential suppliers and customers because of their inexperience.

This quartet has also not worked together extensively as a team. The founders could discover that they do not function as a cohesive group when working together on a daily basis.

SUMMARY AND CONCLUSIONS

Zuma SunCare Inc. is a focused firm which can provide added value to sunscreen users and a significant return to investors. Zuma's unique two-chambered bottle concept enables consumers to conveniently carry and use varying levels of sunscreen protection. Furthermore, Zuma plans to combine sunscreen protection along with an after-sun moisturizing product, providing further value and convenience. Zuma will aim its marketing at a niche targeted only lightly by major sunscreen manufacturers: the 15–34 age group. Sunscreens sold by most competitors appear to have little appeal to people in this age group, who frequently enjoy the sun.

Zuma will minimize capital costs by subcontracting research, development, and production of its Blitz SunTan Lotion. This will enable Zuma to concentrate on its area of expertise: marketing. The firm's President and CEO understands sunscreen consumers, in part because he grew up playing volleyball on the beaches of Southern California. Another founder has extensive experience designing and creating companies' marketing and displays at trade shows.

While marketing costs in this industry are high, Zuma will still be able to have substantial margins. Because Zuma is not capital-intensive, owners will be able to make a large return on their investment. By the end of year five, Zuma projects sales of $11.6 million (2.5% of the marketplace) and after-tax profits of about $2.80 million. Zuma plans to allow outside investors to buy a 20 percent ownership stake. Zuma will divide the remaining shares equally among the four founders.

SCHEDULING AND MILESTONES

Before Sept. 1996	Make founders' investments into company
	Incorporate company
	Obtain accountant, legal counsel
During or before Sept. 1996	Acquire initial financing
Oct. 1996	Begin concept test
During or before Jan. 1997	Obtain second round of financing
Jan. 1997	Reach agreements with subcontractors to begin producing Zuma
Feb. 1997	Begin market test
During or before Sept. 1997	Obtain third round of financing
Oct. 1997	Begin nationwide launch of product
During or before Dec. 1997	Reach agreements with manufacturing subcontractors
	Reach agreements with brokers, distributors, retailers
Dec. 1997	Begin repaying investors' debts
During or before Jan. 1997	Make first sales
	Receive initial cash from sales

EXHIBIT 1 The Sun Care Market					
	1991	*1992*	*1993*	*1994*	*1995*
(in millions) Retail Market Share	$500	$520	$593	$600	$630

Retail Market Share–Suntan Products

	1994
Schering-Plough	33%
Banana Boat	11%
Hawaiian Tropic	10%
Bain de Soleil	9%
Vaseline IC	6%
Others	31%
Total	100%

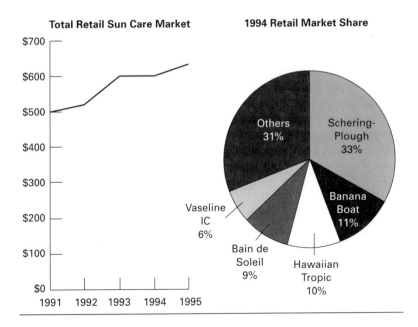

EXHIBIT 2 **Population Trends**

Age Group	1994	1999	2005	% Regular Users
15–19	17.6	19.6	21.0	34.8%
20–24	18.4	17.7	19.8	38.3%
25–29	19.1	18.3	18.1	38.0%
30–34	22.1	19.8	18.4	38.3%
Total 15–34	77.2	75.4	77.3	
Total U.S.	260.2	272.5	286.3	33.0%

Source: Dept of Commerce, Population Series, p. 25.

Age Group	(in millions)
15–19	6.1
20–24	7.0
25–29	7.3
30–34	8.5
Total User Base	**28.9**
Average Annual Retail $ spent	$ 11.00
Estimated Young Adult Segment ($ retail)	**$318**

Population Trends by Age Group

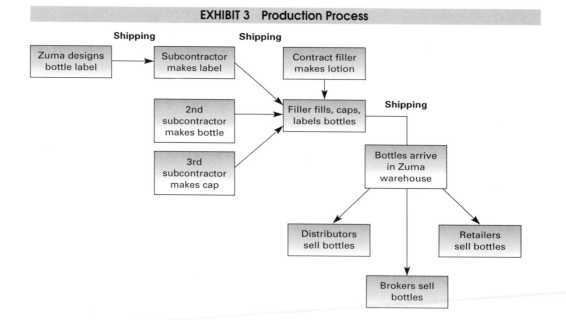

EXHIBIT 3 **Production Process**

EXHIBIT 4 Initial Sales and Costs Forecasts

Sales and Costs Estimate by Category
Based on Estimated Average Monthly Sales in the First Year

Cost per ounce	SPF4	SPF8	SPF15	SPF30	Aloe Vera Gel
Active ingredient	$0.05	$0.08	$0.16	$0.25	$0.25
Inactive ingredients	$0.05	$0.05	$0.05	$0.05	$0.00
Bottle	$0.20	$0.20	$0.20	$0.20	$0.20
Caps	$0.15	$0.15	$0.15	$0.15	$0.15
Label	$0.08	$0.08	$0.08	$0.08	$0.08
Cost per 8 oz. Bottle	1.23	1.47	2.11	2.83	2.43

Per unit Cost for Bottle Sold

Costs per bottle	SPF4 & SPF8	SPF4 & SPF15	SPF8 & SPF15	SPF8 & SPF30	SPF15 & SPF30	SPF4 & Aloe	SPF8 & Aloe	SPF15 & Aloe	SPF30 & Aloe
Active ingredients	$0.52	$0.84	$0.96	$1.32	$1.64	$1.20	$1.32	$1.64	$2.00
Inactive ingredients	$0.40	$0.40	$0.40	$0.40	$0.40	$0.20	$0.20	$0.20	$0.20
Bottle	$0.20	$0.20	$0.20	$0.20	$0.20	$0.20	$0.20	$0.20	$0.20
Caps	$0.15	$0.15	$0.15	$0.15	$0.15	$0.15	$0.15	$0.15	$0.15
Label	$0.08	$0.08	$0.08	$0.08	$0.08	$0.08	$0.08	$0.08	$0.08
Total unit costs	$1.35	$1.67	$1.79	$2.15	$2.47	$1.83	$1.95	$2.27	$2.63
Estimated unit sales amount	2000	2500	6900	6700	6700	4000	12500	13500	9500
Estimated retail price	$7.25	$7.49	$7.95	$8.49	$8.95	$7.49	$7.95	$8.49	$9.49
Estimated unit sales price	$3.99	$4.12	$4.37	$4.67	$4.92	$4.12	$4.37	$4.67	$5.22
Margin per bottle	$2.64	$2.45	$2.58	$2.52	$2.45	$2.29	$2.42	$2.40	$2.59

Total number of sales	64300
Weighted average retail price	$8.38
Weighted average sales price	$4.61
Weighted average cost	$2.14
Weighted average profit per bottle	$2.47

EXHIBIT 5 Concept Test Funding Requirements

Additional Funds Needed
Year 0 Concept Test
In Months 1–5

Use of funds:	
Production & start-up expenses	$10,000
Research & development	$15,000
Package design	$10,000
Bottle mold	$10,000
Market research expenses	$5,000
Travel expenses	$5,000
Advertising development	$50,000
Logo & artwork development	$10,000
Legal fees	$2,000
Salary and wages	$40,000
Total	$157,000
Plus contingency	$15,700
Total funds needed	$172,700
Founder's initial investment	$30,000
Total outside funding required	$142,700

EXHIBIT 6 Market Test Funding Required

Year 0
Additional Funds Required
Market Test In Months 6–12

Use of funds:	
Product production	$10,000
Package design	$5,000
Research & development	$5,000
Travel expenses	$10,000
Advertising development	$25,000
Media expense	$20,000
Legal fees	$2,000
Salary and wages	$80,000
Total	$157,000
Plus contingency	$15,700
Total funds needed	$172,700
Founder's additional investment	$30,000
Total outside funding required	$142,700

EXHIBIT 7 Seasonality Market Trends*

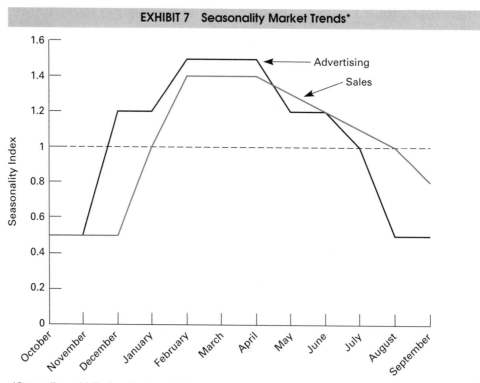

*Seasonality multiplier baseline is equal to 1.

EXHIBIT 8 Monthly Sales for Year 1997

	October	November	December	January	February	March	April	May	June	July	August	September
Number of bottles sold	32,150	33,758	33,758	67,515	94,521	94,521	94,521	87,770	81,018	74,267	67,515	54,012
Number of cases sold	1,340	1,407	1,407	2,813	3,938	3,938	3,938	3,657	3,376	3,094	2,813	2,251
Revenues												
Sales	$148,234	$155,646	$155,646	$311,292	$435,808	$435,808	$435,808	$404,679	$373,550	$342,421	$311,292	$249,033
Cost of goods sold	$68,753	$72,190	$72,190	$144,380	$202,132	$202,132	$202,132	$187,694	$173,256	$158,818	$144,380	$115,504
Gross profit	$79,482	$83,456	$83,456	$166,911	$233,676	$233,676	$233,676	$216,985	$200,294	$183,602	$166,911	$133,529
Operating expenses												
Interest expense	$7,665	$7,700	$7,700	$8,421	$8,999	$8,999	$8,999	$8,855	$8,710	$8,566	$8,421	$8,133
Rent	$833	$833	$833	$833	$833	$833	$833	$833	$833	$833	$833	$833
Utilities	$417	$417	$417	$417	$417	$417	$417	$417	$417	$417	$417	$417
Salary	$13,333	$13,333	$13,333	$13,333	$13,333	$13,333	$13,333	$13,333	$13,333	$13,333	$13,333	$13,333
Wages	$1,600	$1,600	$1,600	$1,600	$1,600	$1,600	$1,600	$1,600	$1,600	$1,600	$1,600	$1,600
Broker expense	$2,965	$3,113	$3,113	$6,226	$8,716	$8,716	$8,716	$8,094	$7,471	$6,848	$6,226	$4,981
Travel and entertainment	$3,333	$3,333	$3,333	$3,333	$3,333	$3,333	$3,333	$3,333	$3,333	$3,333	$3,333	$3,333
Shipping costs	$5,000	$5,000	$5,000	$5,000	$5,000	$5,000	$5,000	$5,000	$5,000	$5,000	$5,000	$5,000
Depreciation	$333	$333	$333	$333	$333	$333	$333	$333	$333	$333	$333	$333
Advertising												
Television advertising	$0	$0	$0	$0	$0	$0	$0	$0	$0	$0	$0	$0
Radio advertising	$4,167	$4,167	$10,000	$10,000	$12,500	$12,500	$12,500	$10,000	$10,000	$8,333	$3,333	$3,333
Print advertising	$1,042	$1,042	$2,500	$2,500	$3,125	$3,125	$3,125	$2,500	$2,500	$2,083	$833	$833
Billboard advertising	$1,042	$1,042	$2,500	$2,500	$3,125	$3,125	$3,125	$2,500	$2,500	$2,083	$833	$833
Promotions												
Sponsorships	$3,125	$3,125	$7,500	$7,500	$9,375	$9,375	$9,375	$7,500	$7,500	$6,250	$2,500	$2,500
In-store promos	$1,479	$1,479	$3,550	$3,550	$4,438	$4,438	$4,438	$3,550	$3,550	$2,958	$1,183	$1,183
Free samples	$208	$208	$500	$500	$625	$625	$625	$500	$500	$417	$167	$167
Trade shows	$2,083	$2,083	$5,000	$5,000	$6,250	$6,250	$6,250	$5,000	$5,000	$4,167	$1,667	$1,667
Office supplies	$292	$292	$292	$292	$292	$292	$292	$292	$292	$292	$292	$292
Insurance	$500	$500	$500	$500	$500	$500	$500	$500	$500	$500	$500	$500
Miscellaneous expenses	$1,250	$1,250	$1,250	$1,250	$1,250	$1,250	$1,250	$1,250	$1,250	$1,250	$1,250	$1,250
Total operating expenses	$50,667	$50,850	$69,254	$73,089	$84,044	$84,044	$84,044	$75,390	$74,623	$68,598	$52,056	$50,522
Income before tax	$28,814	$32,606	$14,202	$93,822	$149,632	$149,632	$149,632	$141,595	$125,671	$115,005	$114,856	$83,007
Taxes	$10,085	$11,412	$4,971	$32,838	$52,371	$52,371	$52,371	$49,558	$43,985	$40,252	$40,200	$29,053
Net income	$18,729	$21,194	$9,231	$60,985	$97,261	$97,261	$97,261	$92,037	$81,686	$74,753	$74,656	$53,955
Break-even volume (bottles)	20,495	20,569	28,013	29,564	33,996	33,996	33,996	30,495	30,185	27,747	21,056	20,436
Excess volume sold (bottles)	11,655	13,189	5,744	37,951	60,525	60,525	60,525	57,275	50,833	46,519	46,459	33,576

EXHIBIT 9   Quarterly Sales for 3 Years

	1997				1998				1,059,921 1999			
	Q1	Q2	Q3	Q4	Q1	Q2	Q3	Q4	Q1	Q2	Q3	Q4
Number of bottles sold	99,665	256,557	263,309	195,794	129,565	333,524	342,301	254,532	174,912	450,258	462,106	343,618
Number of cases sold	4,153	10,690	10,971	8,158	5,399	13,897	14,263	10,605	7,288	18,761	19,254	14,317
Revenues												
Sales	$459,526	$1,182,908	$1,214,037	$902,746	$621,279	$1,599,292	$1,641,378	$1,220,512	$872,275	$2,245,405	$2,304,495	$1,713,599
Cost of goods sold	$213,133	$548,645	$563,083	$418,703	$288,155	$741,768	$761,288	$566,086	$404,570	$1,041,442	$1,068,849	$794,785
Gross profit	$246,393	$634,263	$650,954	$484,043	$333,123	$857,524	$880,090	$654,426	$467,705	$1,203,963	$1,235,646	$918,814
Operating expenses												
Interest expense	$23,064	$23,820	$25,120	$26,419	$29,578	$43,186	$43,772	$37,915	$33,070	$52,176	$52,998	$44,776
Rent	$2,500	$2,500	$2,500	$2,500	$2,600	$2,600	$2,600	$2,600	$2,704	$2,704	$2,704	$2,704
Utilities	$1,250	$1,250	$1,250	$1,250	$1,300	$1,300	$1,300	$1,300	$1,352	$1,352	$1,352	$1,352
Salary	$40,000	$40,000	$40,000	$40,000	$41,600	$41,600	$41,600	$41,600	$43,264	$43,264	$43,264	$43,264
Wages	$4,800	$4,800	$4,800	$4,800	$14,976	$14,976	$14,976	$14,976	$26,997	$26,997	$26,997	$26,997
Broker expense	$9,191	$23,658	$24,281	$18,055	$12,426	$31,986	$32,828	$24,410	$17,446	$44,908	$46,090	$34,272
Travel and entertainment	$10,000	$10,000	$10,000	$10,000	$10,400	$10,400	$10,400	$10,400	$10,816	$10,816	$10,816	$10,816
Shipping costs	$15,000	$15,000	$15,000	$15,000	$20,800	$20,800	$20,800	$20,800	$21,632	$21,632	$21,632	$21,632
Depreciation	$1,000	$1,000	$1,000	$1,000	$1,000	$1,000	$1,000	$1,000	$1,000	$1,000	$1,000	$1,000
Advertising												
Television advertising	$0	$0	$0	$0	$95,333	$182,000	$169,000	$78,000	$99,147	$189,280	$175,760	$81,120
Radio advertising	$18,333	$35,000	$32,500	$15,000	$19,067	$36,400	$33,800	$15,600	$19,829	$37,856	$35,152	$16,224
Print advertising	$4,583	$8,750	$8,125	$3,750	$4,767	$9,100	$8,450	$3,900	$4,957	$9,464	$8,788	$4,056
Billboard advertising	$4,583	$8,750	$8,125	$3,750	$4,767	$9,100	$8,450	$3,900	$4,957	$9,464	$8,788	$4,056
Promotions												
Sponsorships	$13,750	$26,250	$24,375	$11,250	$14,300	$27,300	$25,350	$11,700	$14,872	$28,392	$26,364	$12,168
In-store promos	$6,508	$12,425	$11,538	$5,325	$6,769	$12,922	$11,999	$5,538	$7,039	$13,439	$12,479	$5,760
Free samples	$917	$1,750	$1,625	$750	$953	$1,820	$1,690	$780	$991	$1,893	$1,758	$811
Trade shows	$9,167	$17,500	$16,250	$7,500	$9,533	$18,200	$16,900	$7,800	$9,915	$18,928	$17,576	$8,112
Office supplies	$875	$875	$875	$875	$910	$910	$910	$910	$946	$946	$946	$946
Insurance	$1,500	$1,500	$1,500	$1,500	$1,560	$1,560	$1,560	$1,560	$1,622	$1,622	$1,622	$1,622
Miscellaneous expenses	$3,750	$3,750	$3,750	$3,750	$3,900	$3,900	$3,900	$3,900	$4,056	$4,056	$4,056	$4,056
Total operating expenses	$170,771	$241,177	$234,057	$171,175	$296,538	$471,060	$451,284	$288,590	$326,613	$520,189	$500,142	$325,745
Income before tax	$75,622	$393,085	$416,897	$312,868	$36,585	$386,464	$428,806	$365,836	$141,092	$683,774	$735,504	$593,069
Taxes	$26,468	$137,580	$145,914	$109,504	$12,805	$135,262	$150,082	$128,043	$49,382	$239,321	$257,426	$207,574
Net income	$49,154	$255,506	$270,983	$203,364	$23,781	$251,201	$278,724	$237,794	$91,710	$444,453	$478,078	$385,495
Break-even volume (bottles)	69,076	97,555	94,675	69,240	119,948	190,542	182,543	116,733	132,114	210,415	202,306	131,762
Excess volume sold (bottles)	30,589	159,002	168,633	126,554	9,616	142,982	159,758	137,798	42,798	239,843	259,801	211,855

EXHIBIT 10	Annual Sales for 5 Years				
	1997	*1998*	*1999*	*2000*	*2001*
Number of bottles sold	815,324	1,059,921	1,430,894	1,860,162	2,232,194
Number of cases sold	33,972	44,163	59,621	77,507	93,008
Revenues					
Sales	$3,759,216	$5,082,460	$7,135,774	$9,647,567	$11,577,080
Cost of goods sold	$1,743,563	$2,357,298	$3,309,646	$4,474,641	$5,369,570
Gross profit	$2,015,653	$2,725,163	$3,826,128	$5,172,925	$6,207,510
Operating expenses					
Interest expense	$98,424	$154,450	$183,021	$134,239	$161,087
Rent	$10,000	$10,400	$10,816	$11,249	$11,699
Utilities	$5,000	$5,200	$5,408	$5,624	$5,849
Salary	$160,000	$166,400	$173,056	$179,978	$187,177
Wages	$20,000	$62,400	$112,486	$126,532	$148,024
Broker expense	$75,184	$101,649	$142,715	$192,951	$231,542
Travel and entertainment	$40,000	$41,600	$43,264	$44,995	$46,794
Shipping costs	$60,000	$83,200	$86,528	$67,492	$70,192
Depreciation	$4,000	$4,000	$4,000	$4,000	$4,000
Advertising					
Television advertising	$0	$524,333	$545,307	$562,432	$584,929
Radio advertising	$100,833	$104,867	$109,061	$112,486	$116,986
Print advertising	$25,208	$26,217	$27,265	$28,122	$29,246
Billboard advertising	$25,208	$26,217	$27,265	$28,122	$29,246
Promotions					
Sponsorships	$75,000	$78,000	$84,365	$94,899	$111,018
In-store promos	$35,500	$36,920	$39,933	$44,919	$52,549
Free samples	$5,000	$5,200	$5,624	$6,327	$7,401
Trade shows	$50,000	$52,000	$56,243	$63,266	$74,012
Office supplies	$3,500	$3,640	$3,786	$3,937	$4,095
Insurance	$6,000	$6,240	$6,490	$6,749	$7,019
Miscellaneous Expenses	$15,000	$15,600	$16,224	$16,873	$17,548
Total operating expenses	$817,181	$1,507,471	$1,672,690	$1,735,191	$1,900,414
Income before tax	$1,198,472	$1,217,691	$2,153,438	$3,437,734	$4,307,096
Taxes	$419,465	$426,192	$753,703	$1,203,207	$1,507,484
Net income	$779,007	$791,499	$1,399,735	$2,234,527	$2,799,612
Break-even volume (bottles)	330,547	609,767	676,597		
Excess volume sold (bottles)	484,777	450,155	754,297		

EXHIBIT 11 Quarterly Cash Flows for 3 Years

	1997				1998				1999			
	Q1	Q2	Q3	Q4	Q1	Q2	Q3	Q4	Q1	Q2	Q3	Q4
Operating activities												
Net Income	$49,154	$255,506	$270,983	$203,364	$23,781	$251,201	$278,724	$237,794	$91,710	$444,453	$478,078	$385,495
(Increase) decrease in accounts receivable	($37,769)	($59,456)	($2,559)	$25,586	($51,064)	($80,385)	($3,459)	$34,592	($71,694)	($112,860)	($4,857)	$48,567
(Increase) decrease in inventories	($17,518)	($27,576)	($1,187)	$11,867	($23,684)	($37,283)	($1,604)	$16,044	($33,252)	($52,346)	($2,253)	$22,526
Increase (decrease) in accounts payable	$4,379	$6,894	$297	($2,967)	$5,921	$9,321	$401	($4,011)	$8,313	$13,086	$563	($5,631)
Increase (decrease) in notes payable	$44,758	$70,458	$3,032	($30,320)	$60,513	$95,259	$4,099	($40,992)	$84,960	$133,743	$5,755	($57,553)
(Increase) decrease in prepaid rent	($7,500)	$2,500	$2,500	$2,500	($7,800)	$2,600	$2,600	$2,600	($8,112)	$2,704	$2,704	$2,704
Increase (decrease) in interest payable	$23,064	$23,820	$25,120	($72,005)	$29,578	$43,186	$43,772	($116,535)	$33,070	$52,176	$52,998	($138,244)
Increase (decrease) in accumulated depreciation	$1,000	$1,000	$1,000	$1,000	$1,000	$1,000	$1,000	$1,000	$1,000	$1,000	$1,000	$1,000
Net cash from operations	$59,569	$273,145	$299,186	$139,026	$42,244	$284,899	$325,532	$130,491	$113,994	$481,957	$533,989	$258,862
Investment activities												
(Purchase) sale of equipment	$0	$0	$0	$0	$0	$0	$0	$0	$0	$0	$0	$0
Net cash from investing												
Financing activities												
Issuance of equity	$0	$0	$0	$0	$0	$0	$0	$0	$0	$0	$0	$0
Issuance of long-term debt	$0	$0	$0	$0	$0	$0	$0	$0	$0	$0	$0	($485,400)
Payment of dividends	$0	$0	$0	$0	$0	$0	$0	$0	$0	$0	$0	$0
Net cash flows from financing	$0	$0	$0	$0	$0	$0	$0	$0	$0	$0	$0	($485,400)
Beginning cash balance	$200,000	$259,569	$532,714	$831,900	$970,926	$1,013,169	$1,298,068	$1,623,601	$1,754,091	$1,868,086	$2,350,042	$2,884,032
Ending cash balance	$259,569	$532,714	$831,900	$970,926	$1,013,169	$1,298,068	$1,623,601	$1,754,091	$1,868,086	$2,350,042	$2,884,032	$2,657,494

EXHIBIT 12 Annual Cash Flows for 5 Years

	1997	1998	1999	2000	2001
Operating activities					
Net Income	$779,007	$791,499	$1,399,735	$2,234,527	$2,799,612
(Increase) decrease in accounts receivable	($74,198)	($100,316)	($140,844)	($57,394)	($39,648)
(Increase) decrease in inventories	($34,414)	($46,528)	($65,325)	($26,620)	($18,389)
Increase (decrease) in accounts payable	$8,603	$11,632	$16,331	$6,655	$4,597
Increase (decrease) in notes payable	$87,928	$118,878	$166,905	$32,666	($26,848)
(Increase) decrease in prepaid rent	$0	$0	($0)	($0)	$0
Increase (decrease) in interest payable	$0	$0	$0	$0	$0
Increase (decrease) in accumulated depreciation	$4,000	$4,000	$4,000	$4,000	$4,000
Net cash from operations	$770,926	$779,166	$1,380,803	$2,193,834	$2,723,325
Investment activities					
(Purchase) sale of equipment	$0	$0	$0	$0	$0
Net cash from investing	$0	$0	$0	$0	$0
Financing Activities					
Issuance of equity	$0	$0	$0	$0	$0
Issuance of long-term debt	$0	$0	($485,400)	$0	$0
Payment of dividends	$0	$0	$0	$0	$0
Net cash flows from financing	$0	$0	($485,400)	$0	$0
Beginning cash balance	$200,000	$970,926	$1,754,091	$2,657,494	$4,851,328
Ending cash balance	$970,926	$1,750,091	$2,649,494	$4,851,328	$7,574,653

451

EXHIBIT 13 Quarterly Balance Sheets for 3 Years

	1997				1998				1999			
	Q1	Q2	Q3	Q4	Q1	Q2	Q3	Q4	Q1	Q2	Q3	Q4
Assets												
Cash and marketable securities	$259,569	$532,714	$831,900	$970,926	$1,013,169	$1,298,068	$1,623,601	$1,754,091	$1,868,086	$2,350,042	$2,884,032	$2,657,494
Accounts receivable	$37,769	$97,225	$99,784	$74,198	$51,064	$131,449	$134,908	$100,316	$71,694	$184,554	$189,411	$140,844
Inventories	$17,518	$45,094	$46,281	$34,414	$23,684	$60,967	$62,572	$46,528	$33,252	$85,598	$87,851	$65,325
Other assets	$15,000	$10,000	$5,000	$0	$23,681	$18,481	$13,281	$8,081	$32,639	$27,231	$21,823	$16,415
Equipment	$20,000	$20,000	$20,000	$20,000	$20,000	$20,000	$20,000	$20,000	$20,000	$20,000	$20,000	$20,000
Less depreciation	$1,000	$2,000	$3,000	$4,000	$5,000	$6,000	$7,000	$8,000	$9,000	$10,000	$11,000	$12,000
Net equipment	$19,000	$18,000	$17,000	$16,000	$15,000	$14,000	$13,000	$12,000	$11,000	$10,000	$9,000	$8,000
Total assets	$348,855	$703,033	$999,965	$1,095,538	$1,126,598	$1,522,965	$1,847,361	$1,921,016	$2,016,671	$2,657,425	$3,192,116	$2,888,077
Liabilities												
Accounts payable	$4,379	$11,274	$11,570	$8,603	$5,921	$15,242	$15,643	$11,632	$8,313	$21,399	$21,963	$16,331
Notes payable	$44,758	$115,215	$118,247	$87,928	$60,513	$155,771	$159,871	$118,878	$84,960	$218,703	$224,458	$166,905
Prepaid rent	$7,500	$5,000	$2,500	$0	$7,800	$5,200	$2,600	$0	$8,112	$5,408	$2,704	$0
Interest payable	$23,064	$46,885	$72,005	$0	$29,578	$72,763	$116,535	$0	$33,070	$85,246	$138,244	$0
Other liabilities	$0	$0	$0	$0	$0	$0	$0	$0	$0	$0	$0	$0
Long term debt	$485,400	$485,400	$485,400	$485,400	$485,400	$485,400	$485,400	$485,400	$485,400	$485,400	$485,400	$485,400
Total liabilities	$565,102	$663,774	$689,722	$581,931	$589,211	$734,377	$780,048	$615,910	$619,855	$816,156	$872,769	$183,236
Owner's equity												
Common stock	$80,000	$80,000	$80,000	$80,000	$80,000	$80,000	$80,000	$80,000	$80,000	$80,000	$80,000	$80,000
Equity in excess of par	($296,246)	($40,740)	$0	$0	$0	$0	$0	$0	$0	$0	$0	$0
Retained earnings	($216,246)	$39,260	$230,243	$433,607	$457,387	$708,589	$987,313	$1,225,106	$1,316,816	$1,761,269	$2,239,346	$2,624,841
Total owner's equity	($216,246)	$39,260	$310,243	$513,607	$537,387	$788,589	$1,067,313	$1,305,106	$1,396,816	$1,841,269	$2,319,346	$2,704,841
Total liabilities and owner's equity	$348,855	$703,033	$999,965	$1,095,538	$1,126,599	$1,522,965	$1,847,361	$1,921,016	$2,016,671	$2,657,425	$3,192,115	$2,888,077

EXHIBIT 14	Annual Balance Sheets for 5 Years				
	1997	*1998*	*1999*	*2000*	*2001*
Assets					
Cash and marketable securities	$970,926	$1,754,091	$2,657,494	$4,851,328	$7,574,653
Accounts receivable	$74,198	$100,316	$140,844	$198,238	$237,885
Inventories	$34,414	$46,528	$65,325	$91,945	$110,334
Other assets	$0	$8,081	$16,415	$35,665	$66,941
Equipment	$20,000	$20,000	$20,000	$20,000	$20,000
Less depreciation	$4,000	$8,000	$12,000	$16,000	$20,000
Net equipment	$16,000	$12,000	$8,000	$4,000	$0
Total assets	$1,095,538	$1,921,016	$2,888,077	$5,181,175	$7,989,813
Liabilities					
Accounts payable	$8,603	$11,632	$16,331	$22,986	$27,583
Notes payable	$87,928	$118,878	$166,905	$134,239	$161,087
Prepaid rent	$0	$0	$0	$0	$0
Interest payable	$0	$0	$0	$0	$0
Other liabilities	$0	$0	$0	$84,581	$62,162
Long term debt	$485,400	$485,400	$0	$0	$0
Total liabilities	$581,931	$615,910	$183,236	$241,806	$250,832
Owner's equity					
Common stock	$80,000	$80,000	$80,000	$80,000	$80,000
Equity in excess of par	$0	$0	$0	$0	$0
Retained earnings	$433,607	$1,225,106	$2,624,841	$4,859,368	$7,658,981
Total owner's equity	$513,607	$1,305,106	$2,704,841	$4,939,368	$7,738,981
Total liabilities and owner's equity	$1,095,538	$1,921,016	$2,888,077	$5,181,175	$7,989,813

The original research for this case was prepared by Tom Kinney, Eric Olson, Pat Dunne, and Kurt Moeller under the supervision of Marc Dollinger. The data in the case are real. Some of the names and places have been disguised.

Case 6   Bright Ideas

In early April 1992, Ben Harrison, Jim Floberg, Mark Widmar, and Ken Wilson rushed to revise the business plan they had written the previous semester. Why the hurry? Because later that month they would be presenting the plan at the North American Invitational Business Plan Competition at San Diego State University. Not only was a $5,000 first prize at stake, but the audience would be filled with potential investors looking for first-rate risk capital opportunities and energetic young talent to implement the plans.

This was their last chance to revise before the judging, and the competition looked tough. (See Appendix 1, Program Agenda.) In fact, they had already met one of these groups, Expert Application Systems, in a competition in March and lost. They were determined to finish first this time and were prepared to do whatever was required. (See Appendix 2, Evaluation Criteria.)

Their business plan described a new venture called Bright Ideas. Bright Ideas, Inc., would manufacture an innovative lighting system to be installed underneath carpet tiles. This system consists of a series of colored lights placed on sheets of conductive Mylar. The lights are then positioned in holes in the carpet tiles. The lights are highly visible, and they do not present a safety hazard because they do not break the plane of the carpet. This system can be used to provide emergency lighting, traffic control information, and a decorative accent, and the lights can be sequenced for enhanced effectiveness. No other product then on the market could perform all three of these roles.

The plan called for the four founders of the company, Jim Floberg, Ben Harrison, Mark Widmar, and Ken Wilson, to manage the company. John Harrison, Ben's father and owner of the patent, would have a seat on the board, would have 10 percent equity, and would provide technical expertise. The founders planned to retain a 65 percent share of the equity and sell 25 percent to outside investors.

ORIGIN OF THE IDEA

The Bright Ideas system was originally developed by John Harrison (Ben's father) in the early 1980s. John Harrison worked for Collins and Aikman (C&A) at the time as manager of new product development. C&A called the product Safe-Lite, and it was successfully installed in a variety of structures, including the Miami International Airport, the Atlanta Merchandise Mart, and branches of First Tennessee Bank. Casinos expressed interest in the system for use as decorative lighting. Underwriters' Laboratories certified the product and mandated that it be installed with a carpet tile floor-covering system.

But the product's potential was never reached at C&A. Unfortunately, C&A was taken over by Wickes Corporation in the merger frenzy of the 1980s. Wickes later declared bankruptcy, and the Safe-Lite system was lost in the shuffle and never fully exploited.

John Harrison quit C&A to start his own company. He left with the patent rights to several products, including the Safe-Lite system. But he launched his new company with another product that was closer to a full-scale rollout, and once again the Safe-Lite system was on the shelf.

THE ENTREPRENEURSHIP CLASS

Ben Harrison knew when he enrolled in the MBA entrepreneurship class that he wanted to develop the business plan for the Safe-Lite system, now renamed Bright Ideas. He recruited the other three members of his team, and their prospectus was approved by the professor. After a number of drafts, they submitted their "final version" of the Bright Ideas plan. After a meeting with and feedback from the professor, they produced the next "final" version, which was distributed to the other teams in the class for evaluation. This led to further revisions. Eventually they produced a draft that was submitted to the two business plan competitions. In March, they were notified that they were finalists in two separate contests: the International Business Plan Competition held in New Haven and the North American Competition in San Diego. The International Competition date was on them in no time, and they prepared very little. They were shocked to see how polished and well prepared their opponents were. They resolved then not to be outworked in the next competition.

TABLE 1   Bright Ideas Business Plan

THE BUSINESS PLAN

Following is an abridged version of the business plan they presented at the competition at San Diego State University. The table of contents is presented in Table 1. The cover page, history, and background sections have been omitted. A brochure outlining the product's benefits accompanied the plan and is presented in Appendix 3.

III. MARKET ANALYSIS

The market in which Bright Ideas will compete is not easily defined. The product potentially fulfills three roles, as outlined in Exhibit 1. It can be used as a revolutionary emergency-lighting system, a traffic control device to direct errant shoppers and hospital patients, or a decorative-lighting system for casinos and night clubs. It can also fulfill more than one of these roles simultaneously.

The market for Bright Ideas is a combination of the emergency-lighting, traffic control/display signage, and decorative-lighting markets. While Bright Ideas' niche is largely undefined, its potential is untapped. The Bright Ideas lighting system is an independent product, and it is most likely to be installed when new carpeting is installed. Therefore, even though it is not a carpeting product, it is closely tied to the carpet industry.

The Carpet Industry

For the past several years, growth in the U.S. carpet industry has been slow and steady. A mature industry, it is characterized by relatively stable demand and little product innovation. The industry sold approximately $11 billion ($10,911,000,000) worth of carpet in 1990, a 2.3 percent increase over 1989.[1] About 45 percent of this total was sold to nonresidential customers. Bright Ideas' primary market of public and office buildings accounted for approximately $2.82 billion worth of carpet in 1990.[2]

The demand for carpet tiles (which are required for the Bright Ideas system) has grown significantly over the past several years. Because they are easy to install and create little waste, the demand for carpet tiles has grown by nearly 20 percent per year. This market segment now accounts for about 15 to 18 percent of the entire commercial carpet market.[3]

Most of the demand for carpet is the result of two factors: new construction and retrofitting. Retrofit purchases occur when old carpet wears out, about every three to five years in the high-traffic areas of commercial buildings. This segment is expected to grow strongly over the next ten years as the pace of new construction slows. It is estimated that 90 percent of the commercial buildings to be occupied by 2000 are standing now.[4]

Currently, much of the demand for carpet is tied to the pace of new construction. In the next decade, nonresidential construction is expected to stagnate. Office building, hotel, and other commercial construction is expected to slump by 4 to 8 percent in the next five years. However, a few segments of the industry are expected to grow. Hospital, airport, and educational construction is predicted to grow by 2 to 4 percent per year.[5]

Thus, while the prospects for the entire carpet industry seem stagnant, many of Bright Ideas' target segments should grow strongly.

Most of the carpet produced is sold directly to retailers. Some carpet is sold through wholesalers, and some is sold directly to large customers, but the dominant distribution channel is direct sale from the mills to retailers.

In the carpet industry, there are many competitors. They range in size from $700 million companies all the way down to small operations with only a few hundred thousand in sales. The majority of the carpet mills are located in Dalton, Georgia, and all are located in the eastern United States. No company dominates the market.

Emergency Lighting

In function, Bright Ideas also fits into the $150 million emergency-lighting market. Fire codes require that all public and commercial buildings be equipped with lighted exit signs and emergency lights. Currently, most emergency lights are wall-mounted, battery-operated strobe light systems.

However, the great majority of these products are installed near the ceiling, where they are quickly obscured by smoke during a fire. Since smoke rises, the most logical place to mount emergency-lighting or exit information systems is near the floor. Currently, very few emergency-lighting products are designed to be mounted near the floor.

Loctite Luminescent Systems and Chloride Systems both manufacture an electroluminescent lamp that is mounted near the floor. Their systems consist of a long tube that is mounted either on the wall or at the intersection of the wall and the floor. These systems only operate during emergencies, however. While they are an improvement over ceiling-mounted products, they are bulky, intrusive, and not very aesthetically pleasing.

The other competing product is currently being used in movie theaters and airplanes. It is smaller than the Loctite system and is mounted above the carpet in slim metal housings. Mounted on either side of an aisle, the raised strips provide light in emergencies and during normal use. However, this system makes carpet installation more difficult. More importantly, the raised strips create an obstacle that must be stepped over. Therefore, while it helps solve a safety concern, it creates a safety hazard and restricts movement, especially for wheelchairs. The costs of both purchasing and installing this system are high. Airplane manufacturers are paying about $6,500 to outfit a single airplane with this system.

In addition, none of these competing products is "intelligent." While they all offer a low-level lighting source and some means of path marking, none can vary the escape route to suit the situation. One of Bright Ideas' competitive advantages is its ability to communicate with smoke detectors. Once a detector is activated, the system will strobe the lights in the other direction, guiding occupants all the way to a safe exit.

The emergency-lighting market is expected to grow strongly in the next decade. Across the nation, fire codes are being strengthened. Officials in major cities have recognized that the life protection systems of public and commercial buildings, especially high-rises, need to be improved. Present legislation is being rewritten to require universal use of sprinklers, fire retardant materials, and fire control systems. Although most of these laws are aimed at new construction, many include retrofit provisions as well.

It is only logical that the push to improve safety will eventually include lighting systems. In Japan, current fire codes require an emergency lighting system to be installed within 18 inches of the floor. In California, a stringent 1989 state fire code calls for lowlevel exit signs and exit path marking. Eventually, all state and federal legislatures may require a floor-mounted emergency-lighting system as well. Even without a retrofit provision, this would provide Bright Ideas with a huge captive market.

The primary customers for a Bright Ideas emergency-lighting system include hotels, health-care facilities, public buildings, cruise ships, public transportation, and recreation facilities. Not only will these customers improve their buildings' safety, but they may be able to reduce their costs while doing so. Several insurance companies have indicated that they might reduce the premiums of the policyholders who install a Bright Ideas type of system.

With little competition and huge potential, the emergency-lighting market seems ideal for the Bright Ideas system.

Traffic Control

Another need met by the Bright Ideas system is in the area of traffic control. With the ability to embed illuminated signs and colored rows of lights in the carpet itself, this system provides a unique information delivery system. Wall and ceiling signs are limited in the amount of information they can present. At present, no information system can direct customers all the way to their destination.

In complex structures, such as hospitals, cruise ships, airports, nursing homes, convention centers, amusement parks, and retail outlets, Bright Ideas can provide an optimal solution. Even the most confused patron should have no trouble following a colored stream of lights to the emergency room or departure gate. The stream of lights can also be configured to light in sequence, creating the illusion of movement and making it even easier to find the intended destination. By pressing a few buttons, the system can be reconfigured, reversing the sequence or even directing the patrons to a completely different destination.

No product currently on the market can provide such a simple and flexible directional aid. As in the emergency-lighting market, the competition is currently minimal.

The potential size of this market is quite large. The system is currently installed in the Miami International Airport and the Atlanta Merchandise Mart and is performing up to expectations.

Airport construction is one of the few construction segments that is still growing. It is conservatively estimated that an average airport would require approximately 5,000 feet of the product. If Bright Ideas is installed in only 5 percent of all new airport and convention center construction or in one retail chain, this segment would yield over $1 million annually in sales.

Decorative Lighting

A third potential application for Bright Ideas is in the decorative-lighting market. With many different colors and an almost infinite variety of designs, the Bright Ideas system can be used to create a distinctive statement in the carpet. Potential customers would include retail outlets, hotels, night clubs, exhibition centers, displays, and casinos.

This product uniquely provides the customer with the means to create an extra decorating splash. Casinos, which use their decor to gain competitive advantage, have already expressed interest in this product.

Currently, competition and substitutes in this market are virtually nonexistent. Potential customers are numerous, and most should be willing to pay a great deal for the extra decorating punch, given the increasing importance of lighting design in many retail, hospitality, and entertainment concepts. Initially, however, demand would come from a very small portion of the $1 billion commercial-lighting market.

Bright Ideas' Market

The Bright Ideas product does not fit solely into any single market. It is closely tied to the $11 billion carpet market. However, the system also draws it customers from the $150 million emergency-lighting market and a small segment of the $1 billion commercial-lighting market. Even if it includes only small parts of these gigantic markets, Bright Ideas' potential sales are substantial.

Currently, this system faces very little direct competition. In each market, there are few competitors. No products meet all these needs or are able to compete in all these markets.

Entry into this unique market is relatively simple. Some expertise in the carpet and lighting industry is required, as well as some technical proficiency. Production equipment is specialized, but not expensive or complicated, and capital requirements are relatively small.

We will attempt to make further entry into this market much more difficult. Bright Ideas will enjoy first-mover advantages and the protection of the patent for another 14 years. While this will not completely block competitors, it will slow them substantially, allowing us to achieve a dominant early market position. If large competitors enter before this dominance is achieved, Bright Ideas will concentrate on those niches that have proven most profitable.

Inputs for the system are relatively simple. The Mylar/Capton sheets, bulbs, and other supplies are readily available from many sources. This limits the power that suppliers will exercise in the area of price and quality. If a chosen supplier attempts to extort a higher price, the switching costs should be relatively insignificant.

Potential purchasers of this product are neither organized nor geographically concentrated. They include large contractors, commercial buyers, and carpet retailers. They are currently unaware of the product and its possibilities. If their awareness level is raised, or if safety legislation is passed, demand should increase dramatically.

IV. MANUFACTURING OPERATIONS

We will purchase all the product's components in their final form. The basic component is a flexible ribbon of plastic sheet material. It is important that this material be relatively stiff to ensure that it lies flat on the floor surface. Two suitable materials are Capton and Mylar. Both of these products are manufactured by Du Pont, which has agreed to meet our demand for them. Du Pont is just one of a number of potential suppliers of material. The remaining components required are copper strips coated in tin, low-voltage, low-amperage incandescent bulbs, plastic globes to cover the bulbs, and a low-voltage control box with 6-volt A.C. power supply and 6-volt D.C. battery backup. These products are readily available from a number of suppliers who will be able to meet our demand.

Based on our discussions with suppliers, we have negotiated the per-unit cost of these components. Mylar or Capton can be purchased for $2.17 per foot, copper strips for $0.12 per inch, incandescent bulbs for $0.35 each, plastic globes for $0.32 each, and control boxes for $200 each. Quantities and the costs of the components, labor, and shipping are detailed further in Exhibit 2. Our planned selling price is $13.65 per foot, giving us a gross profit margin of 50 percent. We want to charge a price that reflects our commitment to quality. There is a strong perceived correlation between price and quality, as consumers believe that they get what they pay for.

We will assemble the end product in-house rather than subcontract the work in order to protect the confidentiality of our production process. A special machine is required for assembly. This machine will take the Mylar or Capton in its raw form and process it through a strip let-off, a punching station, a semiautomatic bulb feeder, a welding station, a pick-and-place system for the insulators and globe covers, and a take-up reel system. The assembly details are described further in Exhibit 3 [omitted].

We have negotiated the requirements of this machine with three suppliers and have agreed to initially purchase from one supplier two machines at a cost of $50,000 each. The capacity of one of these machines is 150,000 feet per year, assuming 255 sixteen-hour workdays per year. Given the capacity of each machine, two machines will be more than adequate to meet our anticipated demand in year 1 (these are extremely conservative estimates). As sales start to grow, we anticipate purchasing a total of eight more machines over the next four years in order to increase capacity to meet demand. As part of the requirements for the machine, we have requested that the supplier use interchangeable parts where applicable to help control the cost of repair and maintenance. The supplier has also guaranteed timely on-site maintenance. Because of the uniqueness of these machines and the relatively small size of our supplier, we will purchase these machines rather than lease them.

The operation of the machine is fairly simple and can be performed by a single individual. The majority of the work is performed by the machine. The operator's main concern is that the machine is properly supplied and functioning during each production run. After each run, the operator will use a handcart to move the final product to the packaging and shipping area. At this point the final product will be readied for shipment. This area, as well as the other points where inventory will be temporarily stored, will be locked when not in use.

For each shift, we will need to hire two individuals to operate the machines and one for the packaging and shipping area. Also, one supervisor will be hired to oversee the operations. The supervisor will be responsible for verifying the quality of the product and handling simple equipment repairs. This individual will perform the initial inspection while the production run is in process and then again when the goods are moved to the packaging area. The supervisor has the authority to stop the run if a defect is found. This is deemed appropriate because of the repetitive nature of the process.

For the first six months, when two shifts are running, one of the founders will act as supervisor. This will allow us to avoid hiring a second supervisor right away and to stay close to the operations.

Labor skill requirements for the machine operator are low. Nonetheless, given the need for accuracy in the production process, we will hire only semiskilled workers for these positions. We will be able to attract these workers by paying them an hourly wage of $9.50, which we believe is slightly above the wage these workers normally receive. The labor skill requirements for the shipping and packaging area are also low. However, the exposure in this area is lower, so an unskilled worker is appropriate. We will pay this individual an hourly rate of $6.25.

The role of the supervisor is essential in our operation. Therefore, we will hire an individual skilled in operations management and with previous experience in the manufacturing process. This individual will be compensated on a salary basis of $32,000 per year.

Outside the production process, we will need to hire an electrical engineer to oversee the installation. This individual will be compensated on a salary basis of $35,000 per year. The product installation is simple for an electrician. Therefore, our customers will be able to hire electricians of their choice, and we will provide only an electrical engineer to inspect the installation. Installation and replacement procedures are given in Exhibit 4 [omitted].

Training of workers should not be difficult because of the simple nature of the production process. The training will be performed by the management team. Workers should be up to full speed within two or three weeks.

All employees will be evaluated quarterly, with special emphasis on quality of work and attendance record. Management will emphasize total quality manufacturing and evaluate employees according to this philosophy. Based on each employee's evaluation and on the company's performance, bonuses will be given as deemed appropriate.

At each stage of the production process, the movement of raw materials, work in process, and finished goods will be accounted for by the supervisor, who will enter the transaction into the company's computer system. The system will be a local area network linking the individual PCs currently being used by the management team and will, therefore, not require a cash outlay. Management will play an active role in this process by reconciling the daily records of raw materials receipts, material work orders, merchandise entered into finished goods inventory, and shipping documents back to the daily computer report. All material exceptions will be reconciled immediately.

Based on our estimated production levels, we anticipate total manufacturing and office space needs of 5,000 square feet. The manufacturing operations would consist of 3,000 square feet, mainly for assembly equipment, workstations, and inventory storage. The remaining 2,000 square feet will be used for office space, a reception area, and a conference room. This facility will be more than adequate to meet our future needs as we start to grow.

This facility will be located in Dalton, Georgia, "the carpet capital of the world."

Our product is a perfect complement to the carpet industry, and, thus, the Dalton location will enable us to gain certain synergies. Real estate brokers in the Dalton area have indicated to us that the average lease cost per square foot is $4.50 per year. Given the size of our facility, we estimate our monthly rent will be approximately $1,875.

Dalton has an excellent labor supply, which should be able to meet both our current and future requirements. Over the next five years we anticipate adding shifts in order to step up production to meet demand. This, coupled with the purchase of additional machines, will require the hiring of additional machine operators, package area workers, and supervisors. During this period we anticipate hiring a total of 18 machine operators, 3 packaging area workers, and 1 supervisor. Considering our compensation plan and the strong labor force in the Dalton area, we do not foresee any problems meeting our needs.

V. MARKETING

The Bright Ideas marketing plan will use a two-pronged approach. As with any new product, the primary task will be to build customer awareness in the target market. Simultaneously, a lobbying effort will attempt to persuade legislatures to require the use of floor-mounted emergency-lighting systems in all commercial and public buildings.

Lobbying Effort

The lobbying effort will target local and state governments as well as federal agencies. Even though most of the fire and building codes are legislated at the local level, the lobbying effort will initially solicit state and national agencies. Brochures, information packets, and other awareness-building materials that stress the benefits of Bright Ideas emergency lighting will be sent to the California, New York, Massachusetts, Texas, and other progressive state fire marshals. The information packets will stress research showing the benefits of a floor-mounted lighting system, including the number of (eligible voters') lives that could be saved by the widespread use of such a system. It will stress the ease of installation and the minimal costs in relation to these benefits. Finally, it will stress the U.L. listing and the system's reliability and visibility.

The information packets will be followed by telephone and/or personal interviews. The lobbyist will attempt to solicit an endorsement and possible sponsorship for legislation. This procedure has proven successful with the Tennessee state fire marshal, who has endorsed the product and is anxious to proceed with legislation.

This same procedure will be used to appeal to national safety organizations such as the National Institute of Building Sciences, the National Fire Protection Research Foundation, the National Fire Protection Association, and the National Fire Safety Board. Bright Ideas will attempt to gain their endorsement for the system.

Typically, fire safety legislation is enacted by the domino approach. If an opinion leader such as New York or California adopts a new fire code, many other states are likely to follow suit. Often, however, it is local governments that decide specifically where, when, and how the code will be enforced. This suggests that local governments (at least in the major cities) should eventually be solicited as well.

Another lobbying effort will target the insurance industry. The same type of information/awareness campaign will be presented to the major commercial property insurers. The desired result of this campaign will be to have the insurance companies offer a discount to policyholders who install a floor-mounted emergency-lighting system in their buildings. Several insurance companies have expressed a willingness to consider such a proposal.

A full-time lobbyist will be hired to conduct this campaign. Her duties will include fire safety speeches and meetings with national safety board officials and insurance companies.

The most positive result of this lobbying would be the immediate, universal endorsement of the Bright Ideas system, the enactment of strict fire codes requiring the installation of a floor-mounted emergency-lighting system in all new public and commercial buildings, and a retrofit provision requiring all older buildings to install such a system within five to seven years.

Even a few endorsements with no immediate legislation would set the process in motion and serve to increase awareness among the general public. This would dovetail with the second prong of the marketing effort.

Consumer Marketing

As shown in the market analysis section, the product can compete in several different markets. Consumers in each of these markets have distinct needs. The emergency-lighting customers are primarily concerned with a simple, reliable means of improving the safety of their buildings. The traffic control market will respond to a foolproof, improved means of conveying directional information. The decorative-lighting market needs a new way to create an exciting and distinctive atmosphere.

These markets are not entirely separate, since a single customer may possess several of these needs. For example, an airport may be required to install an emergency lighting system but may want to improve its traveler information system as well.

Initially, Bright Ideas will concentrate on the emergency-lighting and traffic control markets. Both of these markets are large enough to overwhelm a company the size of Bright Ideas. Focused and controlled growth is essential to ensure success.

The first task will be to build awareness of the product with architects/interior designers, large contractors, hotel chains, airlines, retail outlets, the government, and other large purchasers of carpet. Advertisements in such magazines as *Interior Design, Facilities Design & Management, Progressive Architecture, Sweet's Catalogues,* and *Buildings,* as well as direct mail, will be used. Two founders will follow up on leads with calls and personal appointments to demonstrate the product.

Even though it is not a carpet product, the prime opportunity to sell Bright Ideas is during a carpet-buying decision. Until the system achieves the reputation to become a stand-alone product, it will be easiest to piggyback on carpet sales. To further this end, awareness-building brochures will be sent to the large carpet manufacturers and retailers (Exhibit 5—[omitted]). A standard Bright Ideas commission will be paid to any manufacturer or retailer that generates a successful lead.

During the first year, Ben, Ken, and two others will constitute the direct sales force. They will concentrate on large, highly visible locations such as airports and convention centers. This will increase product awareness while reducing the number of individual sales required to reach the first-year sales targets.

The use of independent sales representatives is currently being investigated. While independent reps would dramatically increase the reach of the sales efforts at minimal cost, it would also result in a loss of control and possible image and service problems. We would prefer to maintain our own sales force, but cash flow problems or sluggish growth could induce us to make limited use of independent sales representatives.

Once a sale has been made, the sales rep will work with the client to design the lighting scheme, measure the premises, and determine how much and what type of materials are needed for the job. The specifics of the order will be sent via laptop computer to the factory in Dalton for manufacture.

When the order is ready to be installed, a Bright Ideas engineer will travel to the job site to supervise installation. She will work with the customer's electrician to install the product.

Throughout the sale, an effort will be made to build a good relationship with the client. If Bright Ideas is to succeed in the emergency-lighting market, it must be positioned as a premium product. An image of high quality throughout the manufacturing, sales, and service processes is essential to build trust in the product. Clients must believe that the product is reliable if they are going to depend on it for emergency-lighting purposes.

In keeping with this philosophy, a five-year parts and service warranty will be included with the product. Customers will then have the option to purchase several additional years of protection if they desire. The costs of this program should be minimal, since the bulbs have a 100,000-hour (11.4-year) life, and the majority of the system is essentially maintenance free.

Eventually, it will be possible to differentiate service levels if we are forced to compete at different price points. This may be more applicable for entry into the traffic control and decorative-lighting markets. We plan to maintain the skimming strategy until the threat of competition causes us to change.

The price of the installed system will be $13.65 per foot. This represents a 50 percent gross margin. It is estimated that an average retail outlet would require 150 to 500 feet of the product, a hotel or conference center would require 2,000 to 3,000 feet, and an airport would require 5,000 feet to light all its concourses.

We have estimated first-year sales at 200,000 feet. Our first emphasis will be to pursue the First Tennessee Bank account, a previous test customer that has been receptive to installation of the system in all its 100 branches (approximately 30,000 feet). If we are successful with this sale, each salesperson would need to sell only about 42,500 additional feet of the product during the year, an extremely conservative target. As awareness builds, endorsements increase, and some legislation is ratified, we expect sales to reach 400,000 feet in year 2, followed by 850,000, 1.2 million, and 1.5 million feet in year 5. All sales will require full payment 30 days after shipment.

To give sales an initial boost, we will offer to install a free system in a limited area of one location of large hotel and retail chains. This will allow the clients to evaluate the product on a risk-free basis. If a single organization such as Holiday Inn adopted the system in all its locations, this would easily pay for hundreds of free installations.

As demand grows, it will be necessary to add additional salespeople. The direct sales force will continue to target the large accounts. As this segment becomes saturated, the salespeople will begin to target smaller establishments within a given geographic area. However, we may find that we can offer better service by categorizing the sales force by industry or market segment. If demand threatens to outstrip the reach of our sales efforts, independent sales reps will be used for selected markets.

The sales, distribution, and installation procedures for larger customers will remain the same, even as demand grows. The salesperson will help design the system, the product will be shipped by a carrier such as UPS, and a Bright Ideas technician will supervise the installation.

When the product becomes well known, or if widespread emergency-lighting legislation is passed, the distribution channels will be expanded. The direct sales force will still be used for large and custom jobs. Smaller customers will be able to purchase the system through qualified contractors and retail outlets. Bright Ideas will provide these retail outlets with promotional information and training to maintain our high-quality image. Since the installation procedure is relatively simple, Bright Ideas will conduct regional training seminars to certify independent technicians in the installation of the system.

If the design process can be simplified, it may be possible for small establishments to design, order, and install a system on their own by direct-ordering it from the factory. If and when this distribution channel becomes an option, it will be necessary to expand the marketing and advertising efforts dramatically.

After two or three years, if domestic sales reach their targets, the product will be introduced internationally. Bright Ideas holds the European and Asian patents, so competition should be minimal. Since each order must be custom produced, it may be necessary to locate another factory closer to the end users if shipping costs are exorbitant. This will necessitate a large increase in personnel and capital equipment.

Throughout the marketing efforts, Bright Ideas must remain focused. Given the size of the markets and the number of different uses for the system, management must not try to do too much too soon. If the system is to be sold effectively, and if its quality standards are to be kept high, the company must keep its growth under control.

VI. FINANCIAL PLANS

Financial projections for the first four years beginning in 1993 appear in Exhibits 6 and 7. Exhibit 6 shows the projected income statement, balance sheet, and cash flow statement on a monthly basis for 1993. Exhibit 7 provides the same statements on a quarterly basis for years 1994 through 1996. As can be seen in Exhibit 6, the company requires $625,000 in start-up financing. This includes $25,000 in equity contributed by the founders and $100,000 obtained through a line of credit with a bank. Therefore, $500,000 in equity, representing 25 percent ownership, is still required. The cash flow statement in Exhibit 6 shows that the cash raised will be used to fund working-capital requirements such as inventory and accounts receivable, and equipment purchases.

The projections in Exhibit 8 show an internal rate of return of 109 percent on the investors' $500,000 investment. The net present value of the $500,000 investment is calculated as well, at discount rates ranging from 45 to 60 percent. The substantial cash flow generated by the business allows for the payment of dividends of $800,000 in 1995 and $1,600,000 in 1996. Harvesting occurs at the end of 1996, at an assumed value of ten times 1996 earnings. This is a conservative estimate, given both the actual (projected to be 81.7 percent annually through 1996) and potential growth of the business.

Two pessimistic scenarios were calculated as well to demonstrate the attractiveness of the investment even under "worst-case" scenarios. The first scenario, demonstrated at the bottom of Exhibit 9, includes sales figures 20 percent lower than projected and a market value of eight times earnings in 1996. Under these conditions, cash generated is still sufficient to pay the same dividends, and income remains positive from the first year. The internal rate of return on the investors' investment is 86 percent. Even under very pessimistic conditions, shown on the top of Exhibit 9, the internal rate of return remains an attractive 62 percent. This assumes sales revenue of only 60 percent of that projected and a market value for the common stock of just six times earnings in 1996, which is very unlikely. Under both of these pessimistic scenarios, dividend payments would be half of those projected under the most likely scenario. In all scenarios, income is positive, even in the first year.

Total sales in linear feet for 1993 through 1996 are projected to be 200,000, 400,000, 850,000, and 1,200,000, respectively. These numbers can easily be obtained. The product has already been installed in two branches of First Tennessee Bank, and the customer has expressed interest in having the rest of its more than 100 branches outfitted in the same manner. Similarly, the acquisition of just one major retail chain as a customer would generate enough volume to equal second-year sales projections. As noted in the marketing section, large customers such as airports and hotels will be targeted, providing opportunities for large amounts of business with every sale.

The sales price per linear foot is estimated to be $13.65. This figure is less than what was charged on past installations at the First Tennessee Bank and the Atlanta Merchandise Mart. Similarly, the cost-of-goods-sold figure of 50 percent of sales revenue provides room for cost increases, since previous production had considerably higher margins—around 65 percent. Selling, general, and administrative expenses include the salaries of the founders ($30,000 for each of the four individuals), two engineers ($35,000 for each, with the second person not hired until after the first $500,000 in business has been generated), two salespersons ($35,000 each), and an administrative assistant at $18,000 per year. We have allotted $50,000 to cover the lobbyist's salary and have allowed for generous travel expenses. Rental cost estimates included in this figure were quoted from an experienced commercial real estate executive. The increases in these figures through the years reflect the salaries of hired salespersons, commissions on sales, and other increased selling costs such as travel.

Interest expense on the bank line of credit is calculated at a conservative 12 percent. It is anticipated that the full $100,000 line of credit will be drawn down immediately to meet early start-up needs. With the substantial cash surplus generated, this loan will be paid off by the middle of 1994 at the latest. Fixed-asset purchases consist of the machinery to produce the product. The projected purchase of ten machines by the end of 1996 will provide more than enough capacity to meet demand, given the capacity of each machine, as noted in the production section.

Analysis reveals that Bright Ideas, Inc., needs to sell only 89,915 linear feet of the product to break even. This number represents only 45 percent of the projected first-year sales of 200,000 linear feet. At a selling price of $13.65 per linear foot (yielding a contribution margin of 50 percent), the $613,667 of fixed costs will be covered by $1,227,333 in sales. It is projected that this sales target will be reached in the ninth month of operation.

Because the sales of the product are anticipated to closely track those of carpet sales, which remain relatively constant throughout the year, there are no projected seasonal fluctuations to the business.

Because the company wishes to maintain good relations with its suppliers, accounts payable were projected to be paid off in 30 days. Similarly, credit will be granted to customers on a net 30-day basis. To be conservative, the projections show a month's sales not being collected for two months during the first year and for 45 days in later years.

Mark Widmar, CPA and one of the company founders, will have chief responsibility for controlling the company's funds. Widmar has over three years' experience as an accountant with a Big 6 accounting firm.

VII. ORGANIZATION AND MANAGEMENT

The management team will consist of the four founders: Ben Harrison, Jim Floberg, Mark Widmar, and Ken Wilson. All four of these individuals will have completed their MBA degrees at Indiana University by May 1992. Ben has an undergraduate degree in architecture to go with his MBA degree in marketing. He spent over two years working on large-scale mixed-use commercial developments in the Washington, D.C., metropolitan area. He has a number of contacts with East Coast developers who may be prime targets for our initial marketing efforts. Ben is also comfortable with the design process and can act as a liaison with architectural engineering firms. His experience has already contributed to the accuracy of estimating potential job sizes.

Ken has a double major in marketing and entrepreneurship. He has owned and operated several small businesses. As a partner in Desktop Compositions, he learned the skills that will enable us to design and produce most of our own advertising and promotional materials. Both Ben and Ken will be responsible for promoting and marketing our product. Jim has a major in finance. He has over three years' experience in the insurance industry, with several contacts at both his former employer and with various brokers and agents throughout the country. Jim also spent the previous summer working at a superregional financial institution, which will provide the company with access to potential sources of credit.

Mark majored in finance and is a licensed CPA. He has three years of public accounting experience with Crowe Chizek & Co. and Ernst & Young. He was a senior auditor at the time he left to pursue his graduate degree. Jim and Mark will be responsible for the company's accounting records and preparation of the tax return. Individual resumes are provided in Exhibit 10.

Each member of the management team will receive a salary of $30,000 per year. This compensation level is considered fair given the management team's active role in the company's day-to-day operations. Moreover, each member will be forgoing other traditional and considerably higher-paying job opportunities.

John M. Harrison, Ben's father and product inventor, will be given the chairman position on the board of directors. Even though Harrison will not be active in the day-to-day decision-making process, he will be available for consultation when specific issues require his experience.

VIII. OWNERSHIP

The organization will be formed as a corporation under the name of Bright Ideas, Inc. This form of business was chosen because of its limited liability provision for the owners, making it attractive to all equity investors. Furthermore, S corporation status was not selected because it would make the investment less attractive to more wealthy investors and because dividends will not be paid at all the first year and only partially thereafter. This is because of the organization's need for some cash to fund future equipment purchases as the business expands and the founders' desire to maintain some cash for safety purposes and short-term opportunities that may arise.

The four founders of the company will contribute $25,000 in total to the equity of the business, demonstrating their commitment to the firm's success and their belief in the attractiveness of the investment. This investment will represent 65 percent of the ownership of the company. As noted in Section VI, $625,000 total will be necessary for the start-up of the business. This includes the founders' $25,000 plus $100,000 from a bank line of credit, leaving $500,000 in equity to be secured. No further financing will be needed. As can be seen from the cash flow projections in Exhibits 7 and 9, funds will be used to acquire two machines at $50,000 apiece in the first year and eight additional machines throughout the next three years as demand requires. Total capital expenditures will therefore be $500,000 through 1996.

The board of directors will include each of the founders of the company and John Harrison, who contributed the patent on the Bright Ideas technology in return for 10 percent of the equity and the chairman position on the board. Three other business and university leaders are being selected for board seats on the basis of needed experience. The two remaining seats on the board will be elected by the remaining investor(s). Stock ownership, contribution, and percentage ownership are shown in Table 2.

TABLE 2 Ownership Positions

Investor	Number of Shares	Contribution	Price/Share	Percent of Ownership
Founders	65,000	$25,000	$ .3846	65
Harrison	10,000	Patent	—	10
Investors	25,000	$500,000	$20.00	25

Projected return for the investors is calculated in Exhibit 10.

IX. CRITICAL RISKS

Although we feel that the business has a high probability of success, it is not without its risks. Even though the system will enjoy the protection of a patent for 14 more years, this will not completely block competitors from entering this market. A large, well-funded, and quick-moving competitor would pose a sizable risk to our plans. We hope that by the time a competitor created an alternate design, tested it, and implemented full-scale production, Bright Ideas would be established in a dominant market position. If not, Bright Ideas would focus its efforts on the most profitable niches. Given the gigantic size of the markets, even these relatively small niches would provide ample room for profitable growth.

Patent infringement also poses a potential risk. In the early stages, the firm would not have the financial resources to bring a protracted patent infringement suit against a large corporation. Therefore, we will approach the business as if the patent did not exist, seeking competitive advantage through superior products, quality, and service. We will fight patent infringement wherever possible, but we will not rely solely on the patent for competitive protection. We will also seek patents for closely related designs (such as the fiber-optics patents we already hold). By erecting this "sphere of protection," we hope to help maintain our patent protection.

Another potential risk is the possibility that legislation requiring floor-mounted emergency lighting might not be passed. This risk is not critical, however. Although the lack of legislation certainly would slow Bright Ideas' growth, there would still be a substantial market for such an innovative product.

The few fixed assets required for this business are product specific, and banks may be hesitant to loan against them because of their low resale value. This may present a minor inconvenience during start-up or during any unforeseen periods of slow cash inflows.

Fluctuations in the business cycle pose another risk. Without legislation requiring the use of this product, many businesses may elect not to incur the added expense during recessions and depressions. The Bright Ideas market is closely tied to the very cyclical construction and carpeting industries. However, neither carpeting nor emergency lighting are seasonal products.

We are essentially trying to cause a paradigm shift by making people think about emergency lighting and information presentation in a new way. The success of such efforts is often subject to the whims of influential opinion leaders. If these opinion leaders do not endorse the system, the information and awareness-building campaigns may take considerably longer, slowing initial sales and causing cash flow problems.

Unstable interest rates over the first year and a half of operation could raise interest expense, since our credit line has a variable interest rate. Substantial increases in the rate of inflation or other changes in the economic climate could cause the cost of machinery to rise significantly higher than projections.

Significant delays in receiving payments from customers could threaten the survival of the company in the first year, given its projected cash needs in the first six months. Since customers will be much larger than the company, there is no leverage to collect from the customers once the product is installed.

Notes

1. *U.S. Industrial Outlook*, 1991, p. 9–5.
2. *Manufacturing USA*, 1991, p. 235.
3. Holly Sraeel, "The Carpet Tile Industry Matures," *Buildings*, November 1988, p. 80.
4. Sraeel, p. 81.
5. *U.S. Industrial Outlook*, p. 5–1.

Bibliography

"1990's Top Product Picks," *Buildings*, December, 1990, p. 24. *Manufacturing USA*, 1991, p. 235.

Monroe, Linda K., "Focus on Carpeting Products," *Buildings*, May 1990, p. 64.

Ricketts, Chip, "A $100 Million Company Overnight. (Carpet Services Inc.)," *Dallas Business Journal*, October 23, 1989, p. 1.

Sraeel, Holly, "The Carpet Tile Industry Matures," *Buildings*, November 1988, p. 80.

U.S. Industrial Outlook, 1991, p. 9–5.

Wilson, Frank C., "The 90's: Opportunities for U.S. Carpet Producers," *Textile World*, May 1990, p. 47.

APPENDIX 1

Program Agenda: North American Business Plan Competition

BUSINESS PLAN PRESENTATIONS
8:30 a.m.–11:30 a.m., April 24
Carmel Room III

STUDENT PARTICIPANTS & FACULTY SPONSORS

AMERICAN BIO-TECH BAMBOO, INC.
Simon X. Liao   Don Charest   William Hornaday   Matthias Tomenendal
Professor Charles Hofer
The University of Georgia

BRIGHT IDEAS, INC.
Jim Floberg   Ben Harrison   Mark Widmar   Ken Wilson
Professor Marc Dollinger
Indiana University

CONCRETE CRUSHERS, INC.
Mark Athey   Scott Finch   Delia Prather
Masahiko Shinada   Don Travis   Larry Wescott
Professor Charles Hofer
The University of Georgia

CORE MEDICAL TECHNOLOGIES, INC.
Lawrence M. Hanrahan   Timothy A. Skansi
Professor Raymond Smilor
The University of Texas

EXPERT APPLICATION SYSTEMS, INC.
Margarita Ash   David Beuerlein   Patricia Mack   Deborah Sallee
Professor Raymond Smilor
The University of Texas

JUDGES' DELIBERATIONS
11:30 a.m.–12:30 p.m.
Conference Room 205

Don Bauder, Financial Editor   Carlton J. Eibl, Attorney at Law
San Diego Union Tribune   Brobeck, Phleger & Harrison

Pamela Coker, Chief Executive Officer
ACUCOBOL

Alan J. Grant, Ed. D.   Bob Root, Chief Executive Officer
Grant Venture Management   V1 Sales and Marketing Design

RECEPTION
11:30 a.m.–12:30 p.m.

LUNCHEON & KEYNOTE SPEAKER
Robert J. Lichter   12:30 p.m.–2:00 p.m.
President and Chief Executive Officer   Carmel Room II
John Burnham & Co.   Ballrooms

PRESENTATION OF AWARDS

APPENDIX 2

Evaluation Criteria

SAN DIEGO STATE UNIVERSITY
Entrepreneurial Management Center

NORTH AMERICAN INVITATIONAL BUSINESS PLAN COMPETITION

Spring 1992

EVALUATION CRITERIA

Feasibility of the Business Plan. The winner(s) will be the individual or team whose plan conveys the most promising combination of significant capital gains potential, attractive investment possibilities, and actual implementation; i.e., the more likely the plan is to become a going venture, the better.

Product/Service Description. The business plan should provide a clear description of the proposed product or service offering.

Marketability of the Product or Service. The business plan should be able to demonstrate that there is a viable market for the product or service. It would be helpful to use the results of market surveys and demographic studies to support your argument. Specifically, the plan should focus on size of the market, growth potential of the market, and strategies to enter the market.

Strength of the Management Team. The business plan should profile the key members of the firm's management team. You must demonstrate to the reviewers that the management team possesses the necessary skills, drive, and desire to carry out the plan in an effective and efficient manner.

Description of Operations. The business plan should present a logical approach to resource procurement, product development, and distribution. Plans for layout and design of facilities should also be included in this section.

Assessment of Risk. The business plan should recognize the types and nature of risks associated with starting the new venture.

Sales Analysis and Forecasts. The business plan should include sales forecasts for at least the first three years of operation. Heavy emphasis will be placed upon your ability to present a logical argument in support of the projections.

Capital Requirements. The financial projections contained in the business plan should demonstrate that the firm will have sufficient capital to implement the idea.

Return on Investment. The financial projections should be able to demonstrate that equity investors will be receiving a satisfactory return on investment over a three- to five-year period.

Organization of the Business Plan. The final business plan should be put together in a professional and logical fashion. Writing style and overall appearance are important. Each business plan should contain a two-page executive summary that highlights the critical elements of the overall plan.

APPENDIX 3

Bright Ideas Brochure

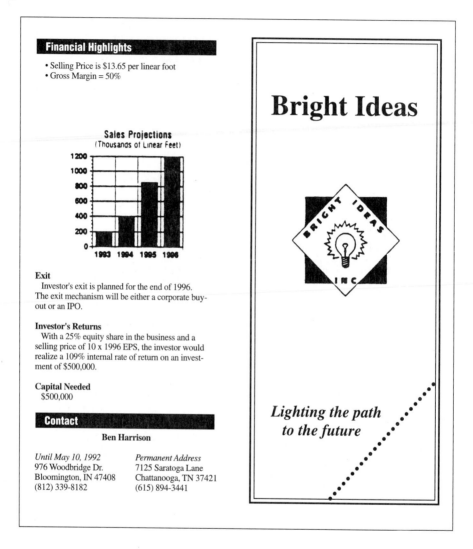

Financial Highlights

- Selling Price is $13.65 per linear foot
- Gross Margin = 50%

Sales Projections
(Thousands of Linear Feet)

Exit
Investor's exit is planned for the end of 1996. The exit mechanism will be either a corporate buyout or an IPO.

Investor's Returns
With a 25% equity share in the business and a selling price of 10 x 1996 EPS, the investor would realize a 109% internal rate of return on an investment of $500,000.

Capital Needed
$500,000

Contact

Ben Harrison

Until May 10, 1992
976 Woodbridge Dr.
Bloomington, IN 47408
(812) 339-8182

Permanent Address
7125 Saratoga Lane
Chattanooga, TN 37421
(615) 894-3441

Bright Ideas

Lighting the path to the future

The Concept

Bright Ideas will produce and market a revolutionary lighting system which was designed to be mounted underneath carpet tiles. The system uses a proprietary flat cabling system which is embedded between two thin sheets of mylar. Small bulbs are then attached to the mylar every three or six inches.

To install the system, the mylar sheet is simply unrolled, affixed to the floor and wired up. Small holes are punched in the carpet tiles, which are then placed over the lights.

The installed system is completely unobtrusive. The bulbs them-

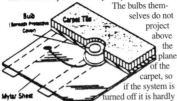

selves do not project above the plane of the carpet, so if the system is turned off it is hardly visible. Unlike current systems in movie theaters and airplanes, there are no metal housings to trip over.

The system is aesthetically pleasing as well. The bulbs can be produced in many different colors, and unlike other emergency lights, the system can actually enhance the decor.

The Bright Ideas system is mounted on the floor, which is the last place to be obscured by smoke. It has the standard battery backup, and uses only six volts of electricity – so it is not a fire hazard itself. It also has a control box which can illuminate the bulbs in sequence, providing the illusion of movement. When the system is connected to smoke detectors located throughout a structure, it becomes quite intelligent.

If smoke is detected in one area of the building, the lights can be programmed to sequence in the opposite direction, guiding occupants to a safe exit (see fig. 2).

No other system can offer all these benefits.

The Process

We have identified three primary markets which can be served by this product.

Emergency Lighting

State and national fire codes mandate that every public structure have some sort of emergency lighting and exit marking system in place. The trend, of course, is to strengthen these codes. Some states already require floor-mounted lighting and path marking systems. To date, this has involved the use of bulky wall-mounted units or photoluminescent paint.

Traffic Control

Complex structures such as airports and hospitals have a growing need to provide efficient directions for their occupants. As globalization increases, the need to provide simple, multilingual communications is increasing as well. Our colorful stream of lights leads even the most bewildered with authority.

Decorative Lighting

Casinos, night clubs, hotels and retail outlets often depend on their decor for competitive advantage. With this system decorators will find it easy to create that necessary visual excitement.

EXHIBIT 1 Bright Ideas Target Markets

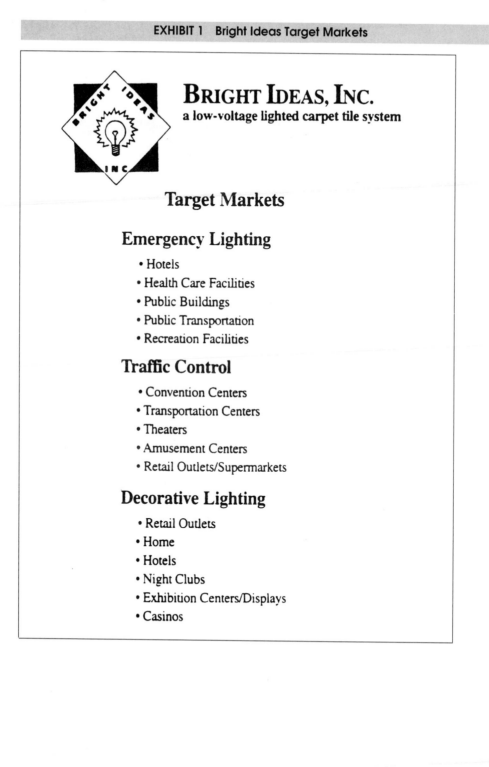

BRIGHT IDEAS, INC.
a low-voltage lighted carpet tile system

Target Markets

Emergency Lighting

- Hotels
- Health Care Facilities
- Public Buildings
- Public Transportation
- Recreation Facilities

Traffic Control

- Convention Centers
- Transportation Centers
- Theaters
- Amusement Centers
- Retail Outlets/Supermarkets

Decorative Lighting

- Retail Outlets
- Home
- Hotels
- Night Clubs
- Exhibition Centers/Displays
- Casinos

EXHIBIT 2	Bright Ideas: Unit Costs

Unit Cost (6″ Centers)

Materials:		Price	
Per Foot Quantity	*Item Description*	*Each*	*Total*
1	Mylar/Capton element	$2.17	$2.17
12	Copper strips	.12	1.44
2	Bulbs	.35	.70
2	Globes	.32	.64
2	Miscellaneous	.18	.36
		Total	$5.31

Labor:

Machine operator		$ .26
Packaging and shipping worker		.10
Supervisor		.24
FICA @ .0765		.06
	Total	$ .66
Total assembly cost per foot		$5.97

Fixed Materials Cost Per 300 Feet:

Control box		$200.00
Line cable		1.35
Letters		24.00
Connector		26.00
Rivets		7.00
	Total	$258.35
	Total fixed cost per foot	$.86
	Total cost per foot	$6.83
	Selling price per foot	$13.65
	Gross margin %	50%

Note: Per unit labor costs were based on production of 37 feet of finished product per hour.

EXHIBIT 6 Bright Ideas: Financial Statements, 1993

Projected Income Statement

	Jan	Feb	Mar	Apr	May	Jun	Jul	Aug	Sep	Oct	Nov	Dec
Units (linear ft.)	8,000	9,000	9,000	9,000	10,000	10,000	14,000	17,000	22,000	24,000	32,000	36,000
Net sales	$110,867	$124,725	$124,725	$124,725	$138,583	$138,583	$194,017	$235,592	$304,883	$332,600	$443,467	$498,900
Cost of goods sold	55,433	62,363	62,363	62,363	69,292	69,292	97,008	117,796	152,442	166,300	221,733	249,450
Gross margin	55,433	62,363	62,363	62,363	69,292	69,292	97,008	117,796	152,442	166,300	221,733	249,450
Operating expenses:												
S, G&A	45,833	45,833	50,000	50,000	50,000	50,000	50,000	50,000	50,000	50,000	50,000	50,000
Depreciation	833	833	833	833	833	833	833	833	833	833	833	833
Operating income	8,767	15,696	11,529	11,529	18,458	18,458	46,175	66,963	101,608	115,467	170,900	198,617
Interest expense	1,000	1,000	1,000	1,000	1,000	1,000	1,000	1,000	1,000	1,000	1,000	1,000
EBT	7,767	14,696	10,529	10,529	17,458	17,458	45,175	65,963	100,608	114,467	169,900	197,617
Taxes	3,107	5,878	4,212	4,212	6,983	6,983	18,070	26,385	40,243	45,787	67,960	79,047
Net income	$4,660	$8,818	$6,318	$6,318	$10,475	$10,475	$27,105	$39,578	$60,365	$68,680	$101,940	$118,570
Dividends	$0	$0	$0	$0	$0	$0	$0	$0	$0	$0	$0	$0

Projected Balance Sheet

	Jan	Feb	Mar	Apr	May	Jun	Jul	Aug	Sep	Oct	Nov	Dec
Assets												
Cash	$425,863	$310,789	$304,081	$311,925	$309,375	$309,597	$288,107	$220,885	$171,678	$146,031	$111,145	$65,080
Inventory	15,591	15,591	15,591	17,323	17,323	24,252	39,265	50,814	55,433	73,911	83,150	91,465
Acc/rec.	110,867	235,592	249,450	249,450	263,308	277,167	332,600	429,608	540,475	637,483	776,067	942,367
Net fixed assets	99,167	98,333	97,500	96,667	95,833	95,000	94,167	93,333	92,500	91,667	90,833	90,000
Total assets	$651,487	$660,304	$666,622	$675,365	$685,840	$706,015	$754,139	$794,640	$860,087	$949,092	$1,061,195	$1,188,912
Liabilities												
Payables	21,827	21,827	21,827	24,252	24,252	33,953	54,971	55,895	60,977	81,302	91,465	100,612
Bank debt	100,000	100,000	100,000	100,000	100,000	100,000	100,000	100,000	100,000	100,000	100,000	100,000
Total liabilities	$121,827	$121,827	$121,827	$124,252	$124,252	$133,953	$154,971	$155,895	$160,977	$181,302	$191,465	$200,612
Equity												
Paid-in capital	525,000	525,000	525,000	525,000	525,000	525,000	525,000	525,000	525,000	525,000	525,000	525,000
Ret. earnings	4,660	13,478	19,795	26,113	36,588	47,063	74,168	113,745	174,110	242,790	344,730	463,300
Total equity	529,660	538,478	544,795	551,113	561,588	572,063	599,168	638,745	699,110	767,790	869,730	988,300
Total liab & eq	$651,487	$660,304	$666,622	$675,365	$685,840	$706,015	$754,139	$794,640	$860,087	$949,092	$1,061,195	$1,188,912

Projected Cash Flow

	Jan	Feb	Mar	Apr	May	Jun	Jul	Aug	Sep	Oct	Nov	Dec
Net income	$4,660	$8,818	$6,318	$6,318	$10,475	$10,475	$27,105	$39,578	$60,365	$68,680	$101,940	$118,570
Dividends	0	0	0	0	0	0	0	0	0	0	0	0
Depreciation	833	833	833	833	833	833	833	833	833	833	833	833
Inventory	(15,591)	0	0	(1,732)	0	(6,929)	(15,013)	(11,549)	(4,619)	(18,478)	(9,239)	(8,315)
Receivables	(110,867)	(124,725)	(13,858)	0	(13,858)	(13,858)	(55,433)	(97,008)	(110,867)	(97,008)	(138,583)	(166,300)
Payables	21,827	0	0	2,425	0	9,701	21,018	924	5,081	20,326	10,163	9,147
Cash from opers.	($99,137)	($115,074)	($6,707)	$7,844	($2,550)	$222	($21,490)	($67,222)	($49,206)	($25,647)	($34,886)	($46,065)
Capital exp:												
Fixed assets	100,000	0	0	0	0	0	0	0	0	0	0	0
Cash generated:												
Surplus/(deficit)	($199,137)	($115,074)	($6,707)	$7,844	($2,550)	$222	($21,490)	($67,222)	($49,206)	($25,647)	($34,886)	($46,065)
Financing:												
Equity	525,000	0	0	0	0	0	0	0	0	0	0	0
Bank debt	100,000	0	0	0	0	0	0	0	0	0	0	0
Net cash flow	425,863	(115,074)	(6,707)	7,844	(2,550)	222	(21,490)	(67,222)	(49,206)	(25,647)	(34,886)	(46,065)
Beginning cash	0	425,863	310,789	304,081	311,925	309,375	309,597	288,107	220,885	171,678	146,031	111,145
Ending cash	$425,863	$310,789	$304,081	$311,925	$309,375	$309,597	$288,107	$220,885	$171,678	$146,031	$111,145	$65,080

EXHIBIT 7 Bright Ideas: Projected Financial Statements

Projected Income Statement (in thousands, except units)

	1994				1995				1996			
	Qtr 1	Qtr 2	Qtr 3	Qtr 4	Qtr 1	Qtr 2	Qtr 3	Qtr 4	Qtr 1	Qtr 2	Qtr 3	Qtr 4
Units (linear ft.)	90,000	97,000	105,000	108,000	154,000	210,000	226,000	260,000	270,000	300,000	312,000	318,000
Net sales	$1,247	$1,344	$1,455	$1,497	$2,134	$2,910	$3,132	$3,603	$3,742	$4,158	$4,324	$4,407
Cost of goods sold	624	672	728	748	1,067	1,455	1,566	1,802	1,871	2,079	2,162	2,203
Gross margin	624	672	728	748	1,067	1,455	1,566	1,802	1,871	2,079	2,162	2,203
Operating expenses:												
S, G&A	200	215	233	239	331	451	485	558	561	624	649	661
Depreciation	2	2	3	3	5	6	7	8	8	10	10	11
Operating income	422	455	491	506	732	998	1,073	1,235	1,301	1,446	1,504	1,532
Interest expense	2	2	0	0	0	0	0	0	0	0	0	0
EBT	420	453	491	506	732	998	1,073	1,235	1,301	1,446	1,504	1,532
Taxes	168	181	197	202	293	399	429	494	521	578	601	613
Net income	$252	$272	$295	$303	$439	$599	$644	$741	$781	$867	$902	$919
Dividends	$0	$0	$0	$0	$200	$200	$200	$200	$400	$400	$400	$400

Projected Balance Sheet (in thousands)

	1994				1995				1996			
	Qtr 1	Qtr 2	Qtr 3	Qtr 4	Qtr 1	Qtr 2	Qtr 3	Qtr 4	Qtr 1	Qtr 2	Qtr 3	Qtr 4
Assets												
Cash	$551	$779	$922	$1,219	$1,107	$1,077	$1,375	$1,594	$1,916	$2,136	$2,565	$3,005
Inventory	56	61	62	89	121	130	150	156	173	180	184	202
Acc/rec.	624	672	728	748	1,067	1,455	1,566	1,802	1,871	2,079	2,162	2,203
Net fixed assets	138	136	183	179	225	269	312	353	345	385	376	415
Total assets	$1,369	$1,648	$1,895	$2,235	$2,520	$2,931	$3,403	$3,905	$4,305	$4,780	$5,286	$5,825
Liabilities												
Payables	78	85	87	124	170	183	210	171	191	198	202	222
Bank debt	50	50	0	0	0	0	0	0	0	0	0	0
Total liabilities	$128	$135	$87	$124	$170	$183	$210	$171	$191	$198	$202	$222
Equity												
Paid-in capital	525	525	525	525	525	525	525	525	525	525	525	525
Ret. earnings	716	988	1,283	1,586	1,825	2,224	2,668	3,209	3,589	4,057	4,559	5,078
Total equity	1,241	1,513	1,808	2,111	2,350	2,749	3,193	3,734	4,114	4,582	5,084	5,603
Total liab & eq	$1,369	$1,648	$1,895	$2,235	$2,520	$2,931	$3,403	$3,905	$4,305	$4,780	$5,286	$5,825

Projected Cash Flow (in thousands)

	1994				1995				1996			
	Qtr 1	Qtr 2	Qtr 3	Qtr 4	Qtr 1	Qtr 2	Qtr 3	Qtr 4	Qtr 1	Qtr 2	Qtr 3	Qtr 4
Net income	$252	$272	$295	$303	$439	$599	$644	$741	$781	$867	$902	$919
Dividends	0	0	0	0	(200)	(200)	(200)	(200)	(400)	(400)	(400)	(400)
Depreciation	2	2	3	3	5	6	7	8	8	10	10	11
Inventory	35	(5)	(2)	(27)	(32)	(9)	(20)	(6)	(17)	(7)	(3)	(18)
Receivables	319	(49)	(55)	(21)	(319)	(388)	(111)	(236)	(69)	(208)	(83)	(42)
Payables	(22)	6	2	37	45	13	27	(39)	19	8	4	20
Cash from opers.	$586	$228	$243	$296	($62)	$20	$348	$269	$322	$270	$429	$490
Capital exp:												
Fixed assets	50	0	50	0	50	50	50	50	0	50	0	50
Cash generated:												
Surplus/(deficit)	$536	$228	$193	$296	($112)	($30)	$298	$219	$322	$220	$429	$440
Financing:												
Equity	0	0	0	0	0	0	0	0	0	0	0	0
Bank debt	(50)	0	(50)	0	0	0	0	0	0	0	0	0
Net cash flow	486	228	143	296	(112)	(30)	298	219	322	220	429	440
Beginning cash	65	551	779	922	1,219	1,107	1,077	1,375	1,594	1,916	2,136	2,565
Ending cash	$551	$779	$922	$1,219	$1,107	1,077	$1,375	$1,594	$1,916	$2,136	$2,565	$3,005

EXHIBIT 8   Cash Flow, IRR, and NPV to Investors (25%)

	1992	1993	1994	1995	1996
Investment	(500,000)				
Dividends (25%)	0	0	0	200,000	400,000
Share of est. mkt value @ 10x inc					8,673,250
Net CF—investor	($500,000)	$0	$0	$200,000	$9,073,250
Annualized IRR	109%				

Discount Rate	NPV
45%	$1,618,140
50	1,351,506
55	1,125,648
60	933,296

EXHIBIT 9   Cash Flow, IRR, and NPV to Investors (25%): Pessimistic Scenarios

Sales = 60% of projected
Values = 6 × income

	1992	1993	1994	1995	1996
Investment	(500,000)				
Dividends (25%)	0	0	0	100,000	200,000
Share of est. mkt value @ 6× inc					3,108,570
Net CF—investor	($500,000)	$0	$0	$100,000	$3,308,570
Annualized IRR	62%				

Discount Rate	NPV
45%	$281,261
50	183,174
55	100,063
60	29,262

Sales = 80% of projected
Value = 8 × income

	1992	1993	1994	1995	1996
Investment	(500,000)				
Dividends (25%)	0	0	0	100,000	200,000
Share of est. mkt value @ 8× inc					5,541,600
Net CF—investor	($500,000)	$0	$0	$100,000	5,741,600
Annualized IRR	86%				

Discount Rate	NPV
45%	$831,657
50	663,773
55	521,586
60	400,513

EXHIBIT 10 Bright Ideas' Founders' Resumes

BENJAMIN J. HARRISON

Current Address:
976 Woodbridge Drive
Bloomington, IN 47408
(812) 339-8182

Permanent Address:
7125 Saratoga Lane
Chattanooga, TN 37421
(615) 894-3441

CAREER OBJECTIVE

Seeking a marketing position that allows broad exposure to a variety of functional areas, including promotion and market research. Ultimately aspire to marketing management position within an organization.

EDUCATION

INDIANA UNIVERSITY—Bloomington, IN, MBA, Marketing, 1990–1992, GPA 3.1, Receiving strong marketing instruction from one of the top MBA programs in the country.

UNIVERSITY OF VIRGINIA—Charlottesville, VA, BS, Architectural Design, 1984–1988, GPA 3.0, Excelled in one of the most rigorous areas of undergraduate study at UVA. Earned minor in History.

ACTIVITIES AND HONORS

Graduate: Editor, Indiana MBA Journal; Marketing Club; Finance Guild; Member of Capital Area PC Professional User's Group while employed in Washington, DC. **Undergraduate:** Member of Atlantic Coast Conference Academic Honor Roll; Letter Winner on University of Virginia's nationally ranked Varsity Track and Cross Country teams; Finisher, 1987 Boston Marathon; Theta Delta Chi—social fraternity.

WORK EXPERIENCE

PLEASANTS AND ASSOCIATES Falls Church, VA May 1991–Aug. 1991
General Management Intern Prepared and edited contract documents. Constructed database to increase accuracy of job cost estimating and enhance efficiency of bidding process. Reviewed potential candidates for full-time employment within the organization.

HOLLE, LIN AND SHOGREN ARCHITECTS—Washington, DC May 1988–Aug. 1990

Design Assistant Office technical expert in implementation of computer-aided design systems (CAD). Provided training to office staff. Produced entire sets of working drawings, including a 54-million dollar mixed-use high-rise development and a 60,000 square foot corporate headquarters. Designed company advertisements for local and trade publications. Participated in layout design for promotional brochures. Established construction schedules, priced out building phases, performed site inspections, and prepared cost estimates for U.S. government leasing. Presented and reviewed designs with clients, engineering consultants, and subcontractors.

ALDERMAN LIBRARY, UNIVERSITY OF VIRGINIA Charlottesville, VA Sept. 1986–May 1988

Archivist's Assistant Compiled collections of historical correspondence, documents, and drawings for the Department of Archives and Manuscripts. Wrote summaries and guides for further research.

DB ASSOCIATES Charlottesville, VA Winter 1987

Architectural Intern Assisted in preparation for visual presentation of design for suburban shopping center.

REFERENCES

MR. STEVE LIN Vice President, Holle, Lin, and Shogren Architects, 4125 MacArthur Blvd. NW Washington, DC 20016, (202) 686-1190
MS. MARGARET WHALEN Manager, internal accounting department, USAir, Inc., 2345 Crystal Drive Crystal Park Four, Arlington, VA 22227, (703) 418-5744
MR. DAVID PFEFFER Vice President, Central Loan Administration, Comerica Incorporated, Detroit, MI 48275, (313) 496-6208
MR. ROBERT SHOGREN Vice President, Holle, Lin, and Shogren Architects, 5125 MacArthur Blvd. NW Washington, DC 20016, (202) 686-1190

EXHIBIT 10 (continued)

JAMES R. FLOBERG

Current Address:
3361 Acadia Court
Bloomington, IN 47401
(812) 332-6014

Permanent Address:
6240 Grand Avenue South
Richfield, MN 55423
(612) 869-3494

CAREER OBJECTIVE
CORPORATE FINANCE Seeking a position as a financial analyst that will provide exposure to a broad range of responsibilities as an analyst and manager, including such areas as cash flow, capital budgeting, tax evaluation and cost control. Desire a position that involves interaction with others both inside and outside the organization and requires strong interpersonal skills.

EDUCATION
INDIANA UNIVERSITY Bloomington, IN, MBA, Finance, 5/92, GPA 3.9, High achievement in all classes as a graduate student. Coursework includes a variety of elective courses in finance.
UNIVERSITY OF MINNESOTA Minneapolis, MN, BS, Economics, 6/87, GPA 3.3, Maintained a GPA of 3.43 over the final two years and a GPA of 3.84 in major courses.

ACTIVITIES AND HONORS
Graduate Outstanding Graduate Intern Scholarship from PNC, MBA Toastmasters, MBA Association, Finance Guild.
Professional Chartered Property Casualty Underwriter Program.
Undergraduate Treasurer of the Economic Student Organization, Dean's List three quarters.

EXPERIENCE
PNC-PITTSBURGH NATIONAL BANK Pittsburgh, PA 5/91–8/91
MBA Intern. Developed a system for analyzing financial data on the Bank's largest commercial credit. Coordinated and ran the undergraduate intern program, consisting of over thirty students. Received a scholarship as the Outstanding Graduate Intern.

INDIANA UNIVERSITY Bloomington, IN 8/90–Present
Graduate Assistant. Serve as a Quality Control Coordinator in the Econometrics Department of the Indiana Business Research Center. Monitor the accuracy of the STATIS database and make efficiency recommendations. Developed and currently revising a five-year plan for data verification.

ST. PAUL SPECIALTY UNDERWRITING, INC. St. Paul, MN 6/87–7/90
Director and Officer Liability Insurance Underwriter. Evaluated management. Analyzed corporate earnings performance, financial condition, shareholder satisfaction and plan of growth all within the context of that industry's trends and environment. Educated insurance brokers and agents. Interpreted and negotiated insurance contracts. Represented The St. Paul in client meetings and seminars. Acted as a liason with other departments within The St. Paul to provide an entire insurance package for targeted industries. Had total responsibility for managing a number of underwriting territories.

UNIVERSITY OF MINNESOTA Minneapolis, MN 4/86–6/87
Undergraduate Teaching Assistant. Graded homework and exams and proctored exams for a variety of economics courses. Tutored students in introductory and intermediate level economics courses.

REFERENCES
MR. JAMES WAY Manager, St. Paul Specialty Underwriting, Inc., 385 Washington Street, St. Paul, MN 55102, (612) 228-8803
MR. NORMAN ENGEL Controller and Vice President, St. Paul Specialty Underwriting, Inc., 385 Washington Street, St. Paul, MN 55102, (612) 228-8987
PROFESSOR WILLIAM SARTORIS Finance Department, Indiana University, 10th and Fee Lane Office 370B, Bloomington, IN 47405, (812) 855-8568

EXHIBIT 10 (continued)

MARK RICHARD WIDMAR, C.P.A.

1201 Carson Way, Apt. #313
Greenwood, IN 46143
(317) 889-8049

52125 Brookview Court
South Bend, IN 46637
(219) 272-9483

CAREER OBJECTIVE Seeking a position that will provide initial exposure to all areas of corporate financial analysis and planning. Desire to utilize my analytical and communication skills in analyzing various financial projects such as cash flow, financial statement analysis, etc. Goal is to use my knowledge of finance and accounting concepts to manage a financial department during advancement to senior management positions.

EDUCATION INDIANA UNIVERSITY Bloomington, IN, MBA, Finance, 5/92, GPA 3.81

Supplemented my finance courses with electives in decision and information systems, entrepreneurships, and strategic management to provide breath of knowledge required of upper management.

INDIANA UNIVERSITY Bloomington, IN, BS, Business-Accounting, 12/87, GPA 3.6

ACTIVITIES AND HONORS

GRADUATE ACTIVITIES/MEMBERSHIPS	UNDERGRADUATE ACTIVITIES/HONORS
• MBA Association—Orientation Mentor	• Dean's List (6 semesters)

• Finance Guild
  -Fund Raising Committee Chair
  -Shadow Day Committee Co-Chair
	• Internship through Professional Practice program
	• Participated in program to acclimate foreign exchange students

• Toastmasters International Speech Club	
• B.E.S.T. Organization	• Beta Alpha Psi
• Junior Achievement	• Intramural Sports

EXPERIENCE INDIANA UNIVERSITY Bloomington, IN, 08/90–05/92
Graduate Assistant, School of Business Library Worked 12 hours per week as library reference consultant assisting students in their research efforts and acclimating them to the services provided by the library.

ERNST & YOUNG Indianapolis, IN 01/88–08/90
Senior Accountant Responsible for audit engagement's initial planning and coordination of client assistance, direction of day to day progress of the fieldwork, including the supervision and development of two/three staff members, and preparation of audited financial statements and tax returns. Consistently met or improved engagement's budgeted expectations. Worked closely with management advising them on technical, as well as system efficiency, issues.

CROWE, CHIZEK AND COMPANY South Bend, IN 09/86–01/87
Audit Intern Worked as a member of audit team assisting in preparation of audited work papers and financial statements. Developed interpersonal communication skills through interaction with other group members and client personnel.

REFERENCES MR. HOWARD SHEARON Partner in Charge of Audit, Ernst & Young. One Indiana Square, Suite 3400 Indianapolis, In 46204, (317) 236-1100
MR. BRUCE BALDWIN Senior Manager, Ernst & Young, One Indiana Square, Suite 3400 Indianapolis, In 46204 (317) 236-1100
MR. GARY BRICK Senior Manager, Ernst & Young, One Indiana Square, Suite 3400 Indianapolis, In 46204 (317) 236-1100

EXHIBIT 10 (continued)

Kenneth Lee Wilson

Current Address:
417 E. 1st Street
Bloomington, IN 47401
(812) 331-2695

Permanent Address:
4382 Poole Rd.
Cincinnati, OH 45251
(513) 385-2220

CAREER OBJECTIVE   Seeking a position with a small organization or an entrepreneural venture that utilizes my communication, computer and management talents.

EDUCATION   **Indiana University** Bloomington, IN, MBA, Dual concentration: Entrepreneurship and Marketing, May 1992, GPA 3.77/4.0

Miami University, Oxford, OH, BS, Interdisciplinary Studies, Dual concentration: philosophy and creative writing, May 1988, GPA 3.62/4.0

ACTIVITIES AND HONORS

Graduate	Undergraduate
• MBA Association	• Honors Program
• Real Estate Club	• Dean's List (5 semesters)
• Habitat for Humanity	• Studied in Luxembourg 1 semester
• Carpet Appreciation Society	• Marching Band-section leader
	• WYCC student radio disc jockey

EXPERIENCE   **Desktop Compositions,** Bloomington, IN 4/89–present
Owner/Operator Manage a freelance design and production firm. Use desktop publishing equipment to write, design, format and produce all types of printed documents. Won a national design award, 6/91. In 1990, acting as junior partner, the firm grossed over $115,000. In 1991, on a part-time basis, grossed $27,000.

Institute for Research on MIS (IRMIS), Bloomington IN, 9/90–5/91, 9/91–5/92
IU Graduate Assistant Responsible for preparing marketing plan for the institute. Write, design, and produce all of the promotional materials for the institute. Performed a research project analyzing the present and future role of information technology in a range of Indiana organizations.

Omega Properties, Cincinnati, OH, 6/91–present
Owner/Operator Created a real estate rehabilitation firm. Research, locate and purchase undervalued properties. Supervise the rehabilitation of the properties. Manage the rental and/or resale of the properties. Currently showing profit of $18,900 after 4 months of operation.

REFERENCES   **Dr. Daniel W. DeHayes,** Professor, Business Administration; Executive Director, IRMIS, Bloomington, IN 47405, (812) 855-7330

Ms. Karen Linch, Owner, Desktop Compositions, Cincinnati Ohio, 45202, (512) 522-4166

Ms. Mev Soller, Director, Public Relations, Cincinnati Bell Telephone, Cincinnati, OH 45202, (513) 397-7731

The people and circumstances of this case are real. The business plan is presented with the permission of its authors. I acknowledge with gratitude the hard work and effort of Ben Harrison, James Floberg, Mark Widmar, and Ken Wilson. A video of the Bright Ideas presentation is available.

Case 7   Rubio's: Home of the Fish Taco

Rubio's Restaurants Inc., formerly known as Rubio's Deli-Mex, is a family-owned and operated Mexican restaurant located in southern California. Rubio's specializes in authentic, fresh-tasting Mexican food using authentic Mexican recipes. Rubio's is best known, however, for its fish tacos, which were relatively unknown in San Diego prior to Rubio's entry in 1983. Although Rubio's is known as the "Home of the Fish Taco," the menu also offers a variety of other, more traditional Mexican favorites such as burritos and carnitas. Designed as a fast-food restaurant, the food may be ordered for consumption on the premises or for carryout. Rubio's offers an alternative to the full-service Mexican restaurant without sacrificing quality. The success of this concept has been phenomenal. After opening in 1983 with one location near Mission Bay. Rubio's has, in just nine years, grown to include 12 restaurants extending from San Diego to Orange County.

HISTORY

The concept for Rubio's restaurants was first developed in the late 1970s during one of Ralph Rubio's camping adventures in San Felipe on the Baja peninsula, Mexico. According to the legend, it was on one of these excursions that Ralph observed numerous American tourists lined up to purchase fish tacos from the San Felipe beach vendors. Over the years, taco stands proliferated in San Felipe. Figuring that fish tacos would be as popular in San Diego as they were in the Baja, Ralph solicited one of the veteran beach vendors, "Carlos," to move to San Diego and open a restaurant that featured these tacos. Although Carlos declined, he provided Ralph with his "secret family recipe" for fish tacos. Ralph carried this recipe with him for five years after his 1978 graduation from San Diego State University. Armed with his liberal arts degree, eight years' experience in the restaurant industry, and $30,000 from his father, Ralph opened the first Rubio's on January 25, 1983. It was located on East Mission Bay Drive in the Pacific Beach area of San Diego, California, on the site of a previously failed hamburger restaurant. Despite Ralph's lack of a menu just two days before the restaurant's scheduled opening, the first week's sales averaged $250 a day and the restaurant was packed. Within three years, sales at the restaurant grew to $2,000 a day. Based on the success of the first restaurant, in March 1986 a second location was opened on College Avenue near San Diego State University. Shortly thereafter, in August 1987, Rubio's opened its third location near Pacific Beach. Rubio's expansion has continued at a rapid rate. Rubio's now has 12 locations from as far south as Chula Vista to as far north as Irvine.

THE FAST-FOOD INDUSTRY

The United States food service industry estimates its 1991 sales at $248.1 billion. The second-largest category of restaurants in the food service industry are the limited-menu outlets, which consist largely of fast-food restaurants such as Rubio's. Sales in this category of food providers are estimated for 1991 at $74.1 billion. According to the National Restaurant Association (NRA), fast-food restaurants have enjoyed rapid growth. In fact, from 1970 to 1990, sales in these limited-menu restaurants have increased at an estimated 12.9 percent compound rate, compared with 7.9 percent for the remainder of the U.S. food service industry.

The success of the fast-food industry, a relatively mature, highly competitive business, is believed to be the result of changing demographics and lifestyles. Over the past several decades more Americans have been turning to restaurants for their meals. Dual-income families made the option of dining out a necessity because of the families' lack of spare time. At the same time, additional income made dining out more affordable. The fast-food industry has also managed to sell its customers on the value and convenience their products and services offer. This perception has been enhanced by the addition of drive-through windows, which enable customers to order and be served in their cars. Restaurants have further catered to customers' idea of convenience by adding delivery to the current list of services offered. Despite these positive indicators, Rubio's, as a competitor in the fast-food industry, faces several challenges in the imminent future. The relatively weaker economy of 1991 and 1992 has led to higher unemployment and an increase in meals prepared and consumed in the home. The fast-food industry is also threatened by several other factors, including environmental pressures, increased nutritional awareness, the AIDS scare, and governmental legislation. As a player in the fast-food industry, Rubio's must monitor the arena in which it participates and respond to the following opportunities and challenges.

Changing Demographics

Aging Population   The United States is simultaneously experiencing a rise in life expectancy and a decline in the number of people aged 15 to 34. The net effect of these trends is an aging U.S. population. This change in demographics is likely to have a significant impact on the fast-food industry. First, as the population of consumers grows older, it is likely their tastes will shift toward midscale restaurants and away from the fast-food industry. In fact, according to a 1988 study conducted by the NRA, customers aged 18 to 24 spend 79 percent of their time attributed to eating out at fast-food restaurants, while individuals aged 45 to 54 spend only 60 percent of their time eating out at fast-food restaurants. The difference between these age groups is allegedly the result of older patrons' higher disposable income and their desire for additional amenities.

The Baby Boomers   The second impact from the changing demographics results from the recent rise in birth rates. Although double-income families have less time for food preparation, baby boomers are now having families of their own. As a result, there are more households with small children who are less likely to dine out. Instead, these families are utilizing such conveniences as microwaves and take-out and delivery services.

The Decline in Teenagers   Finally, the decline in the birth rate in the early 1970s has resulted in a decrease in the number of youths between the ages of 16 to 20. The fast-food segment of the restaurant industry has traditionally relied on this category of individuals as its main source of labor. As a result, fast-food restaurants have had a harder time attracting and retaining employees. This has, to a degree, been alleviated by the vast amount of unemployment resulting from the current recession. However, the overall change in demographics is forcing the fast-food industry to adjust accordingly.

Nutritional Concerns

In addition to the changes associated with an aging population, the fast-food industry must also respond to changes in customers' needs and concerns. Baby boomers are becoming preoccupied with healthier eating, and fast-food restaurants are responding accordingly. Individuals are now concerned not only with value and convenience, but also with the fat and cholesterol content of the items offered by fast-food restaurants. As a result, restaurants are changing their menus and product offerings to emphasize, or deemphasize, the benefits of their products.

In an effort to lure customers, McDonald's launched the new McLean Deluxe, a burger that boasts only 9 percent fat because of the use of seaweed substitutes. Although purportedly healthier, the new item costs the consumer a $0.20 premium over the usual quarter-pounder, which has twice the fat. McDonald's also followed the lead of other fast-food restaurants by switching to 100 percent vegetable oil from a blend containing beef tallow for cooking fries and hash browns. Encouraged by consumer acceptance of these products, McDonald's replaced its ice cream with lowfat yogurt, introduced lowfat milk shakes, and even added cereal and bran muffins to its menu. In June 1991, McDonald's introduced, as limited time promotional items, a 90-calorie Diet Coke float and a 275-calorie grilled chicken sandwich. Other fast-food restaurants, such as Burger King and KFC, have also changed their product offerings to cater to consumers' health concerns. These changes reflect the need of fast-food restaurants to change in response to the needs and concerns of a changing population.

Governmental Legislation

Teen Labor Laws   The fast-food industry must also deal with changes in the legislation that affects it. One such area of legislation is teen labor laws. Current legislation prohibits 14- and 15-year-old persons from working on school nights after 7:00 PM, a time when restaurants usually need a full staff to deal with the dinner crowd. Representatives in the industry have been advocating changes in these restrictions to permit teenagers (1) to work a maximum of four hours on days preceding school days, one hour more than currently allowed, and (2) to work until 9:00 PM on school nights, two hours past the current restriction. Industry advocates are also seeking an extension of the cooking and baking activities these workers are legally permitted to perform. These proposed changes would help ease the pressures on restaurant managers who are attempting to deal with the limited work force. However, the industry's lobbyists met much resistance. In fact, several legislators were seeking to enact certain bills that would increase the pressures on the fast-food industry's hiring practices. One proposed bill would substantially increase penalties for serious infractions of federal teen labor laws to include prison terms for employers whose willful violations resulted in the serious injury of a teenage employee. Another provision of the bill sought a requirement that all applicants under the age of 18 secure a state-issued work permit if they do not possess a high school diploma. Industry representatives believe that regulations such as these would decrease the number of teenagers hired, thereby hurting the exact individuals whom the laws were designed to protect.

Federal Minimum Wage Hike   Legislation in other areas may also affect the fast-food industry. On April 1, 1991, the federal minimum wage rose from $3.80 to $4.25, with a subminimum exception for persons who have never before held a job. Payroll expenses generally account for 26 percent of all sales dollars. According to a survey conducted by Oregon State University, fast-food outlets were relatively unscathed because the majority of their employees already earn between $5.50 and $6.00 an hour. Although full-service restaurants were hit the hardest by this legislation, labor is the second-biggest cost for all restaurant operators.

Mandated Health Plans   The food service industry also faces an increase in labor costs from legislation related to mandated health plans. Legislators are pushing for a bill that would require employers to provide all their employees with health insurance or face a special payroll tax of 7 to 8 percent. The special payroll tax would then be used to fund a federally administered insurance program for low-income Americans. If enacted, the industry fears that many small restaurant operations will be forced out of business by the expensive plan. As an alternative, industry advocates are seeking tax breaks and other incentives designed to encourage restaurant owners to voluntarily provide health insurance to employees.

Discrimination in the Workplace   The fast-food industry is also monitoring proposed legislation intended to curtail job discrimination by allowing workers the right to have juries decide lawsuits against employers suspected of discrimination in the workplace. The act would permit the victims of discrimination to seek both compensatory and punitive damages, an option previously restricted to persons charging racial discrimination. Industry advocates contend that this legislation would shift the burden of the culpability test to require a business to prove its innocence rather than requiring the plaintiff to prove its guilt. As such, restaurants would be forced to resort to hiring persons because of their demographic traits rather than their abilities. Although the original form of the act would not have passed, proponents have negotiated a compromise with the White House guaranteeing its passage.

AIDS, *E. Coli*, and Customer Health   The fast-food industry cannot escape the effects of the AIDS controversy. According to the executive vice-president of the NRA, Bill Fisher, a number of restaurants are identified as employing individuals either suffering from AIDS or infected with HIV. Once identified, the restaurants suffer a rapid decline in business and are often forced to close. As of July 1990, food service lobbyists were attempting to revive the Chapman Amendment (as it was known in the House), a measure that would exempt food service operators from providing employees with AIDS the same rights and privileges as their healthy peers. Employers would then be able to reassign infected employees to positions of comparable salary that did not involve any food handling. Contrary to the food industry's desires, the Senate enacted the Hatch Amendment, which is similar to the Chapman Amendment with one added qualification. It provides that the secretary of the U.S. Health and Human Services Department specify annually the diseases that can be transmitted through food. The Hatch Amendment further provides that only persons with a designated illness may be reassigned. According to Dr. Louis Sullivan, former Secretary of the U.S. Health and Human Services Department, AIDS cannot be spread through food or beverages. The net effect of enacting this law is that food handlers with AIDS may retain their posts, and restaurants are virtually defenseless against consumers' fears.

The winter of 1993 saw an outbreak of illness caused by *E. coli* bacteria infection. A total of 475 cases of illness and three deaths were reported in the West, predominantly in the state of Washington. The cause has been attributed to tainted hamburger meat served at fast-food establishments operated by Foodmaker, Inc. (Jack in the Box). Review of meat vendor qualifications and cooking procedures was immediately undertaken, but a precipitous decline in sales could not be avoided. Whether a full recovery by Foodmaker is possible and what sort of regulations may emerge at the state or federal level are as yet unknown.

Environmental Pressures

The fast-food industry has also been facing increasing pressure from environmental groups to become more concerned over the ecological effect of its products and packaging. According to these environmental groups, chlorofluorocarbons (CFCs), used in the production of the plastic packaging used by the fast-food industry, are responsible for damage to the ozone layer, which protects life on earth from the harmful effects of the sun's ultraviolet rays. Environmentalists also contend that the plastic packaging made of polystyrene foam takes up valuable space in landfills, takes decades to decompose, and has no viable recycling market. Despite some studies that indicated that the packaging is environmentally sound, McDonald's, the world's largest restaurant chain, began replacing plastic packaging in favor of paper. Although the paper is not recyclable and requires tremendous chemical and industrial processes to create it, it is biodegradable if composted and requires less space than foam packaging when discarded. McDonald's explained some of the factors leading to its switch, citing its lack of success at recapturing the packaging that leaves its restaurants and the lack of an infrastructure in the plastics-recycling industry. However, it appears that the company's 1990 annual report explains the real impetus for McDonald's change: "Although scientific studies indicate that foam packaging is sound, customers just don't feel good about it." Several other fast-food companies have also initiated environmental policies that involve recyclable polystyrene and compostable paper and plastic. McDonald's plan, however, is the most sweeping in the industry. The company will also replace its large white take-out bags with brown recyclable ones, convert to smaller napkins, install stainless steel condiment dispensers to eliminate the need for packets, compost eggshells and coffee grounds, and test starch-based spoons, knives, and forks as substitutes for current plastic versions. The company is further challenging its vendors to recycle and will require periodic progress reports that evidence the suppliers' use of recycled material in containers.

Suppliers

Food and beverage suppliers to the fast-food industry exert power on the participants by raising prices or reducing the quality of their products and/or services. One way a restaurant may deal with its suppliers is through backward integration. McDonald's entertained such a move and entered the business of raising cattle. Naturally, the environmentalists who condemn the use of plastics also condemn the raising of cattle—their grazing habits cause erosion and their waste pollutes the ground and air.

Rivalry among Competitors

As a member of the fast-food industry, Rubio's competes with numerous types of restaurants, ranging from individual independent operations to franchises and chains. Rivalry among competitors results from a number of factors, including fixed costs. Fixed costs in the restaurant industry, which include labor costs, utility bills, and the interest expense on buildings, land, and equipment, are quite high. Restaurants have developed a variety of alternatives to compete by reducing their fixed costs.

Contract Services   PepsiCo Inc.'s Taco Bell has adopted one way to reduce high fixed costs. Since the mid-eighties, Taco Bell has been shifting as much of the food preparation to outside providers as possible. By contracting with these outside suppliers, Taco Bell has been able to reduce not only labor costs but kitchen space as well. This reduction in fixed costs has allowed Taco Bell to slash its menu prices, thereby attracting 60 percent more customers and reaching sales of $2.6 billion, a 63 percent increase.

Robotics   The desire of fast-food restaurants to reduce the labor costs has resulted in several more imaginative alternatives. Taco Bell is investigating whether robotics in the kitchen will increase savings by reducing space and labor requirements. Within two years, they are expected to adopt automatic taco makers and soft-drink dispensers. Carl's Jr. restaurant is utilizing an automated ordering system, dubbed Touch 2000, which allows customers to enter their own selections on a touch-sensitive countertop menu. The menu is connected to an IBM computer that checks the order and prompts the customer for more specific information if it is not satisfied. When satisfied, the computer relays the order automatically to the kitchen and the cashier. Burger King is currently evaluating the system as well. Although robotics reduce labor costs, increase productivity, and virtually eliminate boring jobs, not all fast-food restaurants are converting to their use. Today's economy has made human labor more available, reduced restaurant profits, and forced cutbacks in spending on research and development.

Reduced-Size Restaurants   Restaurants are also developing downsized units in an effort to reduce costs and gain access to towns that were previously dismissed because of their inability to generate sufficient sales to sustain a full-size outlet. McDonald's new prototype, called the Series 2000, is 50 percent smaller and costs 30 percent less to build. These new units seat 50 patrons and employ only 20 persons per shift. McDonald's traditional units seat twice as many customers and require, at a minimum, 40 employees per shift. These downsized units will not only allow the chain to enter small towns but will also allow the company to secure locations in congested markets that were previously inaccessible because of the limited size of available sites.

Value Menus   Fast-food restaurants have also explored a variety of strategies to attract customers during hard economic times. In an attempt to compete for the consumer's dollar, Red Lobster, a dinner house, launched a value menu that boasts numerous entrées for less than $10. In addition, the chain upgraded its china, uniforms, and napkins to enhance its image of providing the customer with value. Although fast-food restaurants must proceed cautiously to ensure that the customer's need for quick service is satisfied, many fast-food restaurants are also opting for expanded menus to attract customers. McDonald's has also unveiled new menu selections designed to boost sales. Of particular concern to Rubio's is the addition of two Mexican items, the breakfast burrito and the chicken fajita. McDonald's is also testing turkey and pizza as other menu options. U.S. president Ed Rensi does not anticipate that the addition of these new products will dilute the company's concept of serving hot fast food in a pleasant environment at a low cost. In fact, new technology should enable McDonald's to broaden its menu while maintaining good service times. Other fast-food restaurants have responded to this threat by promoting time-intensive products on a limited basis only.

Taco Bell, the nation's leading Mexican fast-food restaurant, is credited with having started these discount wars with the addition of its 59- and 39-cent value menu items. As operating profits for the third quarter of 1991 decreased, analysts wondered whether Taco Bell's value menu had discounted the chain out of a profit margin. However, according to Taco Bell president John Martin, the chain will not need to raise prices for at least five years because of its systemic restructuring and cost-saving technological changes in operational methods.

Marketing Strategies   Restaurants have also explored other marketing strategies in an attempt to attract customers. Burger King developed a Kids Club to capitalize on the power of children to influence the purchases of their parents. Burger King entices its 2.7 million members with six newsletters "written" by well-known cartoon characters. The members also receive iron-on T-shirt logos and activity booklets. Burger King analysts credit the club for a recognizable increase in the chain's business. Burger King is also investigating other marketing alternatives to increase consumer spending. To further reach its teenage market, Burger King is buying time on Channel One, a satellite service that beams 12 minutes of programming and commercials each day into school classrooms. It is believed that a 30-second commercial on Channel One reaches 40 percent more teens than a commercial on MTV. Finally, Burger King is spending a portion of its advertising budget on local tie-ins to help build traffic at its franchises.

Delivery Service   Fast-food restaurants such as Burger King are also attempting to prod the dinner crowd, who would ordinarily select a midrange restaurant, by offering limited table service during the dinner hour. Customers place their orders at a walk-up counter, serve themselves a drink, and select a seat. When ready, their order is served to them at their table. Although Burger King does not intend to raise its prices as a result of this new service, the effects remain to be seen.

Acknowledging that the 1990s will be a decade dedicated to convenience, pizza restaurants may not be alone in their home delivery service. Although KFC franchisees are reluctant and anticipate operational difficulties, KFC is planning to add delivery service to all 500 of its domestic units. Since no other chicken segment player offers home delivery, it is an opportunity to preempt its competitors and gain a competitive edge.

Payment Convenience   Fast-food restaurants are also experimenting with the use of bank cards and ATM cards as alternative methods for payment. MasterCard, which wants people to use its card for everyday transactions, estimates that 70 percent of the people who eat at fast-food restaurants have a bank card. Arby's tested the system and discovered that bank card transactions exceed cash purchases by 30 to 60 percent. As a result, Arby's will install the system in all company-owned stores. McDonald's is also experimenting with a McCharge card for use in its outlets.

Expanding Distribution Channels   In addition to expanding product lines, restaurants are also looking for new points of distribution. Aided by new technology, fast-food restaurants have moved into many nontraditional outlets. PepsiCo, which owns Taco Bell, Pizza Hut, and KFC, will expand into any outlet where it may tempt hungry consumers. As a result, PepsiCo's food service brands may now be seen in supermarkets, convenience stores, movie theaters, student unions, amusement parks, fairs, hospitals, airports, and sports arenas. Taco Bell is also entertaining the possibility of selling packaged meals on supermarket shelves, a potentially lucrative market given that a quarter of the people aged 35 to 44 are single.

THE RUBIO'S CONCEPT

Product Line

Rubio's main draw is its $1.49 fish tacos. A fish taco consists of a soft corn tortilla, pieces of deep-fried fish fillet, salsa, white sauce, cabbage, and a lime. The white sauce is made up of a mixture of mayonnaise and yogurt. Although the basic ingredients in the fish taco are known, because of local taco wars Rubio's batter for the fish remains a company secret. As a result, the batter is now packaged at a location other than the individual restaurants. Rubio's also offers a fish taco especial, which costs a little more but is prepared with such extras as guacamole, jack and cheddar cheese, cilantro, and onion. For those patrons who do not savor the idea of a fish taco, Rubio's menu offers such other traditional Mexican favorites as burritos, tostadas, nachos, and nonfish tacos. Consistent with the company's desire to satisfy the needs of its customers, menu items have been added or modified in response to customer input. All these items, including the fish tacos, are prepared to order using authentic Mexican recipes and fresh ingredients. A copy of Rubio's current menu is attached as Exhibit 1.

In addition to providing authentic, fresh-tasting Mexican food, Rubio's differentiates itself by offering a cold food menu enabling customers to purchase select ingredients to prepare their own meals at home. In essence, customers may purchase the makings for almost every item on the menu.

Facilities

Rubio's original restaurant locations were selected based on Ralph Rubio's knowledge of the areas and the characteristics of their population. Although Rubio's target market varies to some extent by store location, on the whole its market consists of young and middle-aged upscale professionals and students. Members of these groups typically value their health and enjoy such social activities as the beach, athletic competition, musical entertainment, and dining out. As a result, the facilities are typically located in fast-growing retail areas with high traffic and visibility. Rubio's also considers the land use mix within a three- to five-mile radius. As a result, the restaurants are located in areas with high percentages of residential and office or industrial uses. Unlike the typical inaccessible mall location, these locations provide a greater number of customers with the characteristics of Rubio's target market and more flexible operating hours.

Under the Rubio family's direction, the exterior style and interior design of each of Rubio's restaurants is consistent throughout their 12 locations. The typical unit features a walk-up order counter with a large red-and-white-lettered menu behind it. Paper menus, which detail the company's phone-in order policy, are also provided. The units' decor is contemporary, with light wood, green wallpaper, color framed prints, and Mexican tile tables. A mural of the company mascot, Pesky Pescado, usually appears on one wall. (Pesky is an animated fish, standing upright on his tail, with a taco shell wrapped around his body.) The typical unit also features decorations that emphasize a beach theme, including surfboards, palms, green-and-white walls, ceiling fans, and beach scenes. This upscale atmosphere is further enhanced by a sound system that plays authentic mariachi music.

Although the units vary slightly by location, most have 2,200 square feet, with a cooking area, a dining area for approximately 50 people, and an outdoor patio. Each restaurant features an area where customers may purchase deli items and/or a variety of promotional items, such as T-shirts, bumper stickers, and decals. All units, other than the original one near Mission Bay and the SDSU location, have beer and wine licenses, a feature intended to strengthen Rubio's image as a fast-food alternative to fine Mexican restaurants. Consistent with the company's emphasis on service and convenience to the customer, one restaurant site also features a drive-through facility.

Each Rubio's location also has a designated receptacle for recycling bottles and cans used in the restaurant. Given that there is no consensus on whether plastic or paper is better for the environment, Rubio's will continue to use clamshell containers, which have better thermal retention. Rubio's has, however, switched to tray service to reduce the amount of paper used in each facility. Therefore, each facility also has an area designated for tray storage. As the recycling infrastructure grows, Rubio's continues to monitor plastic recycling. Once the decision to recycle is made, each facility will also have to designate space for plastics recycling.

In addition to these 12 restaurant locations, in April 1990 Rubio's joined the concession lineup at Jack Murphy Stadium. By May, Rubio's had expanded to the plaza level in an effort to meet the enormous demand at the stadium for its product. More recently, Rubio's joined the concessions at the Irvine Meadows Amphitheater.

Unit Operations

The typical unit has 15 to 25 employees, depending on the amount of customer traffic. Each unit has one general manager, two assistant managers, a cashier, an expediter, a prep clerk, four line clerks, a shift leader, and a customer service employee. To ensure uniformity throughout its facilities, the company has developed job descriptions for each of these positions. A sample of these descriptions is contained in Exhibit 2.

Despite the increase in the federal minimum wage rate, Rubio's employees have not been affected. On average, the employees make an hourly wage that already exceeds the new federal minimum. Unit structure and wage scales are presented in Exhibit 3.

In addition to a higher minimum wage, full-time employees are also offered various benefits, such as health insurance. Although Rubio's offers its full-time employees health insurance, only 30 percent currently take advantage of this benefit. Rubio's believes that this may result from cultural differences. As a result, Rubio's is currently engaged in direct marketing of its health insurance plan to its employees in an effort to increase participation rates to 70 percent. Rubio's is making this effort despite the anticipated increase in costs to the company.

Marketing Strategy

Despite the fact that San Diego shares a border with Mexico, Ralph Rubio recognized that no other restaurant in the area was serving authentic Mexican food. By offering fresh-tasting, authentic Mexican food in a contemporary, clean atmosphere, Rubio's is targeting a key segment of the market: young, upscale professionals and students, aged 18 to 49, with a taste for better food. Rubio's success is therefore the result of carving out a special niche in an otherwise crowded fast-food market.

During the first couple of years of operation, Rubio's rarely advertised. Instead, early efforts were concentrated on ensuring that the total concept, from the menu to the decor, was designed to satisfy the customer's needs and desires. Yet despite this lack of advertising, Rubio's was attracting new and repeat customers. Rubio's now promotes its business in at least three media—print, radio, and television—that appeal to consumers within its targeted market. Rubio's is currently investigating the idea of poster panels and billboards as an additional medium to access its target market. Current advertising objectives and strategies are:

ADVERTISING OBJECTIVES:
- Increase "trial" visits to Rubio's within target audience, adults 18 to 49.
- Encourage repeat visits to Rubio's.
- Increase overall awareness of Rubio's.
- Generate awareness of Rubio's new location(s).

ADVERTISING STRATEGIES:
- Implement a consistent, chainwide media plan in San Diego that will effectively reach target market.
- Execute local store marketing efforts in San Diego for grand openings and locations with special needs.
- Implement a localized media and promotions plan in Orange County with emphasis on the Irvine location.
- Administer sales promotion during heavy advertising periods.

As in the past, Rubio's utilizes local cable television channels and radio stations to promote its products. Although the commercials have been relatively simple, they are designed to increase consumer awareness of Rubio's products. By tying the commercials to specific promotions, the effect is to increase regular foot traffic in Rubio's facilities as well as to attract first-time customers unfamiliar with fish tacos. Current advertising also seeks to generate awareness not only for Rubio's products but for its new locations as well.

Rubio's also uses direct mail to attract customers. With direct mail, Rubio's has been able to identify potential customers within a five-mile radius of a new or existing restaurant. Rubio's believes that if it is able to persuade potential customers to try its product once, they will become repeat customers.

In addition to direct promotions, Rubio's participates in numerous indirect promotions. Rubio's has sponsored local athletic events such as the San Diego International Triathlon. Rubio's has also sent a 15-foot inflatable version of Pesky Pescado to local parades, sporting events, and restaurant openings. Pesky, Jr., an inflatable human-size costume, also makes local appearances. These marketing efforts represent 2 ½ percent of sales, or $256,000. As Rubio's expands throughout southern California, it will continue to educate its potential customers through the use of these media and promotions.

Management

Despite its growth from one small restaurant in 1983 to over 12 locations throughout southern California, Rubio's remains a closely held corporation with ownership split among the family members. Ralph and Ray Rubio (Ralph's father) are the founders and majority stockholders. Ralph Rubio is acting president of the company. Ralph's brothers and sister fill the other key positions in the company: Robert is vice-president of operations, Richard is vice-president of expansion, and Gloria is vice-president of training. The youngest Rubio, Roman, assists Gloria at corporate headquarters with training. Although Rubio's has brought in outside people to fill management positions, the family intends to maintain ownership and control for as long as possible.

As a relatively young, family-owned organization, Rubio's is characterized by centralized management and control. The company offers extensive training programs for its managers and employees to ensure efficiency and standardization in the production of its products. This policy is evidenced by its thorough and detailed operations manual. As the business expands, managers are provided with a sufficient degree of flexibility to handle day-to-day operations tailored to the needs of each individual store. Ultimate authority, however, remains with the Rubio family.

Finances

As a privately held company, the majority of Rubio's growth has been achieved with funds generated from within. Recent expansion has also been assisted by bank financing. The company's growth has been relatively slow and cautious. Sales, however, have not been slow. The combined sales from the 12 restaurant locations average over 10,000 fish tacos per day.

Including sales of other menu items, the average Rubio's store had sales of $700,000 during 1991. This figure represents a decline from 1990, when the average store had sales of $745,000. Each store unit is, however, designed , to handle $1 million in annual sales, leaving plenty of opportunity for an increase in sales. Rubio's goal for the next several years is to increase the average store's sales to over $800,000.

Even with the current decrease in sales, the stores are quite profitable. To break even, the typical store must achieve monthly sales of approximately $30,000 to $35,000. The main cost difference among Rubio's facilities results from different lease costs. Labor and material costs remain the same across facilities. Food ingredients represent about 16 percent of the sales price of menu items. The ingredients breakdown for the fish taco and the fish taco especial are presented in Exhibit 4.

A LOOK TO THE FUTURE

Ralph's belief that the fish taco would be as popular in San Diego as it was in the Baja was correct—and judging from the amount of sales and the number of imitators, it is here to stay. Although Rubio's already has 12 restaurant locations, its goal is 50 company-owned restaurants in southern California averaging sales of $40 to $50 million annually. Fast-food industry figures also show that the Mexican food segment is still experiencing lucrative growth nationwide. Rubio's plans, therefore, to continue its expansion into new geographic markets. While Rubio's has already expanded into Orange County, it will continue its investigation of northern California.

Yet as Rubio's approaches its tenth anniversary, the company faces many decisions and challenges that will affect their future. First, the company must determine issues related to future expansion:

1. Is there a market on the East Coast for fish tacos?
2. Is international expansion a viable alternative?

Assuming that such expansion is feasible, the company must then determine how to establish operations in distant locations:

3. Should the company consider franchising, licensing agreements, partnerships, or even joint ventures?
4. Should the company attempt to remain a closely held, family organization?

Alternatively, Rubio's may focus its attention on expanding its distribution channels:

5. Should Rubio's manufacture its fast-food products for distribution in nontraditional outlets?
6. Should Rubio's offer a packaged version of its product in supermarkets and grocery stores?

Moreover, given the importance of limiting or reducing costs, Rubio's must also consider the feasibility of assorted cost-saving investments:

7. Should Rubio's centralize the preparation of some or all of its food products once the company reaches a specified number of outlets?
8. Should Rubio's integrate into its own sources of supply? ∎

EXHIBIT 1   Rubio's Menu

Menu...

Welcome to Rubio's... Home of the Fish Taco! Founded in January of 1983, we have since served over 6 million of our delicious San Felipe style fish tacos to happy customers all over San Diego. Our philosophy is to provide delicious Mexican food served in a clean attractive atmosphere, while maintaining that original Baja flavor. Please enjoy your visit and come back soon!
¡Hasta Luego! *Perky*

Los Otros

QUESADILLA   we spread guacamole on your flour tortilla, sprinkle with cheddar cheese and top it with salsa, we fold it, then heat until it's hot and melted.................**$2.09**

TAQUITOS   three tacos deep-fried and topped with guacamole, salsa and cheese **$1.79**

NACHOS REGULAR   our own homemade chips topped with a melted jalapeno cheese sauce..**88¢**

NACHOS GRANDE   the mas mucho o' nachos. over a bed of chips, you'll find cheese sauce, beans, salsa, guacamole, sour cream, and a black olive at the very top.......**$2.95**

CHIPS   a bag of our fresh tortilla chips, we cut them and fry them right here, every day.....**60¢**

BEANS   a plate of our spicy delicious baked pintos, sprinkled with cheese..............**75¢**

PALETAS   frozen fruit sticks...............**75¢**

CHURROS   ....**75¢**

Combinations

all served with homemade chips and beans

#1   any two tacos
beef carnitas or fish...........................**$2.29**

#2   chicken burrito, beef taco..........**$3.89**

#3   carnitas, burrito, fish taco........**$3.00**

#4   beef burrito, carnitas, taco.........**$3.70**

#5   fish burritos, fish taco................**$3.27**

 #6   carne asade, burrito, fish taco.....**$3.89**

PESKY COMBO   two fish tacos especiales with beans and chips........................**$2.09**

Tacos

FISH TACO ESPECIAL   for the supreme of fish tacos we provide one of our regular fish tacos dressed with guacamole, cheddar cheese and cilantro/onion. go ahead try one..................................**$1.79**

SHREDDED BEEF   in a soft-shell corn tortilla with guacamole, salsa, cilantro/onion and shredded with lettuce........................**$1.59**

CARNITAS   shredded pork, served on a soft-shell corn tortilla with salsa, cilantro/ onion and lettuce.............................**$1.94**

FISH   tacos san tempe-style, a strip of fish battered and deep-fried then placed in a soft-shell corn tortilla with salsa, our special white sauce and cabbage, add a squeeze of lime and you have an authentic fish taco........**$1.00**

CARNE ASADA*   marinated chunks of steak, seasoned, skillet-seared and placed in a soft-shell corn tortilla with guacamole, salsa, cilantro/onion and cabbage, es deliciosa..**$1.34**

Burritos

BEEF   a soft flour filled tortilla with guacamole, beans, spicy shredded beef, salsa, cilantro/onion and a little lettuce. Moo-y delicious.....**$2.49**

CARNITAS   shredded pork on a flour tortilla with beans, salsa, cilantro/onion, and lettuce. one of our specialties........................**$2.44**

CHICKEN   chicken simmered in a spicy tomato sauce with onions and peppers, then served on a flour tortilla sprinkled with cheddar cheese, cilantro/onion, and lettuce **$2.49**

FISH   a local favorite. fish filets in a flour tortilla and guacamole, beans, salsa, white sauce, cilantro/onion and cabbage. so mucho tasty...**$2.54**

BEANS AND CHEESE   beans on a bed of cheese with salsa and cilantro/onion.......**$1.09**

MACHACA   our shredded beef and egg with salsa and cilantro/onion, a great way to start the day...**$1.98**

CHORIZO   mexican pork sausage scrambled in egg with cilantro/onion and salsa, good and spicy...**$1.98**

CARNE ASADA*   from the streets of Mexico City, a recipe that includes tasty chunks of steak marinated and skillet-seared served on a flour tortilla with beans, slasa, cilantro/onion and guacamole...**$2.55**

Tostadas

BEEF   a deep-fried tostada shell covered with beans, salsa, lettuce, chopped tomato, onion, cheese, sour cream, and garnished with a black olive...............................**$2.18**

CHICKEN   our shredded chicken on a bed of beans, salsa, lettuce, chopped tomato, onion, cheese, sour cream and an olive......**$1.05**

BEAN   beans cover the tostada shell and are then topped with salsa, lettuce, chopped tomato and onion, cheese and an olive.........**$1.49**

SALAD MEXICANA   our spicy shredded chicken on a bed of fresh lettuce and tortilla chips covered with chopped tomatoes, jack cheese and sour cream. add our special salsa dressing and you have a light tasty meal that is "mucho" healthy!................**$2.95**

Drinks

pepsi. diet pepsi. rootbeer. orange slice. slice. iced tea. coffee. lowfat milk. big kahuna fruit juice.

cerveza available at most locations

EXTRA ITEMS   guacamole, cheese or sour cream on any item.....................................**25¢**

- all orders packaged to go
- phone in orders welcome

Cold Food Menu

Corn Tortillas.................. .80 Doz
Flour Tortillas..................1.20 Doz
Beans............... 1.00 Pt 1.80 Qt
Taquitos................... 1.00 set (3)
Guacamole...................... 3.75 lb
Cilantro & Onion.............. 1.00 lb
Shredded Beef.............. 3.75 lb
Carnitas...................... 3.75 lb
Chicken....................... 3.75 lb
Shredded Cheese (Jack Ched)....... 3.00 lb
Shredded Mexican Cheese........... 3.00 lb
Chips............................. 1.75 lb
Quesadillas.................... 2.09 each
Salsas...................... 1.60 Pt 3.00 Qt

Note: We do not sell our cold food products in increments less than a pound, pint or dozen.

CALL – IN ORDER POLICY

- Please call in your orders before 1:30 am. No call-in orders will be accepted between 11:30 am and 1:30 pm.
  Note: No call-in or pick-up orders between 11:30 am and 1:30 pm at our Kearney Mesa and University City stores
- Be aware of our two locations in Pacific Beach to avoid misplaced orders
- Customer phone numbers will be required on all orders over $10.00
- When picking up your order, please stand and pay in the cashier line.
- Please allow 24 hours notice for any large deli orders over $25.00

Thank you, Rubio's

Locations

MISSION BAY	CHULA VISTA
4504 Mission Bay Dr	789 N. El Camino Ave
272-2801	427-3811
S.D.S.U.	ENCINITAS
5187 Colten Ave	481 Hemingway St.
206-3844	632-7395
PACIFIC BEACH	EL CAJON
925 Grand Ave	298 Magnum Ave
270-4800	440-3325
POINT LOMA	KEARNEY MESA
McCloud & Vista Blvd	1420 Cameron Mesa Blvd
223-2631	268-5770
SAN MARCOS	UNIVERSITY CITY
Vine & Mesa Way	8935 Towne Center Rd
745-2962	453-1606

Our Fish Tacos are now featured at
JACK MURPHY STADIUM!

Now in Tustin & Irvine

*Available all stores June 15
Prices may vary according to location and are subject to change without notice

Rubio's
Home of the Fish Taco©

EXHIBIT 2	Rubio's Job Descriptions
Prep	Responsible for prepping all the food product, cleanliness and organization of walk-in, and care of equipment.
Line 3	Under the direction of Line 1; Line 3 heats the tortilla, fries fish, taquitos, and churros, and cooks machaca and chorizo.
Line 2	Under the direction of Line 1; Line 2 works the condiment table, wraps the food, keeps the condiment table stocked and his area clean.
Line 2B	Works alongside Line 2. Responsibilities are mainly the wrapping of food to help expedite the food more quickly. This position is implemented during peak hours.
Line 1	The "Quarterback"—sets the pace in the kitchen, reads the ticket, works the steam table and gives direction to Line 2 and Line 3. Line 1 is directly responsible for how smooth the shift goes. He/she is the leader.
Expediter	Responsible for bagging orders correctly and putting out orders. Responsible for restaurant cleanliness. Restocks throughout the day. Always says "thank you" to customers. Must wear the tag provided by the company.
Cashier	Greets the customer, takes the order, and cashiers throughout the day. Responsible for the cash drawer. Keeps area clean and, along with the expediter, helps clean the dining area. If time, helps put out orders. Must wear the name tag provided by the company.
Shift Leader	Responsible for upholding the company's standards and procedures to the highest possible level in every aspect of the restaurant operations. Responsible for the maintenance of the restaurant's operations while under the direction of the management crew. Shift leaders will adhere to the management demeanor and dress policies.
Customer Service Employee	Hired by the Special Service organizations for the disabled to meet the needs of our customers during the busy lunch. Responsible for bussing, wiping tables, restocking, sweeping, getting napkins and utensils for customers already seated, and any other duties specified by the particular store.

EXHIBIT 3   Typical Rubio's Store Structure

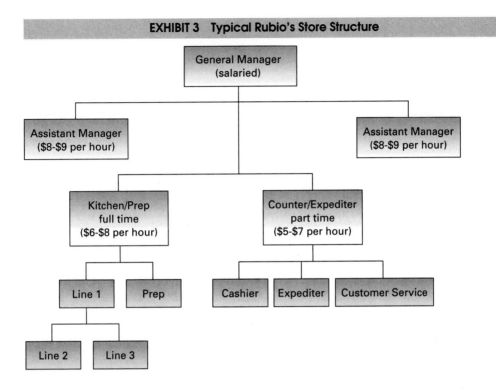

EXHIBIT 4   Menu Recipe File

		Fish Taco	
Ingredients	**Portion**	**CPU**	**Cost**
Fish (pollack)	1.25 oz	0.1031250	0.1289063
White sauce	0.50 oz	0.0215625	0.0107812
Cabbage	0.75 oz	0.0133547	0.0100160
Limes	1.00 slice	0.0069179	0.0069179
Corn tortilla	1.00 each	0.0291667	0.0291667
Fish batter	0.75 oz	0.0218750	0.0164063
Salsa	0.75 oz	0.0227422	0.0170566
		Cost	$0.2192510
		Menu price	$1.44
		Item cost (%)	15.226%
		Gross profit	$1.2207490

EXHIBIT 4   (continued)

| Ingredients | Portion | Fish Taco Especial | |
		CPU	Cost
Corn tortilla	1.00 each	0.0291667	0.0291667
Fish (pollack)	1.25 oz	0.1031250	0.1289063
Fish batter	0.75 oz	0.0218750	0.0164063
Salsa	0.75 oz	0.0227422	0.0170566
White sauce	0.50 oz	0.0215625	0.0107812
Cabbage	0.75 oz	0.0133547	0.0100160
Guacamole	0.50 oz	0.0641875	0.0320937
Cheese	0.50 oz	0.0812500	0.0406250
Cilantro/onion	0.25 oz	0.0248750	0.0062187
Limes	1.00 slice	0.0069179	0.0069179
		Cost	$0.2981885
		Menu cost	$1.79
		Item cost (%)	16.659%
		Gross profit	$1.4918115

This case was prepared by Professor Kenneth E. Marino of San Diego State University with the assistance of graduate student Linda Kelleher Carter. It is intended as a basis for class discussion rather than to illustrate effective or ineffective handling of an administrative situation.

Case 8   Suzy's Zoo

I. INTRODUCTION

Suzy's Zoo, a closely held greeting card company located in San Diego, California, is in its twenty-fifth year of operations. Owner and president Suzy Spafford is the creative and driving force behind the menagerie of characters that make up Suzy's Zoo. The company has managed to secure a profitable and safe niche with a devoted following among its customers. The "Zoo" consists of approximately 35 cartoon characters that come and go; however, a few characters have proven to be especially long-lasting. For example, the most popular character is Suzy Ducken, a fluffy, yellow bird with Mary Jane shoes and white ankle socks. Also popular is the laid-back Jack Quacker, who sports rubber sandals. Other popular zoo characters are Ollie Marmot, Corky Turtle, and D. J. Ducken. Each character has a distinctive personality, and characters are eventually retired when they lose their appeal in the marketplace.

The company and its products are conservative, appealing to middle-American, homespun tastes. As Spafford would say, "Suzy's Zoo cards are G-rated."

Although the beginning was entirely in greeting cards, the company has expanded into a variety of products, including balloons, rubber stamps, and party supplies. Through licensing agreements, the characters appear on needlework, sleepwear, baby gifts, and mobiles. Other licensed goods that have been in the product line but are presently awaiting new licensees are stuffed animals, coffee mugs, and figurines. By finding a market niche, and with a philosophy of slow growth, Suzy's Zoo has always operated profitably. It has also expanded into international markets; currently, Suzy's Zoo products are sold in 46 countries worldwide.

II. HISTORY

Suzy's Zoo founder and president Suzy Spafford started the business in the mid-1960s when she was working toward her bachelor of fine arts degree at San Diego State University. To earn extra money for school, she worked summers and weekends at local artmarts creating colorful pastel and water-color drawings, particularly cartoon characters custom-designed to buyers' tastes. She sold her drawings for $3 apiece, generating $3,000 to $4,000 per summer. During her senior year in college (1967), Bill Murr, a Berkeley, California, medical instrument manufacturer, saw Spafford's work at an artmart in San Diego. He proposed they team up and start a small greeting card business. Murr provided $600 in funding, and Spafford created eight card designs and agreed on a 90 percent (Murr) to 10 percent (Spafford) split. Suzy's Zoo was officially launched.

Spafford worked out of her home, creating designs that were shipped to Murr in Berkeley, who supervised the printing, then boxed and distributed them to local stationery stores. The cards immediately sold well in the Bay Area and on a smaller scale in Washington and Oregon. Within two years, the cards were selling throughout California. Sales increased steadily through the first several years. In the early 1970s, Murr decided he no longer wanted to handle the day-to-day operations. Spafford bought Murr's inventory and reversed the financial arrangement, with Murr retaining 10 percent ownership and no involvement in the actual running of the company. Suzy's Zoo was incorporated in 1976.

Suzy feels the key to her early success was in keeping the company small enough to produce on demand. No warehousing costs and low overhead allowed Suzy's Zoo to completely turn its inventory three to four times per year, a routine the company still tries to practice.

By the mid-1970s Suzy's Zoo cards were being distributed nationally, and her characters were appearing on novelty items such as calendars. During the next several years, new products were added to the Suzy's Zoo line: invitations in 1977, gift wrap and party goods in 1985, Mylar balloons in 1987. In the late 1980s, Suzy's Zoo expanded into the international arena through European and Far Eastern licensing arrangements.

Until recently, Suzy's Zoo depended solely on Spafford for character and product design. Spafford felt that keeping Suzy's Zoo a one-artist company was central to its success. A conscious policy decision was made to maintain a pattern of slow growth.

III. THE GREETING CARD INDUSTRY

Greeting cards are a $5.6 billion-per-year industry dominated by three companies. As Exhibit 1 shows, Hallmark cards is the leader, enjoying approximately a 46 percent share of the market; American Greetings Corp. has a 30 percent share; and Gibson Greetings has about an 8 percent share. The remaining 16 percent of the market is divided among close to 1,000 other companies.

The effect is that two levels of competition operate. The three big card companies are competing against each other on one level, and all the rest of the card companies are competing with each other on another level; but the small companies are not really competing against the big companies.

Ninety percent of all card purchasers are women. Unit sales growth in greeting cards has been 1 to 3 percent per year. But this is a maturing market that recently has been threatening to stop growing for the first time since 1945.

The late 1980s saw vicious price wars in the greeting card industry. Retailers perceived greeting card companies as all alike; every big card manufacturer's profitability suffered in a discounting frenzy. Greeting card companies are therefore having to develop new strategies to maintain their share, or get a large piece, of a pie that is not growing.

The greeting card market is made even more competitive because barriers to entry are very low. This means that it does not take too much to get into the greeting card business. Anyone with an idea, some talent, and a little start-up money can give it a try. This makes for high turnover, as companies enter the market, fail, exit the market, and are replaced by other newcomers. It should be noted that the above information pertains to entry into that 16 percent share of the market where the smaller card companies compete; barriers to entry into the arena where the three large card companies compete are very high.

In an effort to maintain their market share or boost sales in this static environment, the three big competitors have come up with a variety of strategies. Hallmark is trying to persuade today's too-busy-to-write Americans to let it express their sentiments for them. Midway between Father's Day (in June) and Halloween (October 31) is the worst time of year for American publishers of greeting cards. Retailers sell fewer cards at this time than at any other time of the year. Trying to boost sales during this dry spell gave birth to the "nonoccasion" card. Hallmark has produced a series of 500 nonoccasion cards for adults and in 1989 added a new line of adult-to-child cards, "To Kids With Love," to help children ages 7 to 14 and their parents cope with growing up. Nonoccasion cards now account for more than 10 percent of the 7.3 billion greeting cards sold in America each year.

American Greetings has on staff a psychiatrist and various other experts to help come up with new products. The psychiatrist is good at identifying stressful situations in which people have a "psychological need for a card." To further enhance its competitive position and increase declining earnings, American Greetings instituted a costcutting program and improved its customer service. Unprofitable subsidiaries and excess costs were trimmed. Just-in-time (JIT) processes in manufacturing and card development allowed American Greetings to reduce inventories and decrease the time it takes to bring cards to market. As part of its emphasis on customer service, in 1991 American Greetings established its Retail Creative Services Department. This unit emphasized working with customers to create seasonal displays designed to boost store traffic. In early 1992, American Greetings formed its Information Services Department to develop software to analyze retailers' sales patterns and track inventories for many different products. Apparently these innovations are paying off; sales of American Greetings cards and related products such as wrapping paper grew 10 percent in 1991, while Hallmark reported only a 1 percent increase in revenues for the same goods.

Both Hallmark and American Greetings have gone high-tech with computerized greeting card services that allow customers to choose graphics, write messages, and print their personalized messages on blank cards in minutes. It is presumed that this service would appeal to nontraditional card buyers such as men and younger people. Projections indicate that this could become a substantial portion of both companies' business in the future.

For smaller greeting card companies, other strategies have been useful. Finding a niche in the market is one way to compete. The goal is to develop a unique concept or style that will appeal to a wide segment of the buying public without disappearing into the shadows of the giants. For example, use of a distinctive sense of humor, stylized artwork, or messages that appeal to specific groups such as college students could establish a marketing niche.

Many small cardmakers have found that it is very important to listen to their retailers and sales representatives. To compete in an industry dominated by the big companies, the smaller companies have to be better, turn over more quickly, and be more profitable for the retailer.

IV. SUZY'S ZOO TODAY

Operations

The company is a nonunion operation with approximately 50 employees (see organization chart, Exhibit 2).

Spafford makes all the major decisions regarding the company except for personnel and financial matters. Minority owner and vice-president Ray Lidstrom takes the lead in those areas.

Suzy's Zoo currently operates out of a two-story, 52,000-square-foot warehouse/office suite in the Mira Mesa area of San Diego. The company moved into this facility in February 1990. Operations include product design, marketing, warehousing, and shipping. No manufacturing is done on-site; rather, manufacturing is accomplished through subcontractors.

The facility is set up to ensure the efficient flow of products through the warehouse (see operations diagram, Exhibit 3).

Shipments of manufactured goods arrive at the receiving dock from various locations via common carrier on palletized boxes and in cartons. The boxes are placed into a racked bulk-storage area adjacent to the receiving dock. Handtrucks and forklifts are used to move stock.

As product is needed, cartons are broken down and the shelves are stocked in the "picking" area. The picking area consists of merchandise organized by product number on a shelving system, where pickers fill orders by progressing up and down the aisles pulling items called for in the order. Product is stocked from the backside of the shelves (the alleys) so that workers stocking product do not interfere with workers filling orders. As orders are retrieved, they are placed in cardboard cartons, sealed (shrinkwrapped), labeled, and shipped by common carrier to customers' locations. Machinery used in the above operations consists of a counter/collator and a shrink-wrap oven.

An office staff of approximately 12 is maintained for accounting, purchasing, credit, marketing, and customer service functions.

Although the vast majority of sales are wholesale, a small showroom/retail outlet is operated at the front of the building for walk-in traffic. The receptionist performs her office duties from the sales counter and rings up the sales.

Product Line

Spafford is still very involved in product development, and many of her ideas come, as they always have, from her customers. Greeting cards account for about half of Suzy's Zoo sales. The Suzy's Zoo line has expanded to include coloring books, calendars, gift wrap, and paper party supplies. Most nonpaper goods are sold under licensing agreements. Currently, the company is considering the incorporation of coffee mugs into the product line, since mugs are commonly marketed through retail greeting card outlets. The alternative to this is to license the use of the characters to mug manufacturers.

In the case of Suzy'z Zoo, licensees are renting the artwork for a stated period of time so that they can apply Suzy's Zoo character images to their own products, such as mugs and T-shirts. A typical Suzy's Zoo license has a term of three years with an option to renew for an additional two years. The licensing fee is calculated as a percentage of sales and ranges from 3 to 6 percent. International licensees pay higher fees (10 to 12 percent), but this is split between Suzy's Zoo and its international broker. A list of Suzy's Zoo international brokers, the products they license, and their territories can be seen in Exhibit 4. This approach to international expansion allows Suzy's Zoo to penetrate new markets that it cannot enter in other ways, without assuming much of the risk. No one knows if a product will sell, and with licensing, the licensee assumes the costs of manufacturing and getting the product to the marketplace. The major disadvantage of licensing, from Spafford's point of view, is the loss of creative control; she admits to the need for many compromises in this area. In addition to licensing images for nonpaper products, Suzy's Zoo images are also licensed to other manufacturers of greeting cards, such as Current, a large mail-order house based in Colorado.

Marketing Strategies and Distribution

The most important source of marketing to an organization like Suzy's Zoo is its network of independent sales representatives. These individuals are in continued contact with retailer store owners, who can provide the most accurate information on consumer preferences. A decision was made to go with the mom-and-pop shops as the stores of trade and to stay away from the large department store business. These smaller stores have been Suzy's Zoo's "bread and butter;" they place their orders and pay their bills. According to Spafford, "It's clean business and we make a better profit that way." Some of the larger independent card companies are now encroaching on Suzy's Zoo shelf space in these stores. Some smaller independent card companies have merged to compete against the big companies; Suzy's Zoo is not considering such a move. The company has maintained a simplified merchandising policy for sales—no fancy displays, no giveaways, "just simple, plain, honest business," Spafford says. In today's environment, continuing to operate under this policy is becoming more of a challenge. Retailers expect deals, discounts, merchandising, and guarantees from the manufacturer to take back unsold stock. If Suzy's Zoo does not begin to offer some sort of consideration to the marketplace, maintaining shelf space may become more difficult.

Within the United States, manufacturers' representatives sell Suzy's Zoo merchandise to retailers. These representatives operate on a nonexclusive basis, getting standard commissions of 20 percent on the sales they make. Suzy's Zoo does not employ an in-house sales force. Suzy's Zoo products are sold internationally through international licenses, international distributors, and direct sales.

Marketing strategies have had to change over the years to keep up with the growth. The cards have been a boutique item, but other products such as tablecloths, invitations, cups, and plates are mass-marketed in high-volume stores. Revenues from cards have plateaued, and the overall increases in revenues can be attributed to other products. If people do not want to buy cards with cute images anymore, then Suzy's Zoo will put the artwork on other products that people will buy—that is why you see it on items like children's sleepwear and baby products.

As consumer consciousness has been raised, recycled paper products have become more important. Some consumers will not buy paper goods without the recycling code. Another change in recent years is that all Suzy's Zoo products are barcoded, which has allowed Suzy's Zoo merchandise to be sold in some of the larger retail outlets.

Suzy's Zoo participates in approximately six trade shows per year. The two big national shows are the National Stationery Gift Show in New York and the Los Angeles Gift Show. Participation in trade shows is another way to expose the product line to different types of retailers that sales representatives do not currently call on. Suzy's Zoo also participates in regional trade shows through participation by its sales rep organizations.

Sales

In 1976, the year Suzy's Zoo was incorporated, total sales were $600,000. In 1992, total sales will exceed $6 million. In recent years, total sales have increased 4 to 5 percent annually. Approximately 85 percent of Suzy's Zoo annual revenues come from sales to U.S. retailers, 10 percent come from licensing agreements, and almost 5 percent come from export sales shipped directly from the Suzy's Zoo warehouse. Table 1 shows sales data for the past four years.

	TABLE 1	**Sales Figures for Suzy's Zoo**					
Year	*Total Sales ($000)*	*Sales to U.S. ($000)*	*Percent of Total*	*License Income ($000)*	*Percent of Total*	*Export Sales ($000)*	*Percent of Total*
1989	$5,350	$4,775	89.2	$475	8.9	$100	1.9
1990	5,650	4,977	88.1	500	8.8	173	3.1
1991	5,900	5,090	86.3	550	9.3	260	4.4
1992	5,950	5,083	85.4	600	10.1	267	4.5

Suzy's Zoo fiscal year ends June 30.

V. FUTURE

The company philosophy remains as always to "give them what they want at a reasonable price," says Spafford. This philosophy has given Suzy's Zoo a great reputation in the card industry. Suzy envisions constant growth. Her goal is to keep turning out cards and products people can relate to. One of the biggest impediments to Suzy's Zoo's growth is that there is only one Suzy Spafford. Spafford hopes to one day stop drawing every greeting card herself and has begun work on a character "bible" containing drawings and specifications detailing how each character should look and things they might say. This will enable the continuity of the line's look. Spafford is currently training three artists and likens herself in this respect to Walt Disney in the 1930s. She has hired very talented people but has to teach them how to draw the characters the way she would draw them. Spafford feels the business needs more talented people to push the company to the next level.

Suzy's Zoo will never become a giant in the greeting card industry. "We can't compete with Hallmark or American Greeting Cards, nor do we want to." Greeting Cards, however, will continue to make up a significant percentage of the product line.

Currently, Spafford is looking forward to turning some of the characters from Suzy's Zoo into storybook characters. Spafford plans to develop her characters within a storybook world where they will have names, personalities, and even their own dwelling places—there are endless possibilities for stories. Spafford will be more involved in story-line development and illustration, with other artists doing the drawing for greeting card products. Spafford envisions a series of children's classics similar to "Winnie-the-Pooh." A decision has already been made to publish the first book independently and distribute it through the company's existing distribution base. Then the goal is to find a large publishing house to work with on future projects through some type of joint venture arrangement. In the meantime, Suzy's Zoo is currently consulting with a major licensee in the stuffed-animal market. It is hoped this effort will coordinate with the introduction of the first children's book to enhance character recognition.

After books, Spafford wants to try animation. The plans in this area are still vague, but Spafford hopes to create video either for television broadcast, such as a Saturday morning children's cartoon, or for direct sales to video stores. Her ambition is to attract the attention of the Disney company for a possible joint project. If animation becomes a reality, then, of course, this would necessitate the addition of other artists to create this specialized form of drawing. She is also unsure whether the company will create a book and video division or whether the characters will be licensed to an outside video production company.

In addition to these product development ideas, nurturing and growing the greeting card business and responding to changes in retail requirements is also a priority. Internal issues of succession, organization design, and management development have been highlighted by the continued growth of the business.

In any event, it is hoped that books and video will have a circular effect on Suzy's Zoo business as the increased recognition that will come from these higher-profile exposures will boost sale for all products sporting the Suzy Zoo character images. ∎

EXHIBIT 1 Greeting Cards Industry: Market Share Comparison

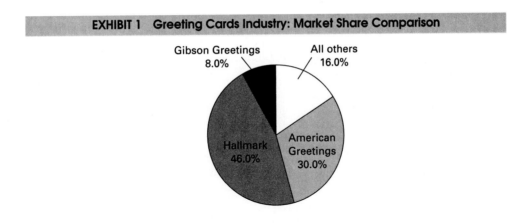

EXHIBIT 2 Suzy's Zoo: Organizational Chart

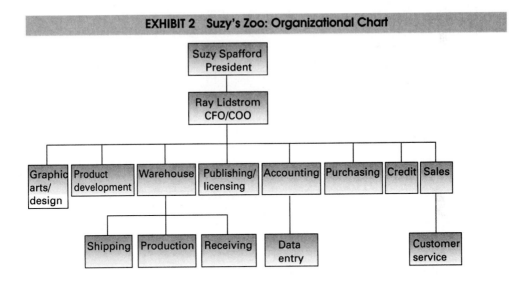

EXHIBIT 3 Suzy's Zoo: Warehouse and Order Assembly Plant Layout

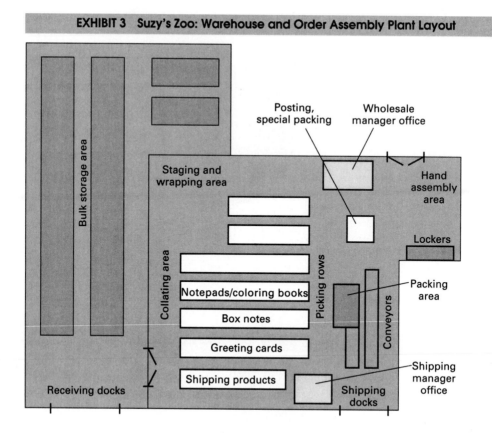

EXHIBIT 4 Suzy's Zoo International Brokers

Name of Co.	Product	Territory
Introduct Holland, BV	Self-adhesive stickers	Finland, Sweden, Norway, Denmark, U.K., N. Ireland, Eire, Belgium, Netherlands, Luxembourg, France, Italy, Spain, Portugal, Greece
Korsh Verlag GmbH & Co.	Kitchen calendars	Germany, Austria, Switzerland
Karto Oy	Greeting cards, postcards, invitations, gift wrap	Finland
Karl Walter GmbH & Co. KG	Photo albums	Europe
AB Pictura Sweden	Gift wrap, carrying bags, gift boxes, greeting cards, postcards	Europe
Reithmuller GmbH	Balloons, lanterns, blow-outs, garlands	Europe

	EXHIBIT 4 (continued)	
Name of Co.	*Product*	*Territory*
Murfett Regency Pty Ltd.	Greeting cards, paper products	Australia, New Zealand, South Pacific
Stanley Newcomb	Greeting cards, paper products	Australia, New Zealand, South Pacific
Trumura Pyxis Intl., Co., Ltd.	Children's products	Japan
Copyrights Europe	Various	All European countries
Alkor GmbH	PVC foil	Europe
George Bruckner GmbH	Cone-shaped paper bags, school friend albums	Germany, Austria, Switzerland

This case was prepared by Professor Kenneth E. Marino of San Diego State University with the assistance of graduate student Terry Wittbrot. It is intended as a basis for class discussion rather than to illustrate effective or ineffective handling of an administrative situation.

Case 9   Potatoquick!

Jim Schafer, president of PotatoQuick!, woke with a start. A glance at the clock revealed that it was 4:30 AM. He had dozed off at his PC while preparing copies of the PotatoQuick! financing proposals. In just four and a half hours Jim was going to meet with his accountant and attorney to decide the future of PotatoQuick!, and he had to be ready. He had not been able to sleep in anticipation of the meeting, but the last few weeks, while exhilarating, had also been exhausting. He poured himself a cup of coffee and began to work on the proposals once again.

As he entered the figures in the spreadsheet, he realized that in three years PotatoQuick! had exceeded even his wildest expectations. And now the timing seemed right to expand. Yet, he was more than a little apprehensive about the options for raising the needed capital. He didn't think he could get a bank loan to cover the full amount necessary for the PotatoQuick! planned expansion. While approaching a venture capitalist for a portion of the capital was another possibility, he didn't know what effect the presence of outside investors would have on his very successful operation. He knew, however, that the time was right for Potato-Quick! to expand into new markets and that expansion would require a great deal of capital.

As he finished printing the final copies of the proposals, a wave of exhaustion swept over Jim. It was now 5:45 AM. He figured that he could sleep until 7:00 and still have time to get ready and drive downtown for the 9:00 meeting. He carefully set the alarm for 7:00 and lay down on the couch. He fell asleep almost immediately.

HISTORY

PotatoQuick! began in 1987, when advanced technology permitted new developments in the storage of food and the packaging used to heat foods in microwave ovens. These developments ushered in a broad array of new opportunities in microwaveable fast food, including popcorn, soups, sandwiches, and baked potatoes. The Potato-Quick! Corporation was formed in California in 1987 by five management partners. The five, including Gary Fuller, the Idaho potato farmer who initially conceived the idea, remain as managers and share all equity interests in the corporation. The first PotatoQuick! potatoes were sold to convenience stores in Los Angeles, California, in January 1987. Six months later, after extensive consumer feedback, toppings were added to the potato packaging, including natural butter, sour cream, chives, and cheddar cheese. In 1988, the company expanded distribution beyond convenience stores in Orange County, California, through contracts with food wholesalers who sold the product to convenience stores throughout southern California. By 1990, PotatoQuick! was offered in 2,000 convenience stores throughout California. Sales to food distributors had increased 50 percent in under three years.

THE PRODUCT

The baked potato is at the core of the company's operation. Generous-sized (10- to 12-ounce) baking potatoes are sourced from quality Idaho packers. The potatoes are transported to the PotatoQuick! California facility, where they are prepared for sale: cleaned, baked, packaged in a microwave container, then refrigerated with a high-quality condiment assortment before shipment. Consumers can thus purchase a nominally processed food product as opposed to highly processed traditional fast-food offerings. Refrigeration keeps the potato from spoiling prior to purchase (average shelf life is two months). The proprietary PotatoQuick! processing technology has not yet been duplicated by other manufacturers; this is because of the company's advanced baking and packaging technologies.

A PotatoQuick! potato retails for $2, the price established from consumer market studies and by comparing competitive fast-food product trends (such as average sandwich price). Forty percent of this retail price is the convenience store margin; this is the industry average for prepared foods. Ten percent of retail is food distributor margin, leaving PotatoQuick! with a 50 percent operating margin of approximately $1 per potato. Gross profit after operating expenses is approximately 10 percent. This is double the food-manufacturing averages of 5 percent, the result in part of directly sourcing the potatoes from packers.

PotatoQuick!'s immediate customers are food wholesalers and distributors, who in turn distribute the product for sale to end consumers in convenience stores. Food distribution in California is highly fragmented by county and region. Sysco Corporation and its subsidiaries are by far the company's leading distributor, accounting for 35 percent of total sales. In-house estimates indicate that through this distribution network, PotatoQuick! is placed in approximately 45 percent of all state convenience stores with microwave/quick food service operations; about 90 percent of all California convenience stores offer fast-food service.

PotatoQuick! has had strong appeal to consumers with nutrition and health concerns who desire the convenience of fast foods without sacrificing product quality. Increasingly, these consumers are seeking low-fat, low-calorie selections and other "lite" alternatives. This group makes up a large percentage of fast-food and convenience store sales. Two key demographic trends are the increasing number of working women who have limited time for cooking and increased levels of per capita income. The product's design, incorporating the health benefits of Idaho potatoes with preparation ease (one- to two-minute microwaving and fast-applying condiments) has been well received among those Californians who make it a regular part of their diets.

PotatoQuick! has been able to maintain high margins because of disciplined management, strong relationships with key distributors, and the wide consumer appeal of its proprietary product. PotatoQuick!'s management team is drawn from several sectors of the potato production and consumption cycle. This has permitted the sourcing of the highest-quality baking potatoes direct from Idaho packers at below-market prices. Management has also established strong relationships with major California food distributors. These agreements have allowed greater predictability of earnings and flexibility in production and hiring decisions. The Sysco Corporation food distributor agreement signed in 1988 permitted PotatoQuick! to distribute in over 1,000 convenience stores in southern California with minimal marginal expense. Contracts with other wholesalers and distributors have allowed the company to control marketing and direct sales expense while maintaining strong product placement in convenience stores.

FUTURE EXPANSION

PotatoQuick! believes that there is potential to expand its quick potato concept beyond California convenience stores, specifically in the northwest United States by 1991. Initial market testing in Seattle, Washington, indicated that response from potential consumers who have tried PotatoQuick!'s product is overwhelmingly positive. Based on the assumption that a penetration level of 50 percent of northwest convenience stores is attainable, the corporation believes it needs additional capacity to profitably meet potential consumer demand. Discussions with area food distributors have resulted in tentative contracts that would allow PotatoQuick! products in half of all food distribution targets. By capturing this base of distributors (and their convenience store customers), and with a predicted convenience store growth rate of 10 to 20 percent per year in densely populated areas, PotatoQuick! believes there is great potential in the northwest United States. Returns are thus projected at two times fast-food industry averages.

THE MEETING

In what seemed to Jim like an instant, the alarm went off. As he struggled off the couch and headed to the shower to get ready for the meeting, he couldn't believe how tired he was. Yet, thinking about the meeting began to get his adrenaline flowing again. At 7:45 he got into his car for the hourlong trip downtown. He checked his briefcase one last time for the proposals and the PotatoQuick! business plan, the blueprint for the company's future. As he started the car he felt confident. PotatoQuick! was a great product, and the expansion program was going to be a success.

Traffic was fairly light, and Jim arrived at the downtown offices of Reese Henry Associates to meet his accountant, Eric Davidson, with fifteen minutes to spare. As they were discussing the recent resurgence of the basketball program at their alma mater, UCLA, Jim's attorney, Carla Nordstrand from the law firm of Davis, Davis, Dimos and Monroe, arrived.

Carla was first to present her views on the proposed PotatoQuick! expansion:

> Jim, I'm really excited about the planned expansion program. Potato-Quick! is a great product and from looking at your business plan, I can tell that you all have done your homework. I recommend that we follow the proposal in your business plan and go for the full $2,000,000. We can get half from your bank and the other half from outside investors. I can set up some meetings with investors who would love to have a piece of PotatoQuick! by the end of the month. I don't see any problem in raising the money.

Jim then turned to Eric to get his views:

> Jim, I agree with Carla that PotatoQuick! is a great product with good potential. While I know that you are anxious to expand into the Northwest, I'd recommend a two-phase approach. First, let's get that $1,000,000 from First Nippon Bank. This should get you on track for the expansion program. If we go slow and do things right, raising additional capital in the future will be easier. I'm sure that Carla could line you up with some investors, but I don't think you're ready for that yet. I've seen too many companies try to grow too fast and lose control. Plus, bringing in outside owners can really change the chemistry of the place. Are you prepared for that?

Jim thanked Carla and Eric for their advice and headed home. He really wasn't sure what to do. On the one hand, he had enough confidence to go for it all and take Carla up on her offer to meet with the venture capitalists. He really wanted to be able to implement the entire expansion program. But he really valued Eric's advice and thought that a more conservative approach might be best in the long run. Potato-Quick! had a great management team, and bringing in outside investors could change that good chemistry. He decided to meet with the other executives and see whether they could come to an agreement on the best approach for funding the expansion.

THE BUSINESS AND ITS FUTURE

Table 1 presents the PotatoQuick! plan's table of contents. The PotatoQuick! corporate offices are located at

> PotatoQuick! Corporation
> 2323 Wilshire Blvd.
> Los Angeles, CA 90045
> U.S.A.
> Telephone: (213) 555–7734
>   (800) 1 P QUICK
> FAX: (213) 555–7728
> Cable: PQUICK
> SIC Code: 1800, Food Service Industries

TABLE 1 PotatoQuick! Business Plan	
Table of Contents	

Summary	[Omitted]
The Business and Its Future	
General	
Nature of the Business	
Business History	[Omitted]
Business of the Future	[Omitted]
Uniqueness	[Omitted]
The Product	[Omitted]
Customers/Purchasers of the Product	[Omitted]
The Market	
Competition	
Marketing	
Production	
Production Characteristics	
Labor Force and Employees	
Suppliers	
Subcontractors	
Equipment	
Property and Facilities	
Patents and Trademarks	
Research and Development	
Litigation	
Government Regulations	
Backlog	
Insurance	
Taxes	
Corporate Structure	
Publications and Associations	
Management	
Directors and Officers	
Key Employees	
Remuneration	
Stock Options	
Principal Shareholders	
Employee Agreements	
Conflicts of Interest	
Accountants, Lawyers, Bankers	
Description of the Financing	
Collateral for the Financing	
Guarantees	[Omitted]
Reporting	[Omitted]
Use of Proceeds	
Ownership	
Dilution	
Fees Paid	
Investor Involvement	

Nature of the Business

PotatoQuick! is a producer and distributor of baked potatoes packaged for sale in convenience stores. Idaho potatoes are prebaked by PotatoQuick!, then packaged and sold in a unique package for microwave use. Included as part of the product packaging are varied toppings that enhance the product's flavor and appeal. The final product is shipped for convenience store distribution to food distributors and wholesalers throughout California.

The Market

The convenience store industry is currently a $54 billion entity that has grown at a compound rate of 12 percent during the past five years. Over this time, the number of convenience stores operating in the United States has increased nearly 6 percent annually to over 78,000 units at year end 1989. On average, these companies have generated sales and earnings growth of 21 percent and 13 percent, respectively. The industry is highly fragmented: In 1989, 12 large companies accounted for only 30.5 percent of total industry sales. Nearly all demographic trends favor the increased use of convenience stores, including (1) more working women, (2) higher levels of per capita income, and (3) smaller families.

Since the mid-1970s, convenience stores have actively tried to increase sales and gross profit margins by implementing fast-food programs. In 1977, fast-food sales at convenience stores totaled $382 million, or 4.1 percent of total sales, while in 1986, this figure rose to $5.1 billion, or 14.4 percent of total sales—an increase of over 1,200 percent. Table 2 details the growth of convenience store fast-food sales.

| TABLE 2 | Additional Industry Data |

Convenience Store Fast-Food Sales

	1977	1979	1981	1983	1984	1985	1986
Sales ($ million)	$382.2	$723.9	$1,157.9	$2,069.0	$2,842.1	$4,349.2	$5,184.0
Percent of in-store total sales	4.1	5.0	5.4	7.5	9.7	13.1	14.4

Fast-Food Sales Breakdown and Gross Margin Analysis

Fast-Food Item	Percent of In-Store Sales	Gross Margin (%)
Sandwiches—fresh	1.3	39
Sandwiches—frozen	1.3	38
Deli services	3.3	47
Food cooked on-site	.4	47
Fountain drinks	3.6	61
Frozen beverages	.9	41
Hot beverages	2.7	66
Other fast food	.9	42
Total	14.4	52

Convenience store operators have aggressively added fast-food items in an effort to broaden their customer base and increase margins. As a result, the convenience store share of all fast-food sales has doubled in the last five years to over 10 percent. Fast-food programs vary widely across chains. Several chains have opted to initiate joint ventures with fast-food chains, and others have decided to use an in-house program. Convenience stores will continue to gain market share in this high-margin category for several reasons. They offer a greater variety of food (such as potatoes), quick service, and the location advantages of convenience stores over fast-food restaurants. Also, convenience stores exhibit greater unit growth than restaurants, and these new stores are constantly improving in appearance and overall quality, making them an acceptable alternative to traditional fast-food restaurants for a larger number of consumers. The PotatoQuick! product is an important source of fast-food revenue in convenience stores and should enable the industry to meaningfully broaden its customer base while increasing margins.

Competition

The PotatoQuick! product competes with food products in convenience stores, but from the broadest perspective, it competes with quick-service eating establishments, mom and pops, take-outs, pizza parlors, coffee shops, delis, supermarket freezers, and microwave ovens. In fact, any establishment serving or selling food is considered competition.

Wendy's International, a $3 billion fast-food company with locations throughout the world, offers several varieties of prepared potatoes with an assortment of toppings. Rax Restaurants, a $500 million fast-food chain located mostly in the southern and midwestern United States, also offers prepared potatoes with toppings such as sour cream, bacon, and cheddar cheese (*AdWeek/Marketing Week*, September 1990, brand report). Nonpotato and other potato derivative products could also be considered in the competitive set; these would include french fries, burritos, sandwiches, nachos, and a mix of other products offered by convenience stores through regional food distributors. Since this market is highly fragmented, competitors vary depending on the region of the country.

Marketing

All marketing efforts are coordinated exclusively around food distribution channels. PotatoQuick!'s marketing manager, Ewa Piwowar, establishes annual and long-term contracts for sale and delivery of the product with California food wholesalers and distributors. These distributors in turn establish tactical in-store marketing and sales support programs for the product. Pricing strategy is most critical in maintaining margins for all elements of the distribution. Thus, distributors also engage in marketing research and share expenses through margin support clauses written in contracts with the corporation.

Owners and managers of convenience stores are also consulted for input and to supplement the direct selling efforts of the food distributors. In-store advertising and point-of-sale promotions for some convenience store chains have been used to increase impulse sales and product awareness. No additional marketing commitments have been made to date.

Production

PotatoQuick! has developed a unique method of packaging potatoes that allows consumers to enjoy a baked potato with minimal preparation. Fresh potatoes from Idaho are delivered to the plant two to three times per week by a trucking firm under contract. The fully automated production process begins by cleaning the potatoes in a high-pressure water bath. Then the potatoes are visually inspected for quality as they pass on a series of belts. Next, the potatoes progress to a large oven for baking, then to a cooling tray, and finally to a packaging machine. The potatoes are packed in a two-part vacuum-sealed container. One section of the container holds the condiments (butter, sour cream, chives, and cheese), and the potatoes are sealed into the second section. The two sections of the package divide easily along a perforation, and the potato container is microwaveable. The production line makes use of moving water, belts, rollers, and sorting equipment to move all potatoes so that potatoes are never handled by the workers, with the exception of the ones that do not pass visual inspection and are discarded.

The condiments may be packed in the containers several days in advance and kept refrigerated, which allows the potato packing machine to operate quickly and efficiently. The finished container is vacuum-sealed and refrigerated in the plant to await shipment.

PotatoQuick! has worked diligently to apply just-in-time inventory techniques. This effort has cut both inventory-holding levels and losses from spoilage. The average inventory on hand is roughly equal to two weeks' sales.

The cost of goods sold (CGS) is calculated from the prices of all inputs to the production process. Direct materials (potatoes, butter, packaging, etc.) account for 70 percent of CGS, direct labor 5 percent, and manufacturing overhead 25 percent.

Production Characteristics

Management has mastered several production procedures critical to the success of the product. One is the baking time and temperature of the potatoes. An underbaked potato is unpopular with consumers because it takes extra time to prepare. However, an overbaked potato has a reduced shelf life, which would limit distribution. The correct baking time and temperature were determined through extensive research and are integral parts of the quality control program.

Labor Force and Employees

PotatoQuick! currently employs approximately 40 people in addition to the five founders. The production facility is running two shifts, with 12 people and a supervisor on each. Two full-time sales representatives manage sales accounts, keeping in contact with key food distributors. One full-time procurement agent works on sourcing for the potatoes, and one other handles all arrangements for transporting them to and from the plant. The remaining employees handle accounting, clerical, maintenance, and general administrative tasks.

Suppliers

PotatoQuick! deals with over 100 suppliers, purchasing items such as direct material, plant maintenance items, and office supplies. The direct materials are potatoes, sour cream, butter, cheese, chives, and packaging material.

The potatoes are purchased from packers in 50-pound boxes. These packers buy potatoes from farmers, clean and sort them, and then package them for shipping. PotatoQuick! works with three packers who can each supply a constant stream of high-quality 10- to 12-ounce potatoes. PotatoQuick! purchases condiments in bulk from local dairy and produce suppliers. The packaging material is purchased under contract from Boise Cascade Packaging Division.

Subcontractors

PotatoQuick! has contracted with Fredrickson Trucking of Aberdeen, Idaho, to transport potatoes from Idaho packers to the California plant. The annual contract with Fredrickson is renegotiated each June.

Another subcontractor is an environmental safety consulting group hired to monitor the wastes emitted from the plant. Manufacturing Monitoring Services takes one sample of emitted water and air each month, analyzes it, and gives feedback on harmful substance levels. Although no harmful samples have been found, it is believed that this monitoring will help PotatoQuick! be safe and preclude any lawsuits.

Equipment

The Los Angeles plant was designed and built by Bingham Contractors, Inc., using the latest advances in food-processing technology. In addition to specially fabricated equipment, the plant also has two General Electric commercial ovens capable of cooking 500 potatoes per hour each, "SureSeal" vacuum-pack sealing machines, and a Mueller cooling system capable of cooling 10,000 feet of warehouse space. Other equipment includes a forklift, a pickup truck, a panel van with cooler, and office equipment.

Property and Facilities

PotatoQuick! owns approximately five acres of land in Los Angeles where the plant is located. The plant is approximately 75,000 square feet, including office space.

Patents and Trademarks

PotatoQuick! has registered the name PotatoQuick! along with its trademark.

Research and Development

PotatoQuick! has contracted with Bingham to perform research on improving flow and processing within the plant. The suggestions from this research have resulted in a 10 percent reduction in throughput time.

Litigation

No litigation is pending at this time.

Government Regulations

The factory and warehouse of PotatoQuick! are subject to an annual inspection by Orange County (California) food inspection authorities. PotatoQuick! has met all local and state government regulations to date and anticipates no problems in the future. The product also falls within guidelines set by the Food and Drug Administration (FDA) regarding the sale, labeling, and packaging of processed foods.

Backlog

PotatoQuick! currently has a two-week backlog of orders that it cannot fill because of full capacity at its California facility. These are firm orders from several northern California food distributors. This two-week backlog should disappear with the planned organization of a third shift of production beginning in 1991.

Insurance

PotatoQuick! is insured by the Allstate Insurance Company of California, Los Angeles. Allstate provides the company with product liability, fire and casualty, fidelity, and business interruption insurance.

Taxes

The company took advantage of a special 1987 California tax incentive package to build its facility in Orange County. Thus, property taxes have been reduced by approximately 50 percent for the first five years of operation, after which the company will pay standard rates. All federal payroll and income taxes as well as California state and local taxes have been paid as scheduled.

Corporate Structure

PotatoQuick! was incorporated in California in 1987. All stock is owned by the five founders of the company: Patrick Gunn, Ewa Piwowar, Doug Camp, Gary Fuller, and Jim Schafer. Each stockholder also has a managerial function with the Potato-Quick! organization. This is outlined in the management section of this document.

Publications and Associations

The Progressive Grocer, Restaurant Business, and *Supermarket News* are the primary trade publications in the food service industry. PotatoQuick! belongs to the Greater California Chamber of Commerce and the Southern California chapter of the Food Manufacturing Association, a trade group serving the food-manufacturing industry. John R. Ready, president of the group, can be contacted to discuss the key strategic issues in the food industry: (213) 555–1334. Frank Stevens, president of the Greater California Chamber of Commerce, will also be available to discuss California's economic climate and local market conditions affecting the PotatoQuick! product: (213) 555–1081.

MANAGEMENT

Directors and Officers

The six members of the PotatoQuick! board of directors are:

Dr. Jackson Pollack
Professor Agricultural Science
California State University

Mr. George Corleone
Chief Executive Officer
Ad-Pac Corporation
San Jose, CA

Ms. Joyce Cheung, Partner
Arthur Andersen Management
  Consulting
Los Angeles, CA

Ms. Kimberly-Ann Greenback
San Francisco, CA

Mr. Noah Setchel
Carmel, CA

Dr. Michael Wonderlicht
Advanced Packaging Group, Ltd.
San Jose, CA

Key Employees

The key employees of the PotatoQuick! Corporation are the company's five founding members:

James Schafer, President   James Schafer (MBA, University of California, Los Angeles) spent two years as controller for MicroProducts Corp., a Menlo Park, California, developer of food products targeted at the microwave convenience market. After two years as controller he was promoted to the position of vice-president of operations and in 1986 assumed the position of president. In 1987 he left MicroProducts to form the PotatoQuick! Corporation.

While at MicroProducts, Schafer oversaw the development and market introduction of several new products. During his tenure as president, the firm's average annual growth rate was 14 percent. Management and the board feel certain that Schafer has the skills and vision necessary to successfully run and expand PotatoQuick!

Gary Fuller, VP Product Development   Gary Fuller (MBA, University of Southern California) conceived the original idea for the product in 1984. He began experimenting with baked potatoes to make them convenient for microwave serving in 1985. In 1986 he perfected the combination of packaging, flavor enhancement, and microwave convenience that is the PotatoQuick! product. Fuller's current projects include refining the PotatoQuick! production process and developing a new mix of flavor enhancement spices to extend the PotatoQuick! product line.

Ewa Piwowar, VP Marketing   Before joining the other founding members in 1987 to form the PotatoQuick! Corporation, Ewa Piwowar (MBA, Warsaw School of Economics and Agriculture) had spent several years as a successful management consultant in her native Poland. She has worked with many companies in the past to bring innovative new products successfully to market.

Piwowar has complete responsibility for development and execution of the company's advertising and marketing strategies. She is currently developing an eye-catching new label and package that she believes has great potential for increasing consumer awareness of the product.

Patrick Gunn, VP Distribution   Patrick Gunn (MBA, San Diego State University) worked in various capacities for the Sysco Corporation between 1982 and 1986 before joining the other founders of PotatoQuick! in 1987. He is very familiar with the food distribution industry and has many contacts within the industry. Gunn is currently working to develop the company's plans for expansion into markets beyond the West Coast.

Douglas Camp, VP Operations   Before joining the PotatoQuick! Corporation, Douglas Camp (MBA, University of Washington) worked for several years as a plant manager for the Frito-Lay Corporation, managing a facility that produced potato chips. He has a broad knowledge of the production processes utilized in the manufacture of fast foods and is currently working to further refine the PotatoQuick! production process.

Remuneration

Remuneration data for the key members of management are outlined below. Figures are for the business year ended December 31, 1989.

	Annual Salary	*Sales Bonus[a]*	*Total Remuneration*
James Schafer	$60,000	$32,000[b]	$92,000
Gary Fuller	50,000	25,000[c]	75,000
Ewa Piwowar	50,000	17,000	67,000
Patrick Gunn	50,000	17,000	67,000
Douglas Camp	50,000	17,000	67,000

[a]All members of key management received a bonus in 1990 of $17,000. This bonus was awarded in recognition of achievement of sales and growth targets.
[b]Schafer received a bonus of $18,000 in recognition of his extraordinary efforts as president to further the growth of the company.
[c]Fuller received an $8,000 royalty from the company on the formula and technology of the PotatoQuick! process.

Stock Options

All outstanding common stock of the company is held in equal amounts by the five founders (see "Principal Shareholders" below). No stock option plans are in place. However, management recognizes the potential need to dilute their holdings in the company to raise growth capital and to attract and retain new employees.

Principal Shareholders

Currently, all of the corporation's common stock is held by the five founders of the company, in the following amounts.

Ewa Piwowar	10,000
Gary Fuller	10,000
James Schafer	10,000
Patrick Gunn	10,000
Douglas Camp	10,000
Total	50,000

These shares were issued at a par value of $10 per share. The company has no other common stock, preferred stock, or any other form of equity outstanding.

Employee Agreements

The five founders of PotatoQuick! Corporation have agreed to remain with the company at least through the end of the calendar year ending December 31, 1995. No other employee agreement exists at this time.

Conflicts of Interest

The company knows of no conflicts of interest between members of management and other entities at this time.

Accountants, Lawyers, Bankers

The company has retained the following professional advisers:

Accountants—
Reese Henry Accountants
Los Angeles, CA 45041

Attorneys—
Davis, Davis, Dimos & Monroe, Attorneys-at-Law
San Francisco, CA 46041

Bankers—
First Nippon Bank
San Francisco, CA 46041

DESCRIPTION OF THE FINANCING

Half the needed capital will be provided through a ten-year bank loan at 14 percent interest. This will supply PotatoQuick! with $1,000,000 to purchase assets that will be used as collateral for the loan (primarily warehouses and land), and allow the retirement of old long-term debt. The remainder of the necessary financing will be provided by venture capitalists. We intend to issue 30,645 shares of common stock at $32.632 per share. This represents a 38 percent ownership stake in the firm. The issuance of this stock will be accompanied by certain rights and privileges transferred to the holders. Venture capitalists will be granted preemptive rights to pro rata participation in any future private offerings. Founders will agree to sell their stock back to the company before selling to any third party, and if the company elects not to purchase, stock will be offered pro rata to investors on a first-refusal basis. Venture capital is subordinated only to indebtedness for borrowed money from banks and other financial institutions.

Collateral for the Financing

Money provided by the venture capitalists will be used primarily to purchase new machines to clean, bake, and package potatoes and a new Mueller refrigeration system. These machines are valued in excess of $650,000 and can be used as collateral for the debt.

Use of Proceeds

The funds generated by the debt portion of this financing proposal will be utilized in the following ways:

Additional machinery	$650,000
Marketing program	75,000
Purchase of inventory	125,000
Payroll expenses	150,000

Ownership

The original owners and founders of PotatoQuick! control 62 percent of the business, with 50,000 shares outstanding. The venture capitalists will be provided with 38 percent of the common stock in the form of 30,645 shares. There are no other owners of PotatoQuick!

Dilution

PotatoQuick! plans to have enough future sales growth and reserve cash to preclude the need for additional financing in the next five years. It will therefore avoid further stock issuances and dilution of outstanding shares.

Fees Paid

PotatoQuick! will pay all fees and expenses of investors' special counsel if the deal is consummated. The company will also bear responsibility for any brokerage fees incurred as a result of this transaction.

Investor Involvement

The venture capitalists will be guaranteed representation with one seat on the board of directors as long as they maintain a minimum of 10 percent ownership of the company. They will also be allowed all voting rights and privileges associated with their proportional control of the firm. Furthermore, PotatoQuick! expects to rely on the financial expertise of these investors intermittently throughout operation of the business.

RISK FACTORS

Limited Operating History

Potential investors should note that the company has a relatively limited operating history. The company has operated for more than three years, building a current level of annual sales of approximately $4,500,000. Management is confident of the company's continued ability to market its current product and to develop new products for the convenience food market. Management believes that the attached financial projections accurately reflect the company's growth potential. However, investors should note that the convenience food market, like any industry, contains uncertainties, and it can be difficult to predict the performance of current and new products. Forces beyond the control of management may act to depress the market or to adversely affect the company's relationship with its distribution network. Past successful operation of the corporation does not ensure future success.

At present, total assets controlled by the corporation equal $1,143,000. Approximately 5 percent of this amount is in the form of cash and marketable securities. The remaining assets are in the form of inventory, accounts receivable, and equipment.

Limited Resources

Investors considering providing capital to the company should note the relatively limited operating resources available to the company at this time.

Limited Management Experience

The company believes its management to be highly skilled and competent to manage current operations and future growth. However, some concern exists that current levels of management may not be sufficient if predicted growth is realized. Management of the company has considered this risk and plans to add personnel with diverse functional backgrounds in the industry as future growth makes these additions necessary.

Persons considering investing in the company should carefully examine the background and skills of members of key management and draw their own conclusions regarding the management of the company.

Market Uncertainties

The market for convenience food items is predicted to grow by 12 percent over the next several years. These forecasts represent the best information available to management at this time. A risk exists that the market will not grow as predicted. Individuals considering investing in the company should examine the convenience food market carefully and draw their own conclusions regarding the uncertainties inherent in this market.

Production Uncertainties

At this time there are no uncertainties in the production process for Potato-Quick! The technology currently used to prepare and package the product is highly reliable and has been in service for three years without presenting more than routine difficulty. President Schafer has extensive experience in the production of microwaveable convenience foods.

However, a substantial portion of the funds the company is seeking will be used to fabricate a new production facility. Although management does not foresee significant difficulties in starting the new production facility, potential investors should carefully consider the difficulties and risks inherent in any production process, and particularly in building and starting a new facility.

Liquidation

In the unlikely event that the PotatoQuick! Corporation should be liquidated, management estimates the following liquidation values for company assets:

Asset	Liquidation Value
Land	$100,000.00
Building	400,000.00
Baking ovens (2)	150,000.00
Other equipment	150,000.00
Inventory (average)	170,000.00
Miscellaneous	30,000.00
Total	$1,000,000.00

Note that the above estimates are subject to interpretation and should not be construed as the exact values the listed items would obtain if sold. All reasonable effort has been made to predict the future value of these items; however, the exact value the market would place on them is beyond the control of management.

Dependence on Key Management

The PotatoQuick! Corporation is not highly dependent on any member of the management team. The company owns all rights to produce and market the product and thus is at no risk of losing any key technology if management were to leave.

RETURN ON INVESTMENT AND EXIT

We can project a sale of the firm at the end of operating year 1995 to a large food processing and distribution corporation with experience in potato products. By this point, the company should be profitable enough and sufficiently ready for further expansion to attract the interest of some large conglomerates. Ore-Ida, Frito-Lay, Pet, and ConAgra appear to be the types of companies that would be likely to consider acquiring the company.

Return on Investment

The venture capitalists will receive 38 percent of the company for $1 million. At the end of 1995 PotatoQuick! is projected to have after-tax profits in excess of $2 million, which, when multiplied by the P/E ratio of 10 for the industry, results in a rough value of the firm of $20 million. This is the amount for which the company is expected to sell to a large conglomerate. Assuming the venture capitalists' share at 38 percent, the value of their share of the company at this point equals $7.6 million. This amount corresponds to an estimated return of slightly over 50 percent.

ANALYSIS OF OPERATIONS AND PROJECTIONS

General

Financial data for the company are presented in Exhibits 1 through 3. The assumptions of the projected data are as follows:

1. Sales growth rate (1991—)	35%
2. Cost of goods sold as percentage of sales	77%
3. Effective tax rate	35%
4. Interest on long-term debts	14%

Results of Operations

In the period 1987–1990 PotatoQuick! enjoyed an average of 26 percent annual growth in sales. However, in the first three years of its existence the company operated at a loss. Beginning in 1990 the company generated cash flows due to dynamic 35 percent sales growth (which brought about economies of scale). Increasing net income will be the result of further expansion and successful sales in new markets. Sales expansion will be possible with the proposed external financing:

- *1991.* $1,000,000 from venture capital for purchases of equipment, plant, and warehouse
- *1991.* $1,000,000 bank long-term loan to pay off $300,000 of original loan, to purchase new working equipment and buildings, and to provide capital

Projected costs are based on previous experience. Costs are expected to decrease due to implementing new efficient equipment. Operating income in the projections conforms to standard practices in the industry.

Financial Conditions

The current balance sheet shows a 2 percent increase of accounts receivable compared with 1989. This was due to 29.7 percent sales growth. Ninety-five percent of sales are sold on account.

This year the company purchased new equipment worth $50,000. Other liabilities include the following year-end balances:

- Salaries and wages payable: $300,000 (accrued bonuses)
- Notes payable: $392,000 (S/T bank loans)

Liquidity of the company has improved as a result of positive net income, but a short-term bank loan was still needed.

Contingent Liabilities

The company had no contingent liabilities at the end of 1990. ∎

This case was written by Alan Ellstrand under the supervision of Marc Dollinger. The events and data in this case are real. Some of the names and places have been disguised. Original research was provided by Patrick Gunn, Ewa Piwowar, Doug Camp, Gary Fuller, and Jim Schafer.

EXHIBIT 1 PotatoQuick! Balance Sheets 1987–1995 (In Thousands)

	Dec. 1986	Actual 1987	1988	1989	1990	1991	Estimated 1992	1993	1994	1995
Cash and marketable securities	$130	$50	$50	$50	$50	$50	$50	$925	$2,300	$4,200
A/R	0	200	245	310	402	607	819	1,106	1,493	2,016
Inventory	20	95	117	148	191	289	390	527	711	960
Total current assets	$150	$345	$412	$508	$643	$946	$1,259	$2,558	$4,504	$7,176
Plant and equipment	$700	$700	$750	$750	$800	$2,200	$2,600	$2,900	$3,150	$3,700
Less accumulated depreciation[a]		($70)	($145)	($220)	($300)	($520)	($780)	($1,070)	($1,385)	($1,755)
Total assets	$850	$975	$1,017	$1,038	$1,143	$2,626	$3,079	$4,388	$6,269	$9,121
Accounts payable	$50	$128	$157	$199	$258	$389	$526	$710	$958	$1,294
Other liabilities[b]	0	329	570	678	692	257	70	50	63	87
Accrued taxes[c]	0	(99)	(179)	(224)	(212)	(182)	(6)	395	705	1,119
Total current liabilities	$50	$358	$548	$653	$738	$464	$590	$1,155	$1,726	$2,500
Long-term debt	$300	$300	$300	$300	$300	$1,000	$1,000	$1,000	$1,000	$1,000
Owners' equity	500	500	500	500	500	1,500	1,500	1,500	1,500	1,500
Retained earnings	0	(183)	(332)	(416)	(394)	(339)	(10)	733	2,043	4,121
Total liabilities and OE	$850	$975	$1,016	$1,037	$1,144	$2,625	$3,080	$4,388	$6,269	$9,121

[a] Depreciation is calculated using straight-line method with a 10-year average life of assets.
[b] Includes wages payable, notes payable, and dividends payable.
[c] Assumes losses are carried forward.

EXHIBIT 2 PotatoQuick! Income Statements 1987–1995 (In Thousands)

| | Actual | | | | | Estimated | | | |
	1987	1988	1989	1990	1991	1992	1993	1994	1995
Sales	$2,000	$2,450	$3,100	$4,020	$6,070	$8,195	$11,063	$14,934	$20,162
Cost of goods sold	1,540	1,887	2,387	3,095	4,674	6,310	8,518	11,500	15,524
Gross profit	460	563	713	925	1,396	1,885	2,545	3,434	4,638
General and administrative expenses	700	750	800	850	1,170	1,240	1,260	1,280	1,300
EBIT	(240)	(187)	(87)	75	226	645	1,285	2,154	3,338
Interest on LT debt	(42)	(42)	(42)	(42)	(140)	(140)	(140)	(140)	(140)
Profit before taxes	(282)	(229)	(129)	33	86	505	1,144	2,015	3,197
Taxes	(99)	(80)	(45)	11	30	177	401	705	1,119
Profit after taxes	($183)	($149)	($84)	$22	$56	$328	$743	$1,310	$2,078

Assumptions:

Sales growth rate (1991–)	35%
CGS as a percentage of sales	77%
Effective tax rate	35%
Interest on LT loan	14%

EXHIBIT 3 PotatoQuick! Cash Flow 1987–1995 (In Thousands)

| | | Actual | | | | | Estimated | | | |
	Dec. 1986	1987	1988	1989	1990	1991	1992	1993	1994	1995
Net income after tax		($183)	($149)	($84)	$21	$56	$328	$744	$1,310	$2,078
(+) Depreciation		70	75	75	80	220	260	290	315	370
(+) Net borrowing	300					700				
(+) New capital	500					1,000				
(−) Dividends						(63)	(63)	(63)	(63)	(63)
Cash available for reinvestment	$800	($113)	($74)	($9)	$101	$1,913	$525	$971	$1,562	$2,385
(−) Capital expenditures	($700)		($50)		($50)	($1,400)	($400)	($300)	($250)	($550)
Net cash flow	$100	($113)	($124)	($9)	$51	$513	$125	$671	$1,312	$1,835

Case 10   Windsor Industries, Inc.

Windsor Industries, of Akron, Ohio, was founded in 1980 by E. L. Gibitz, then 66, to sell an industrial-grade tool board to automobile manufacturers. By 1993, annual sales averaged $405,000 and had seemed to hit their peak. Gibitz felt that there was significant potential for tool board not only in the automotive market but also in the marine service area and, especially, the consumer "do-it-yourself" market. Windsor was originally licensed by a similar company in Great Britain with sales in excess of $5 million a year. Although Great Britain has only one-sixteenth the GNP of the United States, Windsor's sales had never approached that level. Gibitz often wondered what needed to be done to reach a comparable sales level on this side of the Atlantic.

Although 13 years had passed since its founding, the organization still consisted of just three people. Gibitz did everything from making sales calls to packing the product for shipment to placing orders for materials. All manufacturing was outsourced, with material coming from both local and international (Korea and Taiwan) suppliers. Windsor simply designed the tool boards, sold the product, and shipped to the customer. In addition to Gibitz, Windsor employed a sales representative and a receptionist, both of whom participated in the packing function when a large order was to be shipped. Most current customers were automotive manufacturers who bought directly or required their dealers to buy the tool board along with required "essential tools." (Automobile manufacturers require dealers to buy these "essential tools" for each model year of car. Each dealer must retain these tools for five years.) Windsor's recent venture into the marine market was met with positive customer response, but it remained a small portion of sales.

PROBLEM IDENTIFICATION

While there seems to be a strong market for tool board, Windsor Industries has one major problem. At 79, Gibitz does not have the energy level he had when he began the enterprise. Although he enjoys the activity, it is certain that he is not able to maximize the company's potential. It is likely that he would sell the business, given an acceptable offer.

A team of potential buyers emerged. The group was composed of three recently graduated MBA students, one of whom was Gibitz's grandson. But before he could sell the business, and the team could buy it, Gibitz needed to develop a business plan. The business plan proposed the purchase of the company by the team and outlined a strategy for increasing sales to about $3 million in five years. But the plan doesn't address two crucial questions: (1) What is the viability of selling the business? (2) What is the value of the business?

Excerpts of the business plan follow.

THE PRODUCTS

Windsor has two primary products in its tool-board line. The basic tool board, called Loc-Board, is similar to Peg-Board in function but is constructed of reinforced steel and uses a patented screw-in hook that holds up to 160 pounds. With over 100 different hook styles available, the board can hold any tool. The shape of the tool is silk-screened either directly on the board or on an adhesive vinyl overlay that allows easy updating for each new model year. In addition to the hook attachments, the product offers extensive bin storage as well as a tool storage cart developed so that the mechanics' tools are close to the workstation at all times, further increasing the mechanics' efficiency.

A second product, called Forever Peghook, uses the same screw-in philosophy to attach to standard Peg-Board. This is the main product that would be targeted toward the consumer market. Consumers might also be interested in a standard Peg-Board vinyl overlay with shapes of common household tools such as various screwdrivers, hammers, and pliers. This product could also be targeted toward service bays that already use some sort of existing Peg-Board.

The Loc-Board system has two advantages. First, studies have shown that up to 70 percent of an automotive dealer's "essential tools" are either misplaced or missing altogether when audits are conducted. This requires mechanics to spend an average of six to eight hours per month searching for tools. Second, when this search comes up empty, the mechanic may attempt to do the job without the correct tool, possibly leading to unsafe repairs. As a result, this tool board increases both the efficiency of the mechanic and the safety of the repair.

CURRENT MARKETS

Most of Windsor's sales to date have been to automotive manufacturers. Japanese manufacturers Nissan and Subaru have purchased tool-board sets for all their dealers. Other customers are such diverse corporations as Ford (Tractor) and Harley-Davidson. Additional possibilities exist in the marine service market; a recent direct-mail campaign to Mercury Marine dealers has elicited positive response, and a follow-up piece is in the making.

Growth potential exists in two main areas. The first is the industrial and commercial area, primarily foreign automotive manufacturers. Further penetration of the domestic automotive-manufacturing market, the marine-manufacturing market, and other specialty markets (fast oil-change centers, for example) would produce large custom orders.

The second potential growth area is the retail market for individual tool boards. While this is currently being handled by mail order, there is an opportunity to set up distribution channels through national discounters such as Wal-Mart, Kmart, and Sears Roebuck & Co. Additionally, such national and regional hardware discounters as Hechinger and Lowe's are likely prospects. Finally, distribution through auto parts retailers will help reach the retail market.

In addition to steel tool board, Windsor also markets a vinyl overlay designed to cover the traditional Peg-Board that already exists in many applications. Suzuki U.S.A., for example, has recently furnished its 300-dealer network with these overlays combined with the screw-in Forever Peghook designed to secure the hooks to the Peg-Board. The industrial, commercial, and retail potential of this Peg-Board add-on are significant.

PROFIT POTENTIAL AND RESOURCE REQUIREMENTS

As is typical in small businesses, neither revenues nor profits are consistent. Average annual revenues for the past four years (FY 1989 to FY 1992) have been $405,477, with a standard deviation of $78,194. Gross profit as a percentage of sales has averaged 57.0 percent, while net income has averaged $36,229, or 10.3 percent of sales.

Significant improvements can be made in these results. First, the revenues can be substantially higher with additional sales effort, as Table 1 shows. Projections indicate that increased selling effort can produce sales growth of over 650 percent for the first five years of operation. We propose three people in direct sales, each focusing on the automotive market. Second, as is common with entrepreneurial ventures, income may have been understated to avoid federal income taxes. As a result, projected figures will be substantially higher.

Both cost of goods sold and operating expenses will increase to a lesser extent than revenues, as economies of scale in selling and purchasing begin to take place. This yields a pretax net income that grows faster than sales.

After purchasing the company from Gibitz, the new owners' strategy will emphasize sales growth. Automobile manufacturers will play a large part in this expansion effort, as they have traditionally been the largest customers for the product. This will be the focus for the first year and a half. Additionally, a niche exists in the retail market with distribution through large discount retailers (Hechinger, Lowe's) and direct-mail order for a tool board and hook set.

These sales growth targets can be achieved for two reasons. The first is increased sales effort. The second is an increasing trend toward safety in automobiles, as evidenced by such recent additions as the air bag and antilock brakes. A mechanic who cannot find the correct tool with which to make a repair will use a different tool, perhaps resulting in a dangerous repair. The Loc-Board system ensures that the mechanic can find the correct tool.

Capital Requirements

Requirements for capital fall into two categories, the capital to purchase Windsor Industries and the influx of cash necessary to expand the business beyond its current three-person operation. Purchase of the business would include the company and product names, patents, tooling, and other assets. It might also include an annual lease agreement for the existing headquarters facilities at an additional charge.

Growth requirements are difficult to estimate. The first few years of operation will be focused on marketing and sales, resulting in significant advertising and travel

	TABLE 1 Selected Financial Data (Projected)					
	Year 0	*Year 1*	*Year 2*	*Year 3*	*Year 4*	*Year 5*
Sales	$368,919	$725,000	$1,250,000	$1,600,000	$2,100,000	$2,800,000
Cost of goods sold	154,946	304,500	525,000	672,000	882,000	1,176,000
Operating expenses	113,603	305,537	351,794	425,966	604,639	700,842
Pretax net income	$100,370	$ 59,963	$ 318,206	$ 447,034	$ 558,361	$ 868,518

expenditures. With the substantial growth rate that has been projected, the buyers estimate that an additional $200,000 will be required.

THE INDUSTRY

The nearest competitor to the Loc-Board system, although far behind in durability and strength, is standard Peg-Board. The five largest Peg-Board-producing companies produce 50 million square feet of standard Peg-Board annually. At current retail prices of approximately $0.30 per square foot, this is a $15 million market. In addition to these five large companies, hundreds of small local and regional producers exist, multiplying this figure many times. It is also estimated that 500 million hooks are sold annually—an additional $31.25 million.

Market Size and Trends

The two main markets, automotive and residential, are large. The total number of distinct dealer franchises in the United States was 41,368 in 1992. With a historical average of ten tool boards per dealer and an average selling price of $75 per board (including overlays, hooks, etc.), the total automotive market for the product would be $31,026,000. Growth is likely to be zero in the number of automotive dealerships—the number tends to remain relatively constant—so this is an accurate figure for the total market size for later years as well.

Market size for the residential market is not as easy to estimate. A recent survey of households by Rubbermaid, Inc., estimated that about half of the 80 million single-family homes in the United States had some type of Peg-Board. If the market for the Windsor Loc-Hook Starter Set alone (retail price is $14.95) is considered, the total residential market is $598 million.

Customers buy the product for four reasons. First, the Loc-Board system mitigates risk. Mechanics are more likely to use the correct tool for the repair. Second, the product decreases time wasted searching for tools, and thus increases productivity. Third, the screening of the tool on the board improves the likelihood that the tool will be replaced correctly, reducing the dealer's tool replacement expense. Finally, the system organizes the whole work area, increasing the public's perception of the dealership's service quality.

Competition and Competitive Edges

Windsor faces no direct competition. Some indirect competition comes from traditional Peg-Board and from other tool storage systems. Additionally, Kent-Moore and Owatana Tool Company both market a board similar to Windsor's, but they supply the boards only as part of a total package. Both of these companies (which supply to the large domestic automotive manufacturers) buy the accompanying hooks from Windsor.

Competitive advantage comes primarily from the substantial benefits that customers receive. This "value added" consists of increased safety and less down time for mechanics. Tools are not lost nearly as much. As mechanics currently spend seven to eight hours per month looking for tools, this represents significant time savings. Additionally, repairs done without the correct tools can be a safety hazard.

Other competitive advantages come from the following:

1. *Legal aspects.* Patents held for the company's hooks represent a competitive advantage, although it may not be economically feasible to defend these.
2. *Informational aspects.* Current customer lists and historical business information are competitive strengths. The founder's experience with parts outsourcing and low-cost foreign suppliers is also a competitive plus.
3. *Quality characteristics.* The product is highly differentiated. Its level of quality has been consistently high—it is a simple product, but is stronger and more durable than standard Peg-Board.
4. *Market characteristics.* The market is obscure, making competitive entry less likely. Once customer contacts are cemented and the company grows, competitive position will become more defensible. Thus, losing patent protection in a few years becomes less of a factor. Windsor Industries has already established itself as the primary player in this market. Price sensitivity is low, and quality of the product is high compared with standard Peg-Board, the closest form of competition.

Estimated Market Share and Sales

At the current price of $750 for one tool board set (of ten tool boards), the estimated sales level will be 967 sets for year 1. This assumes that if each of the three salespeople obtains only two additional large contracts in the automotive area, with the average contract yielding $100,000 to $150,000 in sales, this sales level can be achieved. Subsequent years' sales will increase further based on resales of overlays and other follow-up sales, and expansion into the retail and direct-marketing (catalog) areas.

ECONOMICS OF THE BUSINESS

Operating margins for the automotive segment of the business dominate the analysis because this is the largest segment of current sales. The new owners will focus primarily on the automotive market during the first year and a half of operation. Table 2 summarizes the pricing margins based on a set of ten tool boards for which the average dealer pays $750. The average purchase cost for a tool-board set is $320, which leaves a $430 gross margin. Profit after taxes is almost $80 per set—over 10 percent of the sales price.

With the infusion of cash from an increase in debt in year 1, sales are expected to grow to $2.8 million in year 5, producing gross profit of $1.624 million and net in-

TABLE 2 Product Costs and Profitability		
	Cost per Unit (set of 10)	*Percent of Sales*
Purchase costs	$320.00	42
Gross margin	430.00	58
Fixed costs	316.00	42
Profit before taxes	114.00	15
Profit after taxes	$ 79.80	10.6

TABLE 3 Fixed Cost Breakdown						
	Year 0	*Year 1*	*Year 2*	*Year 3*	*Year 4*	*Year 5*
Sales	$368,919	$725,000	$1,250,000	$1,600,000	$2,100,000	$2,800,000
Selling expense	9,111	97,000	97,000	126,000	140,000	158,500
Advertising expense	21,689	40,000	50,000	50,000	50,000	50,000
Telephone and utilities	2,724	5,500	5,500	5,500	5,500	5,500
Rent expense	10,000	12,000	15,000	18,000	21,000	24,000
Salaries	41,599	100,000	100,000	120,000	150,000	180,000
Postage	9,620	18,905	32,595	41,722	54,760	73,013
Interest expense	0	55,000	55,000	55,000	55,000	55,000
Total fixed costs	$ 94,743	$328,405	$ 355,095	$ 416,222	$ 476,260	$ 546,013
As percentage of sales	25.70%	45.30%	28.40%	26.00%	22.70%	19.50%

come of $625,000. Additionally, there is ample reason to believe that sales will continue to increase well past the $3 million level.

Durability of the profit stream will come primarily from the momentum that will have been built up by past sales contacts, the reputation of the company and product, and a substantial increase in the selling effort. As has been previously discussed, the threat of new entrants into the specialized segment of the Peg-Board industry that has been created by Loc-Board is minimal because of the relative obscurity of the product offering and perceived barriers to entry. Additionally, Windsor enjoys a significant cost advantage in production of hooks for standard Peg-Board and for the specialized Loc-Board. Last, the depth of Windsor's hook offering will further prevent other companies from attempting to grab market share.

Fixed and Variable Costs

Since past sales trends have fluctuated greatly, the risk of internal manufacturing is currently not outweighed by the economic benefits. Thus the company currently owns few fixed assets, no real estate, and little inventory. Assets to be purchased will be the company name, customer lists, the patents, and the current tooling for hooks. While economies of scale could be attained with in-house production, a significant loss in flexibility would likely result.

Fixed costs beginning in year 1 include selling, advertising, rent, utilities, salaries, and interest expense. These increase after year 1, but they are generally tied to sales. As a result, if sales are greater than or less than expected, these fixed costs will change. These costs are summarized in Table 3.

MARKETING PLAN

Current customers are top prospects for updates in overlays and hooks, and perhaps additional boards as well. Additionally, other import manufacturers are good prospects. Windsor has yet to sell to a Big Three domestic manufacturer. Tapping this market will be a top goal of the sales team during the first year and a half.

The second group of targeted customers are homeowners. Rubbermaid's study estimates that 40 million single-family households in the United States have Peg-

Board. This creates a huge market not only for sales of the Forever Peghook but also for sales of stronger, higher-durability replacement boards.

Marketing strategy will focus on automobile (and other) manufacturers for the first year and a half, as this will be the key to reaching positive cash flow. After this time, the marketing effort will be expanded to include coverage of large discount chains targeted at the homeowner or home improvement market and increased direct mail effort with advertising in national magazines.

Pricing

Current prices are based on the superiority of the Loc-Board system to other available alternatives—namely Peg-Board—and thus leave a comfortable profit margin. The response in volume to changes in price seems to be relatively inelastic, so there is no reason to change the current pricing policy. The new owners may determine in the future that they must drop prices at least temporarily to secure orders from large customers. If this is the case, once the new customer sees the value of the tool storage system, it is likely that he/she will be willing to pay a higher price. At any rate, with the high profit per board, there is substantial leeway available to secure this type of order.

Sales Tactics

Certainly, the sales and marketing function will take priority among all activities during the first few years of the new venture. The new owners expect to travel a great deal, and this is reflected in the comparatively high budgeted expenses for sales activity. Because major customers are located in Detroit and on the West Coast, the directors will likely spend at least 30 to 40 weeks per year on the road selling.

The automotive business will be the first to receive focus. This has been the Loc-Board system's traditional strong area, so it must be saturated by the sales effort. Other large manufacturers will get attention during this first phase of the sales process. Included will be marine manufacturers and other manufacturers with well-developed dealer networks. After the first year and a half, the retail market will be added to the marketing focus, with emphasis on large discount chains and chains specifically targeted to homeowners and do-it-yourselfers.

Service and Warranty Policies

Service and warranties are an important part of the marketing process. The boards are warranted for durability and strength, and the boards are in fact stronger than most customers expect them to be. Additionally, because the hooks are welded, they, too, are much more durable than standard peg hooks. Installation of the boards is simple. Both the shape of the tool and the hook number are silk-screened on the board (or overlay). The installer merely has to match the hook number to the location on the board to install the hook.

Advertising and Promotion

Advertising expense doubles in the first year of the new venture. A focus on creating awareness by significant advertising expenditures in automotive magazines and other trade publications will expand demand in the automotive and retail markets. Also, new product releases will be sent to major product-related publications in an effort to gain publicity at minimal cost.

Distribution

Three channels exist for distribution of the Loc-Board system. First, direct sales will be used to tap the auto-manufacturing market. This will involve a total selling cost of approximately $90,000 in year 1. Subsequent years will focus increasingly on direct sales to major retailers and catalog marketers.

Shipping costs are the main distribution cost. These costs depend on shipment size; smaller orders go through UPS, larger orders through independent freight carriers. Per-unit shipping costs decrease as order size increases. Freight costs have averaged $17,340 over the past five years, roughly 4 percent of revenue.

MANUFACTURING AND OPERATIONS PLAN

A manufacturing plan for the Loc-Board system logically focuses on purchasing because 100 percent of the manufacturing is outsourced to different companies. The actual tool board is made in Ohio, while the hooks that secure the tools on the face of the tool board have been made in Seoul, South Korea, for the last five years. Tooling is being fabricated for a new, lower-cost production facility located in Taipei, Taiwan. Additionally, there are domestic suppliers for the hooks and the vinyl overlays. A freelance graphic artist designs the screens used to silk-screen the tool shapes on the vinyl overlays and boards. No formal order-processing system is being used currently because the nature of the business does not require time- or quantity-based ordering. At present, the different components are ordered when a sale is made to an automobile manufacturer or dealer. When the company grows to the level of multicontractual sales, a formal order-processing system may need to be implemented.

Geographical Location/Facilities and Improvements

Windsor Industries is based in Akron, Ohio. This is where the administrative office and the packaging center are located. All inbound shipments from suppliers are received and repackaged according to order specification. The repackaged items are then shipped to the customer (the dealer or manufacturer). This home base in Ohio will be sufficient to grow the company to the projected level in five years. At that time, further analysis will be conducted to determine whether in-house manufacturing facilities would be less expensive per unit than total outsourcing. Yearly analyses will be conducted to see whether a larger storage facility may be required to handle increased sales levels.

STRATEGY AND PLANS

The strategy that will expand this company from $400,000 in sales to about $3 million in sales in five years will consist of intense selling and marketing efforts to large automobile manufacturers, automobile dealers, and large retail hardware outlets, along with penetration of the do-it-yourself market through direct-mail catalogs. A second strategy is to research all available suppliers of each component that is outsourced. This will reduce the power of the current suppliers, enable Windsor Industries to keep costs as low as possible, and prevent overloading a single supplier with a large order.

The only quality control check Windsor will have on suppliers is the acceptance or rejection of a shipped component lot. This is another reason to research alternative suppliers; if a supplier continually sends poor lots, an alternative supplier can be used. Even if this new supplier has a higher cost, the lost sales resulting from time-consuming and unnecessary reshipping can be minimized. However, supplier relations have been favorable since the business incorporated in 1980. Quality control to the customer is measured in friendly customer service, timely product shipments, and, of course, quality products. Products shipped should be of the highest quality because of the initial quality control check of supplier shipments.

LEGAL ISSUES

The only legal issue pertains to the patent on the screw-in hooks. This patent was granted in 1984 and remains protected until 2001. However, as the company operates in a small market niche with relatively no large-scale exposure, it is doubtful anyone would test the strength of the patent. The patent number is still displayed in current catalogs. More legal issues will arise when the growth of the company leads to large contracts. At this time, consultants and/or lawyers can be hired on an as-needed basis to ensure fair and binding contracts.

ORGANIZATION AND KEY MANAGEMENT PERSONNEL

Windsor Industries is owned and operated by E. L. Gibitz, who would like to sell the business and retire. The incoming entrepreneurial team consists of Jon Littlefield (Gibitz's grandson), Greg Brink, and Tim Middleton. Full ownership (capital stock on the balance sheet) will be transferred to the entrepreneurial team with the following equity split: Littlefield—55 percent; Brink—22.5 percent; Middleton—22.5 percent.

The duties of each team member will overlap considerably. The main focus and effort will be on sales and marketing to each market. For the first 18 months, expansion in the automotive industry will be the goal. After that, each team member will focus on penetrating new markets. Brink will have responsibility for the automotive and industrial business. Because Brink has selling experience as well as a strong interest and background in automobile technology, he is the most qualified to expand in this market.

Middleton will concentrate on developing the direct catalog sales market. Currently this is an ongoing project of Windsor Industries, but it is restricted to advertising in other magazines and limited distribution of company catalogs. Middleton's expertise and experience in conducting reliable market research will be utilized to determine the size of this market, the location of potential customers, and the most cost-effective way to reach them. Customers will be reached by direct mailing of catalogs and increased print advertising in magazines that they frequently read. The goal is to present the product to customers will and often so that they can see and comprehend the value added.

Littlefield will be in charge of a new market area, large retail outlets such as Wal-Mart, Lowe's, and Hechinger. In the first year to two years, he will conduct interviews by phone and in person with purchasing managers in these large stores. If the results of the interviews are positive—and they are projected to be—a test market of stores will be supplied with the products. These stores will be located in towns and cities that are relatively close to Akron but are diverse enough to represent different market areas. The success of these test market stores will determine the rate of expansion in the retail sector.

CRITICAL RISKS, PROBLEMS, AND ASSUMPTIONS

Some risks will exist while trying to grow the venture:

1. Manufacturers (or other customers) may decide to produce their own version of our tool board set. A manufacturer's decision to produce a similar product in-house and distribute it to all dealers could take away a substantial amount of the venture's potential market. By use of suppliers in foreign countries (Taiwan, for example), the management team hopes to keep costs and prices low enough to convince manufacturers that in-house production is not worthwhile.
2. Customer orders have traditionally been sporadic. This is mainly the result of a lack of selling "intensity" by current management. Sales are expected to become more stable and predictable when a dedicated sales force is in place.
3. Sales projections represented in the business plan may be somewhat inaccurate because of the nature of the business. The venture will grow at a rate that depends on the type of customer the entrepreneurial team can attract (manufacturer, independent dealer, or retailer). The entrepreneurial team feels confident that a substantial growth rate can be achieved with an intense selling effort by all members of the venture team.
4. As the venture becomes more lucrative, the market niche will become more attractive to potential competitors. The management team does not feel the market will become large enough to attract major attention for three to four years. By this time, the team hopes to have an extensive customer base and contracts with customers aimed at maintaining business.
5. As sales grow and product demand increases, there is a risk that suppliers to the company may be overwhelmed. The management team plans to prevent any supply problems by close study of supplier capacity and possible alternate supplies. The team will decide in future years if products should be produced in-house.

The company (venture) in question has been a going concern for many years. Although the risks listed are real, they have not presented themselves in any tangible way to the current management of the company. The entrepreneurial team feels confident that these risks are minimal.

THE FINANCIAL PLAN

Pro Forma Income Statement

The income statement contains the company's current-year statement and projections for the first five years of operations under the management of the venture team. For the projected years, several items are held as a constant percentage of sales. These include cost of goods sold, freight, and postage. Other items are held constant or only slightly increased (rent expense, depreciation, etc.). Major expenses to consider are significant increases in selling expense, salaries, and advertising expense. These line items must be emphasized to increase sales. Because of the company purchase recorded in year 1, there is a net income drop from $87,924 to $-13,487 in year 1. Net income and cash flows remain positive in subsequent years.

To test the volatility of earnings with a lower sales projection, the venture team has determined that a 20 percent reduction in sales results in a 35 percent lower net

TABLE 4 Sensitivity Analysis of Net Income (20% Sales Projection Decrease)

Pro Forma Income Statement

	Year 0	Year 1*	Year 2	Year 3	Year 4	Year 5
Sales	$368,919	$580,000	$1,000,000	$1,280,000	$1,680,000	$2,240,000
Cost of goods sold	154,946	243,600	420,000	537,600	705,600	940,800
Gross profit	213,973	336,400	580,000	742,400	974,400	1,299,200
Expenses						
Selling expense	9,111	97,000	97,000	126,000	140,000	158,500
Advertising expense	21,689	40,000	50,000	50,000	50,000	50,000
Telephone and utilities	2,724	5,500	5,500	5,500	5,500	5,500
Freight	13,750	21,617	37,271	47,707	62,615	83,487
Rent expense	10,000	12,000	15,000	18,000	21,000	24,000
Salaries	41,599	100,000	100,000	120,000	150,000	180,000
Depreciation	5,110	5,110	5,110	5,110	5,110	5,110
Early payment of loan	0	0	0	0	100,000	100,000
Postage	9,620	18,905	32,595	41,722	54,760	73,013
Total expenses	113,603	300,132	342,476	414,039	588,985	679,610
EBIT	100,370	36,268	237,524	328,361	385,415	619,590
Interest expense	0	55,000	55,000	55,000	55,000	55,000
EBT	100,370	−18,732	182,524	273,361	330,415	564,590
Taxes (credit)	12,446	−5,245	51,107	76,541	92,516	158,085
Net income	$ 87,924	$−13,487	$ 131,417	$ 196,820	$ 237,899	$ 406,505

*Year 1 and subsequent years are projections.

income figure in year 5. The resulting net income figure is still over $400,000, as shown in Table 4.

Pro Forma Cash Flow Analysis

The company is expected to produce sufficient cash flows in subsequent years to fund operations (funding from cash flows and $200,000 from initial debt financing). If cash flows from operations do not prove sufficient to cover the costs of outsourcing, the company has the ability to establish lines of credit to finance current assets. The company has been successful doing so in the past.

The venture team does not expect any problems with receivables, and the founder's experience would support this. Most of Windsor's customers do not have financial difficulties and are able to pay for products easily. Receivables and inventory are expected to grow in proportion to sales in years 1 through 5. The team does not foresee any major capital equipment purchases because of the outsourcing practices of the company. As sales and cash flows increase, management may decide to purchase a manufacturing facility in the United States to gain some additional control over costs and scheduling. ∎

This case was written under the supervision of Professor James R. Lang by Jon Littlefield. The R. B. Pamplin College of Business. Virginia Polytechnic Institute and State University.

Name Index

Subject Index